THE RIVERSIDE HANDBOOK
AT A GLANCE

THE
RIVERSIDE
HANDBOOK

THE

RIVERSIDE

HANDBOOK

LYNN BEENE

University of New Mexico

WILLIAM VANDE KOPPLE

Calvin College

HOUGHTON MIFFLIN COMPANY   BOSTON   TORONTO

Dallas   Geneva, Illinois   Palo Alto   Princeton, New Jersey

For my parents,
    Roger and Wilma Vande Kopple
    —wjvk

And for our students
    —lb
    wjvk

Senior Sponsoring Editor: Carolyn Potts
Special Projects Editor: Lynn Walterick
Senior Project Editor: Barbara Roth
Assistant Design Manager: Karen Rappaport
Senior Production Coordinator: Renée Le Verrier
Senior Manufacturing Coordinator: Marie Barnes
Marketing Manager: George Kane

Printed in the U.S.A.

Library of Congress Catalog Card Number: 91-72004

ISBN: 0-395-52372-9

BCDEFGHIJ-H-95432

ACKNOWLEDGMENTS

Definition and facsimile of *contemporary*. Copyright © 1985 by Houghton Mifflin Company. Reprinted by permission from THE AMERICAN HERITAGE DICTIONARY, SECOND COLLEGE EDITION.

Robert P. Crease and Nicholas P. Samios. From "Managing the Unmanageable," by Robert P. Crease and Nicholas P. Samios, *The Atlantic*, January 1991, p. 83. Reprinted by permission of the authors.

Arthur C. Danto. Excerpt from "Gettysburg." Originally printed in *Grand Street*. Copyright © 1987 by Arthur C. Danto. Reprinted by permission of the author.

Index facsimile: *Readers' Guide to Periodical Literature*. Copyright © 1991 by The H. W. Wilson Company. Material reproduced by permission of the publisher.

Lewis H. Lapham. Excerpt from "A Political Opiate: The War on Drugs Is a Folly and a Menace." Copyright © 1989 by *Harper's Magazine*. All rights reserved. Reprinted from the December issue by special permission.

Acknowledgments continue on page 855.

C O N T E N T S

Contents ix

PREFACE

The Riverside Handbook is our attempt to create a clear, accessible reference guide for all writers and a text that students and teachers can confidently use in contemporary writing classrooms. Our fundamental goal is that of all writing teachers: We want all writers to learn that the effective use of language is not so much a matter of imposed parameters as it is one of infinite possibilities. Ours is a book with a thesis: All writing presents a writer's perspective on ideas, issues, and subjects; and perspective, when conveyed with confidence, has the power to open eyes and change minds. All parts of this book, large and small, contribute to this thesis. We know that every choice a writer makes— and every awareness of choice a writer has—refines and redefines the writer's perspective. The broader the repertoire of choices, the more fully realized the perspective. Above all we have tried to encourage readers to recognize that they are thinking individuals with much to say and with many options to choose among to make their ideas known.

To these ends, we have anchored our discussions of writing— from the architecture of its processes to the architecture of sentences—in the rhetorical matrix of reading, thinking, and writing. Central to this matrix is *critical thinking*—the active questioning of everything we observe, read, or write, leading each of us to an informed skepticism that does not merely look for "true" or "false." At the crux of the rhetorical matrix is our belief that critical thinking promotes creative ways to solve problems, to reflect on reading, and to stimulate writing processes. This book surveys the many ways writers use critical thinking skills as they work. Three of the most important are the following:

- **Key chapters illustrating the connections among reading, thinking, and writing:** Chapters 1, 13, and 47 in particular involve the student in active consideration of the interrelatedness of these processes. Chapter 1, "College Writing: An Introductory Exercise," presents a provocative dialogue between two cultural critics on the subject of the picture of "reality" presented by television. The chapter takes students step by step through the critical thinking processes of reading, questioning, rereading, and testing that lead to writing about a controversial issue. Designed for use early in a course of study, Chapter 1 reinforces the links among reading, thinking, and writing and suggests the liveliness of these processes as well.

Chapter 13, "The Essay Connection," is a response to a general truth: that many composition instructors use a reader—an anthology of essays—with a handbook. The essay genre (or, more broadly, nonfiction prose) is an important one in writing instruction, and to learn to read, respond to, and analyze essays is a primary accomplishment for any freshman. This chapter tries to build a bridge from the handbook to the reader, offering three analytical perspectives from which to read and analyze essays. We offer a case in point: George Orwell's "Shooting an Elephant," discussed from the three perspectives, with accompanying model analytical essays.

Chapter 47, "Sample Research Reports," highlights the connections among reading to research, questioning issues, and interpreting responses. The chapter presents two research reports that argue opposing positions on the same topic. That topic is television newscasting—"entertainment" to produce revenues, or a serious and reliable source of information? The reports, one documented in MLA style and the other in APA, draw on some of the same sources, but their writers reach sharply differing conclusions about their important and controversial topic. This back-to-back presentation of two arguments underscores the probability—in fact, the inevitability—of divergent perspectives and also reveals the types of reasoning and evidence that writers use in order to persuade readers.

- **Consistent emphasis on the writer's options:** We have tried throughout this book to address the reader as an intelligent co-explorer of language. This means that, although we provide thorough grounding in the standard conventions of using language, we have determined to offer not rules of "shall" and "shall not" but a sense of the rhetorical contexts in which writers realistically work. The "rules" as such are certainly here—the Grammar, Correctness, and Punctuation and Mechanics units attest in depth to that—but they are not offered as immutable dictates. We show the reasons underlying standard practices *and* the options writers have in applying those practices. Unit 9, "Style," is a practicum in recognizing and exercising options. Our perspective in this unit is the same as that throughout the text: Writers make their choices when constructing texts and sentences in the light of what they want to accomplish. Each choice, then, is an act of critical thinking in which the writer weighs what is gained against what might be lost. We believe that this understanding is liberating for students and that it motivates them to do their best work.

• **Research as an integral part of critical thinking and writing:** We see research not as a series of prescribed procedures culminating in the construction of "the research paper" but instead as an investigative process that is the natural outgrowth of critical thinking. To gain the habits and skills of the researcher—search strategies, techniques of inquiry, evaluative judgment, an understanding of synthesis, and above all a sense of informing oneself in support of a perspective—is to write with confidence and authority. Our research unit, Chapters 44–48, concentrates on the thinking strategies, as well as the nuts-and-bolts practices, that researchers need to carry out their tasks. We include a substantial discussion of primary as well as secondary research, and we focus on evaluating sources, developing theses, marshalling sources as evidence, and assimilating these sources into the writer's own, distinct perspective. The unit includes an extensive comparative guide to MLA and APA documentation styles and also includes the two previously mentioned research reports that argue opposite viewpoints on the same issue.

Our primary aims in *The Riverside Handbook* do not end with our emphases on the reading-thinking-writing connection, the options all writers enjoy, and the complementary role research plays in critical thinking. Each discussion, exercise, and suggested strategy further reinforces our thesis. A few of the other areas where our point of view informs our writing are the following:

• **Perspective on issues in English as a Second Language:** In the late twentieth century, writing classrooms are filled with a growing number of students for whom English is a second, or perhaps even third, language. We believe the best tool we can give any writer, no matter what that writer's native language may be, is an understanding of the vast possibilities and promises language offers. Yet we also realize that second-language students sometimes need additional explanations if they are to master certain syntactic constructions or sometimes tricky aspects of usage. Rather than isolating these discussions in a separate chapter, we have chosen to integrate explanations of particular interest to second-language speakers throughout the chapters discussing sentence construction and usage. Sixteen "ESL Consideration" boxes, each listing the major features of a particular syntactic or usage question, appear with the appropriate grammatical and usage discussions. Each of these inserts succinctly states a grammatical or usage issue, provides examples of acceptable and unacceptable uses, and lists helpful ways for writers to remember the acceptable forms. Further, a special ESL-topics index guides readers to the handbook's other discussions of related issues.

● **Extensive discussion of reasoning and argumentation:** If critical thinking informs reading and writing, all writers should understand the formal and informal dynamics of critical thinking. Therefore, Unit 2, "Reading and Reasoning for Writing," surveys accepted strategies for critical reading and contemporary perspectives on critical thinking, argumentation, and inductive and deductive reasoning. Additionally, Chapter 9, "Writing Persuasively," explains and illustrates the most common approaches to persuasion.

● **An entire unit on sentence style:** Believing as we do that style is the writer's exercise of options made visible, we have devoted Chapters 38–43 in Unit 9 to an intensive and—we hope—enjoyable exploration of the dimensions of style. As each chapter title indicates, the chapters examine various ways writers have of "Reviewing and Revising" their sentence subjects, verbs, sentence endings, diction, coordination, and subordination. These chapters are abundantly illustrated with examples and discussions of the kinds of options writers may elect in working with their own sentences. Their emphasis on rethinking as the process that sparks revision links these chapters back to Unit 4, "Revision," which presents the revising of texts and paragraphs.

● **Ease of reference:** A handbook is by definition a reference guide, and we have tried to build into this one a number of features that give the reader easy access to the material he or she needs—and greater access than that usually provided by page tabs that read, for example, **23b cs.** This text has **23b cs,** to be sure, but it also has seven other ways to find information quickly:

Graphic endpapers: Inside the front cover is a schematic "map" of the parts and chapters of *The Riverside Handbook*, all keyed to the tabs on the pages, so the reader can see at a glance the scope and location of coverage.

Lists of key concepts: Each of the rhetorical chapters opens with a list of key concepts discussed in that chapter and succinct definitions of those concepts.

Strategies boxes: All the rhetorical chapters also include boxed presentations of key strategies for the writing process being discussed. These boxes extend rather than distill the related discussions and are quick guides writers can use to remind themselves of salient points.

Special tabs: In addition to providing the usual chapter tabs on every page, this book includes special tabs along the entire outer edge of the pages in Chapters 1, 13, and 47—key chapters in the reading-thinking-writing connection—and on the pages in Chapter 45 featuring the guide to MLA and APA documentation styles.

Quick-reference charts: Recognizing that readers often go to a handbook looking simply and only for a quick answer in order to fix a typical problem, we have included two quick-reference charts on sentence construction and on punctuation and mechanics. Those charts, at the ends of Units 7 and 8 respectively, briefly define common errors and show incorrect examples followed by correct ones.

ESL Consideration boxes: The handbook integrates sixteen boxes discussing certain problem areas for second-language speakers into the already extensive discussions of grammar, style, and usage.

● **Three indexes:** First, *The Riverside Handbook* has a complete subject index that cross-references its major discussions. Second, the text provides an ESL-topics index that locates both the ESL Consideration boxes and information in the text of special interest to second-language speakers. Third, the handbook includes an index to common errors that lists and cross-references the grammar, style, and usage discussions and directs readers to the appropriate quick-reference charts.

In addition to *The Riverside Handbook*, instructors will find a variety of supplementary materials:

● *Options,* by Dean Ward of Calvin College, is a workbook offering intensive practice exercises in composing, revising, sentence construction, punctuation, and style. It may be purchased as a companion text to this handbook; contact your Houghton Mifflin sales representative or regional office for further information.

● **Instructor's Resource Manual/TA Support Package:** The manual offers a thorough crash course in teaching composition, overviews and suggested approaches to the chapters in the main text, answers to exercises in the book, and the answer key to the *Options* student workbook.

● **Cross-Curricular Writing Assignment Booklet:** This booklet provides a design for a cross-curricular approach to teaching composition, as well as assignments and student papers.

● **Printed Diagnostic Tests:** The fifty-five-item diagnostic test is printed as duplicating masters and enclosed in a printed envelope.

● **Computerized ESL-Revision Exercises:** This is an interactive software program with exercises specially designed for ESL students. Available for the IBM.

● **Computerized Developmental Exercises:** These interactive exercises offer students the chance for further practice in sentence correctness. Available for the IBM.

● **Computerized Diagnostic Tests:** These are computerized versions of the diagnostic test. Available for the IBM.

Acknowledgments

Many friends and colleagues helped out with encouraging words—and, at times, discouraging ones—suggestions, and cups of coffee. We don't have the room to thank each one individually. But we do want to make some special acknowledgments.

We thank our many reviewers for their astute and thoughtful responses to our manuscript at various stages of our writing process: Ray Anschel, Normandale Community College (MN); Bruce Ardinger, Columbus State Community College (OH); Poonam Arora, University of Michigan, Dearborn; Guy Bailey, Oklahoma State University; Betty Bamberg, University of Southern California; Frank Beyer, Los Angeles Pierce College (CA); Pearl L. Brown, Quinnipiac College (CT); Mike Bruno, Thomas Nelson Community College (VA); Cheryl Burghdurf, Champlain College (VT); Patsy Callaghan, Central Washington University; Leif Camp, Robert Morris College (IL); Carolyn Channell, Southern Methodist University (TX); Phil Cooksey, Rose State College (OK); Anne Coon, Rochester Institute of Technology (NY); Michael Coulombe, University of Wisconsin; Colonel Joe Cox, U.S. Military Academy (NY); Sara Danglentonio, Frankin Pierce College (NH); Neil Daniel, Texas Christian University; Muriel Davis, San Diego Mesa College (CA); Jim De Saegher, Point Loma Nazarene College (CA); Zita Dresner, University of D.C.; Rick Eden, California State University; Barbara A. Fahey, Scottsdale Community College (AZ); Ann Fields, Western Kentucky University; Mike Fleming, University of San Francisco (CA); Dorothy Friedman, University of D.C.; Irene Gale, University of South Florida; Anita Gandolfo, West Virginia University; William Gibson, University of Minnesota; Sara Guthrie, Mississippi County Community College (AK); Kay Halasek, Ohio State University; Phyllis Hamilton, Frederick Community College (MD); John Hanes, Duquesne University (PA); Patricia Harkin, University of Toledo (OH); Gwen Hauk, Temple Junior College (TX); Mary Lou Hingman, Plymouth State College (NH); Deborah James, University of North Carolina, Asheville; Nadene Keene, Indiana University at Kokomo; Debbie King, Phillips County Community College (AR); James Kormier, Sonoma State University (CA); Pat Knight, Amarillo College (TX); Mike Matthews, Tarrant County Junior College, NE (TX); Bob Mayberry, University of Nevada, Las Vegas; Alice McWaters, Rose State College (OK); Walter Meyers, North Carolina State University; Mike Moran, University of Georgia; Lyle Morgan, Pittsburg State University (KS); William Mowatt, West Valley College (CA); Laura Noell, Northern Virginia Community College; John Pazereskis, Carl Sandberg College (IL); Donna Phillips, Cleveland State University (OH); Randy Popken, Tarleton State University (TX); Lynn Ragar,

Southwestern College (CA); William Reynolds, Hope College (MI); A. John Roche, Rhode Island College; Linda Rollins, Motolow State Community College (TN); Mark Rollins, Ohio University; Mary Rosner, University of Louisville (KY); Leigh Ryan, University of Maryland; Ruth Sabol, West Chester University (PA); Daniel Samide, Hillsborough Community College (FL); Mary Sauer, Indiana-Purdue University; Delores Schriner, Northern Arizona University; Susan Smith, Allegheny College (PA); Jane Stanhope, American University (DC); Mary Jean Steenberg, Metropolitan Community College (NB); John Taylor, South Dakota State University; Donald Tighe, Valencia Community College (FL); Joseph Trimmer, Ball State University (IN); Peggy Urie, University of Nevada, Reno; Barbara Van Camp, Wayne State University (MI); James Vanden Bosch, Calvin College (MI); Karen Vaught-Alexander, University of Portland (OR); Mary Ann Wilson, University of Southwestern Louisiana; Meredith Wilson, Solano Community College (CA); Robert Wiltenberg, Washington University (MO); Richard Zbaracki, Iowa State University.

Douglas Hunt of the University of Missouri wrote Chapter 13, "The Essay Connection: Ways of Reading and Responding." For this compelling contribution to our book we owe him great appreciation.

Special thanks go to Jim Vanden Bosch of Calvin College, not only for writing the Glossary of Usage but equally for unflagging support, which manifested itself in many ways, among them tireless reading of and commenting on manuscript and proof.

Thanks also to Dean Ward of Calvin College for his work both in commenting on our text and in writing its companion workbook, *Options*.

Chris Hall of Wright State University provided invaluable consultation about primary issues in English as a Second Language and created both the ESL Consideration boxes and the ancillary Computerized ESL-Revision Exercises.

Sherry Smith, Alma Walhout, Alicia Jekel, Heather Bouwman, Rachel Berens, and Rebecca Warren, all of Calvin, offered reliable and cheerful clerical assistance.

In New Mexico, Bruce Jaffe willingly supplied his computer expertise on demand. And David W. Frizzell patiently listened and even more patiently read.

We are especially grateful to the staff of Houghton Mifflin Company for their support and assistance throughout this project. Three people in particular must be singled out. First, our thanks to Carolyn Potts, the senior sponsoring editor, who kept the spark of this book alive at all moments. From the beginning she nurtured and clarified the vision of *The Riverside Handbook*. Lynn Walterick, who developed the book, endured many phone calls and letters with professionalism, sensitivity, and understanding. Her guidance and her knowledge of the publishing industry, as well as her keen sense of humor, were invaluable throughout the project. And Barbara Roth coordinated the complex production procedures, large and small, with grace, patience, and wonderful judgment.

L.B.

W.J.V.K.

HOW TO USE THIS BOOK

You may find yourself using this book in two ways in your writing course. First, your instructor may assign certain chapters or parts for you to read, and may ask you to complete some of the exercises. Depending on the structure or emphasis of your class, you may be asked to read chapters in the Writing Process unit, the Revising unit, the Reading and Reasoning unit, or the Research Report unit. Or you may read chapters in the Grammar, Correctness, Punctuation and Mechanics or Style units.

Almost certainly you will use this book as a reference guide when you are working alone on your own writing. The following list details the ways in which you can find and use material in the text:

- **Endpapers and table of contents:** The front endpapers and the table of contents lay out a map of the book, indicating the order of units and chapters and, within chapters, the subjects covered. The units and chapters have simple, clear titles denoting their contents; for example, the Correctness unit (Unit 7) contains chapters concerning common errors in sentence construction.

- **Coded page tabs:** Every page has a tab (a green square) with a code: for example, **22b sf.** This code indicates that you are in Chapter 22, "Sentence Fragments" **(sf)** at **b**, a discussion of correcting fragments.

- **Reading-thinking-writing tabs:** Key chapters discussing the reading-thinking-writing connection (Chapters 1, 13, and 47) are tabbed with a green and black band along the entire outside edge of the pages making up these chapters.

- **MLA and APA documentation guide:** In Chapter 45, this guide, showing how to format bibliographic entries for a research report for MLA and APA specifications, is tabbed with a green band along the outside edge of its pages.

- **Key concepts:** All writing chapters begin with a brief, defined list of the major concepts discussed in the chapter.

- **Strategies boxes:** Within the writing and research chapters, these boxes (tinted light gray and bordered in green and black) present useful hands-on advice that you can refer to when you sit down to write or to do research.

- **Quick-reference charts:** These charts very briefly define and illustrate, with examples of correct and incorrect sentences, the most common errors writers make in sentence structure and punctuation and mechanics. You can refer to these charts to get a quick answer to a problem: For example, if you need to know what a dangling modifier looks like and how to fix it, you can turn to the quick-reference chart at the end of the Correctness unit. Similarly, the chart for punctuation and mechanics is placed at the end of that unit.

- **ESL Consideration boxes:** These boxes, identified by a green band across the top, highlight advice about sentence structure for writers whose first language is not English.

- **Cross references:** A cross reference appears in the text whenever the subject under discussion is treated additionally elsewhere in the text; for example, "see **9b**" means that you are reading something alluding to informal fallacies of reasoning and that there is another discussion at heading **b** in Chapter 9 (which you can find by looking at the page tabs).

- **Terms:** Important terms throughout all chapters appear in boldface type and are defined.

- **Glossaries:** There are two glossaries: one of usage, which offers succinct advice, with examples, about the preferred use of certain words and phrases; and one that offers brief definitions of major grammatical terms.

- **Indexes:** There are three indexes: (1) a **subject** index, in which you can look up any concept or term dealt with in this handbook; (2) an **ESL** index, in which you can look up the ESL Consideration boxes and also further discussion of issues of interest to second-language speakers; and (3) a **common errors** index, in which you can look up such errors as sentence fragments and common splices. These indexes are located at the end of the book.

WRITING AND

THINKING

1

**College Writing:
An Introductory Exercise**

COLLEGE WRITING: AN INTRODUCTORY EXERCISE

S ome students and aspiring professionals believe that serious reading, reflecting, and writing are activities that require extraordinary amounts of effort and commitment—more than anyone can expend in days that are filled with innumerable obligations. When they think about reading, they may think of the latest Danielle Steele novel, because it can be read in snippets, with no need for sustained attention. It seems almost impossible to find the time to contemplate the sophisticated ideas in a complex novel or philosophical essay or to revel in the style, tone, and mood of well-wrought texts. And many people see themselves as just too harried to write down their thoughts, let alone polish their prose.

Yet in today's world we must read and comprehend more information than ever before. And, more than ever, we must be able to convey our own views—our perspectives—about the ideas and issues we encounter. Most ideas, issues, and information are communicated through writing. All of us, students and professionals alike, must write explanations of what we read. We must also make our writing show the scope of our knowledge and our grasp of the continually growing fund of information. Therefore, it is unrealistic for any of us to conclude that we can function *anywhere* without keen reading and writing skills.

Reading and writing require reflection. Reading and writing teach everyone how to reason carefully, analyze closely, recognize

2

conflicting viewpoints on issues, and improve communication skills. This is the principal belief that motivated us to write this handbook, and it underlies the advice and strategies we offer.

This book is based on a number of central assumptions. First, we believe that reading and writing are natural thinking processes, shared by everyone and inextricably linked. Second, we believe that reading, thinking, and writing mean making choices. You have to choose to avail yourself of various analytic strategies, and you have to decide which strategies will work best for you for a given project. In short, you have to practice, experiment, and study to be a better reader, thinker, and writer.

Finally, we take the position that everything you read or write is intended to persuade. All texts present a point of view, which their writers want their audiences to accept. This is another way of saying that all communicative writing has a purpose and that the purpose in writing is to induce the audience to see the world as the writer sees it. When you communicate your ideas to others, you consciously put yourself into a rhetorical situation, sometimes illustrated by a communications triangle like the one below. You identify a problem (or, sometimes, simply the desire to express your opinion), which leads you to compose a text in which you try to persuade an audience to agree with your resolution of the problem or with your point of view. Your readers consider your text and may, if you have reached them, change their own perspectives.

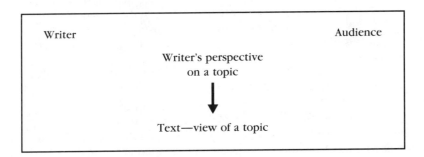

Your text, which presents your view of a topic, links you (the writer), your audience, and the topic you are writing about. And you choose what ideas, appeals, and style best get your perspective across.

1a

Reading as a Road to Writing

When you read someone else's text, you may laugh at its absurdities, wonder at its profound ideas, or argue with its absent author. Whatever your response, you are reacting to its ideas and the way they are presented and supported. When you transfer to your own writing the reasoning skills, knowledge, and sense of style that you develop through reading, you gain greater control over what you write and greater confidence in your ability to write. Writing becomes easier, although it is never effortless.

To help you move along on the road to writing, we ask you to try out an exercise based on the dialogue that appears a little later on in this section and to monitor your initial reactions. The exercise will take you through some of the strategies entailed in reading, critical thinking, and writing. The dialogue we have chosen is an excerpt from a dinner conversation between Neil Postman and Camille Paglia, two cultural critics noted for their strong and sometimes outrageous opinions. Postman, a professor at New York University and author of *Amusing Ourselves to Death: Public Discourse in the Age of Show Business,* was reared in a pre-television world. Books, not visual media, are his preferred medium. Paglia, a professor at Philadelphia College of the Arts and author of *Sexual Personae: Art and Decadence from Nefertiti to Emily Dickinson,* grew up in the 1950s and 60s when virtually every home had a television. Hers is a world of—among other things—Rolling Stones' concerts, half-hour sitcoms, and political sound-bites.

Postman and Paglia lace their conversation with literary references. Because this conversation is an informal, social exchange at dinner, they speak their minds without detailed explanations and evidence and are even slightly flippant. And since they come from different backgrounds, they have different perspectives on the issues that arise.

1 A Note About First Tackling the Text

A quick reading of this excerpt might leave you baffled, particularly if the issues Postman and Paglia banter about are unfamiliar or uninteresting to you. You may ask *What are these people talking about? Where is the structure for their arguments? Where is their support? What am I supposed to understand here?* You will find, though, that working through this exercise will enable you to judge the validity of your initial responses. It will also help you develop a more fully thought-out conclusion about your own perspective on the issues. So don't be discouraged if everything isn't immediately clear.

2 The Postman-Paglia Dialogue

POSTMAN: In *Aspects of the Novel,* E. M. Forster wrote that if you say the king died and the queen died, you don't have a story. But if you say that the king died *because* the queen died, you have a story. I find that television undermines these simple word-based connections. The whole idea of language is to provide a world of intellectual and emortional continuity and predictability. But many of my students no longer understand, for example, the principle of contradiction. I was talking to one student the other day about a paper in which he asserted one thing to be true in the first paragraph and the exact opposite to be true three paragraphs later. He said, "What's the problem?"

This habit derives from television, which tells you that there was a rape in New York and then it tells you there was an earthquake in Chile and then it tells you that the Mets beat the Cardinals.

PAGLIA: Well, Neil, that's life.

POSTMAN: That's insanity.

PAGLIA: Not to me. In your book you say TV is Dadaist[1] in its random, nihilistic compilation of unrelated events. I say it's surrealist[2]— because *life* is surreal! You leave a restaurant and get killed by a falling air conditioner. A tornado hits a picnic. There's no sense to reality. It simply happens. Television is actually closer to reality than anything in books. The madness of TV is the madness of human life.

POSTMAN: Here is what I would like: When our young student is watching Dan Rather say that 5,000 people died in an earthquake in Chile and then Dan says, "We'll be right back after this word from United Airlines," I would like our student to say, "Hey, wait a second, how could he ask me to make such an emotional switch?"

---

1. *Dadaist:* Paglia actually goes on to define this term as she speaks of a "random, nihilistic compilation of unrelated events." Dadaism was an early-twentieth-century artistic and literary movement devoted to total freedom and opposed to tradition, rules, and ideals; one of its recurrent forms was the collage, a random presentation of unrelated objects or words. *Nihilistic* refers to the belief that values are baseless and nothing is knowable.

2. *surrealist:* representing the workings of the unconscious mind. Surrealism was a movement that developed from Dadaism; one of its primary concerns was the study of dreams and the relationship between unconscious and conscious states of being.

1a
cw

PAGLIA: My answer is this: Buddha smiles. He sees the wheel of rein-carnation and accepts the disasters of the universe. That's the way it should be. There's no way we can possibly extend our compassion to 5,000 dead people. By juxtaposing such jarring images, TV is creating a picture of the world that is simply true to life. We are forced to con-template death the way farmers do—as just another banal occurrence, no big deal. Nature can crack the earth open and swallow thousands, and then the sun shines and the birds sing. It's like going from an airplane crash to a hemorrhoids ad. In TV, as in nature, all have equal weight.

POSTMAN: What I am focusing on is our emotional response to those things. We all know that nurses who work in hospitals make jokes. They see the absurdity of death routinely. But they don't see anywhere near the number of deaths the television viewer sees. What I see as dangerous here is a discontinuity of emotion that television promotes, its unnatural evocation, every five minutes, of different and incompat-ible emotions.

PAGLIA: By moving from disaster to commercial, TV creates the effect of Greek tragedy: emotion, then detachment; contemplation of loss, then philosophical perspective. At the end of *Hamlet,* there are four corpses strewn all over the stage.

POSTMAN: But no one is laughing—although I will admit that in the graveyard scene, when Hamlet makes the "Alas, poor Yorick" speech, he *is* laughing. But my point is, just after Horatio's final soliloquy,[3] at least on television, we would then see [a] Hebrew National spot, or perhaps a commercial for Danish pastry.

PAGLIA: To make that radical switch from disaster to detachment is, I think, a maturing process. If you fully responded emotionally to every disaster you saw, you'd be a mess. In fact, you'd be a perpetual child, a psychological cripple. Wisdom by definition is philosophical detach-ment from life's disasters.

POSTMAN: Injecting humor into other insane catastrophes is comic relief. It is what we must do unless we want to go mad. But the effect I am talking about on the television news is different.[4]

---

3. *Horatio's final soliloquy:* Horatio's last words, upon Hamlet's death, are "Now cracks a noble heart. Good night, sweet prince, / And flights of angels sing thee to thy rest!"

4. This dialogue is an excerpt from "She Wants Her TV! He Wants His Book!" *Harper's* March 1991: 54–55.

3 Responding to the Text

1b
CW

What you have just engaged in during your quick first reading is a rather complex process. You asked questions of the text and compared what you know from the brief introduction about the subject and the critics with what they actually said—that is, with what you read. To understand how you move from initial reactions to critical thinking and, eventually, to clear writing, continue this exercise as follows.

Write Down Your Reactions

On a piece of paper, jot down your first reactions to the excerpt. In one column, write your overall responses, including whether you liked the excerpt and which critic's position was more understandable or acceptable to you. In the other column, write down the major issues or questions that you think these critics are discussing. What central controversies do these two people find compelling, and how clearly do they state their positions?

Reread the Dialogue

After you have finished writing this initial response, reread the excerpt. This second reading will involve you more actively with the ideas in the text, for now you have a sense of the context in which they are introduced, as well as a sense of the two critics' personalities. You will begin to read between the lines, to infer connections that neither Postman nor Paglia states directly. You will generalize your initial reactions to the excerpt and the critics and judge both as either good or bad, fair or unfair, interesting or boring. In other words, in rereading you will give the passage more attention and thought and, consequently, form some tentative conclusions about it.

After this second reading, take a new sheet of paper and fill in the two columns again. This time, make your list of reactions reflect whether you agree or disagree with what Postman and Paglia say. To your list of issues, add notes about what personal relevance, if any, those issues have for you.

1b

Reasoning and Writing About a Text

Let us look at what your two readings have yielded. Perhaps you noted that Postman and Paglia raise, at least indirectly, a number of large issues, including the following:

- The picture of "reality" that television newscasts present
- The role of television news in shaping viewers' emotional reactions to life in general
- The best ways of acquiring and grasping information in a visual age
- The disparity between television's random, unconnected images and the habits of mind developed through reading
- The irrationality of events in everyday life
- The appropriate psychological development in contemporary society
- The ways in which surrealism fosters philosophical detachment
- The role that humor plays in maintaining psychological balance

Furthermore, your readings probably made you aware of these critics' individual styles. If you consider who these two critics are, you can see how their styles match their educational experiences. Postman, a critic accustomed to printed material, explains his ideas in longer sentences and weaves into his comments references to literature, theories of language, current events, and specific television newscasts. Paglia, a critic who often concentrates on nonprint media, juxtaposes images and topics, creating with her jumps and starts a sort of verbal collage very much like the view of reality she ascribes to television.

Now return to your listed reactions. Your two columns are really lists of **hypotheses,** or assumptions you make by proposing tentative responses to and explanations for things that you find unexpected or puzzling at first. To examine those hypotheses and move toward understanding your own perspective, take this exercise a few steps further.

1 Testing Your Responses

Return to the excerpt and compare your lists with it. Where *precisely* did the excerpt suggest the issues you wrote down and the reactions you had? What words did Postman and Paglia use that triggered your thoughts? Next, compare your lists with those your friends or peers wrote after they read the excerpt. Did you have the same reactions, or were yours more generous or more cynical than theirs? Now compare your lists with what you know about television, reading, newscasts, and daily living. Does Postman make a point that strikes you as true or reasonable? Does Paglia suggest anything about life that agrees with your experiences?

What you have been doing in this process is testing the framework of your hypotheses against the text, the reactions of others, and your own experience. This testing can help you decide what are the consequences of your initial assumptions. What you want to know is how your framework holds up and whether you can reasonably accept your initial reactions or must modify them in the light of any additional insights that your experience and the reactions of others provide.

2 Explaining Your Reactions—in Writing

Finally, think of someone with whom you enjoy having lively discussions (and perhaps friendly arguments). Considering that person as your audience, write a short explanation (three hundred to five hundred words) of your reactions to one of the issues raised in the dialogue. To do so, look over your lists of ideas, and re-examine your impressions. Consider, for example, what issue either Postman or Paglia presents most clearly and whether that issue is—or should be— a concern for you. Or consider which critic persuaded you. Who made "points" by making the most sense? Ask yourself, too, whether there is another way to look at any of the issues these critics bring up. What would that way be? Why would that way provide a better slant on the issue? To explain your reaction, draw on your understanding of what you have read, your sense of what really happens in the world, and your beliefs about what should happen.

Review what you have written with the same questioning technique you brought to the Postman-Paglia dialogue. Do you find your own response persuasive? Do you think your audience will? How close is your written response to your initial impressions? What did you learn about your own beliefs in the course of doing this exercise?

By engaging in this exercise, you have experienced reading, thinking, and writing as dynamic learning strategies. They require from you an attitude of inquiry and a reflective skepticism, and they move you to solve problems, gain an understanding of spoken and written texts, increase your store of knowledge, and improve your ability to communicate. In short, they lead you beyond the current boundaries of what you know into new arenas of thought and into new ways of presenting your views.

1b
cw

READING AND REASONING FOR WRITING

READING TO UNDERSTAND AND EVALUATE

Reading: The process of finding meaning in written characters or symbols and of interpreting and analyzing texts. Reading is the complement of writing.

Reading preparation: Preliminary steps, which include gathering necessary tools, scanning key material (that is, preface, abstract, table of contents, index), and skimming a text.

Reading critically: Reading a text and analyzing its contents, its impact on you, and the writer's perspective.

Annotation: A reader's critical commentary on or glossing of a writer's text.

Why Read?

All writers read. Professionals read to become more informed about their subjects or their society. They read research documents, proposals and evaluations, advertisements, memorandums and committee reports, abstracts and summaries, recommendations, applications, and letters of all types. Students read textbook assignments, research articles and critiques, novels, laboratory manuals, notices, school newspapers, local and national newspapers, special-interest magazine articles, "crib" sheets, and outlines.

Writers also read outside their fields to gain experience and understanding. Most types of reading teach you to reason. The experiences you have while reading influence both how you react when you have to write and how well you write a text.

2a
ru

1 Assumptions About Reading

As they start reading a text, some writers are hampered by preconceptions about what they are reading and why they are reading. For example, you may expect that informative texts will give you only facts and will not be entertaining. But informative texts can excite feelings, stimulate thought, and draw attention to writing style. Stephen Jay Gould, Carl Sagan, Barbara Tuchman, and Shelby Foote are examples of current writers who inform and entertain.

If you begin reading about an unfamiliar subject or one that does not interest you, you are likely to stumble along and misunderstand concepts. Reading may seem a frustrating chore. If a text is indeed boring, it may be because the writer fails to communicate clearly. Poor communication results when the writer is careless, rushed, or inattentive to the audience.

Writers also read to sharpen their analytic skills. Reading critically leads to a greater understanding of other texts and the improvement of one's own writing. **Critical reading** involves far more than scanning words on a page. Like writing, it is a recursive activity (its processes overlap and repeat). Critical reading requires preparation for reading, skimming for basic information, and rereading to analyze and, often, to prepare to write.

The remainder of this chapter explains the strategies you use in all critical reading, whatever the text. In your composition course—and beyond, very likely—you will frequently need or choose to read a particular type of text, the nonfiction prose essay. For a discussion of reading, analyzing, and writing in response to essays, see Chapter 13, "The Essay Connection."

2b

Preparing to Read

You should lay a groundwork for critical reading by bringing your curiosity and skepticism—as well as a dictionary and a pencil—to a text. With planning, you can understand even very difficult material. **Preparing to read** means determining why you are reading a particular text, what you expect to gain from it, and whether you are the author's intended audience; it also means gathering the right tools to annotate the text.

1 Why Are You Reading the Text?

Ask yourself why you are reading a text: What do you expect to get out of the process? Pay close attention to the subject matter, reread the work, take notes, analyze the reasoning patterns, and write your interpretation of the material.

2 Find Out About the Writer

Knowing something about the writers you read helps you judge their authority or evaluate their reasons for writing on a topic. Knowing a writer's background and biases enriches your appreciation of a text. Many texts begin with short biographical statements. If a text does not introduce a writer, check standard references such as *Current Biography* or any of the various editions of *Who's Who* for information. (For more on biographical sources, see **44c**.)

3 Learn About the Context

Knowing something about the cultural, historical, or social context of a text can tell you about a writer's purposes. Some magazines, for example, publish only essays or stories that meet a certain partisan or professional bias. *The National Review* prints more politically conservative articles than does *The New Republic*. *The American Journal of Physical Anthropology* presents current research to professionals, but *Nature* is accessible to interested novices. Other publications can approach the same topic with different purposes. *The Humanist's* essays consider the wide-ranging impacts of technological, political, and social changes, whereas those in *Newsweek* and *Time* offer primarily factual accounts of those changes.

Are You the Intended Audience?

Determine who the intended audience is and whether you fit the profile. Look at the preface, for example, or the introductory pages. The author may have flatly stated who the intended audience is.

> I wrote this book as an answer to the hundreds of people who have asked me over the years, "Where can I learn to copy edit?" Up till now the answer has been, "You can't." Sure, there are night and summer courses at many colleges, but they concentrate mostly on the Maxwell Perkins tearing-apart-and-rewriting-into-brilliant-prose kind of editing. Although many course teachers are copyeditors themselves, they rarely bring the publisher's point of view to their work. I represent the publisher, and, after all, it's the publisher you have to please. Whether you're currently a teacher, a student, a typist, or even someone who would just like to work at home, you can learn copyediting from this book.
>
> Karen Judd, *Copyediting: A Practical Guide*

5 Gather the Tools to Help You Read

Readers—like artists, craftspeople, and scientists—know that the right tools make any job easier and more rewarding. Have a **pen** or **pencil** ready to write comments in the text's margins, a **notebook** to jot down new concepts or argue with the text or its writer, and a **dictionary** to look up unfamiliar words or terms. With these tools in hand, you're ready to turn to the text.

2c

Skimming a Text

Skimming a text is reading quickly to get just the gist of a work rather than all the information it has to offer. The strategies are obvious. Read the text's title, table of contents, chapter headings, preface, and index. These sections usually highlight major issues and help you identify support for the main points. Look at the abstract, if there is one, and conclusions. Notice any **boldfaced** or *italicized* words. Alert yourself to the questions you will need to ask in subsequent, critical reading. Don't get discouraged if a work still seems difficult after this quick overview. Remember, rereading brings understanding.

1 Look at the Title

2c
ru

The **title** of a work often implies a writer's perspective on a topic. For this reason, titles are good clues to the text's general subject and, sometimes, the writer's approach in a text. You can gather from the titles that *The Story of My Life* by Helen Keller is autobiographical, that *Lifeboat Ethics: The Case Against Helping the Poor* by Garrett Hardin is a work of political economics, and that *The Accidental Tourist* by Anne Tyler implies irony and ambiguity. Similarly, the titles tell you that *Civil Disobedience* by Henry David Thoreau addresses political ethics, and *Cleopatra's Nose, the Twinkie Defense, & 1500 Other Verbal Shortcuts in Popular Parlance* by Jerome Agel and Walter D. Glanze focuses on humorous ties among language, history, and popular culture.

2 Review the Table of Contents
and Index

Because it lists the main headings in a text, a **table of contents** is a condensed outline that reveals the major topics of a work or its organizational skeleton. An **index,** on the other hand, consolidates information located throughout the text; it lists, in alphabetical order, the key terms, topics, names, and titles discussed in a work and the page numbers where these discussions begin. By merely scanning the table of contents of Humphrey Carpenter's *Secret Gardens,* which is a study of the golden age of children's literature in England, you learn that the author organized the book by chapters devoted to particular writers and their contributions to the genre.

The index lists the pages where the author discusses specific writers and their works.

3 Read the Preface

The **preface** outlines a text's content or identifies a writer's intentions. Notice how the following paragraph from the preface to Robert Adams's *Bad Mouth* lays out the order of his ideas by chapter, allowing you to turn at once to a relevant chapter if you want to study only one aspect of his topic.

> Though the studies making up this little collection were not written to fit any particular schema—growing, rather, as a set of free variations on a gradually emerging theme—they do in fact form a pattern of sorts. The first two focus on the idea of counter-language, language used to hinder people or hurt them in a variety of symbolic and practical ways, mostly quite familiar. The next two are concerned with language that deliberately violates standards of decency and standards of truth (such as survive); emphasizing the

**2c
ru**

general prevalence of such language, they look into the consequences of its no longer being exceptional. The last two pieces, departing from a direct concern with language, devote themselves to what I sense as a new and autonomous status for the ugly in modern life, and with the frequent metaphors of rags, garbage, and excrement in which that ugliness finds expression.

Robert M. Adams, *Bad Mouth:
Fugitive Papers on the Dark Side*

4 Look for Headings, Key Words, and Visual Aids

Chapter headings and **subheadings** subdivide topics or sections within a text and work like an outline, guiding you from one point to another. Repeated **key words** indicate a writer's main points and can direct you to the topic sentence in a paragraph. Scan the beginnings and endings of paragraphs looking for words that are in boldface print or italics. Also look briefly at any illustrations, diagrams, tables, or charts. These visual aids often summarize a writer's perspective on the topic.

5 Review the Abstract

The **abstract,** common in research and technical reports, summarizes main points, identifies the major sections, and presents in an abridged form a writer's results, conclusions, and recommendations. For a reader, these features make it one of the most useful forms of summary. Abstracts are found at the beginning of a text and enable readers to decide whether they should read the entire text. (For more on abstracts, see **46c.**) Notice how the following abstract sets out the problem (first sentence) that researchers Rodney D. Wood and J. M. Smith investigated, their methods (second sentence), and their results (third sentence):

Unusual heat transfer phenomena have been observed between solid surfaces and fluids near their thermodynamic critical point. To understand better these phenomena, temperature and velocity profiles and local heat transfer coefficients were measured for turbulent flow of carbon dioxide in a tube at 1,075 lb./sq. in. abs. . . . The results indicate a severe flattening of the radial temperature profiles, a maximum in the velocity profile between the wall at the tube axis, and a maximum in h' when the bulk fluid temperature passes through the transposed critical temperature.

Rodney D. Wood and J. M. Smith, "Heat Transfer in the Critical Region—Temperature and Velocity Profiles in Turbulent Flow"

6 Skim Any Conclusion or Recommendation Sections

Concluding sections do more than tie a writer's main points together. They also re-emphasize significant points, clarify judgments, and recommend action or further reading. **Recommendations,** the focal point of many research reports, are calls to action: The writer tells the audience what it should do about a situation or problem. The specifics of the problem and the evidence for the recommendations should be in the rest of the text.

Reading only the concluding section, however, does not tell you whether the hypotheses are reasonable or the conclusions well supported. Use the concluding section as a guide to judge the information in the text and its organization and presentation.

7 Skim for Literal Meaning

Read rapidly, without stopping or interrupting yourself. Your goal is to absorb the literal meaning—to look at the words, the generalizations, and the basic information. Put a check mark in the margin next to difficult passages and go on. You can return to these sections later.

Notice the devices emphasizing key concepts: boldfaced or italicized words and phrases; sentences, tables, or figures that summarize information; and cross-referenced information. Proceed through the text once so you can explore it again from other vantage points. This way you will be less likely to mistake the digressions for central ideas.

8 Look up Unfamiliar Words and Terms

As you read the text for key words and concepts, pay special attention to unfamiliar words. If you come across a word or term that you don't know, circle it, look up the word in your dictionary, and write its definition in the margin of the text. Large, hardbound dictionaries like the *American Heritage Dictionary,* the *Oxford English Dictionary,* or *Webster's Universal Dictionary* are excellent tools to refer to as you read although you may find a paperbound version of a reputable dictionary useful to carry with you. Turn to dictionaries such as *Van Nostrand's Scientific Encyclopedia* or *The Encyclopedia of Philosophy* to find the definitions of "professional jargon"—words that have specialized meanings in certain disciplines.

2c
ru

Sometimes the literal, dictionary (or **denotative**) meaning of a word does not help. In this case, try to figure out how the writer is using it in context. Decide what the overall meaning of the sentence is and whether the sentence makes clear what the word means. Then look at the paragraph. Ask yourself what the sentence generally means and how the term fits the paragraph's basic information.

Questions for Previewing a Text

- What clues do the titles, headings, and key words give about the main topic and the writer's perspective on that topic?
- What clues do the titles, headings, and key words give about the subtopics and how they relate to the main topic?
- What do the illustrations, diagrams, tables, and charts tell about the main topic and the writer's perspective on that topic?
- What does the information about the writer imply about his or her perspective on the topic?
- Who wanted this article written? Why?
- What situation or issue prompted this writer to create this text? How much do I know about this situation? Where can I find out more information about it?
- Where does the writer state his or her purpose for writing the work? How is the intended audience identified?
- What do I already think about this issue? Are these informed reactions?
- How do I differ from the writer's intended audience? How am I like those readers?

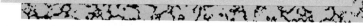

Exercise 1

Skim the following passage, note its main topic and viewpoint, identify its intended audience, and define any unfamiliar words.

The knight was originally the companion of his lord or king, formally admitted to fellowship with him. Around the year 1200 the church took over the dubbing of the knight and imposed its ritual and obligations on the ceremony, making it almost a sacrament. The candidate took a symbolic bath, donned clean white clothes and a red robe, and stood or knelt for ten hours in nightlong silence before the altar, on which his weapons and armor lay. At dawn mass was said in front of an audience of knights and ladies. His sponsors presented him to his feudal lord and gave him his arms, with a prayer and a blessing said over each piece of equipment. An essential part of the ceremony was the fastening of the spurs; our phrase "he has won his spurs" preserves a memory of the moment. An elder knight struck the candidate's neck or cheek a hard blow with the flat of the hand or the side of his sword. This was the only blow a knight must always endure and never return. The initiate took an oath to devote his sword to good causes, to defend the church against its enemies, to protect widows, orphans, and the poor, and to pursue evildoers. The ceremony ended with a display of horsemanship, martial games, and mock duels.

Morris Bishop, The Middle Ages

2d
ru

2d

Analyzing by Rereading

Analyzing is looking for meaning in the words and sentences, as well as discovering meaning between the lines and in what initially seems insignificant. Rereading causes you to evaluate how a text's parts create a whole. As you reread, pose questions about the text and its writer, note what you disagree with, focus on details and evidence, and respond to a writer's ideas by jotting down your own ideas. In short, read critically: Take the work apart to grasp how its generalizations relate to its particulars.

1 Identify Thesis Statements and Topic Sentences

Narrow your focus as you reread by moving from your initial, general response to specific criticisms. Having absorbed the gist and the literal meaning of the work, look for the **thesis statement** (a text's controlling or purpose statement) and **topic sentences** (the paragraph's controlling statements). (For more on thesis statements and topic sentences, see Chapters 8 and 12.)

2 Distinguish General Ideas from Specific Points

You can separate the main ideas from their supporting points by recognizing when writers are generalizing and when they are citing specific details. The writer Adam Smith (a pseudonym) begins the following passage with several factual statements that support the generalization he expresses in sentence 4, the topic sentence of the paragraph. (For more on facts, see **3d**.) Sentence 4 states a subpoint of the essay's thesis that ordinary investors rightly suspect economists and their predictions.

(1) The Hopi language, an American Indian language, contains no words, grammatical forms, constructions, or expressions that refer to what we call "time," or to past, present, or future. (2) The whole structure we base on "time"—wages, rent, credit, interest, depreciation, insurance—cannot be expressed in Hopi and is not part of that world view. (3) The main Eskimo language has twenty-seven different words for snow, each connoting another nuance of texture, utility, and consistency, so the Eskimo's ability to communicate about snow is far greater than ours. (4) The picture of the universe, of "reality," shifts from language to language. (5) The economists whose counsel we seek—as do presidents and prime ministers—speak from a world within the world, just as the Hopi spoke from a world without time, credit, wages, and rent. (6) That cold, neat, elegant world of mathematics views a different reality than blunt, ambiguous English.

Adam Smith, "Why Not Call Up
the Economists?"

Each detail clarifies a generalization and sets up the paragraph's balanced structure:

SENTENCE 1:   Supporting detail—Hopi language

SENTENCE 2:   Supporting detail—English versus Hopi

SENTENCE 3:   Supporting detail—Eskimo language

SENTENCE 4:   Generalization/topic sentence—reality varies by language

SENTENCE 5:   Supporting detail—economists' language

SENTENCE 6:   Supporting detail—economists' language versus everyday English

Moreover, Smith links sentences together by repeating the key words *Hopi, language, time, credit, wages,* by keeping his verbs in the present tense, and by repeating certain sentence structures.

Strategies for Recognizing Main Ideas

1. Find the writer's thesis statement.
2. Find the topic sentence of each paragraph.
3. If a paragraph lacks a topic sentence, express as best you can the writer's general point. (This inference will be the writer's main point or idea for the paragraph.)
4. Determine whether specific details in a paragraph confirm, explain, or contradict its topic sentence.
5. Determine whether individual topic sentences confirm, explain, detail, or contradict the writer's thesis.

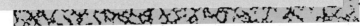

Exercise 2

Using the strategies suggested above, identify the main ideas expressed or implied in the following passages. Also identify the key words and the specific support.

When I was in public high school in Texas in the 1950s, one of the last things a girl wanted was a reputation as a good student. Girls who got good grades were "brains," and brains were socially handicapped. Most girls strived to cultivate the June Allyson image: a follower, not a leader; cute but not too smart, or at least not so smart that the guys felt threatened.

Apparently—despite the women's movement and the presence of significant numbers of successful women as role models—it is still considered inappropriate in most schools and colleges for girls to seem "smart." As a female student at Hunter High School in New York City recently explained, "I make straight A's, but I never talk about it. . . . It's cool to do really badly. If you are interested in school and you show it, you're a nerd." In elite institutions, where students are chosen for their academic ability, girls are more willing to challenge the boys academically than they are in non-selective schools and colleges. But with the demise of most single-sex girls' schools and colleges, there are now even fewer institutions where girls can be leaders and achievers without feeling like freaks. The popular culture—through television, movies, magazines, and videos—incessantly drums in the message to young women that it is better to be popular, sexy, and "cool" than to be intelligent, accomplished, and outspoken. Madonna has replaced June Allyson.

Diane Ravitch, "Back to Basics"

If a projectile is launched with a speed less than orbital speed (which for the earth's gravitational field is about 17,000 miles per hour), then its path will always resemble a parabola, the slowly curving arch usually followed by an arrow, a bullet, or a thrown rock. If, however, the object is launched with a speed between orbital speed and escape speed (which for the earth's gravitational field is about 25,000 miles per hour), then its path will always be an ellipse or a circle. Such is the case with all the planets orbiting the sun and with all the satellites circling the earth. And, finally, if an object is launched with a speed equal to or greater than escape speed, then its path will be a hyperbola, which looks like a parabola with its arch more severely bent. This is the path that was followed by American astronauts to the moon and by spacecraft traveling to other planets. The discovery of these categories was considered as revolutionary in its day as [René] Thom's categorization of abrupt change is today.

Michael Guillen, "The Familiar Faces
of Change"

3 Annotate What You Read

As a child, you might have been scolded for scribbling in books, and, as a young student, you were probably told never to write in a library book. Those lessons are still sound if the copy of a work you are reading belongs to someone else. However, if the text is your property, you should annotate it if you are going to find its nuances. **Annotating** a text—writing on it and about it—prepares you to evaluate. As you read—pen, pencil, or highlighter in hand—underline key words, phrases, and sentences. Highlight examples used as supporting evidence and noticeable repetitions. Fill in definitions of unfamiliar words and dates. Connect related ideas and facts by a line or circle.

Identify allusions, anecdotes, images, metaphors (see Chapter 41). Look for varieties of language such as clichés, colloquialisms, jargon, and formal or informal diction. Mark significant transitions between ideas. Identifying these stylistic devices helps you assess, among other things, whether a writer is appealing to your emotions or your intellect.

Put brackets around striking images or sentences, and briefly note in the margins why they are memorable. Memorize a key sentence, a summarizing word or concept, or a metaphorical phrase. Memorizing key material lets you ponder an idea even when you don't have the text directly before you. Memorizing can also help you think of examples that you can use in your own writing, although to avoid plagiarism, you must be careful to credit them properly.

Challenge everything you read. Ask what purposes a writer has and why the text persuades, delights, or offends you. Test whether the writer's evidence is believable, factually credible, rhetorically persuasive, or merely in line with your preconceptions. Look for the ways in which **tone**—the expressive manner in which a writer communicates a perspective on a topic—influences the overall texture of a work and your judgments of it. (For more on tone, see **10b**.) Notice, for example, the differences in word choice, punctuation, and sentence length that contribute to the satiric tone in Mark Twain's advice to youth, to the emotionalism of Etty Hillesum's letter, and to the academic distance in Noam Chomsky's speculations on language theory.

> Being told I would be expected to talk here, I inquired what sort of talk I ought to make. They said it should be something suitable to youth—something didactic, instructive, or something in the nature of good advice. Very well. I have a few things in my mind which I have often longed to say for the instruction of the young; for it is in one's tender early years that such things will best take root and be most enduring and most valuable. First, then, I will say to you, you young friends—and I say it beseechingly, urgingly—
>
> Always obey your parents, when they are present. This is the best policy in the long run, because if you don't they will make you. Most parents think they know better than you do, and you can generally make more by humoring that superstition than you can by acting on your own better judgment.
>
> Be respectful to your superiors, if you have any, also to strangers, and sometimes to others. If a person offends you, and you are in doubt as to whether it was intentional or not, do not resort to extreme measures; simply watch your chance and hit him with a brick. That will be sufficient. If you find that he had not intended any offense, come out frankly and confess yourself in the wrong when you struck him; acknowledge it like a man and say you didn't mean to. Yes, always avoid violence; in this age of charity and kindliness, the time has gone by for such things. Leave dynamite to the low and unrefined.
>
> Mark Twain, "Advice to Youth"

> When I think of the faces of that squad of armed, green-uniformed guards—my God, those faces! I looked at them, each in turn, from behind the safety of a window, and I have never been so frightened of anything in my life as I was of those faces. I sank to my knees with the words that preside over human life: And God made man after His likeness. That passage spent a difficult morning with me.
>
> I have told you often enough that no words and images are adequate to describe nights like these. But still I must try to convey something of it to you. One always has the feeling here of being the ears and eyes of a piece of Jewish history, but there is also the need sometimes to be a still, small voice. We must keep one another in

touch with everything that happens in the various outposts of this world, each one contributing his own little piece of stone to the great mosaic that will take shape once the war is over.

> Etty Hillesum, "Letter from a Nazi
> Concentration Camp"

Intuitive arguments concerning essential properties must account for the whole range of our intuitions, including the ones just offered if they are indeed correct. An account of the full range of intuitions seems simple enough, if we explain the intuitive force of the argument that such-and-such is an essential property of a thing on the basis of the systems of language and common-sense understanding that we bring to bear in such judgments. . . . A study of human judgments concerning essential and accidental properties may give considerable insight into the cognitive structures that are being employed, and perhaps beyond, into the nature of human cognitive capacity and the range of structures that are naturally constructed by the mind. But such a study can carry us no further than this.

> Noam Chomsky, "The Object of Inquiry"

Finally, consider your reactions to the text. Jot down what you think you know about a writer's subject, as well as your impressions, disagreements, and comments. This is **brainstorming,** a strategy you use in writing. (For more on brainstorming, see **6d**.) Or try asking yourself the questions journalists often address (*Who?, What?, When?, Where?, Why?,* and *How?*) about the subject of a text you are going to read. Your answers will not only tell you what you already know about the writer's topic; they will also help you decide whether you are the writer's intended audience.

Organize your annotations, brainstorming lists, and answers into a summary or a paraphrase that you can compare with the original. A **summary** condenses a writer's assertions into notes or a sort of index of the text. A **paraphrase** recasts in your own words a writer's ideas, methods of organization, and primary evidence. (For more on writing summaries and paraphrases, see **45c**.) When you compare what you have written with the original, you will be evaluating the text's ideas and tying them into your experiences.

2e

An Annotated Example

In the introduction to his populist guide to English writing called *American Tongue in Cheek,* poet, satirist, and *Philadelphia Magazine* columnist Jim Quinn states his purpose as entertaining while lambasting the excesses of "pop grammarians." Here is one of Quinn's impressions about a famous would-be grammarian:

"The Joys of Watergate"

One of the most sacred of all the sacred cows of pop grammar is its insistence that there is a connection between clear thinking and good grammar—that bad thinking, and especially bad political thinking, produces bad writing. This proposition was stated with much pop certitude in George Orwell's essay "Politics and the English Language." But it goes back even further, at least as far as 1927, when Ezra Pound wrote:

> The individual cannot think and communicate his thought, the governor cannot act effectively or frame his laws, without words, and the solidity and validity of these words is in the care of the damned and despised *literati*. When their work goes rotten—by that I do not mean when they express indecorous thoughts—but when their very medium, the very essence of their work, the application of the word to thing goes rotten, i.e., becomes slushy or inexact, or excessive or bloated, the whole machinery of social and of individual thought and order goes to pot.

This is brilliant pop grammar writing—the simple declaration of the connection is itself so well written that we believe it immediately. But it's not true.

A critical reader might annotate this passage as follows:

SUMMARY: Contending that bad politics means bad writing may have historical precedent, but it is a wrong-headed assumption made by amateur grammarians.

PARAPHRASE: One unquestioned belief about language connects bad political thinking to bad writing. George Orwell and, before him, Ezra Pound eloquently made this assertion. But the clear expression of this belief does not make it correct.

REACTION: Quinn's point is well taken. Many eloquent and sophisticated writers—major stylists all—argue for wrong-headed political strategies.

2f

Reading and Writing

Annotating a text and analyzing its meaning are on-going processes, and they resemble the processes you go through when you write. These processes include reasoning critically, integrating new and old information, and responding to a text—the one you are creating—with your thoughts and words. Writing and reading are dynamic inter-actions through which you discover meaning.

Deep, reflective reading expands your understanding and makes you grow as a writer. Well-read writers recognize equivocation, faulty reasoning, inappropriate conclusions, and turgid prose. They appreciate succinctness, logical reasoning, precise generalizations, and stylistically graceful texts. Irony no longer escapes them; satire hits its mark. Through reading, writers learn to recognize the merits of differing opinions and arguments. They also discover a wealth of possible options for organizing their ideas.

C R I T I C A L
T H I N K I N G

Critical thinking: The process of actively questioning and reasoning about ideas, statements, evidence, and actions. Critical thinking combines psychological reasoning with logical reasoning.

Psychological reasoning: The process of proposing solutions to problems, often those that occur in everyday life.

Logical reasoning: The process of analyzing arguments and viewpoints using the tools and conventions provided by formal logic.

Inferring: The process of drawing conclusions and making connections between events or propositions and past experiences or knowledge.

Belief: A conviction that something is true.

Hypotheses and theories: The working assumptions from which reasoning proceeds. Usually, the reasoning process is concerned with providing evidence to accept or refute such assumptions.

Factual statement: An assertion that can be verified by authoritative sources or objectively quantified by observation or experimentation.

3a

What Is Critical Thinking?

Critical thinking can refer to virtually every mental process, including daydreaming, joking, regretting, remembering, problem solving, judging, or interpreting. One type of thinking—musing—is a psychological process that helps us make sense of our world, form our beliefs, and confirm our opinions. Another, perhaps more dynamic type— analytic thinking—requires objectivity and interpretation and is the mainstay of evaluating, reasoning, arguing, or persuading. Throughout this book, we will focus on the relationship of analytic thinking to reading and writing. Above all, we want to emphasize that critical thinking is a process of questioning—of asking *Why?* and *How?* and of carefully weighing the ideas and opinions you encounter, rather than simply accepting them at face value.

3b

Psychological Reasoning

Much of the time our thinking is centered on problem solving. The strategies you use vary with the situations you face. You use **psychological reasoning** for most simple problems, such as figuring out, mostly through trial and error, why your alarm clock refused to work this morning. Without being aware of the mental processes you are employing and without using formal logical procedures, you recognize the problem, speculate about the possible causes, and eliminate the incorrect solutions until you come up with a satisfactory answer.

The alarm clock breakdown is a fairly straightforward example of a situation calling for psychological reasoning. At other times, psychological problem solving may seem more like sheer inspiration or imagination run wild. You worry over a problem, put it aside, and suddenly discover the solution. The process is not magical; you are just not aware of your mental processes.

Thus, the seemingly capricious reasoning you use in everyday life to solve problems is far from simple. Psychological reasoning is a highly complex, often emotional, and typically indefinable mental activity in which you try to bring form and meaning to a situation that does not initially seem to have either form or meaning. Your conclusions are more subjective than objective: that is, they are colored by your experiences, values, and biases rather than arrived at by impartial or logical means. Subjective evaluations are not necessarily less careful than objective evaluations. But they can be less persuasive and harder to communicate because they often lack consistency.

3c

Logical Reasoning

A special aspect of ordinary reasoning, **logical reasoning** has to do with formal or generally recognized patterns of argument. Some of these patterns connect the ideas expressed in specific statements to ideas expressed in other statements in conventionally accepted ways. Logical reasoning is a process, used as an evaluative or interpretive tool, that has

> **objectivity** as its prerequisite,
>
> **insight** as its goal, and
>
> **analysis** as its preferred method.[1]

1 Drawing Inferences

Whether you are setting an alarm clock, writing a travel brochure, or contemplating the national debt, you are thinking critically and starting to reason logically by drawing initial inferences. When you connect one event or perception with another, you infer a relationship between events. In other words, you connect what you see with what you know by **inferring,** or supposing, that what you already know has some bearing on the situation you now face. From this basic inference, you ask questions until you are satisfied that you have associated all the parts into a reasonable pattern.

2 Logical Reasoning and Formal Logic

Applying logical reasoning to the conclusions you propose or to those advanced by another writer requires you to consciously draw on your knowledge of a subject or discipline and on your ability to be

1. Ray Kytle, *Clear Thinking for Composition,* 5th ed. (New York: McGraw-Hill, 1987), p. 3.

skeptical and reflective. Like a detective or a scientist, you are connecting facts into acceptable patterns in order to analyze why you find a perspective persuasive or unpersuasive.

Logicians and writers have proposed several generalized patterns as interpretative tools for analyzing texts. (These patterns are discussed in Chapters 4 and 5.) However, you cannot use logicians' tools like templates: You cannot lay the "correct" tool over your own rough draft or another writer's text and obtain an automatic evaluation of how strong your discussion is or how acceptable the other writer's position is. Logical reasoning does not exist in a vacuum. It depends, in part, on what you know. Therefore, it requires that you inform yourself about an issue, subject, or discipline through reading, observing, experiencing, studying, or discussing.

3 Logical Reasoning and Consistency

Whereas psychological reasoning relies on subjective processes, logical reasoning is said to depend on objective processes and rules, such as the one invalidating contradictory claims. Unlike psychological reasoning, logical reasoning demands *consistency*—conflicting positions on a topic cannot logically support one another. By convention and by definition, a proposition may not be true at one place in an argument and false at another place in the same argument. Such inconsistent propositions are said to be contradictory, and they make the argument invalid.

If you have sufficient information about a subject, evaluate how your statements are connected, and if you draw your final claims clearly from evidence and close reasoning, you can detect inconsistencies in your writing or quickly grasp their implications. You maintain your credibility with your audience and, typically, win others to your perspective because they will see that you have reasoned logically.

Exercise 1

Find a copy of a college catalogue and read the descriptions for the individual programs of study within a major field that you find interesting or about which you have some firsthand knowledge. (For example, what are the various majors offered by the biology department?) Decide what the stated and implied standards are for completing the individual programs. Write a paragraph or two identifying the standards and explaining whether these standards are applied consistently or inconsistently to each major.

3d

Dimensions of Critical Thinking

1 Belief

Beliefs are convictions that we are willing to act on. Traditionally, a *belief* about something becomes *knowledge* about something when there is proof or certainty that the "something" is true.

Beliefs may be abandoned in the face of conflicting evidence. In that respect, they are like hypotheses. However, their psychological impact is different. The holder of a belief is expected to *act* consistently with that belief; the person who proposes a hypothesis is not expected to act in any particular manner at all.

Beliefs initiate many persuasive arguments because they trigger critical thinking. You distinguish your beliefs from competing ones and then propose logical systems to support what you presuppose. Justification of a stand for or against abortion, capital punishment, euthanasia, or any other debatable issue stems from beliefs held as articles of faith. A belief then proceeds to more or less informed opinions and finally to arguments using sophisticated inductive and deductive reasoning patterns. The same process applies to less obvious and unprovable assumptions, such as the uniformity of nature of Heisenberg's uncertainty principle. Indeed, the process is so common that it often goes unnoticed. Yet the beliefs from which logical reasoning, analysis, and argument originate are irreplaceable. Without beliefs such as ethical and scientific postulates, for example, philosophers, scientists, and writers would be unable to theorize, suggest practical applications from hypotheses, or speculate about anything.

2 Hypotheses and Theories

As already noted, having a hypothesis is not likely to prompt a person to act in any particular way. **Hypotheses** and **theories** are the assumptions you use when you reason, think, or calculate. Although often unidentified and taken for granted, they are the starting point for most reasoning and research. It is important to identify and evaluate any assumptions you imply in your writing.

There is no clear-cut distinction between a hypothesis and a theory. Generally, a hypothesis is a more tentative, less critical assumption than is a theory. A theory is usually the product of more evidence and greater deliberation. You can call a hypothesis a "hunch," whereas a theory is more an informed guess.

3 Facts

Claiming that something is a "fact" is often equivalent to claiming that it is "true." The person making such a claim is using persuasion based on the special status that facts have in our culture: They are deemed better than theories. The writer who has "facts" to support his or her conclusion will usually persuade the reader.

When used carefully, facts should refer to that which is verifiable: Someone else will confirm it under the same circumstances. Usually, verifiable facts involve empirical evidence—that is, evidence we perceive through our senses.

Factual statements are often made in quantifiable terms. Most of the time you think of facts as immutable truths, statements that represent reality directly and that form the core of what you claim to know about the world. You accept—without much argument—that "The sun is 93,000,000 miles from earth" or that "If the U.S. President is unable to govern, the Vice President assumes all official duties." But these are factual statements only because someone has, in some way, verified them.

Generally, factual statements fall into one of three categories, depending upon the type of verification. Some factual statements are easily confirmed by **personal observation;** others are factual generalizations based on **statistics;** and others are documented by second- or third-party sources considered **authorities** on a subject.

Writers arguing for a position are likely to make one of the following claims about the so-called facts they use to support their argument:

1. My research indicates that X is true.   (personal observation)
2. Generally, research in the field confirms that X is true.   (factual generalization)
3. It is well accepted by authorities in the field that X is true.   (appeal to authorities)
4. All right-thinking people agree that X is true.   (nonfactual statement)

You should be very careful in weighing the credibility of any such claims and sources.

One particular type of reported fact that claims special persuasive power is **statistics.** Statistics originally meant the collection and tabulation of data concerning the state. Today statistics refers to any data recorded, organized for easy interpretation, and reported as factual evidence to support various hypotheses or speculations or used to argue for the correctness of decisions. It has gained special status because its use of numbers makes it seem precise and scientific.

The most common sources of facts are authoritative materials, such as publications (newspapers, periodicals, and books of various kinds—especially reference books); news programs on television and radio; laws; and recognized authorities (for example, research doctors on medical issues or elected officials on campaign issues). Often you accept statements from authoritative sources as factual because time does not allow you to test everything you hear or read. When you hear a newscaster report that a hostage was released in Lebanon or read that "O. Henry" was William Sidney Porter's pseudonym, that the Xi is a three-hundred-mile-long river in southeast China, or that Abraham Lincoln was President of the United States from 1861 to 1865, you are trusting the accuracy and reliability of various authorities. Again, careful scrutiny is important.

3d
ct

To enhance your capacity for critical thinking and logical reasoning, you need to become an informed reader and take the time to discern how information is stated and what perspectives are implied in any text. To read better, evaluate more carefully, and write competently, you must learn to recognize what the parts of a text are and how these parts are related to one another and to the complete text. You also need to learn about various patterns of reasoning (for instance, inductive versus deductive) and how writers sometimes create logical fallacies by ignoring these patterns (see **9b**). Chapter 4 defines and discusses structured, logical reasoning in detail. It also links the types of reasoning and rational thinking that everyone does to the tools that logicians have proposed and the forms that writers use.

Exercise 2

Sometimes beliefs show up in the most unusual places and often sound more like reasoned theories or factual statements than beliefs. Read the following definition of *belief,* and separate the subjective assertions from any hypotheses and objectively factual statements. Then write your own definition of belief.

To believe is to think, in one very limited sense of the latter versatile verb. To believe that beauty is truth is to think that beauty is truth. To believe so is to think so. The two verbs are thus interchangeable before *that* and *so,* but they diverge elsewhere. We can think hard, but we cannot believe hard. We can believe something, but we cannot think something. Grammar forbids. . . . to believe something is to believe that it is true; therefore, a reasonable something is to believe that it is true; therefore a reasonable person believes each of his beliefs to be true; yet experience has taught him to expect that some of his beliefs, he knows not which, will turn out to be false. A reasonable person believes, in short, that each of his beliefs is true and that some of them are false. I, for one, had expected better of reasonable persons.

W. V. Quine, *Quiddities*

ARGUMENTATION
AND REASONING

Argument: The claim that one proposition or conclusion is a likely or certain consequence of other propositions or premises.

Argumentation: The art of influencing an audience, through reasoning and other appeals, to believe or act as the writer wants the audience to believe or act.

Implicit argument: An argument that lies behind another, more obvious purpose, such as explaining, defining, describing, or informing.

Explicit argument: A direct statement to an audience of a writer's perspective and of the writer's intention to use logical reasoning to advance that perspective.

Proposition: Informally, a statement of fact. Formally, an assertion in which the subject term is affirmed or denied by the predicate term; this assertion is judged true or false in the course of the argument.

Conclusion: The proposition that an argument seeks to support or prove.

Premise: A proposition that supports a conclusion.

Chain of reasoning: A linked series of arguments in which a conclusion of one argument stands as a premise in a subsequent argument.

Argument in Reading and Writing

When you read and analyze texts, you are actually looking for the conviction or thesis that a writer holds and for the ways in which that writer urges you as the reader to accept the thesis. Writing is a complementary process of taking a position and supporting it with evidence so that readers will accept your point of view. Thus, whatever text you read or whatever writing assignment you face, you will find that all writing is argumentative because all writers create prose from their individual perspective.

Although our discussion in this section centers on writing, the information applies equally to critical reading. To analyze what you read *and* to write persuasive texts, you need to understand argumentation and logical reasoning and how they promote informed skepticism—that is, an approach that questions and examines ideas rather than taking them at face value. Informed skepticism—the essence of critical thinking—prepares you to read beyond a literal level and to draft and revise with greater success.

4 b

Defining Argument

An **argument** is a line of reasoning that presents a set of **propositions,** including **premises** and a **conclusion,** that claim that the premises support the conclusion. In narratives, the conclusion is the writer's *theme* (stated directly or indirectly) and the premises are the descriptions, implications, and consequences of the characters' actions. Other types of writing persuade with emotional appeals, informed opinions, and convincing evidence. In descriptive and persuasive writing, for example, the conclusion represents the writer's perspective, and the premises often link facts with appeals to readers' emotions or self-interest.

Whether they take the form of speeches or written texts, arguments contain certain well-defined features. For one, all arguments have **content.** That is, an argument proposes evidence to support a position; the position is made more or less persuasive by the strength of that evidence. Persuasive arguments move from agreed-upon basic positions to a conclusion that the writer hopes the audience will accept. The clearer these arguments, the more persuasive they are likely to be.

In written arguments, you cannot make points with vocal emphasis, gestures, and visual animation. Instead, you set up a dialogue with an imagined audience and rely on reasoning, evidence, and other persuasive means to get that audience to accept your position as sensible. Without immediate responses from an audience, you have to ask yourself the same questions you ask when you read: *What evidence is needed to make the position effective?* and *What would the probable criticisms of the argument be?*

1 Implicit Arguments

Written arguments abound. You find them in obvious sources, such as newspapers, journals, history books, and philosophical treatises, as well as in somewhat less obvious sources, such as government reports, memos, letters, advertisements, instructional manuals, brochures, and even literature.

If a text does not seem to dispute any specific points, you may not realize at first that it is nevertheless an argument. A description of a scene or an emotion or even a memoir is actually an effort to make readers see that scene, experience that emotion, or relive that event as the writer saw, felt, lived, or imagined it. In such cases, argument may not be the primary goal, and the appeals may be to readers' senses and imagination. But even descriptions and narratives contain **implicit arguments,** which ask readers to agree with the description or to believe that the story could have happened the way it is told. Notice, for example, how Lincoln Steffens's obvious purpose in the following passage is to describe his college experience, but his unstated argument is that students learn best when they take control of their education.

> I listened attentively to the first introductory talk of Professor William Cary Jones on American constitutional history. He was a dull lecturer, but I noticed that, after telling us what pages of what books we must be prepared in, he mumbled off some other references "for those that may care to dig deeper."
>
> When the rest of the class rushed out into the sunshine, I went up to the professor and, to his surprise, asked for this memorandum. He gave it to me. Up in the library I ran through the required chapters in the two different books, and they differed on several points. Turning to the other authorities, I saw that they disagreed on the

same facts and also on others. . . . I called on Professor Jones for more references. He was astonished, invited me in, and began to approve my industry, which astonished me. I was not trying to be a good boy; I was better than that; I was a curious boy. He lent me a couple of his books, and I went off . . . to read them. They only deepened the mystery, clearing up the historical questions, but leaving the answer to be dug for and written.

4b
ar

The historians did not know! History was not a science, but a field of research, a field for me, for any young man, to explore, to make discoveries in and write a scientific report about. I was fascinated.

Lincoln Steffens, "I Go to College"

Implicit arguments also underlie apparently straightforward explanations. Your stated intention may be to inform your readers about a product, mechanism, project, or technical situation, but your implied thesis argues for following your procedures or for agreeing with your interpretation. For example, Zenon Pylyshyn uses the term *artificial intelligence* as a bridge to argue implicitly that computers have intelligence:

Using the term *artificial intelligence* gives recognition to the fact that studies of symbolic processes in computer science, and the attempts to understand that elusive quality known as "intelligence," are, at some level, inseparable. This recognition, which has indirectly been responsible for much misunderstanding and criticism, is, in fact, fundamental to the integrity of the field, since a pillar of the artificial intelligence field is the belief that tasks requiring what we would call "intelligent action," can, to some extent, be studied independently of such organisms as humans and the way in which they perform such tasks. In addition to shedding light on these tasks, as well as the class of processes capable of dealing effectively with them, research in A.I. has produced techniques and working systems for dealing with areas previously considered the sole province of human intelligence.

"Artificial Intelligence Systems"

Exercise 1

Identify the claims implicitly argued in the following paragraphs.

1. Good sense is of all things in the world the most equally distributed, for everybody thinks himself so abundantly provided with it, that even those most difficult to please in all other matters do not commonly desire more of it than they already possess.

René Descartes, *A Discourse on Method*

2. John and Mary fall in love and get married. They both have worthwhile and remunerative jobs which they find stimulating and challenging. They buy a charming house. Real estate values go up. Eventually, when they can afford live-in help, they have two children, to whom they

are devoted. The children turn out well. John and Mary have a stimulating and challenging sex life and worthwhile friends. They go on fun vacations together. They retire. They both have hobbies which they find stimulating and challenging. Eventually they die. This is the end of the story.

Margaret Atwood, "Fiction: Happy Endings"

3. We must rely on our scientists to help us find the way through the near distance, but for the longer stretch of the future we are dependent on the poets. We should learn to question them more closely, and listen more carefully. A poet is, after all, a sort of scientist, but engaged in a qualitative science in which nothing is measurable. He lives with data that cannot be numbered, and his experiments can be done only once. The information in a poem is, by definition, not reproducible. His pilot runs involve a recognition of things that pop into his head. The skill consists in his capacity to decide quickly which things to retain, which to reject. He becomes an equivalent of a scientist, in the act of examining and sorting the things popping in, finding the marks of remote similarity, points of distant relationship, tiny irregularities that indicate that this one is really the same as that one over there only more important. Gauging the fit, he can meticulously place pieces of the universe together, in geometric configurations that are as beautiful and balanced as crystals. Musicians and painters listen, and copy down what they hear.

Lewis Thomas, "A Trip Abroad"

2 Explicit Arguments

In contrast to implicit arguments and simple persuasive statements, **explicit arguments** state their argumentative purposes directly and use appeals to reason, not pure emotion. (See Chapter 9 for information on persuasion.) Although all arguments involve persuasion, many formal written arguments structure groups of *propositions* so that one proposition from the group is claimed as a consequence or *conclusion*. The writer structures the other propositions as the *premises* or grounds for accepting that conclusion. (*Proposition* and *premise* are generally interchangeable terms.) The arguer also asserts or implies that all the propositions are relevant to a central issue, the topic or question on which the argument rests.

Propositions and Conclusions

Propositions are expressed in **assertive** sentences (sentences that declare a position); **non-assertive** sentences—such as questions, commands, or exclamations—are neither true nor false and do not figure when you evaluate written arguments. The query *Will you fix sushi for dinner tonight?* neither asserts nor refutes that the family will eat raw fish this evening. Likewise, the command *Just win one for the Gipper!* exhorts support rather than affirms or denies anything. But

Eating sushi leads inevitably to salmonella infections and *We can't win ball games if we don't get a seven-foot center* assert concepts that can be designated as true or false.

Propositions are the **premises** and **conclusions** in an argument that are affirmed (judged true) or denied (judged false). Simple assertions, even if they have different grammatical form, can express the same proposition. For example, these two sentences mean the same thing even though their wording differs:

> Lee trusts Mary.
>
> Mary is trusted by Lee.

When searching texts for their premises and conclusions, you will likely find that the argument has several generalizing sentences: sentences that assert a concept and set up subsequent premises. But you will also find many more sentences that support those generalizations with specific evidence.

Assertive sentences figure as the basic elements of most persuasive discourse because they shape premises into logical arguments. That is, they take positions that can be supported or refuted.

Exercise 2

Identify the premises in the following passages. One sentence does not necessarily equal one premise.

1. Everyone's seen a Western. Most people like them, some do not, but no American and few in the world can escape their influence. (Will Wright, *Six Guns and Society*)

2. All great scientists have used their imagination freely, and let it ride them to outrageous conclusions without crying "Halt!" (Jacob Bronowski, "The Reach of Imagination")

3. Many years ago, mathematicians and logicians were confounded by a certain paradox for which their intellectual habits could produce no solutions. The paradox, which had been known for centuries, is easily stated in the following way: A Cretan says, "All Cretans are liars." If the statement is true, then it is also false (because at least one Cretan, the speaker, has told the truth). We have a proposition, in other words, that is both true and false at the same time. . . . Bertrand Russell and Alfred North Whitehead solved this paradox in their great work, published in 1913, *Principia Mathematica.* They called their solution The Theory of Logical Types, and it, also, may be easily stated: A class of things must not be considered a member of that class. Or, to quote Russell and Whitehead, "Whatever involves *all* of a collection must not be one of that collection." And so, a particular statement by one Cretan about all of the statements made by Cretans is not itself to be considered part of what he is talking about. It is of a different logical type, a different order of things. (Neil Postman, "Confusing Levels of Abstraction")

4 c

4c
ar

Connecting Premises and Conclusions

Whether you are reading someone else's writing or evaluating your own, you can easily spot individual assertions. The question is how to tell a premise from a conclusion or identify the links that connect them. Usually, the answers are either in certain transitional words or in the context.

1 Key Connective Words

Texts frequently contain words that signal which propositions are premises, which are conclusions, and how the premises relate to the conclusion. Words such as *consequently, moreover, so,* and *therefore* signal conclusions; words such as *because, should,* and *since* signal premises. The following table contains many of these common transitional words.

Connector Words for Arguments

Key Words for Conclusions	Key Words for Premises
accordingly	all (this) is (that)
all things considered	as illustrated by
apparently	because
beyond a doubt, beyond question	for
	given (that)
clearly	if
consequently	inasmuch as
entails that	in view of
hence	on the ground that
implies that	should
it follows that, seems clear that	since
	suppose that
it would seem (that)	we can deduce from
obviously	we can infer from
points out that	
proves that	
that being so	

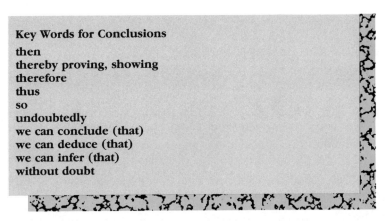

Key words allow you to identify the parts of arguments because they overtly state the proposed connections between the premises and conclusion.

Premises and conclusion connected by *so:*

Premise/evidence	Connector	Immediate conclusion
I don't want to be a doctor, and live by men's diseases; nor a minister to live by their sins; nor a lawyer to live by their quarrels.	*So,*	I don't see there's anything left for me but to be an author. (Nathaniel Hawthorne)

Conclusion and premises connected by *because:*

Immediate conclusion	Connector	Premise/evidence
[Ezra Pound] was a marvelous critic	*because*	he didn't try to turn you into an imitation of himself. He tried to see what you were trying to do. (T. S. Eliot)

Remember, a conclusion may follow the premises, as it does in Hawthorne's assertion, or precede the premises as it does in T. S. Eliot's statement.

Exercise 3

Using key connective words as clues, identify the premises and conclusions in the following passages.

1. It is illogical to reason thus, "I am richer than you, therefore I am superior to you," "I am more eloquent than you, therefore I am superior to you." It is more logical to reason, " I am richer than you, therefore, my property is superior to yours," "I am more eloquent than you, therefore my speech is superior to yours." You are something more than property or speech.

Epictetus, Discourses

2. In modern society power rests extensively on persuasion. Such reverse incentives as flogging, though there are law-and-order circles that seek their revival, are in limbo. So, with increasing affluence, is the threat of starvation. And even affirmative pecuniary reward is impaired. For some, at least, enough is enough—the hope for more ceases to drive. In consequence, those who have need for a particular behavior in others resort to persuasion—to instilling the belief that the action they need is reputable, moral, virtuous, socially beneficent or otherwise good. It follows that what women are persuaded to believe about their social role, and more important, what they are taught to overlook are of prime importance in winning the requisite behavior. They must believe that consumption is happiness and that, however onerous its associated toil, it all adds up to greater happiness for themselves and their families.

John Kenneth Galbraith, "The Higher Economic
Purpose of Women"

3. There was once a lion who was too lazy to go out and hunt for his food, so he decided to use his wiles to feed himself by pretending to be sick. When the other animals came to see him, he invited them into his cave, grabbed them, and ate them.

Nearby, a fox sat and observed the animals entering but saw none leaving. When he went to pay his respects to the lion, the fox remained at the cave entrance.

"Come in closer that I may see you," said the lion. "No," replied the fox. "I see many tracks entering your cave, but none leaving."
Moral: Wise people carefully observe what goes on around them and thus avoid danger.

Aesop's Fables

2 Context

Even in an explicit argument, all the premises may not be directly stated but must be inferred from the text. Sometimes premises are omitted because they are commonly accepted or because stating them

directly might offend the audience. At other times unnecessary information or unstated connections may obscure the arguments. A little
common sense will help you figure out which assertion is the conclusion and which the supporting premise. For instance, consider Somer-
set Maugham's assertion about art:

> Art, if it is to be reckoned as one of the great values of life, must
> teach men humility, tolerance, wisdom, and magnanimity. The value
> of art is not beauty, but right action.

By asking yourself what word would connect Maugham's two statements and which statement supports the other, you can infer which
statement is the conclusion, which the premise, and the causal connection that joins them.

Premises and conclusions connected by inference:

Immediate conclusion	Inference	Premises/evidence
Art, if it is to be reckoned as one of the great values of life, must teach men humility, tolerance, wisdom, and magnanimity.	{*since*}	The value of art is not beauty, but right action.

Writers who omit propositions and premises or cause their audience to puzzle out a conclusion are arguing from **enthymemic** arguments, a rhetorically powerful form of argumentation. Enthymemic
reasoning, discussed in the next chapter, can be most persuasive if
the audience accepts the suppressed propositions as true. But such
arguments lack the conclusive nature that valid deductive arguments
possess.

4d

Chains of Reasoning

Most texts rely on chains of reasoning that set up several successive
arguments in support of a final conclusion. Chains of reasoning occur
when a conclusion in one argument becomes the premise of a subsequent argument. In the example that follows, Martin Luther King, Jr.,
first defines "just laws" as morally defensible and "unjust laws" as morally and socially indefensible. He immediately turns his conclusion
against segregation into a premise for his subsequent argument for civil
disobedience.

4d
ar

Conclusion/premise	Inference/ connector	Conclusion/second premise
So segregation is not only politically, economically, and sociologically un-sound,	*but*	it is morally wrong and sinful.

		Conclusions become premises
Conclusion	**Inference/ connector**	**Second premise**
So I can urge men to obey the 1954 decision of the Supreme Court	*because* *and*	(Restated as positive) it is morally right,
Conclusion		**Second premise**
I can urge them to disobey segregation ordinances	*because*	(Restated as negative) they are morally wrong.

Exercise 4

Using your understanding of propositions and chains of reasoning, iden-tify the premises, conclusions, and connections in the following pas-sages. Remember, you'll have to "read between the lines" to find the assumed propositions in some passages.

1. "If you move I strike, and if you do not move I strike."

Rudyard Kipling, "Rikki-Tikki-Tavi"

2. During the school period the student has been mentally bending over his desk; at the University he should stand up and look around. For this reason it is fatal if the first year at the University be frittered away in going over the old work in the old spirit.

Alfred North Whitehead, *The Aims of Education*

3. Everyone who deals with children these days has heard the dictum that children need to be loved, must be loved. But even to those who like them most, children are not always a joy and delight to be with. Often they are much like older people, and often they are exasperating and irritating. It is not surprising that there are many adults who do not like children much, if at all. But they feel that they ought to like them, have a duty to like them, and they try to discharge this duty by acting, particularly by talking, as if they liked them. Hence the continual and

meaningless use of words like *honey, dearie,* etc. Hence, the dreadful, syrupy voice that so many adults use when they speak to children.

John Holt, How Children Fail

4. The recently rediscovered insight that literacy is more than a skill is based upon knowledge that all of us unconsciously have about language. We know instinctively that to understand what somebody is saying, we must understand more than the surface meanings of the words; we have to understand the context as well. The need for background information applies all the more to reading and writing. To grasp the words on a page we have to know a lot of information that isn't set down on the page.

E. D. Hirsch, Cultural Literacy

5. Sherlock Holmes had been bending for a long time over a low-power microscope. Now he straightened himself up and looked round at me in triumph.

"It is glue, Watson," said he. "Unquestionably it is glue. Have a look at these scattered objects in the field!"

I stooped to the eyepiece and focussed for my vision.

"Those hairs are threads from a tweed coat. The irregular gray masses are dust. There are epithelial scales on the left. Those brown blobs in the centre are undoubtedly glue."

"Well," I said laughing, "I am prepared to take your word for it. Does anything depend upon it?"

"It is a very fine demonstration," he answered. "In the St. Pancras case you may remember that a cap was found beside the dead policeman. The accused man denies that it is his. But he is a picture-frame maker who habitually handles glue."

Arthur Conan Doyle, "The Adventure of
Shoscombe Old Place"

INDUCTIVE AND

DEDUCTIVE

REASONING

Induction: A reasoning process in which the premises provide some, but not irrefutable, evidence for the conclusion. Induction is typically used in arguments concerned with empirical matters (that is, the real world).

Induction by enumeration: A form of induction claiming that since the previously observed members of a class have a particular characteristic, every member of that class that will ever be observed must have the same characteristic. A complex form of enumerative induction, **statistical induction** derives conclusions about populations from evidence of a representative sample; the conclusions are usually stated in terms of probabilities.

Deduction: A reasoning process in which the premises are claimed to provide irrefutable evidence for the conclusion. Deductive arguments are usually concerned with a limited set of items and need have no relation to empirical facts.

Validity and soundness: Deductive arguments are evaluated by the possible relationships between the premises and conclusion; a proper deductive

48

argument is valid. Inductive conclusions are usually
evaluated by how they conform with accepted
empirical fact; a good inductive conclusion is sound.

Categorical proposition: A proposition containing a
subject term, a **predicate term**, and a **quantifier**
(that is, "all," "some," or "no"). It is concerned with
the relationship between the subject class and the
predicate class.

5a
idr

Syllogism: A form of deductive argument in which
the conclusion is inferred from exactly two premises,
one major and one minor. A **categorical syllogism**,
the standard form of the syllogism, contains two
premises and a conclusion, all of which are categorical
propositions. A **disjunctive syllogism** contains a first
premise stating alternatives, a second premise denying
one of those alternatives, and a conclusion asserting
the remaining alternative. A **hypothetical syllogism**
contains two conditional premises (that is, "if . . .
then") and asserts a conditional conclusion. A **mixed
hypothetical syllogism** (that is, *modus ponens* or
modus tollens) contains one hypothetical premise and
one premise that affirms or denies something about
the antecedent or consequent of the hypothetical
premise, and a conclusion that asserts the consequent
or denies the antecedent.

Enthymemic reasoning: A rhetorical rather than
logical form of reasoning resulting in an **enthymeme**,
which exploits an audience's assumptions about an
issue (as well as the writer's credibility and the text's
reasoning patterns) to create a persuasive argument.

5a

Patterns of Logical Reasoning

Induction and **deduction** are the two basic patterns of logical reasoning that writers use to structure their judgments and to convince
others to accept their perspectives. A popular belief about induction
and deduction is that they create order where none previously existed.

In fact, applying inductive and deductive reasoning to a text makes evident the order already present. If that order is faulty, induction and deduction are dependable tools for identifying the text's oversights.

Inductive and deductive reasoning patterns take the various propositions (the *premises*) asserted in a text, along with any factual evidence supporting these premises, and present them in sensible, connected patterns. The two patterns are evaluative tools, not absolute yardsticks of truth. Each pattern claims that its premises should be accepted, either because the conclusion incorporates all of its supporting premises *(induction)* or because the premises point directly to the conclusion *(deduction)*.

5a
idr

Induction and Deduction Patterns

Inductive Reasoning	Deductive Reasoning
First premise/ instance or observation	Major premise (A is B)
Second premise/ instance or observation	Minor premise (B is C)
Nth premise/ instance or observation	
Conclusion based on generalization common to all instances or observations	Conclusion based on distribution of terms in major and minor premises (A must be C because the premises permit no other assertion)

Perhaps, after you have tested a conclusion or gathered more evidence, you will confidently claim the conclusion as valid and reasonable. You may, on the other hand, reject it or accept another one as more convincing, or you may replace one schematic line of reasoning with a better one. Whatever the outcome of your analysis, your ability to identify the elements of an argument and to recognize that some arguments and their conclusions present more convincing possibilities than others relies on the logical reasoning processes known as induction and deduction.

5b

Inductive Reasoning

Inductive reasoning grows out of what you learn and what you experience in real life. If you are driving and your car begins to sputter and stall, and the gas gauge is nearly on empty, you assume that you are running out of gas. You head toward the gas station, reasoning inductively from your observations (the gas gauge is on E) and your previous experiences (cars without gas sputter, stall, and eventually stop) to the conclusion that to continue driving you have to refuel, even though there may be other causes for your car's poor performance.

Inductive reasoning is usually based on practical knowledge. Hence, the more you observe through reading, study, investigation, and experience, the more likely you are to recognize recurring relationships and the more confidently you can assert probable conclusions about events, persons, or ideas. Because induction is a practical form of reasoning, it is all too easy to ignore its subtleties and find yourself making unfounded assertions, which logicians call the fallacies of *post hoc, ergo propter hoc* and hasty generalization. (See **9b** for a list and discussion of informal fallacies.) Careful examination, however, may well indicate that you were too quick to leap from specific instances to a generalized conclusion. Prejudice and intolerance represent the most extreme forms of jumping to unwarranted conclusions from insufficient information.

Exercise 1

Identify the inductive arguments in the following passages.

1. A recent survey of people who had colds asked whether they had taken Dr. Feelgood's Magic Elixir. More than 80 percent of the people responding said that their colds went away within five days of taking this elixir.

2. According to the Warren Commission Report on the assassination of President John F. Kennedy, 2.3 seconds are required to operate the rifle that killed Kennedy. Kennedy's alleged assassin, Lee Harvey Oswald, is alleged to have fired three shots within 5.6 seconds or less. Oswald could not be Kennedy's assassin because he could not have fired his rifle three times within 5.6 seconds.

3. The decline in return for a college degree within the last generation has been substantial. In the 1950s, a Princeton student could pay his expenses for the school year—eating club and all—on less than $3,000. When he graduated, he entered a job market which provided a comfortable margin over the earnings of his agemates who had not been to

college. To be precise, a freshman entering Princeton in 1956, the earliest year for which the Census has attempted to project lifetime earnings, could expect to realize a 12.5 percent return on his investment. A freshman entering in 1972, with the cost nearing $6,000 annually, could expect to realize only 9.3 percent, less than might be available in the money market. This calculation was made with the help of a banker and his computer, comparing college as an investment in future earnings with other investments available in the booming money market of 1974, and concluded that in strictly financial terms, college is not always the best investment a young person can make. (Caroline Bird, "Where College Fails Us")

1 Induction by Enumeration

The most obvious form of inductive reasoning is **induction by enumeration,** or the claim that because all members of an observed class have a certain property every member of that class must have that property. This argument follows the form

All observed A's are B's.
Therefore, all A's must be B's.

The "enumeration" can be anything from simple counting—that is, inferring a conclusion from a series of observed phenomena—to complex statistics. For instance, you can reason in the following way:

DATA:	The first Venusian I saw had three eyes.
DATA:	The second Venusian I saw had three eyes.
DATA:	The third Venusian I saw had three eyes.
DATA:	Every Venusian I've ever seen had three eyes.
CONCLUSION:	Therefore, even though I haven't seen every resident of Venus, I contend that all Venusians have three eyes.

Your conclusion is not irrefutable—it could be discredited at any moment by new, contrary evidence—but it is **sound,** the term used to describe a dependable inductive argument.

Akin to enumeration is **analogy,** the use of data that are not absolutely identical. This type of inductive analogy follows the general form

All A's observed in one context have the property B.

Therefore, a particular unexamined A in a similar
context will also have the property B.

By convention, if you limited the conclusion of the Venusian example to assuming only that a fourth as yet unseen Venusian will have three eyes, you would have been arguing by inductive analogy.

You should scrutinize arguments supported by inductive evidence, not to prove that the arguments are necessarily unsound or invalid, but to test their strength. Ask yourself, *Is the record sufficiently complete? Does my conclusion cover all the instances or only most of them? Is there an exception to the enumerated class?*

2 Statistical Induction

Government, medical, and technical reports rely heavily on a complicated form of inductive reasoning known as **statistical induction.** Statistical induction asserts that because a sample of a general population has certain properties, the whole population probably has those same properties *in the same proportions* as the sample. This argument follows the general form

All observed A's have the property B.
Therefore, all A's probably have the property B.

Inductive reasoning based on statistical induction underlies most arguments for AIDS counseling and for appeals for increased funding for drug research or therapies to prevent or lessen the impact of various ailments.

Reasoning by statistical induction poses some problems. For one, if your sample is too small, you cannot draw reliable conclusions. By the same token, you can bias your statistics by asking biased questions, ones designed to elicit a certain response. Understanding induction means that you will be less likely to accept statistical reports on faith, and more likely to appreciate a conclusion based on large numbers of phenomena.

Exercise 2

Identify the general type of inductive reasoning in the following passages.

1. Obviously, the real work revolution won't come until all productive work is rewarded—including child rearing and other jobs done in the home—and men are integrated into so-called women's work as well as vice versa. But the radical change being touted by the *[Wall Street] Journal* and other media is one part of that long integration process: the unprecedented flood of women into salaried jobs, that is, into the labor force as it has been male-defined and previously occupied by men. We

are already more than 41 percent of it—the highest proportion in history. Given the fact that women also make up a whopping 69 percent of the "discouraged labor force" (that is, people who need jobs but don't get counted in the unemployment statistics because they've given up looking), plus an official female unemployment rate that is substantially higher than men's, it's clear that we could expand to become fully half of the national work force by 1990.

Gloria Steinem, "The Importance of Work"

2. It has long been assumed that a diet low in saturated fats (meaning mostly animal fats) can reduce the risk of cardiovascular disease. Direct evidence for this assumption, however, has been scarce. Such evidence is now provided by a study made at a veterans' hospital in Los Angeles. The study shows that the incidence of cardiovascular disease in a group of 424 veterans with a diet high in unsaturated fats for eight years was 31.3 percent, whereas a control group of 422 men with a normal diet high in saturated fats had a cardiovascular disease rate of 47.7 percent.

"Science and the Citizen," *Scientific American*

3. "I've always reckoned that looking at the new moon over your left shoulder is one of the carelessest and foolishest things a body can do. Old Hank Bunker done it once, and bragged about it; and in less than two years he got drunk and fell off of the shot tower, and spread himself out so that he was just a kind of a layer, as you may say; and they slid him edgeways between two barn doors for a coffin, and buried him so, so they say, but I didn't see it. Pap told me. But anyway it all come of looking at the moon that way, like a fool."

Mark Twain, *The Adventures of*
Huckleberry Finn

3 Applying Inductive Reasoning

You can infer conclusions from data in several ways.[1] Suppose, for example, that you attended a banquet where the menu included salad with choice of dressing, fried whitefish or broiled salmon, and dessert. The next day you and many of the diners are ill with nausea, diarrhea, and overall weakness. When you contact several of your fellow sufferers, you find that one of them had salad with Italian dressing, whitefish and cake. Another had salad with blue cheese dressing, whitefish, and pie. A third had salad with Italian dressing, whitefish, and no dessert, and a fourth had no salad, whitefish, and no dessert. You

1. The methods described here are three of the five canons of inductive inferencing that John Stuart Mill describes in his *System of Logic*. Mill and subsequent logicians call these three the method of agreement, the method of disagreement, and the joint method of agreement and disagreement.

notice a consistency: Each person you interviewed who became ill had eaten the fried whitefish for dinner.

Person/Instance	Antecedent Circumstances			Effect
	S/Dre	*WhF*	*Sal*	
1	Ita.	X	—	S
2	B.C.	X	—	S
3	Ita.	X	—	S
4		X	—	S

It is reasonable to infer that circumstance "WhF" (whitefish) contributed to the effect "S" (becoming sick). As is true with any inductive argument, your survey does not *conclusively* prove that the whitefish was the culprit but does suggest a strong probable cause.

To have all data conveniently pointing to one conclusion, as they do in this example, is a rare occurrence. More frequently, the participants share two or more circumstances, leaving you with at least two possible reasons for the observed phenomenon. For instance, suppose that all the participants you survey who became ill ate both the whitefish and salad with blue cheese dressing. Although you cannot safely assert that the fish alone or the dressing alone caused the illness, you can reasonably eliminate the salmon and dessert.

Exercise 3

Identify the antecedent circumstances and the effects in the following examples; then discuss what, if any, consistencies and inconsistencies exist in the situations. Decide whether the consistencies and inconsistencies strengthen or weaken the inferences you draw by induction.

1. To test the truth of the old quotation, "Paint the dungeon red and drive the prisoner mad," he [Faber Birren] painted the walls, floor and ceiling of his room vermilion, curtained the windows with red glassing, and installed red light bulbs. He spent weeks in this room and found the red surroundings only made him feel "Quite comfortable and cheerful."

Felix Morrow, introduction to *Color Psychology and Color Therapy* (Faber Birren)

2. There is a deep-red dye, well known to analytical chemists, which is used for the analysis of aluminum and to a lesser extent for beryllium and which, on paper, seemed to meet our requirements. This dye is known by the trade name "aluminon," and by the chemical name aurintricarboxylic acid, or simply ATA. In the first test of ATA we injected mice with enough beryllium salt to kill them within a few days. We then injected half the animals with a small dose of ATA and left the others untreated. The results were dramatic: virtually every animal treated with ATA survived and lived on normally, while all of the untreated animals

died. We have repeated this experiment with hundreds of animals of different species, with the same high degree of protection.

Jack Shubert, "Beryllium and Berylliosis"

3. The earliest theoretical attempts to describe and explain the universe involved the idea that events and natural phenomena were controlled by spirits with human emotions who acted in a very humanlike and unpredictable manner. These spirits inhabited natural objects, like rivers and mountains, including celestial bodies, like the sun and moon. They had to be placated and their favors sought in order to ensure the fertility of the soil and the rotation of the seasons. Gradually, however, it must have been noticed that there were certain regularities: the sun always rose in the east and set in the west, whether or not a sacrifice had been made to the sun god. Further, the sun, the moon, and the planets followed precise paths across the sky that could be predicted in advance with considerable accuracy. The sun and the moon might still be gods, but they were gods who obeyed strict laws, apparently without any exceptions, if one discounts stories like that of the sun stopping for Joshua.

Stephen W. Hawking, *A Brief History of Time: From the Big Bang to Black Holes*

Evaluating the Soundness of Inductive Reasoning

1. Are your observations limited to verifying the hypothesis you started with? Have you ignored observations because they don't fit your position instead of basing your conclusion on all your observations on an issue?

2. Are your observations relevant to your conclusion—that is, have you drawn your conclusion from evidence directly tied to it?

3. Are there obvious exceptions that challenge your conclusion? Can you think of an incident, event, or instance sufficiently different from those you observed so that it can't fit your generalization?

4. How large was the sample? Were there enough observations to justify the generalized conclusion?

5. Was the sample representative? That is, was it typical of the broader population?

6. Were the questions stated objectively? Did they allow a variety of opinion on one topic or only a certain response on the issue?

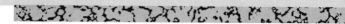

4 Limitations of Inductive Reasoning

Induction forms the mainstay of much scientific writing. The scientific method—the process of gathering data, drawing inferences from the data, and presenting hypotheses based on those data and inferences—is, after all, supremely inductive in spirit. Yet writers who rely on inductive reasoning cannot claim that they have conclusively proven a point, but merely that they can confirm an assertion based on their numerous observations or experiences. No matter how many observations you make or how extensive your experience is, any argument you pose based solely on induction can be decisively refuted by only one counterexample.

If someone finds just one Venusian who *does not* have three eyes, you cannot conclude fairly that all inhabitants native to Venus have three eyes. But you can conclude the negative claim: Any one- or two-eyed Venusians make the assertion *not all Venusians have three eyes* impossible to refute. With this "ironclad" conclusion, you have entered the area of deductive reasoning.

5c

Deductive Reasoning

When Sherlock Holmes re-evaluates for his flabbergasted admirers how he solved a crime, Arthur Conan Doyle's detective maintains that everyone must accept his perspective because he has supported it through clear, deductive reasoning. If you pick Holmes's logic apart, his persuasiveness, like his claim to deduction, looks suspiciously like bravado and induction.

Conan Doyle wants to persuade you that Holmes is credible, and so he labels Holmes's reasoning processes as deductive. Deductive reasoning is given a special "status." You, as a reader and writer, benefit if you understand what deductive reasoning actually is, how it works, and how it can be an effective writing strategy.

Although everything you read or write has premises that provide *some* grounds for accepting a conclusion, only arguments based on deductive reasoning claim to provide *conclusive* grounds for doing so. An argument reasoned deductively is considered correct, or **valid**, when the premises and conclusion are so tightly related that if an audience accepts the premises as true it must also accept the conclusion. The argument is considered **invalid** when errors in its form make it illogical or fallacious. You can see in **9b** that some informal fallacies are little more than flawed deductive arguments. The crucial element in evaluating the validity of deductive arguments is understanding the relationships between the propositions and the conclusion.

1 Categorical Syllogisms

The oldest form of deductive argument is the **categorical syllogism.** The categorical syllogism is an argument based on the relationships of its premises, called **categorical propositions.** Categorical propositions, which resemble simple assertive sentences, have two "terms," or classes, that have a specific relationship in the proposition. In the assertion *Lawyers are educated professionals,* the proposition is about the relationships of the class "lawyers" to the class of persons known as "educated professionals." Categorical propositions, unlike hypothetical propositions or alternatives, assert that certain things are unequivocally true: All or some members of the subject class either *are* or *are not* members of the predicate class. In actual texts, sentences vary structurally, and you will seldom find propositions explicitly stated one to a sentence. Because they can be awkward to use and apply to ordinary language, categorical syllogisms are of more historical than practical interest.

2 Disjunctive or Alternative Syllogisms

Another type of syllogism, the **disjunctive syllogism** or "either . . . or" syllogism, depends not on the relationship of three categories but on considering alternatives. Consequently, it is easier to use in contemporary textual arguments. Consider, for instance, this contention: Either financial speculator Bunker Hunt is a secure billionaire, or he is in financial trouble. Recent news reports imply that Hunt's financial empire is shaky. Therefore, you can conclude that he is financially strapped. Broken down into its constituent parts, this disjunctive syllogism states two components as alternatives in the first premise,

either A or B,

denies or contradicts one of the alternatives in the second (categorical) premise,

not A,

and draws a valid conclusion by asserting the remaining alternative,

therefore, B.

Notice that, even though the alternatives asserted in the first premise may both be true, the premise does not assert that both are categorically true.

3 Hypothetical or Conditional Syllogisms

Another syllogism, the pure **hypothetical**, or **conditional, syllogism,** is more interesting and common than either categorical or disjunctive syllogisms because you compare contingent ideas more often when you argue than you compare categories or simple alternatives. Hypothetical syllogisms depend on propositions linked by the **logical connectors** "if" and "then" in the same way that disjunctive syllogisms depend on alternatives linked by "either" and "or." Some "if . . . then" propositions express causal connections, as when you argue that "If southern California gets relief from the heat and substantial rain, then there is a good chance firefighters can contain the Glendale fires." Others predict a result based on a sequence of related events, as when you argue that "If the university reconsiders its recent appointment of an unqualified administrator to its branch campus, then it will lose face with the faculty, staff, and community leaders."

When you use a second proposition to affirm or deny an "if . . . then" clause, you are setting up a hypothetical syllogism. A pure hypothetical syllogism relates its two "if" (or **antecedent**) clauses and two "then" (or **consequent**) clauses to arrive at a contingent (possible) conclusion. The first premise and the conclusion share antecedents; the second premise and the conclusion share consequents. For example, the argument that

1. If it rains heavily, then the umpire will call for the tarmac to cover the playing field.
2. If the umpire calls for the tarmac to cover the playing field, then the ball game will be called off.
3. Therefore, if it rains heavily, then the ball game will be called off.

fits the form

> If A, then B.
> If B, then C.
> Therefore, if A, then C.

and is a valid hypothetical syllogism.

Other hypothetical syllogisms mix conditional premises with categorical ones. These **mixed hypothetical syllogisms** are among the easiest to identify and use in contemporary texts. When you argue that

1. If southern California gets relief from the heat and substantial rain, then there is a good chance that firefighters can contain the devastating fires in Glendale.
2. Southern California temperatures dropped by 20 degrees yesterday, and the weather forecast is for rain.
3. Firefighters have a good chance of containing the Glendale fires.

you are affirming the "if," or antecedent, clause and have, therefore, an argumentative form that logicians call *modus ponens* (literally, "affirming the antecedent"). It has the valid form

> If A, then C.
> A
> Therefore, C.

A final type, called *modus tollens,* denies the consequent (or "then") clause, as when you argue that

1. If the university reconsiders its recent appointment of an unqualified administrator to its branch campus, then it will lose face with the faculty, staff, and community leaders.
2. The university will not do anything that might cause it to lose face with the faculty, staff, or community leaders.
3. Therefore, the university will not reconsider its appointment.

Expressed formally, this argument follows the pattern

> If A, then C.
> Not C.
> Therefore, not A.

Exercise 4

Identify the premises and conclusions found in the following passages, and, using the information summarized above, determine what form the syllogisms fit. Discuss whether they are valid or invalid, reasonable or unacceptable.

1. No movie actors are practicing attorneys, but all practicing attorneys are people of good legal sense. It therefore follows that no movie actors are people of good legal sense.

2. All child abusers are maladjusted individuals, many of whom suffered themselves in abusive, broken homes. Therefore, many maladjusted individuals are the products of abusive, broken homes.

3. All political action aims at either preservation or change. When desiring to preserve, we wish to prevent a change to the worse; when desiring to change, we wish to bring about something better. All political action is then guided by some thought of better or worse. (Leo Strauss, *What Is Political Philosophy?*)

4 Applying Deductive Reasoning

A working knowledge of the formalities of deductive reasoning allows you to read analytically. An introductory text in logic, or a course in basic logic, would give you a good foundation. Furthermore, knowing deductive reasoning patterns can help you channel your own thinking in logical rather than emotional directions. You will be more persuasive, for example, if you can rationally present the evidence and set up the premises and conclusions.

5 Limitations of Deductive Reasoning

When you analyze a work to discover its reasoning patterns, you should rightly be impressed by the writer's facility with deductive reasoning and syllogistic argument. But in working out what the syllogisms are and whether they are valid and sound, you soon discover their limitations. First, categorical syllogisms are fixed at three propositions and follow technical patterns that are not intuitively obvious. Second, you will probably find in much of your reading that explicitly stated conclusions and premises are the exception rather than the rule; writers want to engage you actively in their arguments by filling in their probable concepts, unstated assumptions, and incompletely stated arguments from your knowledge of the subject area or topic. Writers who omit propositions and premises or oblige their audience to puzzle out a conclusion are arguing not from formal logic but from **enthymemic** reasoning, a rhetorically more powerful form of argumentation discussed on pages 62–63.

Finally, when you do locate the propositions, premises, and conclusions and structure them into clear syllogisms, the argument may well be valid by the technical rules outlined here and yet still not be acceptable. A good example is the Cheshire Cat's rationale to Alice in Lewis Carroll's *Alice in Wonderland:*

"How do you know I'm mad," said Alice.
"You must be," said the Cat, "or you wouldn't have come here."

This rationale meets the criteria for a valid syllogism, but few would accept it as sound or reasonable, for it rests on the Cheshire Cat's unspoken major premise that people who come to Wonderland's forest must be mad—a premise Lewis Carroll intended his audience to see as humorous.

6 Comparing Induction
and Deduction

Knowing something about inductive and deductive reasoning adds to your store of strategies for reading, thinking, and writing critically. Some discussions of induction and deduction presume that these reasoning patterns are simple opposites: that inductive reasoning argues from specific circumstances to generalities, and deductive reasoning argues from generalities to specific circumstances. Such explanations also suggest that a valid or logically correct argument by definition meets the standards of argument form and of common sense. These classic definitions are oversimplified and misleading. You could set up a *valid* deductive pattern that is not sound because it will not stand the test of common sense. For instance, if you argue that

1. All unmarried men are unhappy.
2. My brother is unmarried.
3. Therefore, my brother is unhappy.

your reasoning would be suspect because the initial assertion is not factual.

5d

Enthymemic Reasoning

Most arguments rely on reasoning patterns that do not explicitly state their premises and conclusions. This type of reasoning, called **enthymemic reasoning,** encourages readers to assume the omitted propositions. The core of this reasoning pattern, an **enthymeme,** is an abbreviated or incompletely stated argument. Its premises are typically implied assumptions about human nature, actions, and their consequences, or information that most people accept as probably or commonly accurate. For example, the argument *All Presidents are Commanders in Chief; therefore, George Bush is Commander in Chief* assumes that you will supply the information: *George Bush is currently President.*

Although enthymemes rely directly on formal patterns such as syllogisms, enthymemic reasoning is more widely used in all types of writing, including scientific texts, than fully stated inductive or deductive reasoning. Enthymemic reasoning invites readers to take part in creating the argument and is more persuasive for most audiences. Audiences willingly accept certain propositions as common wisdom and are grateful not to be bored by the obvious.

5d
idr

The question you should ask yourself when you are determining whether to include a premise or omit it is this: *Can I safely presume that my audience knows this information and accepts it as true?* If your answer to either part of this question is no, state the proposition openly.

Exercise 5

Make a list of the assumptions you find in the following perspectives. Then determine whether the perspectives are more or less persuasive because you can state their assumptions.

1. All students oppose the sanctions levied against Sigma Chi fraternity for its discriminatory comments about women; therefore, all female students oppose the sanctions.

2. Inanimate objects are classified scientifically into three major categories—those that break down, those that get lost, and those that don't work.

Russell Baker, "The Plot Against People"

3. If President Bush's September [1989] address to the nation on the topic of drugs can be taken as an example of either his honesty or his courage, I see no reason why I can't look forward to hearing him declare a war against cripples, or one-eyed people, or red geraniums. It was a genuinely awful speech, rooted at the beginning in a lie, directed at an imaginary enemy, sustained by false argument, proposing a policy that already had failed, playing to the galleries of prejudice and fear. The first several sentences of the speech established its credentials as a fraud. "Drugs," said Bush, "are sapping our strength as a nation." "The gravest domestic threat facing our nation," said Bush, "is drugs." "Our most serious problem today," said Bush, "is cocaine." None of the statements meets the standards either of minimal analysis or casual observation. The government's own figures show that the addiction to illegal drugs troubles a relatively small number of Americans, and the current generation of American youth is the strongest and healthiest in the nation's history.

Lewis H. Lapham, "A Political Opiate: The War on Drugs Is a Folly and a Menace"

[Note: Lapham's first sentence is a type of hypothetical syllogism.]

THE WRITING

PROCESS

DISCOVERING

IDEAS

Writing process: The production of writing. It includes **inventing, drafting, revising,** and **editing** and is influenced by such factors as **context, purpose, audience,** and the writer's **experience** with the subject.

Subject: A general area of inquiry from which a writer selects an issue or **topic.**

Writer's block: A temporary impasse that writers experience when they apply unsuitable criteria to their writing, set unrealistic goals, or lack the knowledge or the strategies for planning and revising their work.

Brainstorming: An unstructured technique for generating ideas about a topic whereby a writer creates an unedited list of any and all ideas associated with the topic.

Mapping or clustering: A visual form of brainstorming. A writer starts with a central idea or topic and records, through free association, any thoughts, specific details, or implications linked to that idea or topic.

66

Asking journalistic questions: A structured technique to generate ideas about an issue, considering its *who, what, when, where, why,* and *how.*

Keeping a journal: A technique for generating ideas about a topic. A writer thinks on paper, recording the development of his or her reflections and observations.

Freewriting: A technique of private, nonstop writing used to generate topics and ideas about those topics. A writer puts down whatever topics, reactions, random impressions, or thoughts come to mind.

6a

di

6a

Understanding the Writing Process

Writing would be a simple task if it were a set procedure that could be performed the same way every time. All you would have to do is follow carefully a standard list of required steps. However, writing is not a single procedure but several intertwined operations.

Writing is first and foremost an intellectual activity. It combines intuition with deliberation and inspiration with perseverance. It is the "hard copy" of your thinking: your thoughts committed to paper. At the same time, writing is a discovery process. You seldom come to a writing task with all the necessary ideas—and only those ideas—neatly set out. By the time you draft a final version, some ideas you started with may have completely disappeared, and others may have been entirely transformed. Still other ideas, which you had not even considered before you started to write, may become central to your text. This discovery of meaning as you write has to do with how you interpret or narrow a **general subject** by finding a **topic**—a particular issue within that subject—and how you define your perspective on that topic.

Writing is also a social process. It puts one mind (the writer's) in touch with other minds (those of the **audience**) and creates a community. Inexperienced writers often react defensively when someone criticizes their writing; they interpret negative comments as attacks on their intellects, not on their texts. In truth, anyone who takes the time to review your writing closely is telling you that your words deserve serious attention. Far from being confrontational, the exchange confirms the social and cooperative aspects of the writing process.

There is a close connection between your **purpose,** or objective, in writing and how you compose. A grocery list, for example, is a memory device. Its purpose is plainly informative, and you, as its writer and primary audience, can fill in any missing details as you shop; it does not have to be "right" the first time. A job application letter, on the other hand, is both an important communication and a one-time opportunity. You will want to rewrite the letter several times to get it just right. Your purpose is both to inform and to persuade. As you write, you select information and weigh alternative means of presenting that information. Your own purpose—to secure the job—and your audience's purpose—to match your credentials to their needs—guide your writing process as you decide exactly what to say about yourself and how to say it.

6a
di

The **writing process** is a way of exploring possibilities, realizing your concerns and hopes, working out problems, presenting arguments, and entertaining, informing, and persuading others. To be done well, writing, like all activities, requires practice. Rewriting is not a punishment but rather a chance to gain greater proficiency, flexibility, and understanding.

Like reading and reasoning, writing is a recursive process: It involves overlapping and repetition. You begin with an idea, write it down quickly, then perhaps draw a blank on what to write next. As you expand what you have just written, you detect a related idea to pursue. You jot down this idea and hit another blank or, perhaps, race on to elaborate a thought. You are moving recursively toward your goal, a first draft.

The process varies with individuals and with tasks. You may be the type of writer who dashes off a first draft before you can write its introduction. Or you may slave over an introductory paragraph, unable to proceed until that paragraph is clear. You may see yourself as the type of writer who composes hurriedly and never looks back, only to discover that, in fact, you are constantly rereading what you have written, changing words and rethinking ideas.

Most writers revise as they write because most writers rethink as they write. You will find that you are revising when you look over your first paragraphs, mark intriguing ideas for further thought, and discard other ideas. Each pass lures you to reconsider your topic, audience, or purpose and leads you to another draft.

You may find that you like reading what you have written. But such satisfaction comes only occasionally. Much more often, your writing will strike you as not even close to what you wanted to say. When you rework it, you may discover that the idea you have struggled with either comes quickly or becomes even more obscure. You continue developing, supporting, and clarifying what you think and may repeat the process several times. It is a process of reasoning, drafting, rethinking, and revising.

Exercise 1

List fifteen or more of your beliefs about writing. They can range from "Writing is something my secretary will do for me" to "Good writing is grammatically correct writing" and "Writing as a profession must be the hardest job anyone could have." Get together with two or three of your classmates and compare lists. Try to think of reasons for and against each belief. Then write a paragraph defining one belief and explaining whether that belief is a misconception, a realistic estimation, or a unique interpretation of how writers compose.

6b
di

6b

Coping with Writer's Block

Everyone who writes faces times when the normal frustrations of expressing ideas temporarily freeze the writer into **writer's block.** Thoughts do not come promptly or seem to evaporate before they are written down or emerge as jumbled sentences, unclear words, false starts, and disconnected or repetitious fragments. The anxiety that produces writer's block usually stems from several inappropriate assumptions.

When these often conflicting assumptions become inflexible rules, they immobilize the writing process. You can lessen your anxiety about writing if you realize what causes this anxiety and what remedies you can apply. Both the apprehension about writing and the struggling to write are part of your natural mental processes. The anxiety is your creative "edge," so to speak. When you feel blocked, your intellect is actually gauging what material you need or what freedoms or restrictions the task implies.

You handle writer's block by rejecting some of your beliefs, adopting different writing strategies, and reconsidering the project at hand, its audience, and your purposes. Ask yourself or your audience exactly what the topic is, what the text needs to accomplish, what the audience expects, what information is primary and what secondary, and when a final draft is due. If you lack information about a subject, find out about it. (See Chapters 44 through 47 for suggested research strategies.) If you know too much about a topic, focus on what interests you, what you think your audience would most like to learn about it, or what you are sure they do not know.

False Assumptions That Can Block the Writing Process

- Writers always have a plan or outline, composing an introduction first, then the body, and finally a conclusion.
- Writers never plan what they are going to write.
- Writers always fashion grammatically correct sentences.
- Writers never experiment with language before correcting grammatical errors.
- Writers always edit their ideas, sentences, and words as they write.
- Writers never change the way they write; they always use the same strategies.
- Writers can compose only when they are inspired and must wait for inspiration to strike them.
- Writers who "know their stuff" always write easily, without needing to revise; only people who can't write have trouble composing.

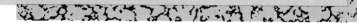

Also try changing some of your habits or beliefs. If you write in a noisy room, seek out a quiet place. If you tend to procrastinate, try breaking the pattern: Start writing the minute you get a project. You may be surprised at how inventive your first thoughts are. Or try breaking the project into smaller steps and setting realistic deadlines for each step.

Above all, *write.* Expect frequent stops and starts and dry periods punctuated by spurts of writing. Write uncritically at first, and wait until you finish writing to analyze your prose. By using this approach, you will be less likely to accept assumptions that limit your writing.

Exercise 2

Writer and teacher Donald M. Murray has suggested that "writing is easy; it's *not* writing that's hard." For him, simplicity is receiving a thought that strikes like a lightning bolt; "what's hard is to create conditions that cause lightning to strike—morning after morning—and then wait for the bolt to hit." List your ideal conditions for writing. Consider what assumptions about writing underlie your list. Then write a paragraph or two stating those assumptions clearly and explaining whether they stand up as realistic assessments of writing or are just myths about the process.

6c

Four Components of a
Writing Process

Writers generally follow a sequence of **inventing, drafting, revising,** and **editing.** Each of these activities is discussed in more detail in the chapters indicated:

6c
di

INVENTING: Choosing a subject (Chapter 6)
Generating ideas about a subject (Chapter 6)
Narrowing a subject to a topic (Chapter 7)
Shaping ideas about a topic (Chapter 7)

DRAFTING: Formulating a thesis statement (Chapter 8)
Developing thesis statements (Chapter 8)
Arguing persuasively (Chapter 9)
Writing a first draft (Chapter 10)

REVISING: Revising drafts (Chapter 11)
Rethinking paragraphs (Chapter 12)

EDITING: Correcting grammar and punctuation (Chapters 14 through 37)
Revising for style (Chapters 38 through 43)
Proofreading (Chapters 11 and 29)

Inventing, a prewriting stage, involves generating ideas and giving them preliminary shape. Writers who simply fill in set formats (such as laboratory reports, questionnaires, prescribed outlines, or examination questions) spend less time generating ideas. But writers who compose papers assigned in college (from undergraduate essays to doctoral dissertations), company reports, business analyses, memorandums, or legal briefs must come up with ideas and provide a structure for their ideas and analyses.

Drafting includes proposing a thesis statement, deciding on your tone, and outlining your ideas—everything involved in actually writing your first draft. Most writers find that inventing and revising take the most time, whereas composing a first draft takes the least.

Revising includes rethinking the content, organization, and level of formality of your text. For most writers, revising is the key to success because they know that the process of rewriting gives their work originality and substance. You have to finish drafting before you can judge your ideas adequately and revise them.

Editing includes checking your revised draft for misspellings, grammatical confusion, clichés, or incoherence and putting your text in a format suitable for your audience. You have turned your ideas into text; now you are turning text into presentable copy.

Remember, though, that dividing this complex process into four components is merely a convenient way to give it form. There is no single proper composing method. Each writing situation dictates its own methods and its own series of integrated activities, which you, like all writers, repeat at different points during your writing.

6d

Inventing

Inventing is the crafting you do *before* you write a first draft. It includes choosing a topic or issue, discovering what you think about that topic, narrowing and shaping your ideas into a plan, and framing a generalization that sets forth your perspective on your topic and suggests how your text will present your perspective and ideas.

1 Choosing a Subject and a Topic

Sometimes you may feel the urge to write; in that case, you choose the subject and terms for the writing. More often, though, someone else will dictate a general subject, and you will need to figure out a topic or approach to that subject. For example, as a college student, you write to fulfill assignments. These tasks seem straightforward—the instructor sets the **writing context,** or situation, and the assignment limits your options. You may be told the subject area, the purpose (for example, to inform, persuade, or affect the readers), the audience (that is, the instructor), and the required guidelines (such as format, length, tables, figures, illustrations, quotations, and references). For instance, a narrow assignment may require you to "Evaluate the economic factors that led Napoleon to invade Russia." The *context* is clearly educational: Your *purpose* is to persuade an already knowledgeable *audience* that you can interpret factual information in a way that shows how the information is now part of your academic *experience.*

CONTEXT: History or political science course
SUBJECT: Evaluation of factual material

PURPOSE: Persuasive—convincing the audience that you
            grasp the facts, can interpret them, and can cause
            the audience to accept your view

            Informative—interpretation of factual material

AUDIENCE: History or political science instructor who
            assigned the topic

GUIDELINES: Quotations, citation of figures, and possibly
            references to other evaluations

6d
di

A broader, more challenging assignment requires that you choose your own topic and write on it. If you have trouble thinking of a topic, here are some general strategies to try.

Strategies for Identifying Subjects and Topics

- Consider a subject you know little or nothing about and research it. To begin to identify one topic within it, ask yourself why you want to know more about that subject. Another topic could be what your audience would find interesting about it.

- Consider a subject you know a great deal about. Choose as a topic why a person unfamiliar with this subject would want to know about it.

- Read about a subject with which you are somewhat familiar and identify the major debate in that area. Research the various sides of the debate.

- Consider a subject about which you have strong opinions, and question your reactions—that is, ask why you hold your particular view, then consider the opposite view. By entertaining the idea that your opinions are changeable, you introduce yourself to both a new topic and a new perspective.

- Consider a subject ordinarily charged with emotion or, conversely, one ordinarily discussed only in logical terms. Or consider an event that you or someone close to you experienced. Does the emotional subject have a logical side and the logical one an emotional side? Is there a way to describe the emotional event using detached logic?

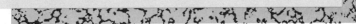

In situations when you are left essentially on your own to find your subject, topic, purpose, and guidelines, you should still be careful to consider what your audience might expect. All you really know is that the audience is your instructor—and that is a good place to begin this type of writing project. (Audience is discussed in Chapter 7.) Consider your audience's stated and unstated purposes. For instance, if a college economics instructor has required you to write on consumerism, an essay detailing why you have trouble balancing your checkbook may not satisfy the spirit of the assignment. The economics professor expects an analysis of economic trends and will accept a review of your spending habits only if your evaluation shows something about the public's general buying patterns. In other words, a college assignment assumes that you will identify an issue and advance and support your opinion on that issue with reasoning and specific evidence.

6d
di

2 Generating Ideas About a Topic

Starting to write is never a simple task. Merely knowing a general subject or identifying a topic within it does not guarantee that your writing experience will be easy or your prose effective. To communicate well in writing, you need to stimulate your mind and make an assignment your own. You should start by collecting ideas about a topic.

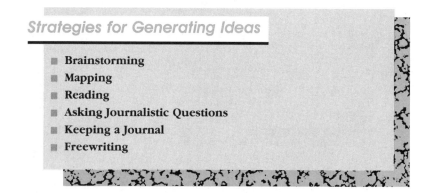

Strategies for Generating Ideas

■ Brainstorming
■ Mapping
■ Reading
■ Asking Journalistic Questions
■ Keeping a Journal
■ Freewriting

Brainstorming

Brainstorming is an unstructured invention strategy that maximizes free association of ideas. When you brainstorm, you let your mind run wild, registering ideas as they come rather than censoring your thoughts. If several people are working on the same project, brainstorming in a group can open up all sorts of new ideas. One person's insight triggers a different view in another person, whose idea, in turn, suggests something to a third person.

Whether you are listing ideas by yourself or in collaboration with others, brainstorming consists of two basic steps. First, list in single words and phrases whatever concepts come to your mind about a topic, no matter how obvious, obscure, pedestrian, or weird the comments or ideas might seem. (If you are working in a group, designate someone to record the ideas that others shout out.) Let one idea suggest another and another and another. Avoid writing full sentences or editing the list. Don't be discouraged if the list seems chaotic or your first thoughts seem to be superficial observations, clichés, ramblings, or repetitions. Force yourself to list more. Eventually, you will move beyond the obvious.

Second, organize your list so you can use it like a subject index in a library catalog. Look for related groups of words, phrases, and ideas. Sort the listed thoughts into patterns. Then write summarizing generalizations that tie sets of ideas together. Remember that the individual entries within a group need not be in any specific order, but they must all relate in some way to your unifying generalization. Set aside ideas that do not seem to fit conveniently anywhere, or create headings for them. Check to see which groups have the greatest number of entries and which have the fewest. Ask yourself questions to stimulate more ideas about the entries on the shorter lists, or discard any groups about which you have little information or interest. Expect the unexpected. Locked in your mind are original ideas—some that you are not aware of yet—that can give your writing depth and interest.

Exercise 3

The following is an incomplete list of ideas created around the general subject of *advertisements*. Organize the list into patterns, and add ideas where needed. (Remember, some of the ideas may not fit anywhere.)

—male/female stereotyping
—men aggressive, in control
  interested in nothing but sex
  soliciting human bodies
  sex, sex, sex
—billboards
  window displays
  sides of buses
  girl watching
—Violence against women
—TV, magazines, films
  sculptures
  murder, burglary

—Women as sex objects, at
  home

Strengths of argument:
  Bo Derek
  Whistler's mother
  avocado commercial
  Black Velvet
  Marlboro Man

—Is the argument strong?
  Why do I believe this?

6d
di

Mapping

Mapping is a visual form of brainstorming that helps you explore a central topic by picturing your thoughts as ideas linked or clustered together in a pattern somewhat like a spider's web. Start with a main idea—the topic of your text— and place it in a circle in the middle of a page. Then, as specific ideas occur to you about that topic, write each one down, draw a circle around it, and connect it to the main idea or loop it with a line to a closely related topic. Each idea represents one subtopic of your central idea. Write down any specific examples the subtopic suggests and draw lines connecting them to the subtopic. Each of these examples extends a subdivision of your main topic.

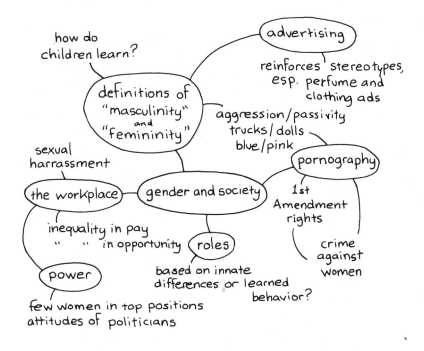

Mapping, like brainstorming, lets loose your creativity. Freely associate every idea you can, no matter how tentative or far-fetched each may seem at first. When you have filled the page with connected ideas, subtopics, and examples, go back and decide—given your intended audience and purposes—which ideas look most profitable for your assignment. As you look over your diagram, you will notice another advantage of mapping: Your ideas are already grouped around specific subdivisions. The subtopic that sparked your thinking can become the generalized heading for that group of ideas, although you may have to restate it. (For more on levels of generality, see **12b.**)

Exercise 4

Read a magazine article, a story, a short report, or a chapter from a textbook, and create a map for an essay that will explain your reaction to your reading. Your main topic could be your response to the writer's perspective, a related idea that the text suggests to you, or even your responses to the text's general subject.

6d
di

Reading

Reading, the most common structured means that students and professionals use to gather new ideas, helps you both before and after you begin a project. You may be asked to analyze or react to something you have read. In this case, you have to read systematically, look for clues to content and perspective, reread for full understanding, annotate, and record salient factors. You may also want to consult other sources after writing a first draft if you need additional factual support or want to review conflicting positions. (See Chapter 2 for critical reading strategies.)

Even when reading is not a stated part of a writing assignment, you are still influenced by what you read or observe. For instance, an essay or story may have impressed you so much that you refer to its main points in a later assignment. Because reading influences your thinking, the more you read, the larger your store of ideas.

Another type of reading—doing library research—also influences your thinking and perspective on a subject. Before you begin a formal research project, you investigate books, articles, reports, or newspapers for ideas that stimulate your thinking or expand your knowledge about your topic. Chapter 44 discusses this type of investigative reading in detail.

Asking Journalistic Questions

Another structured way of generating ideas is to ask yourself the questions you would expect editorial writers or journalists to ask.

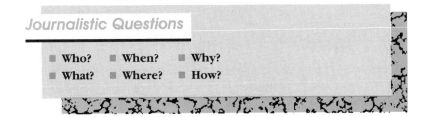

Journalistic Questions

- Who?   ■ When?   ■ Why?
- What?   ■ Where?   ■ How?

Though they are a suggestive way to generate ideas, journalistic questions do not fill in everything. Single-word answers, for instance, lead to superficial discussions in the same way that single-word responses only help reporters compose lead sentences to news stories but do not provide explanations or motives. You have to probe a topic by refining these questions. Propose several responses to each—even if your first responses seem preposterous—and venture tentative answers. These preliminary questions should lead you to related questions and, in turn, to more investigation and ideas. After you have specific reactions to work with, you can organize them and write the text. (For general organizing patterns, see Chapter 7; for specific patterns of development, see Chapter 12.)

**6d
di**

Elaborated Journalistic Questions

Chronological Order

Questions suggesting *narrative structure*	What started the event? Where could this event happen? What would prevent it from happening again? What conditions must exist for it to happen again?

Spatial Order

Questions suggesting *descriptive structure*	What terms best describe this item? What does it look like? Which senses does it appeal to? What is its size, color, and composition? Where is it most likely found?

Climactic and Anticlimactic Orders

Questions suggesting *definition, process, or classification structures*	What definitions are assumed? What other definitions are possible? What clarifies the item's meaning? What are its parts, qualities? How do the parts interact? How are the parts ordered or grouped? What distinguishes this item? How is it used?

Questions suggesting *comparison and contrast structure*	What does it resemble? What differs from it? What analogy fits it best? What does it correspond to? Why is this contradictory? Why is or isn't this so?
Questions suggesting *cause and effect structure*	What are the origins of this? Why could or couldn't this happen? Why should or shouldn't this happen? What consequences are important? How can I bring this about? What influences work here?
Questions suggesting *argumentative structure*	Why should or shouldn't this be so? What are the benefits or drawbacks? What is the recommendation? Why is or isn't this true? Why is this problem a problem? Why is this solution a solution? Why should a reader trust me? Why do I believe this? If this weren't so, what would result?

Expanding the basic *who, what, when, where, why,* and *how* questions can also help you organize your material: In-depth questions suggest ways to structure a discussion. Questions such as "Why did this event happen?" or "What is this event's outcome?" imply a climactic order, such as an evaluative or cause and effect structure. But if questions such as "How did this event happen?" or "Who benefited from the event?" or "How did the setting influence what happened?" spark your interest, you should consider a chronological order, like narration. The more you question yourself and your subject, the larger your list of ideas becomes and the more readily you can find the specific topic that you will want to address.

Exercise 5

Using the questions listed above, formulate ideas for an essay on one of the following general subjects:

Euphemisms	Technical jargon
Psychology of clothing	Destructive criticism
Value of time-sharing condos	Poetry of Robert Frost
Psychic advisers	Terrorism
Manned exploration of Mars	Medicare
Euthanasia	Nuclear power

Keeping a Journal

Few writers remember their every thought. Consequently, many write down their impressions in a convenient place and return to their notes when they need inspiration, confirmation, or additional material. **Writers' journals** are registers of writers' ideas and opinions, and writers who keep journals return to them often, filling in ideas, modifying their notions, and working out their thoughts on paper.

6d
di

The easiest part of keeping a journal is getting started: Just buy a notebook and a pen and begin writing. Your journal writing is private because you are its primary, and perhaps its only, reader. Write out your observations, descriptions, theories, fantasies, experiments with language, and speculations about anything and everything, as well as your reactions to what you read and learn. Journals encourage you to write whatever you please in an informal style, to contend with new ideas, and to reflect on your opinions before you have to present them to a public audience.

Maintaining a journal is harder than starting one because regular writing requires discipline. Keep your journal with you during the day so you can take a few minutes to write in it. Or set aside a definite time for writing. Try organizing your journal into sections. (A notebook you can add paper to helps here.) Make a section for daily events and tasks, a section for recording interesting or provocative statements from others, a section for personal reactions, and a section for academic or professional responses. Try creating headings so that when you write something down you will have a pattern for playing with the idea. Whatever plan works best for you, stick with it. After several weeks' worth of journal entries, you will be intrigued with what you have thought and how many ideas you find.

Exercise 6

Locate in your library several journals and diaries by different kinds of writers. (You may want to look for *The Diary of Anne Frank,* Woody Allen's "Reminiscences: Places and People" (in *Side Effects*), Joan Didion's "On Keeping a Notebook," Lillian Hellman's *Pentimento,* or the notebooks of Charles Darwin, Margaret Mead, or Werner Heisenberg. What seems similar to you about these journals? What is unique about each of them? In your own journal, write your reflections on the values and drawbacks of journals.

Freewriting

Freewriting is just what it sounds like: freely writing whatever comes into your mind without stopping to consider punctuation, spelling, or grammatical constructions. To freewrite, put your pen on the paper and write nonstop for ten, fifteen, up to twenty minutes. Change topics, scribble nonsense sentences, or write "I can't think of what to write" until you think of something to write. If the word you want does not come readily to mind, draw a squiggly line and come back to it when you are through. But don't stop the flow of words and ideas. In freewriting, you are following your writing (and your mind) wherever it takes you rather than forcing yourself to stay with one subject or to pay attention to grammatical correctness.

Such writing may leave you with scrawled notes on several topics and perhaps with a text that does not always make sense. While you freewrite, don't worry about the seeming disorder. You are writing to put down on paper all the ideas churning in your head. You can organize and improve them later.

At the end of a freewriting session, you could have as many as 350 to 500 words. Look over what you have written, pick out a sentence or an idea that interests you, and try another session. You will end up with another 350 to 500 words. If you repeat the exercise, you will have written more than a thousand words in about forty-five minutes—a substantial start on any writing project. Freewriting gives you the opportunity to exercise your writing muscles before any reader's eyes peruse your writing.

6d
di

Exercise 7

Set your alarm for ten minutes and try freewriting on one of the following topics. When you finish, put your writing aside for a day or so. Then return to it, and, without reading what you have previously written, write for another five to ten minutes on the same topic. Compare the two exercises, and list the ideas and perspectives you discover.

1. The matter-of-fact meaning of an event is always or never matter-of-fact.
2. Everyone should know something about biology because . . .
3. Everyone should know something about literature because . . .
4. A college education is primarily for vocational advancement.
5. A college education is primarily for humanistic advancement.

Exercise 8

Choose one of the following general subjects and try a freewriting session for thirty minutes. Then look over what you have written and write a one-sentence statement of your perspective on the subject.

1. Writer's block
2. Students taking required courses
3. Professionals working for a supervisor about whom they have strong feelings
4. Inexperienced writers facing an unpleasant writing project
5. Women being better doctors than men are

7

KEY CONCEPTS

Defining a topic: Identifying a topic or an issue for a writing task.

Narrowing a subject: Limiting a subject area to a defined topic.

Organizing a topic: Organizing ideas into a pattern. The pattern may be based on **chronological order** (grouping by time), **spatial order** (grouping by place), **climactic order** (grouping from the least to the most important), or **anticlimactic order** (grouping from the most to the least important).

Audience: The person or persons who react to, study, or act on a piece of writing.

Evoked (general) audience: The person or persons who eventually read a piece of writing. When directing their work to this audience, writers usually take care to organize clearly and avoid technical jargon.

Identified (specific) audience: The person or persons, known to a writer, who read the writer's

82

work. Specific audiences expect organizational patterns and vocabulary appropriate to their discourse communities.

Audience analysis: How writers pinpoint an audience's needs for and requirements of a text.

Discourse community: A group that by virtue of its cultural, professional, regional, or personal ties shares a common vocabulary and use of language.

7a

Defining a Topic

If you want to write a book, a broad subject such as "the art of fiction writing," "Chinese philosophy," or "fishing in the Great Lakes" may be fine. But for essays, memorandums, and reports, you will have to focus on specific areas or single aspects of the subject. Limiting your subject, restricting the scope of what you are going to write, makes sense for many reasons. First, you don't have enough time to write everything that could be said about a particular subject. Second, audiences usually want writers to get directly to the point, offer a thorough discussion of that point, and provide supplementary sections that an audience can read or ignore. Your "slant" enlivens the writing for your readers because you have given them something new: your interpretation of a clearly defined topic.

7b

Narrowing a Subject to a Topic

The fundamentals of any writing task—situation, purpose, and audience—dictate how you narrow a defined topic. Select the most interesting ideas you have produced using invention strategies. Then take these ideas and see how they match your situation, purpose, and audience. Questions such as those in the box on the next page can guide your thinking about narrowing your topic to workable proportions.

7b
dt

Questions for Narrowing a Subject

Narrowing a subject by using a writer's situation and experience	Why do I care about this subject? What do I know about this subject? What features of this subject do I find most intriguing, important, or disturbing? Why?
Narrowing a subject by using a writer's sense of purpose	Why am I writing on this subject? What perspectives about this subject would persuade me? What change do I want to stimulate by writing about this subject? What salient aspect of this subject excites my interest? If I can present only one circumstance about this subject, what would it be? Why is that circumstance memorable?
Narrowing a subject by using a writer's sense of audience	Why does my audience need to read this work? What would be important about this subject for my audience? What can I assume my readers already know? What impression of myself do I want to leave with this audience? What slant can I give this subject that would seem unique to my audience? What aspect of this subject will my readers identify with? What can I say about this subject that my readers don't already know?

Another way to narrow a subject to a manageable topic is to consider the parts or features of the subject as though each were a single entity. When you examine a subject as a single entity, you look for its distinguishing parts or features. For example, the general subject of *botany* includes such areas as "plant physiology," "taxonomies of plants," "morphology of plant design," and "geographic distribution of plant life." You could take any one of these specific areas and discover dozens of subareas by asking questions about it. "The geographic distribution of plants" is a narrower area than "botany." You might ask: Why do certain similar groups of plants appear in widely separated regions? How do plant seeds and spores travel? What is the impact of introducing nonnative plants into certain regions? If the last subarea interests you, but you need to narrow the topic still further, you might focus on the impact of introducing a specific nonnative plant into a specific region.

7b
dt

Narrowing Subjects: Some Examples

General	Specific	More specific
politics	political influence	the standards for determining the ethical behavior of political leaders
sex	sexual attitudes	the ways advertisers exploit current attitudes toward sex in television commercials
music	rock and roll	justifications for labeling or not labeling rock musicians' albums
athletics	nonprofessional athletes	educational benefits promised by college athletic programs
botany	radishes	significance of studying the reproductive cycle of wild radishes

Exercise 1

Narrow the generality in each of the following quotations to a specific topic suitable for an eight hundred- to fifteen hundred-word essay.

1. There is in us a tendency to judge a race, a nation, or an organization by its least worthy members. (Eric Hoffer)

2. As soon as a child begins to move about and explore, he begins to ponder the problem of his identity. (Bruno Bettelheim)

3. Oh, [advertising] needs for us to do or be many things: workers, technicians, executives, soldiers, housewives. But first of all, last of all, it needs for us to be buyers; consumers; beings who want much and will want more—who want consistently and insatiably. (Randall Jarrell)

7c

Organizing Ideas About a Topic

Undoubtedly, you know—or may be yourself—a person whose desk looks like the aftermath of a typhoon. Often the person who made this chaos knows where to find everything in it; unfortunately, no one else can find anything in the desk.

Chaos in a text can be equally annoying. Therefore, once you have some ideas and have initially limited the subject, turn your attention to organizing your ideas. Writers who are familiar with methods of organizing—who know various ways to structure ideas and the advantages and disadvantages of each—increase their chances of communicating effectively.

Organizing the ideas you have generated is somewhat like taking a vacation: If you don't plan your itinerary, you can end up wandering aimlessly and wasting too much time. The vacation falls apart, and you are discouraged. In the same way, if you launch into a writing project without an organizational plan, your readers will not be able to follow your thinking. After you have considered various ways to organize your ideas, your next steps should be to eliminate unsuitable patterns and to select the beneficial ones.

Be aware that some organizational plans are not useful because, though they fit your material, they may not be suitable for your audience. For example, if you are tracing the history of a theory, it may seem logical to order your discussion sequentially—that is, by the published dates of the research documents you are reviewing—but your audience might gain more from a least-to-most-important type of organization. Before drafting, shuffle your major ideas around until you find the structural patterns that help you express these ideas appropriately.

Once you have rearranged your ideas into groups and given them summarizing headings, you are ready to decide on a plan. If you structure your ideas on a topic into a preliminary plan, you avoid the problem of not being able to start the essay or of writing different beginnings without ever getting to your point. Best of all, a plan helps you avoid just staring at a blank piece of paper.

1 Chronological Order: Ordering Ideas by Time

Chronological order commonly underlies descriptions of processes, experimental procedures, instructions, histories, progress reports, and adages such as

> For want of a nail, the shoe was lost. For want of the shoe, the horse was lost. For want of the horse, the battle was lost.

For such texts, a time sequence dictates how you arrange ideas. Chronological order is an obvious way to make a text coherent because most readers can follow information set out in a time sequence. It is also easy to think of transitional elements to enhance this coherence—for instance, words and phrases such as *before, after; in the first place, in the second place; yesterday, today*; and *subsequently, finally*. Imperative verbs *(put, move, start)* also link events and ideas in an accessible, linear order.

Chronological order has its disadvantages. It can be tedious if every event is listed. You have to limit yourself to details that fit your purpose and switch from a sequential discussion to another type when your purpose and audience dictate. Furthermore, sequencing by time can overemphasize some ideas and shortchange others. An initial event, for example, may have triggered subsequent events or may be only coincidental. Finally, audiences expect informative texts to state major points immediately. Taking them step by step through your thinking can prove so monotonous that they lose the essence of what you are writing.

2 Spatial Order: Ordering Ideas by Position

Another good device for organizing descriptions, procedures, and some definitions is **spatial order,** or arranging ideas by relating them to a geographical plan or the physical space they occupy. Astronaut Neil Armstrong used spatial order in describing the first American moon landing as "one small step for man; one giant leap for mankind." Like chronological order, spatial order has a built-in coherence: It proceeds naturally from top to bottom, from bottom to top, from left to right, right to left, front to back, and so on. Certain transitional words and phrases—such as *here, there, in the front, in the back, moving from left to right, one meter above* or *below,* or *to the east of*—also make spatial organization obvious to your audience.

Spatial ordering has the same disadvantages as chronological order. Too many details can get monotonous if you are not selective about which features you report. You can overemphasize some elements because of their position while slighting others that are critically important to your viewpoint. To avoid this imbalance, introduce other organizational patterns into smaller units within a spatial pattern. Finally, you can lull a reader into inattention by consistently beginning your sentences with an orienting word or phrase (for example, *on the first level, on the second level, on the third level*). Avoid this problem by replacing some of the more obvious connectives.

7c dt

3 Climactic Order: Ordering Ideas from Least to Most Important

Climactic order, or positioning ideas from the least to the most important, is a structure familiar to anyone who has told an exciting story, reported a solution to a problem, or argued a stance. It is best illustrated by Julius Caesar's understatement when he vanquished Gaul: *Veni, vidi, vici,* or "I came, I saw, I conquered." The primary advantage of climactic order is that it grips readers' attention and lures them on to the next section by highlighting previous elements. Furthermore, it is the expected organizational pattern for technical, scientific, or critical audiences, who anticipate that a knowledgeable writer will save the deciding point—the clincher, so to speak—for the end.

However, imposing climactic order on a topic that does not lend itself to such order can prove confusing. Some mechanisms, literary texts, and procedures, for example, demand chronological discussions, or sequential descriptions of their operations, events, and steps, or spatial renderings of their parts, locales, or approaches. Moreover, impatient readers resent waiting until the end of a text to get essential information. Finally, an unengaged audience will not stay with your text to discover your perspective. Begin your text with an intriguing element but not one so absorbing that it eclipses your final idea.

4 Anticlimactic Order: Ordering Ideas from Most to Least Important

Anticlimactic order reverses climactic order by beginning with the most important point and ending with the least. It is a pattern commonly used in newspaper and television news reports, scientific and professional abstracts, some types of technical reports, and certain deftly crafted arguments. For example, the first sentence of an essay by Charles Kenney and Robert Turner on the current generation is this: "The generation of Americans who are now young adults has been, as odd as it sounds, deprived of the adversity that has been so valuable in shaping the American character."

Impatient readers appreciate this ordering because they can get striking material first and skim—or even ignore—the rest of an article or report. However, that very advantage has its drawbacks. Audiences are less inclined to finish long documents with anticlimactic organizations. For this reason, you might want to consider the most-to-least-important organization as unsuitable for many of the texts you have to write.

Exercise 2

Identify the different structuring patterns that Arthur Danto weaves together in the following passage.

To visualize the terrain [outside Gettysburg], draw a vertical line and label it Seminary Ridge. This is where the Confederate Army formed its line, along the crest. They seized it after a heated battle with [General] Buford's forces, which, despite reinforcements, were driven fourteen hundred yards east to Cemetery Ridge. Now draw a line parallel and to the right of Seminary Ridge, only curve it to the right at the top, to form a sort of fishhook. This was the shape of the Union line, indeed called "The Fish-hook," on July 2 and 3 [1863]. (Gettysburg is a dot between the lines, just about where the hook begins its curve.) Where the barb would be is Culp's Hill. Farther back along the shaft is Cemetary Hill. At the eye of the hook is Big Round Top, at a distance of about four miles from Cemetery Hill. About half its height, and upshaft, is Little Round Top. The four hills served as battle towers. The rampart itself slopes to the west to form what is designated a *glacis* in the vocabulary of fortification. It was a formidable defensive position, but Seminary Ridge too would have been a formidable defensive position. "If we could only take position here and have them attack us through this open ground!" [General Robert E.] Lee's chief of artillery, Porter Alexander, recalled having thought. "We were in no such luck—the boot, in fact, being upon the other foot." A defensive war was not what had brought Lee north and onto enemy territory. He had to attack if there was to be a battle.

[General James] Longstreet did not think there needed to be a battle. Standing beside Lee, he surveyed the Union position with his field glasses for a very long time, turned to Lee and said "If we could have chosen a point to meet our plans of operation, I do not think we could have found a better one than that upon which they are now concentrating. All we have to do is throw our army around by their left, and we shall interpose between the Federal Army and Washington [D.C.]. We can get a strong position and wait, and if they fail to attack us we shall have everything in condition to move back tomorrow night in the direction of Washington."

"No," said General Lee—the words are famous and fateful—"the enemy is there and I am going to attack him there."

Arthur C. Danto, "Gettysburg"

Understanding Audience

The claim that writing conveys perspective implies that there is a person—perhaps only you—willing to read what you have written and capable of being informed or challenged by your perspective. Anything you write will be read by someone, whether it is notes on your refrigerator for your roommate or your spouse, instructions for repairs, requests for information, résumés for jobs, or memos. Any writing situation, therefore, presumes a writer with a goal, an audience with stated or unstated expectations, and a text that satisfies—more or less—both the writer's purpose and the audience's demands.

But the complexities of audience analysis far exceed this simple description. Audiences vary from nameless individuals to those we know well and from superficial readers to very demanding ones. Expectations differ from one audience to another; sometimes readers change their expectations midway through your text or presume that you will present something you never intended to say. Understanding that you are writing for a specific type of audience and realizing that an audience influences what you write are, perhaps, the two most important principles to consider as you begin any writing project.

Writer—text—Audience

When you draft, you set out to compose a text whose purpose is to communicate your perspective on a topic. Your audience expects to be informed without having to decipher your ideas, persuaded without being coerced or offended, impressed without being overwhelmed, or entertained without being taxed. Your written text is never the direct transfer of ready-made knowledge—it is not, that is, a snapshot of your ideas. Instead, it is a dynamic interaction between you and your audience in which you, the piece of writing, and your audience meet to create meaning.

One way to visualize the interaction among writer, text, and audience is to see writing as an overlapping process that at different junctures favors you, your audience, or your piece of writing.[1]

**7e
dt**

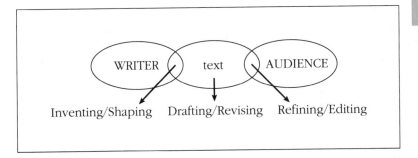

WRITER / text \ AUDIENCE

Inventing/Shaping   Drafting/Revising   Refining/Editing

1 Writer—Inventing/Shaping

You may want to believe that professional writers compose a final, perfect draft dictated primarily by the needs of their intended audiences, and that they compose straight through from beginning to end. But they don't, and you won't either. All writers engrossed in an assignment are more aware of false starts, procrastination, agonizing paralysis, or diffuse overwriting than they are of the dialogue they have entered into with their eventual audience. You explore ideas, approaches, controversies, and reasons through different invention strategies. You gradually discover your meaning, define and narrow your topic, and shape your ideas into a rough draft. When you are inventing and shaping, your attention focuses directly on the ideas in the text and secondarily on your intended audience's needs. At this stage, you will ask yourself—sometimes repeatedly—questions having to do with content: "What do I know?" or "What do I mean?" These questions show how your initial concerns center on your knowledge. Only later do you ask, "Am I making sense?"—a question that focuses on how well you are getting your knowledge across to others.

---

[1]Scott P. Sanders suggests this diagram in his "Toward a Poststructural Audience Analysis" (in press).

7f
dt

2 Text—Drafting/Revising

If you favor your subject matter over your audience or your perspective over its presentation, your work will be poorly designed and ineffective. If, on the other hand, you refine your initial thoughts, make audience a central interest, and revise your draft, your resulting text should be communicative.

As you draft and revise, you assess what you think your audience needs, and you make choices about how best to meet these requirements. You rethink ideas, experiment with different approaches, recast sections, scratch out unproductive parts, and shape productive ones into coherent prose. Drafting and revising open up optional ways to clarify your meaning and adapt your intentions to your audience's requirements.

3 Audience—Refining/Editing

Finally, when you recast sentences, substitute words, and check for grammatical correctness, spelling, and mechanical precision, your audience and their expectations take precedence over the content of your text. Other readers replace you as the audience, and your private dialogue becomes a public exchange in which they now engage.

Exercise 3

Think about the last writing assignment you had to do for a history, science, or literature course. Make a list of what you did to prepare for the assignment, how you went about writing the assignment, and what your reactions were to your instructor's criticisms. Compare your list with those of others. Then write a brief explanation of why your lists were or were not similar.

7f

Determining Audience Types

Whether your purpose in writing is to inform, effect a change, or provoke a response, you need to identify your audience and determine how to adapt your content, organization, style, and tone to fit various audiences and situations. Adapting to an audience's needs requires you to make some assumptions about the relationships various types of audiences can have to you and your topic.

1 General and Identified Audiences

One common way to analyze your audience is to consider all readers as either fictionalized, unknown people or specific, identifiable persons. An **evoked audience,** sometimes called a **general audience** or the **common reader,** is any person who could pick up your writing and read it. This audience brings diverse backgrounds, purposes, and interests to texts as varied as magazine articles and essays, political pamphlets, fiction, advertisements, and historical treatises. When you write for a general audience, you favor your opinions, prejudices, and attitudes about your subject matter over your audience's need for facts. Your intention may be to inform this audience, but it is the information about *your* impressions more than the information they can act on that is important.

7f
dt

If you elevate your beliefs and judgments over your readers' concerns, your audience may entertain your perspective only temporarily. To hold the attention of a general audience, you must kindle their interest by making your perspective compelling. You have to insist that they listen to you, see it your way, and change their minds.

Since you don't know them specifically, you must guess as best you can about what your evoked, or general, audience may want to know and how to capture their interest. Getting other persons to see the significance of your ideas and perspective means trusting that your readers are intelligent and curious and carrying out your writing strategies accordingly. General audiences demand a startling lead, unusual anecdote, or some eye-catching first few lines that will "hook" them into your writing. They also need definitions for specialized terms, concise reasoning, and an assortment of short, specific examples and illustrations. General readers expect a tone that animates the substance of a writer's ideas. They also expect prose that shows your command of a topic and relates your viewpoint to their interests—sometimes a difficult task since you cannot be sure what these individual interests are.

Most of all, general audiences expect to hear your voice—the distinct character that you project or, more accurately, that your readers construct. This voice will come across most effectively if you imagine that you are writing not to a mass of readers, but to one person who has engaged you in an especially animated conversation. By writing to a particular person, real or imagined, you improve the chances that your writing will interest almost anyone who reads it.

Sometimes you know precisely who is going to read your writing, and your knowledge of this **identified,** or **specific, audience** shapes what and how you write. You will be responding to your readers' professional, vocational, and informational needs or perhaps just fulfilling an assignment made by your instructor. In either case, your readers' knowledge limits your purpose. College students, for instance, write to demonstrate their abilities and their grasp of a subject to their instructors. Specialists draft technical reports to guide operators through procedures. Employers in various fields provide manuals to their workers to inform them about benefits.

Even when you have fairly precise information about an audience, you must make assumptions about your readers' goals that are very similar to the guesses you make with evoked audiences. Although you may know your readers' first names, you still have to imagine what they are thinking, what pressures they are facing, how they will react to what you write, and who else is likely to read it.

Exercise 4

Make a list of the audiences you have written for in the last six months and of what you have written. Include every type of writing—even notes passed in class. Determine who the audience was for each text. What traits or needs of your audiences influenced how you wrote a text? What did your audiences understand? What did they misinterpret?

Exercise 5

Read the following passages and decide whether the writer intended to address an evoked audience, a specific audience, or both. Then list the reasons for your answer.

1. Imagine my delight when I spotted your new science-fiction magazine on the newsstands. I have been a fan of yours for many, many years and I naturally wasted no time in buying a copy. I wish you every success in this new venture.

In your second issue I read with interest your plea for stories from new authors. While no writer myself, I have had a time traveler living with me for the past two weeks (he materialized in the bathtub without clothes or money, so I felt obliged to offer him shelter), and he has written a story of life on earth as it will be in the year 5000.

Before he leaves this time frame, it would give him great pleasure to see his story in print—I hope you will feel able to make this wish come true.

                              Patricia Nurse, "One Rejection Too Many"

2. I've never been one for inaction. Everything I've ever felt strongly about, I've done something about. I guess that's why, unable to do anything else, I soon began writing to people I had known in the hustling world, such as Sammy the Pimp, John Hughes, the gambling house owner, the thief Jumpsteady, and several dope peddlers. I wrote them all

about Allah and Islam and Mr. Elijah Muhammad. I had no idea where most of them lived. I addressed their letters in care of Harlem or Roxbury bars and clubs where I'd known them.
    I never got a single reply.

Malcolm X, *Autobiography*

3. Your recent entry put you in the Final Group where we'll find our next millionnaire. Now here's a chance to go for $1,000,000.00 every month for a whole year.   (Publishers Clearinghouse Sweepstakes offer)

7f
df

2 One-to-One and Group-to-Group Audiences

Another way to see your audience is to understand that you can write for yourself, for one other specific person, for a group of persons with similar backgrounds or shared interests, or for a group of persons with dissimilar backgrounds and few shared interests. The trick is classifying your audience.

Students typically write for an audience of one—themselves or their instructors; professionals write for multiple audiences. When you write for yourself, your purposes are often immediate. You write class notes, summaries, or paraphrases so you can remember the information that you will need in order to pass an examination or complete a writing assignment. On the other hand, when you brainstorm for an essay, draft a short story or poem, or write in a journal, you are writing as much to amuse and inform yourself as to remember.

Messages home, business letters, and memorandums are usually written for an audience of one—the person addressed in the message, letter, or memo—although others may, unexpectedly, join that audience. As a student, you are familiar with writing for instructors, who ease some of your concern about writing by furnishing guidelines. For instance, a teacher of a Western civilization course who asks you on an examination whether St. Augustine would support contemporary pro-life or pro-choice positions does not want an essay chronicling St. Augustine's life or discussing his position in theological history, even though you may feel you know this material better. Your knowledge of the teacher's pedagogical objectives determines your purpose, and the specific terms of the question limit the topic and suggest your audience's expectations.

When you write for an audience of many readers, you need to ascertain whether that audience belongs to a **discourse community** familiar to you. As a speaker and writer, you belong to several groups, or discourse communities, who communicate with each other about their outlooks, concerns, or goals in a shared dialect or jargon. As a citizen in a Western democracy, you belong to large-scale discourse communities, which share cultural values, ideological or economic convictions, religious tenets, and social affiliations. As an aspiring professional, you show your familiarity with the particular discourse community by using its specialized terminology, research methods, and standards. You may also belong to discourse communities that include dissimilar people united by a goal such as environmental action or by a common interest such as rock music.

7f
dt

If you are new to a type of writing, such as the academic discourse expected at college, one way to discover how to win your audience's attention is to try to imagine your potential readers' backgrounds, attitudes, and language preferences. Then speculate about how closely these aspects of your audience match what you are familiar with. The closer the identification, the more likely it is that you know your audience's discourse community; the farther apart you are, the more you have to learn about this discourse group in order to communicate with it effectively.

Questions for Analyzing Audience

Questions about background

1. What are my audience's names, (approximate) ages, educational levels, and economic and social statuses?
2. What are this audience's interests and concerns? Are these professional or personal interests? Are they my interests and concerns?
3. What position does my audience hold in relation to my position? (Does my audience include my instructor or fellow students, relatives or friends, supervisors or subordinates, administrators or workers?)
4. What are their political biases, ethical convictions, and moral beliefs? What bearing, if any, do these beliefs have on my topic? What influence, if any, do they have on my approach to my topic?
5. What aspects of my audience's concerns could influence how that audience reacts to my text?

Questions about knowledge

1. Why would my audience be interested in my topic?
2. What does my audience know about my topic? What attitude does it have toward my topic?

3. Do the people in my audience share specialized knowledge, interest, and concerns that relate to my topic?

4. Does my audience share the professional, community, or personal experiences that are part of my topic?

5. What do I want my audience to think of me and of my perspective?

Questions about needs

1. Why do I want my audience to read my text?

2. What do I want my audience to learn about my topic? What attitude do I want my audience to have after reading my writing?

3. How will the individuals reading my writing use it?

4. Does my text include *all* the information my audience needs and *only* the information it needs? What types of overviews, definitions, examples, evidence, or arguments do I need in order to convince this audience to accept my perspective?

5. If others were writing on this topic, what would I want them to say to me as their audience?

7f
dt

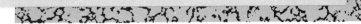

Even though you may not be able to answer all these questions for a given audience, asking them will help you determine where your audience stands in relation to you and your perspective on a topic. Your answers will also help you discover your meaning and thesis (inventing); organize your ideas; integrate evidence and arguments, as well as anticipate and address objections or controversies (drafting/ revising); and select and refine the diction and tone of your text (refining/editing).

Exercise 6

Make a list of the discourse communities you belong to. What characteristics distinguish each of them? Write a brief description of the discourse community you find the most familiar. In your essay, include information about the topics that this community prefers to discuss and the language that it uses.

Exercise 7

Rewrite an essay you wrote at least a year ago for (a) yourself, (b) an audience of one such as a relative or close friend, or (c) a particular discourse community that you define.

7f
dt

Exercise 8

Even though the general topic may be the same, different audiences call for different information and techniques. Using the questions about audience, take one of the following topics and explore how you would address the needs of the various audiences suggested in each topic.

1. Your high school's football coach, a man you believe single-handedly caused your school to lose most of its games, is retiring. How would you write about him (a) in your journal, (b) for your college composition instructor, (c) for your local newspaper, and (d) for a presentation about him at his retirement dinner?

2. Your sister—a newly commissioned lieutenant just graduated from college ROTC—is about to enter an air force training program for missile guidance. How would you write about her (a) to her, (b) to your grandparents, (c) to your college composition instructor, and (d) to your local newspaper?

3. After you studied the crib notes for it, you finally read a long novel (for example, *Moby Dick, War and Peace, Bleak House*) for the first time. How would you write a comparison of the crib notes and the actual book for (a) your best friend, (b) your instructor in an introductory literature course, (c) your classmates in the introductory literature course, and (d) the people attending an open discussion of literature at your local library?

CREATING THESIS STATEMENTS AND OUTLINES

Thesis statement: A generalization summarizing a writer's perspective on an issue. Thesis statements (**theses** or **themes**) can be stated (**explicit theses**) or implied (**implicit theses**).

Working thesis statements: A writer's initial assertions of a perspective. Working thesis statements are commonly modified when writers revise their drafts.

Outline: A general description of main points of a topic, which also summarizes a writer's approach to that topic. **Informal outlines** are loosely constructed lists of proposed divisions and subdivisions of a written work. **Formal outlines** are carefully structured lists that use indentations, Roman and Arabic numerals, and upper- and lower-case letters to distinguish major headings from corroborating details. **Topic outlines** describe primary divisions of a text in single words, phrases, and clauses. **Sentence outlines** describe subdivisions of a text in complete sentences. **Paragraph outlines** summarize each paragraph of a text in single sentences. **Combination outlines** mix elements of topic, sentence, and paragraph outlines.

8a

What Is a Thesis Statement?

The analytical core of a text is your **thesis,** or **forecasting,** statement: It is the central generalization from which you develop your discussion. The thesis statement asserts your attitude toward a topic, summarizes your conclusion, and projects your organization. A basic thesis statement is a bargain with your intended audience: You promise to support a perspective, and, ideally, your readers agree to follow your lead. You owe it to your readers to indicate your position or purpose and to show how you intend to develop that point of view. Your readers, in turn, should temporarily give up their preconceptions about the topic to entertain your perspective. An elaborated thesis statement gives the audience additional information: It tells what steps you will follow in presenting your evidence. But whether your thesis statement is basic or elaborated, your audiences are likely to use it in evaluating your presentation.

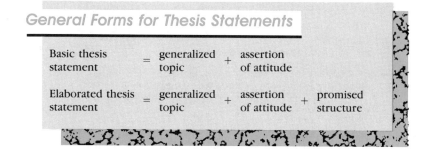

General Forms for Thesis Statements

Basic thesis statement	=	generalized topic	+	assertion of attitude		
Elaborated thesis statement	=	generalized topic	+	assertion of attitude	+	promised structure

Most one-sentence thesis statements have two parts: a topic, usually indicated by the subject of the sentence, and an observation or comment about that topic, usually indicated by the predicate. The topic states the issue that you are tackling; the observation asserts your attitude toward that issue.

Thesis statements can be, but seldom are, rhetorical questions, fragments, or a series of sentences. While rhetorical questions pinpoint the situation or problem that inspired your perspective, they do not define that perspective. However, they can help you formulate a working thesis, and they can also be persuasive, nudging the reader to consider your perspective with increased open-mindedness. For example, Virginia Woolf begins an essay about the writing of biography with a rhetorical question that hints at her thesis:

The art of biography, we say—but at once we go on to ask, Is biography an art? The question is foolish perhaps, and ungenerous certainly, considering the keen pleasure that biographers have given us. But the question asks itself so often that there must be something behind it. There it is, whenever a new biography is opened, casting its shadow on the page; and there would seem to be something deadly in that shadow, for after all, of the multitude of lives that are written, how few survive!

"The Art of Biography"

8a tos

Sentence fragments can emphasize a point but lack either the topic or the observation. Therefore, they read more like mottoes than informative forecasting statements. Multisentence theses, on the other hand, are valuable mainly in longer, complicated discussions. Detailed or complicated texts require that you build a context, guide readers through that context, and gradually reveal to them the complexities of your perspective. These tasks are best accomplished with a multisentence thesis statement whose elements are distributed throughout the text. They are generally less confrontational than a statement delivered at the outset.

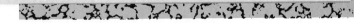

Characteristics of a Thesis Statement

- **Contains a generalization about a topic. Writers change tentative (working) thesis statements as they develop their viewpoints.**
- **Expresses a perspective that can be argued rather than a self-evident one.**
- **Announces the writer's purpose and defines the limits of the supporting evidence.**
- **Often forecasts reliably the content and organization of a text.**
- **Is usually written in complete sentences rather than rhetorical questions or suggestive but uninformative fragments.**

Exercise 1

Another way to generate ideas and discover meaning is to start with a topic and restrict it with fantastic, antagonistic, irresponsible, or ridiculous comments rather than reasonable qualifications. Proposing an outlandish thesis statement can spark your critical thinking, open up your understanding of an issue, and, eventually, lead to a sound thesis. Take the following list of topics and experiment with this strategy. Then limit several of these extreme theses to defensible statements.

1. Style is merely . . .
2. Technical training must try to satisify . . .
3. Slightly modifying Rodin's sculpture "The Thinker" leaves you with . . .
4. Recent environmental scares are . . .
5. Chimpanzees, like humans . . .
6. Contemporary business practices vividly illustrate . . .
7. Many of America's military leaders are subscribing to . . .
8. Increases in violent crime on this city's streets guarantee . . .
9. Capital punishment and abortion effectively risk . . .
10. The biological qualities of antibodies are harmful because . . .

1 Implicit Thesis Statements

Writers sometimes imply their theses instead of directly stating them. **Implicit thesis statements** hint at judgments rather than openly presenting them. Implicit thesis statements, or **themes,** are common in fiction, but they also appear in other types of writing. For example, when you design a form letter encouraging individuals to pay their association fees, your purpose is to raise money for the group. Reminding participants of the numerous membership privileges implies the persuasive thesis *This organization benefits you and deserves your financial support.*

Implicit theses are not persuasive in awkwardly written texts. Moreover, unstated theses are inappropriate for many kinds of informative texts because readers expect these documents to state a position clearly and to explain the knowledge presented.

2 Explicit Thesis Statements

More readers are familiar with **explicit thesis statements,** which provide information in a straightforward, unequivocal fashion and indicate plainly both your topic and your perspective. Explicit theses discipline a writer's thinking about a vague topic and save time, for they dictate a sort of mini-outline of the viewpoint to be presented. And they also provide a clear standard for revision.

Exercise 2

The sentences in each of the following pairs are possible explicit thesis statements. For each pair, decide which assertion could be an effective thesis statement and what changes you would have to make to turn it into a workable thesis. Be prepared to justify your answers.

1a. I intend to discuss my Border terrier's idiosyncratic behavior.

b. Border terriers, far more than other breeds, endear themselves to their often suffering owners because their idiosyncrasies mitigate the frustrations they provoke.

2a. Euphemisms substitute vagueness for specificity.

b. Although they argue that euphemisms are mostly harmless, people who rely on euphemisms are substituting vagueness for specificity and are attempting to make unpleasant or even immoral realities disappear.

3a. Frank Zappa contends that labeling or rating records alleged to contain explicit sexual lyrics is "the equivalent of treating dandruff by decapitation."

b. Labeling records that contain explicit lyrics won't work because people will always buy records they are not supposed to have.

4a. We should quit fighting the drug lords and legalize drugs because legal drugs are cheap and won't leave any reason for the drug lords to fight.

b. Drugs—as well as guns and poison—can cause death if misused, but that is not sufficient reason to make them illegal.

5a. Given today's precarious economic situation, unionizing a shop guarantees permanent unemployment.

b. Form a union, lose your job.

Exercise 3

List five of your "pet peeves"—situations or conditions guaranteed to anger you and raise your blood pressure. These could range from inconsiderate people to imprisonment for violating local censorship rules. Then decide which ones would be best handled in an essay with an implicit thesis statement and which in an essay with an explicit thesis. List the details you would use for an essay with an implicit thesis, and draft the thesis for the essay with an explicit statement.

8b

Formulating a Thesis Statement

Generating a thesis forces you to move from a hypothetical stance on a topic to a conclusion that you will be able to back up with appropriate and credible evidence. Individual writers have their own methods of coming up with theses. Some discover their thesis statements when they are not writing but doodling or musing or engaging in some different activity. Others are methodical, inferring a thesis from their assembled evidence. Still others set out deliberately to challenge accepted positions with a brand-new slant on the topic. If you are having difficulty finding your thesis on a topic, try following this reasoning sequence:

1. Narrow a subject to find a topic by asking yourself what interests you about this subject.
2. Ask yourself what you believe about the topic or take on the persona of your readers and ask yourself what beliefs, opinions, or judgments they hold.
3. Draft a statement expressing that belief, opinion, or judgment.

You will have identified a topic within a broad subject, focused on an aspect of that topic by suggesting a possible perspective, and drafted the perspective into a flexible working thesis. This strategy is productive if you remember that it is a way to start—not an end in itself.

There are some pitfalls in this elementary approach. If your thesis sets forth a perspective that few would find objectionable, you have left yourself little to write about. Likewise, failing to anticipate possible objections leaves you with a superficial thesis, which you won't be able to justify. Proposing a perspective that you don't understand or fully accept suggests that you are uninterested in the topic or unconvinced by your own perspective. Test the significance of your thesis and be ready to re-examine and change the thesis if necessary.

Thesis statements answer the question *What do I, the writer, need and want to say about this topic?* They can take several forms. One elementary way to shape a thesis statement is to write *The purpose of this essay is* _____. Finishing this statement helps get your thinking—and writing—started. Later, when you have completed a rough draft, you can delete the unneeded announcement of intention ("The purpose . . . is") and construct a new focused thesis.

A variation on this strategy is to include justifications. Assert a perspective toward a topic, define your reasons for holding that perspective, and list (forecast) your justifications in the order in which you will discuss them. Your thesis statement would follow this form:

Topic:	danger of theft in this community	Reducing *the danger of theft in this community*
Perspective:	impossible	is *impossible*
Justifications:	police budget apathy	because we have an *insufficient police force,* a *shrinking municipal budget,* and a *generally apathetic view* toward crime.

If you are analyzing causes, effects, and trends, recommending a position, or challenging accepted wisdom, using this strategy to propose a preliminary thesis statement can focus your thinking and show your readers how you will justify your position. Notice, however, that the formulaic phrasing "Assertion is true/false because of 1, 2, and 3" can impose a pedestrian order on your text instead of making it an engaging defense.

Yet another strategy is to use the problem-solution model. Ask yourself what problems a topic suggests and what solutions—either legitimate or fantastic—might resolve those problems. For example, the topic *reducing crime in our community* suggests solutions ranging from the mundane (more police intervention, exploiting community resources) to the preposterous (locking people up in their homes by 8 P.M.). Simple questions about a topic lead to more complex ones, such as the following: *What causes criminal activity in a community? Who is responsible for reducing crime in a neighborhood?* or *When do the solutions become more restrictive than the problem?* This thesis-forming strategy is another means of generating ideas.

8c
tos

Strategies for Drafting Working Thesis Statements

- Infer a thesis from accumulated evidence, factual statements, or supporting data.
- Challenge a thesis gleaned from accepted wisdom.
- Finish the statement *My purpose is . . .*
- Assert a topic and perspective; list plausible or questionable justifications.
- State a topic as the problem in a situation; provide a perspective as the solution.

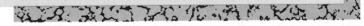

8c

Keeping a Thesis Statement Flexible

As you write, you may find that you do not accept or cannot defend your working thesis. Your examples may not be strong enough, your initial opinion changes, your thesis statement both affirms and denies your viewpoint, or your thesis lacks an argumentative edge. Whatever the situation, you will need to modify your working thesis.

Don't despair, and don't stop writing to revamp your working thesis. Stay flexible. Write a full first draft, and, as you write, think candidly about your reaction to your topic. Remember that writing is not inscribing preconceived ideas but a process of discovering meaning and shaping viewpoints. Seize the opportunity during the act of writing to determine why you hold certain opinions on the given topic. Recognize that you may not even know what your opinions are until you have written them and that one way you can revise your writing is by refining your working thesis.

8d

Developing Multiple Thesis Statements

What you think about a topic, as well as how you think about it, can lead you to several different yet feasible thesis statements. Each thesis, in turn, can suggest a different organization for your text. One way to identify different working theses is to divide a sheet of paper in half, label one column "Topic" and the other "Observation," and propose various observations about a topic. For instance, the topic *affirmative action policies* could have these observations:

Topic	**Observation**
1. Affirmative action policies	are difficult to detect when they function honorably and equally difficult to overlook when they are abused.
2. Affirmative action policies	historically have given various ethnic groups and others better access to training and jobs.
3. Affirmative action policies	have prompted substantial changes in the country's social values and political structure.
4. Affirmative action policies	are wrongheaded because they are costly, time-consuming, and end up favoring the unqualified.
5. Affirmative action policies	jeopardize our ability to protect the individual rights of all citizens.

If your audience is a college professor and your purpose is to demonstrate your knowledge of affirmative action policies, thesis 2 would display your historical knowledge, whereas thesis 3 would reveal your ability to analyze this knowledge. If you want to criticize recent court rulings, theses 1, 4, and 5 express these concerns, although thesis 4 is more dramatic and controversial than the other two.

Productive thesis statements also implicitly suggest various methods of development for the text. Thesis 1 points to an essay detailing specific policies and comparing and contrasting their impact on certain populations or geographic areas. The essay could include chronological, spatial, or climactic orders. Thesis 2 proposes a description or definition of certain policies, possibly ordered chronologically or climactically. The use of the adverb *historically* implies that the essay will have an objective tone and numerous factual statements. Thesis 3 could set up a causal analysis or implied argument advanced by spatial, chronological, or least-to-most-important organization. Thesis 4 would require numerous specific details and carefully integrated reasoning, or it might become an unconvincing tirade. Thesis 5 could be developed as an argument based on deductive reasoning (see Chapter 5) or Rogerian persuasion (see Chapter 9) and ordered chronologically, anticlimactically, or climactically.

8e
tos

8e

Positioning a Thesis Statement

You can position your thesis statement anywhere in your text. Determining the best place to put a thesis statement is a decision based on your sense of where the statement will have its greatest effect. You can make your decision any time while you are drafting. Start by putting your thesis statement in the first paragraph. Later, when you revise, consider moving the thesis statement to another, possibly more promising, location.

1 Thesis Statements in Introductions

A thesis statement in an introduction immediately gives your perspective and the organization of your document. Placed at the beginning of a text, a thesis statement can pique readers' curiosity. It can also reduce impatience in readers who want to know right away what you intend to do. As Adrienne Rich shows in the following address to Doug-lass College graduates, placing the thesis statement in the introduction reminds you of what you are writing about and gives you a ready standard for judging how well you are developing your main point.

> For this convocation, I planned to separate my remarks into two parts: some thoughts about you, the women students here, and some thoughts about [those] who teach in a women's college. But ultimately, those two parts are indivisible. If university education means anything beyond the processing of human beings into expected roles, through credit hours, tests, and grades (and I believe that in a women's college especially it *might* mean much more), it implies an ethical and intellectual contract between teachers and students. This contract must remain intuitive, dynamic, unwritten; but we must turn to it again and again if learning is to be reclaimed from the depersonalizing and cheapening pressures of the present-day academic scene.
>
> Adrienne Rich, "Claiming an Education"

2 Thesis Statements in Conclusions

Placing your thesis statement at the end of a text is a natural consequence of drafting your text in a climactic structure (see **7c**), of using inductive or deductive reasoning patterns (see **5b** and **5c**), or of tracing a cause from various effects (see **12b**). In all these cases, you are allowing your audience to follow you through the mental journey or through the data that lead you to a final statement of your perspective. Holding a potentially objectionable thesis statement until the end of a text is also an effective tactic if your purpose is persuasion.

Niles Eldredge uses this tactic in the following argument concerning creationism. His conclusion, introduced by the summarizing transition *So,* follows as an obvious judgment from his numerous examples.

> So the creationists distort. An attack on some parts of Darwin's views is equated with a rejection of evolution. They [the creationists] conveniently ignore that Darwin merely proposed one of many sets of ideas on *how* evolution works. The only real defense against such tactics lies in a true appreciation of the scientific enterprise—the trial-and-error comparison of ideas and how they seem to fit the material universe. If the public were more aware that scientists are expected to disagree, that what a scientist writes today is not the last word, but a progress report on some very intensive thinking and investigation, creationists would be far less successful in injecting an

authoritarian system of belief into curricula supposedly devoted to free, open, rational inquiry into the nature of natural things.

Niles Eldredge, "Creationism Isn't Science"

3 Thesis Statements Elsewhere in Texts

Positioning a thesis statement in the middle of a text or inserting parts of it throughout a text are complicated strategies. You should use them only if you are reasonably sure about your audience or find yourself presenting interlocking perspectives. Delaying a statement of your thesis lets you describe the conditions leading to your viewpoint. After you set the context, your audience will more readily accept the consequences of your thesis.

If your perspective is complicated, you may need to partition it and introduce it piecemeal. In this case, you will probably need to reassemble the parts in a concluding summary. If your perspective is controversial or your audience is impatient, placing a thesis statement anywhere but in the introduction or conclusion can be a problem. A reader who begins an essay only to ask by the second or third paragraph *So what?* will not see the subtle benefits of your efforts at strategic placement.

8f

Creating an Outline

You have grouped the ideas that you have produced, considered various ways to arrange the groups, and drafted a working thesis statement. Before you start drafting your text, consider drawing up an **outline,** an overview or blueprint of the writing project, so you can test various organizational patterns to find the one that best fits your perspective. Outlining provides an opportunity to adapt and rearrange evidence before writing a text. In that sense, some people find it a valuable preview for what is to come.

1 Outlines as Blueprints for Writing

For some writers, an outline may be superfluous or the equivalent of a verbal straitjacket. Yet when used judiciously as a functional planning strategy, outlines save many writers time and effort. Seasoned writers draft outlines in the same way that they draft working thesis statements—they expect to modify, embellish, or depart from them. Useful outlines allow you to arrange main ideas and supporting points in the best way possible. They enhance your thinking by forcing you to define a thesis clearly. They can improve the coherence of your text and show you what to emphasize and what to downplay.

**8f
tos**

Steps in Drafting an Outline

- **Narrow your topic to a working thesis statement.**
- **Divide your ideas into groups and create descriptive general headings for each group.**
- **Arrange the ideas into a logical pattern (chronological, spatial, least-to-most important, most-to-least important, or problem-solution).**
- **Fill in gaps under general headings by inventing ideas, examples, and details. Err on the side of too much information rather than too little.**
- **Rethink the outline's logical pattern.**
- **Rethink the outline's general headings and supporting information. Eliminate statements you can't prove, or find information to support them.**
- **Transform your outline into a rough draft.**

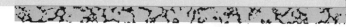

2 Choosing an
Appropriate Outline

If you study the various types of outlines and ask writers how they typically proceed, you will find that personal preference dictates most writers' outline styles. Some writers feel intimidated by the Roman numerals, capital letters, parallel topics, and tight balance of a formal outline. They prefer indenting information of less importance or listing major points on separate pieces of paper. Others need the formal structure to see their way through a topic. Still others use different colors of ink or styles of lettering to distinguish levels of prominence (for instance, all capitals for major points, upper- and lower-case lettering for secondary points, and script for examples). Basically, though, there are two types of outlines: informal outlines, which are unpolished synopses of your ideas, and formal outlines—topic, sentence, paragraph, and combination outlines—which are all very structured.

Formal outlines can be **topic, sentence,** or **paragraph outlines** or a **combination** of these types. A topic outline distills major points into single clauses and secondary topics into abbreviated phrases. For example, a topic outline for a short paper discussing women and detective fiction might begin this way:

I. The new breed of female detective novelist

   A. In the "hard-boiled" tradition

      1. Sue Grafton

         a. Private eye: Kinsey Millhone, a loner

         b. Southern California setting

      2. Sara Paretsky

         a. Private eye: V.I. Warshawski (different style from Kinsey Millhone)

         b. Chicago setting

Whichever type of outline clarifies your thinking and helps you arrange your thoughts is the right one for you to use.

Informal Outlines

Informal outlines sketch your working intentions into rough divisions and subdivisions. They are also valuable invention tools. When you have made a preliminary list of ideas, drafted general headings for those ideas, and sorted concepts under those headings, you have created an informal outline. This initial restructuring of your ideas should highlight one unifying idea—the core of your thesis statement. You can expand from this list of ideas and working thesis statement by freewriting, mapping, or asking journalistic questions. The particular value of an informal outline is its looseness: You can shape your thoughts while you are still coming up with details, examples, subordinate ideas, or tighter reasoning patterns.

Formal Outlines

Formal outlines systematically present parallel ideas and subordinate details. This type of outline is called "formal" partly because it follows an established format, a hierarchy of indentations using Roman numerals, upper- and lower-case letters, and Arabic numbers. Formal outlines indicate an exact, intelligible relationship between major points and secondary ideas or supporting examples. Each numbered or lettered indentation indicates a level of subordination.

8f
tos

A topic outline can be tricky if you have not thought out your ideas completely or recognized which divisions parallel other divisions. Vague headings, such as "Introduction" and "Conclusion," and broad terms, such as "Historical review," lead to undeveloped, largely unusable outlines. For these reasons, you should not rely entirely on a topic outline as a blueprint for a complicated text.

Conventions of Formal Outlining

I. Roman numerals are flush with the left margin of the page and denote the major divisions of a text.

   A. Upper-case letters are the first indentation and denote the secondary ideas that will support a major division in a text.

      1. Arabic numerals are indented under upper-case letters.

      2. Arabic numerals denote significant examples that support a writer's ideas and general thesis.

         a. Lower-case letters are indented under Arabic numbers.

         b. Lower-case letters denote specific details or an explanation of an example's main points.

   B. Except for single examples of specific points, individual divisions generally have two or more subpoints.

II. Formal outlines contain more than one major division.

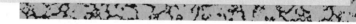

   A **sentence outline** is an expanded topic outline in which each division is a complete sentence that expresses an idea developed in a paragraph of the text. Sentence outlines are more demanding because most writers have to think ideas through before they can convey them in complete sentences. In the long run, however, such outlines can save you time because you can directly transfer many of the sentences from the outline to your text. Here is the earlier example, considerably expanded in a sentence outline:

I. A new breed of female detective novelist, representing a departure from the Agatha Christie type, has gained considerable popularity in recent years.

   A. For the first time, women are writing in the "hard-boiled" tradition made famous by such male novelists as Raymond Chandler and Dashiell Hammett.

      1. Sue Grafton is perhaps the most popular example.

         a. Her private eye is the likeable loner Kinsey Millhone, who uses her considerable wits to get herself out of highly dangerous situations.

         b. Her novels are set in southern California (a fictionalized version of Santa Barbara), recalling in some ways the atmosphere of Chandler's novels.

      2. Sara Paretsky, who worked for years as the advertising manager of an insurance company, is also becoming very well known.

         a. Her private eye, V.I. (for "Victoria Iphigenia") Warshawski, is somewhat more social than but equally as tough as Kinsey Millhone.

         b. The novels are set in Chicago and reveal an extensive and compelling knowledge of that city.

8f
tos

The drawback of sentence outlines is that they can become monotonous. To achieve parallel development of ideas, some writers end up repeating the same sentence structures, a practice that becomes distracting. Additionally, some subcategories of an outline simply don't deserve full sentences; lists, individual examples, and inventories of facts are better expressed as phrases. Forcing these elements into sentences only creates awkward and unwieldy subcategories and can give minor ideas too much significance.

A **paragraph outline** usually has no subdivisions beyond first-level Roman numerals because each division is a sentence-length summary of a paragraph:

I. A new breed of female detective novelist, very different from the Agatha Christie type, has become popular. Some of these novelists work in the "hard-boiled" mode of Chandler and Hammett. Two of the most popular are Sue Grafton and Sara Paretsky. Grafton's private eye, the loner Kinsey Millhone, lives in southern California, where she constantly gets into dangerous situations and gets out of them by using her wits. Paretsky's novels, set in Chicago, feature private eye V.I. Warshawski. Warshawski is more social than Millhone, but she is equally tough when faced with danger, which she often is.

Explaining every secondary point and specific detail would be the same as writing the essay. Consequently, paragraph outlines tend to be less substantial than topic or sentence outlines. They also obscure precisely those relationships between ideas that an outline is designed to underscore.

The most flexible kind of outline is the **combination outline**— a hybrid of topic, sentence, and paragraph outlines. Here is the example one more time:

8f
tos

I. A new breed of female detective novelist, representing a departure from the Agatha Christie type, has gained considerable popularity in recent years.

   A. Women writing in the "hard-boiled" tradition made famous by such male novelists as Raymond Chandler and Dashiell Hammett

      1. Sue Grafton

         a. Private eye Kinsey Millhone (loner)

         b. Southern California setting

      2. Sara Paretsky

         a. Private eye V.I. Warshawski

         b. Chicago setting

Main topics appear as full sentences, giving them the emphasis and development they deserve, and secondary topics and examples appear in single words, phrases, or clauses. In this arrangement, you can easily move ideas around and add or delete information until you have collected your thoughts into a workable blueprint.

WRITING

PERSUASIVELY

Writing persuasively: A writer's effort, through logical reasoning or other appeals (emotional, ethical, or fallacious) to influence an audience to accept a claim.

Persuasion: A writer's presentation and elaboration of logical and other appeals in an effort to convince readers or move them to action. In practice, persuasion and argumentation are not independent of one another.

Dialogue argument: An argumentation (invention) strategy that sets up alternative reasons for a position, assesses supporting and rebutting evidence, and creates chains of evidence by using specific transitional elements to suggest pro and con ideas.

Practical reasoning: An argumentation strategy based on **claims** (stated conclusions), **data** (grounds that form the evidence supporting a claim), and **warrants** (general principles that underlie claims and connect them to their supporting data). An expanded version of this model adds **qualifiers,** which acknowledge that claims are probabilities, **reservations,** which state possible rebuttals, and

115

9a
wp

backings, which give reasons supporting a warrant's authority.

Rogerian persuasion: An argumentation strategy without a conventional structure. A writer moves from a neutral explanation of a situation to a demonstrated understanding of an audience's point of view and, finally, to a statement of the writer's aims, goals, or analyses and how they mutually benefit the writer and audience.

Fallacies: Logically flawed but, at times, persuasive reasoning patterns. **Informal fallacies** are unsound arguments because their content, not their form, is flawed by ambiguity, presumptions, or lack of relevance.

9a

Strategies for Persuasive Writing

There is an appealing tidiness about inductive and deductive reasoning, especially syllogisms (see **5c**); if you are skilled in analyzing arguments and texts, it is relatively simple to find and judge these patterns. The patterns are so simple that some writers purposely exaggerate them for stylistic or humorous reasons. Lewis Carroll in *Alice in Wonderland,* for example, consciously sets up misleading syllogisms, such as the Pigeon's retort to Alice, to make his audience laugh:

> "I *have* tasted eggs, certainly," said Alice, who was a very truthful child; "but little girls eat eggs quite as much as serpents do, you know."
>
> "I don't believe it," said the Pigeon; "but if they do, why, then they're a kind of serpent: that's all I can say."

By and large, however, the texts that you will read or write will not depend solely on deduction or induction. These patterns are not always practical or persuasive. In ordinary discourse, you use a variety of reasoning strategies and appeals depending on your audience and purposes. The following argumentative strategies and appeals, though discussed separately, seldom occur in isolation. More often, writers combine them with one another or with inductive or deductive reasoning to make their texts persuasive. You as the writer determine which combination works best in your text.

1 Dialogue as Argument

According to rhetorician Sheridan Baker, writers can productively organize their perspectives through **dialogues.** This approach
allows you to discover alternative reasons for a viewpoint, assess
opposing assertions and evidence, and build chains of ideas and evidence. Dialogues, in this sense, are a kind of strategy in which you
"create" an opponent and debate each assertion with that opponent.
For a pro and con dialogue, start with a topic that can be argued from
either a "yes" or a "no" position. Assert one side. Think of your opponent as a person who disputes your every statement. Then challenge
your assertions by zigzagging back and forth between their pros and
cons and making sure that you explain any abstract words and define
any terms that are fundamental to your position. Baker's terminology,
listed below, promotes this back-and-forth dialogue.

9a
wp

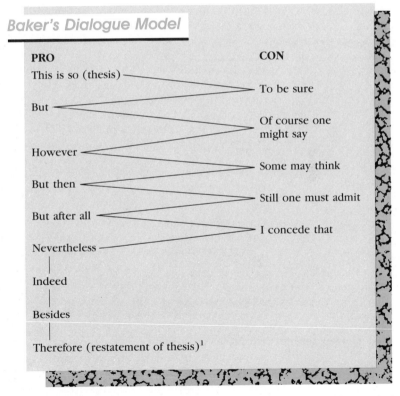

Baker's Dialogue Model

PRO	CON
This is so (thesis)	To be sure
But	Of course one might say
However	Some may think
But then	Still one must admit
But after all	I concede that
Nevertheless	
Indeed	
Besides	
Therefore (restatement of thesis)[1]	

[1]This diagram represents an adaptation of the model in Sheridan Baker, *The Practical
Stylist,* 4th ed. (New York: Thomas Crowell, 1977).

Baker's suggested model helps you pinpoint opposing perspectives. Confronting these viewpoints strengthens your writing by enhancing its persuasiveness. Additionally, this model helps you draft topic sentences and jot down, perhaps in outline form, supporting evidence and obvious counterclaims.

2 Practical Reasoning

In the 1950s, philosopher Stephen Toulmin criticized formal, or analytic, reasoning as too abstract and unwieldy, particularly for discussions that address "real world," or debatable, issues. He argued that, in making daily decisons, absolute truth is not possible and sometimes not even desirable. In place of the indisputable conclusions of syllogistic logic, he proposed **practical reasoning,** a system that, in Toulmin's view, more realistically reflects human behavior and thinking.

Basic Divisions of Practical Reasoning Model

DATA (Evidence)	CLAIM (Assertion)
The Robber Baron Paper Company was built fifty years ago, and a steamy, sulphurous sludge flows out of its outlet pipes into the river.	The Robber Baron Paper Company is polluting the Deep Muddy River.

WARRANT

Since

The discharge of old paper plants includes acids and bleaches, which are the most dangerous waste materials to rivers.

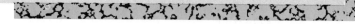

The key term in the practical reasoning strategy is *reasonable.* A claim made in a thesis statement is "reasonable" because people generally accept it or because a writer sufficiently supports it, not because it survived the restrictive scrutiny of the mathematical proofs demanded by formal logic. Texts using practical reasoning set forth feasible claims for accepting the writer's viewpoint. This is a particularly important way to present a viewpoint when you remember that specific fields of study or situations you may find yourself in create their own standards for judging claims as reasonable.

Practical reasoning has a terminology distinct from that of formal logic. At its most basic, practical reasoning consists of a **claim, data,** and a **warrant.** A claim asserts your conclusion, thesis, or perspective. It is signaled by words such as *therefore* or *so.* Data are the proofs and evidence supporting the claim, and warrants are the general principles that connect a claim to its evidence.

9a
wp

For most types of argumentation, you will find that this basic model does not indicate what evidence is most persuasive or how your thesis can sound objective. It also does not tell you how to suggest a warrant rather than state it openly or how to modify a possibly controversial perspective. Expanding the basic model for practical reasoning adds the elements **qualifiers, reservations,** and **backing** and blends enthymemic with practical reasoning to fill in the gaps. (See **5d** for a discussion of enthymemic reasoning.) A qualifier (such as a phrase beginning with *presumably* or *chances are*) modifies a claim by acknowledging that it is probable but not indisputably true. A reservation states possible exceptions or rebuttals—the conditions under which the claim is not reasonable. A backing states reasons that support a warrant's application to a particular argument. With these additions, an essay detailing the environmentally questionable activities of the Robber Baron Paper Company could be developed along the lines of the diagram on page 120.

Most texts that you will write will back up claims about future events with references to data or past events, generalize a consequence with references to similar circumstances, or justify a hypothesis with substantial reasons or facts. Whatever you write, you constantly have to weigh evidence for and against claims, assert conclusions based on assumptions and probabilities, and pay attention to the rules or principles that connect facts and knowledge to your conclusions. (See **4c** for a related discussion of premises and conclusions.) By using the dynamic structural categories of practical reasoning, you can adapt what you know to new information that you gain as you write. Additionally, as a writing strategy, practical reasoning puts you in your audience's place and suggests what they may think about your assertions.

9a
wp

Expanded Practical Reasoning Model

DATA – – – – – – – (Qualifier) – – –CLAIM
So, presumably

The Robber Baron Paper Company was built fifty years ago, and a steamy, sulphurous sludge flows out of its outlet pipes into the river.	The Robber Baron Paper Company is polluting the Deep Muddy River.

WARRANT   **RESERVATION**

Since   *Unless*

The discharge from old paper plants includes acids and bleaches, which are the most dangerous waste materials to rivers.	The Robber Baron Paper Company has spent several million dollars to retrofit recovery systems on its discharge pipes.

BACKING

Because

Research indicates that chemicals that change pH levels in rivers kill both plants and animals and make the rivers inhospitable to future organisms.

Exercise 1

The following passage contains some of the structural categories of practical reasoning. Identify these categories and how they are connected.

The Environmental Protection Agency, Consumer Product Safety Commission, Food and Drug Administration, consumer groups, and home owners' associations have responded to—and indeed contributed to—this escalating fear of environmental sources of disease by demanding the banning of pesticides, food additives, urea formaldehyde foam insulation and other products of modern industrial know-how. In the case of the Love Canal, President Carter went so far as to declare an official state of emergency and order the costly relocation of more than 700 homeowners. In Missouri, the EPA was the subject of bitter criticism, and damning press coverage, for not evacuating families sooner from the dioxin-contaminated areas.

It is no surprise, then, that national surveys indicated that, in the 1980s, Americans are significantly more supportive than ever before of environmental legislation, efforts to clean up toxic wastes, and more stringent government control of food additives, pesticides, and a vast array of consumer products. All of this is *allegedly* in the interest of promoting health through the application of preventive measures to remove the suspected disease-causing agents. . . .

It is in this context that the cigarette stands out as the ultimate paradox in American society. While magazines, newspapers, and the electronic media focus almost daily on *hypothetical* risks posed by environmental chemical contamination and the techniques of modern food production and processing, and the American public is demanding that the government "do something" to prevent environmentally induced disease, there is a near complete lack of interest in the leading cause of premature death in the U.S.—the cigarette. *While no one died at Love Canal or Three Mile Island* [Pennsylvania], *some 400,000 Americans this year alone will die prematurely from disease directly associated with cigarette smoke.*

Elizabeth M. Whelan, "Big Business vs. Public Health: The Cigarette Dilemma"

9a
wp

Exercise 2

Review something you recently wrote and see if you have organized your information by following the strategies of practical reasoning. If you find gaps, make a list of the types of information that you would include if you revised the work.

3 Rogerian Persuasion

For psychologist Carl Rogers, communication is listening with understanding. You can communicate better if you and your audience share some common ground. These observations are the basis of a writing strategy called **Rogerian persuasion.** One value of Rogerian persuasion is practicality: You arrange information in your text from neutral explanations of a topic to discussions of it centered on your audience's concerns. This progression lets your audience see your viewpoint as one that also matches their interest.

Rogerian persuasion begins with a neutral statement of a situation that gives rise to an issue and an impartial statement of this issue as a problem. First, focus attention on the problem without evaluating it. This technique invites your audience to judge the problem impartially, establishes you as a credible, objective source, and establishes your credibility as the writer.

Next, discuss the problem, using your audience's interest as the context. Demonstrate that you understand the audience's probable viewpoint and can state it fairly and accurately. To do so, you will have to analyze your audience carefully. Building this bridge to your audience gains their trust.

In the last stage, invite your audience to see the problem from a new perspective—yours. Your goal is to convince them that their interest coincides with yours. Show your audience that accepting your perspective benefits them. Finally, state your conclusion as if you and your readers completely agreed on it.

4 Logical, Emotional, and Ethical Appeals

To refine its points further, Rogerian persuasion makes use of three time-honored modes of persuasion: logical, emotional, and ethical appeals. **Logical appeals,** called *logos* in classical Greek rhetoric, center on the nature of your message and include sound reasoning and relevant evidence. Practical reasoning or deductive strategies, such as those used in the following passage, are appropriate in framing a logical appeal:

> Today [Alvin] Weinberg's phrase is unfortunately associated with an unproductive debate about science funding policy in which "Big Science" often carries connotations similar to those of "Big Business." The suggestion is that large scientific projects unfairly monopolize scientific capital, squeezing out the little guy who might make valuable innovations if given a chance. But the analogy is false. Knowledge generated by large scientific projects, unlike the profits of large corporations, becomes the property of the entire community and restructures the scientific background against which research teams large and small plan and execute new ventures. Moreover, "Big Science" is a general term whose meaning varies from one branch of science to another. It can refer to the construction of large instruments used by only a small fraction of the community at once, as in astronomy; large equipment complexes serving many individuals simultaneously, as in materials science; or the coordination of the work of numerous small research teams, as in biology. In each case the funding needs, the size and role of research groups, and the information flow between project users and the wider scientific community is different. It is thus meaningless to debate the value of Big Science in general; projects must be judged on an individual basis.
>
> Robert P. Crease and Nicholas P. Samios,
> "Managing the Unmanageable"

Emotional appeals, called *pathos* by classical rhetoricians, stir your audience's emotions. In a text structured by Rogerian principles, you appeal to your audience's emotion by showing them the potential benefit of accepting your viewpoint or by playing on their feelings. For example, the writer of the following passage uses emotionally charged language in both the title, "Penniless Widow Robbed by Rich Corporation," and the text to sway readers, even though the corporation may have a legitimate claim:

9a
wp

> A penniless widow might be booted out of her house by her heartless multimillionaire landlord even though she's senile and helpless.
>
> Transamerican Corp [sic] which uses the slogan "Our heart is everywhere," doesn't seem to be moved by the sad plight of 77 year old [sic] Lennie Williams.
>
> The financial giant wants to sell Lennie's tidy home out from under her because she can't make the $500 monthly payments on a loan taken out by her son-in-law.
>
> *Albuquerque Street News*

Note that the distinction between reasonable persuasion and informal fallacies, discussed on pages 124–134, may become blurred with some emotional appeals.

Finally, **ethical appeals,** called *ethos* in classical studies, invite an audience to accept a position because the writer's character is outstanding. Ethical appeals are persuasive only if you can establish yourself as knowledgeable about a topic. In the following passage, note how the writer, a registered nurse and patient advocate, combines an emotional appeal with an ethical appeal, based on her occupation and her experiences in geriatric care facilities, to argue for the rights of the elderly:

> The elderly suffer quietly. They are afraid they will be punished if they speak up for themselves. Most of them can't speak for themselves. They just want to escape this hell. I do too. They need a place to stay; I need a job. We're trapped.
>
> I am one little nurse, in one little care facility, living with this terrible secret. If [the administrators] knew I was telling on them, I wouldn't have a job. What about my rent? What about my needs? But I need to tell. I confess to my participation in these crimes. I can't keep this secret any longer.
>
> Judy Frawley, "Real Life: Inside the Home"

As with emotional appeals, distinctions between legitimate persuasion by ethical appeal and some informal fallacies of relevance may be hard to maintain.

Writing that claims to be objective seems persuasive because it sounds "objective." However, no text is ever completely objective because every piece of writing expresses its writer's perspective. Consequently, a text that sounds neutral does so because its writer has impersonally cited data, not because it lacks a viewpoint. Personal experiences, for example, can give your writing an objective tone if those experiences are relevant, show your knowledge of your topic, and speak well of you. The effect is to make you "credible." So you should consider carefully the type of evidence you provide for your readers.

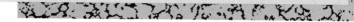

Rogerian Persuasion Compared with Persuasive Appeals

1. State the situation neutrally as a problem. Avoid any evaluation.	Logical appeal Emotional appeal Ethical appeal
2. Discuss the problem from the audience's point of view.	Ethical appeal
3. State your position directly and support it with plausible evidence.	Logical appeal Ethical appeal
4. Summarize how accepting your position benefits your audience or explains the situation and problem better.	Logical appeal Emotional appeal Ethical appeal

Exercise 3

Review an essay examination you wrote for a college course. Mark the appeals to logic, emotion, and your character. Decide which type of appeal dominates.

Informal Fallacies

The general term **fallacy,** from the Greek *phelos* for "deceitful," means a flaw in logical reasoning that leads to an unsound argument. All fallacies are *non sequiturs:* The conclusion does not follow logically from the premises. There are two broad classes of fallacies. Formal fallacies arise from flaws in the structure or arrangement of premises in arguments. A conclusion cannot be accepted because the rule does not apply. **Informal fallacies,** common in everyday writing, result from flaws in content, such as vague language, prejudice, or information unrelated to the conclusion. Informal fallacies, in particular, are often subtle and complex, yet, at a cursory glance, very persuasive.

Informal fallacies fall into three broad categories: (1) language used ambiguously, (2) a certain reasoning being presumed, or (3) irrelevant material being introduced. The following definitions and examples briefly survey the kinds of fallacious reasoning that fall within these categories.

9b
wp

Informal Fallacies

Ambiguity	Presumption	Relevance
Accent	Begging the question	Appeal to authority
Composition	False cause	Appeal to force
Division	False dilemma (Either-or fallacy)	Appeal to ignorance
Equivocation	Hasty generalization	Argument to the person (Ad hominem)
Personification	Irrelevant thesis	Bandwagoning
	Sweeping generalization	False analogy

1 Informal Fallacies
of Ambiguity

Fallacies of ambiguity come about when you use words with multiple meanings. The vagueness of your terminology lures readers into believing they have understood a point when, in fact, you meant something else entirely.

Accent

Fallacies of accent create an ambiguous tone. A statement taken out of context, such as "Money is the root of all evil," is a fallacy of accent. The original quotation, "The love of money is the root of all evil," accents the *love of money;* the fallacious statement isolates *money* as the culprit. Accent fallacies also occur where words are inaccurately stressed to give different meanings. Asserting that a neighbor should "get what he deserves" may mean that the neighbor merits praise for acting kindly or harsh criticism for antisocial behavior. Accent fallacies often occur in writing when certain words in a passage are italicized or italics are deleted from an original quotation. Both changes alter the meaning of the passage by changing the emphasis.

9b
wp

Composition

If you assert that whatever is true about a part must also be true about the whole, you have engaged in a **fallacy of composition.** Stated less formally, composition fallacies assume that the value of an individual member of a group definitively proves the value of the whole group. Many fallacies of composition hinge on the word *all.* An obvious example of fallacious composition is arguing that because the Ford Escort gets excellent gas mileage, all Ford cars get excellent mileage. It is unreasonable to generalize from one Ford product to every car the company produces.

Division

The **fallacy of division,** the reverse of the composition fallacy, argues from generalities to specifics. Division asserts that what is true of a whole is also true of its individual parts. It is fallacious to argue that because the San Francisco 49ers (the team) have won consecutive Super Bowls, each player is an exceptional athlete. Some 49er players excel, but it is the teamwork of all the players, whether spectacular or merely skilled, that wins the games.

Equivocation

Equivocation, from the Latin *equi* for "equal" and *vox* for "voice," means using different meanings for the same word. Most terms have a denotative, or dictionary, meaning and a connotative, or emotionally colored, meaning. (See **41c** for more on denotation and connotation.) There is no difficulty as long as you keep the different senses of a word separate and consistently use one meaning throughout a text. If you confuse the denotative and connotative meanings of a word in a single context, you are equivocating. Puns such as Richard Hughes's on the word *baited,* are humorous equivocations: "Presently she told Dick she had a cat so smart that it first ate cheese and then breathed down the mouseholes—with baited breath—to entice the creatures out."

Personification

Used imaginatively, **personification** creates metaphor, as Shakespeare does in *Julius Caesar* when Antony says to Brutus: "Nature might stand up/And say to all the world, 'This was a man!'" (V.v. 74–75). Nature cannot literally stand up or speak; it is an abstraction to which Shakespeare gives human qualities for the purpose of his play. However, personifications can lead to erroneous thinking. Asserting that "Technology will save the earth" or that "The facts speak for themselves" takes an abstraction (technology) or a collection of data (facts) and endows each with human attributes that neither has. This sort of personification amounts to a form of careless thinking. Advertisers, for example, frequently personify science to sell products. Students rail against "the system" as some kind of single entity, which confuses registration processes or sends out incorrect notices, in the same way that fanatics and political critics blame "the system" rather than responsible elements or people in a bureaucracy.

9b
wp

2 Informal Fallacies of Presumption

Fallacies of presumption can be persuasive because they resemble sound formal arguments. However, they are flawed because they have some groundless or refutable assumptions buried in them. These fallacies cause trouble because we do not realize that we, too, are assuming some data or principles.

Begging the Question

Begging the question, or *petitio principii,* is broadly circular argumentation: It confuses a premise in an argument with the argument's conclusion. There are at least three versions of begging the question. One version asserts a premise and then restates it, in slightly different words, as the conclusion. Arguing that war is inevitable because it can't be avoided illustrates this simple version of *petitio principii.* However, this type of question begging is not always so obvious. Theorist Richard Whately, for example, uses circular reasoning when he writes that "To allow every man unbounded freedom of speech must always be, on the whole, advantageous to the state; for it is highly conducive to the interest of the community that each individual should enjoy a liberty, perfectly unlimited, of expressing his sentiments."

A somewhat more complex variation of this basic form asks that we accept one statement on the basis of a second *and* accept the second on the basis of the first. That way the conclusion is true because its premise is true and, likewise, the premise is true because the conclusion is. Arguing, for example, that Vice President J. Danforth Quayle is qualified for his government post because President George Bush selected him and Bush selects only qualified individuals for office creates a sophisticated form of this circular pattern.

A third form of begging the question is a type of enthymemic reasoning. In this case, an unstated, problematical generalization is used to support a conclusion that is itself problematical. For instance, arguing that someone is obviously uneducated because he is a carpenter presumes that an audience accepts the broader generalization "All carpenters are uneducated." Openly stating the underlying assumption quickly points out the fallacy; however, sometimes an unstated presumption is an ingrained belief, which people don't think to question.

False Cause

Chronological arguments sometimes imply that, because one event precedes another event, the first event caused the second. This **fallacy of false cause,** or *post hoc ergo propter hoc* (literally, "after this, therefore because of this"), underlies many superstitions but cannot reasonably justify a conclusion. Some incidences of *post hoc* thinking are obvious and amusingly harmless. When you wash your car on the weekend and wake up Monday morning to a rainy day, how many times have you said, "If I hadn't washed the car, it wouldn't have rained!" Advertisers use false cause skillfully, implying that if you wear designer jeans by So-and-So, you will be more attractive, or if you drive a particular model of luxury car, you will have "made it" in society.

False Dilemma

False dilemmas, also known as *black-and-white fallacies, bifurcation,* or *fallacies of the excluded middle,* oversimplify argumentation by forcing the reader to accept an either-or conclusion. The bumper sticker "America: Love it or Leave it" is a simple example of such a bogus dilemma. Writers presenting a true dilemma seek to explain as many solutions and uncover as many presumptions as they can before deciding. The bumper sticker, however, presumes only one conscientious option *(Love it)* and one expedient avenue for protest *(or Leave it).*

Black-and-white fallacies occur frequently in writing, particularly in analyses that exclude shades of meaning and in recommendations that unfairly limit choices. Once recognized, false dilemmas always become suspect. Therefore, exposing a false dilemma, as former Secretary of Education William Bennett does in the following example, can be very persuasive in itself. Bennett outlines a false dilemma posed in values-education classes. His implicit purpose is not to limit the options possible for resolving the situation but to point out that, by limiting options, these courses are shams.

9b
wp

> All right class. Your husband or wife is a very attractive person. Your best friend is attracted to him or her—presumably one or the other. How would you want him to behave? The choices are: (a) maintain a clandestine relationship so you wouldn't know about it; (b) be honest and accept the reality of the relationship; or (c) proceed with a divorce.
>
> "What Value Is Values Education?"

Hasty Generalization

We recently heard someone say the following: "After watching that senator on television this past weekend, I think of senators as the biggest hypocrites on earth." One or more senators may be a hypocrite, but to call all senators hypocrites on the basis of watching one senator on television would be to make a **hasty generalization.** Generalizing is an inductive process that starts with a careful review of evidence, proceeds through the posing of questions about any relationships implied by the evidence, and ends by proposing generalities. If, however, a generalization rests on a single piece of evidence or on an unusual rather than a typical incident, the generalization is hastily drawn and, therefore, suspect.

Irrelevant Thesis

A thesis statement presents a writer's perspective on a topic. It is the generalization that a writer supports through evidence, explanation, and reasoning. A thesis statement is logically like a conclusion: It states a reasoned, supportable position. But using a line of reasoning to support one thesis when, in fact, you are arguing for another is a *non sequitur* called **irrelevant thesis,** or *ignoratio elenchi.*

Irrelevant thesis fallacies are also called "red herrings," after a means of distracting hunting dogs from their quarry—dragging smoked fish (red herrings) across their trails to confuse the scent. Such fallacies are not always easy to identify and can sometimes be very persuasive. Arguing that television is not harmful because it keeps you out of trouble is an example of an irrelevant thesis because suggesting that "staying out of trouble" is good diverts attention from the real issue of actual harm television might cause. A more subtle example would be the argument that former President Richard M. Nixon should not be denounced for jeopardizing U.S. citizens' civil rights because he opened U.S. diplomatic relations with China and successfully negotiated arms control reductions with the Soviet Union. This argument, in part, uses Nixon's rightly praised accomplishments to argue an irrelevant thesis. The issue is *not* Nixon's stature in international relations but his complicity in the Watergate break-in and cover-up, a violation of guaranteed civil rights.

9b
wp

Sweeping Generalization

A **sweeping generalization,** or the *fallacy of accident,* reverses the terms of a hasty generalization: The generalization is reasonable, but it is applied to an atypical case and, therefore, fallaciously sweeps the particular case aside. Arguing that, because the Constitution guarantees the right to bear arms, assassins like Lee Harvey Oswald and James Earl Ray or mentally unbalanced people like Charles Manson should own guns is an example of sweeping generalization.

Hasty generalizations are typically found in evaluations based on factual reports and are easy to recognize because the stated evidence does not support a generalization. Sweeping generalizations, on the other hand, are used frequently in emotional and ethical appeals and seem persuasive because individual cases are regularly subsumed under widely accepted generalities.

3 Informal Fallacies of Relevance

Still other fallacies introduce irrelevant material into arguments: Their premises do not relate to the conclusions that they supposedly support. Some emotional appeals may be indistinguishable from fallacies of relevance, particularly if the writer's perspective lacks other reasoning to support it.

Appeal to Authority

A fallacious **appeal to authority,** or *argumentum ad verecundiam* (literally, "an argument addressed to our sense of modesty"), can be confused with citing sources, which you do when you write research reports. Legitimate appeals to authority are based on the competence and experience of experts in specialized fields. Fallacious appeals to authority rely on the opinions of an expert from one field about a topic in another field to influence an audience. Citing Detroit manager Sparky Anderson's opinions or the published statements by major league baseball umpires as evidence that the infield fly rule is inconsistently applied is a legitimate use of authoritative material. Arguing that one brand of tennis shoe is superior to all others because Bo Jackson endorses it is an amusing—and, for many sports enthusiasts, persuasive—*argumentum ad verecundiam.*

There are several types of fallacious appeals to authority. The advertising endorsement just mentioned is an **appeal to the one:** It suggests that a person's competence in one field automatically transfers to another field. A second type, also common in advertising, is an **appeal to the consensus;** it depends on the idea that, because many people buy a product or accept a theory, the product must be superior or the theory reasonable. (This is similar to the "bandwagoning" appeal, discussed on pages 133–134.) The statistic that more hospitals use a brand of acetaminophen than aspirin makes "authority," in the form of consensus, the reason for buying the product.

A variation on a fallacious appeal to consensus is the **appeal to a select few.** Discerning women recarpet their homes in Stainmaster carpeting; the marines are looking for "a few good men." In both examples, the appeal is an emotional one to prestigious authority, the authority of the elite. Prestige reinterpreted historically creates a fallacious **appeal to tradition,** a fourth type of fallacious appeal to authority: Maxwell House coffee must be good because it captures that great hometown flavor from years ago. Likewise, trying to discredit a new approach solely because it departs from conventional practices is fallacious.

Appeal to Force

"Might makes right" epitomizes the fallacious **appeal to force,** or *argumentum ad baculum.* This is the "strong arm" method sometimes used in lobbying for a cause. Intimidating a city's residents into voting against gun control by reminding them of the large financial contributions rightful gun owners make to the city does not address the merits of gun control for that city. Instead, it implies that gun owners may withdraw their financial support if their wishes are not obeyed.

In general, appeals to force are the most obvious fallacies and the easiest to discredit. They can, nevertheless, be subtle and very persuasive. In the recent Persian Gulf war, for instance, Desert Storm commander General Norman Schwarzkopf informed his defeated Iraqi counterpart that Iraq could not fly its planes because United Nations guidelines prohibited such flights and because American and coalition forces would shoot them down. Technically, Schwarzkopf practiced an

9b
wp

appeal to force. The U.N. resolutions provided sufficient grounds, based on international and political support, for Schwarzkopf's statement. His additional reason, while obviously persuasive, was nonetheless fallacious to the argument at hand.

Appeal to Ignorance

The fallacious **appeal to ignorance,** or *argumentum ad ignorantiam,* proposes that a thesis is reasonable because there is no definitive evidence against it. Arguments for extraterrestrial life, ghosts, psychic phenomena, and some miraculous occurrences all appeal to lack of proof. Subtly used, appeals to ignorance can be persuasive. For example, arguing that people should not begin to make judgments about genetic experiments *solely* because genetic engineering is still too new is a fallacious appeal to ignorance.

Appeals to ignorance, however, are acceptable in courts of law. Consider a situation in which a prosecutor has only circumstantial evidence against a defendant. Our legal system assumes that a defendant is innocent until evidence proves guilt beyond a reasonable doubt. Without incontrovertible proof of guilt, the defendant is legally considered innocent. This judgment is not a fallacy of ignorance because it is standard policy to take an absence of proof as evidence that the defendant is not guilty.

Argument to the Person

A fallacious **argument to the person,** or *argumentum ad hominem,* is perhaps the most complex, fascinating, and potentially persuasive of all the logical fallacies. Found in arguments, arts criticisms, and recommendations, *ad hominem* arguments attempt to refute an opponent's position or ideas by making irrelevant attacks, usually by innuendo, on that individual's personal traits or character.

Broadly, *ad hominem* appeals are either abusive attacks or circumstantial charges. *Ad hominem* abusive arguments ignore the evidence supporting a conclusion and instead attack the person, asserting a conclusion by means of reference to his or her actions, character, or personal features. A crude example is an insult such as "you can't trust Professor Standfast's teaching. She's a communist." More sophisticated versions, however, can be engaging. During the 1980 presidential debates, the Republican candidate, Ronald Reagan, joked that he would not discriminate against his opponent, Vice President Walter Mondale, on the basis of age. The joke was an *ad hominem* appeal turned against Mondale's own attempt at *ad hominem* abusive arguments. Mondale had earlier implied that Reagan's political decisions would not be acceptable because Reagan, then in his seventies, was too old to make effective policy. Reagan's quip that he would not hold Mondale's youth against him pointed out Mondale's fallacious argument.

One form of *ad hominem* abusive appeal goes by the Latin name *tu quoque,* or the "you also" argument. *Tu quoque* appeals try to refute a position by showing that the person advocating it is guilty of the offense that he or she is campaigning against. Suppose that the spokesperson for an antidrug campaign were caught taking an illegal drug. While an adverse response to the spokesperson's arguments seems natural, it is fallacious. The spokesperson's argument is not worthless simply because the person presenting it failed to practice what he or she preached.

The other broad category of *ad hominem* appeals is insinuations that set up an irrelevant connection between a person's actions or associations and the position being argued. Informally called guilt by association, *ad hominem* circumstantial arguments assume that an individual accepts all the values of a group. Arguing, for example, that it is useless to ask welfare clients how much money they need because, as welfare recipients, they will want as much money as they can get, is a fallacious appeal to the circumstances. As you might expect, *ad hominem* circumstantial appeals are quite persuasive and abound in political debates.

The last type of *ad hominem* circumstantial appeal, called "poisoning the well," is an attempt to refute an argument by claiming that a person holding a position can't present evidence rationally because he or she stands to benefit from it personally or would be exempt from its negative outcomes. Arguing, for example, that someone opposing a tax bond for education does not have the welfare of a community in mind "poisons the well" of discourse. Suggesting that a person opposing a military draft is doing so because his age or medical condition assures him an exemption is fallacious in the same way. The accusations label the opponents as prejudiced and their arguments as mere rationalizations for self-interested conduct. Although blatantly fallacious, this form of *ad hominem* circumstantial appeal makes it difficult, if not impossible, for the persons so attacked to state their cases fairly.

Bandwagoning

Bandwagoning, or *ad populum,* appeals are emotional attempts to secure agreement by implying that a position must be accepted, regardless of the evidence for or against it, because everyone with credibility holds it. Bandwagoning offers the popular position, not the most reasonably argued or completely supported one, as the trustworthy one. The appeal is common in advertising, where potential customers are assured that every thinking adult wants a company's product, and in political propaganda, where public opinion polls, not reasoned arguments, are used to confirm a politician's stand on an issue.

Bandwagoning appeals are persuasive in part because they mirror the legitimate concerns of the majority. Democratic societies work by majority rule, making the opinion of the many an important factor. However, supporting candidates because they are popular does not mean that the candidates are necessarily the best persons for an elected position. The same holds true for issues. Because a poll reports that 90 percent of a representative sample supports a position does not mean that the position is objectively correct. Voters have been known to pick the wrong candidate, and the judgment of the majority is not infallible. Impartial evidence should override appeals to popularity.

False Analogy

False analogy, a reasoning error closely related to *false dilemma,* a fallacy of presumption, occurs when irrelevant circumstances are used to arrive at a conclusion drawn by analogy. Analogies can be used to support arguments because they make pertinent comparisons between items. But an analogy pushed too far often breaks down because a hidden assumption does not stand the test of relevance. The argument that you should not have to balance your budget or pay your bills because the federal government fails to do so is a false analogy. A complex version of false analogy is Francis Bacon's frequently reprinted argument in support of war.

> No body can be healthful without exercise, neither natural body nor politic; and, certainly, to a kingdom, or estate, a just and honorable war is the true exercise. A civil war, indeed is like the heat of a fever; but a foreign war is like the heat of exercise, and serveth to keep the body in health; for in a slothful peace, both courages will effeminate and manners corrupt.
>
> Francis Bacon, *Of the True Greatness of Kingdoms*

9c

A Final Note on Logical Fallacies

Two central points about fallacious reasoning need stressing. First, fallacies overlap one another. For instance, the Richard Nixon example of irrelevant thesis (page 130) overlaps into a subtle *ad hominem* circumstantial fallacy that defends Nixon for his actions rather than his arguments. By the same token, using Bo Jackson to sell tennis shoes (page 131) is a subtle bandwagoning appeal, as well as a fallacious appeal to authority. This point leads to a second, equally significant one: It is less important to know how to label a fallacy than to recognize fallacious reasoning in your writing. Logicians and rhetoricians have classified and named these faulty reasoning structures for you. Rather than memorizing names, your wisest course is to absorb this collective knowledge and use it to check and analyze your own thinking and writing.

9c
wp

Exercise 4

Remembering that informal fallacies are not always discrete examples in the ordinary language texts, check the reasoning in the following passages. If you find fallacious arguments, suggest more logical ways to make the writer's point.

1. [T]he lack of accountability and the naiveté of relying on the market to protect children is alarming. In the 19th century the slogan was "let the buyer beware," and meat packers sold tainted meat to consumers. In the 20th century deregulation produced the savings and loan debacle. Nobody seriously proposes rescinding environmental safeguards—why should our children not be similarly protected?

Bill Honig, "Why Privatizing Public
Education Is a Bad Idea"

2. [T. S. Eliot's placement of Jews in his poetry], however, is a problem in literary criticism, which for the moment is not my main interest. My main interest is the response of Jewish literary people to writers who indulge in or brush against anti-Semitism. It was the fashion some years ago to say that we need not be concerned with the personal beliefs of writers, deplorable as these may sometimes be; those beliefs, it was said, become troublesome only if they form a significant presence in the writer's work. Mimicking my elders, I used to say this too, but recently I have begun to wonder. Now I find myself as strongly offended by the explicitly anti-Semitic remarks of writers as I am by troubling representations of Jews in works of literature that, because they do appear in works of literature, must necessarily be ambiguous and open to multiple readings.

Irving Howe, "An Exercise in Memory"

3. However, it matters very little now, what the King of England either says or does; he hath wickedly broken through every moral and human obligation, trampled nature and conscience beneath his feet; and by a steady and constitutional spirit of insolence and cruelty, procured for himself an universal hatred.

Thomas Paine, Appendix to *Common Sense*

4. To my generation—the children of the fifties—these [high school history] texts appeared permanent just because they were so self-contained. Their orthodoxy, it seemed, left no handholds for attack, no lodging for decay. Who, after all, would dispute the wonders of technology or the superiority of the English colonists over the Spanish? Who would find fault with the pastorale of the West or the Old South? Who would question the anti-Communist crusade? There was, it seemed, no point in comparing these visions with reality, since they were the public truth and were thus quite irrelevant to what existed and to what anyone privately believed. They were—or so it seemed—the permanent expression of mass culture in America.

Frances FitzGerald, *America Revised*

5. Whether or not practitioners of "oppression studies" have actually achieved theoretical unity, they do share a single purpose, which Peter Shaw has termed "intellectual dis-equilibrium." It is, in effect, a substitute for radical political action in that it attempts to alter reality by changing its description.

Prohibitions on free speech (in the name of protecting the "oppressed" and promoting sensitivity) are imposed de jure and de facto; first by rules, frequently referred to as "anti-harassment" codes, and then by fear, usually as willing (sometimes unwilling) conformity with "politically correct" thinking.

Charles J. Sykes and Brad Miner,
"Sense and Sensitivity"

C O M P O S I N G   A

F I R S T   D R A F T

First draft: An often messy, chaotic version of a writer's text.

Tone: A writer's **voice,** or **attitude,** toward a text's subject matter or audience. Word choice and syntax determine the tone of a text. There are three main types of tone: **informal,** or **casual; middle,** or **consultative;** and **formal,** or **academic.**

First Drafts as Sketches

First drafts are just that—the beginning or skeletal version of texts. They are neither ultimate expressions of your thoughts nor direct transcripts of spoken language. First drafts are seldom last drafts. They are messy, sometimes unsystematic, awkward prose. They may begin with one perspective and end with another. They become final drafts only when you rethink and reorganize your ideas, reconsider your supporting information, and edit your sentences for tone, correctness, and style.

You can approach writing a first draft from several angles. For example, you can freewrite a draft by writing without referring to your notes until the draft is complete. Let your pen make whatever connections your mind allows as you are writing. Later restructure this draft in conjunction with your notes and outlines. Remember that lists, notes, and outlines by themselves represent only your preliminary thinking. When you begin to draft, you may make further discoveries about your topic.

You could, however, write a more structured draft from an expanded formal outline or write the middle or body of the text first and compose the introduction and conclusion later. Or you could use a somewhat less formal approach. Print your thesis statement boldly on the top of several sheets of paper, state individual generalizations about the thesis on the separate sheets, order your notes around the generalizations, and make each generalization a paragraph or a section of your draft. These strategies may prove less structured than they seem. With each you may find that your methodical approach looks more like freewriting as new ideas enrich some sketchy points but also introduce new complexities.

The best general advice is to write your first draft quickly, without interruption. Don't marvel over particularly skillful sentences and clever nuances or worry about fragmentary introductions, faulty diction, lapses in grammar, inconsistent evidence, or weak conclusions. You may find that writing without interruption will produce a draft with fewer errors and greater unity and coherence than you expected. Additionally, you will have finally written something. Resist the temptation to answer extraneous questions about your thesis, refine the draft's sentences, or polish your style. Rethinking or revision and rewording or editing usually come after, not before, the process of drafting. Keep yourself writing by asking leading questions such as the following:

- What do I ultimately want to accomplish with this work of prose? How will this first draft start me toward those goals?
- What is my perspective? How does my thesis statement feature that perspective?
- What am I saying in this section?
- What details, factual statements, and specific incidents should I remember to use in this draft to make my perspective vivid and persuasive?

Above all, remember that the most effective texts do not begin fully formed; they evolve, over time, from sketchy first drafts.

1 Acknowledging Your Rhetorical and Practical Considerations

Openly acknowledge your rhetorical and practical considerations. Rhetorical considerations include the subject with which you are concerned, the audience that you are addressing, and your own perspective. Practical considerations include what you want to accomplish by writing a text, the type of text you are writing, and your deadline. As you write your draft, these considerations merge. Close attention to these points guides your writing strategy and dictates how much you can hope to accomplish during each writing session.

The writing process varies not only according to the individual, but also according to rhetorical and practical considerations. If you are writing a report on a subject you know well, you may not need to do any research. If you do need to research a topic, be warned: Researching can be seductive because it is often an easier and less daunting chore than writing. Devoting 95 percent of your time to research but only 5 percent to writing will not leave you enough time to draft, reassess, and revise your report. All your research will be useless if you have not communicated it effectively. (For more on researching, see Chapters 44 through 47.)

Audience, the type of writing, and your attitude toward the project also influence how you compose a first draft. If you know your readers well, you will use tactics that will sway them and avoid ineffective ones. If you are unfamiliar with your audience, you should, if possible, learn about them before you start your first draft. The type, or **genre,** of document also influences how you write a first draft. If you must draft an apology, you may compose and revise at one sitting. If, however, you are writing a speculative essay or a formal report for a college course, you will probably write several drafts that you painstakingly review, revise, integrate, and edit.

10b

Discovering Your Tone

Tone is the elusive quality that readers perceive as a writer's voice. Style creates tone, and tone conveys to your audience how you feel about the topic and them. (See discussions on style and tone in Chapters 38 through 43.) In speaking, you can easily indicate your tone by means of emphasis. For instance, on the face of it, the sentence "Do you appreciate what he did for you?" requests information. However, consider how the message changes if you emphasize different words when you say the sentence:

1. *Do* you appreciate what he did for you?
2. Do *you* appreciate what he did for you?
3. Do you *appreciate* what he did for you?
4. Do you appreciate *what* he did for you?
5. Do you appreciate what *he* did for you?
6. Do you appreciate what he *did* for you?
7. Do you appreciate what he did *for* you?
8. Do you appreciate what he did for *you?*

That changed or added meaning—your voiced **attitude**—is tone.

1   Influences on Tone: Subject Matter and Audience

Tone reflects your attitudes toward your topic and your audience. If your subject matter is factual, your tone will vary depending on whether you are reporting those facts, evaluating them, or persuading others to accept them. Your attitude toward your audience, even more than your attitude toward the subject matter, influences the tone of your text. Through your tone, you tell an audience if you are their ally, their opponent, or are indifferent to them. Whether your audience is close and personal or distant and unfamiliar also affects what and how you write. You recount what you did at a party in different ways to a family member, a close friend, and a co-worker.

Even though they are central to determining tone, neither subject matter nor audience alone dictates the tone of a discourse. It is the interplay of the two—your view of the topic and your estimate of your audience—that suggests the appropriate tone for a given discourse. Limiting yourself by considering only subject matter or only audience may mean that your text does not achieve a suitable tone.

2   Choosing an Appropriate Tone

Tone is more difficult to achieve in writing than in speech because written text does not allow for fluctuations in vocal pitch, gestures, or body language. Your choice of words, phrases, sentences, and punctuation communicates your tone. A further complication with tone in writing is that tone exists along a continuum from intimate and personal to highly formal and authoritative. Some pieces you write will run the gamut of this continuum because, at different places in a text, your approach to subject matter and audience may have to change. In general, however, writing situations call for an **informal, or casual, tone;** a **formal, or academic, tone;** or, most frequently, a **middle, or consultative, tone.**

Informal Tone

10b
fd

An **informal tone** is essentially a personal tone, not intended for all readers. It avoids filling in background and context, relies on words enriched with private definitions, and incorporates elements such as personal pronouns, contractions, slang, colloquialisms, and regional dialect terms. An informal tone closely parallels casual conversation. An informal tone, such as Calvin Trillin uses to describe a crawfish-eating contest, invites readers to share personal thoughts on a topic.

> The oyster-eating champion, a specialist away from his specialty, was the first contestant to drop out. "I'm not full. I could have a hotdog," he said, when I asked him what happened. "But these things don't taste right." The first female contestant in the history of the contest, a trim secretary, dropped out some time later. ("I'm not as hungry as I thought I was," she said.) The winner, Chester McGear, looked like one of the fraternity boys everyone had been so worried about, although he had actually graduated a couple of years before. He wore a sweatshirt emblematic of having consumed ten pitchers of beer in some tavern in Chicago, and he had a small rooting section that chanted "Go Chester, Go!" or *"Allons, Chester, Allons!"* or "Come on, Chester, Eat That Meat!" He was on his twenty-second pound of crawfish when his opponent dropped out. I was pleased to see that McGear acted the part of a traditional eating champion. They never admit to being full. My father always used to tell me about a boy who won a pie-eating contest in St. Joe by eating thirty-three pies and then said, "I wooda ate more but my ma was calling me for supper." When the reporters went up on the stand to interview McGear, he remained in his place, and as he answered the questions he absently reached toward the platter in front of him and peeled crawfish and popped them into his mouth, like a man working on the peanut bowl during a cocktail party.
>
> Calvin Trillin, "The Crawfish-Eating Contest"

Formal Tone

A **formal tone** is a detached tone. The text is appropriately dignified, and its writer assumes that the reader will remain a social stranger. Writers of texts intended to convey information, for example, frequently adopt a formal tone. As Edwin Scott Gaustad's definition of dissent shows, formal texts tend to use formal pronouns like *one* and *he* rather than more personal ones like *I, me,* or *mine.* They rely on multisyllabic words or professional jargon rather than commonplace terms and on compound-complex sentences rather than simple sentences. Their tone draws attention to the text's content and not its writer.

10b
fd

> While it is true that restraint and oppression frequently give dissent its cohesion and therefore its strength as a mass movement, it is not true that, apart from these external forces, the dissenter is without aim or energy or nerve. Rather, the dissenter is a powerful if unpredictable engine in the service of a cause. Though he is prone to many sins, sloth is not his crime. The path of greatest resistance is frequently the very one that the dissenter sets himself upon. He may chase out demons dwelling in others; himself he cannot save.
>
> One might argue that the above describes not the dissenting man but the religious man, *homo religiosus.* This observation has some validity. Religion in its essence is already offbeat, irregular, asymmetric. It confronts and attempts to cope with the unexpected and the unexplained. That which conforms, that which is balanced, that which is orderly and precise does not require the ministrations of cult or clergy, of ritual or myth. The profoundly religious man resists the routine, defies the machine, confounds the computer. In Abraham Heschel's words, he is concerned not with process but with some event.
>
> Edwin Scott Gaustad,
> "A Delineation of Dissent"

Consultative Tone

A **consultative,** or **middle, tone** blends informal and formal into a casual straightforwardness that is appropriate for correspondence, most reports and proposals, and much academic writing. The writer supplies information, guides readers through the problem and suggested resolutions, and helps readers feel that they are a part of the process. Texts written in a middle tone, like Barry Lopez's passage below, address intimates and strangers alike with generally accepted slang, some personal pronouns, and variations in sentence structure and complexity—with some sentences interrupted by dashes or parenthetical material. The consultative tone draws attention to the writer, as well as to the content. The writer becomes a credible source of information with a unique voice expressing a personal, often rational, perspective on a topic of concern to both writer and audience.

> One of the problems that comes with trying to take a wider view of animals is that most of us have cut ourselves off from them conceptually. We do not think of ourselves as part of the animal

kingdom. Indians did. They thought of themselves as The People
(that is a translation from the native tongue of most tribal names)
and of animals as The Wolves, The Bears, The Mice, and so forth.
From here on in this chapter, the line between Indians and wolves
may fade, not because Indians did not perceive the differences but
because they were preoccupied with the similarities. They were
inclined to compare and contrast their way of living with, say, the
weasel's way or the eagle's way. They would say, "We are like the
wolves in that we . . ." They were anthropomorphic—and animistic.
Highly so. We aren't talking, really, about our wolf anymore. We are
talking about their wolf. We are, in a sense, in a foreign country.

Barry Lopez, *Of Wolves and Men*

**10b
fd**

When you first compose a draft, elements of tone slip in unnoticed because you have not yet turned your critical reader's eye on
your own work. Yet the persuasiveness of your writing rests on how
successfully you manage tone. Tone is primarily a matter of judicious
selection of content and style to accommodate a particular audience.
By choosing a coolly rational tone when your readers require thought-
fulness or a candidly persuasive one when they need convincing, you
use tone as a compelling rhetorical tool.

Exercise 1

Read the following passages once quickly, and decide which tone—
informal, formal, or consultative—predominates. Then reread each
carefully, picking out the words, phrases, and sentences that create the
tone.

Baseball is a highly literary game. Its reader, knowing that the players
need not be superlative athletes as in tennis or soccer, feels no bar to
identifying with them—a necessity of literature. The rules are intricate
to the point of inscrutability; the events are various enough to simulate
the complexity of life itself. Then our normal reluctance to face complexities can equalize the comprehensions of life and of baseball. Facil-
itating the just balance of text and feelings for continuing joint recon-
sideration: by definition, then, baseball text is dedicated prose. The lex-
icon is rich and strictly organized, yet with ample room for tropes—
which are not slang because the business is known to be serious. The
same event may be narrated with immense variety, the same patch of
text will cover an infinite number of events—for who can doubt that
baseball will endure as long as apple pie?

Martin Joos, *The Five Clocks*

American baseball may be one nation, indivisible, with free agency and
juggled tax depreciations for all; but from Yankee Stadium and Fenway
Park to Chavez Ravine and the Big A, it doesn't seem that way. Each
major league park is persistently and confidently unique. Does baseball,

10b
fd

like a liquid, take the shape of its container? In every case, the stadium, and even the seat, seasons the game. Consequently I imagine that each park has one best place to perch. That's why the first three innings are *mine.* Each day, to keep my taste buds alive, I follow my whims in search of that game's best spot. If that means a stroll to the bleachers or a visit to the scouts with their radar guns in the box seats, then that's what I do; if the sundown, all crimson and lavender, seems more promising than the game, then I hike to the upper deck and watch them both. I've even been known to sit above the dugout and bench-jockey players in what I hope is an unidentifiable voice.

Tom Boswell, *Why Time Begins
on Opening Day*

A suspended game shall be resumed at the exact point of suspension of the original game. The completion of a suspended game is a continuation of the original game. The lineup and batting order of both teams shall be exactly the same as the lineup and batting order at the moment of suspension, subject to the rules governing substitution. Any player may be replaced by a player who had not been in the game prior to the suspension. No player removed before the suspension may be returned to the lineup.

A player who was not with the club when the game was suspended may be used as a substitute, even if he has taken the place of a player no longer with the club who would not have been eligible because he had been removed from the lineup before the game was suspended.

Official Baseball Rules

IV

REVISING

R E V I S I N G   A S
R E T H I N K I N G

Revising: A process of literally "re-seeing" a text; it includes rethinking the argument, evaluating the evidence, reorganizing the ideas, and reconsidering the perspective.

Revising for logic: A writer's reassessment of viewpoint and the thesis statement and evidence expressing that viewpoint.

Revising for organization: A writer's re-evaluation of the patterns that shape a text and the organization that structures the ideas of the text.

Revising for content: Rethinking the content of a text by performing four activities: **adding information** to clarify generalities through specifics; **deleting information** to eliminate repetitious or extraneous material; **substituting information** to replace weaker points with stronger ones and to change tone; and **rearranging information** to tighten a text's structure.

Editing: Revising for sentence style and diction.

146

11a

Revising as Rethinking

No one writes a flawless text in the first draft. Generally, writers record their initial thoughts as a rough draft and, through multiple revisions, turn this draft into polished text. **Revising** is neither a penalty for having written poorly the first time nor a less important step than writing the rough draft. It is a chance to **rethink** your argument and its evidence, reorganize your ideas, and reconsider your perspective. In short, it is an opportunity for you to manage your own words.

Moreover, revising is not something you do only after you have completed a first draft. Writers revise at all points in the writing process. They cross out words, insert sentences, rephrase ideas, and sometimes tear up a page or two. You cannot separate the activities of thinking, writing, and revising, even though we have divided this text into chapters and subchapters on these topics. Thinking, writing, and revising are integrated parts of a single process geared to make your written work fit your intentions.

To achieve your purpose and communicate your ideas clearly and convincingly, you will usually need to write several drafts, and each draft will require revisions. Your goal as you revise is to express your perspective in a way that meets your own and your intended audience's requirements.

11b
rr

11b

Levels of Revising: Logic, Organization, and Content

In the broadest sense, revising is a two-stage operation: first, rethinking the entire project and, second, reviewing individual words, phrases, and sentences. This latter type of revising, called **editing,** focuses on style (see Unit 9 for a complete discussion). The first part is concerned with revising the whole essay for its content, logic, and organization. **Revising for logic,** an evaluative process tied to critical reading, consists of reassessing your perspective and the thesis statement that expresses that perspective. **Revising for organization** involves improving the order of your ideas in your text. **Revising for content,** discussed in detail below, means reconsidering the information you put in a text and adding, deleting, replacing, or rearranging that information for clarity and readability.

11b
rr

Basic Strategies in Revising for Content

Addition: Add arguments, details, paragraphs, sentences, phrases, or words to delineate or simplify a point or argument.

Deletion: Omit arguments, details, paragraphs, sentences, phrases, or words to eliminate repetition and to strengthen the focus of your writing.

Substitution: Replace certain arguments, details, paragraphs, sentences, phrases, or words with others to change the tone, explain the meaning, improve the style, or focus readers' attention on a point.

Rearrangement: Move certain arguments, details, paragraphs, sentences, phrases, or words around to clarify your logic and to fit your purpose and concept of audience.

1 Adding Information

If you step back and look at your text as though someone else had written it, you will usually find that you have skipped vital points and need to add more information. The following are examples of the kinds of information writers frequently omit in first drafts: all the steps in a process; the consequences of a recommendation you are making; a relevant comparison; a cause for a predicted effect; the logic underlying an argument; or even something as obvious as a clear statement of your purpose.

Specific examples are perhaps the most common addition you will make when revising. Anecdotes, analogies, character portrayals, descriptions, expert opinions, factual statements, and statistics create emphasis, and drama. They clarify generalizations, give concrete support to arguments, and contribute to the text's overall persuasiveness.

There are many ways to introduce examples besides the familiar transition words such as *an example is, for example, for instance,* or *X is an example of.* You can use introductory words or phrases, including *another way, like, specifically, such as, some examples of this, think of it this way,* and you can also rely on verbs such as *tell* and *exemplify,* or any verbs indicating the senses (*look, see, hear,* and so on).

Transitions alone will not automatically blend added information into a text, however. As you revise, you should check whether the added information is accurate. Consider whether your examples and details clearly relate to the generalizations you have proposed. If examples and ideas are sufficiently integrated, you have probably communicated your perspective to your audience.

Exercise 1

The following passage uses examples to defend the writer's perspective. Identify the perspective, how it is expressed, and the examples that support it.

11b
rr

It is hard, on the other hand, to blame the policeman, blank, good-natured, thoughtless, and insuperably innocent, for being such a perfect representative of the people he serves. He, too, believes in good intentions and is astounded and offended when they are not taken for the deed. He has never, himself, done anything for which to be hated—which of us has?—and yet he is facing, daily and nightly, people who would gladly see him dead, and he knows it. There is no way for him not to know it: there are few things under heaven more unnerving than the silent, accumulating contempt and hatred of a people. He moves through Harlem, therefore, like an occupying soldier in a bitterly hostile country; which is precisely what, and where, he is, and is the reason he walks in twos and threes. And he is not the only one who knows why he is always in company: the people who are watching him know why, too. Any street meeting, sacred or secular, which he and his colleagues uneasily cover has as its explicit or implicit burden the cruelty and injustice of the white domination. And these days, of course, in terms increasingly vivid and jubilant, it speaks of the end of that domination.

James Baldwin, *Nobody Knows My Name*

2 **Deleting Information**

Perhaps the most difficult revision for any writer to make is to cut out material once it is safely down on paper. But your prose will greatly benefit if you delete redundancies, obscure points, and digressions. Consider whether every fact, idea, and argument you have put in your draft directly relates to your audience, purpose, and perspective. If some of the information seems irrelevant, look at it carefully before you eliminate it. Digressions may signal that you changed your original perspective on the topic as you wrote. If so, redraft your thesis statement and consider what you might need to do to make the rest of your text support this new thesis statement. If you have not changed your perspective, cut out any material that is outside your topic or inappropriate to your perspective and continue revising.

3 Substituting Information

Replacing information is a matter of considering your audience. Substitute when you sense that your audience will react more positively to the new idea, sentence, phrase, or word. Explain complex matters by substituting familiar examples for less common ones. Likewise, make definitions clearer where possible by substituting ordinary words for overly technical, abstract, or uncommon terms. This kind of strategic replacement lets you avoid redundancies, supply relevant support, tighten organization, and set an appropriate tone.

4 Rearranging Information

One of the most effective guidelines for revising is a simple one: *Keep reorganizing information until you are satisfied that your audience can easily follow your purpose and perspective.* Cut, move, and paste sentences from a section—or move them in a computer—until they follow your intended order. Decide where new information fits best and insert it there. Reconsider the way you shaped your ideas. Discovering in a subsequent draft that a climactic order suits your purpose better than an anticlimactic order leads you to reverse the order of your points and move blocks of text around to fit this new order.

11c

Strategies for Revising

1 Basics of Revising

The basic rule for revising any text is to *challenge everything*. Resist the temptation to change only individual words. Pay attention to your whole draft, and remember that the changes you make in one part may require changes in other parts. You may choose from a number of revision techniques; they are discussed in the rest of this section. Note that these strategies focus on logic and organization, as well as content.

2 Revising from Introductions and Outlines

One way of revising is to concentrate on your introduction. Scrutinize your essay's first few sentences with your audience's background in mind. Ask yourself whether these sentences will capture your audience's attention. Look at your outline to see if you have exhausted its ideas in your draft. If not, think over the omitted ideas and mark the draft to add pertinent details.

11c
rr

3 Revising from an Outline of Your Draft

Another strategy is to put away your working outline and to re-outline your draft as you read it. (Be sure to outline what you have actually written—not what you hoped to write.) Underline the topic sentences that trace your main points. Check to see if each topic sentence consistently relates to the thesis and if each transition consistently connects one sentence to the next. If a topic sentence strays from the thesis statement, rewrite the topic sentence to fit. If the topic sentences do not fall into a logical sequence, juggle them first in your new outline. Then compare this outline with your original one. Note what is missing, what has been added, and what has been moved around. Then reorganize the draft on the basis of your evaluation of the new outline.

4 Revising with a Notational System

Still another methodical way of revising is to mark the text using your own notational system and then revise from that system. Try using *OK* for sections that read well, √ for sections that need rethinking, *thin* for sections that need more detail, *move to #X* and *#X* for units that should be moved and where they will go, and *ugh!* for sections that might best be omitted. Use underlining for thesis statements and squiggly lines or brackets for topic sentences. Then rewrite your text using your marks as a guide.

Suggested Revising Marks

thin [add more information]	*reorder* [chronological, most to
clarify	least important, etc.]
drop this	*OK!*
move to #	*ugh!* [omit or rewrite all this]
wordy [delete information]	*identify*
? [check accuracy]	√ [rethink this]
?? [something is missing]	⁋ [new paragraph]
∧ [insert here]	⌀ [delete this]

5 Revising Through Questioning

Starting with the first paragraph, reread your draft straight through and annotate with specific questions in mind: What do your first and last paragraphs accomplish? Where and how clearly does your thesis statement appear? What main points develop that thesis statement? What points should be omitted? What ideas added? What creates interest? Give yourself credit for what you have done well by identifying your strongest paragraphs and your best sentences; then ask yourself: Why are they satisfying? Compare these convincing passages with the rest of your writing and ask yourself: What's lacking? Rewrite the less persuasive sentences and paragraphs.

6 Revising with a Checklist

Some writers find that a worksheet or checklist guides them efficiently while they revise. Devise a worksheet (like the one suggested on pages 154–155) for yourself. Make your goal an evaluation of what you wrote, and do not let filling in the form make you lose sight of that goal.

Exercise 2

Using the suggested worksheet or one of your own making, revise a text you wrote for a general audience. Then list the changes you would want to make if you were to submit that document to a specialized audience.

7 Revising by Reconsidering Intention

A complementary revising technique focuses on the purpose of your text. How did you want the audience to respond? Categorize the information in your text using your intentions, or motives, as the criteria. Scan your text for words, phrases, or sentences that signal your intentions, set up the responses, and move readers from one response to another. If you do not find any, you know where to start revising. Intentions create different modes of writing, and explanations are meant to teach. Therefore, in an informative text, look for definitions, instructions, procedures, or words that interpret ideas for your readers. Arguments move an audience to action. You will want to highlight the reasoning patterns, sections that dramatize your viewpoint, and transitional terms such as *consequently* and *therefore*. Fiction and speculative nonfiction are for enjoyment. Look for descriptive terms, narrative passages, time markers, and the like.

11c
rr

None of these categories exists entirely in isolation, however. Do not be surprised if you find that you introduce your explanation with a narrative or that you precede an argument with a set of instructions. You had several intentions when you wrote, and you combined methods to present your perspective. For instance, in proposing a solution to a problem, you must provide the following:

- Definition of the situation that gave rise to the problem. (definition)
- Explanation of the problem, with a discussion of its possible effects. (instructional section)
- Statement of the proposed solution. (definition)
- Application of the solution to the problem, with a discussion of the possible effects. (procedure)
- Appeal to the audience to accept the proposed solution. (persuasion)

Exercise 3

Your intentions sometimes change as you rewrite a text. Take an essay you have written recently and list your purposes in writing the text. Examine what you have written and decide what type of text it is: informative, persuasive, entertaining, or a combination. Mark the passages that met your intentions. Decide what you would add to the text to make your purpose clearer and what you would delete in a rewritten version.

Revision Worksheet

1. Audience and Purpose
   My audience is ————————————————————————
   My audience knows ———————————————————————
   My audience can't know ——————————————————
   ——
   ——

   I wrote this text because ——————————————————
   ——

   The impression I want to leave with my reader about my text
   is ——————————————————————————————————————
   ——
   ——

2. Thesis Statement and Introduction
   The first paragraph says ——————————————————
   ——

   The thesis statement is ———————————————————
   ——

   It accomplishes ——————————————————————————
   ——

   It needs ————————————————————————————————
   ——

3. Main Points and Support

1st point is	Effective because	Support needed	Keep/omit?
————	————	————	————
————	————	————	————

2nd point is	Effective because	Support needed	Keep/omit?
————	————	————	————
————	————	————	————

3rd point is	Effective because	Support needed	Keep/omit?
————	————	————	————
————	————	————	————

11c
rr

4th point is	Effective because	Support needed	Keep/omit?
_____	_____	_____	_____
_____	_____	_____	_____
_____	_____	_____	_____

5th point is	Effective because	Support needed	Keep/omit?
_____	_____	_____	_____
_____	_____	_____	_____
_____	_____	_____	_____

Additional points	Needed because	Support for	Put in
_____	_____	_____	_____
_____	_____	_____	_____

4. Reasoning Patterns and Style

Strongest paragraph is _____

Reasoning pattern	Type of support	Transitions used
_____	_____	_____
_____	_____	_____
_____	_____	_____

Convincing because _____

Weakest paragraph is _____

Reasoning pattern needed	Support needed	Transitions needed
_____	_____	_____
_____	_____	_____
_____	_____	_____

5. Conclusion, Audience, and Purpose

My conclusion is _____

It ties in with my thesis statement/introduction because _____

It accomplishes/doesn't accomplish my purpose because _____

My audience now should know _____

My audience should now see me as _____

11c
rr

8 Revising with a Friendly Audience

Another technique is to let a friend or an instructor read your draft and react to it. (Note: Letting a friend *rewrite* your work is plagiarism.) If your friend reacts mostly to your style, you need to redirect his or her criticisms. Ask your friend to tell you what your thesis statement is, what your main points are, and what supporting evidence is impressive. Then ask if any sections seem unnecessary. However, do not automatically cut what someone else sees as unnecessary. Instead, consider whether you need to connect these points more obviously to your thesis. If you determine for yourself that they have no connections, then delete the "padding."

11c
rr

9 Revising with a Computer

Because a computer lets you perform all the basic revision strategies and print out numerous clean "hard copies," it is a convenient tool for rethinking, revising, and even rewriting your text. You can add specifics to clarify generalities, eliminate repetitious or extraneous information, substitute stronger points for weaker ones, replace imprecise words or inappropriate diction, and move words, phrases, sentences, or even whole sections around to strengthen the reasoning and organization of a text. You can easily correct typographical errors and check for spelling errors or duplicated words, for consistent punctuation, and for jargon. You can "search and replace" vague references (i.e., *this* or *it*) or frequently confused words (e.g., homonyms such as *accept* and *except* or *who's* and *whose*). And, best of all, you can mark any changes you want to make on the hard copy and then return to the screen and enter the revisions quickly.

10 Proofreading a Final Draft

The purpose of proofreading is to catch content, typographical, and format errors before your reader does. Although you can proofread your text yourself, the easiest and best strategy is to get another person (usually called a *copyholder*) to slowly read your text out loud while you mark you own copy. Proofread in stages, each time looking for specific items. First read for content accuracy. Make sure that the numbers in tables or figures are correct and that headings are informative and in the right place.

Next, proofread for grammatical accuracy. Locate typographical errors by reading lines backward. Consult your dictionary about the differences in meaning among related words like *affect/effect, personal/personnel, stationary/stationery, to/two/too, threw/through/thorough. wear/were/where.* (For a list of homonyms, see **29b**.) Check for double letters, silent letters, capitalization, and punctuation.

Third, proofread for format and appearance. Make sure you have left adequate margins around your text, spaced sentences precisely, indented paragraphs, and correctly placed your title, name, and any other identifying information.

11d

Revising: A Case in Point

The following is a student's essay written for a first-year writing course. The instructor asked students to read William Zinsser's essay "College Pressures" and write a response to its thesis. Zinsser says that college students have to juggle academic demands with the pressures of living on their own for the first time. This student, PennyLee Rieger, agreed with Zinsser but felt that Zinsser ignored college athletes, who face more of these stresses than other students do. She composed her first draft by jotting down ideas in an informal outline. Then she turned on her computer but left her monitor off. With the screen dark, Rieger could fill out the ideas from her brief outline without interrupting herself, changing her thoughts, or editing her first draft before she completed it.

1 Revision for Content

Rieger printed her rough draft (reproduced below), read it, and began revising by thinking about her audience and purpose. She marked the draft with questions and circled her punctuation, spelling, and grammatical errors so she could return to them later.

Recipients

```
      William Zinsser tries to describe
the pressures Yale Students face, but he
misses the pressures athlethes face,         vague
maybe because Yale doesn't have much of
an athletic program. Student athletes
enjoy learning, competing, and studying
but pressures get heavy on them. Not all
```

althletes are "dummies." Scholarship
althletes, for exmple, have to keep their
grades up and still compete strongly if
they are to hold on to their financial
support. The pressures they face trying
to live two lives at one time really
mount up. Their classmates get on their
case, and so do their parents. Worst of
all they get on their own cases when they
aren't perfect students and perfect   ← ?
competitors.

    Athletes stand out from other
students on any campus because their
different from all the other students.
This difference causes peer pressure to
happen every day of their lives. They are
always competing and trying to beat out
everyone else because they think their
supposed to do that. Competing against
their teammates and other students can
get heavy. Everyone is always competing   slang
to do better than the other guy. Zinsser,
who sounds like he was a student athlete,   ← need ?
describes how every Yale student thinks
every other Yale student is working   too much
harder and doing better. They really   Yale ?
don't know what's going on. They think
they have to work harder all the time
just to keep up. He wishes students could
forget what they're doing and go to a
flick. Trying to 'keep a head of the
Joneses' all the time is'nt healthy. But
they do it anyway. But zinsser forgets
that athletes put more pressure on
themselves than even Yale students do. If a   tone too
jock sees another student write a 10-page   casual
paper, he thinks he has to write a longer   throughout ?
one. If she sees another student get a B
on a text, she has to get a B+ or an an
A. My friend Jane Roberts plays tennis
and she has to play in challenge matches   Sense ?
that are real hard. She gets nervous real   This
quick and really doubts that she can play   goes on
as good as she wants to. Then some other   too long
player like Stacey McFarland comes along

and tells Jane that she can beat her
because Stacey beat her 6-0, 6-0, 6-1 the
day before. All of a sudden Jane gets
more tense and upset. She has to be
better than the other girl and better
than Stacey! She better relax and realize
that if she has confidence she can win.
     Next is the most horrifying pressure
of all pressures, parents. Athletes never
feel that they can do enough to please
their parents even when their parents
aren't there to watch them all the time.
Are they letting their parents down
somehow? These thoughts fly through their
heads all the time. Zinsser sums up the
problem pretty well when he write [put in
Zinsser's exact words here]. Pleasing
your parents and coaches seems to be the
goal for many athletes. Parents spend
money to you into school and you have to
do something to show your folks that your
working. Competition and parental
pressure come together too. For example,
if twleve basketball players are all on
tthe same team but only five can play,
there's a problem. Bob Rainer felt
nervous about the big game last month
because he wanted to start because his
parents were coming to the game. When he
got word that he could start, he was real
happy. But then his dad called and told
Bob that he expected his son to score big
in the game. That depressed Bob even
more. His parents just put added pressure
on him, which he doesn't know what to do
with. It will finally snap sometime, but
the time is unforseen.
     Not all athletes feel this way, but
most do. Paul spneds all his time
worrying about tests, assignments,
practice, matchs, and being the best. He
runs on the track team and want the team
to be number one in the next meet. So he
runs five miles more each day and doesn't
eat so he'll weigh less and can run

get

best way to
put it ?

this is a type
of pressure
too

faster. His body gets stressed out   *slang*
tenfold. He never relaxes or entertains
himself. The idea of being number one is
everything. And he always has on-going
butterflies which seem to sit in the
bottom of his stomach. When the big meet
finally happens, he's so weak from
overwork and sick from stress that he
can't even compete. He loses and the team
loses. Yet all his tension came from the
constant "song and dance" that keeps
playing in his head as long as he's an
athlete.

**11d
rr**

Zinsser sums up the pressures for
students when he writes that [put in
Zinsser's words. Something about students
getting too goal-oriented at a young age
Better find out if I have to footnote the
guy?] Athlethes who make mistakes in
their studies and in sports and who can
accept that mistakes won't damn them will
be a winner in the end. Accepting that
something is wrong is the first step.

2 Revision for Content and Organization

Before writing her second draft, Rieger outlined what she had
written by composing a sentence for each paragraph that summarized
what the paragraph was about.

1. Thesis: Student athletes feel the same types
   of pressures other students do but to a
   greater degree because they're athletes. The
   pressures are peer pressure, parental
   pressure, and self-induced pressure. [Didn't
   clearly state this anywhere]

2. Athletes are always competing against their
   classmates, other schools' athletes, and
   their teammates.

3. Parental pressure is really awful. Athletes
   feel it because they think they owe their
   parents great performance in sports.

4. The idea of being number one in your sport is most important to any athlete.

5. All this worrying about competing can hurt student athletes, and it would be best if they learned to accept some setbacks.

The outline helped Rieger see why her organization and reasoning might confuse a reader. Not all her paragraphs had clear topic sentences, not all the topic sentences developed her thesis statement, and not all the sentences in each paragraph related to one another. Further, the connections between ideas were not always plain, and her examples and comments did not always fit her topic or its tone. She had not explained to her reader why and how student athletes feel these pressures more than other students. She redrafted her ideas into a new outline.

11d
rr

1. Thesis: Even though scholarship athletes receive their grants as reward for their sports and academic talent, they feel peer pressure, parental pressure, and self-induced pressure more than many other students.

2. Both classroom and athletic competition can get intense because everyone is trying to do better than other students and players.

3. Example: A good example of peer pressure is Jane, who attends college on a tennis scholarship and has to play a challenge match with her teammate Sara.

4. A more horrifying type of pressure is parental pressure.

5. Finally, the worst pressure in any athlete's life is self-induced pressure.

6. Conclusion: Any athlete who can recognize and deal with these additional pressures and who knows that mistakes aren't examples of fatal character flaws and pressures aren't necessarily good will be a winner in the end.

From her marked-up draft and this new outline, she began restructuring and rewriting.

3 Revision for Logic

Completing her next draft, Rieger turned her attention to the logic in the individual paragraphs and sentences. She immediately saw that some of her statements were flippant, so she deleted some and substituted a more formal tone for others.

She gave particular attention to her introduction and conclusion. She wanted her introduction to state her position directly and immediately interest her reader. She decided to rearrange the paragraph and start with a statement about Zinsser's essay that would lead to an explicitly stated thesis.

In his essay "College Pressures" William Zinsser describes the ~~tenstion~~ *tensions* Yale students face. Zinsser is right about~~y~~ these ~~pressures~~, but he doesn't go far enough ~~maybe because Yale doesn't have much of an athletic program~~. He forgets the special ~~pressures~~ *way* student athletes face ~~and how they~~ *these* understand ~~pressure~~ *athletic students* Many enjoy learning, competing, and studying but pressures get heavy on them. However, sometimes the~~ir~~ ~~pressures~~ *competitiveness* ~~they face~~ *that makes them athletes* can almost defeat them. Even though scholarship athletes receive their grants as reward for their talent, they feel more pressures *and create* than *for themselves* many other students. ~~The pressures on student athletes can be classified as~~ (peer pressure, parental pressure, and self-induced pressure.)

Rieger wanted her conclusion to reaffirm her thesis, convince her reader that she had covered her topic fully and fairly, and signal to that reader that she had finished her discussion. She decided that mentioning the names of her student examples (Jane, Bob, and Paul) and renaming the three types of pressure created the best ending because it tied the conclusion to the introduction. She then reconsidered her concluding sentence. She thought it should sum up her position *and* leave her reader impressed. But, since she could not think of a strong "punch line" to end the essay, she bracketed the last sentence and resolved to revise it later. Finally, she shortened the conclusion by deleting some repetitive material, sentences, and words.

Not all athletes feel pressured the way Jane, Bob, and Paul do, but most do. ~~Competitors~~ create their own feelings of

[handwritten insertions: "many tend to" above "the"; "Athletes who are ~~very~~ strongly competitive" below]

tension, frustration, and agony. Peer pressure, parental pressure, and self-induced pressure make an athlete's life worse. And the constant "song and dance" that these pressures cause keeps on playing as long as an athlete keeps on competing. Zinsser sums up the pressures ~~directly~~ when he writes that "it's why I think we should all be worried about the values that are nurturing a generation so fearful of risk and so goal-obsessed at such an early age." An athlete ~~who can make a mistake academically or in sports,~~ who can recognize and deal with these additional pressures, and who can accept that mistakes aren't examples of fatal character flaws or that pressures aren't necessarily good will be a winner in the end. [Accepting that pressures can make something go wrong and that they don't have to act better than everyone else just because they are athletes is their first step to walking away from those pressures.]

[handwritten annotations: "this?" above "these"; "a thing" inserted above "necessarily good"; "ugh! Do something here" in right margin]

4 Last Revision and Proofreading

Rieger rewrote her essay two more times, each time rearranging information, smoothing the tone, and reviewing each paragraph for a topic sentence, a clear organization, and adequate supporting evidence. Satisfied with its content, logic, and organization, she asked a friend to help her proofread the revised draft. They checked the punctuation, spelling, and grammar and corrected the formatting. Finally, she entered all her proofreading changes into her computer and printed the following essay.

Forgotten Recipients of Pressure

In his essay "College Pressures" William Zinsser describes the stresses Yale students face. Zinsser is correct about these tensions, but he doesn't go far enough when he writes about them. He forgets the special way student athletes make these pressures worse. Most athletic students enjoy learning, studying, and, especially, competing. However, sometimes the competitiveness that makes them athletes can almost defeat them. Even though scholarship athletes receive their grants as reward for their talent, they feel peer pressure, parental pressure, and self-induced pressure more seriously than many other students.

The peer pressure starts off every day of an athlete's life. All students have to compete against other students in their classes, but athletes also compete against other schools' athletes and their own teammates. Both classroom and athletic competition can get intense because everyone is trying to do better than other students and players. Zinsser argues that college students may not even know how great the pressure is. He believes every student thinks every other student is working harder and doing better than she is. The student thinks the only solution is to work harder still, to writer longer papers, and to score higher than anyone else on the tests. If students could forget about their peers for a while and go to a movie, Zinsser feels they would be healthier.

A good example of peer pressure is Jane, who attends college on a tennis scholarship and has to play a challenge match with her teammate Sara. She has to keep her grades up, so when she sees another student writing a 10-page paper she tries to write a 15-page paper. Right before the big match, she starts to have doubts if she can beat Sara. Stacey, another teammate, tells Jane, "Oh, you can beat her. I beat her 6-0, 6-0, 6-1, yesterday." Now Jane's body tenses. She has to win because Stacey won yesterday, and she wants to be a better player than both Sara and Stacey. The pressure keeps building in Jane's mind and could cause her to lose the match. If she would realize that the pressure could hurt her, Jane could learn how relaxation and confidence can ease peer pressure.

11d
rr

A more horrifying type of pressure is parental pressure. Athletes always want to do well for their parents. They're asking themselves at least once a week "Am I letting my parents down?" Zinsser sums up the parental pressure athletes feel when he writes about all students: "But the pressure on students is severe. They are truly torn. One part of them feels obligated to fulfill their parents' expectations; after all, their parents are older and presumably wiser. Another part tells them that the expectations that are right for their parents are not right for them." Athletes who don't have scholarships feel that their parents have spent extra money on them and that they should pay their parents back in some way. Studying and working harder aren't enough. They have to be the best on the team. For example, Bob is feeling nervous about the big basketball game because he wants to be one of the starters but only five of the twelve players can start. He is very nervous the week before the game, and then his parents call to wish him luck. They tell him he is the best basketball player the team has, and they expect that he will score at least 20 points because he is the best. Now Bob is more nervous; he has the pressure not only of starting but also of scoring 20 points. He doesn't know what to do with the pressure his parents just added on him. Each time this happens, Bob gets more anxious. At some unforeseen time, he may "snap."

Finally, the worst pressure in any athlete's life is self-induced pressure. For any athlete, excellence and performance are everything. However, being the best and wanting to be the best are two totally different areas. Zinsser describes what self-induced pressure can lead to when students try to--but cannot--get everything done perfectly. "They will get sick. They will get 'blocked.' They will sleep. They will oversleep. They will bug out." Athletes push their bodies to the limit to be the best. They worry about tests, assignments, and essays like other students, but they also worry about practice, matches, and being the best competitor. For example, Paul wants to be number one on his running team by being the big winner at the next meet. So he doesn't eat and runs five miles more a day for the week before the meet. He keeps thinking about running in every event and being the star at the meet. The stress level in his body exceeds its normal limits tenfold. He never has time to relax or entertain himself because all he can do is practice and think about being the best. When the day for the big meet finally arrives, Paul is so sick from stress that he breaks down and can't compete at all. In his eyes, he's failed everyone, but particularly himself. Yet all his tension came from himself.

Not all athletes feel these pressures as strongly as Jane, Bob, and Paul, but many tend to. Athletes who are strongly competitive create their own feelings of tension, frustration, and agony. Peer pressure, parental pressure, and self-induced pressure make an athlete's life worse. And the constant "song and dance" that these pressures cause keeps on playing as long as an athlete keeps on competing. Zinsser sums up the pressures directly when he writes "It's why I think we should all be worried about the values that are nurturing a generation so fearful of risk and so goal-obsessed at such an early age." An athlete who can make a mistake academically or in sports, who can recognize and deal with these additional pressures, and who can accept that mistakes aren't examples of fatal character flaws or that pressures aren't necessarily good will be a winner in the end. Accepting that pressures can make something go wrong is an athlete's first step to walking away from those pressures.

12

P A R A G R A P H S

Paragraph: A physical unit within a text that is concerned with one topic or an aspect of a topic or that serves as a transition between complex points. The size, organization, and function of paragraphs vary greatly.

Paragraphing: A method of guiding readers through a text. Where paragraphing imitates the writer's thought patterns, the reader is more disposed to accept the writer's conclusions.

Coherence: The overall effect of unity and comprehensibility that a communicative text imparts. Coherence arises from a clearly logical structure, recognizable organization, and various cohesive elements (such as transitions) that connect ideas and make them relevant to the whole.

Topic sentence: A generalization that unifies the information in a paragraph. Topic sentences are the thesis statements for paragraphs.

Patterns of development: The multiple organizations for paragraphs and texts that reflect a writer's thinking about a topic or subject. Common patterns of development include analysis and

167

classification, cause and effect, comparison and contrast, definition, description, listing, narration, and question and answer.

12a

Flexible Paragraphing

There are numerous conventions and formal devices for identifying and constructing paragraphs. The truth is that a *paragraph* is not as clear-cut an entity as a *sentence* or a *word*. The common definition, which we use in this chapter, is that a **paragraph** is a textual unit covering one topic or an aspect of a topic or serving as a transition between complex points. But paragraphs come in an array of shapes and sizes. Moreover, most writers draft their texts with purpose, audience, and information primarily in mind: The finer points of paragraphing come later. Consider, as an example, how you determine whether the following eleven sentences make one paragraph or several:

> (1) I suggest that the introductory course in science, at all levels from grade school through college, be radically revised. (2) Leave the fundamentals, the so-called basics, aside for a while, and concentrate the attention of all students on the things that are *not known*. (3) You cannot possibly teach quantum mechanics without mathematics, to be sure, but you can describe the strangeness of the world opened up by quantum theory. (4) Let it be known, early on, that there are deep mysteries, and profound paradoxes, revealed in their distant outlines, by the quantum. (5) Let it be known that these can be approached more closely, and puzzled over, once the language of mathematics has been sufficiently mastered. (6) Teach at the outset, before any of the fundamentals, the still imponderable puzzles of cosmology. (7) Let it be known, as clearly as possible, by the youngest minds, that there are some things going on in the universe that lie beyond comprehension, and make it plain how little is known. (8) Do not teach that biology is a useful and perhaps profitable science; that can come later. (9) Teach instead that there are structures squirming inside all our cells, providing all the energy for living, that are essentially foreign creatures, brought in for symbiotic living a billion or so years ago, the lineal descendants of bacteria. (10) Teach that we do not have the ghost of an idea how they got there, where they came from, or how they evolved to their present structure or function. (11) The details of oxidative phosphorylation and photosynthesis can come later.
>
> Lewis Thomas, "Humanities and Science"

Thomas himself divides this information into three paragraphs: sentences (1) through (5), (6) and (7), and (8) through (11). He introduces the topic in (1), suggesting that that sentence is the first paragraph's topic sentence. The ideas in all three paragraphs cluster around the generalization in the second sentence that what is *not known* will interest curious young minds more than what is supposedly known.

Notice that you looked for these paragraphs not by using an arbitrary number of sentences or words that should be in a paragraph but by examining their content. You may have divided the paragraph the same way that Thomas did, or you may have used another organizational strategy because the pattern seemed more consistent with your understanding of Thomas's purpose and sentences. What is important to realize is that paragraphing is both individualistic *and* systematic: Writers, not arbitrary conventions, set the system for audiences to interpret.

12a
par

Exercise 1

Decide where paragraph divisions should logically fall in the following passage. List the reasons for your decision.

(1) New York—I'm in the writing racket, see. (2) It used to be a nice little living, the writing racket, until the English Mafia moved in on it. (3) I mean, it didn't pull in the really big bucks, but then, it wasn't something you had to sweat either. (4) I'd lie around the house sleeping till noon, then roll out of the sack, drink a few pots of coffee, then go out in the back yard and split infinitives for a few hours. (5) If I got tired of splitting infinitives, maybe I'd dangle a few participles. (6) Or if the widow next door was peeking at me from behind her curtains I might give her an eyeful of committing a solecism. (7) One sunny day, I was out there writing up a storm about parameters. (8) To be honest with you, I have no idea what parameters are. (9) I've picked up enough Latin to know that "meter" means "measure," and enough Greek to know that "para" means "near" or "beside," so maybe parameters are measures of a beside, all of which is neither here nor there. (10) The thing is, you see, in the writing racket when you're pinched for something to write about, you can always write about parameters. (11) Don't ask me why. (12) People like to read about parameters is all I know, and writing about parameters makes you feel smart, especially if you are writing about the parameters making a quantum leap, and don't ask me what kind of leap the quantum variety is either, because all I know is that quantum leaps are the only kinds of leaps that are made anymore, at least by parameters.

Russell Baker, "The English Mafia"

Paragraph Coherence

Coherence is that quality of a text or its paragraphs that unifies the text and makes it comprehensible. To achieve coherence, the individual elements must be connected in ways that make them relevant to the thesis and produce a unified, comprehensible result. Coherent paragraphs are about one thing, the topic, and they contribute to a larger something, the thesis of the text. Achieving coherence involves paying close attention to such basic matters as pronominal reference, modification, and conjunctions (for example, *and, then, however,* and *consequently*) and more sophisticated ones such as repeating key words and ideas, logically ordering ideas, and clearly indicating patterns of development.

1 Topic Sentences

Central ideas or main points are summarized in **topic sentences**, which orient readers to the paragraph's purpose in the way that thesis statements direct them to a text's argument. In the following paragraph from one of his speeches, Martin Luther King, Jr., begins with the topic sentence (in italics) and then repeats the sentence's three key words—*violence, impractical,* and *immoral*—in the paragraph to remind listeners of his topic:

> *Violence as a way of achieving racial justice is both impractical and immoral.* It is *impractical* because it is a descending spiral ending in destruction for all. The old law of an eye for an eye leaves everybody blind. It is *immoral* because it seeks to humiliate the opponent rather than win his understanding; it seeks to annihilate rather than to convert. Violence is *immoral* because it thrives on hatred rather than love. It destroys community and makes brotherhood impossible. It leaves society in monologue rather than dialogue. Violence ends by defeating itself. It creates bitterness in the survivors and brutality in the destroyers. A voice echoes through time saying to every potential Peter, "Put up your sword." History is cluttered with the wreckage of nations that failed to follow this command.
>
> Martin Luther King, Jr.,
> "Stride Toward Freedom"

Topic sentences, which typically begin paragraphs, are present because paragraphs tend to have unifying generalities—not because

12b
par

there is a rule mandating that every paragraph must have a topic sentence.

Identify the topic sentences in the following paragraphs.

Many American universities have diluted or displaced their "core curriculum" in the great works of Western civilization to make room for new course offerings stressing non-Western cultures, African-American studies, and women's studies. There is little argument about the desirability of teaching the greatest works written by members of other cultures, by women, and by minority-group members. Many academic activists go beyond this to insist that texts be selected primarily or exclusively according to the author's race, gender, or sexual preference, and that the Western tradition be exposed in the classroom as hopelessly bigoted and oppressive in every way. "What we have now in universities is a kind of liberal closed-mindedness, a leveling impulse," says the sociologist David Riesman, of Harvard University. "Everybody is supposed to go along with the so-called virtuous positions." Because race and gender issues are so sensitive, several professors who have crossed the boundaries of what may be said in the classroom have found themselves the objects of organized vilification and administrative penalties. These curbs rarely apply to professors who are viewed as the champions of minority interests—they are permitted overly ideological scholarship, and immunized from criticism even when they make excessive or outlandish claims with racial connotations.

Dinesh D'Souza, "Illiberal Education"

Certainly, the academy changes those from alien cultures more than it is changed by them. While minority groups had an impact on higher education, largely because of their advantage in coming as a group, within the last few years students such as myself, who finally ended up certified as academics, also ended up sounding very much like the academics we found when we came to the campus. I do not enjoy making such admissions. But perhaps now the time has come when questions about the cultural costs of education ought to be delayed no longer. Those of us who have been scholarship boys know in our bones that our education has exacted a large price in exchange for the large benefits it has conferred upon us. And what is sadder to consider, after we have paid that price, we go home and casually change the cultures that nurtured us. My parents today understand how they are "Chicanos" in a large and impersonal sense. The gains from such knowledge are clear. But so, too, are the reasons for regret.

Richard Rodriguez, "Going Home Again: The
New American Scholarship Boy"

Consider what has happened to two of our largest and most important companies, Du Pont and General Electric, over the past

12b
par

decade. Du Pont has a well-deserved reputation, going back more than 175 years, for being one of America's most innovative companies. Its long record of success was due almost entirely to the quality of its research in the basic sciences. But during the 1970s, Du Pont, for the first time in its history, appointed as chief executive officer (CEO) an attorney who lacked any scientific training. Under the leadership of Irving Shapiro, the company has cut back on its R[esearch] and D[evelopment] budget rather than on shareholders' dividends. R and D expenditures as a percentage of sales declined from 6.6 percent in 1970 to a little over 3 percent in 1979. Because of these budget cuts, the company failed to develop new product lines to reduce their dependence on synthetic fibers. The result: the company was hit harder by the recession of the late 1970s than almost any other chemical company. While Shapiro's legal skills were an asset in Du Pont's dealings with the government, it now remains for Du Pont's new CEO, a chemist named Edward Jefferson, to see if he can restore the company to its leadership role in science and technology.

David Vogel, "Business Without Science"

2 Levels of Generality

One way to identify topic sentences and judge how well they are supported is to outline a paragraph and identify its **levels of generality**—the hierarchy of ideas in the paragraph. Some paragraphs have only two levels: the topic sentence and its immediate support. This organization, called *coordinating structure,* is the pattern Bruce Catton uses in the following paragraph:

1. So [Ulysses S.] Grant and [Robert E.] Lee were in complete contrast, representing two diametrically opposed elements in American life.
    2. Grant was the modern man emerging; beyond him, ready to come on the stage, was the great age of steel and machinery, of crowded cities and a restless burgeoning vitality.
    2. Lee might have ridden down from the old age of chivalry, lance in hand, silken banner fluttering over his head.
    2. Each man was the perfect champion of his cause, drawing both his strengths and his weaknesses from the people he led.

Bruce Catton, *A Stillness at Appomattox*

Other paragraphs narrow continually: Each sentence following the topic sentence develops only one point from the previous sentence, creating a *subordinating structure.* Katherine Kuh uses subordinating structure in discussing the impact of technology on art:

1. How natural, then, that artists reflect this pressure by showing all sides of an object, its entire motion, its total psychological content in one concerted impact.
    2. It is almost as if the pressures of time had necessitated a visual speed-up not unlike the industrial one associated with the assembly line and mass production.
        3. Speed with its multiple overlays transforms our surroundings into jagged, interrupted images.

Katherine Kuh, *Break-Up:*
The Core of Modern Art

Mary E. Mebane uses the same structure in examining how stereotypes handicap some individuals, but she puts her topic sentence at the end, rather than at the beginning, of the paragraph:

12b
par

2. This woman [that is, the chairman's wife] had no official position on the faculty, except that she was an instructor in English; nevertheless, her summons had to be obeyed.
    3. In the segregated world there were (and remain) gross abuses of authority because those at the pinnacle, and even their spouses, felt that the people "under" them had no recourse except to submit—and they were right except that sometimes a black who got sick and tired of it would go to the whites and complain.
        4. This course of action was severely condemned by the blacks, but an interesting thing happened—such action got positive results.
            5. Power was thought of in negative terms: I can deny someone something, I can strike at someone who can't strike back, I can ride someone down; that proves I am powerful.
1. The concept of power as a force for good, for affirmative response to people or situations, was not in evidence.

Mary E. Mebane, *Mary*

Another type of paragraph blends coordination and subordination, creating a *mixed structure*. William Zinsser, for instance, begins with a topic sentence, adds two specific illustrations of his point, then details his second supporting point:

1. My particular hang-up as a writer is that I have to get every paragraph as nearly right as possible before I go on to the next paragraph.
    2. I'm somewhat like a bricklayer: I build very slowly, not adding a new row until I feel that the foundation is solid enough to hold up the house.

2. I'm the exact opposite of the writer who dashes off his entire
first draft, not caring how sloppy it looks or how badly it's
written.
3. His only object at this early stage is to let his creative motor
run the full course at full speed; repairs can always be made
later.
3. I envy this writer and would like to have his metabolism.
3. But I'm stuck with the one I've got.

William Zinsser, *Writing with a
Word Processor*

**12b
par**

Aileen Pace Nilsen balances information similarly but, like Mebane, ends her paragraph with the topic sentence:

2. We see similar differences in food metaphors.
3. Food is a passive substance just sitting there waiting to be
eaten. Many people have recognized this and so no longer
feel comfortable describing women as "delectable morsels."
3. However, when I was a teenager, it was considered a
compliment to refer to a girl (we didn't call anyone a
woman until she was middle-aged) as *a cute tomato, a
peach, a dish, a cookie, honey, sugar,* or *sweetie-pie.*
3. When being affectionate, women will occasionally call a
man *honey* or *sweetie,* but in general, food metaphors are
used much less often with men than with women.
3. If a man is called *a fruit,* his masculinity is being
questioned.
3. But it's perfectly acceptable to use a food metaphor if the
food is heavier and more substantive than that used for
women.
4. For example, pinup pictures of women have long been
known as *cheesecake,* but when Burt Reynolds posed for
a nude centerfold, the picture was immediately dubbed
beefcake, c.f. *a hunk of meat.*
1. That such sexual references to men have come into the general
language is another reflection of how society is beginning to
lessen the differences between their attitudes toward men and
women.

Aileen Pace Nilsen, "Sexism in English:
A 1990s Update"

Exercise 3

Try your hand at outlining a paragraph. Identify the topic sentences in
the following passage and state whether the paragraphs follow a coordinating, subordinating, or mixed structure.

The flats took on a mysterious quality as dusk approached and the
last evening light was reflected from the scattered pools and creeks.

Then birds became only dark shadows, with no color discernible. Sanderlings scurried across the beach like little ghosts, and here and there the darker forms of the willets stood out. Often I could come very close to them before they would start up in alarm—the sanderlings running, the willets flying up, crying. Black skimmers flew along the ocean's edge silhouetted against the dull, metallic gleam, or they went flitting above the sand like large, dimly seen moths. Sometimes they "skimmed" the winding creeks of tidal water, where little spreading surface ripples marked the presence of small fish.

The shore at night is a different world, in which the very darkness that hides the distractions of daylight brings into sharper focus the elemental realities. Once, exploring the night beach, I surprised a small ghost crab in the searching beam of my torch. He was lying in a pit he had dug just above the surf, as though watching the sea and waiting. The blackness of the night possessed water, air, and beach. It was the darkness of an older world, before Man. There was no sound but the all-enveloping, primeval sounds of wind blowing over water and sand, and of waves crashing on the beach. There was no other visible life—just one small crab near the sea. I have seen hundreds of ghost crabs in other settings, but suddenly I was filled with the odd sensation that for the first time I knew the creature in its own world—that I understood, as never before, the essence of its being. In that moment time was suspended; the world to which I belonged did not exist and I might have been an onlooker from outer space. The little crab alone with the sea became a symbol that stood for life itself—for the delicate, destructible, yet incredibly vital force that somehow holds its place amid the harsh realities of the inorganic world.

Rachel Carson, The Edge of the Sea

12b
par

A misconception about paragraphs is that they must have topic sentences. While most paragraphs contain an explicit unifying generality and its supporting information, not all paragraphs require a topic sentence. Sometimes a paragraph elaborates a topic sentence that was stated in the preceding paragraph. Paragraphing in narratives and descriptions can begin when a different character speaks or when the point of view shifts in a description. Writers composing expositions, explanations, and arguments will, at times, suppress a paragraph's central idea so that readers can infer it—a paragraph strategy that depends on enthymemic reasoning. (See **5d**.) At other times paragraphs are simply a way to break up long passages visually, as you often see in newspaper columns, and thus have no explicit topic sentences. Finally, transitional paragraphs that move an audience from one complex idea to another usually lack topic sentences.

3 Transitions

You can achieve coherence in paragraphs by clearly presenting the connections and relationships between ideas in sentences. Pronouns, for example, tie parts of paragraphs together through reference. Adjectives such as *some* or *many* imply a progression through a paragraph, and conjunctions tell readers what connections they should see. Repeating words, phrases, or synonyms throughout a paragraph, relying on parallel grammatical constructions, using short paragraphs as transitions, and other stylistic devices are all ways of aiding coherence in paragraphs.

12b
par

Selected Transitional Devices

Pronouns: *this, that, these, those, her, hers, him, his, it, its, them, their, theirs, one, everyone, none*

Adjectives: *another, each, either, every, many, neither, others, some*

Conjunctions indicating time: *after that, at once, at the same time, briefly, finally, first (second, third, and so forth), from this point on, meanwhile, just then, later, next, previously, then, up to now*

Conjunctions indicating addition: *also, alternatively, and, and also, besides, for example, for instance, further, furthermore, in addition, in the same way, likewise, moreover, next, nor, or else, similarly, specifically*

Conjunctions indicating contrast: *but, despite, however, in contrast, nonetheless, on the contrary, on the other hand, still, yet*

Conjunctions indicating reason: *as a result, because, consequently, for this reason, hence, in conclusion, it follows that, otherwise, since, so, that being so, therefore, thus, to conclude, to sum up, to this end, under the circumstances, with this in mind*

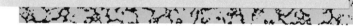

4 Patterns of Development

Coherent paragraphs also have discernible **patterns of development,** which tell readers how you put information together as you thought about the topic. The general methods you typically use to develop ideas in a text are simple. You assert a point and comment on it, give a reason or series of reasons for it, or combine commentary with reasons. Paragraph by paragraph, your presentation usually falls into patterns that are described with labels like *definition, comparison* and *contrast,* or *narration.* Paragraphs using primarily classification, definition, details, or explanation patterns comment on an assertion, whereas paragraphs using analysis and classification, listing, and question and answer developments give reasons for an assertion. Paragraphs using narration, description, and comparison and contrast patterns often combine commentary with proof.

Though one pattern or another tends to dominate a paragraph, many paragraphs show a combination of patterns. It is difficult, in fact, to find a single text or paragraph that relies solely on one organizational strategy. When you are drafting, ask yourself: *What am I going to say about this point?* and *What have I already said about this idea?* Answers to the first question suggest a pattern in which to develop a thought, and answers to the second confirm whether to continue your original pattern or change it and your thinking about a point.

The most common patterns of paragraph development are discussed in the rest of this section. Remember that it is unusual to find only one pattern in a paragraph. Expect to read and write paragraphs that contain, for example, metaphoric definitions within evaluations, narration within evaluations, or comparisons and contrasts within cause and effect paragraphs.

Analysis and Classification

Analysis breaks down a complex idea into logical parts and states, or classifies, those parts in some ordered manner. It is a good tool for defining difficult terms and evaluating arguments by judging their parts, as H. L. Mencken does in this passage:

> Unluckily, there are three flaws in the argument [for abolishing war through legal systems]. The first, which is obvious, lies in the circumstance that a system of legal remedies is of no value if it is not backed by sufficient force to impose its decisions upon even the most powerful litigants—a sheer impossibility in international affairs, for even if one powerful litigant might be coerced, it would be plainly impossible to coerce a combination, and it is precisely a combination of the powerful that is most to be feared. The second lies in the fact that any legal system, to be worthy of credit, must be administered by judges who have no personal interest in the litigation before them—another impossibility, for all the judges in the international court, in the case of disputes between first-class powers, would either be appointees of those powers, or appointees of inferior powers that were under their direct influence, or obliged to consider

the effects of their enmity. The third objection lies in the fact, frequently forgotten, that the courts of justice which now exist do not actually dispense justice, but only law, and that this law is frequently in direct conflict, not only with what one litigant honestly believes to be his rights, but also with what he believes to be his honor. Practically every litigation, in truth, ends with either one litigant or the other nursing what appears to him as an outrage upon him. For both litigants to go away satisfied that justice has been done is almost unheard of.

H. L. Mencken, *Minority Report*

Cause and Effect

Cause and effect paragraphs, commonly found in descriptions of processes, are deceptively simple. It is difficult to state with confidence exactly what caused something to happen or what resulted from a series of events. Multiple causes can bring about a single effect or multiple effects, and a single cause or event can lead either to a single effect or to multiple ones. Another problem is distinguishing between immediate or apparent causes for an effect and distant or underlying causes. In discussing the effects that television violence may have on children, Marie Winn presents what seems like an immediate cause:

> . . . the number of juveniles arrested for serious and violent crimes increased *1600 percent* between the years 1952 and 1972, according to FBI figures. Since this is the very period in which television became ascendant in the lives of American children, and since the programs children watch are saturated with crime and destruction, it has long seemed reasonable to search for a link between the two.

But she goes on to tell readers that underlying causes make the connection between juvenile violence and television more complex:

> And yet this link continues to elude social scientists and researchers, in spite of their great efforts to demonstrate its existence. The truly repugnant, sadistic, amazingly various violence appearing on home screens must surely have subtle effects upon children's behavior, but it clearly does not cause them to behave in seriously antisocial ways. After all, the majority of American children are regularly exposed to those violent programs that have been proposed as a causative factor in the increase of juvenile violence, and yet the children involved in the FBI statistics are but a small proportion of the viewing population. And while a number of research studies *do* indicate a relationship between viewing violence on television and subsequent aggressive behavior, that behavior as seen in the research laboratory obviously does not involve rape or murder, the serious crimes included in the FBI report, but rather ordinary childish aggression— pushing, shoving, hitting, and so on.

Marie Winn, *The Plug-in Drug*

Because cause and effect analysis is demanding, you should consider carefully how you organize information when you write paragraphs using this pattern. Some writers use a chronological or spatial
pattern of development (for instance, narration or description) for
individual paragraphs and arrange those paragraphs in an order that
suggests a cause and effect organization for the entire text. However,
this arrangement can lead you to assume that because one event happened before another it must have caused the second event. (See **9b**
for a discussion of the fallacy of false cause.)

Comparison and Contrast

Comparisons present similarities, and contrasts state differences.
You can restrict a paragraph to only a comparison or only a contrast, as
Marie Winn does in the following passage, which compares reading
and watching television:

> The pace of reading, clearly, depends entirely upon the reader. He
> may read as slowly or as rapidly as he can or wishes to read. If he
> does not understand something, he may stop and reread it, or go in
> search of elucidation before continuing. The reader can accelerate his
> pace when the material is easy or less than interesting, and slow
> down when it is difficult or enthralling. If what he reads is moving,
> he can put down the book for a few moments and cope with his
> emotions without fear of losing anything.
>
> The pace of the television experience cannot be controlled by the
> viewer; only its beginning and end are within his control as he clicks
> the knob on and off. He cannot slow down a delightful program or
> speed up a dreary one. He cannot "turn back" if a word or phrase is
> not understood. The program moves inexorably forward, and what is
> lost or misunderstood remains so.
>
> Marie Winn, *The Plug-in Drug*

However, you may find it easier to put both similarities and differences
in one paragraph, particularly if you are using comparison and contrast
to define a term or explain a concept. For example, Winn chooses this
pattern for her first paragraph, where she implicitly compares reading
for enjoyment with reading critically. She continues the pattern in the
second paragraph with the implicit contrast between television viewing and reading.

Definition

Definition paragraphs answer the implicit question *What is*
_____ ? A **formal definition** states a term, the class it belongs to,
and the distinguishing characteristics that separate it from other mem-

12b
par

bers of that class. These characteristics are the details, anecdotes, and illustrations that complete the paragraph. Charles Earle Funk puts *white elephant* in the class *items* and uses humorous examples to distinguish it from other items:

> That large portrait of your wealthy Aunt Jane, given by her and which you loathe but do not dare to take down from your wall; that large bookcase, too costly to discard, but which you hope will be more in keeping with your future home; these, and a thousand other like items are "white elephants"—costly, but useless possessions.
>
> Charles Earle Funk, *A Hog on Ice & Other Curious Expressions*

12b par

Informal definitions omit a part of a formal definition or change the way the definition is stated:

> What [writing] involves is one person earnestly attempting to communicate with another. Implicitly, then, it involves the reader every bit as much as the writer, since the success of the communication depends solely on how the reader receives it. Also, since more than one person is involved, and since all people have feelings, it has to be as subject to the basic rules of good manners as any human relationship. . . . Far from writing in a vacuum, [the writer] is conversing, in a very real sense, with another human being, just as I am conversing right now with you, even though that person—like you—may be hours, days, or even years away from him in time.
>
> John R. Trimble, *Writing with Style: Conversations on the Art of Writing*

Metaphorical definitions rely on a comparison or analogy to something your audience already knows. They paint a picture for your readers that can clarify a point more quickly and sharply than several explanatory paragraphs. Michael Harrington, for instance, defines *poverty* in part by describing the psychological suffering it creates and in part by comparing it to a type of prosperity:

> Related to this technological advance is the social definition of poverty. The American poor are not poor in Hong Kong or in the sixteenth century: they are poor here and now, in the United States. They are dispossessed in terms of what the rest of the nation enjoys, in terms of what the society could provide if it had the will. They live on the fringe, the margin. They watch the movies and read the magazines of affluent America, and these tell them that they are internal exiles.
>
> Michael Harrington, "A Definition of Poverty"

Description

Descriptive paragraphs follow a chronological, spatial, least-to-most-important, or most-to-least-important pattern. Though using primarily chronological order, E. B. White mixes it with other patterns in the following description of a week he and his son spent fishing:

> We had a good week at the camp. The bass were biting well and the sun shone endlessly, day after day. We would be tired at night and lie down in the accumulated heat of the little bedrooms after the long hot day and the breeze would stir almost imperceptibly outside and the smell of the swamp drift in through the rusty screens. Sleep would come easily and in the morning the red squirrel would be on the roof, tapping out his gay routine. I kept remembering everything, lying in bed in the mornings—the small steamboat that had a long rounded stern like the lip of a Ubangi, and how quietly she ran on the moonlight sails, when the older boys played their mandolins and the girls sang and we ate doughnuts dipped in sugar, and how sweet the music was on the water in the shining night, and what it had felt like to think about girls then. After breakfast we would go up to the store and the things were in the same place—the minnows in a bottle, the plugs and spinners disarranged and pawed over by the youngsters from the boys' camp, the Fig Newtons and the Beeman's gum. Outside, the road was tarred and cars stood in front of the store. Inside, all was just as it had always been, except there was more Coca-Cola and not so much Moxie and root beer and birch beer and sarsaparilla. We would walk out with a bottle of pop apiece and sometimes the pop would backfire up our noses and hurt. We explored the streams, quietly, where the turtles slid off the sunny logs and dug their way into the soft bottom; and we lay on the town wharf and fed worms to the tame bass. Everywhere we went I had trouble making out which I was, the one walking at my side, the one walking in my pants.
>
> E. B. White, "Once More to the Lake"

Listing

One of the simplest and most effective patterns of development, listing inventories facts, events, details, or reasons in support of or as explanation for the assertion in the topic sentence. Neil Postman lists example after example to support the thesis he expresses in the first two sentences of this paragraph:

> Human intelligence is among the most fragile things in nature. It doesn't take much to distract it, suppress it, or even annihilate it. In this century, we have had some lethal examples of how easily and quickly intelligence can be defeated by any one of its several nemeses: ignorance, superstition, moral fervor, cruelty, cowardice,

12b
par

neglect. In the late 1920s, for example, Germany was, by any measure, the most literate, cultured nation in the world. Its legendary seats of learning attracted scholars from every corner. Its philosophers, social critics, and scientists were of first rank; its human traditions an inspiration to less favored nations. But by the mid-1930s—that is, in less than ten years—this cathedral of human reason had been transformed into a cesspool of barbaric irrationality. Many of the most intelligent products of German culture were forced to flee—for example, Einstein, Freud, Karl Jaspers, Thomas Mann, and Stefan Zweig. Even worse, those who remained were either forced to submit their minds to the sovereignty of primitive superstition, or— worse still—willingly did so: Konrad Lorenz, Werner Heisenberg, Martin Heidegger, Gerhardt Hauptmann. On May 10, 1933, a huge bonfire was kindled in Berlin and the books of Marcel Proust, André Gide, Emile Zola, Jack London, Upton Sinclair, and a hundred others were committed to the flames, amid shouts of idiot delight. By 1936, Joseph Paul Goebbels, Germany's Minister of Propaganda, was issuing a proclamation which began with the following words: "Because this year has not brought an improvement in art criticism, I forbid once and for all the continuance of art criticism in its past form, effective as of today." By 1936, there was no one left in Germany who had the brains or courage to object.

Neil Postman, Conscientious Objections

Narration

Stories are not the only type of writing that relates events according to time. Various texts that include processes, descriptions, and some types of arguments have paragraphs that follow a chronological ordering, which is a typical narrative pattern. Caroline Sutton uses narration to trace the steps required to put stripes in toothpaste:

Although it is intriguing to imagine the peppermint stripes neatly wound inside the tube, actually stripes don't go into the paste until it's on its way out. A small hollow tube, with slots running lengthwise, extends from the neck of the toothpaste tube back into the interior a short distance. When the toothpaste tube is filled, red paste—the striping material—is inserted first, thus filling the conical area around the hollow tube at the front. (It must not, however, reach beyond the point to which the hollow tube extends into the toothpaste tube.) The remainder of the dispenser is filled with the familiar white stuff. When you squeeze the toothpaste tube, pressure is applied to the white paste, which in turn presses on the red paste at the head of the tube. The red then passes through the slots and onto the white, which is moving through the inserted tube—and which emerges with five red stripes.

Caroline Sutton, How Do They Do That?

12b
par

Question and Answer

This pattern poses a question to readers that they cannot answer and provides answers for it in the rest of the paragraph. Question and answer paragraphs are very effective because they engage readers quickly in the writer's topic. In a one-sentence paragraph, P. S. Wood sets out the three questions that his essay answers:

> As women rush into athletic competition, certain questions are being raised: How good are women as athletes? How do they compare with men? Are women's bodies strong enough, tough enough, to take the battles?
>
> P. S. Wood, "Sex Differences in Sports"

Stephen Jay Gould poses and partially answers his own question:

> One such question, with an obvious and incorrect answer, lies close to our biological lives: why, in humans (and in most species familiar to us), are males and females produced in approximately equal numbers? (Actually, males are more common than females at birth in humans, but differential mortality of males leads to a female majority in later life. Still, the departures from one to one ratio are never great.) At first glance, the answer seems to be, as in Rabelais's motto, "plain as the nose on a man's face." After all, sexual reproduction requires a mate; equal numbers imply universal mating—the happy Darwinian status of maximal reproductive capacity. At second glance, it isn't so clear at all, and we are drawn in confusion to Shakespeare's recasting of the simile: "A jest unseen, inscrutable, invisible, as a nose on a man's face." If maximal reproductive capacity is the optimal state for a species, then why make equal numbers of males and females? Females, after all, set the limit upon numbers of offspring, since eggs are invariably so much larger and less abundant than sperm in species familiar to us—that is, each egg can make an offspring, each sperm cannot. A male can impregnate several females. If a man can mate with nine females and the population contains a hundred individuals, why not make ten males and ninety females? Reproductive capacity will certainly exceed that of a population composed of fifty males and fifty females. Populations made predominately of females should, by their more rapid rates of reproduction, win any evolutionary race with populations that maintain equality in numbers between sexes.
>
> Stephen Jay Gould, "Death Before Birth, or a Mite's Nunc Dimittis"

As you revise, evaluate every paragraph's coherence by how well it suits your purpose and intended audience. Look at individual elements such as conjunctions, patterns of development, and emphasized points. Determine what words or phrases identify the connections

12b par

between sentences and the flow of ideas among paragraphs. Supply the connections that will help your readers follow your thoughts easily. Judge patterns of development by how well the details amplify a topic sentence and whether the pattern suits your thesis statement and purpose. Use short, even single-sentence, paragraphs for emphasis, but only when the surrounding paragraphs clarify the abbreviated paragraph. Break overly long paragraphs just before transitional elements such as conjunctions, when you shift from commentary to giving reasons, or when one development pattern gives way to another.

12b
par

Exercise 4

Sometimes a pattern of development effectively carries a writer's ideas; at other times, it goes astray. Underline the words and phrases that link ideas in the following paragraphs, decide what pattern of organization each follows, and evaluate the paragraph's effectiveness.

The bus stopped at Little Five Points and one black got off. A young white man was getting on. I tensed. What would happen now? Would the driver ask the black man to get up and move to the empty seat farther back? The white man had a businessman's air about him: suit, shirt, tie, polished brown shoes. He saw the empty seat in the "colored" section and after just a little hesitation went to it, put his briefcase down, and sat with his feet crossed. I relaxed a little when the bus pulled off without the driver saying anything. Evidently he hadn't seen what had happened, or since he was just a few stops from Main Street, he figured the mass exodus there would solve all the problems. Still, I was afraid of a scene.

Mary E. Mebane, *Mary*

I have collected, in my time, derringers, snowstorm paperweights, and china and porcelain dogs, and perhaps I should explain what happened to these old collections before I go on to my newest hobby, which is the true subject of this monograph. My derringer collection may be regarded as having been discontinued, since I collected only two, the second and last item as long ago as 1935. There were originally seventeen snowstorm paperweights, but only four or five are left. This kind of collection is known to the expert as a "diminished collection," and it is not considered cricket to list it in your *Who's Who* biography. The snowstorm paperweight suffers from its easy appeal to the eye and the hand. House guests like to play with paperweights and to slip them into their luggage while packing up to leave. As for my china and porcelain dogs, I disposed of that collection some two years ago. I had decided that the collection of actual objects, of any kind, was too much of a strain, and I determined to devote myself, instead, to the impalpable and the intangible.

James Thurber, "What a Lovely Generalization!"

When Muhammad Ali flunked his army intelligence test, he quipped (with a wit that belied his performance on the exam): "I only said I was the greatest; I never said I was the smartest." In our metaphors and fairy tales, size and power are almost always balanced by a want of intelligence. Cunning is the refuge of the little guy. Think of Br'er Rabbit and Br'er Bear; David smiting Goliath with a slingshot; Jack chopping down the beanstalk. Slow wit is the tragic flaw of a giant.

Stephen Jay Gould, "Were Dinosaurs Dumb?"

12c

Rethinking Paragraph Boundaries

One principal question writers face in revising their texts is *Where does a paragraph begin and end?* Paragraphing is a matter of individual choice: You have to decide what makes a paragraph in your writing. As you wrote a first draft, you essentially ignored the details of paragraphing and concentrated on ideas. Now, as you revise, identify the paragraphs by looking for units of information that address your readers' demands and by using indentation as a visual guide for your audience to recognize those units.

Determining paragraph boundaries by intuition is not an easy or usually successful strategy. A consistent plan works better. Highlight the sentences that present important generalizations about your perspective or that restate an aspect of your thesis statement. These are likely to be your topic sentences. Put the symbol ¶ before each topic sentence even if you have been indenting for paragraphs as you wrote the draft. You may have changed your mind about what belongs in a paragraph as you wrote the draft, and these ¶ markers alert you to the shifts in topic. Look for sentences that add information to a topic sentence, complete its thought, or amplify its theme. These are probably the sentences that make up the rest of a paragraph. As an alternative, look for changes in direction in groups of sentences. If, for example, several sentences seem to be outlining the steps of a process, you may want to start a new paragraph with each step. That way you give your readers clear visual cues about the importance of each stage.

The primary function of any paragraph is to contribute to the structure of the whole text. Taken individually, paragraphs should be purposeful, unified, adequately developed, and rational. As you revise individual paragraphs, challenge every sentence: Each should support, restate, or illustrate the paragraph's main idea. If a sentence does not fit, reject it as a digression, or check if it is the topic sentence for, or belongs in, another paragraph. Furthermore, each paragraph should have enough material to make the topic sentence convincing and keep the audience interested. The sentences in specific paragraphs should link information sensibly, making the paragraphs internally coherent. Each paragraph must also contribute to your perspective and develop your controlling idea coherently. Coherence comes from organizing information in patterns, providing transitions, and showing readers how that patterning fits the purpose of an individual paragraph as well as the overall purpose of your text.

Exercise 5

When rearranged, the following series of sentences is a paragraph from Deborah Tannen's *You Just Don't Understand.* Rearrange the jumbled sentences into a coherent paragraph. Identify the transitional markers and implied connections that create the paragraph's coherence, and decide what pattern of development controls the information.

(1) Second, they often said they had not spoken to that friend in a while—days, weeks, months, or even longer—but they knew that if they needed him, he would be there.

(2) Most of those who said they did told me they tended to discuss them with women friends.

(3) Most women were in constant touch with their closest friends, and frequently discussed even minor decisions and developments in their lives.

(4) But there were differences that indicated they were somewhere farther on the continuum from the pole of intimacy than most women.

(5) Some of the men I interviewed said they did not discuss their problems with anyone.

(6) One man told me he does have a friend that he tells his troubles to, but if he does not have a serious problem, he does not call his friend; that's why so much time can pass without their talking.

(7) First of all, they had one friend, at most two, with whom they discussed problems, not several, or even many, as was the case with many women I talked to.

(8) Some men said that they had a man friend with whom they discussed problems.

Exercise 6

Find an essay you really enjoyed and, using the explanations given in this section, analyze several paragraphs from it. Look closely at each paragraph's main idea, use of detail, use of transitional elements, and connection to the other paragraphs. Then choose a different subject and write a paragraph that imitates the structure and language of one of the paragraphs you analyzed.

V

THE ESSAY

CONNECTION

13
**The Essay Connection:
Ways of Reading and Responding**

13

In a typical composition class, students use both a handbook like this one and a reader, which is a collection of essays by professional writers. This chapter should help you find ways to respond to such essays with essays of your own. Let us begin with two observations about the essay as a form of writing.

The first observation is that the essay is an action intended to provoke a reaction. It is easy to look at the essay as dead words on a page, but we would do better to think of it as a jab, a tickle, a challenge, a fist waved in a face, a finger pointed in accusation, or a reassuring pat on the back. If we remember that the essayist is *doing* something to us as readers and attempting to get us to *do* something in turn, then we approach the essay with our guard up. We may need to jab back.

The second observation is slightly more complicated, and involves three dimensions in which the essayist may attempt to provoke a reaction.

13a

Three Dimensions of an Essay

The three dimensions we will consider here are the objective, emotional, and moral dimensions. To illustrate them, let us consider a sentence from George Orwell's essay "Shooting an Elephant":

188

With one part of my mind I thought of the British Raj as an unbreakable tyranny, as something clamped down, in *saecula saeculorum,*[1] upon the will of prostrate peoples; with another part I thought that the greatest joy in the world would be to drive a bayonet into a Buddhist priest's guts.

The sentence refers to a time when Orwell served as a policeman in Burma, then a colony of England, and so was an agent for the British "Raj" (lordship) over that country. What does the sentence do to the reader? It makes an objective statement, creates an emotion, and encourages us to consider the morality of a course of action.

The **objective dimension** has to do with the most obvious way that an essay can address the reader: to make an objective statement. In making such statements, the writer is an instructor—informing, reporting experience, building ladders of logic to lead us to conclusions about the way things are. The objective content in Orwell's sentence is his report that at a certain period in his life he felt certain emotions. As readers, we can accept the truth of this report or reject it. Most of us are probably inclined to accept it, but it may be a lie—an issue that comes up later in this chapter.

An essay's **emotional dimension** is its emotional effect on the reader. An essay's emotional content may not match its objective content: The way that a writer reports a dull fact may excite our feelings. Few of us are inclined to react one way or another to the mere fact that, several decades ago, George Orwell hated both British imperialism and the people of Burma. But when we read "I thought that the greatest joy in the world would be to drive a bayonet into a Buddhist priest's guts," we *do* react emotionally. The image of a bayonet being driven into a man's stomach is disturbing to us. That the man is a priest makes it more disturbing. That Orwell uses the word *guts* adds to the emotional impact. Most of us feel revulsion and are appalled that Orwell could think bayoneting a priest would be "the greatest joy in the world." If we were hooked up to the right laboratory equipment, an experimenter could probably show that the sentence can raise our blood pressure and lower our galvanic skin response. It will get to us if we let it.

An essay also has the potential to affect the principles by which we live. That is its **moral dimension**. Essays have helped turn liberals into conservatives (and vice versa) and believers into skeptics (and vice versa). Thomas Paine's essay "Common Sense" recruited supporters for the Revolutionary War, Henry David Thoreau's essay "Civil Disobedience" helped Mahatma Gandhi develop the non-violent principles in his battle against British authority in India, and (to come down

---

1. "For ages of ages"; until the end of time.

to the domestic scale) Frances Moore Lappé's introduction to *Diet for a Small Planet* kept thousands of Americans from eating meat for several years.

If we take Orwell's sentence in isolation, it is hard to see a particular principle behind it, but we sense the writer's moral concerns: the split between conscience (which rejects imperialism) and emotion (which is ready to kill Burmese priests), and the dangers of treating other people as subhuman.

13b

The Key Questions to Ask for Each Dimension

An awareness of the three dimensions helps us understand one way that the essays typically collected in a reader differ from much of the other material we read: They engage the audience in all three dimensions. A physics textbook rarely concerns itself with our emotions or morals. A romance or a crime novel gives us few objective statements to consider. But the typical essay in a reader operates strongly in all three dimensions. The fact that it uses the full keyboard, so to speak, is one reason that it is particularly worth studying in a composition class.

One way that we can make ourselves better readers of essays and better writers about them is to ask ourselves a series of questions that will fix our attention on each dimension in turn.

1. What statement does the writer want us to accept as true? How does he or she attempt to persuade us to accept it? How fully should we allow ourselves to be persuaded?

2. What emotions does the writer encourage us to feel? How does he or she encourage us to feel them? How fully should we surrender to them?

3. How does the writer encourage us to act? By what means does he or she encourage us to act this way? How willing should we be to act this way?

The questions can be applied to whole essays, to sections or paragraphs, and sometimes (as we have done) to individual sentences. The rest of this chapter shows how these questions can make us more conscious of the action of an essay on an audience and how this consciousness can provide ways of writing papers responding to the essay. Our specimen essay is George Orwell's "Shooting an Elephant," reprinted on pages 191–196. If you have not read the essay, you should do so before continuing the chapter.

Shooting an Elephant

GEORGE ORWELL

In Moulmein, in Lower Burma, I was hated by large numbers of   1
people—the only time in my life that I have been important enough
for this to happen to me. I was sub-divisional police officer of the
town, and in an aimless, petty kind of way anti-European feeling was
very bitter. No one had the guts to raise a riot, but if a European
woman went through the bazaars alone somebody would probably
spit betel juice over her dress. As a police officer I was an obvious
target and was baited whenever it seemed safe to do so. When a
nimble Burman tripped me up on the football field and the referee
(another Burman) looked the other way, the crowd yelled with
hideous laughter. This happened more than once. In the end the
sneering yellow faces of young men that met me everywhere, the
insults hooted after me when I was at a safe distance, got badly on
my nerves. The young Buddhist priests were the worst of all. There
were several thousands of them in the town and none of them
seemed to have anything to do except stand on street corners and
jeer at Europeans.

All this was perplexing and upsetting. For at that time I had   2
already made up my mind that imperialism was an evil thing and the
sooner I chucked up my job and got out of it the better. Theoreti-
cally—and secretly, of course—I was all for the Burmese and all
against their oppressors, the British. As for the job I was doing, I
hated it more bitterly than I can perhaps make clear. In a job like
that you see the dirty work of Empire at close quarters. The
wretched prisoners huddling in the stinking cages of the lockups,
the grey, cowed faces of the long-term convicts, the scarred but-
tocks of the men who had been flogged with bamboos—all these
oppressed me with an intolerable sense of guilt. But I could get
nothing into perspective. I was young and ill-educated and I had to
think out my problems in the utter silence that is imposed on every
Englishman in the East. I did not even know that the British Empire
is dying, still less did I know that it is a great deal better than the
younger empires that are going to supplant it. All I knew was that I
was stuck between my hatred of the empire I served and my rage
against the evil-spirited little beasts who tried to make my job
impossible. With one part of my mind I thought of the British Raj as
an unbreakable tyranny, as something clamped down, in *saecula
saeculorum,* upon the will of prostrate peoples; with another part I
thought that the greatest joy in the world would be to drive a bayonet into a Buddhist priest's guts. Feelings like these are the normal
by-products of imperialism; ask any Anglo-Indian official, if you can
catch him off duty.

One day something happened which in a roundabout way was   3
enlightening. It was a tiny incident in itself, but it gave me a better
glimpse than I had had before of the real nature of imperialism—the
real motives for which despotic governments act. Early one morning the sub-inspector at a police station the other end of the town
rang me up on the 'phone and said that an elephant was ravaging the
bazaar. Would I please come and do something about it? I did not
know what I could do, but I wanted to see what was happening and I
got on to a pony and started out. I took my rifle, an old .44 Win-
chester and much too small to kill an elephant, but I thought the
noise might be useful *in terrorem*. Various Burmans stopped me on
the way and told me about the elephant's doings. It was not, of
course, a wild elephant, but a tame one which had gone "must." It
had been chained up, as tame elephants always are when their attack
of "must" is due, but on the previous night it had broken its chain
and escaped. Its mahout, the only person who could manage it when
it was in that state, had set out in pursuit, but had taken the wrong
direction and was now twelve hours' journey away, and in the morning the elephant had suddenly reappeared in the town. The Burmese
population had no weapons and were quite helpless against it. It had
already destroyed somebody's bamboo hut, killed a cow and raided
some fruit-stalls and devoured the stock; also it had met the munic-
ipal rubbish van and, when the driver jumped out and took to his
heels, had turned the van over and inflicted violences upon it.

The Burmese sub-inspector and some Indian constables were   4
waiting for me in the quarter where the elephant had been seen. It
was a very poor quarter, a labyrinth of squalid bamboo huts,
thatched with palm-leaf, winding all over a steep hillside. I remember that it was a cloudy, stuffy morning at the beginning of the rains.
We began questioning the people as to where the elephant had gone
and, as usual, failed to get any definite information. That is invariably
the case in the East; a story always sounds clear enough at a distance,
but the nearer you get to the scene of events the vaguer it becomes.
Some of the people said that the elephant had gone in one direction,
some said that he had gone in another, some professed not even to
have heard of any elephant. I had almost made up my mind that the
whole story was a pack of lies, when we heard yells a little distance
away. There was a loud, scandalized cry of "Go away, child! Go away
this instant!" and an old woman with a switch in her hand came
round the corner of a hut, violently shooing away a crowd of naked
children. Some more women followed, clicking their tongues and
exclaiming; evidently there was something that the children ought
not to have seen. I rounded the hut and saw a man's dead body
sprawling in the mud. He was an Indian, a black Dravidian coolie,
almost naked, and he could not have been dead many minutes. The

people said that the elephant had come suddenly upon him round the corner of the hut, caught him with its trunk, put its foot on his back and ground him into the earth. This was the rainy season and the ground was soft, and his face had scored a trench a foot deep and a couple of yards long. He was lying on his belly with arms crucified and head sharply twisted to one side. His face was coated with mud, the eyes wide open, the teeth bared and grinning with an expression of unendurable agony. (Never tell me, by the way, that the dead look peaceful. Most of the corpses I have seen look devilish.) The friction of the great beast's foot had stripped the skin from his back as neatly as one skins a rabbit. As soon as I saw the dead man I sent an orderly to a friend's house nearby to borrow an elephant rifle. I had already sent back the pony, not wanting it to go mad with fright and throw me if it smelt the elephant.

The orderly came back in a few minutes with a rifle and five 5 cartridges, and meanwhile some Burmans had arrived and told us that the elephant was in the paddy fields below, only a few hundred yards away. As I started forward practically the whole population of the quarter flocked out of the houses and followed me. They had seen the rifle and were all shouting excitedly that I was going to shoot the elephant. They had not shown much interest in the elephant when he was merely ravaging their homes, but it was different now that he was going to be shot. It was a bit of fun to them, as it would be to an English crowd; besides they wanted the meat. It made me vaguely uneasy. I had no intention of shooting the elephant—I had merely sent for the rifle to defend myself if necessary—and it is always unnerving to have a crowd following you. I marched down the hill, looking and feeling a fool, with the rifle over my shoulder and an ever-growing army of people jostling at my heels. At the bottom, when you got away from the huts, there was a metalled road and beyond that a miry waste of paddy fields a thousand yards across, not yet ploughed but soggy from the first rains and dotted with coarse grass. The elephant was standing eight yards from the road, his left side towards us. He took not the slightest notice of the crowd's approach. He was tearing up bunches of grass, beating them against his knees to clean them and stuffing them into his mouth.

I had halted on the road. As soon as I saw the elephant I knew 6 with perfect certainty that I ought not to shoot him. It is a serious matter to shoot a working elephant—it is comparable to destroying a huge and costly piece of machinery—and obviously one ought not to do it if it can possibly be avoided. And at that distance, peacefully eating, the elephant looked no more dangerous than a cow. I thought then and I think now that his attack of "must" was already passing off; in which case he would merely wander harmlessly about until the mahout came back and caught him. Moreover, I did not in the least want to shoot him. I decided that I would watch him for a little while to make sure that he did not turn savage again, and then go home.

But at that moment I glanced round at the crowd that had 7 followed me. It was an immense crowd, two thousand at the least and growing every minute. It blocked the road for a long distance on either side. I looked at the sea of yellow faces above the garish clothes—faces all happy and excited over this bit of fun, all certain that the elephant was going to be shot. They were watching me as they would watch a conjurer about to perform a trick. They did not like me, but with the magical rifle in my hands I was momentarily worth watching. And suddenly I realized that I should have to shoot the elephant after all. The people expected it of me and I had got to do it; I could feel their two thousand wills pressing me forward, irresistibly. And it was at this moment, as I stood there with the rifle in my hands, that I first grasped the hollowness, the futility of the white man's dominion in the East. Here was I, the white man with his gun, standing in front of the unarmed native crowd—seemingly the leading actor of the piece; but in reality I was only an absurd puppet pushed to and fro by the will of those yellow faces behind. I perceived in this moment that when the white man turns tyrant it is his own freedom that he destroys. He becomes a sort of hollow, posing dummy, the conventionalized figure of a sahib. For it is the condition of his rule that he shall spend his life in trying to impress the "natives," and so in every crisis he has got to do what the "natives" expect of him. He wears a mask, and his face grows to fit it. I had got to shoot the elephant. I had committed myself to doing it when I sent for the rifle. A sahib has got to act like a sahib; he has got to appear resolute, to know his own mind and do definite things. To come all that way, rifle in hand, with two thousand people marching at my heels, and then to trail feebly away, having done nothing—no, that was impossible. The crowd would laugh at me. And my whole life, every white man's life in the East, was one long struggle not to be laughed at.

But I did not want to shoot the elephant. I watched him beat- 8 ing his bunch of grass against his knees, with that preoccupied grandmotherly air that elephants have. It seemed to me that it would be murder to shoot him. At that age I was not squeamish about killing animals, but I had never shot an elephant and never wanted to. (Somehow it always seems worse to kill a *large* animal.) Besides, there was the beast's owner to be considered. Alive, the elephant was worth at least a hundred pounds; dead, he would only be worth the value of his tusks, five pounds, possibly. But I had got to act quickly. I turned to some experienced-looking Burmans who had been there when we arrived, and asked them how the elephant had been behaving. They all said the same thing; he took no notice of you if you left him alone, but he might charge if you went too close to him.

It was perfectly clear to me what I ought to do. I ought to walk up to within, say, twenty-five yards of the elephant and test his behavior. If he charged, I could shoot; if he took no notice of me, it would be safe to leave him until the mahout came back. But also I knew that I was going to do no such thing. I was a poor shot with a rifle and the ground was soft mud into which one would sink at every step. If the elephant charged and I missed him, I should have about as much chance as a toad under a steamroller. But even then I was not thinking particularly of my own skin, only of the watchful yellow faces behind. For at that moment, with the crowd watching me, I was not afraid in the ordinary sense, as I would have been if I had been alone. A white man mustn't be frightened in front of "natives"; and so, in general, he isn't frightened. The sole thought in my mind was that if anything went wrong those two thousand Burmans would see me pursued, caught, trampled on and reduced to a grinning corpse like that Indian up the hill. And if that happened it was quite probable that some of them would laugh. That would never do. There was only one alternative. I shoved the cartridges into the magazine and lay down on the road to get a better aim.

The crowd grew very still, and a deep, low, happy sigh, as of people who see the theatre curtain go up at last, breathed from innumerable throats. They were going to have their bit of fun after all. The rifle was a beautiful German thing with cross-hair sights. I did not then know that in shooting an elephant one would shoot to cut an imaginary bar running from ear-hole to ear-hole. I ought, therefore, as the elephant was sideways on, to have aimed straight at his ear-hole; actually I aimed several inches in front of this, thinking the brain would be further forward.

When I pulled the trigger I did not hear the bang or feel the kick—one never does when a shot goes home—but I heard the devilish roar of glee that went up from the crowd. In that instant, in too short a time, one would have thought, even for the bullet to get there, a mysterious, terrible change had come over the elephant. He neither stirred nor fell, but every line of his body had altered. He looked suddenly stricken, shrunken, immensely old, as though the frightful impact of the bullet had paralysed him without knocking him down. At last, after what seemed a long time—it might have been five seconds, I dare say—he sagged flabbily to his knees. His mouth slobbered. An enormous senility seemed to have settled upon him. One could have imagined him thousands of years old. I fired again into the same spot. At the second shot he did not collapse but climbed with desperate slowness to his feet and stood weakly upright, with legs sagging and head drooping. I fired a third time. That was the shot that did for him. You could see the agony of it jolt his whole body and knock the last remnant of strength from his legs. But in falling he seemed for a moment to rise, for as his hind legs collapsed beneath him he seemed to tower upward like a huge rock toppling, his trunk reaching skywards like a tree. He trumpeted, for the first and only time. And then down he came, his belly towards me, with a crash that seemed to shake the ground even where I lay.

I got up. The Burmans were already racing past me across the mud. It was obvious that the elephant would never rise again, but he was not dead. He was breathing very rhythmically with long rattling gasps, his great mound of a side painfully rising and falling. His mouth was wide open—I could see far down into caverns of pale pink throat. I waited a long time for him to die, but his breathing did not weaken. Finally I fired my two remaining shots into the spot where I thought his heart must be. The thick blood welled out of him like red velvet, but still he did not die. His body did not even jerk when the shots hit him, the tortured breathing continued without a pause. He was dying, very slowly and in great agony, but in some world remote from me where not even a bullet could damage him further. I felt that I had got to put an end to that dreadful noise. It seemed dreadful to see the great beast lying there, powerless to move and yet powerless to die, and not even to be able to finish him. I sent back for my small rifle and poured shot after shot into his heart and down his throat. They seemed to make no impression. The tortured gasps continued as steadily as the ticking of a clock. 13

In the end I could not stand it any longer and went away. I heard later that it took him half an hour to die. Burmans were bringing dahs and baskets even before I left, and I was told they had stripped his body almost to the bones by the afternoon.

Afterwards, of course, there were endless discussions about 14 the shooting of the elephant. The owner was furious, but he was only an Indian and could do nothing. Besides, legally I had done the right thing, for a mad elephant has to be killed, like a mad dog, if its owner fails to control it. Among the Europeans opinion was divided. The older men said I was right, the younger men said it was a damn shame to shoot an elephant for killing a coolie, because an elephant was worth more than any damn Coringhee coolie. And afterwards I was very glad that the coolie had been killed; it put me legally in the right and it gave me a sufficient pretext for shooting the elephant. I often wondered whether any of the others grasped that I had done it solely to avoid looking a fool.

13c

The Objective Dimension: The Thesis and Other Statements

1 Focusing on a Statement

Because it so deeply involves facts and arguments, the objective dimension is the one where research can be most useful. The more you know about the subject and the author, the better equipped you are to appreciate and perhaps to question the statements being made. But since the research essay is covered elsewhere in this handbook (Chapters 44–47), we concentrate here on responses that require only a close scrutiny of the essay and a minimal amount of research.

Minor Statements

Virtually any statement that a writer makes can be the subject of an interesting response. A biology student reading "Shooting an Elephant" might be struck by Orwell's assertion that the elephant had had an attack of "must," which had passed off by the time he arrived on the scene. What exactly is "must"? Does Orwell's diagnosis seem correct? Or someone interested in religion might notice in Orwell's statement that the street corners in Burma were crowded with Buddhist priests who "seemed to have nothing to do except . . . sneer at Europeans." Why were they there? Given the emphasis on passiveness in Buddhism, how do we account for the political activism of the priests? Responses to such minor statements in an essay can lead to fascinating papers, but they require a good deal of research, and some instructors might complain that they are not responses to the essay as a whole. It would be prudent to talk with your instructor before you undertake an essay responding to a minor statement in an essay.

The Thesis

To respond to the whole essay, we ordinarily look for more central statements—probably the most central statement, the thesis. Since essayists don't always state their thesis in a single sentence, we sometimes have to formulate it for ourselves. In Orwell's seventh paragraph, however, we find a clear statement of the central proposition: "I perceived at this moment that *when the white man turns tyrant it is his own freedom that he destroys* [emphasis added]."

Testing the Centrality
of a Statement

How do we determine that this is the thesis? There are two good indicators.

First, all (or virtually all) the parts of the essay contribute support to it. If we examine the essay carefully, we see that

1. paragraphs 1 and 2 reveal the unhappy (and unfree) lives of the English "tyrants" in Burma.
2. paragraphs 3 through 13 report on an incident in which Orwell, because he is "playing the tyrant," kills an elephant that he does not want to kill.
3. the final paragraph finishes the discussion of the incident, reminds the reader that British colonists see themselves as superior to their Burmese subjects, and reiterates that Orwell killed the elephant "solely to avoid looking a fool."

The second indicator is related to the first: The writer takes several opportunities to prepare us for his thesis or remind us of it. In paragraph 3, Orwell notifies us that the "tiny incident" he is about to share with us gave him a "glimpse . . . of the real nature of imperialism." In paragraph 6, he tells us: "As soon as I saw the elephant I knew with perfect certainty that I ought not to shoot him" (though we know with perfect certainty that he will). In paragraph 9, he tells about his fear that the Burmese will laugh at him if he fails to shoot the elephant. And, of course, he ends the essay with the sentence about avoiding "looking a fool." Orwell is an artful writer, but he won't risk letting us miss his point.

2 Alert Surrender to the
Essay's Thesis

Skepticism is a useful tool, but when we are reading essays, it should be used later rather than sooner. The best approach is to *start* by taking the author's side—not only suspending our disbelief but actively working at being persuaded. By such an alert surrender, we open our eyes to what is valuable in the writer's argument, and we may discover techniques we can use in our own writing. The factors that help us accept a writer's propositions are innumerable. Here we deal with two: the quality of the evidence and the trustworthiness of the writer.

Finding the Strength of the Evidence

We might divide evidence into three types: logical deduction, demonstration by weight of examples, and what we will call "empathetic plausibility." Few essays use all three types equally, and one of your tasks in managing your "alert surrender" is to recognize the type of evidence that the essayist primarily relies on. At this stage, you want to overlook weaknesses in order to get a clear view of strengths.

Logical Deduction

Logical deduction (see **5c**) is nearly as impossible to resist as mathematical proof, and essays that use it successfully are sometimes very influential. One famous example is Thomas Robert Malthus's *Essay on Population* (1798), which argues that the tendency of population to increase geometrically and of food supply to increase only arithmetically *must* lead to catastrophe. Garrett Hardin's "The Tragedy of the Commons" (1968) is another; it widely influenced both economic and environmental thought. Deductive logic, however, is a specialized tool. Few "personal" or "informal" essays use it as the primary method of backing statements, and "Shooting an Elephant" uses it hardly at all. To do justice to Orwell's essay, we won't weigh it on the scales of deductive logic; we should look elsewhere for opportunities to be persuaded.

Demonstration by Weight of Examples

A more common way for essayists to support their propositions is demonstration by weight of examples (see the discussion of induction, **5b**). Orwell might have attempted to prove his point that "when the white man turns tyrant it is his own freedom he destroys" by studying the lives of a number of typical white tyrants and demonstrating from his data that these people are less free than the dark-skinned people they pretend to govern. If he accumulated a large *number* of examples, and if we believed that his examples were truly *representative* of the whole class of white tyrants, then we might find his case persuasive. Orwell, however, does not do this. Instead, he relies largely on one example, himself. We won't find the persuasiveness of Orwell's essay in the number of examples and their representativeness, but since we are reading to surrender, we should look for it elsewhere.

Empathetic Plausibility

The strength of Orwell's essay lies in empathetic plausibility. Like many essays, this one does its persuasive work by giving us an "inside" view of a mode of life we have previously known only from the outside. It takes us into the mind of an imperial policeman and encourages us to understand—to empathize with—his view of the world. If it convinces

13c
es

us that *we* would feel unfree in the policeman's situation, then it has gone a good way toward proving Orwell's statement that "when the white man turns tyrant it is his own freedom he destroys." For a discussion of how Orwell achieves empathetic plausibility, see the sample essay at the end of this section.

Finding the Writer Trustworthy

Even if the evidence in an essay seems compelling, we are unlikely to accept the propositions of a writer we distrust. To win our trust, the writer must seem knowledgeable and forthright. Otherwise, we may view some of the "facts" given as mistaken or suspect that they are being offered with the intention of deceiving. Alert surrender to an essay requires that we at least note what the author says about himself or herself in the essay. We may also need to use such sources as encyclopedias, the various volumes of *Who's Who,* and *Contemporary Authors* in order to obtain more information.

In "Shooting an Elephant," Orwell shows that he has knowledge pertinent to the statement that "when the white man turns tyrant it is his own freedom he destroys": He explains that he was a "sub-divisional police officer" in Burma and experienced the loss of freedom that he is talking about. He also writes like a forthright man, a plain speaker who does not use the smoke screen of a fancy vocabulary to cover his meaning. We trust him even more because, when he describes his own actions in the essay, he does not attempt to make himself look good. In fact, he seems eager to show us his faults. If we make the effort to read about his life in the readily available biographical sources, we will find that he was very honest and moral.

3 Resistance to the Thesis

Even in the process of consciously cooperating with the essay—searching for acceptable evidence and finding reasons to trust the writer—we sometimes find ourselves eager to resist. After the first, friendly study of the essay, we can productively unleash this resistance.

Finding Weakness in the Evidence

As one philosophy professor has said, finding weaknesses in the support of propositions is about as easy as finding loose teeth in six-year-olds. Dozens of characteristic weaknesses have been studied and labeled. For economy's sake, we limit ourselves here to two of the most common: the *post hoc* fallacy and hasty generalization.

The Post Hoc *Fallacy*

The *post hoc* fallacy (see Chapter 9, page 128) draws its name from the Latin phrase *post hoc, ergo propter hoc:* "after this, therefore because of this." It is a pattern of thinking that confuses sequence with causation. The fallacy seems easy to detect and avoid, but connections between cause and effect are so complicated that *post hoc* reasoning may appear even in a sophisticated essay. Some economists, for example, charge that other economists commit the *post hoc* fallacy when they claim that the Great Depression was caused by panic selling in the stock market. When an essayist asserts that X was caused by Y, skeptical readers almost reflexively look for the possibility of *post hoc* reasoning.

Such readers might react by showing that the supposed cause was not *necessary* to the supposed effect. If youth and inexperience were enough to make Orwell succumb to the pressure of a large crowd of onlookers, the skeptic says, then his role as a white "tyrant" was not necessary to his loss of freedom. Even if a cause is necessary, some readers might believe that it is not *sufficient* to the supposed effect: Orwell might not have experienced his loss of freedom if he were merely a tyrant; he had to be young and inexperienced as well.

Hasty Generalization

Hasty generalization (see Chapter 9, page 129) means drawing a broad conclusion from too few examples or from examples that are not representative of a whole class. It is closely related to stereotyping. We might want to assume that a writer as skillful as Orwell would avoid this weakness, but personal essays like "Shooting an Elephant" are not written to please logicians. Examined critically, Orwell's generalization about European colonists is suspect, since it is supported by a single example (himself).

Finding the Writer Untrustworthy

There are three fairly obvious reasons for finding a writer untrustworthy: a history of dishonesty; some vested interest on the writer's part in the statement under discussion; and incredible statements made in the essay itself. Orwell passes the first test admirably; he has a reputation as an honest seeker after truth, and some sources even call him a "secular saint." We might, however, raise an alarm on both the second and the third test. Does Orwell have a vested interest in the statement that "when the white man turns tyrant it is his own freedom he destroys"? In a sense, he may. "Shooting an Elephant" was written eight years after he resigned as a policeman and changed from a supporter of British imperialism to a critic. Might he have written the essay partly in order to vindicate his resignation and his changed politics? And are his statements in the essay always credible? Do we really believe that this sensitive man who would spend a large part of his life as a champion of the poor and oppressed ever "thought that the greatest joy in the world would be to drive a bayonet into a Buddhist priest's guts"? There is room to suspect that the essay exaggerates the bad effects imperialism had on the characters of white men in the colonies.

4 Writing About the Objective
Dimension: Sample Essay

Since every essay has strengths and weaknesses, deciding whether to accept the truth of the thesis may require careful balancing. Papers about the objective content tend to be most effective when they make plain the difficulty of achieving a balanced judgment. In the sample essay that follows, you will find evidence of the struggle between alert surrender and alert resistance.

The Slavery of the Masters

In "Shooting an Elephant," George Orwell, reflecting on his experience as a British policeman in colonial Burma, asserts that "when the white man turns tyrant it is his own freedom he destroys" (194). This is a remarkable proposition. Readers may want to believe it both because it is surprising and because it strengthens the case against oppression. Yet Orwell doesn't prove that the proposition is true.

Orwell's evidence would have been sufficient if his purpose had been to help us understand how a European colonist, even one with good intentions, could feel compelled to become "a sort of hollow, posing dummy, the conventionalized figure of a sahib" (194). Orwell makes us understand this through a story he tells from his own perspective--or from the perspective he had as a younger man. We sympathize with him when he is tripped and laughed at on the soccer field and jeered at on street corners. We understand how his desire to maintain his dignity in front of the Burmese crowd forces him to violate his own

conscience. More than that, we empathize, for we
have all been desperate at times "to avoid looking
a fool" (196). Orwell's narrative must convince
many readers that if they were in the role of the
"sahib," they, too, might act "like an absurd
puppet" (194).

But Orwell's argument has a great weakness.
Understanding what made him behave as he did in
Burma (and what might have made us behave the same
way) is not the same as understanding the
psychology of all the European colonists. Orwell
may have felt ashamed because he was supporting "a
tyranny . . . clamped down . . . upon the will of
prostrate peoples" (191), but this does not mean
that most Europeans did. Because he was relatively
young and inexperienced, he may have been very
sensitive about seeming foolish. But this does not
mean that veteran colonists felt the same emotions.
Therefore, even though Orwell was acting against
his will when he shot the elephant, we can't
conclude that every European was so unwilling to
play his or her role. Orwell, who left Burma in
disgust and spent the rest of his life opposing
colonialism, is not a representative colonist. To
conclude that his psychology typifies the
psychology of other men in his position is a very
hasty generalization.

In the final paragraph of the essay, Orwell
tells us how other Europeans reacted to the
shooting of the elephant:

> The older men said I was right, the
> younger men said it was a damn shame to
> shoot an elephant for killing a coolie,
> because an elephant was worth more than
> any damn Coringhee coolie. (196)

These don't seem like men with sensitive
consciences who "play the tyrant" against their
will. From what we see of them, they seem to be
happy bullies, free from regrets. And they may be
more representative of European colonizers than
Orwell is.

13d

The Emotional Dimension: Situation and Style

Some essays act on our emotions hardly at all, concentrating on statements and treating us as entirely logical creatures. Essays collected in readers, however, usually include passages that create anger, irritation, fear, relief, joy, sorrow, terror, anxiety, or other emotions. Actually, most essays create a stream of changing emotions in those who read them. We may be amused by the first paragraph, alarmed by the second, and saddened by the third—with the contrast in emotions making us feel each more distinctly. To study all the emotional changes in even a short essay like "Shooting an Elephant" would be a complex project. As a practical matter, it is better to focus on a short passage that seems crucial to the emotional impact of the essay.

1 Choosing a Passage for Analysis

To those deeply interested in the way essays work, almost any passage might reward analysis, but for most readers, the best passages to study are the ones with these characteristics:

1. Such emotional force that we remember our response after the details of the passage have been forgotten
2. Manageable length, for a passage shorter than two or three hundred words may provide little material for study and one longer than a thousand words may be too long to examine fully in a short paper
3. A close enough connection with the thesis of the essay so that we can explain the relation between the objective content of the essay and the emotional content of the passage

An appropriate passage from "Shooting the Elephant" is the shooting itself, from the beginning of paragraph 11 ("When I pulled the trigger . . .") to the end of paragraph 12 ("The tortured gasps continued as steadily as the ticking of a clock").

2 Accounting for the Emotional Impact

The objective content of a passage should be evaluated through several readings. We might be convinced of a thesis on a first reading and then, on second thought, find reason to doubt it. For emotional content, though, it is usually best to trust our first impression, provided we read the passage carefully. If a passage alarmed us then, we can believe that it is an alarming passage. The fact that we are not alarmed when we return to it for the tenth time, subjecting it to close analysis, should not make us mistrust our first impression. The intriguing question is why we felt what we felt.

The sources of emotional impact are complex enough to baffle psychologists. Here we concern ourselves with only three: stereotypical emotional situations, imagery, and charged language.

Stereotypical Emotional Situations

Ordinary experience tells us that some situations evoke little emotion in most people (for example, sitting in a physics class); some evoke strong, but variable, emotions (for instance, embarking on a journey); and some are charged with strong, predictable emotions (for example, funerals). Situations in this last category are often useful to writers because they move readers quickly in a given emotional direction.

Orwell makes use of such an emotionally charged situation when he tells the story of shooting the elephant. The killing of a large animal is something that alarms most of us, particularly if the animal is "tame," as pets are tame. The alarm is greater if the animal is one we associate with intelligence and kindliness. And if the killing is unnecessary and painful, we feel shock and pity. It is hardly a situation about which half of Orwell's readers would feel one way and half another.

Imagery

Many images carry a strong emotional charge, even in isolation. The image of a smiling baby tends to make us smile. The image of a pistol may alarm us vaguely. But if we put the pistol into the same picture with the baby, the juxtaposition of the two images raises the level of alarm dramatically. Advertisers know that putting two emotionally charged images side by side can create dramatic impact, and writers know this too.

In "Shooting an Elephant," Orwell is constantly creating and juxtaposing images that evoke strong emotional responses. Consider, for example, two images involving the elephant. Before he is shot, we see him "tearing up bunches of grass, beating them against his knees to clean them and stuffing them into his mouth" (paragraph 5). It is an image that suggests peace and harmony. After Orwell's third shot, we see the elephant crash to the ground and lie "breathing very rhythmically with long rattling gasps, his great mound of a side painfully rising and falling" (paragraph 12). The tranquility of the first image makes the second more distressing.

Charged Language

The *denotation* of a word or phrase is its objective meaning, stripped of emotional overtones and associations we call the *connotation* of the word. Obviously, connotation and denotation are not truly separable: To call someone a murderer is to make an objective and an emotional statement at the same time. The connotative charge of some words is nonetheless stronger than that of others. During the Cold War, for example, the word *Russian* had powerful negative connotations for most Americans: emotions that President Ronald Reagan captured in the phrase "the evil empire." During the same period, the word *Canadian* carried no equivalent emotional charge, positive or negative. To say that someone was "an agent of the Canadian government" would hardly have raised the same suspicion and hostility that calling the person an agent of the Russian government would have.

In the eighth paragraph of "Shooting an Elephant," Orwell describes the animal "beating his bunch of grass against his knees, with that preoccupied grandmotherly air elephants have." The denotative meaning of the phrase might be roughly expressed like this: The animal was "beating a bunch of vegetation against its forelimbs; its attention was apparently unfocused." But the connotations, which depend heavily on our emotional associations with the word *grandmotherly* and *preoccupied* (and, to a lesser degree, *grass* and *knee* and *his*), would be missing in such a paraphrase. We would have lost overtones that connected the elephant with innocence, humanness, and advanced age.

Description of this sort provides an opportunity for the writer to introduce charged language into an essay. Metaphor, simile, analogy, and personification provide other opportunities. When Orwell describes the dying elephant, he says that "the thick blood welled out of him like red velvet." On the denotative level, the comparison to red velvet is useful for helping us imagine the thickness of the blood. On the connotative level, "red velvet" brings to mind the world of overstuffed chairs and elegant dresses. These associations seem jarringly inappropriate in the violent scene, and so make the violence more shocking. It is as if we had seen a killing in our grandmother's living room.

3 Questioning the Pertinence of the Emotion

The alert reader pays close attention to the ways that the emotional and objective dimensions of an essay interact, especially in cases where strong emotion may cloud judgment. Unscrupulous writers sometimes deliberately cover the weakness of their arguments by introducing highly charged language, imagery, and stereotypical situations, and even well-intentioned writers sometimes let their own emotions confuse their reasoning.

A key to maintaining a clear head is to ask: What is the pertinence of the emotion generated to the writer's argument? Is the emotional passage merely a "red herring"[2] without any logical relation to the writer's key statement? Or does it add force to a statement that is also being supported by logic and evidence? In the case of Orwell's essay, the shock and pity we feel when the elephant is killed is logically connected to the statement, as we will see in the next sample essay.

4 Writing About the Emotional Dimension: Sample Essay

Writing about the emotional dimension of an essay can be especially demanding because it requires us to use both the analytic and the emotional parts of our minds. There is danger of one kind if we read insensitively and so miss the emotional impact. There is danger of another kind if we leave our intelligence behind and merely emote. One key to success in writing about the emotional dimension is to find persuasive evidence for your statement in the text of the essay you are discussing. Another is to stress the responses that a typical reader would have, rather than the responses that are peculiar to you.

A highly personal response, one that is less about the essay than about the feelings the essay inspired in you, may produce a valuable paper, but it is not the type of paper we are discussing here.

A Fair and Powerful Use of Emotion

Long after readers forget the thesis of George Orwell's essay "Shooting an Elephant," they are likely to remember his two-paragraph description of the elephant's death (paragraphs 11 and 12, pages 195–196). We react strongly to this passage because we are naturally upset by the killing of a large, tame, intelligent animal. In this case, too, our natural repulsion increases because the animal dies "very slowly and in great agony."

---

2. Bogus emotional content in an argument is called a red herring because it confuses the reader's mind in the same way that a smelly fish might confuse a bloodhound's nose.

Though Orwell is the killer, as well as the writer, he does nothing to diminish the horror of the scene. Instead, he uses imagery and language that heighten our sympathy for the elephant and make his own action look all the worse.

The way Orwell describes the elephant makes us see the animal in human terms. The elephant is referred to as he, never as it. When the first bullet hit him, Orwell reports, "he looked suddenly stricken, shrunken, immensely old." Since very few of us could tell an "immensely old" elephant from one in the prime of life, the image that comes to our minds will almost certainly be that of an old man, perhaps one with graying skin sagging on his face. And the words "suddenly stricken" also have human associations. In reality, the elephant has been suddenly stricken--by the bullet. But this cannot be what Orwell means. What the phrase suggests is something like this: "The elephant looked as if he had been suddenly stricken by a disturbing thought." The impression that the elephant thinks like a human is reinforced by Orwell's saying that "an enormous senility seemed to have settled upon him," for senility is not a word usually associated with animals. After the third shot, Orwell describes the elephant as "dying, very slowly and in great agony, but in some world remote from me where not even a bullet could damage him further." The language suggests not only a human consciousness, but a mystic's capacity for turning inward.

This mystical note is another important aspect of Orwell's description. He links the elephant with religion and the supernatural. When Orwell fires his first shot, he hears a "devilish roar of glee" from the crowd, and at once ("in too short a time . . . even for the bullet to get there") a "mysterious, terrible change" comes over the elephant. The prose provides more than a literal description: It suggests cheering devils and a killing by supernatural means. The indications that the event is more mysterious than the simple killing of a simple beast are reinforced when Orwell tells us that "one could have imagined him [the elephant] thousands of years old."

When the elephant goes down for the last time, he seems "for a moment to rise" and "tower upward like a huge rock toppling, his trunk reaching skywards like a tree." The imagery associates the elephant with nature but at the same time suggests something spiritual. When the kneeling elephant raises its trunk "skywards" and trumpets once before its death, we surely (even if half-consciously) associate the gesture with prayer.

The result of Orwell's associating the elephant with both human and spiritual life is to make us feel some of the shock and pity that Orwell must have felt when he acted in a way that he knew was wrong. The appeal to emotion is a fair one because Orwell is not manipulating readers into false feelings. Instead, he is helping them share in an emotion he felt himself. The appeal is also logically connected to Orwell's thesis in the essay: that a European colonist tends to lose his freedom in the colonies, since "in every crisis he has got to do what the 'natives' expect of him," no matter how loathsome he finds it. Because we experienced some of the revulsion Orwell felt when he shot the elephant, we are more likely to understand and accept this claim.

13e

The Moral Dimension: The Writer's Values and Your Own

1 Clarifying the Writer's Values

Some essays, regardless of their thesis, bristle with statements about how life should be led. In "What I Believe," for example, E. M. Forster writes, "I hate the idea of causes, and if I had the choice between betraying my country and betraying my friend, I hope I should have the guts to betray my country." Though he uses the pronoun "I," he must wish that all people would take the same stand: It is a question of principle with him. Other essays are less direct in stating principles, but it is unusual (if not impossible) for an essay to be perfectly neutral on the question of how we should live. Orwell's essay is less direct than Forster's. It refrains from any sweeping statements of principles, but we know that the principles are there, underlying the apparently objective report of actions and their causes.

Identifying the Action Urged on the Original Audience

One productive way of examining the principles of the essayist is to recall the circumstances in which the essay first appeared. Most of the essays collected in readers were originally published in magazines or newspapers, and like other journalistic pieces, they were intended for an audience steeped in the events and concerns of the moment. Often the best way to grasp the principle is to imagine ourselves in the original audience and consider what dilemmas in human values we face.

Orwell's essay was published in 1936, in *New Writing,* a British magazine. Common knowledge and a half-hour of research in the library might tell us this much about the moral dilemma of the times:

1. In 1936, Britain was still a great colonial empire. Though some of its colonies (such as Canada, Australia, and Ireland) were becoming essentially independent nations, it continued to exercise in its African and Asian colonies what Orwell calls "an unbreakable tyranny . . . clamped down . . . upon the will of prostrate peoples." Wealth stripped from these colonies directly or indirectly benefited most of the British middle class, including most of Orwell's readers.

2. Since the eighteenth century, one of the commonplace justifications for European colonialism had been that the dark-skinned people in Asia, Africa, and the Americas were inferior to whites and so would naturally benefit by having white rulers governing their lives.

3. In 1936, many Britons questioned the justifications for colonialism and thought it was morally outrageous.

Orwell's readers, then, were people facing a choice between two political positions: one favoring colonialism in Africa and Asia and one opposing it. Their pocketbooks favored colonialism, and so did the racism common in English society at the time. If they were going to choose against colonialism, they needed something on the other side of the balance.

Putting ourselves in these readers' place when we look at Orwell's essay, we get a clearer view of what course of action the essay was urging. The essay is designed to make the colonial system seem less justifiable. It presents the British colonizer not as an enlightened administrator, coolly managing the affairs of the "natives," but as a "hollow, posing dummy," a "conventionalized figure of a sahib" doing "what the 'natives' expect of him." And it presents the colonists as people who believe that the life of a "coolie" is less valuable than the life of a "working elephant" and that the life of the elephant is less valuable than the pride of a white official. Orwell does not need to tell us that these values are perverse. When they are stated as frankly as Orwell states them, their perversity is clear. So to Orwell's intended audience the essay was a call for action that might be phrased this way: "Faced (as you are) with the choice between maintaining colonialism or abandoning it, you should abandon it for the sake of your own freedom and dignity."

Identifying the Timeless Moral Theme

Not being English people of Orwell's generation, we don't face the same dilemma his original audience faced. But Orwell's essay has not lost all its moral importance. As often happens with a great essay, the need for the specific action called for may pass, but the *basis* for deciding on a moral course of action remains important. Learning to find the basis of the proposed course of action is crucial to understanding the moral dimension of an essay.

We can look for the basis (the moral theme) by determinedly asking ourselves "why?" and seeing what answer the essay gives. When we reach the insight into moral life that lies behind the whole essay, we have found the basis. Often the basis in a classic essay will be something we would not have expected. Consider Orwell's essay. Why (we ask) should we abandon colonialism? Because (Orwell tells us) it is an oppressive system. Why (we ask) shouldn't we participate in an oppressive system? We might expect the answer to be "because it harms innocent people." But this is *not* the answer Orwell gives. The Burmese are not presented as innocents, and the shooting of the elephant benefits more of them (by providing food) than it harms.

So we have to return to the question. Why shouldn't we participate in an oppressive system? As we can see in the third sample essay, Orwell gives a surprising answer.

Identifying Values Embedded in the Style of the Essay

Thus far, we have been dealing with the principles underlying the content of the essay, but we should remember that the style also reveals the writer's principles. Writers may present their ideas fairly or unfairly, insensitively or humanely, arrogantly or modestly. *How* writers write may express their values as clearly as *what* they write. We sometimes read an essay that urges us to take a moral stance but uses shameful means of persuasion, or an essay that urges an action we feel is wrong but urges it in a way we find honorable and admirable. In the case of "Shooting an Elephant," the manner in which Orwell writes encourages the most severe self-scrutiny. He does not allow himself to treat racism as an evil that infects the thinking of other men only. Instead, he presents himself as a specimen racist: someone capable of wanting to "drive a bayonet into a Buddhist's priest's guts" and of being "very glad that the coolie had been killed" because it put him "legally in the right." If there is a moral basis present in *how* Orwell writes as well as in *what* he writes, it is that we must remove the beam from our eyes before we attempt to remove the mote from the eyes of others.

13e
es

2 Maintaining an Awareness of Alternative Values

Most of us learn our most basic values early in life, so it is rare for an essayist to teach us something entirely new about morality. Sometimes an essay forcefully reminds us of a value we have accepted but not acted on. Martin Luther King's "Letter from Birmingham Jail," for instance, reminds a group of clergymen of the Judeo-Christian values that should have brought them to the aid of Birmingham's black community. Sometimes an essay reveals a conflict in our values that we had not been aware of before. Joan Didion's "Marrying Absurd" reminds us of the conflict between wanting to enjoy the new world of instant gratification and wanting to retain the old world, in which things are done "right" and everything is "just as nice" as we "hoped and dreamed it would be."

Even though essays more often remind us of familiar values than they argue for new ones, we ought to keep our guards up and consider whether the writer's values really match our own. Orwell takes a stand for individual conscience against the pressure of groups. This may at first seem to be a stand that no one could object to. But is it? Is it always true that the individual placed in a position of responsibility should be concerned first with keeping his or her conscience clean? After all, if Orwell had done what his conscience dictated, not only he, but one or more bystanders, might have been "trampled on and reduced to a grinning corpse"; and respect for the forces of law and order might have been weakened without any change in the colonial system. It is not clear that anyone would have been better off. Won't some readers believe that the happiness of others is more valuable than private feelings of righteousness? Even if we finally agree with Orwell—or any essayist—we should learn to look at the other side of a moral question.

3 Writing About the Moral Dimension: Sample Essay

Responding to the questions of principle that underlie an essay sometimes seems to bring us face to face with the writer, creating a two-way conversation. We listen very closely to make sure we understand precisely what the writer's moral stance is, and then we scrutinize it carefully, knowing that accepting someone's morality as our own can be a serious business. The essay below accepts, with some hesitation, what its writer takes to be Orwell's underlying rationale for urging a British withdrawal from the colonies.

A Selfish Call for Good Behavior

It is natural to think of George Orwell's essay "Shooting an Elephant" as part of a propaganda war. At the time of its publication, Britain was still a major colonial power. It imposed on such colonies as Burma "an unbreakable tyranny . . . clamped down, in saecula saeculorum, upon the will of prostrate peoples" (191). By publishing his essay in a British magazine, Orwell clearly intended to weaken the position of those who wanted Britain to keep these colonies forever. He also wished to strengthen the position of those who wanted to end colonialism.

The surprising thing about the essay is the rationale Orwell offers for ending colonialism. We might have expected him to emphasize the damage done to the good people of Burma by British rule, but he doesn't do this. Instead, he presents the Burmese in a bad light: Rather than bravely engage in political resistance, they spit on helpless European women (191); their priests are idle and unpleasant (191); they seem incapable of getting the facts about the elephant straight; and they eventually become a "devilish" (195) mob, making a holiday out of the killing of the elephant. Those who wanted to oppose colonialism because the Burmese would be better off ruling themselves would have found little to support their position in Orwell's essay.

Orwell's emphasis is on the damage Europeans do <u>to</u> <u>themselves</u> by being tyrants in their colonies. The damage takes two forms. First, the European colonist (Orwell uses himself as an example) loses his freedom. He is forced to behave like a "sahib" rather than an individual: "He wears a mask, and his face grows to fit it" (194). In Orwell's case, his own will was not to kill the elephant, but the mob of Burmans expected him to act decisively, and he "could feel their two thousand wills pressing me forward, irresistibly" (194). The loss of freedom is related to the second kind of damage, a coarsening of conscience. Orwell tells us that he felt an "intolerable sense of guilt" about participating in the British tyranny, but at the same time he wanted to "drive a bayonet into a Buddhist priest's guts." He felt emotions of which he knew he should be ashamed. And when he acted against his conscience in killing the elephant, the result was yet another round of shameful emotion: "afterwards I was very glad that the coolie had been killed; it put me legally in the right and it gave me a sufficient pretext for shooting the elephant" (196). To be glad that another human being has been crushed to death in enormous agony is almost a form of madness.

Orwell's moral principle, removed from its historical context, is that <u>for</u> <u>our</u> <u>own</u> <u>sake</u> we should refrain from behaving against our conscience. Conscience is a delicate tool, and we blunt it whenever we abuse it. Some people might object that it is insensitive of Orwell to say so little about the suffering of colonized people and concentrate instead on the psychological and moral damage done to the colonizers. But Orwell's point is that the damage is done to the colonist's <u>conscience</u>, which is numbed by the role of "sahib." To protect their conscience, to free people to act on moral principle, is in the interest of the weak, as well as the strong.

13f

Other Ways to Respond to an Essay

In this chapter we have concentrated on analytic responses to individual essays. Such responses can be valuable in their own right and are good training for the critical reading and writing typical of college work. There are, of course, many other ways to respond to an essay, and it is worthwhile for us to look quickly at five of these.

1 Using the Same Form with a Different Purpose

Essays take so many "forms" that it would be impossible to make a comprehensive list, but some forms strike almost every reader as familiar. Orwell's essay, for example, is a first-person narrative of an event that changed the author's life. Thus, one possible response to it is to write your own first-person narrative about an event that changed *your* life.

Presumably, your aim will not be to show your readers the moral dangers of colonialism, but, like Orwell's narrative, your essay should have a clear purpose. You might want to follow Orwell's pattern of providing enough information at the start of the essay to show the reader the significance of the event that you will focus on. You might, like him, focus on an event that occupied about an hour and so can be described in great detail.

2 Close Stylistic Modeling

To get a fuller appreciation of the structure and rhythm of the writer's prose, imitate a brief passage (about 250 words is as much as most of us can sustain) as closely as possible. Match the writer phrase by phrase, trying to use the same grammatical structures and marks of punctuation, but writing on a different subject. Parody is legitimate here, and for pure fun it is sometimes worthwhile to pick a subject your author never would have. The following example was modeled on Orwell's eleventh paragraph.

> When I opened the oven I did not smell the burning or feel the heat—I never do when a thermostat goes haywire—but I saw the smoke that shot out toward the ceiling. At 300 degrees, too low a

temperature, you would have thought, even for the turkey to cook safely, a weird, thermonuclear disaster had destroyed the bird. It wasn't melted or vaporized, but every ounce of the carcass was charcoal. It looked entirely blackened, hardened, almost mineral, as though the heat . . .

3 Using Similar Subject Matter but Taking a Different View

What people mean by the subject matter of an essay is rather vague. Let us say that it is the raw material of experience before the writer makes anything of it—develops a thesis, creates or re-creates an emotional response, takes a moral stand. In Orwell's case, we might say that the subject is "shooting an elephant" or "acting out the role of a 'sahib' " or "dealing with a crisis in a foreign country." If the subject matter of an essay interests you, you may want to write a parallel essay about it, one that makes your own point rather than the author's. Though your subject matter should be similar, your meaning might differ from Orwell's in any of the three dimensions. For example, here are three possibilities:

1. Present an episode in which you (as a dormitory counselor, perhaps, or as a supervisor at work) had to exert your authority over others. You might use this essay to demonstrate the proposition that being a "sahib" sometimes makes you more rather than less free.

2. Present a scene in which you kill, deliberately or accidentally, an animal. Your might use this essay to create an emotional response different from Orwell's.

3. Present an episode in which you acted against your conscience or instinct. You might use this essay to show that such actions sometimes lead to good results.

4 Taking a Similar View but Using Different Subject Matter

Agreeing intelligently with the writer's views can be as challenging as disagreeing with them. One way of actively agreeing is to write an essay that adopts the writer's attitude and shows that it applies to another subject. You might take one of these approaches:

1. Write an essay demonstrating that the "tyrant" does enslave himself, but concentrate on an episode far different from Orwell's shooting of the elephant. You might, for instance, write about being

a merely social "sahib," someone looked up to because of your family's status in the community.

2. Write an essay which, like Orwell's, re-creates the heightening of emotion that we sometimes feel when we know that we have done wrong. Again, your episode could be very different from Orwell's. Even in a shoplifting episode from childhood, there can be a similar heightening of emotion.

3. Write an essay demonstrating that acting wrongly makes the conscience less sensitive. Your wrongdoing will presumably not involve elephant guns and Burmans.

5 Comparing Two Essays

A comparison of two essays often sharpens our understanding of both. If your reader contains essays organized by theme, you may find it easy to make productive comparisons, since related essays are collected side by side. The editor of your reader, however, is not the only one with a mind for comparisons: You will probably discover some comparisons that he or she could not have anticipated. An essay comparing "Shooting an Elephant" and James Baldwin's "Fifth Avenue, Uptown" might be interesting. One involves a British overseas colony; the other involves an American ghetto—sometimes called an "internal colony." We naturally wonder what similarities there are in the natures of the two colonies. Or "Shooting an Elephant" might be compared with another of Orwell's famous essays, "Politics and the English Language." "Politics" discusses rules of effective writing, and we could determine how well Orwell follows his own rules in "Shooting an Elephant." No doubt, you will think of other comparisons. The possibilities are limitless.

Unlimited possibilities are the note on which to end this chapter. Every response you have to an essay can be productive. Sometimes you react almost entirely to the style and begin to imitate it in your own work. Sometimes a single phrase sticks in your mind and becomes the germ for an essay of your own. Enthusiasm for what you read is obviously a powerful spur to writing a response, but boredom or irritation can be a stimulant, too—especially if you explain precisely what it is that makes an essay irritating. The key is to get your brain and your words moving. When you move, you find your own direction.

VI

GRAMMAR

14

I n this book, we use the word *grammar* to refer to the principles that guide people as they combine words into sentences. Knowing these principles for the English language gives you some practical advantages. First, if others note problems with a piece of your writing, these principles should help you focus on and correct many of the problems. Second, these principles might lead you to discover some sentence structures that you have rarely used and to understand more specifically when it would be appropriate and effective to use them.

Knowing these principles might also increase your appreciation of language. Without the ability to combine words into sentences, people could never communicate their perspectives on the world to others. In fact, they probably would not be able to formulate those perspectives. Therefore, examining English grammar can shed light on what it means for human beings to be language-using creatures.

14a

The Simple Sentence and Standard Edited English

The simple sentence allows writers to make a predication, to assert something about something else. Such assertions are the basic units that writers use to express ideas and that readers use to process those expressions.

When we describe the various forms that the simple sentence can take, we do so in terms of the conventions for Standard Edited English. This variety of English appears in major newspapers across the United States and in magazines such as *Time* and *The Atlantic*. And most people who write on the job use this variety in their work.

Standard Edited English is not the only variety of English in the United States. Many nonstandard varieties of English, which are usually called regional or social dialects, flourish in different regions and among different social classes. If you were to travel across the United States and pay close attention to varieties of English, you would probably hear and read sentences such as these:

The car needs fixed.

We might could win.

They done been gone all night.

Such sentences are regular parts of the English language for many people, and, in the appropriate region or social setting, they should be able to use such sentences without scorn or condemnation from others. However, by relying on a nonstandard variety of English in situations where Standard Edited English is expected, a person might not communicate well with others. And even a partial failure in communication could lead to negative consequences, such as not being admitted to certain colleges or not landing an attractive job.

These comments are not meant to suggest that Standard Edited English is inherently superior to all other varieties of English or that Standard Edited English will never change. They simply point out the fact that, because of certain social and historical developments, Standard Edited English has come to be accepted as the variety in which most public documents in the United States are written. Consequently, unless you need to use a nonstandard variety of English to achieve some special effect, you should write your essays for college classes in Standard Edited English.

14a
ss

Exercise 1

List five to ten words, groups of words, or sentences that you have heard or read and that you believe are not parts of Standard Edited English.

EXAMPLE: It ain't nobody I remember.

14b

Identifying the Simple Sentence

Most traditional definitions hold that a simple sentence has both a subject and a predicate. The **subject** names what the sentence is about. The **predicate** makes a statement about the subject, asks a question about the subject, or tells the person or persons named in the subject to do something. The predicate always includes a verb—a word naming an action, process, occurrence, or state of being. Finally, the simple sentence is grammatically independent. In other words, the simple sentence is an independent clause (see **14f**). *The diplomats took them to Jamaica* is an independent clause; it can stand alone as a simple sentence. *Although the diplomats took them to Jamaica* is a subordinate clause; it cannot stand alone as a simple sentence (see **14f**). Here are two examples of simple sentences. In each case, the subject appears first and is separated from the predicate by a slash (/):

**14b
SS**

> He / wrote about a river.
>
> Ernest Hemingway / wrote a story about the Big Two-Hearted River.

Exercise 2

Form as many simple sentences from each of the following lists of words as you can. Then indicate which sentence you think was actually used by the author named.

> EXAMPLE: idiom lie difficulties with deeper than comparison but (original from Mina Shaughnessy, *Errors and Expectations*)

From this list, you could derive at least the following simple sentences:

> But deeper than idiom lie comparisons with difficulties.
>
> But comparisons with idiom lie deeper than difficulties.
>
> But comparisons lie deeper than difficulties with idiom.
>
> But difficulties with comparisons lie deeper than idiom.

The last sentence is the one that Shaughnessy wrote.

1. the him caught there tanner (original from Roger Shattuck, *The Forbidden Experiment*)

2. national his law became whim (original from Robert Waite, *The Psychopathic God: Adolf Hitler*)

3. its also agriculture legal has aspect (original from Bronislaw Malinowski, *Coral Gardens and Their Magic*)

4. have fact a the of region the rains always life throughout been (original from Fernand Braudel, *The Mediterranean and the Mediterranean World in the Age of Philip II*)

5. as we possible behind leave thought must far as patriarchal (original from Gerda Lerner, *The Creation of Patriarchy*)

14c

Identifying the Subject in Simple Sentences

Most traditional definitions of the subject describe it as what the sentence is about. This definition is based on the function that the subject usually fulfills for readers. But it is possible to be more specific about the subject by looking at a different kind of definition.

1 Typical Meanings of Subjects

Subjects can also be described in terms of meanings or the roles that the persons or things named by subjects play. The subject usually names who or what acts, experiences something, is described, is identified further, or is acted upon:

Babe Ruth pointed to the bleachers. [The subject, *Babe Ruth,* names the one who acted.]

Bartleby felt lonely. [The subject, *Bartleby,* names the one who experienced something.]

They are brilliant. [The subject, *They,* refers to those who are described.]

Garth is the new accidental tourist. [The subject, *Garth,* names the one who is identified further.]

The portrait was stolen. [The subject, *The portrait,* names that which was acted upon.]

Most subjects are either nouns or pronouns (see Chapter 15). Often the subject is the first noun or pronoun in a sentence. Occasionally, though, the first noun or pronoun is not the subject. Consider this sentence:

Into the arena marched the matadors.

The first noun in this sentence is *arena*, but it is not the subject. The easiest way to find the subject is to ask, "Who or what marched?" The answer is that the matadors marched; *the matadors* is the subject.

Exercise 3

In each of the following sentences, the subject is italicized. Indicate whether the subject names a thing or person who acts, experiences something, is described, is identified further, or is acted upon.

EXAMPLE: *Helen Keller's parents* hired a new teacher. [The subject names those who acted.]

1. *That new teacher* was Anne Sullivan.
2. *Anne* held Helen's hand under a stream of water.
3. *Anne's technique* was brilliant.
4. *The water* was directed over Helen's hands.
5. *Helen* felt the thrill of returning thought.

2 Identifying Simple and Complete Subjects

14c ss

The **simple subject** is usually the single noun or pronoun that names what or who acts, experiences, is described, is identified, or is acted upon:

simple subject ___ verb
The older people from the delta saved the village.

The **complete subject** includes the simple subject and all the words that modify it or one of its modifiers:

complete subject
The older people from the delta saved the village.

If a simple subject stands alone, the simple subject and the complete subject are identical:

simple subject and complete subject
They saved the village.

Exercise 4

In each of the following sentences, underline the complete subject and circle the simple subject.

EXAMPLE: Helen's inner (life) was a blank with absolutely no sense of time.

1. A serious illness had destroyed her sight and hearing.
2. She did not understand the secrets of language.

3. Her mental processes were mainly natural impulses.

4. Her dormant being did not understand the connection between words and things.

5. Her experience with the water on her hands changed her life profoundly.

3 Identifying Compound Subjects

In some sentences, two or more complete subjects are joined to form a **compound subject.** Sometimes these subjects are joined by coordinating conjunctions *(and, but, or, for, nor, so, yet)*:

```
                compound subject
     first subject          second subject
```

The school board and a community group raised money for a new playground.

In some compound subjects, three or more subjects are linked, usually by commas and a coordinating conjunction:

```
                 compound subject
    first subject      second subject      third subject
```

The concertmaster, an oboe player, and a cellist were practicing.

And sometimes the subjects are joined by correlative conjunctions *(both . . . and, either . . . or, neither . . . nor, not only . . . but also, whether . . . or)*:

```
                compound subject
     first subject          second subject
```

Both her teacher and her friends consider her poem "Recursions" unfinished.

14c
ss

Exercise 5

Indicate whether each of the following sentences has a compound subject. If a sentence has a compound subject, specify what individual complete subjects are parts of it.

EXAMPLE: Helen's parents and her friends were amazed. [This sentence has a compound subject. The two individual complete subjects are *Helen's parents* and *her friends.*]

1. The smell of the lilacs and the warmth of the sun took on new significance for her.

2. Her mind raced to learn new words.

3. Anger, pain, and joy had names now.

4. Her vague feelings and natural instincts now changed into definite thoughts.

5. Neither wonder nor joy would ever again be absent from her life.

Identifying the Predicate in Simple Sentences

In most sentences, the predicate includes all the elements that are not parts of the complete subject. The predicate includes a verb. It may also include one or more auxiliary verbs and elements that modify the verb, that modify a modifier of the verb, or that complete the meaning of the verb.

The verb in a simple sentence must be a finite verb; that is, it must describe a definite and limited action, process, experience, or state of being. In *the sun rising,* for instance, *rising* is not finite; *rising* does not name a definite and limited action. In *The sun rises,* however, *rises* is a finite verb; *rises* names a definite and limited action.

1 Typical Meanings of Predicates

The predicate usually indicates what the subject does, tells what the subject experiences, describes the subject, identifies the subject further, or indicates what is done to the subject:

Babe Ruth pointed to the bleachers. [The predicate, *pointed to the bleachers,* indicates what Babe Ruth did.]

Bartleby felt lonely. [The predicate, *felt lonely,* tells what Bartleby experienced.]

They are brilliant. [The predicate, *are brilliant,* describes those to whom *They* refers.]

Garth is the new accidental tourist. [The predicate, *is the new accidental tourist,* identifies Garth further.]

The portrait was stolen. [The predicate, *was stolen,* indicates what was done to the portrait.]

Exercise 6

In each of the following sentences, the predicate is italicized. Indicate whether the predicate tells what the subject does, tells what the subject experiences, describes the subject, identifies the subject further, or indicates what is done to the subject.

EXAMPLE: The wolves *raised the two abandoned children.* [The predicate tells what the wolves did.]

1. The two abandoned children *were raised by the wolves.*
2. They *felt comfortable among the wolves.*
3. They *adopted some of the wolves' habits.*
4. They *were the famous children abandoned in the forest of India.*
5. They *were incapable of uttering sentences.*

2 Identifying Simple and Complete Predicates

The **simple predicate** of a sentence includes all the verbs in the sentence. Sometimes a sentence contains only one verb, the main verb:

main verb
The principal of that school carries a baseball bat.

But often, besides the main verb, a sentence contains auxiliary verbs, such as forms of *be* (*is* carrying), forms of *do* (*did* carry), and forms of *have* (*have* carried). It may also contain forms of modals, which are auxiliary verbs that show degrees of possibility and obligation (*might* carry, *must* carry).

The **complete predicate** includes the simple predicate and all the words that modify or complete the meaning of the main verb; it also includes all the words that modify these modifiers:

complete predicate
The road from Cedarville surprised them.

complete predicate
The road from Cedarville winds along the Paris River for fourteen miles.

If a sentence has only a main verb, that verb is considered both the simple and the complete predicate:

simple and complete predicate
The rear brakes squeaked.

**14d
ss**

Exercise 7

In each of the following sentences, underline the complete predicate and circle the simple predicate.

EXAMPLE: The child (had spent) much of his youth in the forests of southern France.

1. The boy sneaked into the garden of a tanner.
2. He dug for vegetables.
3. The tanner grabbed him firmly.
4. The boy fought.
5. The tanner might keep him from escaping.

3 Identifying Compound Predicates

Like subjects, predicates can be joined—to form a **compound predicate**—and they can be linked in the same ways as subjects. They can be linked by means of coordinating conjunctions *(and, but, or, for, nor, so, yet)*:

first predicate   second predicate

Julie dipped her net into the water and caught a minnow.

Predicates can also be linked by means of commas and a coordinating conjunction:

first predicate   second predicate

Jack started across the log, lost his balance,

third predicate

and fell into the stream.

Finally, predicates can be compounded by means of correlative conjunctions *(both . . . and, either . . . or, neither . . . nor, not only . . . but also)*:

first predicate   second predicate

Nick either walked from Seney or hitched a ride with a logging crew.

Exercise 8

Indicate whether or not each of the following sentences has a compound predicate. If a sentence has a compound predicate, specify what individual complete predicates are parts of it.

> EXAMPLE: The villagers stared at the boy and considered him wild. [This sentence has a compound predicate. The two individual complete predicates are *stared at the boy* and *considered him wild.*]

1. The boy could not speak and made only strange noises.
2. The villagers crowded around the boy and gaped at him.
3. Some of them saw him as subhuman or as something supernatural.

14d
SS

4. The boy was obviously frightened and tried to escape.
5. But one villager was kind and made the boy his responsibility.

Identifying the Kinds of Simple Sentences

So far we have described a kind of simple sentence called the **declarative**. Its main function is to convey information, and readers and listeners generally respond to it by absorbing the information it conveys.

Three other kinds of simple sentences occur in English. One is the **interrogative**:

Did you march on their headquarters?

Its main function is to request information. Readers and listeners generally respond to it by providing the information requested.

Another kind of simple sentence is the **imperative**:

Be happy!

The traditional assumption is that the subject for such imperatives is *you*. The main function of imperatives is to express a command. Readers and listeners generally respond to imperatives by performing the appropriate actions.

The final kind of simple sentence is called **exclamatory**:

What a wonderful test those instructors have devised!

How well you sang the high notes!

The main function of such sentences is to express how much a speaker or writer is impressed with something. Readers and listeners generally respond by thanking others for compliments, by agreeing or disagreeing with the substance of the sentence, or by taking some form of action.

Distinguishing Independent Clauses from Subordinate Clauses

Independent clauses have both a subject and a predicate and are grammatically independent. **Subordinate clauses** have subjects and predicates and are therefore true clauses. But they are subordinate to other grammatical constructions.

Perhaps the easiest way to spot a subordinate clause is to recognize the kinds of words that usually introduce such clauses. These words are subordinating conjunctions (such as *if, since,* and *unless*), relative pronouns (such as *that, who,* and *whoever*), some adjectives (such as *whose, which,* and *what*), and some adverbs (such as *when, where, whether, why,* and *how*). When words such as these introduce a clause, they signal that the clause is subordinate:

> If you take one more step . . .
>
> . . . who seized the day . . .
>
> . . . whose book on meditation and motorcycles was captivating . . .

If a coordinating conjunction *(and, but, or, for, nor, so, yet)* introduces a group of words that has a subject and a predicate, the group is an independent clause:

> . . . but they saw debate as a kind of warfare.

Most people do not usually read a subordinate clause without a pertinent question rising in their minds. When they read *If you turn one more page,* they probably wonder, "Well, what? What if I turn one more page?" Therefore, if you were to present a group of words such as *If you turn one more page* as a sentence—that is, punctuated to end with a period—you could expect to be told that you have created a sentence fragment (see **22a**). A subordinate clause is usually accompanied by one or more independent clauses.

14f
ss

Exercise 9

Indicate whether each italicized clause in the following sentences is independent or subordinate.

> EXAMPLE: *When people are young,* they often can learn to speak several languages fluently. [The italicized clause is a subordinate clause.]

1. Some people claim *that those acquiring several different languages should receive consistent exposure to those languages.*

2. *If children get consistent exposure to several languages,* the children will probably acquire all the languages.

3. Some children *who are fluent in several languages* say that they dream in more than one language.

4. *But they usually think primarily in one language,* although thinking in other languages is possible.

5. The language *that people acquire first* is usually the one most deeply rooted in them.

Identifying Phrases

Phrases are words or groups of words without a subject or a predicate or both; they usually function in a sentence like single words. The phrases most pertinent to the focus of this chapter are noun phrases and verb phrases. Every **noun phrase** has a noun or a word that acts as a noun (such as *speculating* and *to guess*) as its head word. Sometimes this is all that a noun phrase contains. Often, however, the head word is preceded by an **article** *(a, an,* or *the)*. Besides, the head noun is often modified before, after, or both before and after, and the full noun phrase includes the article, the head word, and all the modifiers. Here are some examples (with the head word in italics):

quiet *desperation*

pickerel in a pond

some *patterns* in the mud

widening concentric *circles* on the surface of the pond

In sentences, noun phrases function like single nouns. You could write *The widening concentric circles on the surface of the pond made him speculate about time* or *Circles made him speculate about time.* The difference lies in how much information you think your readers need or would enjoy.

A **verb phrase** has a main verb as its head word. Sometimes this is all that a verb phrase contains. But often the main verb is accompanied by one or more auxiliary verbs. The full verb phrase includes the main verb and all of the auxiliary verbs. Here are some examples (with the main verb in italics):

has *ambled*

might have *ambled*

could have been *ambling*

Verb phrases can serve as predicates of simple sentences, but they do not contain a subject. Therefore, they are neither independent nor subordinate clauses, but phrases.

ESL Consideration

ARTICLES WITH PLACE NAMES

There are three things to remember about using articles with place names:

1. In most cases, no article is used with a geographical name: *Europe, France, Rome, Lake Baykal.*

2. Collectives and plurals take *the: the Baltic Republics, the United States, the People's Republic of China, the Rocky Mountains, the Alps, the Great Lakes.*

3. Bodies of water, land masses, and regions of the world usually take *the: the Pacific Ocean, the Black Sea, the Gulf of Tonkin, the Bay of Biscay, the Amazon River, the English Channel, the Erie Canal, the African Continent, the Nile Delta, the Yucatan Peninsula, the Gobi Desert.*

Exercise 10

Indicate whether each italicized word or group of words in the following short excerpt from William A. Nolen's *The Making of a Surgeon* is an independent clause, a subordinate clause, or a phrase.

> EXAMPLE: *If you study for five years*, you will be ready to take that examination. [*If you study for five years* is a subordinate clause.]

Removing a stomach, a gall bladder or an appendix *can be* a difficult job. If the ulcer is stuck to the pancreas, the gall bladder acutely inflamed, the appendix ruptured, it takes *a smooth technician* to do the job safely. Still, *a reasonably intelligent, moderately adept individual* might learn to do any of these jobs in a few months. If you can cut, sew, and tie knots, you *can operate. When you get down to fundamentals,* that's really all there is to the mechanical phase of surgery.

Then what is there about surgery that makes it necessary for a doctor to study for five years? *The answer, in a word, is 'judgment.'*

It takes a long time and *a lot of hard work* for a doctor to acquire sound judgment. Every time he sees a patient he has to be able to assess and evaluate the history *of the patient's illness,* the findings on physical examinations, the chemical studies of the blood, the results of X-rays and a multitude of other factors; and often after weighing all these factors, he has to decide whether to operate or not, what procedure to use, whether to do them immediately or later. And *he* has to be right. It takes at least five years for a doctor to acquire the knowledge and experience he *needs* to do the job. It's much more difficult to decide if a patient needs to have his stomach removed than it is to do it.

Subjects and Predicates: Further Distinctions

1 Words That Are Not Parts of the Subject or the Predicate

Some words in simple sentences lie outside the bounds of both the subject and the predicate. Perhaps the most common example of such words is the **sentence adverb,** an adverb that modifies the entire sentence:

sentence   simple   simple
adverb   subject   predicate

Fortunately, they survived.

Especially in direct quotations of speech, you will also see **vocatives,** words that indicate to whom a sentence is addressed:

simple   complete
vocative   subject   predicate

"Mrs. Robinson, he was very surprised."

You may also encounter **interjections,** which are words and groups of words that express intense emotions:

complete   complete
interjection subject   predicate

Goodness, they are singing an alluring song.

Often interjections are followed by an exclamation mark and are therefore formally separated from the subsequent sentence.

Sometimes you will see **responsives,** words such as *yes* and *no*:

simple   complete
responsive subject   predicate

No, they moved their funds out of the stock market before October.

Responsives occur most often in direct quotations of speech.

Finally, you may sometimes see an absolute phrase written as part of a simple sentence. An **absolute phrase** consists of a noun or pronoun followed usually by a participle (see **17c**) and possibly by some modifiers. In the sentence *The stock market having crashed, they looked for a new line of work,* there is an absolute phrase: *The stock market having crashed.* An absolute phrase is not connected by any word to the sentence with which it appears, nor does it modify any word in that sentence. Rather, it stands in an absolute, or independent, relationship to the rest of the sentence and modifies all of it.

2 Material Between the Complete Subject and the Verb

The verb does not directly follow the complete subject in all sentences:

14h
ss

simple   modifies
subject   the verb   verb

Grete obviously won the race without taking any short cuts.

The modifier *obviously* stands after the subject and before the verb, but, since it modifies the verb, it is part of the complete predicate.

15

NOUNS AND PRONOUNS

T his chapter focuses on the words that most commonly appear as the simple subject in simple sentences: nouns and pronouns.

15a

Identifying Nouns

1 Some Ways to Identify Nouns

Traditionally, **nouns** have been defined as the words that refer to persons *(Mrs. Robinson)*, places *(Brooklyn)*, things *(trees)*, qualities *(softness)*, actions *(collecting)*, events *(game)*, and concepts *(justice)*.

You can often identify nouns on the basis of their form or possible form, for many nouns take a slightly different form when they change from singular to plural. Singular nouns refer to one thing: *mitten, boot, boss*. Plural nouns refer to more than one thing: *mittens, boots, bosses*. As these examples show, many nouns are made plural by the addition of *-s* or *-es*. However, when some nouns are made plural, their final consonant must also be changed (for example, *leaf* becomes *leaves*, and *loaf* becomes *loaves*).

If you do not know whether a word is a noun or not, a generally reliable test is to ask whether it has a plural form. *Belt* does, but *into, skillfully,* and *although* do not.

Finally, many nouns can be identified through their distinctive suffixes. Suffixes are clusters of letters added to the ends of words or bases for words. For example, adding the suffix *-ster* to the word *young* produces the noun *youngster.* Being aware of the following suffixes, all of which are commonly used to create nouns, should help you identify many different words as nouns:

-ance (as in *annoyance*)	*-ism* (as in *truism*)
-ancy (as in *flippancy*)	*-ist* (as in *leftist*)
-ation (as in *fluctuation*)	*-ity* (as in *activity*)
-dom (as in *kingdom*)	*-let* (as in *ringlet*)
-eer (as in *auctioneer*)	*-ment* (as in *shipment*)
-ence (as in *excellence*)	*-ness* (as in *darkness*)
-ency (as in *currency*)	*-ship* (as in *friendship*)
-ess (as in *lioness*)	*-sion* (as in *scansion*)
-ery (as in *foolery*)	*-ster* (as in *youngster*)
-ice (as in *cowardice*)	

2 Some Categories of Nouns

Nouns are usually divided into several different categories.

Common nouns refer to a member or to members of a general group or class of things: *person, city, cars.*

Proper nouns refer to a specific and namable member of a group or class. Usually, these nouns begin with a capital letter: *Elizabeth Cady Stanton, Seattle, Volvo.* Sometimes the names of people are preceded by a title: *Professor Fox.* In such cases, the title and the noun together are considered a proper noun.

Collective nouns refer to collections of people, places, and things in their entireties: *team, committee, jury.*

Concrete nouns refer to things that people can perceive with their senses: *weed, needle, basketball.*

Abstract nouns refer to concepts. People cannot perceive these with their senses; they create and reflect on them in their minds: *mercy, justice, righteousness.*

Some nouns can be either concrete or abstract, depending on how they are used in context. In the statement *William and Harold wanted to join a fraternity,* the noun *fraternity* refers to a group of

---

ESL Consideration

GENERIC CATEGORIES AND ARTICLES

There are five structural patterns in English for indicating generic categories, which show that people or things are members of groups. The patterns are listed here, showing when articles are used with nouns:

> PATTERN 1: *THE* + SINGULAR NOUN   *The possum* is nocturnal.
>
> PATTERN 2: PLURAL NOUN   *Possums* are nocturnal. (no article)
>
> PATTERN 3: *A/AN* + SINGULAR NOUN   *A baby* will cry.
>
> PATTERN 4: MASS NOUN   *Cholesterol* occurs in animal fats. (no article)
>
> PATTERN 5: *THE* + PLURAL NOUN   *The Spaniards* love children.

Pattern 1 is the most formal and is often used in technical or informative writing. Pattern 2 is the complement of Pattern 1, yet less formal. It is preferred when discussing simple inanimate objects ("Forks were a novelty in the Middle Ages."). Pattern 3 is the most informal and frequently occurs in speech or writing containing personal observations. Pattern 4 is restricted to mass nouns in formal and informal settings. Pattern 5 is rarely used: It is reserved mainly for discussing information about religious, political, national, social, or professional groups.

15a
np

---

people housed in a building. Here *fraternity* refers to something concrete; people frequently speak of seeing fraternities or fraternity houses. On the other hand, in *William and Harold enjoyed the fraternity among the delegates,* the noun *fraternity* refers to something like collegiality and good cheer, both abstractions.

Count nouns refer to things that can be separated into individual units and counted: *toes, speeches, days.*

Mass nouns refer to things or substances that cannot be separated into individual units and counted. People think of such things in terms of undifferentiated wholes: *mud, slime, gravy.*

Again, depending on how they are used in context, some nouns can be either count nouns or mass nouns. In *They are having difficulty,* the noun *difficulty* is a mass noun and refers to an undifferentiated whole. On the other hand, in *The research team faced two further difficulties with fusion,* the noun *difficulties* is a count noun.

ESL Consideration

ARTICLES AND NOUNS

Here is a chart that can help you decide when to use *a* or *an, the,* and *some* with nouns:

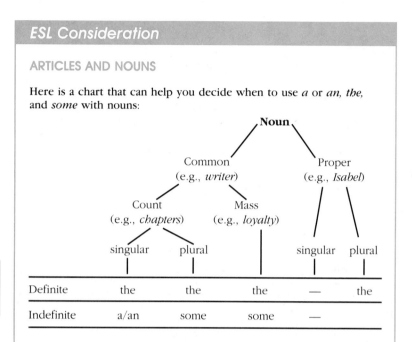

	Count (e.g., *chapters*) singular	Count plural	Mass (e.g., *loyalty*)	Proper singular	Proper plural
Definite	the	the	the	—	the
Indefinite	a/an	some	some	—	

Exercise 1

Indicate whether each of the following italicized nouns refers to a person, place, thing, quality, action, event, or concept.

> **EXAMPLE:**   Did Rousseau actually sign that *contract?* [The noun *contract* refers to a thing.]

For many years, *Professor Tommi* has collected people's names that are interesting in the *light* of what those people do for a living. He has learned of a Reverend Cant, who was a canon of *York.* He has a reference to a Susan Staves, who wrote a *book* called **Players' Scepters.** Once on a trip during *vacation* through Indiana, he noticed a sign for Courtney P. Justice, Attorney at Law. He has a letter about *justice* from the president of a college of law, William B. Lawless. And he has an advertisement for a book that traces the revelation of God's *greatness;* the book is **The Glory of God** by J. Dwight Pentecost. And Professor Tommi's *collecting* goes on. He has heard of an orthopedist named Bonebreak, a Rolls Royce salesperson named Brakewell, a pianist named Keys, and an archivist named *H. E. Peek.* One recent addition to his collection is the *name* of the author of **What People Eat,** Dr. Isaias Raw.

Identifying Pronouns

Traditionally, **pronouns** have been defined on the basis of their function within sentences: They substitute for nouns. Consider the following:

Currer saw Ellis and thanked her.

In this sentence the pronoun *her* substitutes for *Ellis.* In the following short passage, the pronoun *He* substitutes for the noun phrase *The boy on the raft:*

The boy on the raft warned the others to stay away. He had smallpox.

Whatever a pronoun substitutes for is called its antecedent. In the examples above, *Ellis* is the antecedent for *her,* and *The boy on the raft* is the antecedent for *He.* Both of these antecedents appear before the pronouns that substitute for them, but this is not always the case:

On his arrival, Jaggers produced a legal document.

Jaggers is the antecedent for *his,* even though it appears after *his.*

One good question about pronouns is why a language would have them. Why not just repeat nouns and noun phrases? The answer lies in the efficiency of language. In most cases, once a noun or a noun phrase is written, repeating it usually calls more attention to what the noun or noun phrase names than is necessary. You can sense this even in short sentences such as the following:

Hester lost Hester's embroidery needle.

It is especially easy to sense this in the case of longer noun phrases:

Although the man with the waxed mustache attended all of Professor Sweet's articulation classes, the man with the waxed mustache could never properly say the sentence about rain in Spain.

Repeating *the man with the waxed mustache* is not necessary; the language works more efficiently by substituting *he* for it.

We begin with the personal pronouns, since they have most of the characteristics that grammarians associate with pronouns. That is, they have forms showing distinctions in person, which can best be understood in terms of an imagined speaking situation. The first-person forms refer to the speaker or speakers, the second-person forms refer to the hearer or hearers, and the third-person forms refer to the persons or things spoken about. In addition, personal pronouns have forms reflecting distinctions in gender: masculine, feminine, and neuter.

1 Identifying Personal Pronouns

Most of the **personal pronouns** take the place of nouns and noun phrases that refer to people. Besides showing distinctions in person and in gender, these pronouns show distinctions in case. *Case* refers to the form that a noun or pronoun takes in order to show how it relates to other parts of sentences. A personal pronoun takes one form if it serves as the subject of a sentence *(I)* and a different form if it names what receives the action referred to by the verb *(me)*. Personal pronouns have three case forms: the subjective, the possessive, and the objective. The subjective case is used when the pronoun serves as a subject, among other possibilities. The possessive case is used when the pronoun signals ownership of (*their* farm) or close association with something (*his* portrait). The objective case is used when the pronoun serves as the receiver of the action referred to in the verb, among other possibilities.

The **subjective forms** of the personal pronouns are as follows:

	Singular	**Plural**
First person	I	we
Second person	you	you
Third person masculine	he	they
Third person feminine	she	they
Third person neuter	it	they

The **possessive forms** of the personal pronouns are as follows:

	Singular	**Plural**
First person	mine	ours
Second person	yours	yours
Third person masculine	his	theirs
Third person feminine	hers	theirs
Third person neuter	its	theirs

The possessive pronouns are similar or identical to members of another set of words: *my, our, your, his, her, its, their.* These words do not stand alone, as pronouns do; they are associated with nouns (as in *your skill* and *their interpretation*). These words do not function as pronouns but as adjectives modifying nouns (see **17a**). The pronouns such as *mine* and *theirs* appear on their own:

The committee considered two approaches.

Theirs was interesting but costly.

Mine was dull but cheap.

The **objective forms** of the personal pronouns are as follows:

	Singular	Plural
First person	me	us
Second person	you	you
Third person masculine	him	them
Third person feminine	her	them
Third person neuter	it	them

2 Identifying Reflexive Pronouns

Reflexive pronouns have forms showing distinctions in person, number, and gender. The reflexive pronouns are as follows:

15b
np

	Singular	Plural
First person	myself	ourselves
Second person	yourself	yourselves
Third person masculine	himself	themselves
Third person feminine	herself	themselves
Third person neuter	itself	themselves

Reflexive pronouns often reflect back upon the subject of the sentence, indicating that the action passes back to the one or ones named in the subject:

After each racquetball match, the challenger congratulates *himself.*

They congratulated *themselves.*

3 Identifying Intensive Pronouns

The reflexive pronoun forms also serve as **intensive pronouns.** To function as intensive and not reflexive pronouns, these forms have to emphasize or intensify the focus on a noun or pronoun, not show how action passes back to that noun or pronoun. In the following, *himself* functions as an intensive pronoun:

Henry himself prefers blackened redfish.

In the following sentence, the same form functions as a reflexive pronoun:

> Henry ordered himself some blackened redfish.

Usually, intensive pronouns appear immediately after the noun or pronoun they intensify. But they can appear before that noun or pronoun, especially in a more informal style:

> Myself, I prefer broiled king salmon.

And they can appear at some distance after the noun or pronoun:

> I prefer broiled king salmon myself.

The point of such sentences is usually to stress contrasts:

> Henry likes blackened redfish.
> I prefer broiled king salmon myself.

4 Identifying Reciprocal Pronouns

The **reciprocal pronouns** are *each other* and *one another*. Both of these have a possessive form: *each other's* and *one another's*. These pronouns mark reciprocal actions. If someone writes *The two contestants congratulated each other,* he or she means that each one of the contestants congratulated the other contestant. Conventionally, writers use *each other* to refer to two people and *one another* to refer to three or more people.

5 Identifying Relative Pronouns

The most common **relative pronouns** are *who* (with the possessive form *whose* and the objective form *whom*), *which,* and *that*. *Who* refers to persons, *which* refers to objects, and *that* refers to both persons and objects.

Relative pronouns often introduce a particular kind of subordinate clause called the adjective or relative clause (see **21b**). They get their name because they relate or link the subordinate clause to the word or phrase in the independent clause that the subordinate clause is connected to. But relative pronouns also play a role in the subordinate clause. Consider the following:

> The French lieutenant wrote to the woman who lived on the coast.

Here the relative pronoun *who* relates the subordinate clause *who lived on the coast* to the independent clause *The French lieutenant wrote to the woman.* In the subordinate clause, *who* is the subject of the verb *lived.*

6 Identifying Demonstrative Pronouns

There are four **demonstrative pronouns,** all of which carry a sense of pointing to someone or something: *this, that, these, those. This* and *that* refer to singular persons or things. *These* and *those* refer to more than one person or thing. *This* and *these* refer to persons or things nearer the writer in space or time. *That* and *those* refer to persons or things more distant from the writer in space or time. Referring to paintings, someone could write the following:

Those on the west wall have to be moved.

These here should not be touched.

7 Identifying Indefinite Pronouns

15b
np

When writers refer to indefinite persons or things, they often use **indefinite pronouns.** For example, a college bulletin might include the following sentence:

Anybody wishing to drop a course must notify the registrar before the tenth week of the semester.

The writers of the bulletin have no way of knowing which individual or individuals will want to drop a course. Thus, they use the indefinite pronoun *anybody.* Here are some indefinite pronouns:

all	each	less	no one
anybody	either	more	nothing
any	everybody	most	one
anyone	everyone	nobody	somebody
anything	everything	naught	some
aught	few	neither	someone
both	least	none	something

8 Identifying Interrogative Pronouns

Writers use **interrogative pronouns** when they do not have enough information to refer to indefinite persons or things but must ask about them:

what   who   whose   whom   which

Who, whom, and *whose* are used to ask about persons:

>Who will fight the Minotaur?
>
>Whom did the Minotaur chase?
>
>Whose is this?

What is used to ask about things:

>What caused such a huge crater in northern Quebec?

Which is used in questions involving choices among a limited number of alternatives. *Which* can ask about either persons or things:

>Which of your two friends is assertive?
>
>Which of the ten baseball cards did you lose?

**15b
np**

Exercise 2

Find the pronouns in the following sentences and indicate what kind of pronoun each one is.

>EXAMPLE: Tantalus was greatly honored by the gods since they
>allowed him to eat at their table. [*they* (personal
>pronoun); *him* (personal pronoun)]

1. The gods did even more for Tantalus; they themselves came to a banquet in his palace.

2. But he acted abominably, and no one knows why.

3. He had his son, Pelops, killed and served to the gods.

4. This was a most sacrilegious act.

5. But most of the gods, who had come down from Olympus at his request, were not fooled.

6. They drew back from the table in disgust, looked at one another, and decided to devise a punishment for him that would be more terrible than his banquet.

7. What was it?

8. They set Tantalus in a pool in Hades, but when he bent over to try to take a drink, the water disappeared into the ground.

9. Above the pool hung branches full of delicious fruit, but when he reached for a piece of it, the wind blew the branches out of his reach.

10. From the punishment that Tantalus had to endure, speakers of English derived for themselves a new verb: *tantalize.*

15c

Nouns and Pronouns: Further Distinctions

1 Possessive Case Before Gerunds

Gerunds are verb forms that function as nouns in sentences (for example, *skiing, racing, practicing;* see **16b**). Often when writers of Standard Edited English use a noun or pronoun immediately before a gerund, they use the possessive case form of the noun or pronoun:

> possessive
> case   gerund
> We are not afraid of her winning the tournament.

> possessive case   gerund
> Becky Sharp's gossiping caused trouble.

2 The Double Possessive

Occasionally, writers use the **double possessive:** that is, they use two signals of the possessive case together—an apostrophe plus *s* and an *of* phrase. They do so particularly in sentences beginning with *This* or *That,* especially if the style is quite informal:

> That serve of Maggie's is a winner.

Using both signals of the possessive helps to avoid the ambiguity in such phrases as *Acton's picture.* Is this a picture of Acton or a picture that belongs to Acton? *The picture of Acton* means that the picture is an image of Acton; *The picture of Acton's* means that it is a picture belonging to Acton.

3 The Zero Relative Pronoun

The **zero relative pronoun** is a relative pronoun that has been omitted from a sentence. You could write the following:

> This is the mystery novel that I like best.

But you could also omit the relative pronoun:

> This is the mystery novel I like best.

In the second example, you can speak of a zero relative pronoun.

16

V E R B S

T his chapter focuses on the verb or verb phrase, without which a group of words does not have a predicate.

16a

Identifying Verbs

Traditionally, **verbs** are defined as the words that refer to mental or physical actions *(think, evade)*, processes *(melt)*, occurrences *(fall)*, or states of being *(am)*.

Verbs can also be identified on the basis of their form or possible form. All verbs except *be* have five different forms:

The infinitive or base form:	receive	give
The past-tense form:	received	gave
The past participle:	received	given
The *s*-form for present tense:	receives	gives
The present participle:	receiving	giving

The first three of these forms are traditionally called the principal parts of a verb. The principal parts of *give* are *give, gave,* and *given.*

The verb *be* has eight different forms:

The infinitive or base form:	be
The past-tense forms:	was, were
The past participle:	been
The present-tense forms:	am, is, are
The present participle:	being

You can assume that a word is a verb if you can think of at least five different forms for it. In fact, if the word has an *s*-form and a present participle (the *-ing* form), you can assume that it is a verb. *Tolerate* has the forms *tolerates* and *tolerating;* it is a verb. *Through* has no *s*-form or present participle. Nor does *gingerly*. These two words are not verbs.

The prefix *en-* often marks verbs: *enact, enchant, encircle, enclose, encode, endear, enforce, enlighten,* among others. Some suffixes, too, usually turn other parts of speech into verbs:

-ify, -fy	vilify
-en	darken
-ate, -iate	activate
-ize	trivialize

Exercise 1

Use each of the following words in one sentence as a noun and in another sentence as a verb.

EXAMPLE:	air (noun)	The air in the valleys was humid.
	air (verb)	The dissidents aired their grievances.

1.	amount	6.	side
2.	book	7.	station
3.	corner	8.	summer
4.	elbow	9.	weather
5.	counter	10.	word

16b

Identifying the Classifications of Verbs

Here are four ways in which verbs are classified.

16b
V

1 Main Verbs and Auxiliary Verbs

a. Main Verbs

A simple sentence has at least one **main verb,** which refers to the primary activity in the sentence. If a simple sentence has only one verb, that verb will necessarily be the main verb:

main verb

The retired postal workers sprinted.

b. Auxiliary Verbs

The main verb can be accompanied by one or more **auxiliary verbs.** Together, the auxiliary verbs and the main verb in a sentence make up a **verb phrase.** Auxiliary verbs express shades of meaning having to do with such matters as the time of actions, processes, occurrences, and states of being. There are four general categories of auxiliary verbs:

Forms of **Be**

Forms of *be* can be main verbs:

main verb

The professor of management is a perfectionist.

But they can also appear as auxiliaries:

verb phrase

The bear was tagged by the researchers.

verb phrase

The team from Delta House is winning the game.

Forms of **Have**

Forms of *have* can appear as main verbs:

main verb

The Greeks had a gift for the Trojans.

But forms of *have* can also appear as auxiliaries:

verb phrase

They have slaughtered the seals.

verb phrase

They had slaughtered the seals.

verb phrase

They will have slaughtered the seals.

Forms of **Do**

Forms of *do* can be main verbs:

main verb

Bart did the dirty deed.

But forms of *do* also appear as auxiliaries, as when writers emphasize the action of a verb, make negative statements, and ask yes-no questions:

verb phrase

The phantom did save her.

verb phrase

They did not find any silver fleece.

verb phrase

Do steroids cause acne?

Modal Verbs

Modal verbs help show how the writer views the action or event depicted in a sentence. Modal verbs appear only as auxiliaries. The most common modal verbs are *can, could, shall, should, will, would, may, might, must,* and *ought to.* Modals convey subtle shades of meaning within two realms. One is the realm of possibility and probability:

The Cubs might win the pennant this year.

The other is the realm of permission, ability, and obligation:

The manager of the Yankees must lead them to the pennant.

Two modal verbs, *will* and *shall,* also help form the future tense (see **16c**):

verb phrase

The sun will rise in the southeast.

Exercise 2

In each of the following sentences, circle the main verb and underline the entire verb phrase.

     EXAMPLE: Many people had (expressed) concern about abuses of language.

   1. The National Council of Teachers of English has formed a Committee on Public Doublespeak.

16b

v

2. For the past several years, this committee has presented a Double-speak Award.

3. The word *doublespeak* was derived from the words *doublethink* and *newspeak*, both from George Orwell's novel *1984.*

4. The Doublespeak Award is given to people guilty of deceptive and confusing language.

5. In the past, the award has been presented to several prominent public figures.

6. The Committee on Public Doublespeak also publishes a newsletter about cases of doublespeak.

7. Readers of the newsletter can find phrases such as *energetic disassembly.*

8. This was used for the possibility of an atomic explosion in an armaments plant.

9. Or readers will find such phrases as *predawn vertical insertion.*

10. This is military language for an invasion by paratroopers.

2 Transitive and Intransitive Verbs

a. Transitive Verbs

Transitive verbs signal the transfer of action from the subject noun or pronoun to another noun or pronoun (an object noun or pronoun) that usually follows the verb (see direct object, **19b**).

subject	transitive	object
noun	verb	noun

Stradivarius made a violin.

Only transitive verbs can be expressed in the passive voice (see **16c**).

b. Intransitive Verbs

Intransitive verbs do not signal the transfer of action from a subject noun or pronoun to another noun or pronoun. There are two different kinds of intransitive verbs.

Intransitive complete verbs can make a complete predication on their own. They refer to actions, but these actions are not transferred to an object:

intransitive complete

Caged birds never sing.

Some verbs can function either as transitive verbs or as intransitive verbs, depending on their contexts. In *They sing,* the verb *sing* functions as an intransitive complete verb. In *They sing ribald camp-*

fire songs, however, *sing* functions as a transitive verb; it signals the transfer of action over to songs.

The second kind of intransitive verb is the linking verb. A **linking verb** connects a subject noun or pronoun to a word in the predicate that either renames it *(Benedict is the traitor)* or describes it *(Ulysses was crafty).* *Be* is the most common linking verb, but there are other verbs very similar to it in meaning that often function as linking verbs: *appear, continue, prove, remain, seem, stand,* and *stay.* Another very common linking verb is *become.* The following verbs are similar to it in meaning and often function as linking verbs: *come, get, grow, turn, turn out, wear,* and *work.* Finally, several verbs that convey meanings related to the senses commonly function as linking verbs: *feel, look, smell, sound,* and *taste.*

Exercise 3

Indicate whether each of the following italicized verbs is a transitive verb, an intransitive complete verb, or an intransitive linking verb.

EXAMPLE: He *drove* a van. [*Drove* is a transitive verb.]

Our beginnings do not *foreshadow* our ends if one judges by the Hudson River. A few miles east of the Bad Luck Ponds, the Hudson came down between the ridges to race alongside route 28; it was a mountain stream: clear, cold, shallow, noisy. A few miles from its source in Lake Tear-in-the-Clouds a mile up on Mount Marcy (the Indian name for the mountain is better: Tahawus, "Cloud-splitter") and three hundred river miles from the thousand oily piers of Hoboken, Weehawken, and Manhattan, here it *was* a canoer's watercourse. Above the little Hudson, spumes of mist *rose* from the mountains like campfire smoke.

Route 8 dropped out of the Adirondacks to Lake George, the way lined with resort homes and summer camps that *advertise* in the back pages of the *New York Times Magazine.* At Hague, I turned north and *followed* the water up a narrow valley to Ticonderoga and cut through town to the shore of Lake Champlain where, under the dark brow of the fort built by the British against French and Indian raids, I waited for the ferry.

William Least Heat Moon, *Blue Highways*

---

3 Regular and Irregular Verbs

Verbs are divided into two classes on the basis of how their past-tense forms and past participles are derived.

a. Regular Verbs

Most verbs are regular; their past-tense and past-participle forms are derived by adding *d* or *ed* to the base form. *Roll* is a regular verb; its past-tense and past-participle forms are *rolled* and *rolled*. Occasionally, you will have to double the final consonant of a regular verb before you add the *d* or *ed* to make the past-tense and past-participle forms:

plan   planned   planned

b. Irregular Verbs

There are about 250 irregular verbs in English. With these you cannot predict by formula how the past-tense and past-participle forms are produced. The following examples show some of the variations you can expect to see:

cut	cut	cut
beat	beat	beaten
come	came	come
meet	met	met
swim	swam	swum
speak	spoke	spoken
go	went	gone

**16b
v**

The dictionary is an invaluable tool in distinguishing regular from irregular verbs. If it lists only one form for a verb, the verb is regular. If the verb is irregular, the dictionary will list its principal parts.

The following list can help you review the principal parts of irregular verbs. In some cases this list includes two or more forms, both with some currency. The list also shows that some of these verbs are developing regular forms in addition to the older irregular forms.

abide	abode, abided	abode, abided
arise	arose	arisen
awake	awoke, awaked	awoken, awaked
be	was, were	been
bear	bore	borne
beat	beat	beaten
become	became	become
begin	began	begun
behold	beheld	beheld
bend	bent	bent
bet	bet, betted	bet, betted
bid	bad(e), bid	bade, bid, bidden
bind	bound	bound
bite	bit	bitten, bit
bleed	bled	bled
blow	blew	blown

break	broke	broken
breed	bred	bred
bring	brought	brought
build	built	built
burst	burst	burst
buy	bought	bought
cast	cast	cast
catch	caught	caught
choose	chose	chosen
cling	clung	clung
come	came	come
cost	cost	cost
creep	crept	crept
cut	cut	cut
deal	dealt	dealt
dig	dug	dug
dive	dived, dove	dived
do	did	done
draw	drew	drawn
dream	dreamt, dreamed	dreamt, dreamed
drink	drank	drunk
drive	drove	driven
dwell	dwelt, dwelled	dwelt, dwelled
eat	ate	eaten
fall	fell	fallen
feed	fed	fed
feel	felt	felt
fight	fought	fought
find	found	found
fit	fit	fit
flee	fled	fled
fling	flung	flung
fly	flew	flown
forbid	forbade, forbad	forbidden
forecast	forecast	forecast
foretell	foretold	foretold
forget	forgot	forgotten, forgot
forgive	forgave	forgiven
forsake	forsook	forsaken
freeze	froze	frozen

16b
v

get	got	got, gotten
give	gave	given
go	went	gone
grind	ground	ground
grow	grew	grown
hang (suspend)	hung	hung
have	had	had
hear	heard	heard
heave	heaved, hove	heaved, hove
hide	hid	hidden
hit	hit	hit
hold	held	held
hurt	hurt	hurt
keep	kept	kept
kneel	knelt, kneeled	knelt, kneeled
knit	knitted, knit	knitted, knit
know	knew	known
lay	laid	laid
lead	led	led
lean	leant, leaned	leant, leaned
leap	leapt, leaped	leapt, leaped
learn	learnt, learned	learnt, learned
leave	left	left
lend	lent	lent
let	let	let
lie (location)	lay	lain
light	lit, lighted	lit, lighted
lose	lost	lost
make	made	made
mean	meant	meant
meet	met	met
misdeal	misdealt	misdealt
mislead	misled	misled
misspell	misspelt, misspelled	misspelt, misspelled
mistake	mistook	mistaken
misunderstand	misunderstood	misunderstood
mow	mowed	mown, mowed
outbid	outbid	outbid
outdo	outdid	outdone
outfight	outfought	outfought

outgrow	outgrew	outgrown
outrun	outran	outrun
outshine	outshone	outshone
overcome	overcame	overcome
overdo	overdid	overdone
overeat	overate	overeaten
overfeed	overfed	overfed
overhang	overhung	overhung
override	overrode	overridden
overrun	overran	overrun
oversee	oversaw	overseen
overshoot	overshot	overshot
oversleep	overslept	overslept
overtake	overtook	overtaken
overthrow	overthrew	overthrown
pay	paid	paid
prove	proved	proved, proven
put	put	put
quit	quit, quitted	quit, quitted
read	read	read
rebuild	rebuilt	rebuilt
redo	redid	redone
remake	remade	remade
repay	repaid	repaid
reread	reread	reread
rerun	reran	rerun
reset	reset	reset
restring	restrung	restrung
retell	retold	retold
rethink	rethought	rethought
rewind	rewound	rewound
rewrite	rewrote	rewritten
rid	rid, ridded	rid, ridded
ride	rode	ridden
ring	rang	rung
rise	rose	risen
run	ran	run
saw	sawed	sawn, sawed
say	said	said
see	saw	seen
seek	sought	sought

16b
v

sell	sold	sold
send	sent	sent
set	set	set
sew	sewed	sewn, sewed
shake	shook	shaken
shave	shaved	shaven, shaved
shear	sheared	shorn, sheared
shed	shed	shed
shine	shone, shined	shone, shined
shoe	shod, shoed	shod, shoed
shoot	shot	shot
show	showed	shown
shred	shredded, shred	shredded, shred
shrink	shrank	shrunk
shut	shut	shut
sing	sang, sung	sung
sink	sank, sunk	sunk
sit	sat	sat
sleep	slept	slept
slide	slid	slid
sling	slung	slung
slink	slunk	slunk
slit	slit	slit
smell	smelt, smelled	smelt, smelled
sow	sowed	sown, sowed
speak	spoke	spoken
speed	sped, speeded	sped, speeded
spell	spelt, spelled	spelt, spelled
spend	spent	spent
spill	spilt, spilled	spilt, spilled
spin	spun, span	spun
spit	spat, spit	spat, spit
split	split	split
spoil	spoilt, spoiled	spoilt, spoiled
spread	spread	spread
spring	sprang, sprung	sprung
stand	stood	stood
steal	stole	stolen
stick	stuck	stuck
sting	stung	stung
stink	stank	stunk
stride	strode	stridden, strode
strike	struck	struck
string	strung	strung
strive	strove, strived	striven, strived

16b
v

swear	swore	sworn
sweat	sweat, sweated	sweat, sweated
sweep	swept	swept
swell	swelled	swollen, swelled
swim	swam	swum
swing	swung	swung

take	took	taken
teach	taught	taught
tear	tore	torn
tell	told	told
think	thought	thought
throw	threw	thrown
thrust	thrust	thrust
tread	trod	trodden

unbend	unbent	unbent
undergo	underwent	undergone
understand	understood	understood
undertake	undertook	undertaken
undo	undid	undone
unfreeze	unfroze	unfrozen
unmake	unmade	unmade
unwind	unwound	unwound
uphold	upheld	upheld
upset	upset	upset

wake	woke, waked	woken, waked
wear	wore	worn
weave	wove	woven
wed	wedded, wed	wedded, wed
weep	wept	wept
wet	wetted, wet	wetted, wet
win	won	won
wind	wound	wound
withhold	withheld	withheld
withstand	withstood	withstood
wring	wrung	wrung
write	wrote	written

16b
v

Exercise 4

Rewrite each of the following sentences, changing all the verbs into the past tense.

EXAMPLE: The batter walks out of the dugout.
            The batter walked out of the dugout.

1 The batter strides to the on-deck circle.
2. He stretches out his back muscles.
3. He swings three heavy bats vigorously to loosen up his arms and shoulders.
4. Then he drops all but one bat.
5. He inspects the pine tar on this bat.
6. He checks for hairline cracks.
7. He glares at the pitcher.
8. He smiles at the fans behind the dugout.
9. Finally, he struts to the plate.
10. Just then the manager replaces him with a pinch-hitter.

4 Finite and Nonfinite Verbs

16b
v

Finite verbs (such as *rose*) describe definite and limited actions, processes, occurrences, or conditions. **Nonfinite verbs** (such as *rising*) describe unfinished actions, processes, occurrences, or conditions. There are three kinds of nonfinite verb forms, all of which are called **verbals.**

Infinitives

The infinitive generally consists of the word *to* followed by the base form of the verb: *to examine.* The infinitive can show variations in tense, voice, and aspect: *to examine, to have examined, to be examining, to have been examining, to be examined, to have been examined.*

Infinitives function within sentences as several different parts of speech:

As a noun:

To travel would be a pleasure.

As an adjective:

The place *to have been* was Jimmy's.

And as an adverb:

To win, you should memorize your two-hour speech.

When present infinitives follow verbs such as *let, help, make, see, hear,* and *watch,* the *to* of the infinitive is usually dropped:

Did you hear him sing the national anthem?

The *to* that would normally precede *sing* has been dropped.

Infinitives sometimes appear with their own subjects. In *We wanted her to win*, the pronoun *her* is the subject of the infinitive *to win*.

Participles

There are several different participle forms:

The present participle: waving
The past participle: waved
The perfect participle: having waved

The first and last of these have a passive form *(being waved; having been waved)*.

Participles function as adjectives—they modify nouns and pronouns:

Enjoying the productions of the Shaw plays, she felt renewed.

Enjoyed by hundreds of people, the productions of the Shaw plays were repeated.

Having enjoyed the productions of the Shaw plays, they drove to Stratford.

16b
v

Gerunds

There are four gerund forms:

The simple form: waving
The passive of the simple form: being waved
The perfect form: having waved
The passive of the perfect form: having been waved

These forms are gerunds if they function as nouns:

gerund

Enjoying concerts can renew your spirit.

Exercise 5

Indicate whether each italicized verb form in the following sentences is finite or nonfinite. If the form is nonfinite, indicate what kind of verbal it is and what function it fulfills in the sentence.

EXAMPLE: *Fishing* for nearly four hours without a bite, Jonathan began to get discouraged. [*Fishing* is nonfinite; it is a present participle modifying *Jonathan.*]

1. At that point, he *decided* to try casting among the rocks off the north shore of Rutland Island.

2. He pulled the anchor up and headed for Rutland, *hoping* the wind would not intensify.

3. *To get* to Rutland Island most quickly, he had to go through Potaginnissing Shoal.

4. *Navigating* the shoal could be dangerous, but he made it through without any incidents.

5. As he *approached* Rutland Island, he turned the motor off and drifted up close to the rocks.

6. He decided to try casting a diving minnow, *hoping* to fool some of the northern pike that prowled the shallow waters.

7. He made several casts along submerged boulders, but he *had* no strikes.

8. *Wondering* if he would ever catch a fish, he tossed his lure almost on shore.

9. As he retrieved it, he *noticed* a v-like wave forming behind the line; a large pike was following his line.

10. *Catching* this monster, he thought, would make his day.

16c

Modifications of Verbs

The following modifications of verbs convey various shades of meaning.

1 Number

Nouns and some pronouns show distinctions between singular and plural number. To a limited extent, verbs show these same distinctions. Verbs in the present tense (see pages 263–264) have one form to agree with singular nouns and third-person pronouns *(practices)* and another form to agree with plural nouns and all first-person and second-person pronouns *(practice).*

2 Person

Personal pronouns show distinctions between first, second, and third persons (see **15b**). To an extent, verbs change in form to agree with these different pronouns:

	Singular		Plural
First person	I work	First person	we work
Second person	you work	Second person	you work
Third person masculine	he works	Third person	they work
Third person feminine	she works		
Third person neuter	it works		

The verb *be* changes forms more drastically than any other verb:

	Singular		Plural
First person	I am	First person	we are
Second person	you are	Second person	you are
Third person masculine	he is	Third person	they are
Third person feminine	she is		
Third person neuter	it is		

The third-person forms are used to agree with most nouns:

The provost works.   The philosopher is necessary.

The provosts work.   The philosophers are necessary.

16c
V

3 Mood

Mood refers to the changes in the form of a verb that show how the writer regards the action, process, occurrence, or state of being. There are three moods in English—the indicative, imperative, and subjunctive.

a. Indicative Mood

The **indicative** is the mood of fact. Writers use verbs in the indicative mood to make statements of fact (The times *are changing.*) or to ask questions about facts (Where *have* the flowers *gone?*).

b. Imperative Mood

The **imperative** is the mood of command. Writers use verbs in the imperative mood to make commands or very serious requests. Normally, the imperative mood is indicated by the base form of the verb, with a *you* assumed as the subject:

Do not count your chickens.

An exclamation mark often follows such sentences:

Stop it right now!

c. Subjunctive Mood

The **subjunctive** is the mood of the imagined or the hypothesized. Writers use verbs in the subjunctive mood to express wishes, recommendations, speculations, and the like.

Subjunctive verbs can take three primary forms. One is the base form, used in all persons and numbers. This form appears in subordinate *that* clauses after such verbs as *ask, demand, recommend, request,* and *require:*

I recommend that you *be* quiet on that point.

The base form also appears in several set expressions:

be that as it may	suffice it to say
far be it from me	long live the republic
so be it	God save the Queen
so help me God	

Finally, the base form appears in subordinate clauses expressing conditions and concessions:

If that be the case, they will tear up their literature books.

The second common subjunctive form is the past-tense form. Writers use it in connection with hypothetical actions, processes, occurrences, and conditions in the present, usually in subordinate clauses introduced by *if, as if,* or *as though.* Note that *were* is the past-tense form of *be* regardless of whether the subject is singular or plural:

She played that concert as if she *were* inspired.

The third subjunctive form is the past perfect tense form. Writers use it in connection with hypothetical actions, processes, occurrences, and conditions in the past:

If I *had won,* I would be humble.

Note that *would* or *could* is used with the verb in the main clause to show that the full sentence deals with the hypothetical.

Exercise 6

Identify the mood of each of the italicized words in the following.

> EXAMPLE: Dialects *vary* from region to region. [*Vary* is in the indicative mood.]

1. Until Cheryl moved away to college, she *thought* that dialects were what everyone else spoke.

2. She assumed that she spoke the language as it was meant to be spoken, and she would recommend that others *speak* it as she did.

3. She would become slightly irritated when others *called* what she called a "gutter" an "eavestrough."

4. "Why *say* that?" she wondered to herself.

5. Her irritation would grow when others would pronounce "Chicago" as if the **a** *were* flat and hard.

6. "*Make* the **a** full and round," she would demand.

7. The turning point *came* for Cheryl when she made a presentation to a class of second graders.

8. She *told* a short story about a mosquito hawk.

9. "Mosquito hawk!" the class roared. "What in the world *is* a mosquito hawk?"

10. When she realized that they all used the word "dragonfly" instead of "mosquito hawk," she began to suspect that there *are* legitimate different names for things and different ways to pronounce the same word.

4 Tense

The **tense** of a verb relates the time of an action, process, occurrence, or condition to a particular point of reference, often the time of writing.

a. The Present Tense

For most persons and numbers, the form of the verb used for the present tense is the base form. The form for the third-person singular adds an *s* to the base form, or an *es* if the base form ends in *ch, s, sh, x,* or *z* (as in *crunches*). The forms of *work* and *be*, accompanied by personal pronouns, are as follows:

I work	we work	I am	we are
you work	you work	you are	you are
he, she, it works	they work	he, she, it is	they are

The most common use of verbs in the present tense is to describe actions, processes, occurrences, and conditions that are simultaneous with the time of writing:

The soprano shatters several panes of glass on the Prudential Building.

You can also use the present tense for regular occurrences:

Each Monday she boards a ferry for Manhattan.

You can use it to express general truths:

Honesty is the best policy.

You can use it to describe actions in the past if you want to give them dramatic immediacy:

> The car pulls up beside me, and I groan. It is the sheriff.

You can even use the present tense to describe actions that will take place after the time of writing:

> The plane to Rio leaves next Monday.

Finally, by and large you should use the present tense to describe what is happening in a work of art, as well as how a work of art affects the reader, viewer, or listener:

> Throughout the novel, Ahab pursues the whale with great intensity. Some readers find the ending ambiguous.

b. The Past Tense

16c
V

In the past tense, the second principal part of verbs other than *be* is used for all persons and numbers. *Be* requires two different forms, *was* and *were*:

I worked	we worked	I was	we were
you worked	you worked	you were	you were
he, she, it worked	they worked	he, she, it was	they were

With the past tense, you can describe actions, processes, or occurrences that were completed or conditions that ended prior to the time of writing:

> He lived on a pedestal in the desert.

You can also use it to describe actions, processes, or occurrences that happened repeatedly or conditions that existed repeatedly in the past:

> Wars raged throughout the Middle Ages.

c. The Future Tense

The most common forms for the future tense combine *will* with the base form of a verb.

The future-tense forms for *work* and *be* are as follows:

I will work	we will work
you will work	you will work
he, she, it will work	they will work

I will be	we will be
you will be	you will be
he, she, it will be	they will be

ESL Consideration

TIME EXPRESSIONS WITH SIMPLE PAST AND PRESENT PERFECT TENSES

Certain time expressions are often used inappropriately with either the simple past tense or the present perfect tense:

INCORRECT: Since September, I studied in the United States.

INCORRECT: Last week I have watched a TV program on Arab culture.

Use the simple past tense of verbs (e.g., *ran, said, wrote*) with time expressions such as the following:

yesterday   *last week*
the other day   *a month ago*
earlier this week   *two years ago*
at seven o'clock on this past Friday

CORRECT: Two years ago they traveled to Greece to see their relatives.

Use the present perfect tense of verbs (e.g., *has run, has said, has written*) with these time expressions:

since   *so far*
until now   *up till now*

CORRECT: Until now they have not had time to plan for their next trip.

**16c
v**

The future tense is appropriate for actions, processes, occurrences, or conditions that will occur after the time of writing:

Tomorrow the magician will use real doves.

d. The Present Perfect Tense

The forms for the present perfect tense consist of present-tense forms of *have* combined with the past participle of the verb:

I have worked   we have worked
you have worked   you have worked
he, she, it has worked they have worked

I have been   we have been
we have been   you have been
he, she, it has been   they have been

The present perfect tense is used to describe actions, processes, occurrences, or conditions that began before the time of writing but either continue to the time of writing or somehow still affect the time of writing:

> She has followed a plan to travel abroad each summer.

e. The Past Perfect Tense

The forms for the past perfect tense are made up of the past-tense form of *have* combined with the past participle of the verb:

I had worked	we had worked
you had worked	you had worked
he, she, it had worked	they had worked

I had been	we had been
you had been	you had been
he, she, it had been	they had been

16c
V

In thinking about how to use the past perfect tense, you will have to keep three different times in mind: (1) the time of writing, (2) the time in the past when an action, process, occurrence, or condition started, and (3) another time in the past when the action, process, occurrence, or condition ended:

> By last Tuesday, their position in the standings had improved dramatically.

f. The Future Perfect Tense

The most common forms for the future perfect tense consist of *will* followed by *have* and the past participle of the verb:

I will have worked	we will have worked
we will have worked	you will have worked
he, she, it will have worked	they will have worked

I will have been	we will have been
you will have been	you will have been
he, she, it will have been	they will have been

You will also have to keep three different times in mind in thinking about using the future perfect tense: (1) the time of writing, (2) the time in the future when an action, process, occurrence, or condition will begin, and (3) the time in the future when the action, process, occurrence, or condition will end:

> By her fourth birthday, she will have given four piano recitals.

Exercise 7

In each of the following cases, write a sentence with the specified verb in the specified tense.

EXAMPLE: The past tense of *break*
            He broke his arm at a Boy Scout rally.

1. The present tense of *steal*
2. The past tense of *disturb*
3. The future tense of *study*
4. The present perfect tense of *read*
5. The past perfect tense of *compose*
6. The future perfect tense of *retire*

5 Aspect

16c
v

Aspect specifies the character of actions, processes, occurrences, and conditions, particularly their distribution in time. Do they happen sporadically? Do they happen regularly? Do they last a long time? These are questions about distinctions in aspect. Standard Edited English makes extensive use of the progressive aspect. Progressive aspect signals that actions, processes, occurrences, and conditions, no matter when they occur, do not occur in an instant but continue for a while. You can put verbs in all six tenses into the progressive aspect. To do so, add the forms of *be* appropriate for the number, person, and tense to the present participle of the verb:

Present tense, progressive aspect:	*Big Brother is watching you.*
Past tense, progressive aspect:	*Big Brother was watching you.*
Future tense, progressive aspect:	*Big Brother will be watching you.*
Present perfect tense, progressive aspect:	*Big Brother has been watching you.*
Past perfect tense, progressive aspect:	*Big Brother had been watching you.*
Future perfect tense, progressive aspect:	*Big Brother will have been watching you.*

16c
V

ESL Consideration

STATIVE VERBS AND PROGRESSIVE ASPECT

Writers frequently misuse the progressive aspect with *stative* verbs, a special group of verbs that describe "states of being." In most writing contexts, progressive aspect is not used with stative verbs. Here is a list of some common stative verbs:

appear	have	remember
appreciate	hear	see
believe	imagine	seem
belong	know	smell
contain	like	suppose
cost	love	taste
desire	mean	think
dislike	measure	want
doubt	need	weigh
entail	own	wonder
feel	prefer	
hate	recognize	

Some stative verbs, however, include progressive aspect, taking on additional, active meanings. These types of statives have synonyms. Here are examples of some common ones employed in narration or description (the synonym for the italicized stative verb appears in the following sentence):

She *was looking* at herself in the mirror.
(She was staring at herself in the mirror.)

Professor Healy *was seeing* a student.
(Professor Healy was meeting with a student.)

Now, Sonja *is thinking* about a job in electrical engineering.
(Now, Sonja is considering a job in electrical engineering.)

He *was having* problems in his science classes.
(He was experiencing problems in his science classes.)

6 Voice

Voice is a grammatical category that applies only to transitive verbs. With verbs in the **active voice,** the subject performs the action; the focus is on the agent of the action:

Elliot conducted the kazoo band.

With verbs in the **passive voice,** the subject receives the action; the focus is on the recipient of the action:

The kazoo band was conducted by Elliot.

In some situations you may choose to drop the *by*-phrase:

The kazoo band was praised.

The verb *praise* appears in passive form for all six tenses below:

Present tense:	*He is praised.*
Past tense:	*She was praised.*
Future tense:	*It will be praised.*
Present perfect tense:	*He has been praised.*
Past perfect tense:	*She had been praised.*
Future perfect tense:	*It will have been praised.*

(For advice about using passive verbs in your writing, see Chapter 39.)

16c
v

> *Exercise 8*
>
> In the following sentences, change passive verbs into active verbs, and active verbs into passive verbs.
>
> > **EXAMPLE:**   The mail carrier never rings the bell more than once.
> > The bell is never rung by the mail carrier more than once.
>
> 1. Three red marker buoys were rounded by the two competing sailboats.
> 2. The Coast Guard had put these buoys into place before the race.
> 3. But a stiff southerly wind severely hampered the boats' sprint to the finish line.
> 4. Only a few of the local weathercasters had predicted this wind.
> 5. No signs of letting up were shown by the wind.

17

O ne common way to expand a simple sentence is to modify its nouns and pronouns. **To modify** means to describe, identify, or qualify. This chapter focuses on words, phrases, and clauses that modify nouns and pronouns.

17a

Identifying Adjectives

Adjectives are the most common modifiers of nouns and pronouns.

1 Some Ways to Identify Adjectives

With regard to the nouns or pronouns that they modify, most adjectives answer one of the following questions: Which one(s)? What kind? How many?

> Which proposal was accepted? The *Swiss* proposal was accepted.

> What kind of proposal was it? It was a *peace* proposal.

How many amendments were offered? *Sixty* amendments were offered.

Adjectives often appear as parts of adjective phrases. These phrases always contain an adjective, which may have a modifier both before and after it and may be followed by a word, phrase, or clause that completes its meaning. Here are some examples:

Adjective with a modifier before it: *very happy.*

Adjective with a modifier after it: *happy indeed.*

Adjective with modifiers before and after it: *very happy indeed.*

Adjective with modifiers before and after it and an infinitive phrase to complete its meaning: *very happy indeed to see you.*

Some adjectives can be identified on the basis of the suffixes they take. Occasionally, these suffixes appear on parts of speech other than adjectives, so you will have to be somewhat cautious about making judgments on the basis of suffixes alone. But the following suffixes will give you a fairly reliable indication that the words they are attached to are adjectives:

17a adj

-able, -ible	manageable, credible
-al, -ial	normal, racial
-ate	fortunate
-ful	careful
-ic	historic
-ical	economical
-ish	impish
-ive, -ative	definitive, affirmative
-less	restless
-ous, -eous, -ious	famous, erroneous, rapacious
-y	handy

Most adjectives can also be identified because they have a comparative and superlative form. Adjectives such as *green* and *beautiful* are positive forms; they show qualities without comparison. When writers compare two nonidentical things in terms of greenness or beauty, they use comparative forms of the adjectives: One thing is *greener* or *more beautiful* than the other. And when writers compare three or more nonidentical things in terms of greenness or beauty, they use superlative forms of the adjectives: One thing is *greenest* or *most beautiful* of all.

You can recognize many adjectives by the *-er* ending for the comparative form and the *-est* ending for the superlative form. These endings are added to adjectives one syllable long and to some adjectives two syllables long, especially if the two-syllable adjectives end in *-y* (*funny, funnier, funniest*), *-ly* (*lovely, lovelier, loveliest*), *-le* (*simple, simpler, simplest*), *-er* (*tender, tenderer, tenderest*), and *-ow* (*mellow, mellower, mellowest*).

Some adjectives two syllables long and all adjectives three syllables long or longer show the comparative form with *more* (*more beautiful*) and the superlative form with *most* (*most beautiful*).

All adjectives show comparison in the negative direction by adding *less* (*less offensive*). Their superlative forms in this direction include *least* (*least offensive*).

Some adjectives have irregular comparative and superlative forms:

17a adj

Positive	Comparative	Superlative
bad	worse	worst
ill	worse	worst
far	farther, further	farthest, furthest
good	better	best
well	better	best
little	less	least
much	more	most
many	more	most

Exercise 1

Use each of the following adjectives in two sentences, one in which the adjective appears in the comparative degree, the other in which the adjective appears in the superlative degree.

EXAMPLE: crestfallen

(1) Albert was more crestfallen than Marie when their science project exploded.

(2) Of the six people who saw the science project explode, Albert was the most crestfallen.

1. fast   4. stubborn
2. rowdy   5. impressive
3. sallow   6. bright

2 Kinds of Adjectives

Adjectives fall into two groups: descriptive and limiting.

a. Descriptive Adjectives

Descriptive adjectives attribute a quality or condition to nouns and pronouns:

the *paper* moon   the *forlorn* moors

b. Limiting Adjectives

Limiting adjectives point out particular nouns and pronouns or indicate the number of people, places, things, or ideas referred to. The limiting adjectives include some forms that can also function as pronouns. To be adjectives and not pronouns, these words must modify a noun or pronoun. *That* in *That planet is a desert* is an adjective, while *That* in *That is a desert* is a pronoun. Limiting adjectives fall into eight categories:

Possessive Adjectives

The possessive adjectives are as follows: *my, your, his, her, its, our,* and *their.* They appear in contexts such as this:

Our thirst was quenched.

Demonstrative Adjectives

Demonstrative adjectives point things out: *this, that, these,* and *those. This* and *that* are used with singular nouns and pronouns; *these* and *those* are used with plural nouns and pronouns. *This* and *these* modify things closer to the writer in distance or time; *that* and *those* modify things more removed from the writer in distance or time:

This quartz crystal has only recently become valuable.

That agate in the north display case has always been valuable.

Cardinal Adjectives

Cardinal adjectives are the words used in counting (*one, two, three* . . .):

Two guitarists were playing the wrong song.

Ordinal Adjectives

Ordinal adjectives indicate position in a series (*first, second, third* . . .):

The *third* attempt to find the grail failed.

17a
adj

Relative Adjectives

Relative adjectives are words such as *which, whichever,* and *whatever.* They appear in sentences with subordinate adjective clauses:

> They hiked to Ptarmigan Pass or Ouzel Falls, *whichever* place is in Wild Basin.

Indefinite Adjectives

There are many indefinite adjectives, most of which indicate quantities or amounts. Here are some examples:

all	enough	little	several
another	every	many	some
any	few	more	
each	less	much	

Indefinite adjectives appear in contexts such as this:

> *Many* students planned to major in accounting.

Interrogative Adjectives

Interrogative adjectives modify the nouns or pronouns about which writers ask questions: *what, which, whose.* They appear in contexts such as this:

> *Which* quantum physics course did you have the most difficulty with?

Proper Adjectives

Proper adjectives derive from proper nouns and therefore are usually capitalized: *French, Brazilian, Tahitian.* They appear in sentences such as the following:

> Many universities adopted the *German* system of graduate education.

Exercise 2

Indicate whether each of the following italicized adjectives is descriptive or limiting. Also indicate which noun or pronoun each adjective modifies.

> EXAMPLE: The *ominous* clouds appeared from the southwest.
> *Ominous* is a descriptive adjective modifying *clouds.*

1. The *greenish* hue really scared those who noticed it.
2. *Those* golfers certainly should have gotten off the course.
3. They must have abandoned *their* good sense.

17a
adj

4. *Every* minute, thunder would echo across the landscape.
5. Playing in such conditions could have *terrible* consequences.

17b

Identifying Prepositional Phrases That Modify Nouns and Pronouns

Other common modifiers of nouns and pronouns are **prepositional phrases**. **Prepositions** show relationships between words, often relationships of time and space. Here are some examples:

about	behind	for	over
above	below	from	past
across	beneath	in	through
after	beside	inside	throughout
against	between	into	to
along	beyond	like	toward
among	by	near	under
around	despite	of	until
as	down	off	up
at	during	on	with
before	except	outside	without

To function as prepositions, these words have to be followed by a noun, pronoun, or some other element functioning as a noun. This element is called the **object of the preposition:**

with *us*

without *words*

A preposition can have compound objects:

with *clarity* and *grace*

Often the object of the preposition will be modified itself:

with *utmost* seriousness

The preposition and its object or objects and the modifiers of the object or objects make up a prepositional phrase. If the words in the list above appear in a sentence without an object, then they function as adverbs, modifying the verb:

Lone riders were always passing *through.*

A preposition signals a relationship between its object and another word in the sentence, often a noun or a pronoun. (But see also **18c.**) Together, the preposition and its object modify the noun or pronoun. Such prepositional phrases usually appear after the noun or pronoun they modify:

a fellow *in the grass*   a bird *in the hand*

Exercise 3

In each of the following sentences from Stephen Jay Gould's "Were Dinosaurs Dumb?" underline all the prepositional phrases that modify nouns or pronouns and then indicate what noun or pronoun each phrase modifies.

EXAMPLE: In "Cunning is the refuge of the little guy," of the little guy modifies refuge.

1. Slow wit is the tragic flaw of a giant.
2. The discovery of dinosaurs in the nineteenth century provided, or so it appeared, a quintessential case for the negative correlation of size and smarts.
3. The idea of warmblooded dinosaurs has captured the public imagination and received a torrent of press coverage.
4. We have abundant data on the relationship of brain and body size in modern reptiles.
5. But comparison across species, when the differences are large, seems reasonable.

17c
adj

17c

Identifying Participles and Participial Phrases

Participles (see also **16b**) are nonfinite verb forms that function like adjectives. Participles can appear without an object:

Dazed, the challenger got up from the wrestling mat.

But often the participle introduces a participial phrase that includes an object and perhaps one or more modifiers of that object:

Seeing little white stars, he decided to stay on the wrestling mat.

Participial phrases can precede or follow the noun or pronoun they modify:

> *Sitting in the Mariners' Church,* the woman murmured to herself.

> The woman murmured to herself, *sitting in the Mariners' Church.*

Exercise 4

In the following sentences from William Faulkner's *The Hamlet,* underline the participles and participial phrases and indicate what each participle or participial phrase modifies. Then imitate the form of each sentence using material that you invent.

> **EXAMPLE:** In "The men stood at a respectful distance, looking at them," the participial phrase looking at them modifies men.
>
> Imitation: The man collapsed onto the floor, overcome by exhaustion.

1. At that moment Jody Varner, followed by a blacksmith, thrust through them again.
2. The men following had already fallen rapidly back.
3. The other man sitting on the steps with his back against the post was the blacksmith.
4. She crossed the yard, looking toward the lot gate.
5. The other did not move, sitting on the top step, not quite facing them, sitting there beneath the successive layers of their quiet and intent concentrated listening and waiting.

17d adj

17d

Identifying Infinitives and Infinitive Phrases That Modify Nouns and Pronouns

Infinitives (see also **16b**) are nonfinite verb forms that can, among other things, modify nouns or pronouns. An infinitive can appear without an object:

> The place *to go* is home.

> The investment *to have avoided* involved suburbs in swampland.

But often an infinitive introduces an infinitive phrase that includes a complement and perhaps one or more modifiers of that complement:

The best way *to solve that problem* is indescribable.

Infinitives and infinitive phrases used as adjectives usually appear after the noun or pronoun they modify.

Exercise 5

Underline the infinitives and infinitive phrases in the following sentences and indicate what each infinitive or infinitive phrase modifies. Not all sentences include an infinitive or an infinitive phrase.

> EXAMPLE: In "In young Jason's opinion, the game to play is miniature golf," the infinitive to play modifies game.

1. For him, the price to pay is never too high.
2. And the delays to endure are never too long.
3. He loves putting the ball through castles, over suspension bridges, and around embedded bricks on his way to the cup.
4. And he even loves following the yellow bricks from one hole to the next.
5. In his mind, the only thing to hate is the fact that on the last hole his ball disappears down a pipe to a hidden basket.

17e
adj

17e

Identifying Appositives

Appositives are nouns, noun phrases, and noun clauses (see **21b**) that appear after nouns or pronouns in order to rename or further identify what the nouns or pronouns refer to. Appositives further identify by narrowing the field of reference (Tom, *our neighbor*), by providing a broad system of classification (the injury, *an accident*), or by giving specific details (its weight, *three hundred pounds*). If an element is an appositive to a noun or pronoun, you should be able to insert a form of *be* between it and the noun or pronoun and produce a sensible sentence:

> Batman, the Joker's nemesis, saved Gotham City.
> Batman is the Joker's nemesis.

Appositives are often introduced by *namely, that is, such as, for example, to wit,* and *that is to say.*

Appositives are not exactly like other modifiers of nouns and pronouns since renaming or further identifying is not the same as attributing a quality. But appositives are similar enough to these other modifiers that you can classify them with the modifiers of nouns and pronouns.

Exercise 6

Write each of the following sentences over, adding at least one appositive to each.

EXAMPLE: Two students never take morning classes.

Two students, *Ed and Carol,* never take morning classes.

1. Some other students refuse to take classes in the afternoon.
2. They set the early afternoons aside for their favorite soap opera.
3. They say they cannot live through the day without seeing their favorite actors.
4. They have even come to enjoy some of the commercials.
5. Only after the program is over do they go back to their regular assignments.

**17f
adj**

17f

Modifiers of Nouns and Pronouns: Further Distinctions

1 Compound Modifiers

Some modifiers of nouns and pronouns consist of two or more words, yet they still function like one-word adjectives. These **compound modifiers** are usually hyphenated when they precede the word they modify:

cold-blooded animal   *up-to-date* records

cut-and-dried strategy   *up-to-the-minute* reports

If your dictionary lists any such forms with a hyphen or hyphens, then you should hyphenate the forms even when they appear after the word they modify:

The criminal was cold-blooded.

2 Phrasal Prepositions

Some prepositions, often called **phrasal prepositions,** consist of two or three words, yet they function like one-word prepositions. Here are some two-word prepositions:

according to	due to	out of
along with	except for	prior to
apart from	instead of	subsequent to
because of	next to	up to
close to		

And here are some three-word prepositions:

by means of	in case of	in spite of
by way of	in front of	in view of
in addition to	in line with	on behalf of
in back of	in place of	with respect to

17f
adj

18

ADVERBS AND

OTHER MODIFIERS

OF VERBS

I n this chapter, we focus on modifiers of verbs. These modifiers can help you describe actions and processes intensely and vividly. Instead of writing *The lady from Pasadena drove her four-door sedan,* you can add a modifier to show how she drove: *The lady from Pasadena drove her four-door sedan **demonically.*** But you should avoid using such modifiers to add spice to verbs that are less exact and vivid than possible. In most situations, you should prefer a more vivid verb to a less vivid verb with a modifier; for instance, you should use *strut* rather than *walk proudly.*

18a

Identifying the Kinds of Adverbs

The most common modifiers of verbs are adverbs. Since the complete set of adverbs includes words with several different kinds of functions, it helps to distinguish four kinds of adverbs from each other: simple, sentence, conjunctive, and interrogative.

1 Simple Adverbs

Simple adverbs modify individual words within sentences. Often they modify verbs, by adding information about the circumstances of the action the verb describes:

> Bond *nonchalantly* wrestled sixty-six Nile crocodiles.

Simple adverbs also frequently modify adjectives, in which case they indicate the degree of the quality named by the adjective. Sometimes the adverb shows that the quality is greater than an assumed norm:

> *highly* contagious   *incredibly* funny

Sometimes the adverb shows that the quality is less than an assumed norm:

> *slightly* contagious   *somewhat* funny

Simple adverbs also modify other adverbs, often either intensifying or toning down the meaning of the adverb:

> *unusually* quickly   *moderately* quickly

18a adv

2 Sentence Adverbs

A **sentence adverb** comments on the content of the entire sentence it is attached to:

> *Apparently,* they are not reliable proofreaders.

Sentence adverbs often show what the writer's attitude toward the meaning of the sentence is:

> *Fortunately,* the sauna was not fully heated.

3 Conjunctive Adverbs

Conjunctive adverbs put a sentence or independent clause into a logical relationship with an earlier sentence or clause. Conjunctive adverbs often signal relationships of addition *(furthermore),* contrast *(however),* comparison *(similarly),* result *(therefore),* and time *(meanwhile).* Conjunctive adverbs provide a somewhat more formal and explicit logical connection than do the coordinating conjunctions

ESL Consideration

COORDINATING CONJUNCTIONS AND CONJUNCTIVE ADVERBS

Some coordinating conjunctions and conjunctive adverbs have similar meanings. Here is a listing indicating the similarities:

Coordinating Conjunctions	Conjunctive Adverbs	Meaning
and	furthermore, besides, moreover, in addition	addition
but, yet	however, nevertheless, on the other hand, in contrast	contrast
for		reason
or	otherwise	choice
nor		negative choice
so	consequently, therefore, accordingly, thus	result

18a
adv

(and, but, or, for, nor, so, yet). You can probably sense the difference even in these two brief examples:

But the paper was plagiarized.

However, the paper was plagiarized.

Here are some common conjunctive adverbs:

accordingly	furthermore	likewise	otherwise
also	hence	meanwhile	similarly
besides	however	moreover	therefore
consequently	indeed	nevertheless	thus
finally	instead	nonetheless	

Some multiword conjunctive adverbs also appear quite regularly:

as a result   on the contrary
at the same time   on the other hand

4 Interrogative Adverbs

Interrogative adverbs introduce questions about specific bits of information:

Where has all the ozone gone?

These questions are often called *wh*-questions since most of the adverbs that introduce them begin with *wh*-:

when   where   why   how

Exercise 1

Indicate what kind of adverb each of the following italicized words is.

EXAMPLE: *However* in the second sentence is a conjunctive adverb.

William Archibald Spooner was a warden at New College, Oxford, and an ordained priest. *However,* he will probably be remembered more for uttering what are *now* known as spoonerisms. What are spoonerisms, and *where* might they have originated? They *usually* involve transposing initial sounds in two or more words. For example, in one sermon Spooner meant to say that "Our Lord, we know, is a loving Shepherd." *Unfortunately,* Spooner told his surprised congregation that "Our Lord, we know, is a shoving Leopard." *Similarly,* he once told a congregation that "All of us have in our heart a half-warmed fish to lead a better life." Spooner *often* made such mistakes outside of church too. *Surprisingly,* he *once* told friends that he loved to "pedal gently round on a well-boiled icicle." And he *severely* scolded a lazy student with these words: "You have hissed all of my mystery lessons, and completely tasted two whole worms." Because of such slips, *therefore,* Spooner's name will probably remain in the language for a long time.

18b

Identifying Simple Adverbs

Since our focus in this chapter is on modifiers of verbs, we concentrate on simple adverbs, which commonly modify verbs.

1 Identifying Simple Adverbs on the Basis of How They Modify Verbs

In general, **simple adverbs** convey the following specific kinds of information about the circumstances of actions and processes:

a. Manner

Some simple adverbs indicate how an action takes place. Another way to think of their function is to imagine them as answering the question "How?"

How did the messenger run?   He ran *feverishly.*

b. Time

Some simple adverbs indicate when an action takes place or how one action relates to others in time. You can think of them as answering the question "When?"

When did they leave for Shangri La?   They left *yesterday.*

c. Frequency

Some simple adverbs indicate how frequently actions occur. You can think of them as answering the question "How often?"

How often did they bow?   They bowed *repeatedly.*

d. Place

Some simple adverbs indicate where an action takes place. They answer the question "Where?"

Where did he leave his trifocals?   He left them *somewhere.*

e. Direction

Some simple adverbs indicate the direction of an action. You can think of them as answering the question "In what direction?"

In what direction did the oil tanker turn?   It turned *away.*

f. Degree

Some simple adverbs indicate to what degree an action takes place. They answer questions such as "How much?" and "To what degree or extent?"

To what extent did he perspire while doing the news broadcast?

He perspired *profusely.*

Exercise 2

In each of the following sentences from Henry James's *The Europeans,* tell what kind of information—manner, time, frequency, place, direction, or degree—the italicized adverb conveys.

EXAMPLE: In *They walked rapidly,* the word *rapidly* is an adverb of manner.

1. She never dropped her eyes upon his work; she only turned them, *occasionally,* as she passed, to a mirror suspended above a toilet-table on the other side of the room.

2. You may imagine whether, after this, she carried her head less *becomingly.*

3. His companion turned away with an impatient step, but *presently* came back.

4. His sister *slowly* turned in her place, looking at him.

5. "I *never* saw anything so bold."

6. *Superficially,* she was conscious of a good deal of irritation and displeasure; the Baroness was a very delicate and fastidious person.

7. That evening, after dinner, he told his sister that he would go forth *early* on the morrow to look up their cousins.

8. "I was *greatly* moved by it."

9. Eugenia paced the length of the room again, and *then* she stopped before her brother.

10. But almost *immediately* she corrected this movement, and stood still, facing him.

2   Identifying Simple Adverbs on the Basis of Form

Many simple adverbs, especially adverbs of manner, have been derived from adjectives by the addition of *-ly*:

kind   kindly   gentle   gently

If the adjective ends in *-ic,* then *-ally* is added:

geographic   geographically   graphic   graphically

One exception to this guideline is the adjective *public;* the adverb derived from it is *publicly.*

However, you must be careful in associating the *-ly* ending with adverbs. Some adverbs do not have this ending:

fast   here   much   well

And some adverbs have two forms in many dialects of English, one with the *-ly* ending and one without it:

bright, brightly	doubtless, doubtlessly	loose, loosely
cheap, cheaply	fair, fairly	loud, loudly
close, closely	high, highly	low, lowly
deep, deeply	late, lately	near, nearly

quick, quickly	slow, slowly	tight, tightly
rough, roughly	smooth, smoothly	wrong, wrongly
sharp, sharply		

In some of these pairs, the two forms mean slightly different things. *Near* and *nearly,* for instance, are not identical in meaning:

> Stay near, all right?   They are nearly finished.

In the other pairs, the two forms carry the same meaning, but the one with the *-ly* is more formal and would be more appropriate in most of your college writing. For example, *slowly* would be more appropriate than *slow* in a persuasive essay aimed at the administrators of your institution:

> **APPROPRIATE:**   Why is the administration responding so slowly?
>
> **INAPPROPRIATE:**   Why is the administration responding so slow?

Finally, you have to be cautious about associating the *-ly* ending only with adverbs because other parts of speech also end in *-ly*. Some nouns do:

> bully   folly

And some adjectives do:

early	likely	monthly
friendly	lively	masterly

Like adjectives, most simple adverbs have a comparative and a superlative form. A few one-syllable adverbs take *-er* and *-est*:

> fast   faster   fastest

And some two-syllable adverbs take *-er* and *-est*:

> early   earlier   earliest

But many adverbs, including most of those ending in *-ly,* take *more* and *most*:

> quickly   more quickly   most quickly

Some adverbs have irregular comparative and superlative forms:

Positive	Comparative	Superlative
well	better	best
ill	worse	worst
badly	worse	worst
much	more	most
far	farther, further	farthest, furthest

18b
adv

All adverbs that show degrees of comparison in the negative direction do so with *less* and *least:*

abominably   less abominably   least abominably

Simple adverbs do not always appear alone as modifiers of verbs; they are often parts of **adverb phrases.** Such phrases always contain an adverb, which may have a modifier both before and after it and may also be followed by a word or phrase that completes its meaning. Here is an adverb phrase in which the adverb *frankly* has modifiers before and after it and a prepositional phrase to complete its meaning: *very frankly indeed for the butler.*

> *Exercise 3*
>
> Write two sentences for each of the following adverbs, in one sentence using the adverb in the comparative degree and in the other using it in the superlative degree.
>
> EXAMPLE: Well   Eddie skis better than some spectators.
>
> Nikko skis best.
>
> 1. high   4. adroitly
> 2. near   5. carelessly
> 3. badly

18c

Identifying Prepositional Phrases That Modify Verbs

Prepositional phrases (see also **17b**) commonly modify verbs, conveying the same kinds of information that simple adverbs do:

MANNER: She floats through the air *with ease.*

TIME: They sleep *in the morning.*

FREQUENCY: He pays them *on every holiday.*

PLACE: She lectured on Dr. Strangelove *in the Pentagon.*

DIRECTION: She swam *toward Point Pelee.*

DEGREE: He brought photography *to the highest level.*

> *Exercise 4*
>
> Rewrite the following sentences, adding to each an adverbial prepositional phrase conveying the kind of information indicated in parentheses.

EXAMPLE: He worried about his first test in law school. (time)

He worried for weeks about his first test in law school.

1. He looked for a good place to study. (place)

2. When he found one, he spent hours poring over problems in contract law. (manner)

3. He asked fellow students to quiz him about fine points expressed in the textbook. (frequency)

4. He worried because his professor had said that the student with the lowest score on the test would fail. (degree)

5. Last semester, someone had studied and yet had failed with a score of 99 percent. (manner)

Identifying Infinitives and Infinitive Phrases That Modify Verbs

Infinitives and infinitive phrases (see also **17d**) can modify verbs. When they do, they often convey a sense of purpose or result:

You must practice *to improve.*

When infinitives function in this way, they may be preceded by *in order:*

You must practice *in order to improve.*

Many writers customarily use the words *in order* when the infinitive appears at the beginning of a sentence:

In order to improve, you must practice.

Exercise 5

Write down the infinitives and infinitive phrases that modify verbs in the following passage, and indicate what verb each modifies.

EXAMPLE: In *She took an art history course to learn about artistic movements,* the infinitive phrase *to learn about artistic movements* modifies *took.*

She did not speak to her adviser about this choice. In fact, she did not say a word to anyone about her choice. It was a choice to make on her own, she had strongly felt, and it was a choice that has enriched her life. She now takes time on her lunch hour to marvel at Chagall's stained glass. The influence of the course has been so pervasive that she even uses words like *cubism* and *Dadaism* to describe common scenes.

Identifying Nouns and Noun Phrases That Modify Verbs

Occasionally, you will find nouns playing a role that is somewhat unusual for them: modifying verbs. In the following, the noun *mornings* modifies the verb *slept:*

> They slept mornings.

More often you will find a noun phrase—for example, an adjective and a noun *(last week)*—modifying a verb:

> They traveled to Potsdam last week.

Many of these modifiers are like prepositional phrases without the preposition:

> *They performed two hours* is comparable to *They performed for two hours.*

Exercise 6

In the following sentences, indicate which nouns and noun phrases modify verbs or verb phrases, and indicate which verb or verb phrase they modify.

> EXAMPLE: In *Next month Michael will enroll in a class in tai chi chuan,* the noun phrase *next month* modifies the verb phrase *will enroll.*

1. This semester he has experienced a lot of stress.
2. Last semester was nothing like this one.
3. This spring he has more than six students in his class.
4. And they come to his office every day.
5. He says that he has been pulled in so many directions that he needs to take a class to find what he calls his "center."

19

T his chapter focuses on seven different patterns of the simple sentence. These patterns do not apply to all possible simple sentences, but they do apply to many of them. In fact, you could write thousands of different simple sentences on the basis of these seven patterns. And you could write thousands of other sentences on the basis of combinations of these patterns. Knowing these patterns, then, can help you see a wide range of possibilities for conveying meanings in writing.

19a

Identifying Patterns of the Simple Sentence with Intransitive Verbs

Three patterns apply to simple sentences with intransitive verbs, verbs that do not signal the transfer of action from the subject noun phrase to another noun phrase. There are two kinds of intransitive verbs: complete and linking.

Complete verbs combine with subjects to make a complete predication. They do not have to be followed by a noun or pronoun:

The actor *wailed.*   The audience *wept.*

Linking verbs connect the subject to a word in the predicate that either renames the subject or describes it:

The winner *is* M. Bonaventure.   She *was* grateful.

1 Sentence Pattern One

Pattern One sentences have a subject and a complete verb. All of the following are Pattern One sentences:

Caesar came.   He saw.   The formidable warrior conquered.

2 Sentence Pattern Two

Pattern Two sentences have a subject, a linking verb, and a subjective complement. The linking verb, which usually denotes being, becoming, sensing, or seeming, links the subject to the subjective complement.

The **subjective complement** is a word that usually follows the verb and completes the meaning of the subject. It does so by either renaming or describing the subject. If the word renames the subject, it is usually a noun. Therefore, it is called a **predicate noun.**

Diogenes was a cynic. [*Cynic* is a predicate noun.]

It is possible to have compound predicate nouns:

Diogenes was a *cynic* and *scoffer.*

If the subjective complement describes the subject, it is usually an adjective. Therefore, it is called a **predicate adjective.**

Ulysses was cunning. [*Cunning* is a predicate adjective.]

It is possible to have compound predicate adjectives:

Ulysses was *cunning* and *bold.*

3 Sentence Pattern Three

Some intransitive verbs appear in sentences without a predicate noun or a predicate adjective. Yet these verbs do not combine with their subjects to make a complete predication. They need an adverb, an adverb phrase, or a prepositional phrase functioning adverbially in order to make a complete predication. Forms of *be* often function in this way. For example, if you were to read the words *my keys were,* you would not accept them as a complete predication. This group of words

19a
ps

needs an adverbial modifier in order to make a complete predication:

My keys were in the car.

Such adverbial modifiers are called **adverbial complements,** since they complete the meaning of the verb. They are not subjective complements because they do not rename or describe the subject. Most of them complete the meaning of the verb by conveying information about location or time:

That old shipwreck lies *off Whitefish Point.*

But these adverbial complements may convey other information:

Her epic poem is *in its final stages.*   The work is *for her son.*

Exercise 1

Indicate whether each of the following italicized sentences is a Pattern One, Pattern Two, or Pattern Three sentence.

EXAMPLE: *Many names of cities are interesting* is a Pattern Two
sentence (with the predicate adjective *interesting*).

Rudyard is in Michigan's Upper Peninsula. Many people who pass through it wonder how it got its name. A few people know that Rudyard was once a terminus for a railroad track, the other terminus of which was the town of Kipling. The owner of the railway loved to read Rudyard Kipling's books. *The name Marenisco is also interesting.* This town, also located in Michigan's Upper Peninsula, got its name from the first parts of the names of its first woman settler, Mary Relief Niles Scott. Or consider the town named Germfask. *It too is in Michigan's Upper Peninsula.* It got its name from the initials of the surnames of the first eight settlers. Michigan's Lower Peninsula is not without its share of interesting names. *Novi is one.* This name comes from the fact that the city was once stop no. vi on a railway line. Are all these histories correct? Yes, but not all people accept them fully. *They wonder.* And their wondering increases when they hear that Azusa, California—at least according to one story—got its name because some of its inhabitants claimed they grew everything from A to Z in the USA.

19b
ps

19b

Identifying Patterns of the Simple Sentence with Transitive Verbs

Transitive verbs signal the transfer of action from the subject over to a noun phrase in the predicate, which is called the direct object. The following four sentence patterns use transitive verbs.

1 Sentence Pattern Four

Pattern Four sentences have a subject, a transitive verb, and a direct object. The **direct object** is a noun phrase that usually appears after the verb and shows what the subject acts upon.

The direct object often shows whom or what the action of the verb affects:

The children scrubbed *the streets.*

Sometimes, however, the direct object can show what came into existence as a result of the action of the verb:

The group composed *a sonnet.*

In all such cases, the direct object can be compounded:

Eliza made *a choice* and *a commitment.*

Generally, you will be able to identify the direct object in a sentence by asking what? or whom? of the verb. Suppose that you needed to identify the direct object of the following sentence:

Rikki killed the cobra.

You would ask what? of the verb: Rikki killed what? The answer, *the cobra,* is the direct object.

As you try to determine whether a noun phrase is a direct object or not, it will be helpful to know that almost all Pattern Four sentences can easily be made passive. When this happens, the direct object becomes the subject:

Asher made a promise.   A promise was made by Asher.

In a sentence such as *Jenny became captain,* however, the noun *captain* is not a direct object since it cannot become the subject if one tries to make this sentence passive:

INCORRECT: Captain was become by Jenny.

In *Jenny became captain,* the word *captain* is a predicate noun.

In most cases, the noun phrase serving as subject and the noun phrase serving as the direct object refer to different people or things. But when reflexive or reciprocal pronouns function as direct objects, the subject and the direct object can refer to the same people or things:

The *swimmers* pushed *themselves.*

Harry and *Sally* still respect *each other.*

2 Sentence Pattern Five

Pattern Five sentences are identical to Pattern Four sentences except that they contain an adverb, adverb phrase, or prepositional phrase functioning adverbially and serving as an adverbial complement to the verb. Without the adverbial complement, these sentences would not be accepted as making complete predications. For example, the verb *stuck* often appears in Pattern Five sentences:

She stuck her diary under the bed.

If the adverbial complement *under the bed* did not appear in this sentence, the sentence would not make an acceptable predication:

INCORRECT: She stuck her diary.

Other verbs that commonly appear in Pattern Five sentences are *put, keep,* and *place.*

3 Sentence Pattern Six

19b
ps

Pattern Six sentences have two objects after the verb: a direct object and an indirect object. The **indirect object** appears between the verb and the direct object. It indicates to whom or for whom the action of the verb is performed; it names the one or ones who receive the fruits of the action or who feel the results of the action. You can identify the indirect object by asking to whom? or for whom? of the verb. Consider the following:

Scrooge gave them a small gift.

Scrooge gave to whom or for whom? He gave to them; *them* is the indirect object. Some sentences have compound indirect objects:

Scrooge gave *them* and *us* a small gift.

Usually, the subject, the indirect object, and the direct object will all name different people or things. But in sentences in which a reflexive pronoun or some reciprocal pronouns appear as the indirect object, the subject and the indirect object can name the same people or things:

They gave *themselves* a break.

They offered *each other* congratulations.

Indirect objects often appear after such verbs as *ask, tell,* and *give.* Here is a sampling of other verbs that often take both a direct object and an indirect object:

allot	cash	find	point	send
allow	catch	get	pay	sew
assign	color	grant	play	show
award	cut	hum	promise	sing
bring	deny	leave	read	teach
build	design	lend	refuse	throw
buy	draw	make	save	trade
carve	extend	offer	sell	write

In some cases, you can choose how to express references to those for whom something is done. You can express such references as indirect objects:

19b
ps

Oliver sent *Jenny* flowers.

Or you can express such references as the objects of prepositions such as *to* and *for* (and occasionally *with* and *of*):

Oliver sent flowers *to Jenny.*

If the reference appears in a prepositional phrase, then it functions in the sentence not as an indirect object but as the object of a preposition.

This choice is significant, since it allows you to choose what to express at the end of your sentence. The end of a sentence is generally the most emphatic position. If you wanted to stress to whom or for whom an action was performed, you could express that reference in a prepositional phrase at the end of the sentence:

Oliver sent flowers to Jenny.

But if you wanted to stress not the reference to Jenny but the reference to the flowers, you could make *Jenny* the indirect object:

Oliver sent Jenny flowers.

4 Sentence Pattern Seven

Pattern Seven sentences have a subject, a transitive verb, a direct object, and an objective complement. The **objective complement** appears after the direct object and completes the meaning of the direct object, either by identifying or describing the direct object. If the objective complement identifies or names the direct object, it is usually a noun:

> They made David the *champion.*

If the objective complement describes the direct object, it is usually an adjective:

> They considered Goliath *invincible.*

Objective complements can be compounded:

> They made David *the champion* and *their representative.*
>
> They considered Goliath *mighty* and *invincible.*

The relationship between an objective complement and the direct object it names *(They elected Babe manager)* is like that between a subject and a predicate noun *(Babe is manager).* And the relationship between an objective complement and the direct object it describes *(She considered the hills alive)* is like that between the subject and a predicate adjective *(The hills are alive).*

You will sometimes see Pattern Seven sentences with the words *to be* between the direct object and the objective complement:

> They consider detective novels to be fascinating.

Often, too, *as* appears between the direct object and the objective complement:

> They saw him as a traitor.

Here are some verbs that commonly appear in Pattern Seven sentences:

appoint	consider	find	like	prove
believe	declare	hold	make	rule
call	dismiss	judge	name	set
choose	drive	keep	paint	think
color	elect	leave	prefer	view

19b
ps

Exercise 2

Identify the pattern of each of the following sentences by writing the correct number of the pattern on the blank line.

EXAMPLE: _____2_____ Amsterdam is an intriguing city.

1. _____ Amsterdam lies on marshy land.
2. _____ Many canals crisscross the city.
3. _____ Many of its buildings rest on wooden or concrete piles.

4. _____ Some visitors call Amsterdam charming and delightful.
5. _____ They tell others stories of the Rijksmuseum and quaint residential courtyards.
6. _____ And they relish the many different restaurants.
7. _____ Other visitors complain.
8. _____ They find too much vice in the city.
9. _____ They call Amsterdam a modern Vanity Fair.
10. _____ The city, however, seems oblivious to such names.

Exercise 3

Use each of the following verbs in a sentence of the pattern indicated in parentheses.

EXAMPLE: exist (Pattern One)   Black holes exist.

1. sulked (Pattern One)
2. paints (Pattern One)
3. remain (Pattern Two with a predicate noun)
4. proved (Pattern Two with a predicate adjective)
5. was (Pattern Three)
6. paints (Pattern Four)
7. kept (Pattern Five)
8. painted (Pattern Six)
9. called (Pattern Seven with a naming objective complement)
10. consider (Pattern Seven with a describing objective complement)

19c

Sentence Patterns: A Further Distinction

Some sentences have what are called **cognate direct objects.** These are direct objects with meanings that repeat or amplify the meaning of the verb they appear with. A few examples follow; the cognate direct objects appear in italics:

They will sing a *song* of sixpence.

They never sleep the *sleep* of the righteous.

They have fought the good *fight.*

She lived a long and happy *life.*

20

ALTERATIONS OF
THE SIMPLE
SENTENCE

In this chapter, we examine some common ways of altering the seven patterns of the simple sentence. Some of these alterations allow you to use negation and to ask questions. Others allow you to convey special nuances of focus and emphasis.

20a

Forming Negative Sentences

All seven patterns of the simple sentence can be changed from positive to negative forms. If the sentence to be made negative contains a verb phrase, not just a one-word verb, add *not* immediately after the first auxiliary verb:

> The headless horseman has ridden again.
>
> The headless horseman has *not* ridden again.

In more informal contexts, you would probably contract *has not* to *hasn't*.

If the sentence to be made negative has only a one-word verb and if that verb is a form of *be,* add a *not* immediately after the form of *be:*

The mission was impossible.

The mission was *not* impossible.

Again, in more informal contexts, you would probably contract *was not* to *wasn't. Is, are,* and *were* are other forms of *be* that allow such contractions *(isn't, aren't, weren't).*

If the sentence has only a one-word verb and if that verb is not a form of *be,* first add a form of *do* before the verb. This form should be in the same tense, person, and number as the one-word verb originally was. The one-word verb then takes its base form:

Our coach *tossed* a chair onto the basketball court.

Our coach *did toss* a chair onto the basketball court.

Then add *not* after the form of *do:*

Our coach did *not* toss a chair onto the basketball court.

In more informal contexts, you would probably contract *did not* to *didn't.*

You can also use some other words, such as *never* and *no,* to form negative statements:

Those students hand in papers with frayed edges.

Those students *never* hand in papers with frayed edges.

There was room in the inn.

There was *no* room in the inn.

20a
as

Exercise 1

Rewrite each of the following sentences, making the negative ones positive and the positive ones negative.

EXAMPLE: Sometime before 1400, Julian of Norwich did not decide to become an anchoress.

Sometime before 1400, Julian of Norwich decided to become an anchoress.

1. She felt pressure from her peers to make this decision.
2. She did not feel a call from God.
3. And she could not provide for herself.
4. Therefore, the church did not allow her to become an anchoress, or religious recluse.
5. Such people would interact frequently with others.
6. In fact, most were not enclosed in cells.

7. The service of enclosure was playful.

8. It did not consist of the Mass for the dead.

9. For the anchoress was not dead to the world.

10. Thereafter, she would think about earthly things.

Forming Questions

Several different kinds of questions are possible in English: yes-no questions, *wh*-questions, alternative questions, and tag questions.

1 Forming Yes-No Questions

20b
as

Yes-no questions get their name because the response they typically aim for is either a "yes" or a "no." Occasionally, other words (such as *certainly, probably, decidedly, absolutely,* and *surely,* as well as the corresponding negatives) provide the response to yes-no questions.

If a statement has a verb phrase, not just a one-word verb, move the first auxiliary verb before the subject:

They are becoming literate.   *Are* they becoming literate?

If a statement has only a one-word verb and if that verb is a form of *be,* move that form before the subject:

Ahab is alive and well.   *Is* Ahab alive and well?

If a statement has only a one-word verb and if that verb is not a form of *be,* first add a form of *do* before the verb. This form of *do* should be in the same tense, person, and number as the one-word verb originally was. The one-word verb then takes its base form:

She won the marathon.   She *did* win the marathon.

Then move the form of *do* before the subject:

Did she win the marathon?

Have is a special case of a one-word verb, since it allows two possible forms of yes-no questions:

You have spare change.   Do you have any spare change?

Have you any spare change?

The first of these is more common in American English.

2 Forming *Wh*-Questions

Wh-questions are so named because they aim for a specific bit of information and the word in the question that most clearly points to that bit of information often begins with *wh*. Some of these words are interrogative pronouns:

who, what, whatever, which, whichever, whose

Some are interrogative adjectives:

what (approach), which (solution), whose (ideas), whatever (problem), whichever (course)

And some are interrogative adverbs:

when, where, why, how

Consider the statement *Gehrig has hit a long home run.* If you wanted to form a *wh*-question asking about the subject of this sentence *(Gehrig),* you would substitute the appropriate *wh*-word for the subject and leave the other elements in normal order:

Who has hit a long home run?

If you wanted to form a *wh*-question asking about any other element of this sentence, then the *wh*-word and any words modified by it stand first, followed by an inversion of order. The example has a verb phrase *(has hit),* and thus the *wh*-word is followed by the first auxiliary verb and then the subject:

What has Gehrig hit?

If the statement has a one-word verb instead of a verb phrase and if that verb is a form of *be,* then that form follows the *wh*-element and is followed by the subject:

Cobb was healthy.   How was Cobb?

If the statement has a one-word verb other than a form of *be,* the *wh*-word is followed by a form of *do* in the same tense, person, and number as the one-word verb originally was. The form of *do* is followed by the subject and then by the original verb in its base form:

Shoeless Joe played in Chicago.   Where did Shoeless Joe play?

Finally, if the element of a statement that you are asking about is the object of a preposition, you have two choices regarding where to express it in the question: before the *wh*-word or at the end of the sentence:

Dean played for the Cardinals.   1. For whom did Dean play?

2. Whom did Dean play for?

The first version has the advantage of not ending with a preposition, which ordinarily would not carry enough information to deserve the position of greatest prominence in a sentence. But in some contexts— for example, in writing a letter to a close friend—the first version would seem too formal, and you would be wise to follow the pattern of the second sentence.

Because both yes-no and *wh*-questions are really forms of action in that they seek a response, they appear more often in speech than in writing. But that does not mean that you will not be able to use them to your advantage in writing.

They can serve as good introductions, particularly if they are provocative questions. Thomas Hurtmann uses a *wh*-question for the title of an essay ("How Dangerous Is Your Computer?"), and he introduces the essay with two provocative yes-no questions: "Can your home or office computer make you sterile? Can it strike you blind or dumb?"

Questions can also serve as good transitions. At a significant juncture in his essay "Zen Buddhist Monasticism," Thomas Merton asks two important yes-no questions in one sentence:

> Is it enough to say that Zen is a philosophic and existentialist type of spirituality, capable of bringing man into an authentic confrontation with himself, with reality, and with his fellow man, or shall we see in it a degree of religious quality?

Finally, yes-no and *wh*-questions can serve as excellent concluding sentences in essays, especially if the essays make it clear to readers how the questions should be answered. Here is one example of such questions, which Judy Syfers uses to conclude an essay in which she satirizes the expectations that males in Western culture have of wives: "My God, who *wouldn't* want a wife?"

20b
as

3 Forming Alternative Questions

Alternative questions seek a reply that isolates one of two or more options. These questions appear in two different forms. One form is similar to that of yes-no questions:

Should the government raise or lower taxes?

The other form is similar to that of *wh*-questions:

Which do you prefer, a lemon or a lime?

Although alternative questions appear more often in speech than in writing, you will find good uses for them in your writing. In a paper in which you have argued for one approach over another, you could conclude with an alternative question and trust that your readers have found your argument persuasive enough to select the option you advocate:

> After reviewing the evidence, which would you prefer, a technological or a liberal arts education?

4 Forming Tag Questions

Tag questions are used primarily to elicit agreement from others. They are forms such as these:

> He is lord of the rings, isn't he?
>
> Clara doesn't dismiss the argument, does she?

20b
as

In these examples, as in most tag questions, a pronoun that refers to the subject of the statement stands at the end. And if the verb in the statement is positive, the verb in the question will be negative. If the verb in the statement is negative, the verb in the question will be positive.

Tag questions occur most frequently in speech. But they are also useful in writing. You can use them to alert readers that they will be exploring assumptions that they have probably made too quickly:

> Real men do not cry, do they?

You can also use tag questions to conclude essays, nudging readers to agree with you in the end:

> Irony is important, isn't it?

Exercise 2

Change each of the following statements into the kind of question specified in parentheses.

> EXAMPLE: They spent two weeks planning the reunion. (yes-no question)
>
> Did they spend two weeks planning the reunion?

1. They have always enjoyed family reunions. (yes-no question)
2. They are eager to attend this one. (yes-no question)
3. They mailed the invitations in June. (yes-no question)
4. All their great-aunts also plan to attend. (*wh*-question)
5. They often have trouble remembering their great-aunts' names. (*wh*-question)
6. Sometimes they call Aunt Fanny, Aunt Minnie. (*wh*-question)

7. They should memorize the names or request name tags. (alternative question)

8. They dislike only one thing, either playing the silly games or being told how much they have grown. (alternative question)

9. The food never disappoints them. (tag question)

10. They find the Dutch apple pie especially tasty. (tag question)

20c

Forming Passive Sentences

The subject of an active verb names who or what performs the action. Thus, the presentation focuses on the agent, the action, and the object of the action, in that order:

The soldiers destroyed the village.

Verbs in the passive voice present the same actions from a different perspective. The subject of a passive verb names who or what receives the action of the verb. Thus, the presentation focuses on the object of the action, the action, and the agent of the action, in that order:

The village was destroyed by the soldiers.

Or all references to the agent or agents may be omitted:

The village was destroyed.

Verbs in the active voice are made passive through the addition of a form of *be* and a change of the verb into its past participle form:

paints → is painted

throws → is thrown

The verb *find* appears in the passive voice in all six tenses in the following list of sentences:

PRESENT: He is found.

PAST: She was found.

FUTURE: It will be found.

PRESENT PERFECT: He has been found.

PAST PERFECT: She had been found.

FUTURE PERFECT: It will have been found.

Only transitive verbs can be made passive. Therefore, only Sentence Patterns Four through Seven can be changed into passive form.

Pattern Four sentences have a direct object:

Freddie ruined *the neighborhood.*

In the passive form of this sentence, the original direct object, *the neighborhood,* becomes the subject, and the original subject either is expressed at the end of the sentence as the object of the preposition *by* or is deleted:

The neighborhood was ruined by *Freddie.*

The neighborhood was ruined.

Pattern Five:

ACTIVE VERB: Sylvia placed a poem in a jar.

PASSIVE VERB: A poem was placed by Sylvia in a jar.

A poem was placed in a jar.

**20c
as**

Pattern Six:

ACTIVE VERB: The king granted them a wish.

PASSIVE VERB: They were granted a wish by the king.

They were granted a wish.

A wish was granted them by the king.

A wish was granted them.

Most often the indirect object (as in *They were granted . . .*) becomes the subject. Most people view the passive version in which the direct object is made the subject as somewhat formal, sometimes even stilted. In any case, whichever object does not become the subject in a passive sentence is called the **retained object:**

                         retained object
They were granted a wish by the king.

                         retained object
A wish was granted them by the king.

Pattern Seven:

ACTIVE VERB: They elected him secretary.

They consider him unfortunate.

PASSIVE VERB: He was elected secretary by them.

He was elected secretary.

He is considered unfortunate by them.

He is considered unfortunate.

What was the objective complement *(secretary* and *unfortunate)* remains in the sentence, but since it now either renames or describes what has become the subject, it is best to call it a retained complement. (For advice about using passive verbs in your writing, see **39b**.)

Exercise 3

Change all active sentences among the following into passive forms. Change all passive sentences into active forms.

> **EXAMPLE:**   Gordon Smith and Greg Kahn have examined the names of baseball players.
>
> The names of baseball players have been examined by Gordon Smith and Greg Kahn.

1. Sportswriters nickname some players.
2. Fellow players nickname other players.
3. In 1876, National League players nicknamed Bob Ferguson "Death to Flying Things."
4. Players and fans called Joe Harnung "Ubbo Ubbo."
5. We are reminded of other eras by some players' real names, such as Hilly Flitcraft, Zoilo Versailles, and Orville Overall.
6. Smith and Kahn consider the names of many modern players interesting.
7. For example, they have named Elroy Face, Rollie Fingers, and Don Gullett to their All-Anatomy Team.
8. Similarly, they have named Blue Moon Odom, Pinky May, and Champ Summers to their All-Calendrical Team.
9. Such teams could probably be selected by very young fans.
10. An All-Culinary Team with Spud Davis, Coot Veal, and Bake McBride could be assembled by them.

20d

Forming Sentences with Fronted Elements

Sometimes you can take an element that would ordinarily appear fairly late in a sentence and move it to the beginning. In other words, you can "front" an element, leaving the order of the rest of the elements undisturbed. For example, here is a normal Pattern Two sentence:

> He was not charismatic.

Fronting the predicate adjective produces the following:

> Charismatic he was not.

Such a construction works well when the fronted adjective is closely related to the material preceding the sentence. Moreover, the fronted adjective often marks a contrast:

You would have to be intelligent and tactful.

Intelligent you are.

Tactful you most assuredly are not.

It is also possible to front direct objects. Here is a normal Pattern Four sentence:

They enjoyed the aesthetics course.

Fronting the direct object produces the following:

The aesthetics course they enjoyed.

Such a construction functions similarly to the construction with a fronted predicate adjective. The fronted direct object usually connects very closely to information that has already appeared. Moreover, the fronted object or objects often mark a contrast:

Just as it is written: "Jacob I loved, but Esau I hated."

—Romans 9:13, NIV

Exercise 4

Write five pairs of sentences. The second sentence in each pair should contain a fronted element. The first should provide an appropriate context for the fronted element.

EXAMPLE: We bought hiking boots and carabiners.

The carabiners we have never used.

20e

Forming Sentences with Inversions

Sentences with inversions resemble those with fronted elements, for in both an element that usually appears fairly late is moved to the front. However, in sentences with inversions, the order of the subject and verb or the first part of the verb phrase is also switched around:

More pathetic yet were his attempts at wit.

In this sentence, the subject *(his attempts at wit)* and the verb *(were)* appear in inverted order.

You will frequently find adverbs with negative meanings in sentences with inverted subjects and verbs:

Never was she rude to her colleagues.

But other adverbs can also function in this way:

Up went twenty-four right hands.

And you will find adverbial prepositional phrases in such a pattern:

Near the front of the bridge stood the troll.

Almost always the adverbs or the prepositional phrases connect to information already introduced into a story or essay. The last example would probably appear after sentences mentioning the bridge. Furthermore, sentences with inversions allow you to express sentence subjects to which you want to call particular attention at the end of sentences, where they will be in the most emphatic position. In the last example, that is an important reason for waiting until the end of the sentence to refer to the troll.

20e
as

Exercise 5

Write a sentence with an inversion to come after each of the following sentences.

EXAMPLE: For *They will almost certainly be on time,* you could write *Rarely are they late* as the subsequent sentence.

1. The expedition confronted a huge expanse of water.
2. This federal penitentiary is very secure.
3. The sergeant asked for a volunteer.
4. At the end of the wire you will see a small eyelet.
5. They looked up to the large cascade.

21

 f you were to use nothing but simple sentences in your writing, some of your readers might claim that your style is monotonous and does not adequately signal how various sentences relate to each other. They might add that they expected to find some sentences made up of two or more clauses, not just one independent clause, as simple sentences are. This chapter will help you respond to such claims. In it, we examine sentences made up of two or more clauses.

21a

Identifying Compound Sentences

Compound sentences include two or more independent clauses:

> They made a fashion statement, but no one understood it. [two independent clauses]

> They made a fashion statement, and no one understood it, but they were not discouraged. [three independent clauses]

Usually the two or more independent clauses in a compound sentence are closely related in meaning. This is particularly true of the balanced compound sentence, in which the independent clauses contain similar structures and are about equally long:

> Day after day they pour forth speech; night after night they display knowledge.   Psalm 19:2, NIV

Compound sentences are distinct in form from simple sentences that have a compound subject, a compound predicate, or both a compound subject and a compound predicate:

compound subject
Julie and Sherman are loyal to the Cubs.

compound predicate
They skip work and attend games.

compound subject   compound predicate
The players and coaches know them by name and ask for their advice.

1 Commas Linking Independent Clauses in Compound Sentences

Commas appear more often than any other mark of punctuation as the links between the independent clauses of compound sentences. When they function in this way, commas are almost always accompanied by either coordinating or correlative conjunctions.

The **coordinating conjunctions** are *and, but, or, for, nor, so,* and *yet.* A few examples of compound sentences with commas and coordinating conjunctions follow. Note that the comma precedes the coordinating conjunction. Also note that if a compound sentence has more than two independent clauses, only the last two require both a comma and a coordinating conjunction between them; between the others a comma by itself is enough:

> Norman and Paul were avid fishermen, but they never used live bait.

> They especially loved fly fishing, for their father had made no distinctions between fly fishing and religion.

> They tied their own flies, they studied the habits of trout, and each of them dared to fish the big waters alone.

Only occasionally should you consider omitting the comma before a coordinating conjunction linking two independent clauses in a compound sentence. You may consider this when the two independent clauses are short and comparable in rhetorical force:

> We tried and we failed.

The **correlative conjunctions** that commonly link independent clauses in compound sentences are *neither . . . nor, either . . . or, not only . . . but also,* and *just as . . . so.* When these link independent clauses in a compound sentence, generally one member of a pair introduces the first clause and the other member of the pair follows a comma and introduces the second clause:

> Either I will send you a note today, or I will call you tomorrow.

2 Semicolons Linking Independent Clauses in Compound Sentences

In many compound sentences, one independent clause is joined to another with a semicolon:

> They are dashing; we are dependable.

Often the semicolon is followed by a prepositional phrase functioning adverbially:

> We should rest now; *in the morning* we can finish the report.

And often the semicolon is followed by a **conjunctive adverb,** a word or a group of words that modifies the second independent clause at the same time that it connects the second clause to the first (see **18a**). Usually, a comma follows the conjunctive adverb:

> Most of her first serves were good; *however,* all of her opponent's returns were excellent.

3 Colons Linking Independent Clauses in Compound Sentences

Some compound sentences have a colon as the link between two independent clauses. Most often a colon works well when the second independent clause explains or elaborates on material expressed in the first clause:

> The decision was simple: They had to surrender.

Exercise 1

Make a compound sentence out of each one of the following simple sentences by adding one or more independent clauses. Link the clauses in the way that seems best to you.

EXAMPLE: The professor of surgery failed at least one person in each of his classes.

The professor of surgery failed at least one person in each of his classes, for he wanted his students to feel pressure.

1. Sometimes he failed students because of bad attitudes.
2. He never forgot his policy.
3. He made some students nervous.
4. He paid no attention to their opinions of him.
5. After his death, no one mourned him.

21b

Identifying Complex Sentences

A **complex sentence** includes an independent clause and one or more subordinate clauses. Subordinate clauses have subjects and verbs and are thus true clauses, but they cannot stand alone as sentences. Within complex sentences, they modify other words, phrases, and clauses, and they are therefore grammatically dependent on those other words, phrases, or clauses. For example, *while they were on the island* is a clause that cannot stand alone as a sentence. It must modify something else, as it does in *While they were on the island, they heard cannons being shot over the water.* In this sentence, the subordinate clause modifies the verb *heard*.

Complex sentences are excellent for ordering ideas in hierarchies. They allow you to make a main point and then add to it other related but less important ideas. There are three kinds of subordinate clauses that can be parts of complex sentences: adverb clauses, adjective clauses, and noun clauses.

Adverb Clauses

Adverb clauses function within sentences like adverbs: They most often modify verbs, adjectives, adverbs, or entire clauses. One important difference between a single adverb and an adverb clause is

ESL Consideration

VERB TENSES AND ADVERB CLAUSES OF CONDITION

The subordinating conjunctions *if* and *unless* are frequently used to construct adverb clauses of condition, which are important in academic writing. These clauses are used to make predictions, to explain the results in a cause-and-effect analysis, and to speculate on alternative outcomes if historical events had been different. Several types of sentences with clauses of condition require special attention to verb tenses.

Function of the Subordinate Clause	Verb Tense in Subordinate Clause	Tense to Use in Independent Clause
To describe general truths	***present tense***	***present tense***
	If water *is* frozen,	it *expands.*
To describe habitual occurrences	***present tense***	***present tense***
	If I *have* time in the morning,	I usually *ride* my bicycle to school.
	past tense	***past tense***
	If I *had* time in the morning last year,	I *would* usually *ride* my bicycle to school.
To make predictions	***present or future tense***	***future tense***
	If you *give* me a good reason,	I *will reconsider* my decision.
	If you *will give* me a good reason,	I *will reconsider* my decision.
To hypothesize or speculate		
About the Past	***past perfect tense***	***would (or might) + have + past participle***
	If I *had lived* in the 60s,	I *would have made* every effort to meet Martin Luther King, Jr.
About the Present	***"were" subjunctive***	***would + verb***
	If I *were* student body president,	I *would listen* to what international students have to say.

that an adverb clause allows you to express more information than a single adverb does:

single adverb
Afterward, he smoked six Cuban cigars.

adverb clause
After they had discussed the nature of Marxism, he smoked six Cuban cigars.

Many adverb clauses can stand at the beginning, in the middle, or at the end of complex sentences:

While they traveled to Great Falls, they avoided the main issue between them.

The conversation between the two of them, *while they traveled to Great Falls,* was strained and unnatural.

They struggled to find things to say *while they traveled to Great Falls.*

Note that when the adverb clause appears last, it is usually not set off by a comma. But many adverb clauses appear first in complex sentences, reflecting the fact that they carry information that in context is older or less important than the information in their accompanying independent clauses.

Adverb clauses begin with **subordinating conjunctions,** words that link adverb clauses to independent clauses. The general kinds of meaning that adverb clauses can convey, along with some examples of the subordinating conjunctions that help convey these meanings, are listed below:

TIME: after, as, as long as, as soon as, before, once, since, until, when, whenever, while

When the White Rabbit looked at its watch, Alice jumped to her feet.

PLACE: where, wherever

She followed the rabbit *wherever it went.*

CAUSE OR PURPOSE: as, because, in order that, since, so that, that

Alice examined the bottle *because she was wise.*

MANNER: as, as if, as though

Alice ran *as if she were terrified.*

21b
cs

RESULT: that, so that

She grew so tall *that she had to kneel on the floor.*

CONDITION AND CONTINGENCY: as long as, if, in case, once, on the condition that, provided that, unless, whenever

If the Dormouse begins to sing, pinch it.

CONCESSION AND CONTRAST: although, even if, even though, if, though, whereas, while

Although the Queen ordered their execution, the gardeners did not lose their heads.

GENERAL POSSIBILITY: however, whenever, wherever

The Queen bellowed angrily *however Alice responded.*

COMPARISON: as, than

Alice was smarter *than the King.*

21b
cs

Adverb clauses of comparison are frequently elliptical. That is, parts of them do not appear in print, yet readers still interpret the parts that do appear as elements of an adverb clause. For instance, *Alice was smarter than the King* contains the elliptical clause *than the King*. Its full form would be *than the King was smart.* When an action verb is understood but not expressed in the adverb clause, the appropriate form of *do* is frequently used even though no form of *do* appears in the independent clause:

Gels fight cellulite more effectively than lotions *do.*

Exercise 2

To each of the following independent clauses add the kind of adverb clause specified in parentheses.

EXAMPLE: They studied for their biochemistry test. (time)

After they played shuffleboard for four hours, they studied for their biochemistry test.

1. They studied. (place)
2. They agreed to study together. (condition)
3. They took a break. (time)
4. They seemed to review a great deal of material. (concession)
5. They stayed up all night. (result)

2 Adjective Clauses

Within complex sentences, **adjective clauses** function like adjectives, modifying nouns or pronouns. They usually appear immediately after the noun or pronoun that they modify:

adjective clause

I will read the chapter that contains several cartoons.

adjective clause

All those who wish to preserve the dunes will listen.

Most adjective clauses are introduced by **relative pronouns.** The most common of these are *who* (with the objective form *whom* and the possessive form *whose*), *that,* and *which. Who* substitutes for references to persons, *which* substitutes for references to things, *that* substitutes for references to both persons and things, and *whose* is now widely accepted as a substitute for references to objects as well as persons, particularly when it helps avoid long or clumsy prepositional phrases. Instead of writing *We damaged Tom's car, the door of which had already been dented,* you can now write *We damaged Tom's car, whose door had already been dented.*

21b
cs

Some adjective clauses are introduced by **relative adverbs:** *when, where, while,* and *why.* It is important to distinguish the use of these as relative adverbs from their use as subordinating conjunctions. In *When the clock struck midnight, the carriage changed into a pumpkin,* the word *when* introduces an adverb clause that modifies the verb *changed.* But *when* also appears in sentences such as this one:

She remembered a time when she scrubbed floors.

Here *when* functions as a relative adverb; it introduces a clause that does not modify the verb *remembered* but adds descriptive material about the noun *time.*

Whether the relative word is a pronoun or an adverb, it not only links the subordinate clause to the independent clause but also plays a grammatical role in the subordinate clause. For example, in *I will read the chapters that contain several cartoons,* the relative pronoun *that* functions as the subject of the adjective clause.

Occasionally, you will find an adjective clause with a preposition before the relative pronoun:

We saw the room *in which Emerson wrote his most influential essays.*

The preposition is considered a part of the relative clause. You can get a better idea of how the whole prepositional phrase fits into the structure of the adjective clause by rewriting the adjective clause with a more normal word order and substituting a noun phrase for the relative pronoun *which:*

> Emerson wrote his most influential essays in the room.

You might wonder whether *We saw the room in which Emerson wrote his most influential essays* is always preferable to *We saw the room which Emerson wrote his most influential essays in.* Over the years many grammarians have argued against the second form, noting that a sentence should not end with a preposition. They argued that a preposition is really a *pre*-position, or a word that comes before another word, and that at the end of a sentence a pre-position has no words from the sentence to precede. Today many people do not find this argument compelling. It is true, however, that prepositions usually do not carry the most essential or important information in sentences. Therefore, unless moving prepositions to the beginning of relative clauses makes sentences too heavy and formal for your requirements, you will probably not want to end sentences with prepositions.

(Like other modifiers of nouns and pronouns, adjective clauses can be either restrictive or nonrestrictive. For help in identifying and punctuating restrictive and nonrestrictive elements, see Chapter 32.)

21b
cs

Exercise 3

Combine the sentences in each of the following groups into one sentence, keeping the first sentence in each group as an independent clause and making the second and all other subsequent sentences into adjective clauses.

> EXAMPLE: He had put his winning lottery ticket in a manila envelope.
>
> His secretary accidentally shredded the envelope.
>
> He had put his winning lottery ticket in a manila envelope that his secretary accidentally shredded.

1. The absent-minded professor gave a passing grade to a student. That student had never attended class.

2. The hokey-pokey is not what it is all about. We did the hokey-pokey at skating parties.

3. H. L. Mencken ridiculed that notion. H. L. Mencken had a devastating wit.

4. William Shakespeare wrote one particular sonnet. William Shakespeare wrote many famous sonnets. The one particular sonnet was not discovered until the latter part of the twentieth century.

5. The Uncertainty Principle is certain.
The Uncertainty Principle is the source of some people's insecurity.
The Uncertainty Principle is the source of other people's doubt.

3 Noun Clauses

Noun clauses can be introduced by conjunctions (such as *if, that,* and *whether*), pronouns (such as *who, whom, whoever, what, which, whatever,* and *whichever*), adjectives (such as *whose, which,* and *what*), and adverbs (such as *when, where, why,* and *how*).

Within independent clauses, noun clauses function as nouns. For example, very commonly they play the role of subject:

> *Whatever was,* was right.

Very commonly, too, they play the role of direct object:

> I do not believe *what you say about Oz.*

In addition, noun clauses sometimes function as indirect objects, predicate nouns, objective complements, and objects of prepositions.

Occasionally, noun clauses function as appositives. For the most part, such noun clauses are subordinated by *that* and follow such nouns as *fact, belief, hope, statement, news,* and *argument:*

> The fact *that you are smiling* proves my point.

You can identify the clause *that you are smiling* as a noun clause renaming *The fact* (and not as an adjective clause describing *The fact*) because when you insert a form of *be* between *fact* and *that* the noun and the subordinate clause make sense together:

> The fact *is* that you are smiling.

You cannot do this between a noun and an adjective clause that modifies it. For instance, starting with *The car that they stole had faulty brakes,* you could not write *The car is that they stole.*

Exercise 4

Identify the noun clauses in the following sentences and indicate what grammatical role each one plays within its sentence.

> **EXAMPLE:** In *She argued that speakers of different languages see the world differently from each other,* there is one noun clause: *that speakers of different languages see the world differently from each other.* The noun clause is the direct object in the sentence.

21b
cs

1. What she claimed startled some students.

2. They had heard that people's views of the world could differ.

3. The fact that she had specific evidence for her claim did not change their minds.

4. They expressed their beliefs to whoever would listen.

5. What they believed was that they set the standard for views of the world.

21c

Identifying Compound-Complex Sentences

A combination of the compound and complex sentences, the **compound-complex sentence** has two or more independent clauses, just as compound sentences do. It also has one or more subordinate clauses, just as complex sentences do. The following is a compound-complex sentence with two independent clauses and one subordinate clause:

           subordinate clause   independent clause

Although the team was not fully prepared, they debated well,

            independent clause

and the judges complimented them on their skills.

    With compound-complex sentences, you can convey a great deal of information, but the length and complexity of this kind of sentence add to the demands on you to keep all the information clearly related and sharply focused.

Exercise 5

Indicate how many clauses each of the following compound-complex sentences contains, and label each clause as an independent, an adverb, an adjective, or a noun clause.

    EXAMPLE: There are three clauses in *Since they registered late, they were able to get into few of the popular courses, and they became depressed and angry.* [adverb clause *Since they registered late*; independent clause *they were able to get into few popular courses*; and independent clause *and they became depressed and angry.*]

1. The course that focused on the sociology of love was closed, and they could not petition to get into it.

2. What some students looked for were courses that required little writing, but such courses were impossible to find.

3. Some students tried to avoid courses that encouraged collaborative study, but they soon learned that all instructors were requiring collaborative work and study.

4. If students wanted classes that met early in the morning, they had several choices, and their job of putting together a schedule was easy.

5. Students who registered early got all the classes that they wanted, and they walked around campus with satisfied grins on their faces.

21c
cs

VII

CORRECTNESS

22

I n the chapters in this unit, we focus on ways to correct some of the common errors people make in writing. These errors are not all equally serious. In the following sentence, the objective form *whom* is incorrect, yet it would probably not seriously distort the message of the sentence for many readers:

> The committee nominated the student whom many professors said was an eclectic reader.

On the other hand, errors such as incomplete comparisons can make readers wonder what a sentence means:

> The students like harming frogs as much as their teacher.

However serious the different errors are, they should not worry you as you plan and compose essays, for your main concern should be discovering meanings. But as you revise and especially as you edit, you should correct these errors. If you do not, in many situations readers will question your writing ability and be skeptical of your perspective on things.

This unit concludes with a quick-reference chart (see pages 465–468) that very briefly defines and illustrates common errors at the sentence level.

22a

Identifying Sentence Fragments

Imagine reading the following paragraph:

> I can be quiet and reserved, a really respectful person, or I can be really rowdy. I change my behavior, depending on whether I am around my parents or my friends. Always having certain expectations about behavior.

This paragraph could be improved in several ways, but the problem that we will focus on involves the final group of words: *Always having certain expectations about behavior.* This group is a sentence fragment, and it would probably confuse many readers, who would say that they cannot be certain who has the "expectations": the parents, the friends, both the parents and the friends, or the writer. If an essay were to confuse readers repeatedly, sooner or later it would also irritate them. And even if readers could be sure who has the expectations, the fragment might cause them to lose so much respect for the writer that they decide they cannot take the essay seriously.

A **sentence fragment** begins with a capital letter and ends with a period, a question mark, or an exclamation mark. However, a fragment is not a sentence, usually for one or more of the following reasons.

1   The Fragment Might Lack a Subject

Some groups of words are fragments because they lack a subject (see **14c**):

FRAGMENT: And spent all afternoon in a video arcade.

If you were to find such a fragment in an essay, you would probably ask who spent all afternoon in a video arcade. Adding a subject to the fragment produces a sentence:

CORRECTED: And *they* spent all afternoon in a video arcade.

Note that it is legitimate to begin a sentence with a coordinating conjunction. But you will want to avoid beginning several sentences in a row with coordinating conjunctions. Often, this practice does not signal precisely enough how one sentence relates to those around it. It can also make your style monotonous.

Note, too, that imperative sentences generally do not have a subject expressed:

Write this down!

Imperatives are grammatical sentences; in most of them *you* is assumed as the subject:

(You) write this down!

2 The Fragment Might Lack a Verb

Some groups of words are fragments because they lack a verb (see Chapter 16):

FRAGMENT: She and her friends over the years.

Adding a verb to this fragment produces a grammatical sentence:

CORRECTED: She and her friends *mellowed* over the years.

Note that, for a group of words to be a sentence, its verb must be finite. **Finite verbs** refer to definite and limited actions, processes, occurrences, and conditions. Both *rises* in *The sun rises* and *rose* in *The sun rose* are finite verbs. **Nonfinite verbs** (or **verbals**) do not refer to definite and limited actions, processes, occurrences, and conditions. The following two groups of words are fragments because they include a verbal (in italics) rather than a finite verb. They can be corrected as shown:

FRAGMENT: They *to care* about why that student dropped out.

CORRECTED: They care about why that student dropped out.

FRAGMENT: Our group *discussing* different kinds of welfare.

CORRECTED: Our group was discussing different kinds of welfare.

3 The Fragment Might Be a Subordinate Clause

To be a sentence, a group of words has to be an independent clause. That is, it must have a subject and a verb, and it must not be dependent on any other grammatical unit. Some groups of words are fragments because they are not independent but subordinate clauses. For instance, the subordinate adverb clause *When their hair began to turn gray* cannot stand alone as a sentence. It must be attached to an independent clause, as it is in the following:

> When their hair began to turn gray, they saw it as a sign of wisdom.

As you get better at distinguishing fragments from sentences, you will probably also get better at sensing that subordinate clauses punctuated as sentences usually leave one or more pertinent questions in readers' minds. If you were to read *If President Lincoln had signed the treaty,* you would be inclined to ask, "Well, what then? What would have happened?"

Exercise 1

Identify the fragments in the following paragraph, and change each fragment into a sentence.

> **EXAMPLE:** *Or want to look good in front of somebody* is the first fragment in the paragraph. Possible correction: *Or we might want to look good in front of somebody.*

We act differently in different situations because we might want to hide something. Or want to look good in front of somebody. We also act differently so we won't get in trouble. There is a need to change behavior. Because a person always wants to feel accepted and feel liked by others. So he or she has to change behavior to suit others' needs. People are most certainly misled by behavioral changes. Never knowing what the person is really like. Or how the person acts like. In a way behavioral changes can be hypocritical. Yet I think they are needed, and changing behavior comes automatically for most people. Because no one wants to hurt anyone's feelings. If everyone tried to please everyone else, we would all be boring. Everyone would be behaving the same way.

22b

Correcting Sentence Fragments

If you have trouble identifying fragments, try reading your prose aloud. As you read sentences, your voice will probably drop in pitch as you complete them. As you finish reading sentence fragments, however, your voice will probably not drop in pitch as much as it did with the sentences. You can also try reading your papers from the last sentence to the first. This procedure will keep you from assuming that some elements in one sentence can be carried over mentally to the next group of words.

In most cases, there are several ways to correct fragments. The correction you choose should depend largely on how much importance you want to attach to the information conveyed by the fragment. In general, if you want to attach a good deal of importance to that information, you should change the fragment into an independent clause. If you want to attach less importance to the information, you should change the fragment into a subordinate clause and connect it to an independent clause. If you want to attach even less importance to the information, you should change the fragment into a phrase or a word and connect it to an independent clause.

For example, suppose you had to revise this short passage:

> We spent some time tuning our instruments carefully. And then played several popular songs.

This revision attaches a good deal of importance to the information originally expressed in the fragment:

> We spent some time tuning our instruments carefully. And then we played several popular songs.

This revision attaches somewhat less importance to the information:

> Before we played several popular songs, we spent some time tuning our instruments carefully.

And this revision attaches even less importance to the information:

> Before playing several popular songs, we spent some time tuning our instruments carefully.

What follow are some examples of structures that often appear as sentence fragments, as well as some recommendations on how to correct them.

1 Subordinate Clauses as Fragments

Subordinate clauses cannot stand alone as sentences since they modify words, phrases, or clauses. If the subordinate clause *which was never home to me* were punctuated as a sentence, it would be a sentence fragment.

Most of the time, you will probably correct this kind of fragment by attaching the subordinate clause to the preceding or following independent clause:

> I never again thought of Quoncoseeque. Which was never home to me.

> I never again thought of Quoncoseeque, which was never home to me.

But if you wanted to call extra attention to the information originally expressed in the fragment, you could change the fragment into an independent clause:

> I never again thought of Quoncoseeque. It was never home to me.

Or

> I never again thought of Quoncoseeque; it was never home to me.

2 Noun Phrases Plus Adjective Clauses as Fragments

Some fragments consist of a pronoun, noun, or noun phrase followed by an adjective clause:

> **FRAGMENT:**   A coach who thinks only of winning.

The easiest way to correct such fragments is to make the pronoun, noun, or noun phrase part of an independent clause, where it can properly be followed by the adjective clause:

> He is a coach who thinks only of winning.

22b
sf

3 Absolute Phrases as Fragments

Absolute phrases, which are made up of a noun or a pronoun *(the storm),* a participle *(disappearing),* and possibly some modifiers *(in the east),* sometimes appear as sentence fragments:

> We went back into the water for a while. The storm disappearing in the east.

Probably the easiest way to correct this error is to connect the absolute phrase to the sentence with which it makes the most sense. Usually, the absolute phrase will be set off by a comma:

> We went back into the water for a while, the storm disappearing in the east.

Or

> The storm disappearing in the east, we went back into the water for a while.

You would choose the first version if you wanted to stress and perhaps develop the point about the storm's disappearing. You would choose the second version if you wanted to stress and perhaps develop the point about going back into the water for a while.

You can also turn absolute phrases into independent clauses, in most cases simply by changing the participle into a finite verb:

> We went back into the water for a while. The storm was disappearing in the east.

4 Participial Phrases as Fragments

Participial phrases consist of a participle *(retrieving)* and an object of the participle *(the serve),* along with possible modifiers of both the participle and its object *(hastily, wild): hastily retrieving the wild serve.* Sometimes these appear as sentence fragments:

> The ball boy tripped near the net. Hastily retrieving the wild serve.

The easiest way to correct such a fragment is to attach it to the sentence it makes best sense with. Usually the participial phrase will be set off by commas:

> The ball boy, hastily retrieving the wild serve, tripped near the net.

Or

> Hastily retrieving the wild serve, the ball boy tripped near the net.

If you think that the information in the participial phrase is quite important in context, you could turn the participial phrase into an independent clause:

> The ball boy tripped near the net. He was retrieving the wild serve hastily.

5 Infinitive Phrases as Fragments

Infinitive phrases include an infinitive *(to fix),* along with an object of the infinitive *(the tire),* and possibly some modifiers of both the infinitive and its object *(properly, flat): to fix the flat tire properly.* These phrases, too, sometimes appear as fragments. You can correct them by attaching them to the sentence that includes the word or words they modify. If you use an infinitive phrase to introduce a sentence, usually you should follow the infinitive phrase with a comma:

The tour leader had to ask for help. To fix the flat tire properly.

To fix the flat tire properly, the tour leader had to ask for help.

This version stresses the tour leader's having to ask for help.

If you insert the infinitive phrase within the sentence, you will generally need to add a comma both before and after the phrase. You must take care, however, not to make it difficult for your readers to connect the subject and the verb of the sentence. The following begins to strain a reader's ability to connect the subject and the verb:

The tour leader, to fix the flat tire properly, had to ask for help.

Finally, you can also put the infinitive phrase at the end of the sentence. In that case, you would normally not use a comma before the infinitive phrase:

The tour leader had to ask for help to fix the flat tire properly.

This version stresses the fixing of the flat tire.

6 Prepositional Phrases as Fragments

22b
sf

Prepositional phrases include a preposition *(toward)*, its object or objects *(authorities)*, and any possible modifiers of the object or objects *(all): toward all authorities.* Individual prepositional phrases, as well as strings of prepositional phrases, often appear as fragments:

They were always disrespectful. Toward all authorities.

You would usually correct such fragments by attaching the prepositional phrase to the adjoining sentence, after the word that the phrase modifies:

They were always disrespectful toward all authorities.

The prepositional phrase *toward all authorities* modifies the adjective *disrespectful.*

7 Appositives as Fragments

Appositives are words (usually nouns), phrases, or clauses used after a pronoun, noun, or noun phrase in order to rename or further describe the person or thing named by the pronoun, noun, or noun phrase. In the following example, the appositive *Mrs. Fribac* identifies the person referred to by the phrase *The woman next door:*

> The woman next door, Mrs. Fribac, chased the vacuum salesman away.

Sometimes appositives appear as fragments, often apparently as a result of writers' afterthoughts:

> My best friend never had to study very much in high school. Julie.

To correct such a fragment, you should express the appositive immediately after the element it renames:

> My best friend, Julie, never had to study very much in high school.

Since technically you can have only one *best* friend, in this case *Julie* is a nonrestrictive appositive and should be set off within the sentence by commas. If the word that the appositive renames appears near the end of a sentence, you would need only one comma:

> Studying in high school was never very necessary for my best friend, Julie.

22b
sf

Sometimes, especially when you are working with compound appositives of three or more members, you may opt to set them off with dashes:

> Three universities—Clemson, Oklahoma, and Columbia—were recruiting him to play football.

Or

> He was recruited to play football by three universities— Clemson, Oklahoma, and Columbia.

The dash or dashes set the appositives off very clearly from the rest of the sentence and call more attention to them than commas do.

8 Parts of Compounds as Fragments

Sometimes writers leave parts of compound elements of sentences isolated as fragments. They often do this with the second verb and subsequent ones in a compound verb phrase:

> They drove for over fourteen hours. And then looked for a motel in Ely.

But writers also do this with the second and subsequent direct objects in a compound direct object or the second and subsequent elements in a compound predicate noun or predicate adjective:

> They all wrote six essays. And even one long poem.
>
> The chaperones were alert. Also conscientious.

Generally, you would correct such fragments by expressing all the parts of a compound construction together in one sentence:

> They drove for over fourteen hours and then looked for a motel in Ely.

Exercise 2

Correct the fragments in the following paragraph.

> **EXAMPLE:**   The first fragment is *And in different places.* This fragment could be corrected by being attached to the end of the first sentence.

The reasons are simple why people must act differently in different social groups. And in different places. But if people are constantly changing, they will be very unhappy. Changing until they aren't sure who they are. But some people are very insecure about themselves. And unsure how to act. I think that the best solution for that is to just be yourself. Because people should never do things that they normally wouldn't do. Just because they think others will like them for it. Sure, we all act differently in different situations. With a close friend. Or with a big group. But people should always be themselves. Something that is necessary for all of us. Society being as impersonal as it is. In conclusion, I should say that if you are consistent, people will like you more. Probably since you will like yourself a lot more.

22c

Intentional and Justifiable Fragments

Sometimes writers use fragments on purpose and for specific reasons.

1. To answer questions:

> Will we pass? Possibly.

2. To remind readers about material already covered:

> So much for our discussion of fragments.

3. To alert readers about material to be covered:

> Now for the principle of the conservation of mass. (Albert Einstein)

4. To signal shock or excitement:

> Incredible! What courage!

You can use such fragments in your own writing, but you must be certain that your context justifies their purpose to your readers.

Writers also use fragments for less conventional purposes. Often they do so in narrative or descriptive passages. Toward the end of the following selection, for instance, the author uses three fragments to indicate how difficult it was for him to locate the source of a sound:

> All at once there is a barely perceptible noise, a soft rumble as of thunder. The sound dies without discovery of its nature or its source. It returns, seeming to come from all directions at once, like ventriloquy. One moment it is subterranean; the next, it gathers from on high. Is it the wind? Tricking among the roofs and towers? A construction of the water? A vagrant noise from the Piazza San Marco?
>
> Richard Selzer, "Diary of an Infidel"

22c
sf

To the extent that we can generalize about the purpose of less conventional fragments, we would note that they carry special emphasis and drama. Sometimes this emphasis is not immediately apparent because the fragment can seem more casual than the sentences around it. But usually the emphasis becomes all the stronger when readers fully understand the implications of the fragment and contrast those serious implications to the seemingly casual form of the fragment. Consider—and feel—the force that Robert Hughes is able to convey with the fragment that concludes the following short passage:

> It took less than seventy-five years of white settlement to wipe out most of the people who had occupied Tasmania for some thirty thousand years; it was the only true genocide in English colonial history. By the standards of Pol Pot, let alone Josef Stalin or Adolf Hitler, this was a small slaughter. But not to the Tasmanian Aborigines.
>
> *The Fatal Shore*

You will probably want to use such fragments in some of your writing. But you must be cautious with them. If your readers do not experience the effect you are aiming for, or if they do not think that the effect justifies the fragment, they will criticize your use of the fragment.

Exercise 3

Record what effect the fragment or fragments in each of the following short passages has on you.

1. The first in time and the first in importance of the influences upon the mind is that of nature. Every day, the sun; and, after sunset, night and her stars. (Ralph Waldo Emerson)

2. They took no interest in civilized ways. Hadn't heard of them, probably. (Clarence Day)

3. When they are indoors, they sit for a while without doing anything much. Then they suddenly decide to go out again for a while. Then they come in again. In and out—in and out. (Robert Benchley)

4. For twelve years, Max Beerbohm admitted in his valedictory article, Thursdays had been for him the least pleasant day of the week. Why Thursday? Because that was the day, the latest possible one, he set aside each week to get his writing done. (John Mason Brown)

5. The carts were jammed for thirty miles along the Karagatch road. Water buffalo and cattle were hauling carts through the mud. No end and no beginning. Just carts loaded with everything they owned. (Ernest Hemingway)

Exercise 4

Working alone or as a member of a team, find five fragments that appear in print. Formulate an explanation for why each appears where it does. Is each fragment justified?

22c
sf

23

COMMA SPLICES AND FUSED SENTENCES

I magine reading the following group of words in an essay:

> The people at the corner table were ready to order the chef's specialty, the spicy meatballs on the tray near the end of the table were nearly gone.

As you were reading this group of words for the first time, how long did it take you to realize that it contains two distinct independent clauses? You probably could not be certain of this until you reached the verb *were* near the very end. Then you might have had to read the group of words again in order to interpret it properly. This group of words has in it an example of an error called the comma splice.

23a

Identifying Comma Splices

In a **comma splice,** a comma links, or splices, two or more independent clauses, unless the independent clauses make up a series in which the last independent clause is introduced by a coordinating conjunction:

> COMMA SPLICE: Billy could not face his accuser, he could only moan to himself.
>
> CORRECT: Billy stuttered, he moaned, and he turned from his accuser.

As our introductory example about the diners shows, a comma by itself is not sufficient to distinguish independent clauses from each other and to indicate how they are related in meaning. When readers encounter a comma splice, they usually have trouble telling when a predication is complete, and so they must reread parts of the material. If they have to do this often, they are likely to lose patience with the writer.

If you use two or more independent clauses next to each other in an essay, readers will expect to see these clauses expressed and related in one of several possible ways. You can express the independent clauses as separate sentences:

> He rushed to the dictionary. He had to learn what *zeugma* means.

You can link the independent clauses with a comma followed by a coordinating conjunction *(and, but, or, for, nor, so, yet):*

> He rushed to the dictionary, for he had to learn what *zeugma* means.

When the independent clauses are closely related in meaning (for example, by contrast), you can use a semicolon between them:

> He rushed to the dictionary; his friend went in search of a professor of Greek.

Finally, when the second independent clause elaborates on or explains the meaning of the first, you can link them with a colon:

> He is a man of power now: He knows what *zeugma* means.

Exercise 1

Identify the comma splices in the following passage.

> EXAMPLE: The first group of words punctuated as a sentence in the passage is a comma splice.

Most students at the state university have a difficult time choosing a major, the choice is an obstacle to their academic progress. It probably should not be a surprise, then, that many students go about making this choice in questionable ways. Some choose a major on the basis of grades, the program or department that they get the best grades in is the one that they choose. Others choose on the basis of professors. If a program has popular professors teaching in it, they choose that program for their major. Still other students avoid these two approaches, they think they have a better method. They examine the average starting salary of graduates of various programs, they select from among the programs that lead to jobs with high salaries. Too few students try to find a match between their talents and the opportunities a program provides. And too few evaluate programs in terms of how the programs would help them serve others. Probably the strangest reason for a choice is that of a recent male graduate, he is from Rhode Island. He decided to major in ancient religion and theology. His reason was that he liked the academic gowns of professors of religion and theology and hoped to be able to wear such a gown himself.

23b

Correcting Comma Splices

If you have trouble spotting comma splices in your own drafts, you can focus your attention on each comma. Is there an independent clause to the left of the comma? Is there also an independent clause to the right of the comma? And does the independent clause to the right have no coordinating conjunction introducing it? If you respond affirmatively to these three questions, you have spotted a comma splice.

Probably the most important thing to remember about correcting comma splices is that you should strive to relate your ideas in the way most appropriate to what you are trying to accomplish at that particular point in an essay. Different ways of correcting comma splices relate the same ideas somewhat differently.

1   Changing an Independent Clause into a Subordinate Clause or a Phrase

You might find that one of the independent clauses in a comma splice should not be an independent clause at all. In context, the information in one independent clause may be background information or less important information than that in the other independent clause. Therefore, you could correct the comma splice by changing one of the independent clauses into a subordinate clause or a phrase. For example, consider the following short passage:

> One member of the hurricane-tracking team is essential, she is known as the weather officer. She decides how low in the eye of the storm it is safe to fly.

The first group of words punctuated as a sentence is a comma splice. Probably the best way to correct it is to subordinate the information in the second independent clause of the splice. In the context, the title of the singled-out team member is background information, as is clear from the fact that the second sentence elaborates on why the weather officer is essential, not on her title. Therefore, you could express the information carried by the second independent clause in a subordinate adjective clause:

> One member of the hurricane-tracking team, *who is known as the weather officer,* is essential.

Or you could express this same information in a participial phrase:

> One member of the hurricane-tracking team, *known as the weather officer,* is essential.

2 Substituting a Period for the Comma

Substituting a period for the comma in a comma splice is probably the easiest way to correct the comma splice. But it is not always the best way. For instance, if we had corrected the comma splice in our last example in this way, we would have given more prominence to the title of one team member than it probably merited in context:

> One member of the hurricane-tracking team is essential. She is known as the weather officer. She decides how low in the eye of the storm it is safe to fly.

Correcting a comma splice by breaking it into two separate sentences works especially well when the independent clauses are fairly long and deserve roughly equal emphasis:

COMMA SPLICE:	They never wavered in the face of the strafing by the enemy jets, they held their positions and rallied their troops.
CORRECTED:	They never wavered in the face of the strafing by the enemy jets. They held their positions and rallied their troops.

3 Substituting a Semicolon for the Comma

Substituting a semicolon for the comma is another good way to correct a splice. A semicolon works best if the independent clauses are closely related in meaning and if you wish to draw attention to that

23b
csf

close relationship. For example, when one independent clause contrasts with another, a semicolon will draw readers' attention to that
contrast:

> COMMA SPLICE: He called his remark witty, it was an accident.
>
> CORRECTED: He called his remark witty; it was an accident.

A semicolon also works well if the second independent clause in
a comma splice begins with a word or a phrase, usually a conjunctive
adverb, that shows how the second clause is logically related to the
first:

> COMMA SPLICE: The band boosters have sacrificed in order to
> support a kazoo marching band, therefore, we
> students should sacrifice.
>
> CORRECTED: The band boosters have sacrificed in order to
> support a kazoo marching band; therefore, we
> students should sacrifice.

4 Substituting a Colon for the Comma

As a means of correcting a comma splice, the colon resembles the
semicolon. Both draw readers' attention to a close relationship
between the independent clauses. But colons usually signal fewer
kinds of close relationships than semicolons do—primarily relationships of explanation, elaboration, and fulfillment of expectations raised
by the first independent clause. Consider the following:

> COMMA SPLICE: Caesar made up his mind, he was going to
> cross the Rubicon.

A good way to correct this comma splice, in which the second independent clause specifies what Caesar made up his mind about, would
be to substitute a colon for the comma:

> CORRECTED: Caesar made up his mind: He was going to cross
> the Rubicon.

5 Adding a Coordinating Conjunction After the Comma

Finally, you can correct a comma splice by adding an appropriate
coordinating conjunction after the comma between the independent
clauses. Consider the following comma splice:

> COMMA SPLICE: We did not want to intrude, we wanted to say
> a word or two to them.

It is difficult to know how these two independent clauses relate to each other in meaning. Has the intrusion taken place? Did the intrusion include the "word or two to them"? Did the intrusion happen because the speakers said more than a "word or two"? Or did the intrusion involve not saying the "word or two" at all? You cannot tell from this comma splice. But a coordinating conjunction introduced after the comma makes the relationship clearer, particularly if you imagine the sentence as uttered by people about mourners whom they had hoped to comfort:

> **CORRECTED:**   We did not want to intrude, yet we wanted to say a word or two to them.

Exercise 2

Identify the comma splices in the following passage and suggest two ways to correct each one. Be prepared to discuss the advantages of each of your suggested corrections.

> **EXAMPLE:**   The first group of words punctuated as a sentence in the following is a comma splice. It could be corrected by inserting an *and* after the comma. But it would probably be better to turn the first independent clause into a phrase (such as "After extensive research on this campus"). The first clause should probably be subordinated as a phrase since the research itself is not the focus of the rest of the passage.

23b
csf

We have conducted extensive research on this campus, we have found that students have four main approaches to selecting classes.

One can be called the "least-effort" approach, it is quite interesting. Students who adopt this approach ask their peers how much work various courses require. Then they try to register for the easy courses, and they attempt to avoid the demanding courses.

People call the second approach the "remarkable résumé" approach. Students taking this approach choose only those classes taught by Nobel laureates, these students usually hope to go on to graduate school.

The third approach is quite common, it is also irritating to deans and department chairs. It is called the "customer convenience" approach. Some students adopting this approach refuse to take morning classes, they sleep in after watching late-night television. Other students adopting this approach refuse to take afternoon classes, they reserve afternoons for watching soap operas.

Finally, the fourth approach can be called the "egocentric" approach. Students who take this approach will select any class with a title ending with the words *and you.* Therefore, they often take classes called such things as "Social Deviance and You," "Nostratic Love Lyrics and You," and "Black Holes and You."

Are Comma Splices Ever Acceptable?

Comma splices are acceptable in writing, but only occasionally. In such instances, the independent clauses in them are usually short, similar in structure, and closely related in meaning. Reading the first of these independent clauses makes you expect to see a second and perhaps a third independent clause. These later independent clauses often express comparisons, contrasts, amplifications, and explanations.

Commas move readers through such independent clauses more quickly than semicolons and colons. Often this quick movement imitates some quickness in meaning:

> She peered through the crack, then she jumped away.

More often, though, writers will use commas between independent clauses to achieve a kind of crescendo or air of inevitability. One independent clause nudges the reader to move onto the next independent clause in order to learn how things will turn out:

23c
csf

> I held my breath, I closed my eyes.

In sum, you will occasionally see groups of words that are technically comma splices. They will probably be groups such as these:

> He was on first, I was on third.
>
> I came, I saw, I surrendered.
>
> Our team is not aggressive, it is assertive.
>
> We were charming, they were uncharmed.

If you are thinking of using such comma splices in your own writing, proceed with caution. You should be sure that the independent clauses in the comma splice are short, similar in form, and closely related in meaning. You should have a good idea of the effect you are trying to achieve. And you should be confident that the effect justifies including what is technically an error. To achieve this confidence, you must consider who your readers are likely to be. Most readers will accept a comma splice used intentionally to achieve a particular effect. But some will never compromise on technical correctness, and your use of a comma splice will only drive a wedge between them and your piece of writing.

Exercise 3

Find or write five comma splices that you think can be defended in particular contexts, and formulate a defense for each of them.

Identifying Fused Sentences

In a fused (or run-on) sentence, one independent clause follows another with no mark of punctuation between them. Most fused sentences contain two independent clauses; a few contain three or more:

> The park is lovely it is also dangerous after sunset.
>
> The park is lovely it is also dangerous after sunset rival gangs control different parts of it.

Correcting Fused Sentences

You can correct fused sentences as you would comma splices.

1 Subordinating the Material in an Independent Clause

You should decide whether in context the independent clauses in a fused sentence deserve to be independent clauses. Perhaps one should be subordinated to another. Consider the following fused sentence:

> FUSED SENTENCE: I like the fourth sandwich on the menu it is called The Sophomore's Sacrifice.

Unless in context the name of the sandwich becomes the focus of attention later on, it would probably be best to correct this fused sentence by subordinating the information in the final independent clause:

> CORRECTED: I like the fourth sandwich on the menu, which is called The Sophomore's Sacrifice.
>
> OR: I like the fourth sandwich on the menu, called The Sophomore's Sacrifice.

2 Breaking a Fused Sentence into Two or More Sentences

Probably the easiest way to correct a fused sentence is to separate it into two or more sentences:

FUSED SENTENCE: We used to walk over to Ridgewater Park to play baseball the park near our homes was reserved for croquet.

CORRECTED: We used to walk over to Ridgewater Park to play baseball. The park near our homes was reserved for croquet.

3 Adding a Semicolon

When the independent clauses in a fused sentence are closely related in meaning, you can link them with a semicolon:

FUSED SENTENCE: Watching an aerobic dance class will not lower your cholesterol count you have to do some exercise yourself.

CORRECTED: Watching an aerobic dance class will not lower your cholesterol count; you have to do some exercise yourself.

4 Adding a Colon

Especially when the second of the two independent clauses in a fused sentence explains or elaborates the first, you can use a colon between them:

FUSED SENTENCE: The inexperienced climbers were easy to spot they began their climbing lessons by taking new boots out of shopping bags.

CORRECTED: The inexperienced climbers were easy to spot: They began their climbing lessons by taking new boots out of shopping bags.

5 Adding a Comma and a Coordinating Conjunction

Finally, you can correct a fused sentence by inserting a comma and an appropriate coordinating conjunction between the independent clauses:

FUSED SENTENCE: We washed the graffiti off the walls we
                  mopped the floors.

CORRECTED: We washed the graffiti off the walls, and we
             mopped the floors.

Exercise 4

Identify the fused sentences in the following passage, and suggest two
different ways to correct each one. Be prepared to discuss the advantages and disadvantages of each of your suggested corrections.

EXAMPLE: The first group of words punctuated as a sentence is a
           fused sentence. You could correct it by dividing it into
           two separate sentences: *Students at our university
           have a very high default rate on guaranteed student
           loans. It is about 29 percent.* This correction calls a
           good deal of attention to the rate of 29 percent. Or you
           could change the second independent clause into an
           appositive: *Students at our university have a very high
           default rate on guaranteed student loans, about 29
           percent.* This correction saves words and has more
           fluidity in rhythm than the first correction.

Students at our university have a very high default rate on guaranteed
student loans it is about 29 percent. Different professors offer different
reasons for this high percentage. Some professors of social work
describe graduates choosing to live in poverty they want to serve others.
English professors give a different reason, and it strikes many people as
strange. According to these professors, their graduates are very busy
waiting to be inspired to write novels they have no time to think about
debts from the past. According to some business professors, graduates
with an undergraduate business degree tie most of their money up in
stocks and bonds and therefore have no liquid assets with which to
repay loans. This claim is hard to believe. Other professors have a different explanation these are professors in the medical school. In their
view, their former students can hardly afford to purchase malpractice
insurance; therefore, these students are not able to repay their loans.
Whatever the reason for all the defaults, one thing is clear. The university must act and act quickly to avoid severe consequences the government will make less money available to students here.

**23f
csf**

23f

Are Fused Sentences Ever Acceptable?

Some fused sentences are acceptable in writing, but only in truly
extraordinary circumstances. Usually, such fused sentences appear in

narratives, often narratives of an experimental nature. And by and large they appear in order to imitate phenomena not usually imitated in writing. For example, James Joyce concludes *Ulysses* with Molly's soliloquy, a passage of some twenty-five thousand words that contains no mark of punctuation at all. It is a passage made up of clauses and phrases fused to others and then to still others. In the passage, Joyce tries to imitate the stream of Molly Bloom's thoughts as she tries unsuccessfully to fall asleep. Here is a portion from near the end of her soliloquy:

> I love flowers Id love to have the whole place swimming in roses God of heaven theres nothing like nature the wild mountains then the sea and the waves rushing then the beautiful country with fields of oats and wheat and all kinds of things and all the fine cattle going about that would do your heart good to see rivers and lakes and flowers all sorts of shops and smells and colours springing up even out of the ditches primroses and violets nature it is . . .

If you are trying to achieve effects such as Joyce was aiming for, you could consider using fused sentences. But you should be certain that the fused sentences you use actually produce the effects you are seeking. You must also be certain that those effects are worth the risk of introducing structures as unconventional as fused sentences into your work. Otherwise you may convince readers that your writing does not deserve their attention.

**23f
csf**

Exercise 5

Think of three to five effects that could be achieved with fused sentences. Then describe rhetorical situations in which you might be able to use fused sentences to try to achieve such effects.

24

A W K W A R D   O R

C O N F U S I N G

S E N T E N C E S

I n early drafts of essays, most writers include some sentences that are awkward or confusing. Some of these seem to have little wrong with them:

> Rebecca finds the class in nematodes as interesting as Ned.

But this sentence can be read in at least two ways: Either Rebecca finds the class in nematodes as interesting as she finds Ned, or she finds the class as interesting as Ned does. Other sentences go wrong in so many ways that it is difficult to describe their flaws:

> In my view, by too quickly expressing your opinion is never the best idea for relatives with celebrations of holidays together.

If you do not correct all awkward or confusing sentences, you will thwart readers' expectations and try their patience.

24a

Identifying Faulty Predications

Faulty predications are sentences that include elements that do not go together logically. Usually, these elements are the subject, verb, and objects or complements. For example, sometimes writers connect a subject naming a thing to a verb describing an action that only people can perform:

> FAULTY: The rules expect all members of the team to maintain their eligibility.

Rules cannot expect things. To correct such a predication, you would have to find a verb that goes together logically with the subject:

> CORRECTED: The rules stipulate that all members of the team must maintain their eligibility.

24b

Correcting Faulty Predications

The key to spotting and correcting faulty predications is to ask yourself certain questions about your sentences as you revise them. Can the subject actually perform the activity described by the verb? In sentences with passive verbs, can the subject have the activity described by the verb performed on it? In sentences with one or more direct objects, can the subject perform the activity described by the verb on the direct object or objects? And in sentences with one or more predicate nouns, can the subject be equated with the predicate noun or nouns?

Some faulty predications involve an illogical relationship between an inanimate subject and a verb:

> FAULTY: The most recent theory of language thinks about different kinds of bonding.

Theories cannot think; people do. One way to correct this sentence is to use a noun that names people as the subject:

> CORRECTED: The developers of the most recent theory of language think about different kinds of bonding.

Some predications with an inanimate subject are difficult to judge:

> The university states that all freshmen must live on campus.

In the strictest sense, a university cannot state. Yet many people would accept this predication; it saves writers from having to indicate what is probably not an important issue: who from the university does the stating. Reading widely and consulting other well-read people should help you decide which predications that are technically illogical are acceptable.

In other faulty predications, subjects are connected to verbs that produce clumsy pairings or redundancies:

> FAULTY: The use of aspirin, according to all available records, was never used on children under the age of seven.

This sentence states that "The use . . . was never used," which is a clumsy predication. One way to correct this predication is as follows:

> CORRECTED: According to all available records, aspirin was never used on children under the age of seven.

Still another kind of faulty predication appears when writers connect action verbs to direct objects that are illogical for them:

> FAULTY: The teacher complimented the progress in the class.

A teacher cannot compliment progress, but he or she can compliment students for making progress:

> CORRECTED: The teacher complimented the students in the class for making progress.

Finally, many faulty predications include a subject related by a linking verb to a predicate noun that is illogical for the subject:

> FAULTY: A trait that I like a lot is a person with modesty.

A trait cannot be a person, but it can be something like modesty. You could correct the faulty predication as follows:

> CORRECTED: A trait that I like in a person is modesty.

Also in this last category are constructions such as these:

> FAULTY: Code switching is when people switch from one social dialect to another in different contexts.
>
> FAULTY: Prejudice is where people make hasty and unfounded judgments.
>
> FAULTY: The reason for caution is because of the dangerous machines.

All these sentences include a subject and a linking verb. But instead of also including a predicate noun or predicate adjective, elements often

24b
acs

found after a linking verb, these sentences move into elements that usually function as adverbs in modifying verbs. In addition, the last sentence contains a redundancy; since *because* means "for the reason that," a paraphrase of the beginning of the sentence would be "The reason for caution is for the reason that." One good way to correct such sentences is to find an element that can function as a predicate noun after the linking verb:

> **CORRECTED:** Code switching is the *ability* to change from one social dialect to another in different contexts.
>
> **CORRECTED:** Prejudice is the *practice* of making hasty and unfounded judgments.

You could revise the final faulty predication more extensively:

> **CORRECTED:** Caution is important because the machines are dangerous.

Exercise 1

Correct whatever faulty predications occur in the following sentences.

> **EXAMPLE:** *The coach's theory of procedures for practice believes in discipline* is a faulty predication; a theory cannot believe. Possible correction: *With regard to procedures for practice, the coach believes in discipline.*

1. Regulations argue that students who plagiarize must perform one hundred hours of community service.

2. The professor of philosophy, in a talk given last night, contended that truth varies from social group to social group.

3. Aphasia is where an individual suffers a language disorder.

4. Explaining the steps of registration to all new students is the process of this pamphlet.

5. The purpose of the orientation document explains the regulations of the college for students who do not live on campus.

6. The reason our papers are late is because we could not get the laser printer to work properly.

7. A detailed syllabus is a practice in all philosophy courses.

8. Their view sees interesting developments in the theory of history.

9. The graduate students, increasing in number with each day, expanded out of the seminar room and into the hallway.

10. The conference with their advisers deflated their pursuit of those four topics.

24c

Identifying Mixed Constructions

Mixed constructions include elements that do not go together grammatically. In *By hurrying to turn their papers in on time is a practice of many sophomores,* for example, there is no noun phrase to serve as the subject of the verb *is.* But there is a logical relationship lurking below the surface of this sentence, which is apparent when the sentence appears without the introductory preposition: *Hurrying to turn their papers in on time is a practice of many sophomores.* It seems as if the writer of the original sentence began with one strategy for forming the sentence and then shifted to another.

24d

Correcting Mixed Constructions

Some mixed constructions include an unnecessarily doubled subject or an unnecessarily doubled direct object:

MIXED (DOUBLE SUBJECT):   *Tom, he* skipped classes to go hunting.

MIXED (DOUBLE DIRECT OBJECT):   *The girl in the green coveralls,* Tom scared *her* when he shot blindly into a thicket.

Such sentences are usually easy to correct; you have to delete one of the subjects or direct objects:

CORRECTED: Tom skipped classes to go hunting.

CORRECTED: Tom scared the girl in the green coveralls when he shot blindly into a thicket.

Other mixed constructions include as an apparent subject some kind of phrase that cannot serve as a subject:

MIXED: By just accepting that there are different dialects and that each one has value, will help alleviate the negative attitudes in our classrooms today.

The writer tries to make the prepositional phrase starting with *By* the subject. But prepositional phrases usually do not serve as subjects. The

ESL Consideration

MIXED CONSTRUCTIONS WITH SUBORDINATING AND COORDINATING CONJUNCTIONS

Sometimes writers mix subordinating and coordinating conjunctions in sentences, producing ungrammatical constructions:

> *Although* he is a very honored and well-known intellectual at my university, *but* Mr. Singh is not considered an outstanding teacher.

The sentence gives the reader two different structural signals. *Although* introduces a subordinate clause; however, *but* leads to a contrasting statement in a coordinate construction. The sentence should be restructured, eliminating one or the other structural signal:

COMPLEX SENTENCE: Although he is a very honored and well-known intellectual at my university, Mr. Singh is not considered an outstanding teacher.

COMPOUND SENTENCE: Mr. Singh is a very honored and well-known intellectual at my university, but he is not considered an outstanding teacher.

This type of mixed construction often occurs when a writer attempts complex sentences containing subordinating conjunctions of concession and contrast (for example, *although, even though, though, if,* and *even if*).

---

student could correct the construction by dropping the *By*; this produces a gerund phrase, which can serve as the subject:

CORRECTED: Just accepting that there are different dialects and that each one has value will help alleviate the negative attitudes in our classrooms today.

In still other mixed constructions, a subordinate clause, often an adverbial clause, appears where readers expect to find a subject:

MIXED: *Although the team lost in the semifinals* is no reason to call the season a failure.

An adverbial clause cannot serve as a subject. You could change it into a noun clause, which can serve as a subject:

CORRECTED: That the team lost in the semifinals is no reason to call the season a failure.

Or you could keep the adverbial clause and change the original predicate into an independent clause:

CORRECTED: Although the team lost in the semifinals, we have no reason to call the season a failure.

Finally, some mixed constructions have an entire independent clause where readers expect to find a subject:

MIXED: *The Spartans blocked the kick* was the biggest turning point of the game.

To correct many such constructions, you will have to revise them substantially:

CORRECTED: The blocked kick by the Spartans was the biggest turning point of the game.

Exercise 2

Find and correct all mixed constructions in the following passage.

EXAMPLE: The second group of words punctuated as a sentence is a mixed construction (with a double subject). It could be corrected as follows: *As the researchers suggest, women use more tag questions in all conversations than do men.*

24d
acs

Recently, researchers have been studying ways in which the speech patterns of women and men differ. As the researchers suggest, women, they use more tag questions in all conversations than do men. Tag questions are constructions such as "They shoot horses, don't they?" If this suggestion turns out to be a fact poses a large problem for interpretation. Some researchers think that tag questions show that women use the language of submission. By adding a tag to the end of their sentences, which comes in the form of a question, is how they signal to men that they are being submissive. Other researchers have a different interpretation. These tags, the researchers say, women use them to bring more people into conversations. A woman might use a tag with her husband is her attempt to bring him into a conversation with others. Finally, some researchers see tag questions as techniques by which women subtly manipulate conversations. When a woman uses a tag question with a man to show what she wants him to talk about, is a subtle kind of power. Since these different interpretations exist, researchers will have to be much more sensitive to aspects of the conversational situations they study in the future.

24e

Identifying Faulty Parallelism

Parallelism is a principle that applies to coordinated elements in sentences. According to this principle, whenever you have more than one element playing the same grammatical role, you should try to use elements that have the same form. For example, if you wanted to use coordinated direct objects, you should try to use the same kind of word, phrase, or clause in each direct object slot. You could choose gerunds:

> They enjoy *painting* and *sculpting.*

You could choose gerund phrases:

> They try *painting realistic representations* and *sculpting abstract figures.*

Or you could choose noun clauses:

> They depicted *what they had actually seen* and *what they had only imagined.*

When your readers see that you could have filled two or more slots in a sentence with the same kind of form but did not, they will say that your sentence exhibits faulty parallelism. One of the earlier examples can be changed so that it exhibits faulty parallelism between direct objects:

> They try painting realistic representations and to sculpt abstract figures.

Here a gerund phrase *(painting realistic representations)* is coordinated with an infinitive phrase *(to sculpt abstract figures).*

Readers do not expect parallelism between all coordinated elements. They usually do not notice nonparallel forms if those forms are common and closely related in meaning:

> We prefer the metaphors below and in the next chapter.

Here the adverb *below* is coordinated with the prepositional phrase *in the next chapter.* This sentence lacks formal parallelism, but the relationship in meaning between *below* and *in the next chapter* is very close, and the word *below* is common in contexts like this. A writer could change *below* to a phrase such as *below this paragraph* and achieve parallelism. But doing so in this case is probably not necessary, particularly since the phrase adds little that readers do not already know.

Usually, however, if you make coordinated elements parallel in form, you can create pleasant rhythms and can use similarities in form to call attention to similarities and differences in meaning. Here is a sentence lacking parallelism and clarity:

> One teacher favors bidialectalism in her classroom, another striving to eliminate nonstandard social dialects, and for a third teacher almost complete acceptance of nonstandard social dialects.

With parallelism, particularly parallelism between verb forms, the sentence becomes much clearer:

> One teacher favors bidialectalism in her classroom, another strives to eliminate nonstandard social dialects, and a third accepts nonstandard social dialects completely.

In some cases, you may want to draw even more attention to similarities and differences in meaning by making coordinated elements both parallel in form and similar in sound. In the following sentence, one of our students reinforces the parallelism between coordinated direct objects by using three words that begin with *p:*

> Acquiring a foreign language can affect a child's perceptions of others, possibilities for the future, and performance in school.

Remember, though, that you must not use words that are similar in sound if their meanings do not fit your purpose or if the sounds become irritatingly cute.

24f
acs

24f

Correcting Different Kinds of Faulty Parallelism

1 Faulty Parallelism Between Elements Joined by Coordinating Conjunctions

With the coordinating conjunctions *and* and *or,* you can coordinate many different structures. When you do so, you should use identical forms in each of the coordinated slots:

PARALLEL SUBJECTS: *Photographing sunsets* and *finding sand dollars* are their favorite pastimes.

Writers seem especially likely to violate the principle of parallelism when they use coordinated verbs and verb phrases. Sometimes they omit a necessary auxiliary verb:

FAULTY: The proposal has value and influenced the
           committee.

This sentence requires *has* before the verb *influenced.* The first *has* is a main verb, and the sentence needs a second *has* as the auxiliary with *influenced:*

PARALLEL: The proposal has value and has influenced the
           committee.

Sometimes writers omit one of two main verbs, especially if the slots for these two verbs are somewhat distant from each other:

FAULTY: They can, and have been studying, the proposal.

The problem here is that the modal verb *can* does not go with the form *studying.* This sentence can be corrected as follows:

PARALLEL: They can study, and have been studying, the
           proposal.

In other cases, writers coordinate verbs, each of which is closely associated with a particular preposition. The problem arises when they omit one of the prepositions:

FAULTY: They will listen and abide by your rules.

In this sentence, *will listen* is idiomatic with *to,* not *by:*

PARALLEL: They will listen to and abide by your rules.

A similar problem occurs when writers coordinate nouns that are closely associated with particular prepositions. They omit one of the prepositions:

FAULTY: She has knowledge and respect for Mayan artifacts.

The trouble is that *knowledge* is not idiomatic with *for,* as this sentence suggests it is. *Knowledge* is idiomatic with *of* or *about:*

PARALLEL: She has knowledge of and respect for Mayan
           artifacts.

A very closely related problem centers on words that function as adjectives and on the prepositions with which these words are closely linked:

FAULTY: The provost was ashamed and alarmed at their
           demands.

24f
acs

On the basis of this sentence, you might think that since *ashamed* is coordinated with *alarmed,* both of these words are closely associated with *at.* But in this context *ashamed* is idiomatic with *of:*

> PARALLEL: The provost was ashamed of and alarmed at their demands.

Finally, you should take special care when you use adjective clauses beginning *and who, and which,* and *and that.* The best rule of thumb is not to use such a clause in a sentence unless you have already done so or unless you intend to follow such an adjective clause with another like it. If you disregard this rule, you might produce sentences such as this:

> FAULTY: They are scientists with imagination and who are bold.

You could correct this sentence in several ways:

> PARALLEL: They are scientists with imagination and boldness.
>
> They are scientists who have imagination and boldness.
>
> They are imaginative and bold scientists.
>
> They are scientists who have imagination and who have boldness.

The last possibility is correct but would probably strike many readers as unnecessarily long.

2 **Faulty Parallelism Between Elements Joined by Correlative Conjunctions**

The correlative conjunctions that commonly coordinate elements within sentences are *both . . . and, either . . . or, neither . . . nor, not only . . . but (also),* and *whether . . . or.* In coordinations signaled by correlative conjunctions, what appears after the first conjunction should have the same form as what appears after the second. Consider this sentence from one of our students:

> FAULTY: It is not only important for the teacher to know of the problem but also to avoid aggravating the problem.

What appears immediately after the *not only?* An adjective, *important,* does. What appears immediately after the *but also?* An infinitive, *to*

24f
acs

avoid. This sentence could be corrected by coordinating one infinitive with another:

> PARALLEL: It is important for the teacher not only to know of the problem but also to avoid aggravating the problem.

3 Faulty Parallelism Between Elements in a Series

When you form a series of three or more elements, all of the items in the series should be the same form. Here is a sentence with a series of three subjects that are not fully parallel:

> FAULTY: No food, drink, or smoking is allowed in the museum.

The first two subjects are common nouns, and the third is a gerund. It is true that gerunds function as nouns, but you could enhance the parallelism in at least two different ways:

> PARALLEL: No eating, drinking, or smoking is allowed in the museum.
>
> No food, drink, or cigarettes are allowed in the museum.

The first revision may be preferable, since the second one does not explicitly forbid cigars and other smoking materials.

Many writers have trouble with what appears to be a series of verb phrases:

> FAULTY: He was in his late teens, of average height, and spoke with a twang.

The problem here is that a prepositional phrase *(of average height)* occurs between two verb phrases, creating the impression that it was supposed to be a verb phrase too. To achieve parallelism in such a sentence, you must change the prepositional phrase into a verb phrase:

> PARALLEL: He was in his late teens, was of average height, and spoke with a twang.

Sometimes you will have to choose whether or not to repeat words in a series. If you wanted to use three noun phrases as the subjects in a sentence, should you write *the sweat on my forehead, the pain in my jaw, and the blood on my chin?* Or would it be better to omit two instances of *the: the sweat on my forehead, pain in my jaw,*

24f
acs

and blood on my chin? Your decision rests on how clearly you want to signal parallel structures and on how quickly you want your prose to move. The series that repeats *the* signals parallel structures more clearly than the other, but it is also somewhat more slowly paced. Slowness is not necessarily bad; in fact, you may opt for the slower version in order to call more attention to the sweat, pain, and blood.

Exercise 3

Correct all of the following sentences that display faulty parallelism.

EXAMPLE: Money is easier spent than to earn.

Money is easier to spend than to earn.

1. They have and will play a part in our deliberations.
2. Some of these patients have deficiencies in hearing, speech, vision, and cognitive damage.
3. The careers that graduates of this institution select range from teaching to business executives.
4. The academic-standards code will include sections legalizing incompletes and that specify when the incompletes must be removed.
5. They are well and considering a trip to Iceland.
6. They believe that this machine is more hindrance than helpful.
7. The cross-country team trains regularly and with a great deal of rigor.
8. They have knowledge and admiration for the professor's accomplishments.
9. You laughed not only about their proposal but also smirked at their report.
10. The dean is tall, with long dark hair, and smiling cheerfully.

24g
acs

24g

Identifying Faulty Comparisons

Technically, faulty comparisons could be included in the section on faulty parallelism since sentences or parts of sentences that are compared or contrasted should be parallel in form. Faulty comparisons usually go wrong because of incompleteness, ambiguity, or sloppy logic. For example, *Spritz is better* is a faulty comparison since, without help from the context, readers cannot tell what Spritz is better than. Faulty comparisons are numerous enough to warrant having a separate section devoted to them.

24h

Correcting Faulty Comparisons

If you keep the following three concerns clearly in focus, you should be able to correct almost all faulty comparisons.

1 Making Comparisons Complete

Sometimes people write sentences such as this:

INCOMPLETE: Ultrahold lasts longer.

What does Ultrahold last longer than? This question arises because the comparison is incomplete. In order to correct it, you have to add information:

CORRECTED: Ultrahold lasts longer than Staysoft.

24h
acs

A related point is that you should make all double comparisons grammatically complete. Double comparisons involve two points of comparison. For example, you can indicate that you like Proust as much as, if not more than, you like Wilde. The trouble usually arises when writers omit the second *as:*

FAULTY: I like Proust as much, if not more than, I like Wilde.

CORRECTED: I like Proust as much *as,* if not more than, I like Wilde.

A similar problem occurs in the following:

FAULTY: She is one of the smarter, if not the smartest girl, in the class.

The grammar of the sentence leads readers to complete the first comparison as follows: *She is one of the smarter girls.* But the word *girls* never appears in the sentence. You could correct this double comparison as follows:

CORRECTED: She is one of the smarter girls, if not the smartest girl, in the class.

2 Making Comparisons Unambiguous

To introduce this chapter, we used the sentence *Rebecca finds the class in nematodes as interesting as Ned.* This sentence includes an ambiguous comparison, since readers cannot tell whether Rebecca finds the class as interesting as she finds Ned, or whether she finds the class as interesting as Ned does. When writers make ambiguous comparisons, they generally have only one meaning in mind. And often readers suspect what meaning that is. However, readers cannot always be certain that their suspicion is correct on the basis of the sentence they see. Here is a revision that captures the more probable meaning:

> Rebecca finds the class in nematodes as interesting as Ned does.

Sometimes it is impossible for readers even to guess what meaning the writer intended:

FAULTY: Dickens read Shakespeare as much as Samuel Johnson.

To avoid confusing readers, you must spell out precisely what you mean:

CORRECTED: Dickens read Shakespeare as much as Samuel Johnson did.

24h
acs

3 Making Comparisons Logical

Illogical comparisons relate things that are not in the same class, things that are really not comparable:

FAULTY: The British today have an attitude similar to us in America.

The trouble with this sentence is that it compares an attitude with people ("us in America"). The sentence should compare one attitude with another:

CORRECTED: The British attitude today is similar to the American attitude.

OR: The British today have an attitude that is similar to the one we Americans have.

In comparing one item with others in the same class, you should use the word *other* after *any:*

> Chicago is larger than any other city in Illinois.

If you were to omit the *other,* you would be implying that Chicago is larger than itself, since it too is a city in Illinois.

Exercise 4

Find and correct all faulty comparisons in the following passage.

EXAMPLE: The first sentence contains the incomplete comparison *men do more interrupting*. You could correct this comparison by adding *than women* to the end of the sentence.

Researchers have found that in conversations men do more interrupting. In fact, one study found men responsible for 96 percent of the total number of interruptions. Interruptions generally irritate female speakers as much, if not more than, forms of inattention do. Indeed, interrupting is one of the worse, if not the worst trait, of men's linguistic behavior.

Most researchers say that men interrupt others because they see language as competition. These researchers add that the conversational habits of the men you know are probably not significantly different from other men. Why might men see language as competition? Some researchers suggest that the reason lies in the hierarchies that boys establish among themselves in their play. One boy is the leader, and he has more authority. The others find a place lower in the hierarchy and try to work their way up the hierarchy. Other researchers suggest that men's conversational competitiveness comes from their being socialized to act in a "macho" manner. Macho men see life as a challenge to be conquered more than women. Whatever the correct explanation is, most researchers believe that interrupting is more harmful than any aspect of men's speech.

25

W hich present-tense form of *to explore* would you use to fill the gap in the following sentence, *explores* or *explore*?

> The professor, along with several research assistants, _____ literacy in America.

The correct form is *explores.*

This question addresses issues of **subject-verb agreement.** In Standard Edited English (see Chapter 14), subjects agree with verbs in person and number. The word *person* refers to a three-part distinction: First person refers to the writer or writers, second person refers to the one or ones written to, and third person refers to the one or ones written about. The word *number* refers to a two-part distinction: Subjects and verbs can be either singular or plural.

Many people master most conventions of subject-verb agreement as children. If they have a problem, it is usually with one or more of several clearly defined sets of conventions. We will first review some general conventions of subject-verb agreement and then move on to some sets of conventions that occasionally pose challenges for writers. It might be helpful to remind yourself that an *s* or *es* at the end of most nouns (not those such as *children* and *oxen*) means that the noun is plural *(books, quizzes)* but that an *s* or *es* at the end of a verb usually means that the verb is singular *(he dreams, she wishes).*

25a

Some General Conventions of Subject-Verb Agreement

In this section, we refer to first person, second person, and third person only when necessary. Usually, we need to indicate only whether a noun or verb is singular or plural.

1 Agreement with a Singular Subject

You should pair singular subjects with singular verbs.

	With Forms of a Transitive Verb	**With Forms of *To Be***
FIRST PERSON:	subject verb I invent stories.	subject verb I am on a tour.
SECOND PERSON:	subject verb You, Paul, invent new machines.	subject verb You, Paul, are on the cutting edge.
THIRD PERSON:	subject verb He invents rationalizations.	subject verb He is on the brink.

2 Agreement with a Plural Subject

You should pair plural subjects with plural verbs.

	With Forms of a Transitive Verb	**With Forms of *To Be***
FIRST PERSON:	subject verb We write truths.	subject verb We are on the level.
SECOND PERSON:	subject verb You, Leo and Molly, write myths.	subject verb You, Leo and Molly, are on the lookout.
THIRD PERSON:	subject verb They write train schedules.	subject verb They are on the go.

3 Agreement Between a Linking Verb and a Subject

When you write sentences that move from a subject through a linking verb to a predicate noun, the verb should agree with the subject, even when the subject and predicate noun differ in number. The subject is the noun that appears before the verb:

subject   verb

These eyes are the problem.

subject   verb

The problem is these eyes.

4 Agreement with a Phrase as Subject

Different kinds of phrases—for instance, infinitive phrases and gerund phrases—can serve as nouns and therefore as subjects of sentences. When they do, they take a singular verb:

subject   verb

To learn that list of terms is difficult.

But note that a compound subject made up of two or more phrases takes a plural verb:

subject   subject   verb

Learning the list and teaching it to others are our goals.

5 Agreement with a Noun Clause as Subject

When noun clauses are subjects, they take singular verbs, even if they are related by a linking verb to a predicate noun that is plural:

subject   verb   predicate noun

What I want is my two front teeth.

But note that a compound subject made up of two or more noun clauses takes a plural verb:

subject   subject   .   verb

That they cheated and that they did so intentionally are not clearly established.

25a
sva

Exercise 1

Select the correct form in parentheses and write it on the blank line.

EXAMPLE: *continue* Many educators (continues, continue) to argue about essentials in education.

1. _____ Recently, some educators (has, have) suggested that our schools ought to focus on cultural literacy.

2. _____ In their opinion, cultural literacy (is, are) a matter of knowing facts about culture.

3. _____ Their main concern (is, are) aspects of European and American culture.

4. _____ According to them, learning facts such as what Fabian tactics are (is, are) essential.

5. _____ What will happen to Americans without such knowledge (is, are) that they will not be able to bring the proper information to bear on what they read.

6. _____ These educators claim that reading about a Faustian bargain without knowing who Faust was (is, are) a frustrating and shallow experience.

7. _____ Such claims (has, have) been praised by many people.

8. _____ But praise (is, are) not the only response that these claims elicit.

9. _____ Some scholars are concerned about which people (gets, get) to select the list of facts.

10. _____ What kinds of knowledge are left out of school programs (is, are) another matter of concern.

25b
sva

25b

Challenges in Subject-Verb Agreement Posed by Compound Subjects

The conventions covered in this section sometimes pose challenges caused by elements that are or appear to be compound subjects.

1 Agreement with Subjects Linked by *And*

If two or more subjects are linked by *and,* they are considered plural, and they take a plural verb. This is true even when one or both of the subjects are singular:

compound subject   verb

McCoy and Scotty are in the transporter room.

compound subject   verb

Spock and some other officers are in a class in logic.

compound subject   verb

The two ensigns and three ambassadors are in trouble.

2 Agreement with a Compound Subject with a
Part Implied

Sometimes you might write a subject that has two or more parts
but that leaves a word or two implied: *British and American English.*
This is actually a shortened form of *British English and American
English;* two different things are being named. If you were to use
British and American English as a subject, you should make the verb
plural:

compound subject   verb

British and American English are not totally different.

25b
svo

3 Agreement with a Compound Subject with
Parts That Refer to the Same Person or Thing

Sometimes you might choose to write sentences such as the
following:

compound subject   verb

My friend and lover has good taste.

Is the singular verb *has* correct? It is if *friend* and *lover* both refer to
the same person. If they do not refer to the same person, the verb
should be plural, and usually another *my* would appear, just before
lover:

My friend and my lover have good taste.

4 Agreement with a Compound Subject
Introduced with *Each* or *Every*

When you use *each* or *every* before a compound subject, make
the verb singular:

compound subject   verb

Each sophomore and junior helps with the blood drive.

In this case, a convention of subject-verb agreement seems illogical. After all, anyone who reads the example about the blood drive knows that the subject almost certainly refers to many sophomores and juniors. But the convention rests on thinking of *each* as presenting each sophomore and junior individually to readers' attention. The same is true of *every*.

5 **Agreement with a Compound Subject That Includes a Positive and a Negative Construction**

When you use compound subjects that are presented in a positive construction and in a negative construction, make the verb agree in number with the positive construction. If that construction is singular, the verb should be singular:

positive construction   negative construction

The logic of your claims, not your whines for mercy,
verb

leads us to grant your petition.

If the positive construction is plural, the verb should be plural:

positive construction   negative construction

Your whines for mercy, not the logic of your claims,
verb

lead us to grant your petition.

6 **Agreement with Subjects Linked with Correlative Conjunctions or with *Or***

When you form compound subjects using *or* or the correlative conjunctions *either . . . or, neither . . . nor,* or *not only . . . but also,* you will have to examine the subjects carefully before deciding what verb form to use. If both subjects are singular, the verb should be singular:

compound subject   verb

Either Hoover or Smiley is responsible for that.

If both subjects are plural, the verb should be plural:

compound subject

Not only the political dissidents but also the freedom fighters
verb

are serious political threats.

If one subject is singular and the other is plural, the verb should agree with the subject it is nearer to:

compound subject   verb

Neither Smiley nor the two special agents were at the checkpoint.

Or

compound subject   verb

Neither the two special agents nor Smiley was at the checkpoint.

Both of these last two examples are correct, but most writers would regard the first one as more stylistically pleasing.

If you use *or* or *nor* to link compound subjects with parts that are singular but that differ in person, you should make the verb agree with the person of the subject it is nearer to:

compound   compound
   subject   verb   subject verb

She or I am in charge here.   I or she is in charge here.

Exercise 2

In each of the following sentences, use the descriptions in brackets to select the verb form appropriate for the sentence; write that form on the blank line.

EXAMPLE: *are*   Students in urban school districts and students in rural school districts [form of *to be* in the present tense] responsible for taking a cultural literacy test.

1. _____ A teacher who proctors the test and several students [form of *to devote* in the present tense] three consecutive afternoons to the test.

2. _____ The teacher and proctor [form of *to watch* in the present tense] the students as they write the test.

3. _____ Both sacred and profane works of art [form of *to be* in the present tense] the subjects for questions.

4. _____ Each hero of Greek mythology and great American sports figure [form of *to appear* in the present tense] on the test.

5. _____ For example, Aphrodite and Babe Ruth [form of *to be* in the present tense] the subjects of questions.

6. _____ A question about *fin de siècle,* not the questions about the Marquis de Sade, usually [form of *to bore* in the present tense] many students.

25b

SVG

7. _____ But the questions about grammar, not the question on Eros, really [form of *to intrigue* in the present tense] them.

8. _____ Either the name *Medusa* or a reference to a kind of snail [form of *to appear* in the present tense] on every test.

9. _____ Either the name *Werner Heisenberg* or various references to Albert Einstein [form of *to appear* in the present tense] relatively often.

10. _____ Neither terms such as *expletive* nor references to philosophies such as nihilism ever [form of *to appear* in the present tense] on the test.

25c

Challenges in Subject-Verb Agreement Posed by Uncertainties About What the Subject Is

Another set of challenges in subject-verb agreement is posed by sentences for which it can be difficult to decide what the subject is.

1 Agreement with a Modified Noun as the Subject

Sometimes writers make errors in subject-verb agreement when they use long noun phrases as subjects. This is especially true if those noun phrases include nouns that differ in number from the head noun. Here is an example of such an error from one of our students:

> The gaining of a better understanding of the processes of communication in our own language and culture are another social benefit of bilingualism.

The head noun of the subject noun phrase is *gaining.* But since a plural noun, *processes,* appears after *gaining,* the student was apparently tempted to make the verb plural *(are).* However, *gaining* is singular, and therefore the verb should be singular:

> The gaining of a better understanding of the processes of communication in our own language and culture is another social benefit of bilingualism.

If the head noun had been plural, the plural verb would have been correct.

2 Agreement with a Subject Followed by an Additive Phrase

You might sometimes choose to write subjects to which you add phrases introduced by such elements as these:

accompanied by	except	no less than
along with	in addition to	together with
as well as	like	with

Adding such a phrase to a subject can make a singular subject seem plural. But adding such a phrase does not make the subject compound; the phrase modifies the subject. Therefore, if your subject is singular, the verb must be singular, even if several plural nouns appear in the modifying phrase:

> simple subject
>
> The admiral, accompanied by dozens of his cousins and aunts,
>
> verb
>
> sings about the Queen's Navy.

Of course, if you were to change this sentence into one with a compound subject, most simply by substituting *and* for *accompanied by,* then the verb must be plural:

> compound subject   verb
>
> The admiral and dozens of his cousins and aunts sing about the Queen's Navy.

25c
sva

3 Agreement with a Subject in a Question

In many questions (not those such as *They did?*), a part of the verb phrase appears before the subject. If the subject is singular, the first part of the verb phrase should also be singular:

> first part of
> the verb phrase   subject
>
> Does our distinguished panelist wish to respond?

If the subject is plural, the first part of the verb phrase should also be plural:

> first part of
> the verb phrase   subject
>
> Do our distinguished panelists wish to respond?

Keep in mind that since modal verbs do not show distinctions in number, the guidelines given above do not apply to them:

modal verb   subject
Might our distinguished panelist wish to respond?

modal verb   subject
Might our distinguished panelists wish to respond?

4 Agreement Between an Inverted Verb and a Subject

In some sentences with an adverb at the beginning, the verb precedes the subject, but it must still agree with the subject in number:

verb   subject
Here comes old Saint Nicholas.

verb   subject
Here come all his elves.

And whenever you write sentences with a phrase at the beginning, make the verb agree with the subject, not with part of the phrase:

verb   subject
In the box were the two missing pieces.

5 Agreement with a Subject in a Sentence with an Expletive

Expletives can pose some challenges in subject-verb agreement, primarily because they bump the subject to a position after the verb. When you use the expletive *there,* you should locate the subject in order to decide whether the verb ought to be singular or plural. If the subject is singular, make the verb singular:

verb   subject
There is a letter for you.

If the subject is plural, make the verb plural:

verb   subject
There are some letters for you.

When *it* functions as an expletive, it does not pose as many challenges for subject-verb agreement as *there* does. You should make the verb that follows *it* singular, even if the subject is plural:

verb   subject

It is the credit control officers at the door.

Exercise 3

In the following sentences, correct all errors in subject-verb agreement.

> EXAMPLE: The vice principal in charge of discipline on the top two floors in the west and east wings have decided to take the cultural-literacy test along with the students. [The verb phrase should be the singular *has decided,* which agrees with the singular subject, *vice principal.*]

1. The vice principal, together with his three security officers, agree to take the test with the students.

2. Into the room they stride.

3. Suddenly there is smirks and giggles everywhere.

4. One student sitting next to six of the more troublesome students in the school over the last two years sneer that the vice principal should know all about pride and prejudice.

5. A wide range of comments and jokes follow.

6. "He will surely know what *draconian* means," a student hiding behind two football players sneer.

7. The vice principal, along with the security officers, try to ignore the jokes.

8. "There is no reason to get angry," he repeats to himself.

9. "How hard can these questions be, anyway?" he wonders.

10. But upon opening his test booklet, he finds that he knows nothing at all about the phrase "sweetness and light."

25d

Challenges in Subject-Verb Agreement Posed by Uncertainties About Whether the Subject Is Singular or Plural

The last set of challenges in subject-verb agreement involves difficulties in deciding whether particular subjects are singular or plural.

1 Agreement with Words Such as *Who,*
Which, or *That*

Some writers have trouble with agreement in sentences such as
this:

We supported the proposals that were defeated.

The problem is deciding whether the relative pronoun *(that)* should
be considered singular or plural. It should be considered singular if its
antecedent is singular and plural if its antecedent is plural. Since the
antecedent of *that* is the plural *proposals, that* should be treated as a
plural. If the antecedent of *that* is *proposal,* then *that* should be treated
as singular:

We supported the proposal that was defeated.

A special problem centers on why the verb in the adjective clause
in the first sentence below is plural and why the verb in the adjective
clause in the second sentence below is singular:

She is one of those actresses who do research.

She is the only one of those actresses who does research.

The verb in the first adjective clause is plural *(do)* since the antecedent
of the relative pronoun *who* is the plural *actresses.* The easiest way to
see why the verb in the second relative clause is singular *(does)* is to
notice that the sentence claims that she is the only one doing research.
You could omit "of the actresses" and not change the main part of the
message:

She is the only one who does research.

In this case, *one* is considered the antecedent of *who,* and since *one* is
singular, the verb in the adjective clause is singular.

2 Agreement with an Indefinite Pronoun

Some indefinite pronouns—*both, few, many, others, several*—
always take a plural verb:

subject verb   subject verb

Both are difficult.   Few pass them.

But many indefinite pronouns, even though they may bring to
mind several people or things, take singular verbs. Consider *everybody,*

for example. When you write a sentence such as *Everybody was at the party,* you are probably thinking of several people. But the convention is to use a singular verb. One justification for this convention is the claim that words such as *everybody* present each member of a set individually to readers. Here are some additional indefinite pronouns that take a singular verb:

another	each	nobody	something
anybody	everybody	one	whatever
anyone	everyone	somebody	whichever
anything	everything	someone	whoever

3 Agreement with *None*

Many grammarians treat *none* as meaning "not one." In most cases, therefore, *none* should be considered singular:

subject   verb

None of us is likely to escape.

However, if you wish to use *none* to mean "all are not," then you should make it agree with a plural verb:

subject   verb

None of the secretaries are happy about the cuts in pay.

4 Agreement with Words Such as *All* or *Some*

You should treat words such as *all, any, half, more, most, the rest,* and *some* as singular if they refer to something that cannot be counted:

subject   verb

The rest of the sludge is still on the beaches.

And you should treat these words as plural if they refer to more than one of something that can be counted:

subject   verb

The rest of the workers are covered with oil.

5 Agreement with a Collective Noun

When you use a collective noun as a subject and want readers to see the group as a totality, use a singular verb:

<u>   subject   verb </u>

The majority of that department is socialist.

When you want readers to focus not on the group as a totality but on individual members of the group, then you should use a plural verb:

<u>   subject   verb </u>

The majority of department members are specialists in poetry.

If such sentences seem awkward to you, you can revise them:

<u>   subject   verb </u>

Most members of the department are specialists in poetry.

6 Agreement with a Word or Phrase Indicating a Fixed Quantity

You should treat words and phrases indicating a quantity or an amount of something as you do collective nouns. If you want your readers to see the amount as a totality, use a singular verb:

<u> subject   verb </u>

Three miles is too far to sprint.

On the other hand, if you want your readers to focus on each unit in the amount, use a plural verb:

<u>   subject   verb </u>

Three different miles in that race are especially challenging.

You may treat percentages and fractions in the same way. Usually, however, you will probably find it most appropriate to treat percentages as plural:

<u>   subject   verb </u>

Only 40 percent of the rugby team are abstract thinkers.

And you will usually find it most appropriate to treat fractions as singular:

<u>   subject   verb </u>

One-tenth of the book was clear to us.

25d
sva

7 Agreement with References to Processes of Addition, Multiplication, Subtraction, and Division

When you refer to a process of addition or multiplication in a subject, you can make the verb either singular or plural:

subject	verb		subject	verb

Three plus three is six.   Or   Three plus three are six.

subject	verb		subject	verb

Three times three is nine.   Or   Three times three are nine.

The singular verbs are more customary in such sentences.

When you refer to a process of subtraction or division, you should make the verb singular:

subject	verb

Three minus one is two.

subject	verb

Nine divided by three is three.

8 Agreement with Nouns Such as *Statistics*

Many nouns end in s and can give the impression of being plural: *athletics, aerobics, hysterics, politics, statistics.* However, you can treat these words either as singulars or as plurals. For example, you can use *statistics* to refer to several different (hence plural) statistics:

subject	verb

Five different statistics are important in these calculations.

Or you can use *statistics* to refer to one thing:

subject	verb

Statistics is a course of utmost significance.

9 Agreement with Nouns Such as *Linguistics*

Other nouns that end in s and therefore give the impression of being plural, such as *linguistics, mathematics, news,* and *shingles* (the disease), take a singular verb:

subject	verb

Shingles sometimes has serious side effects.

25d
sva

10 Agreement with Nouns Such as *Pajamas*

Some nouns end in *s* but refer to only one thing: *eyeglasses, jeans, pajamas, pants.* Even though these refer to only one thing, they agree with a plural verb:

subject   verb

Her pajamas are plaid.

subject   verb

The pants he wore were flood pants, we agreed.

11 Agreement with *A Number Of* or *The Number Of*

When you use the phrase *a number of* as part of a subject, make it agree with a plural verb:

subject   verb

A number of philosophers are skeptical.

When you use the phrase *the number of* as part of a subject, make it agree with a singular verb:

subject   verb

The number of eagles is encouraging.

12 Agreement with References to Words, Phrases, and Titles

Occasionally, the subjects of your sentences may be words used as words, phrases used as phrases, and the titles of songs, poems, stories, essays, novels, and the like. In such cases, use a singular verb:

subject verb

Children has an interesting history.

subject   verb

On tenterhooks never refers to camping equipment.

subject verb

The Frogs is their favorite play.

13 Agreement with Nouns Such as *Media* and *Criteria*

Some words that have come into English from other languages, primarily Latin, appear regularly in both their singular and plural forms:

Singular	Plural
bacterium	bacteria
criterion	criteria
curriculum	curricula or curriculums
datum	data
erratum	errata
medium	media or mediums
memorandum	memoranda or memorandums
phenomenon	phenomena or phenomenons
stratum	strata

Not all writers have both the singular and the plural forms of all of these words in their working vocabularies. Some, for instance, never use the word *datum*.

We recommend that in formal writing contexts you make the singular forms listed above agree with singular verbs and the plural forms agree with plural verbs:

subject   verb
The criterion was neatness.

subject   verb
The criteria were neatness and timeliness.

As you do so, you show your readers that you are aware of the formality of the situation. You can also signal your awareness of the formality of the situation by using the Latinate plural (such as *memoranda*) if a word has two plural forms.

At the same time, informal situations do not always call for such preciseness. Would the faulty agreement in *The data shows the advantages of oat bran* set off an alarm in a letter from you to your parents? In the cases of most families, the technically correct *The data show* would seem excessively formal and out of place in such writing.

Exercise 4

Feel free to judge whether the following statements are true or false, but before doing so, underline the verb in parentheses that is correct.

EXAMPLE: The Gettysburg Address was one of those speeches that (was, <u>were</u>) shorter than people expected.

1. The Pax Romana was the only one of those diseases of the Middle Ages that (was, were) not fatal.

2. Cybernetics (is, are) the study of how information flows and is managed, in humans and machines.

3. Everyone in Pamplona (knows, know) what an *aficionado* is.

4. The number of quarks seen in laboratories (is, are) large.

5. Five trillion miles (is, are) how far light can travel in a year.

6. *Porgy and Bess* (is, are) an opera from the 1890s.

7. The Ides of March (was, were) on March 15 on the ancient Roman calendar.

8. The phenomenon of mitosis (produces, produce) four cells from one.

9. "Bread and circuses" (refers, refer) to government practices that provide short-term solutions to public problems.

10. A nuclear family (is, are) a family living in the atomic age.

11. A number of critics (considers, consider) 1922 the annus mirabilis of modern literature.

12. None of the utterances by the oracle at Delphi (was, were) easy to interpret.

13. The biological family of hominids (includes, include) the species *Homo sapiens.*

14. "The World Is Too Much with Us" is one of those poems that (laments, lament) our attachment to material things.

15. Several of the paintings in the Sistine Chapel (is, are) frescoes.

26

U S I N G   V E R B

F O R M S

C O R R E C T L Y

W hat would you say is wrong with the following sentence, which Professor Mina Shaughnessy once found in some student writing?

> Then the good father came along and feels he should share the experience.

This sentence contains an unjustified shift in verb tenses, from the past tense *came* to the present tense *feels.*

This shift would probably not cause many readers to lose the message of the sentence. But it might cause them to lose some respect for the writer, making them less willing to trust the writer's perspective.

26a

Problems with Shifts in Tenses

1 Shifts in Tenses Within Individual Sentences

If sentences include more than one verb, those verbs can be in whatever tense the meaning of the sentence requires:

> It looks as if young Herbert will finish writing his first book a few years after his father finished writing his masterpiece.

The first verb, *looks,* is in the present tense since it describes how something appears at the time the sentence was written. The second verb, *will finish,* is in the future tense since it describes a process that is not complete until some time after the sentence was written. The third verb, *finished,* is in the past tense since it describes a process that was completed before the sentence was written. The meaning of this sentence justifies the switch from the present to the future and then to the past tense.

Now consider a sentence from one of our students:

> Many authors support their cause with the same passages but interpreted the passages differently.

The verbs shift from the present tense *(support)* to the past tense *(interpreted).* And there is no good reason for the shift. You should be most on guard for such unjustified shifts of tenses in the following three kinds of situations.

a. Verb Tenses in Complex Sentences

In complex sentences, the tense of the verb in the subordinate clause depends on the tense of the verb in the independent clause.

If the verb in the independent clause is in the present tense, you have several choices for the tense of the verb in the subordinate clause:

1. The present tense to describe a process that occurs at the same time as the process described by the verb in the independent clause:

   independent clause   subordinate clause
   They *escape* to other worlds when they *read* science fiction.

2. The past tense to describe a process that was completed by the time of the process described by the verb in the independent clause:

   independent clause   subordinate clause
   They *are* certain that they *misplaced* their copies of *Dune.*

3. The present perfect tense to describe a process that extends from a point in the past to the time of the process described by the verb in the independent clause:

   independent clause   subordinate clause
   They *claim* that they *have subdued* giant sandworms.

26a
vf

4. The future tense to describe a process that will occur after the process described by the verb in the independent clause:

    independent clause   subordinate clause
They *conserve* water now so that they *will be* ready for the rigors of the desert planet.

If the verb in the independent clause is in the past tense, the verb in the subordinate clause can be in the following tenses:

1. The present tense to describe a general truth:

    independent clause   subordinate clause
They *found* that reading science fiction *is* addicting.

2. The past tense to describe a process that took place at about the same time in the past as the process described by the verb in the independent clause:

    independent clause   subordinate clause
Paul *felt* no fear when he *walked* on the desert.

3. The past perfect tense to describe a process that took place further in the past than the process described by the verb in the independent clause:

    independent clause   subordinate clause
Then the emperor's squadrons *realized* that they *had made* a critical error in judgment the day before.

If the verb in the independent clause is in the present perfect or the past perfect tense, the verb in the subordinate clause will usually be in the past tense:

    independent clause   subordinate clause
This book *has increased* in value since I *bought* it.

    independent clause   subordinate clause
The collectors *had left* before I *reached* the show.

If the verb in the independent clause is in the future tense, the verb in the subordinate clause can be in the following tenses:

1. The present tense to describe a process that occurs at the same time as the process described by the verb in the independent clause:

    independent clause   subordinate clause
They *will read* all night if they *buy* that book.

26a vf

2. The past tense to describe a process that is completed by the time of the process described by the verb in the independent clause:

<table>
<tr><td>independent clause</td><td>subordinate clause</td></tr>
</table>

They *will lose* the city since they *forgot* to guard the mountain passes.

3. The present perfect tense to describe a process that will occur in the future but before the process described by the verb in the independent clause:

<table>
<tr><td>independent clause</td><td>subordinate clause</td></tr>
</table>

They *will feel* more secure when they *have established* an overall plan of defense.

Finally, if the verb in the independent clause is in the future perfect tense, the verb in the subordinate clause usually will be in the present or the present perfect tense:

<table>
<tr><td>subordinate clause</td><td>independent clause</td></tr>
</table>

Before Paul *turns* thirty, his troops *will have conquered* many worlds.

<table>
<tr><td>subordinate clause</td><td>independent clause</td></tr>
</table>

Before the wars *have ceased*, millions of people *will have died*.

26a
vf

Exercise 1

On the blank line, write a form of the verb in parentheses that is in an appropriate tense. In some cases, two or three forms are possible.

EXAMPLE: Linda reads science fiction whenever she _____ (to find) time.

Linda reads science fiction whenever she finds time.

1. Linda is certain that she _____ (to lose) her copy of *Heretics of Dune* two weeks ago.

2. She feels that she _____ (to lose) one of her main sources of meaning.

3. Just last week she lamented that a month ago she _____ (to lose) her copy of *Dune Messiah*.

4. Linda will read a book from cover to cover unless she _____ (to lose) it.

5. At this rate, before Linda graduates from college in two years, she _____ (to lose) dozens of books.

b. Verb Tenses in Indirect Discourse

When you report what others have said or written, you must decide whether to use direct quotations or indirect discourse. With direct quotations, you quote other people's words exactly, enclose them in quotation marks, and often add a tag to indicate the source of the words:

"I can predict the future," the emperor claimed.

With indirect discourse, you report what others have said or written, but you do so without quotation marks and with a different kind of indication of the source of the words:

The emperor claimed that he could predict the future.

As you shift from direct quotations to indirect discourse, you usually also have to shift verb tenses. If the verb in a quotation is in the present tense, the verb in indirect discourse will usually be in the past tense:

QUOTATION: "I *rule* the universe," he claimed.

INDIRECT DISCOURSE: He claimed that he *ruled* the universe.

If the verb in a quotation is in the past tense, the present perfect tense, or the past perfect tense, the verb in indirect discourse should be in the past perfect tense:

QUOTATION: "I *ruled* the universe," he boasted.

INDIRECT DISCOURSE: He boasted that he *had ruled* the universe.

QUOTATION: "I *have commanded* armies," he announced.

INDIRECT DISCOURSE: He announced that he *had commanded* armies.

QUOTATION: "I *had foreseen* the attack," he said.

INDIRECT DISCOURSE: He said that he *had foreseen* the attack.

Finally, if the verb in a quotation is in the future tense, the verb phrase in indirect discourse should be *would* plus the base form of the verb:

QUOTATION: "I *will detect* every rebellious thought," he asserted.

INDIRECT DISCOURSE: He asserted that he *would detect* every rebellious thought.

26a
vf

ESL Consideration

STATEMENTS IN INDIRECT DISCOURSE

To change a direct quotation to a statement in indirect discourse:

1. Change the point of view of the quotation from first person *(I)* to third person *(he, she, it, they)*.
2. Introduce the statement in indirect discourse with the conjunction *that*.
3. Make sure the speaker's words are introduced with a phrase such as *he said that . . ., she stated that . . .,* or *they argued that. . . .*
4. Many verbs in quotations are in the present tense. Change the tense from present to past. If the quotation contains modals, change *will* to *would, may* to *might* or *could, can* to *could, must* to *had to,* and *shall* to *would.*

DIRECT QUOTATION: Professor Zucker, my favorite history professor, once said, "I shall never fully understand Russian history until I experience a winter in Moscow."

INDIRECT QUOTATION: Professor Zucker, my favorite history professor, once said that he would never fully understand Russian history until he had experienced a winter in Moscow.

If the verbs in the quotation are in the past tense, past perfect tense, or future tense, see page 385.

26a
vf

Exercise 2

Rewrite each of the following quotations in the form of indirect discourse.

EXAMPLE: "In those days I read science fiction as a means of escaping reality," the fugitive said.

The fugitive said that in those days he had read science fiction as a means of escaping reality.

1. "I once preferred to read science fiction," Bartleby added.
2. "I too have tried to escape present realities," Proust lamented.
3. "I cannot see using science fiction as an escape," Sappho said.
4. "I had always thought that science fiction was for imagining possible worlds," Kant objected.
5. "At least I will always use it in that way," he added.

c. Shifts in Tenses Between a Verb and One or More Verbals

The verbals—infinitives, gerunds, and participles—can show distinctions in tense. When you write a sentence that includes both a verb and a verbal, you will have to ask how the time of the process described by the verbal relates to the time of the process described by the verb.

If the process described by the verbal occurs at the same time as or later than the process described by the verb, you should use the present tense for the verbal:

> They chose to buy a time machine. [The choosing and the buying occurred at the same time.]

> They want to buy a time machine. [The buying will occur after the wanting began.]

If the process described by the verbal occurs or should have occurred earlier than the process described by the verb, you should use the perfect form of the verbal:

> They were sorry to have failed. [The failing occurred before the being sorry.]

Exercise 3

Fill in the blank line in each of the following sentences with the correct form of the element described in parentheses.

> **EXAMPLE:** _____ (participial form of the verb *hear*) about C. S. Lewis last year, the reading group recently decided to read *The Chronicles of Narnia*.
>
> Having heard about C. S. Lewis last year, the reading group recently decided to read *The Chronicles of Narnia*.

1. _____ (participial form of the verb *see*) *The Lion, the Witch, and the Wardrobe* on public television a week earlier, they decided to read all the books in the series.

2. But some members of the group were not able _____ (infinitive form of the verb *read*) any of the sections about the White Witch.

3. _____ (participial form of the verb *hear*) much earlier that this witch could turn creatures into stone, they became afraid to read any pages containing references to her.

4. After several weeks elapsed, the other members of the group became impatient because by then they expected _____ (infinitive form of the verb *read*) five of the books in the series.

5. "How can you hope _____ (infinitive form of the verb *learn*) about Aslan if you cannot overcome your fear of the White Witch?" they asked the stalled readers.

26a
vf

ESL Consideration

INFINITIVE VS. GERUND AS DIRECT OBJECT OF VERBS

Use an *infinitive* as the direct object to signify that something is hypothetical, unfulfilled, or anticipated:

Many of my friends hope *to study* in an American university.

In contrast, use a *gerund* as the direct object to indicate that something is real, fulfilled, or experienced:

Frankly, I enjoy *studying* for tests.

2 Shifts in Tenses Within Paragraphs

In many paragraphs, most or all of the verbs are in the same tense. However, it is easy to find paragraphs in which the verbs shift from one tense to another. Here is an example from E. B. White's "Walden":

26a
vf

> Stay with me on 62 and it will take you into Concord. As I say, it was a delicious evening. The snake had come forth to die in a bloody S on the highway, the wheel upon its head, its bowels flat now and exposed. The turtle had come up too to cross the road and die in the attempt, its hard shell smashed under the rubber blow, its intestinal yearning (for the other side of the road) forever squashed. There was a sign by the wayside which announced that the road had a "cotton surface." You wouldn't know what that is, but neither, for that matter, did I. There is a cryptic ingredient in many of our modern improvements—we are awed and pleased without knowing quite what we are enjoying. It is something to be traveling on a road with a cotton surface.

Several different verb tenses appear here, but we will focus on just three—the future, the past perfect, and the present. Are these tenses justified? Yes. White uses the future tense (as in *will take*) to describe potential processes in the future. He uses the past perfect tense (as in *had come*) to describe actions completed before the time in the past when he drove on that road. And he uses the present tense (as in *is*) to state a general truth.

So you may vary verb tenses within a paragraph. But you should do so as White does—with good reason. It is difficult to imagine any valid justification for the tense shifts in the following:

> I drive to Parking Lot Q about the same time as always. As I neared my assigned spot, I notice that someone had placed a sign at the head of my spot. The writing on the sign was hard to decipher; the

letters looked like runes. But after a few minutes I can make out
what it said: "Reserved for Hobbits."

Exercise 4

Write a paragraph in which all the verbs are in the same tense. Be prepared to explain why all the verbs should be in that tense. Then write a
paragraph in which you shift from one verb tense to at least two others.
Again, be prepared to justify those shifts.

Problems with Shifts in Voice

When you write sentences that include more than one clause, you will
sometimes need to shift between active and passive verbs. Sometimes
the reason will be that you do not know who performed one action but
do know who performed another:

                  passive verb   active verb

Although the maps had been altered, Frodo still found the
route.

And sometimes the reason will be that you want to keep the subjects in
both clauses identical in order to have a consistent focal point from
one clause to the next:

     subject active verb   subject   passive verb

Gandalf spoke persuasively, and therefore he was elected by
the council.

When writers shift between active and passive verbs for no good
reason, however, they can confuse their readers:

     subject active verb   subject   passive verb

Gandalf thought deeply, and later a decision was made.

The main problem with such a sentence is that readers cannot be
certain who made the decision. Of course, the sentence can be revised
as follows:

Gandalf thought deeply, and later a decision was made by him.

This sentence reveals who made the decision, but it is difficult to imagine how anyone could justify switching from the active to the passive verb when it is clear that Gandalf did both the thinking and the
deciding.

ESL Consideration

FAULTY PASSIVE CONSTRUCTION

Sometimes elements from active and passive structures are mixed, producing an ungrammatical construction:

My country has been studied its lack of modern technology for too many years.

My country is obviously the subject and the agent of this sentence, which means that it should be followed by an active verb form, yet it is followed by a passive form in the present perfect tense. Depending on the context, the sentence can be corrected either by replacing the past participle with a present participle, thus maintaining the active form, or by completely transforming the verb into a passive form:

ACTIVE: My country has been studying its lack of modern technology for too many years.

PASSIVE: My country's lack of modern technology has been studied for too many years.

26b
vf

Exercise 5

Suggest reasons for the shifting between active and passive verbs in each of the following cases. Are any of these shifts justified?

EXAMPLE: A student writes the following in a descriptive essay: "As we trudged up the side of Mount Doom, rumblings could be felt deep in the earth."

This shift could have resulted from haste or carelessness; it could have resulted because the writer had the rumblings so vividly in mind that he or she decided to make them the subject of the independent clause. Since this sentence is not clear about who felt the rumblings, it should be revised:

As we trudged up the side of Mount Doom, we could feel rumblings deep in the earth.

1. A high school student's report of portrayals of Native Americans in fiction includes the following sentence: "Scarlet Plume walked for three days toward the butte, and then a startling vision was seen."

2. A member of the women's volleyball team writes the following to a close friend: "Ever since the gym floor was cleaned, we have improved our defensive play."

3. A university president writes the following in a letter to alumni: "Two English professors made such an interesting proposal that they were asked to formulate a comprehensive plan for the university in the twenty-first century."

4. The head of a secretarial pool writes to a superior: "The cost-recovery diagram was prepared improperly, so next time I will do it myself."

5. A writer includes the following in a descriptive essay: "I crept onto the ledge where the waterfall could be clearly seen."

26c

Problems with Three Pairs of Verbs

The following pairs of verbs often pose problems for writers.

1 Set and Sit

The five forms of *set* are as follows: *set, set, set, sets, setting.* In almost all cases, *set* is a transitive verb (one exception: *The sun set over the lake.*). In the active voice, *set* appears with at least two nouns or pronouns, one to name who does the setting and another to name what that person sets:

The *high lord* set the *dagger* on the table.

Forms of *set* in the active voice are incorrect if they appear without a noun or pronoun naming what is set:

INCORRECT: They set around all day.

The five forms of *sit* are as follows: *sit, sat, sat, sits,* and *sitting. Sit* is an intransitive verb; it does not signal the transfer of action to an object:

The other lords sat respectfully.

Forms of *sit* are incorrect if they appear with a direct object:

INCORRECT: You should not sit *yourself* at the head of the table.

One exception to this generalization is as follows:

She sat the horse like a professional.

26c
vf

2 *Raise* and *Rise*

The five forms of *raise* are as follows: *raise, raised, raised, raises,* and *raising. Raise* is transitive; in the active voice, it appears with at least two nouns or pronouns, one to name who or what does the raising and another to name what that person or thing raises:

The *giant* raised a green *stone* above his head.

Forms of *raise* in the active voice are incorrect if they appear without a noun or pronoun naming what is raised:

INCORRECT: His evil followers raised to cheer.

The five forms of *rise* are as follows: *rise, rose, risen, rises,* and *rising. Rise* is an intransitive verb; it does not signal the transfer of action to an object:

The dust cloud rose ominously.

Forms of *rise* are incorrect if they appear with a direct object:

INCORRECT: They rose the *standard* high.

3 *Lay* and *Lie*

The five forms of *lay* are as follows: *lay, laid, laid, lays,* and *laying.* In almost all cases, *lay* is a transitive verb (one exception: *The little red hen lays best.*). In the active voice, *lay* appears with at least two nouns or pronouns, one to name who does the laying and another to name what that person lays:

They laid their *swords* aside yesterday.

Forms of *lay* in the active voice are incorrect if they appear without a direct object:

INCORRECT: Bodies are laying across the plain.

The five forms of *lie* are as follows: *lie, lay, lain, lies,* and *lying. Lie* is an intransitive verb; it does not signal the transfer of action to an object:

The Great Swamp lies near the Shattered Hills.

Forms of *lie* are incorrect if they appear with a direct object:

INCORRECT: They lie their *provisions* on the raft.

26c
vf

Exercise 6

Indicate whether the verb forms in each of the following sentences are correct or incorrect. If a form is incorrect, write in the correct form.

EXAMPLE: The verb in *They set nervously in the council hall* is incorrect; it should be *sat.*

1. After traveling all the way to Revelstone, Thomas Covenant laid down for a nap.

2. In the past few days his fever had risen slightly.

3. If he could set his problems aside for a while, he thought, he could start to recuperate.

4. But visions of Lord Foul raised before his eyes.

5. Lord Foul had set too great a burden on the people of the land.

6. He had lain the foundation for despair.

7. Signs of disease and woe lay across the countryside.

8. And no one would be able to raise the people's hopes.

9. Covenant decided that when his hosts visited him, he would sit down with them and describe what he had seen.

10. No one could spend time laying around Revelstone.

Problems with Shifts in Mood

When you write sentences that include more than one verb, you must be careful not to shift from one mood to another without good reason. Sometimes writers produce sentences with unjustified shifts from a verb in the subjunctive mood to a verb in the indicative mood, and vice versa:

subjunctive mood   indicative mood

It is imperative that he see the Andelainian Hills and saves them.

The last two verbs should both be in the subjunctive mood:

subjunctive mood   subjunctive mood

It is imperative that he see the Andelainian Hills and save them.

Probably the most common unjustified shift in mood is that between the imperative and the indicative. Often this shift occurs in directions:

imperative mood   indicative mood

Add an ironic twist to your story, and you should avoid smirking as you tell it.

In such cases, it is usually better to stick to the imperative mood:

imperative mood   imperative mood

Add an ironic twist to your story, and avoid smirking as you tell it.

Exercise 7

Correct all unjustified shifts in mood in the following passage.

> EXAMPLE: Covenant requested both that the beggar identify himself and that he stated his purpose.
>
> Covenant requested both that the beggar identify himself and that he state his purpose.

Thomas Covenant asked the beggar what he meant by saying "Be true." In fact, Covenant demanded that the beggar explain this saying and that he told what his name was.

"If I knew who you were," Covenant said, "I will be able to decide how to interpret what you say."

The beggar replied, "I have warned you once. Serve the Land, and you should flee from despair."

26e
vf

26e

Problems with Split Infinitives

A **split infinitive** has an adverbial modifier between the *to* and the base form of a verb: *to really win.* In the history of composition teaching, there is a long tradition of banning all split infinitives. One reason that some people have given for this is that infinitives in Latin are not split. The trouble with this reason is that the one-word infinitives of Latin cannot be split, whereas the two-word infinitives of English can be.

A better reason not to use split infinitives is that they can put a strain on readers. Once readers see a *to* and realize that it is part of an infinitive, not a preposition (as in *to the hills*), they must wait until they see the base form of the verb to process the whole infinitive. If the interrupting material is long, the wait can be irksome:

to fully and without any reservation whatsoever trust

Having to wait to connect *to* and *trust* can frustrate readers and lead them off the track in a sentence. In general, then, it is a good idea to be cautious about split infinitives, especially if the interrupting material is lengthy and hard to interpret.

But advising you to be cautious is not the same as recommending that you never use a split infinitive. Sometimes writers move adverbs before or after infinitives and in so doing call attention to the fact that they are not splitting the infinitive. "Look at me," they seem to say; "I haven't split this infinitive":

It is important clearly to see our common enemy.

Many experienced writers would prefer this version, especially if they had good reasons not to place *clearly* at the end:

It is important to clearly see our common enemy.

Moreover, with some interrupting adverbials, it is difficult to know where to express them if not between the two parts of an infinitive:

We hope to more than triple our force in the next two weeks.

To avoid this split infinitive, you would have to do some fairly extensive revising:

We hope to increase the size of our forces by more than 300 percent in the next two weeks.

Finally, sometimes you will have to use a split infinitive in order to avoid ambiguities:

This routine is designed to better prepare soldiers to fight.

Could you avoid the split infinitive *to better prepare* in this way?

This routine is designed better to prepare soldiers to fight.

No. In this sentence *better* modifies *designed,* not *to prepare.* How about the following?

This routine is designed to prepare better soldiers to fight.

This revision will not work either, since now *better* modifies *soldiers.* Here is still another possibility:

This routine is designed to prepare soldiers to fight better.

26e
vf

This version is almost acceptable, but it, too, changes the meaning, from better preparing to better fighting. In such cases, therefore, the split infinitive is the best option short of recasting the entire sentence.

Exercise 8

Find the split infinitives in the following passage, and then judge whether each is acceptable or not.

EXAMPLE: In the first sentence of the passage, *in the first place* comes between *to* and *depict.* This positioning is not necessary, and it puts a strain on readers. The words *in the first place* could precede *to depict.*

In *The Left Hand of Darkness,* Ursula le Guin tries to in the first place depict a world that is different from ours but not impossible for us to imagine. She calls this world "Winter" or "Gethen." The aspect of this world that many readers find most surprising is that all of its inhabitants are hermaphrodites. Le Guin tries to realistically portray beings who go through a short phase and then emerge with either their male or female hormones dominant. All these beings will be primarily male at some points in their lives and primarily female at other points. When Earthlings first encounter the Gethenians, the Earthlings are too accustomed to seeing sexuality in their own terms to really understand the Gethenians. After a while, however, the Earthlings begin to with some shock of recognition comprehend life on Gethen. They realize that everyone on Gethen can at some time give birth to a child. They also realize that they cannot ever see a Gethenian as only male or only female. This is more than some of them can endure. They try to consciously stop worrying about it, but they are too accustomed to seeing others as either male or female.

26e
vf

27

C areless writers can make many different kinds of errors in using pronouns. Not all of these errors have the same effects on readers. For instance, when writers produce sentences such as the following, they probably confuse some readers but amuse most of them with the use of *it*:

> You should not drive your students crazy with work on metaphors. Let our new program on figurative language do it.

When writers produce sentences such as the following, they leave their readers wondering which person *he* refers to:

> Socrates and Plato entered the cave in the morning, and later he emerged.

These errors are not equally serious. But you will not want to include any such errors in your prose unless you know you are doing so, have a reason for doing so, and are confident that your readers will recognize and accept that reason.

27a

Problems with Pronoun Case

The case of a pronoun is the form it takes to show how it relates to other parts of a sentence. Pronouns can appear in one of three cases: the subjective, objective, or possessive. Only the pronouns *I, we, he, she, they,* and *who* have different forms for all three cases. Others (such as *it*) have the same form for both the subjective and objective case *(it)* and a different form for the possessive case *(its).* (See **15b** for additional information on pronoun forms.)

Pronouns in the subjective case function within sentences most frequently as subjects or predicate nouns. For example, in referring to George Lakoff and Mark Johnson's work on metaphors, as we often do in this chapter, we could write the following:

subjective pronoun as subject

They examine metaphors about debate.

subjective pronoun as predicate noun

The person with the unassailable point is he.

Pronouns in the objective case function within sentences most often as direct objects, indirect objects, and objects of prepositions:

objective pronoun as direct object

Our evidence destroyed them.

objective pronoun as indirect object

He gave me a new plan of attack.

objective pronoun as the object of a preposition

I cannot win an argument with her.

Pronouns in the possessive case function within sentences most often to show relationships of possession or close association. They can appear wherever nouns can appear in sentences. In the following sentence, a possessive pronoun functions as the subject:

possessive pronoun as subject

Juanita's claims are defensible. Yours are not.

In the rest of this section, we examine situations in which writers sometimes make errors with pronoun case.

1 Pronouns as Compound Subjects or Compound Predicate Nouns

Pronouns serving as subjects or as predicate nouns should be in the subjective case. Sometimes writers mix subjective and objective forms of pronouns in producing a compound subject or compound predicate noun:

objective subjective
pronoun   pronoun

INCORRECT: Him and I investigated metaphors about time as money.

The members hoping to stop wasting the

objective subjective
pronoun   pronoun

committee's time are her and I.

Here are the correct sentence forms:

CORRECT: *He* and *I* investigated metaphors about time as money.

The ones hoping to stop wasting the committee's time are *she* and *I.*

Deciding on the case of pronouns serving as parts of a compound subject can be especially difficult if the compound subject appears in a question or subordinate clause:

subjective   objective
pronoun   pronoun

INCORRECT: Do you and them have time left?

subjective   objective
pronoun   pronoun

I think that she and him waste their time.

It may help in revising such sentences to read them through once with one part of the compound and then again with the other part of the compound. For example, take *Do you and them have time left?* You will first read *Do you have time left?* That is correct. Then you will read *Do them have time left?* This reading should alert you that the pronoun should be *they,* not *them:*

CORRECT: Do you and they have time left?

27d
pro

2 Pronouns as Compound Objects

When a sentence has a compound direct object, indirect object, or object of a preposition, some writers mix objective and subjective forms or use only subjective forms:

objective subjective
pronoun   pronoun

INCORRECT: The teacher lectured him and I about wasting time.

objective subjective
pronoun   pronoun

This invention will save them and I many days.

subjective subjective
pronoun   pronoun

You will need to save some time for he and I.

Objective pronouns are called for in all of the three incorrect sentences above:

CORRECT: The teacher lectured *him* and *me* about wasting time.

This invention will save *them* and *me* many days.

You will need to save some time for *him* and *me*.

If you have trouble making such corrections, try reading the sentence with only one part of the compound element in it at a time. Is *The specialists gave them and we a little time* correct? No. *The specialists gave them a little time* is correct. But *The specialists gave we a little time* should almost clang in your ears in its faultiness. The sentence should be revised as follows:

The specialists gave them and us a little time.

3 Pronouns as Subjects and Objects of Infinitives

When you use a pronoun as either a subject or an object of an infinitive, use the objective case of the pronoun:

subject of   direct object of
infinitive   the infinitive

We urged *him* to invest *them* in editorial work.

Sometimes writers use a subjective form of a pronoun in one of these slots, particularly the slot for the subject of the infinitive:

INCORRECT: We asked *she* to spend time on the project.

CORRECT: We asked *her* to spend time on the project.

In addition, sometimes writers use *hear, help, let, make, see,* or *watch* and follow it with an infinitive phrase in which a pronoun in the wrong case appears:

subjective pronoun

INCORRECT: Let she lose that rehearsal time.

The *she* should be *her,* which is correct since in constructions like this, *lose* is an infinitive that appears without the *to* that usually marks it. Therefore, *her* functions as the subject of the infinitive and needs to be in the objective case.

4 *We* and *Us* Followed by Nouns

Sometimes you might choose to attach the pronoun *we* or *us* to a noun: *we rulers, us rulers.* But how do you decide whether to use *we* or *us* with a particular noun? If the noun functions subjectively (for example, as a subject or a predicate noun), you should use *we,* the subjective form:

subject

We kings are running out of time.

If the noun is an object, you should use *us,* the objective form:

object of the preposition

Perhaps you can borrow some time from us rulers.

5 Pronouns Used as Appositives

Appositives follow and rename or further describe other words, usually nouns. When you use one or more pronouns as appositives to a noun, the pronouns must be in the same case as the noun. If the noun has a subjective role, the pronoun or pronouns used as appositives to the noun should be in the subjective case:

complete subject   subjective pronouns as appositives

The two members of the poets' society, he and I, lost a lot of time looking for the cave.

If the noun has an objective role, the pronoun or pronouns used as appositives to the noun should be in the objective case:

object of a   objective pronoun
preposition   as appositive

Put aside some time for a friend, me.

6 Pronouns Following *Than* or *As*

Whenever you use a pronoun after *than* or *as,* you will have to be clear about your meaning in order to decide which form of the pronoun to use. Generally, when you use a pronoun after *than* or *as,* you will be doing so within an elliptical adverb clause, a clause that has material left out of it. When you write *She budgets time as well as I,* you mean *She budgets time as well as I budget time,* but you can omit material without confusing readers. The pronoun in the elliptical clause must be *I* since it is the subject of that clause.

On the other hand, when you write *The exercise cost Dale more time than me,* you mean *The exercise cost Dale more time than the exercise cost me time,* but again you can omit material without confusing readers. The pronoun in the elliptical clause must be *me* since it is the indirect object of that clause.

It is especially important to be clear about your meaning for sentences in which either a subjective or an objective form is possible. Both of the following are correct sentences:

Running short on time bothers him more than I.

Running short on time bothers him more than me.

But these sentences have markedly different meanings. Here is a fuller form of the first:

Running short on time bothers him more than I bother him.

And here is a fuller form of the second:

Running short on time bothers him more than it bothers me.

7 *Who* and *Whom, Whoever* and *Whomever*

Few people today regularly distinguish between the subjective forms *who* and *whoever* and the objective forms *whom* and *whomever.* Many people use a subjective form when an objective form would be technically correct. For this reason, many people think that *whom* and *whomever* will not even appear in speech in the not too distant future.

Whether or not these people are right, some writers still do distinguish *who* from *whom,* and *whoever* from *whomever,* at least in formal situations, and they will expect you to do likewise. That is, they will expect you to use *who* and *whoever* when the pronoun serves as a subject or a predicate noun. And they will expect you to use *whom* and *whomever* when the pronoun serves as some kind of object. Many writers have trouble deciding whether to use subjective or objective forms in one or both of the following two constructions.

a. In Subordinate Clauses

Some writers have trouble with constructions such as this:

They questioned the man (who? whom?) could not put his ideas into words.

Because these writers know that *the man* is the direct object in the main clause (They questioned whom? They questioned the man.), they suspect that the pronoun relating the adjective clause to *the man* must also be in the objective case. But the key here is how the pronoun functions in its own clause. In its own clause, it is the subject, and therefore the proper form is *who.* You can see this more easily by focusing only on the subordinate clause and by substituting the appropriate personal pronoun in the slot where the relative pronoun appears:

who could not put his ideas into words

he could not put his ideas into words

27a
pro

If the relative pronoun functions in its own clause as some kind of object, then you should use *whom* or *whomever:*

They questioned the children whom the ideas had confused.

Again, you can see more easily which form is correct by focusing only on the subordinate clause and by substituting the appropriate personal pronoun for the relative pronoun and rearranging the order of words appropriately:

whom the ideas had confused

the ideas had confused *them*

Such strategies should also help you with subordinate clauses that contain parenthetical elements such as *they think* or *we believe:*

They are the ones (who? whom?) we think force meanings onto inappropriate words.

By focusing on only the subordinate clause, by substituting the personal pronoun that sounds correct to you for the relative pronoun, and by ignoring the *we think,* you can deduce that you need a subjective form in this clause:

(who? whom?) force meanings onto inappropriate words

They force meanings onto inappropriate words.

Since *they* is in the subjective case, you will need a relative pronoun in the subjective case. The relative pronoun is the subject of its clause:

They are the ones *who* we think force meanings onto inappropriate words.

If the relative pronoun functions as an object in its own clause, you should choose the objective case form, *whom:*

They are the ones to *whom* we think the ideas came through.

b. In Questions

Some writers have trouble deciding between the subjective and objective form of the interrogative pronoun when this pronoun introduces a question:

(Whoever? Whomever?) will capture that idea in words?

The key here is to see that the pronoun functions as the subject. You can see this most easily by substituting a personal pronoun for the interrogative pronoun and changing the question into a statement:

(Whoever? Whomever?) will capture that idea in words?

She will capture that idea in words.

Since *she* is a subjective form, you should use *whoever,* another subjective form, in the question:

Whoever will capture that idea in words?

Going through the same process should also lead you to select the objective form *whomever* when appropriate:

(Whoever? Whomever?) would the hollow words offend?

The hollow words offended *them.*

Since *them* is an objective form, you should use *whomever,* another objective form, in the question. In the question, *whomever* is the direct object:

Whomever would the hollow words offend?

8 Possessive Pronouns Before Gerunds

Gerunds are verb forms that end in *-ing* and function as nouns:

Stuffing ideas into a sentence is pointless.

In most cases, when a gerund is preceded by a personal pronoun, the pronoun should be in the possessive, not the objective, case:

QUESTIONABLE: We disapprove of *them* stuffing ideas into a sentence.

PREFERABLE: We disapprove of *their* stuffing ideas into a sentence.

However, you should not use a possessive pronoun before a gerund if doing so produces an awkward sentence. An awkward sentence almost always results when the possessive pronoun is separated from the gerund by several words:

AWKWARD: We disapprove of his, a respected authority on military expenses, stuffing many ideas into one sentence.

In such cases, it would be better to use *him,* an objective form:

IMPROVED: We disapprove of him, a respected authority on military expenses, stuffing many ideas into one sentence.

You may also choose to use an objective form in constructions such as *him stuffing.* When you do, however, *stuffing* no longer functions as a gerund but as a participle modifying *him.* This is correct, but it has a different focus from *his stuffing.* When you use a possessive pronoun before a gerund (*his stuffing*), you focus on the action. When you use an objective pronoun before a participle (*him stuffing*), you focus on the person performing the action. You will have to decide in context what you wish to focus on.

9 Distinguishing Possessive Pronouns from Contractions

Some indefinite pronouns take an apostrophe plus *s* to show possession: *anybody's idea.* However, not all forms that function as pronouns take an apostrophe plus *s* to show possession: *its.* And some related forms that function as adjectives also do not take an apostrophe plus *s* to show possession: *your* (as in *your meaning*), *their* (as in *their*

27a
pro

words). And at least one form that can function both as a pronoun and as an adjective does not take an apostrophe plus *s* to show possession: *whose.*

We focus on these four forms to help you distinguish them from some contractions: *it's* (for *it is*), *you're* (for *you are*), *they're* (for *they are*), and *who's* (for *who is*). When you use one of these contractions, your readers should be able to read in a subject and a verb for it:

> It's hard to get this idea across to you.
>
> It is hard to get this idea across to you.

On the other hand, if you use one of the possessive forms listed above, your readers should be able to see its possessive role and should not read in a subject and a verb for it:

> Its point was hard to get across to you.
>
> The point of that speech was hard to get across to you.

Exercise 1

In each of the following sentences, select the form that is correct and write it on the blank line.

EXAMPLE: ___We___ Lakoff, Johnson, and (we, us) are investigating metaphors involving the directions up and down.

1. _____ Some of these metaphors help (we, us) talk about our emotions.

2. _____ That party boosted the spirits of Fydor and (she, her).

3. _____ (We, Us) sophomores are feeling down.

4. _____ We fell into a deeper depression than (they, them).

5. _____ We commanded (they, them) to be in high spirits.

6. _____ The understudies, Judy and (he, him), felt their spirits rise.

7. _____ They questioned the men (who, whom) they knew felt really low.

8. _____ (Who, Whom) has depression never afflicted?

9. _____ Other of these metaphors help us talk about (us, our) being in various physical conditions.

10. _____ (Its, It's) eyes bright, the spaniel was in peak condition.

11. _____ The only ones here in top condition are Wilma and (I, me).

12. _____ The doctor warned Barney and (I, me) that without regular exercise we would decline in health.

13. _____ Take a hint from (we, us) nurses.
14. _____ He is sinking faster than (I, me).
15. _____ We will pay (whoever, whomever) adds to this list of metaphors.

27b

Problems with the Reference of Pronouns

Many of the pronouns that people use have antecedents. The antecedent is usually a noun or a noun phrase that names what or whom a pronoun refers to.

When writers do not make a clear connection between a pronoun and its antecedent, they have a problem with the reference of the pronoun. Usually, it is one of the following five kinds of problems.

1 The Antecedent Is Too Distant from the Pronoun

Sometimes writers leave so much distance between a pronoun and its antecedent that readers cannot connect the two readily:

> Manipulating people's minds through various skilled uses of metaphors goes along with all the other strategies that dictators have employed through the years. If people can be led to name aspects of situations of their lives in certain ways, their thinking processes can be controlled. Therefore, it is one of the dictators' most feared weapons.

The only noun phrase that the singular *it* can refer to is *manipulating people's minds through various skilled uses of metaphors* in the first sentence. Yet since the pronoun and its antecedent are separated by several words, it can be difficult for readers to connect them readily. It would probably be wisest to replace the *it* with a shortened form of the noun phrase, such as *manipulating people's minds through metaphors.*

Sometimes the problem is not so much the distance between a pronoun and its antecedent as it is the nature of the material between them:

> She rose to power with a bold strategy in a firm that astounded corporate analysts.

What is the antecedent for the relative pronoun *that?* Its most logical antecedent is *strategy.* But could it be *firm?* It could be, although this seems less likely. Firms in themselves probably astound people less often than strategies do. But you should always try to keep readers from wondering what sentences mean. Here is one way to revise the example:

> In her firm, she rose to power with a bold strategy that astounded corporate analysts.

(For additional information on matching relative pronouns with antecedents, see **15b**.)

2 Two or More Antecedents for a Pronoun Are Equally Possible

Sometimes writers produce sentences in which a pronoun could connect to two or more nouns:

> INCORRECT: After Evangeline talked to Fanny, she fell from power.

No matter how much time readers have to think about this sentence, they will not be able to determine to whom *she* refers. Of course, the context of such a sentence might make it clear who fell from power. But you should still correct such a problem, perhaps by repeating the appropriate noun:

> CORRECT: After Evangeline talked to Fanny, Evangeline fell from power.

If such problems come up when you report what someone else says, often the best response is to change the indirect report to a direct quotation:

> INCORRECT: Eustace told Caspar that he was the low man on the totem pole.

If Caspar is the low man on the totem pole, the sentence should appear as follows:

> CORRECT: Eustace told Caspar, "You are the low man on the totem pole."

3 The Antecedent Is Too Broad

Sometimes writers use the pronouns *it, this, that,* and *which* to refer to the information conveyed in an entire sentence or in a series of sentences. Sometimes this practice causes readers little or no trouble.

However, the reference can easily be too broad to be identified:

> INCORRECT: The senator in an inferior political position to John rejected his proposal. This still infuriates several voters.

What infuriates the voters—the fact that the senator rejected John's proposal or the proposal itself? If the writer has the first possibility in mind, the second sentence could be revised as follows:

> CORRECT: This rejection still infuriates several voters.

If the writer has the second possibility in mind, the second sentence could be revised as follows:

> CORRECT: This proposal still infuriates several voters.

4 The Antecedent Might Be Clear to the Writer but Unclear to Readers

Sometimes writers use a pronoun and seem to have a clear antecedent in mind for it, but they do not make that antecedent clear to readers. Sometimes writers do this because they have an antecedent for a pronoun suggested to them by a modifier they have used:

> INCORRECT: I will listen to student responses and test them at a later date.

Is *responses* the antecedent for *them?* Will the writer be testing responses? No, the writer will be testing students, but the modifier *student* made her think that *students* was present as an antecedent for *them.* She should have used the noun *students* instead of the pronoun *them.*

Sometimes this problem arises because writers have an antecedent for a pronoun suggested to them by a noun or noun phrase they have used:

> INCORRECT: I have considered the profession of teaching and have decided not to become one.

Is *profession* or *teaching* the antecedent for *one?* Has the writer decided not to become a profession or a teaching? No, the writer has decided not to become a teacher and apparently had the noun *teacher* brought to mind by the noun *teaching.* The writer should substitute *a teacher* for *one.*

27b
pro

Finally, sometimes this problem arises because writers have an antecedent for a pronoun suggested to them by a verbal they have used:

> "After using your ointment, my face started to clear up at once, and after using two jars, it was gone altogether." (cited in *Fun-Tastic* by Denys Parson)

What is the antecedent for *it?* What was gone? Readers are tempted to think that the writer's face was gone. But here the infinitive *to clear* has apparently brought to the writer's mind an antecedent such as *rash* or *case of acne.* The writer should specify what was gone.

5 The Antecedent Is Unclear to Writers and Readers

Sometimes writers use a pronoun for which neither they nor their readers can have a definite antecedent in mind:

> INCORRECT: In books on metaphor, it shows that greater quantity is associated with higher levels.

The pronoun *it* does not have a clear antecedent, and neither the writer nor readers could say what it might be.

Of course, *it* appears in some constructions without a clear antecedent and is commonly accepted:

> It is true that the number of books written each year continues to rise.

Or

> It is cooler today even though the humidity is still high.

However, the *it* in *In books on metaphor, it shows that . . .* only leads readers to ask who or what shows. Particularly since the sentence already contains a reference to books, the sentence could be revised as follows:

> Books on metaphor show that greater quantity is associated with higher levels.

Finally, consider this sentence:

> In many situations, they use dead metaphors.

To whom does *they* refer? The writer probably has in mind only the vaguest of references to people in general. Whenever you use the pronoun *they,* make sure your readers can clearly identify to whom it refers:

> In many situations, poor poets use dead metaphors.

Exercise 2

If any of the following sentences exhibit a problem with the reference of pronouns, describe the problem as precisely as you can, and then revise the sentence to correct the problem.

> **EXAMPLE:**   In *Metaphors We Live By,* it says that people in many cultures conceive of virtue as up and depravity as down.

It is impossible to tell to whom or what the *it* refers. One way to correct this sentence is as follows:

> The authors of *Metaphors We Live By* claim that people in many cultures conceive of virtue as up and depravity as down.

1. Dean told Gary that he is high-minded.
2. Either the group has very high standards or the work was more difficult than it appeared, which is a most remarkable thing.
3. In many civics books, they tell readers to become good citizens.
4. Gunnar and Griselde considered the sport of professional wrestling, but they decided not to stoop to becoming one.
5. After Stephen consulted with Orson, he decided that directing the film was beneath him.
6. The committee blocked the provost's recommendation; it seemed like a low trick to many faculty members.
7. After a good deed, they usually feel upright.
8. The dean has already surveyed faculty advising practices but has decided that writing about these practices without talking to them would be underhanded.
9. In the student handbook, it says to avoid the abyss of partying.
10. The advancement officer presented a recruitment strategy at a banquet; this offended parents of prospective students.

27c
pro

27c

Problems of Agreement Between Pronouns and Their Antecedents

Pronouns should agree with their antecedents in number (singular or plural), person (first, second, or third), and gender (masculine or feminine).

1 Problems of Agreement in Number Between Pronouns and Their Antecedents

If writers have a problem with agreement in number, that problem is likely to lie in one of the following areas, often because the conventions for the writers' speech do not match the conventions for their writing or because pronouns are separated from their antecedents by several words.

a. Agreement in Number Between a Pronoun and a Collective Noun

If you use a pronoun that has a collective noun as its antecedent (such as *class*), you can make the pronoun either singular or plural, depending on how you want readers to focus on the noun. If you write about a class of students and want readers to focus on it as a unit, you would use a singular pronoun:

> After *the class* worked on the assignment for three days, *it* ran out of steam.

On the other hand, if you want your readers to focus on a class as comprised of many individual students, you would use a plural pronoun:

> After *the class* worked on the assignment for three days, *they* ran out of steam.

A very common error involves shifting between singular nouns such as *person* and plural pronouns such as *they:*

> INCORRECT: Never again will a person experience such a great learning period as they do then.

Our point is not that *person* is a collective noun; obviously it is not. Our point is that some writers apparently see nouns such as *person* as collective nouns referring to a group of people or things, and therefore they make them agree with plural pronouns. This point probably also applies to sentences in which writers use the singular pronoun *one.* Some writers often apparently think that *one* has a collective sense, and therefore they incorrectly make it agree with a plural pronoun. In the following, the writer incorrectly links *one* and *they:*

> INCORRECT: First of all, one cannot use only one's own language when they define elements existing in another language.

27c
pro

In all cases of nouns or pronouns wrongly viewed as having a collective sense, the nouns and pronouns should agree with a singular pronoun, or the nouns and pronouns should be made plural in the first place. The two earlier incorrect examples could be revised as follows:

> CORRECT: Never again will people experience such a great learning period as they do then.
>
> First of all, one cannot use only one's own language when he or she defines elements existing in another language.

(For more advice about such constructions as *one . . . his or her,* see pages 417–419 of this chapter.)

b. Agreement in Number Between Pronouns and Nouns Modified by a Phrase

Sometimes the noun that a pronoun must agree with is modified by a phrase, often a prepositional phrase. Occasionally, this phrase will be long and will contain other nouns. These other nouns can make it difficult to decide whether the pronoun should be singular or plural:

> My mind, *together with my eyes and ears,* is not working as (it? they?) should.

The pronoun must agree with the noun that the prepositional phrase modifies, not with any nouns within that prepositional phrase. Since the modified noun *(mind)* is singular, the pronoun should be singular:

> My *mind,* together with my eyes and ears, is not working as *it* should.

If the modified noun is plural, then the pronoun should be plural:

> My *eyes and ears,* together with my brain, are not working as *they* should.

c. Agreement in Number Between a Pronoun and an Indefinite Pronoun

Indefinite pronouns (such as *both*) often serve as antecedents for other pronouns (such as *they*). Some indefinite pronouns are always considered plural:

> both   few   others   several

27c pro

When one of these is the antecedent for a pronoun, that pronoun should be plural:

> *Both* of the debaters claimed that, as far as *they* could see, the judges' mental wheels were not turning well.

Other indefinite pronouns are considered singular:

another	each one	neither	somebody	whoever
anybody	everybody	nobody	someone	
anyone	everyone	no one	something	
anything	everything	nothing	whatever	
each	either	one	whichever	

When one of these is the antecedent for a pronoun, that pronoun should be singular:

> If *something* in my office seems out of place, *it* can cause my thinking to break down.

In some circumstances it would be awkward to treat *everyone* and *everybody* as singular:

> After everyone arrived, I opened the books for her.

You would probably never write such a sentence, at least if you wanted readers to associate *her* with *everyone*. For this and other reasons, there is great pressure today to use a plural pronoun to agree with *everyone* and *everybody*:

> After *everyone* arrived, I opened the books for *them*.

This pressure is so strong that usually few will object to sentences like the example immediately above. But in more formal contexts, it will usually be wisest for you to revise such sentences so that a pronoun that is singular does not agree with a word that is plural:

> After all the *participants* arrived, I opened the books for *them*.

Finally, some indefinite pronouns can be either singular or plural:

> all   any   most   some

If these pronouns are associated with uncountable things, then generally the pronouns are treated as singular:

> *Most of the journey of love* is surprising since *it* is long and bumpy.

However, if these pronouns are associated with things that can be counted, generally they are treated as plurals:

> *Most of the participants* agreed that *they* talked of love as a journey.

d. Agreement in Number Between a Pronoun and Two or More Nouns or Pronouns Linked by *And*

If you use a pronoun to connect two or more nouns or pronouns linked by *and,* the pronoun should be plural, even if one or all of the nouns or pronouns are singular:

> *Clark and Lois* reached a crossroads as *they* got better acquainted.

> *Mr. Bigmus and his two wives* reached a crossroads as *they* got better acquainted.

> *The men and women on the bus* reached a crossroads as *they* got better acquainted.

One exception to this convention covers the situation in which two or more nouns refer to one person, as when *husband* and *father* refer to the same person. Then the pronoun that agrees with these nouns should be singular:

> *The husband and father* thought of the relationship as a dead-end street that *he* had wandered into.

e. Agreement in Number Between a Pronoun and Two or More Nouns or Pronouns Linked by *Or* or *Nor*

If you use a pronoun to connect to two or more nouns or pronouns linked by *or* or *nor,* you should make the pronoun agree with the noun or pronoun it is nearer to:

> Neither Ernest nor *his father* wanted to admit to *himself* that their relationship was foundering.

> Neither the two girls nor *their mother* wanted to admit to *herself* that their relationship was foundering.

The last example is correct, but it is somewhat awkward, and most writers prefer to express the singular noun before the plural. Then, of course, the pronoun that follows must agree in number with the plural noun.

Exercise 3

If any of the following sentences has a problem with agreement in number between pronouns and their antecedents, describe the problem as

27c
pro

precisely as you can, and then rewrite the sentence in order to correct the problem.

EXAMPLE: When a student studies metaphors for love, they will find that many have to do with a journey. [There is a shift from the singular *a student* to the plural *they*. One way to correct this sentence is to change *a student* to *students* and *studies* to *study*.]

1. The journey metaphor, together with other metaphors for love, is striking because it carries many sad meanings.

2. If anyone is having trouble in a relationship, they might say they are going nowhere.

3. Most people who refer to love as a journey would say that to them the metaphor brings difficulty and despair to mind.

4. Most of the despair does not easily lose their sting.

5. At some point in a relationship, men and women will usually pause and reflect on one's feelings.

6. The journey metaphor, along with several other common expressions, is not as popular as they once were.

7. When a speaker used to refer to love, they talked of flights from enemy advances.

8. Then one could use such expressions and offend few others.

9. Neither the two linguists nor Ms. Liebmann would commit themselves about why the journey metaphor lost some of its popularity.

10. All of them were afraid of the trouble they might stir up.

**27c
pro**

2 Problems of Agreement in Person Between Pronouns and Their Antecedents

Sentences in which pronouns do not agree with their antecedents in person exhibit shifts in person. Writers occasionally make such shifts between nouns, which are considered to be third person, and second-person pronouns:

INCORRECT: When *a person* is in a relationship that is off the track, *you* can feel really depressed.

CORRECT: When *people* are in a relationship that is off the track, *they* can feel really depressed.

Writers more often produce shifts from a first- or third-person pronoun to a second-person pronoun:

INCORRECT: When *one* is spinning wheels in a relationship, *you* can become irritable.

CORRECT: When *people* are spinning wheels in a relationship, *they* can become irritable.

Occasionally, the shift is from the first person to the second:

> **INCORRECT:**   *I* went to a therapist because that is how *you* can find out if a relationship is on the rocks.
>
> **CORRECT:**   *I* went to a therapist because that is how *I* can find out if a relationship is on the rocks.

Exercise 4

Correct all the instances in the following in which pronouns do not agree with their antecedents in person.

> **EXAMPLE:**   In the first sentence, there is a shift from the noun *a person* to the second-person pronoun *you.* Possible correction: change *a person* to *people, uses* to *use,* and *you* to *they.*

Some researchers claim that the metaphors a person uses to refer to others will affect how you treat those people. For example, if one uses metaphors such as *broad* or *tart* to refer to women, you will probably react to them in a limited and limiting way. The same is true if women use metaphors such as *stud* and *hunk* to refer to men. How one refers to others affects how you treat them. And most people find it very difficult to become conscious of the metaphors they use to refer to others.

3 **Problems of Agreement in Gender Between Pronouns and Their Antecedents**

27c
pro

The only pronouns that show distinctions in gender are the third-person singular personal pronouns:

> **SUBJECTIVE CASE:**   he, she, it
>
> **OBJECTIVE CASE:**   him, her, it
>
> **POSSESSIVE CASE:**   his, hers, its

Therefore, at least on the surface, it seems that the matter of making a pronoun agree with its antecedent in gender should be easy. If the antecedent is clearly masculine, use a form of *he:*

> During *Henry's* recent sabbatical, *he* investigated sexist metaphors.

If the antecedent is clearly feminine, use a form of *she:*

> During *Kate's* recent sabbatical, *she* investigated sexist metaphors.

And if the antecedent is clearly neuter, use a form of *it:*

> *The field of metaphor analysis* is attracting more researchers than *it* can support.

The trouble is that some antecedents are not clearly masculine, feminine, or neuter. And the English language has no singular pronoun that connects to antecedents of unknown gender. For example, if you want to relate a personal pronoun to the indefinite pronoun *everyone,* which pronoun should you use? Or what if you want to connect a personal pronoun to a noun of undetermined gender, such as *doctor, teacher,* or *lawyer?*

Not too long ago, most writers used the pronoun *he* or one of its variants in such cases:

> *Everyone* wanted to list a metaphor *he* had found.

> When *the doctor* gave *his* diagnosis, *he* startled people by referring to metaphoric maladaptations.

The claim used to justify such sentences was that words designating masculine gender also included females in their reference. The claim rested more on the power of those who made it than on its logic, and most people today would call such a claim sexist or gender-exclusive. Most writers have come to see that the practice of using masculine pronouns in all cases is unfair and perhaps even harmful to females as they develop their views of themselves and their possibilities in life.

Just as harmful was the practice of selecting pronouns according to stereotypes. All medical doctors must be male, so the stereotype went. Consequently, a sentence such as the following would be correct:

> After *the doctor* made rounds, *he* filled in some charts.

All nurses must be female, so the stereotype went. Consequently, a sentence such as the following would be correct:

> *The nurse* winced when the patient screamed at *her.*

So what should you do when you want to connect a personal pronoun to an indefinite pronoun such as *everyone* or to a noun of unknown gender? We recommend the following three strategies, in the order from most to least preferred. First, see if you can change the personal pronoun to an article. Doing this can rid sentences of gender references:

> Everyone should have *his* dictionary of sexist terms.

> Everyone should have *a* dictionary of sexist terms.

**27c
pro**

Any writer who includes an offensive term deserves to have *his* manuscript rejected.

Any writer who includes an offensive term deserves to have *the* manuscript rejected.

If that strategy does not work, try to change the troublesome singular reference to a plural. For example, changing *Everyone wants to have his own way* to *Everyone wants to have a way* or *Everyone wants to have the way* does not work. But changing *everyone* and *his* to plurals does work:

All people want to have *their* own way.

Finally, if neither of these strategies works, use a variant of *he or she*:

The successful candidate for this position will be able to present his or her views concisely.

This strategy works unless you have to repeat a variant of *he or she* even once in a sentence; such repetition is usually cumbersome:

CUMBERSOME: The successful candidate for this position will be able to present his or her views on whether he or she would welcome teaching undergraduate students as part of his or her responsibilities.

27c
pro

Exercise 5

If any of the following sentences display sexism, rewrite them to correct the problems.

EXAMPLE: When a high school principal examines how students view love, he finds that they see it as a form of warfare.

The writer of this sentence wrongly assumes that a high school principal is male (note the pronoun *he*). Possible correction:

When high school principals examine how students view love, they find that the students see it as a form of warfare.

1. Anyone who has been besieged by admirers can testify to how wary he gets.

2. A person who has to fend admirers off will often find himself the envy of his friends.

3. Everyone who conquers in love wants to tell his tale to others.

4. When one is pursued relentlessly, he tends to grow weary.

5. Whenever a writer notes that "All's fair in love and war," he may be entirely serious.

28

H ow would you describe what is wrong with the following sentence: "Here are some suggestions for handling obscene phone calls from the New England Telephone Company" (adapted from Richard Lederer's *Anguished English*)?

The trouble is caused by the modifier "from the New England Telephone Company." Where it stands, this modifier leads readers, at least for a moment, to think that the obscene calls come from the New England Telephone Company. Upon looking at the sentence more closely, most readers would be able to tell where the modifier should be placed:

> Here are some suggestions from the New England Telephone Company for handling obscene phone calls.

For these readers, the misplaced modifier probably leads to more amusement than confusion.

With other sentences that have modifier problems, readers can have a more difficult time discovering what the writers meant:

> We hoped frequently to set world records.

Did the writers hope frequently, or did they hope that they would frequently set world records? Without being able to ask the writers, readers are left with an unresolvable ambiguity. Whether sentences with modifier problems lead to amusement or ambiguity, if writers do not correct them, readers will probably not read their work with full seriousness.

28a

Problems with Adjectives

If writers have trouble using adjectives, they usually fail to observe the conventions of one or more of the following categories.

1 Using Adjectives After Linking Verbs to Modify the Subject

When you use a linking verb to connect a subject to a modifying word in the predicate, that modifying word should be an adjective:

	subject	linking verb	predicate adjective

CORRECT: The elderly patients felt weak.

You should not use a linking verb to connect a subject to an adverb:

INCORRECT: The elderly patients felt weakly.

2 Using *Good, Bad, Well,* and *Badly* Correctly

Good and *bad* always function as adjectives, so they can be connected with linking verbs to subjects:

	subject	linking verb	predicate adjective

CORRECT: The plans for pollution control were good.

	subject	linking verb	predicate adjective

The execution of those plans was bad.

You should not use *good* and *bad* after verbs that are not linking verbs:

transitive
subject   verb   direct object adjective

INCORRECT: The meter monitored pollutants good.

transitive
subject   verb   direct object adjective

The meter monitored pollutants bad.

Badly always functions as an adverb, so it should never be connected with a linking verb to a subject:

linking
subject   verb   adverb

INCORRECT: The sulfur dioxide smelled badly.

Badly may appear after verbs that show action:

transitive direct
subject   verb   object adverb

CORRECT: The mechanical scrubbers cleaned the air badly.

Well can function either as an adjective or as an adverb. Most often it appears as an adverb modifying a verb that shows action:

complete
subject   verb   adverb

CORRECT: Our agency functions well.

But *well* can also appear as an adjective connected by a linking verb to a subject. When it does, it means "in good health":

linking adjec-
subject   verb   tive   adverb

CORRECT: The patient is   well   now.

3 Correcting Incomplete Comparisons Involving Adjectives

Sometimes writers use comparative and superlative forms of adjectives and leave readers with incomplete comparisons:

INCOMPLETE: Industrial wastes are more dangerous.

You might well ask, "More dangerous than what? And how are they more dangerous?" The sentence provides no answers.

28a mod

ESL Consideration

-ING VS. -EN and -ED PARTICIPLES

-Ing (present) and *-En/-Ed* (past) participles are frequently misused when they are derived from verbs describing emotional qualities such as *amuse, bewilder, disappoint,* and *surprise.*

You should use *-ing* participles when you mean that a person, thing, or idea *causes* the emotion:

The American lifestyle is *amusing* to many international students.

Use *-En/-Ed* participles when you mean that a person *experiences* the emotion:

He is *amused* at Americans' obsession with breakfast cereals.

Unless the situation or other sentences make it clear what you are comparing and how you are comparing these things or people, you should complete the terms of comparisons you make:

28a
mo

COMPLETE: Industrial wastes are more dangerous than heated water as a form of water pollution.

4 Correcting Double Comparative or Superlative Forms of Adjectives

Some adjectives signal the comparative and superlative degrees through the addition of *-er* and *-est:*

warm   warmer   warmest

Other adjectives signal the comparative and superlative degrees through the addition of *more* and *most:*

beautiful   more beautiful   most beautiful

No adjectives have double comparative or superlative forms. That is, no adjectives add both *-er* and *more* or both *-est* and *most:*

	double comparative form	double superlative form
INCORRECT:	more warmer	most beautifulest

5 Correcting Absolute Adjectives That Are Compared

Sometimes people modify nouns by calling them *more round* or *most unique.* The adjectives *round* and *unique* should not be expressed in comparative or superlative degree since the quality they name has no degrees. Roundness is roundness; one thing cannot be more round than another. However, one thing can be more nearly round than another. For something to be unique means that it is one of a kind; one thing cannot be the most unique in the world. However, one thing can be more nearly unique than another. Here are some other adjectives that should not appear in comparative or superlative form:

complete	equal	impossible	parallel	unanimous
dead	eternal	infinite	pregnant	universal
empty	everlasting	invisible	square	vertical
endless	favorite	matchless	supreme	whole

Exercise 1

28a mod

Indicate which of the following sentences contain an error involving adjectives. Then revise each of these so that the errors are corrected.

EXAMPLE: The water tastes badly.   The water tastes bad.

1. Many people hear about the problem of acid rain regularly, but they do not take this problem seriously.

2. The problem of acid rain is more severe.

3. Acid rain forms when moisture in the air interacts good with nitrogen oxide and sulfur dioxide.

4. These chemicals are the products of automobile combustion and industrial processes.

5. The moisture and the chemicals react to produce the very unique compounds nitric acid and sulfuric acid.

6. These acids may not sound too badly, but they fall to earth with each rainfall or snowfall.

7. They are far more worse than many other pollutants since they can contaminate huge bodies of water.

8. When the contamination becomes severe, the fish in those bodies of water feel weakly and die.

9. In some areas, the state of many lakes is not good at all.

10. Some proposed solutions seem more impossible than others.

Problems with Adverbs

If writers have trouble using adverbs, they usually fail to observe the conventions of one or more of the following categories.

1 Using Adverbs to Modify Verbs

Sometimes writers make the mistake of modifying a verb with an adjective:

         verb adjective

INCORRECT: The volunteers worked good.

The adjective *good* should be changed to the corresponding adverb, *well:*

        verb adverb

CORRECT: The volunteers worked well.

2 Using Adverbs to Modify Other Adverbs

Sometimes writers make the mistake of using an adjective to modify an adverb, perhaps because this practice is common in informal speech:

INCORRECT: The council has responded to the problem of

      adjective adverb

    solid wastes real well.

The adjective *real* should be changed to the corresponding adverb, *really:*

CORRECT: The council has responded to the problem of solid

      adverb adverb

   wastes really well.

3 Using Adverbs to Modify Adjectives

Sometimes writers make the mistake of using an adjective to modify another adjective, again perhaps because this practice is common in informal speech:

        adjec-
        tive adjective

INCORRECT: Their plan for recycling plastic is real attractive.

28b
moc

Real should be changed to the corresponding adverb, *really:*

adverb   adjective
CORRECT: Their plan for recycling plastic is really attractive.

Note, though, that *really* is not a strong modifier; in some sentences, you can probably eliminate it.

4 Correcting Double Negatives

You have probably heard someone, perhaps a teacher, correct someone else for using a **double negative,** or two words with negative meaning in the same clause. Some words with negative meaning are indefinite pronouns:

no   none   no one   nothing   neither

And many are adverbs:

barely   hardly   never   nor   not   scarcely

Earlier in the history of the English language, using several negative words in one clause was a way of emphasizing the negative meaning. Therefore, in the twelfth and thirteenth centuries, a scribe could write something like "There nas no man nowhere so vertuous," expressing negative meaning in *nas, no,* and *nowhere.* Similarly, in much informal speech today, you can hear people using two or more negative words in an attempt to convey an especially strong negative meaning:

negative negative
We didn't get no warning about that oil spill.

In more formal situations, double negatives are almost always regarded as errors. Readers typically react as if they were following a rule of mathematical logic: Two negatives make a positive. Therefore, in your own formal writing you should take care to correct double negatives:

negative negative
INCORRECT: The landfill cannot hardly hold more garbage.

negative
CORRECT: The landfill can hardly hold more garbage.

One exception to the convention banning double negatives involves using two negatives to make understatements, which writers sometimes do to move a sentence into a middle ground between very positive and very negative. Writing that candidates for public office are *not unworthy* is claiming that they fall somewhere between unworthy and worthy. At other times writers use understatements to add to the punch of their points:

> The proposal for a waste incinerator is not inexpensive.

Getting readers to relate the meanings of *not* and *inexpensive* can actually be more effective than stating directly that the proposal is expensive.

5 Correcting Incomplete Comparisons Involving Adverbs

Sometimes writers use comparative and superlative forms of adverbs and leave readers with incomplete comparisons:

> INCOMPLETE COMPARISON: The Stiknet filtering system operates more inexpensively.

You are probably inclined to ask, "What does this filtering system operate more inexpensively than?" This sentence provides no answer.

Of course, some contexts show what things are being compared and how they are being compared:

> Our committee considered two filtering systems, the Permflo and the Stiknet systems. We finally decided to buy the Stiknet system, for one main reason. The Stiknet filtering system operates more inexpensively.

However, if the first sentence had not appeared in this paragraph, the last sentence would have to spell out what systems are being compared:

> COMPLETE COMPARISON: The Stiknet filtering system operates more inexpensively than the Permflo system.

6 Correcting Double Comparative or Superlative Forms of Adverbs

Most adverbs signal their comparative and superlative degrees through the addition of *more* and *most*:

> swiftly   more swiftly   most swiftly

28b
mod

ESL Consideration

NOT VS. NO

Not is regularly used to make a verb phrase negative and to modify an entire noun phrase:

verb phrase

She does *not* like tofu.

noun phrase

Not many American tourists visit my country.

No is more typically used like the words *the, this,* and *some* to modify a noun and its associated adjectives:

adjective noun

I saw no fresh fruit in the store.

**28b
mod**

Some adverbs signal their comparative and superlative degrees through the addition of *-er* and *-est:*

fast   faster   fastest

And a small number of adverbs signal their comparative and superlative degrees through more radical changes in form:

well   better   best   badly   worse   worst

No adverb has two ways of signaling the comparative degree or the superlative degree:

double, comparative form   double superlative form

INCORRECT: more faster   most fastest

7 Correcting Absolute Adverbs That Are Compared

Sometimes people write sentences such as the following:

INCORRECT: They delivered their speeches on the benefits of

compared absolute adverb

recycling more matchlessly than ever before.

Matchlessness has no degrees. Therefore, if an action occurs matchlessly, it cannot be equaled. If actions do not occur matchlessly, some of them can occur more nearly matchlessly than others. One possible revision of the incorrect sentence above is as follows:

> CORRECT: They delivered their speeches on the benefits of recycling more nearly matchlessly than ever before.

Here are some other adverbs that should not appear in the comparative or superlative degree:

endlessly	infinitely	uniquely
equally	invisibly	universally
eternally	perpendicularly	
impossibly	straight	

Exercise 2

Indicate which of the following sentences contain an error involving adverbs. Then revise each of these so that the errors are corrected.

> EXAMPLE: Noise levels are becoming real bad.
>
> Noise levels are becoming really bad.

1. A form of pollution that is becoming increasingly serious is noise pollution.
2. This problem is terrible serious for those living in large cities.
3. These people do not hardly have times of tranquility and quiet.
4. Unfortunately for these people, many city governments are working too slow to bring noise levels down to acceptable levels.
5. For the good of all citizens, the city governments will have to learn to respond much more faster.
6. Otherwise the people will suffer real badly.
7. High levels of noise can easy harm people's hearing.
8. And high levels of noise can even lead people to develop high blood pressure and ulcers.
9. One city has responded to its noise problem most uniquely.
10. The plan that the city has developed will very likely work better.

28c
mod

28c

Problems with Dangling Modifiers

In *Anguished English,* Richard Lederer cites the following sentence: "When a small boy, a girl is of little interest." The modifier *When a small boy* is a dangling modifier.

1 The Nature of Dangling Modifiers

When a small boy seems to modify *a girl,* but that is impossible for all except those who have had a sex-change operation. A **dangling modifier** is one in which the implied subject or actor in the modifier is different from the subject of the clause to which it is attached:

dangling modifier

INCORRECT: Covering the patient with a lead vest, the machine took an x-ray.

The introductory modifier *Covering the patient with a lead vest* is a dangler since its implied subject (probably something like *the dental hygienist*) is different from the subject *(the machine)* of the clause that follows. The introductory modifier has nothing to modify; it cannot modify *the machine* or *an x-ray.* This sentence could be revised as follows:

CORRECT: After the dental hygienist covered the patient with a lead vest, the machine took an x-ray.

Most dangling modifiers appear at the beginning of sentences, but some appear within sentences:

28c
nod

INCORRECT: A system has been established whereby,

dangling modifier

by carefully reading the print-outs, high radiation levels can be avoided.

There is nothing in this sentence for the modifier to modify; neither a system nor high radiation levels can read print-outs.

Dangling modifiers also appear at the end of sentences:

dangling modifier

Radiation can be deadly when unwarned.

Here again the modifier has nothing to modify; radiation cannot go unwarned.

2 Correcting Various Kinds of Dangling Modifiers

Several kinds of structures commonly appear in sentences as dangling modifiers.

a. Prepositional Phrases

Prepositional phrases often are dangling:

dangling prepositional phrase

INCORRECT: At sixteen years of age, my family moved away from the nuclear plant.

Since people do not ordinarily talk of families as being sixteen years of age, you can assume that the prepositional phrase does not modify *my family*. A good correction involves changing the prepositional phrase into a clause containing a reference to the writer:

CORRECT: When I was sixteen years of age, my family moved away from the nuclear plant.

Sometimes dangling prepositional phrases have a gerund as their object:

INCORRECT: By moving, the nuclear plant could no longer harm us.

To correct this sentence, after the modifier you could add a reference to who moved and a verb to go along with this reference:

CORRECT: By moving, my parents ensured that the nuclear plant could no longer harm us.

b. Participles and Participial Phrases

Participles and participial phrases sometimes appear as dangling modifiers:

dangling participle

INCORRECT: Moving, the nuclear plant was left behind.

dangling participial phrase

Moving our family, the nuclear plant was left behind.

A good way to correct such sentences is to add words for the modifiers to modify and to change the passive verb *(was left)* to active:

CORRECT: Moving, we left the nuclear plant behind.

Moving our family, our parents left the nuclear plant behind.

28c
moc

c. Infinitives and Infinitive Phrases

Infinitives and infinitive phrases sometimes appear as dangling modifiers:

dangling infinitive

INCORRECT: To survive, the house near the nuclear plant was abandoned.

dangling infinitive phrase

To survive the radiation, the house near the nuclear plant was abandoned.

A good way to correct such sentences is to add words for the modifiers to modify and to change the passive verb *(was abandoned)* to active:

CORRECT: To survive, we abandoned the house near the nuclear plant.

To survive the radiation, we abandoned the house near the nuclear plant.

d. Elliptical Clauses

Sometimes **elliptical clauses** appear as dangling modifiers. They are called elliptical because in them a subject and a verb could appear but do not. For example, *when a baby* is an elliptical adverbial clause. Readers would probably interpret it with a subject and a verb such as *I was: When I was a baby.* In the following sentence, this same elliptical clause appears as a dangling modifier:

dangling elliptical clause

INCORRECT: When a baby, my family moved away from the nuclear plant.

This modifier dangles because it suggests that a family could be a baby.

You could correct such a sentence in at least two ways. You could add the words that originally were left out of the elliptical clause:

CORRECT: When I was a baby, my family moved away from the nuclear plant.

Or you could leave the elliptical clause as it is, add an appropriate word for it to modify, and make a few other changes in wording:

CORRECT: When a baby, I moved away from the nuclear plant with my family.

3 Some Accepted Dangling Modifiers

Some modifiers, many of which function as kinds of signposts in essays, are technically dangling modifiers but are accepted, even in formal situations:

Strictly speaking, radiation is pollution.

Considering the situation, the radiation must be eliminated.

Given the facts, preventing radiation pollution must be a top priority.

Why are these dangling modifiers? Consider the last example. A good way to see why *Given the facts* is a dangling modifier is to ask, "Who is given the facts?" *Given* has nothing in this sentence to modify. Yet readers usually interpret such a modifier as meaning "all those who are considering this matter are given these facts." And with such a general reference, such modifiers are not seen as errors. You would get into trouble with these signposts probably only if you used more of them than your readers needed to follow you through an essay; in such a case, they might feel somewhat insulted.

> *Exercise 3*
>
> Use each of the following groups of words in two sentences: in the first, as a dangling modifier, and in the second, as a correct modifier.
>
> EXAMPLE: seeping from the landfill
>
> a. Seeping from the landfill, the river was full of pollutants.
>
> b. Seeping from the landfill, the toxic chemicals polluted the river.
>
> 1. at ten months of age
> 2. by contaminating the groundwater
> 3. draining acres of farmland
> 4. to find unpolluted water
> 5. when unaware

28d
moc

28d

Problems with Misplaced Modifiers

How would you describe what is wrong with a sentence such as "They have an excellent discussion of pollution in their most recent work"?

The problem is that the modifier *in their most recent work* is misplaced.

1 The Nature of Misplaced Modifiers

The modifier *in their most recent work* is not a dangling modifier because it has something in the sentence to modify, the verb *have: They have an excellent discussion in their most recent work.* The trouble is that, if the modifier appears at the end of the sentence, it seems to modify pollution: *pollution in their most recent work.* You could correct the problem by moving the modifier:

> CORRECT: In their most recent work, they have an excellent
> discussion of pollution.

2 Correcting Various Kinds of Misplaced Modifiers

a. Some Adverbs

28d
mod

Many adverbs can appear in several different positions in a sentence:

> *Gladly* will we fight water pollution.
> We *gladly* will fight water pollution.
> We will *gladly* fight water pollution.
> We will fight water pollution *gladly.*

However, some adverbs should appear directly before the word or phrase that they modify:

almost   exactly   just   nearly   scarcely
even   hardly   merely   only   simply

Note how the meaning changes in the following sentences as *only* changes positions:

> Only the director asked the Boy Scouts to clean up the banks of the river. [The director, no one else, asked them.]
> The director only asked the Boy Scouts to clean up the banks of the river. [The director only asked; he or she did not give an order.]
> The director asked only the Boy Scouts to clean up the banks of the river. [The director asked only the scouts, no one else.]

The director asked the Boy Scouts only to clean up the banks of the river. [The director asked them only to clean up the banks, not plant shrubs on them.]

The director asked the Boy Scouts to clean up only the banks of the river. [The director asked them to clean up only the banks, not the river bed.]

The director asked the Boy Scouts to clean up the banks of only the river. [The director asked them to clean up the banks of only the river, not the banks of a creek.]

These examples show that adverbs such as *only* modify the word or phrase that follows them directly. When adverbs such as *only* precede words that they do not modify, they are misplaced:

MISPLACED: We only gave them one warning.

Is this sentence making a point about only giving? No, it is making a point about the small number of warnings being given. It should be revised:

CORRECT: We gave them only one warning.

It is true that many people misplace such adverbs in their speech. However, in your more formal writing, you should take care to place such adverbs where they will help convey the precise message that you intend.

b. Prepositional Phrases

When writers misplace prepositional phrases, they are likely to do so in one or more of the following situations.

First, sometimes writers put a prepositional phrase after the wrong noun:

misplaced
prepositional phrase

INCORRECT: The issues and the panel members for discussion have been selected.

The prepositional phrase *for discussion* probably does not modify *panel members.* Since the phrase almost certainly modifies *issues,* it should appear immediately after it:

CORRECT: The issues for discussion and the panel members have been selected.

28c
mo

Second, sometimes writers place a prepositional phrase so that it seems to modify a noun, when in fact it must modify a verb:

INCORRECT: They include a thorough examination of the

misplaced prepositional phrase

causes of ecological damage in their last chapter.

You probably sense that *in their last chapter* must modify the verb *include*. But as the phrase stands here, it seems to modify *ecological damage*. There are at least two ways to revise such a sentence:

CORRECT: They include in their last chapter a thorough examination of the causes of ecological damage.

In their last chapter, they include a thorough examination of the causes of ecological damage.

We recommend the second revision, since in it the verb *(include)* and direct object *(a thorough examination)* are not separated from each other.

Finally, sometimes writers place prepositional phrases so that it is not clear whether they modify a main verb or an infinitive:

INCORRECT: The ecologists warn homeowners to avoid

misplaced prepositional phrase

fertilizers in their guidebooks.

The prepositional phrase modifies the main verb *warn,* but it seems to modify the infinitive phrase *to avoid fertilizers.* The sentence could be revised in at least two ways:

CORRECT: In their guidebooks, the ecologists warn homeowners to avoid fertilizers.

The ecologists warn in their guidebooks that homeowners should avoid fertilizers.

c. Participial Phrases

Sometimes writers place a participial phrase too far in advance of the word it modifies:

misplaced participial phrase

INCORRECT: Leaving an oil slick behind, we watched the tanker enter the bay.

The participial phrase appears to modify *we*. But no one thinks of people as leaving an oil slick behind them. The participial phrase should be placed so that it is clear that it modifies the tanker:

> **CORRECT:**   We watched the tanker, leaving an oil slick behind, enter the bay.

In addition, sometimes writers place a participial phrase too far after the word it modifies:

> misplaced participial phrase
>
> **INCORRECT:**   We watched the tanker sitting on the bluffs
>
> overlooking the bay.

Obviously, the tanker is not sitting on the bluffs; the people are. You could revise such a sentence in at least two ways:

> **CORRECT:**   We, sitting on the bluffs overlooking the bay, watched the tanker.
>
> Sitting on the bluffs overlooking the bay, we watched the tanker.

The second revision has the advantage of not separating the subject, *we,* from its verb, *watched.*

d. Adjective Clauses

28d
mod

If a writer does not place an adjective clause right after the word it modifies, readers might think that the clause modifies a different word:

> misplaced adjective clause
>
> **INCORRECT:**   We saw the barrels from the bluffs that had been
>
> dumped by the tanker.

The adjective clause modifies *barrels,* not *bluffs.* To make this clear, you would have to position *barrels* and *that had been dumped by the tanker* next to each other:

> **CORRECT:**   From the bluffs, we saw the barrels that had been dumped by the tanker.
>
> We saw from the bluffs the barrels that had been dumped by the tanker.

The first of these is somewhat smoother than the second in that it does not separate the verb *(saw)* from the direct object *(the barrels . . .).*

e. Adverb Clauses

Many adverb clauses can appear in more than one place in a sentence:

CORRECT: *Although the weather was threatening,* the captain of the tanker left the bridge.

The captain of the tanker, *although the weather was threatening,* left the bridge.

The captain of the tanker left the bridge *although the weather was threatening.*

Some adverb clauses, however, must appear before or soon after the verb they modify or readers will interpret them as modifying a different verb or an infinitive:

INCORRECT: The captain explained to the crew how to

misplaced adverb clause

navigate the ice field before they left port.

In this sentence, *before they left port* has to modify *explained,* not *how to navigate,* since they could not navigate while still in port. Here are two ways to correct this sentence:

**28d
mod**

CORRECT: Before they left port, the captain explained to the crew how to navigate the ice field.

The captain explained to the crew before they left port how to navigate the ice field.

Exercise 4

Revise the following sentences to correct the misplaced modifier in each.

EXAMPLE: The herders put the cows in the barn with a fever.

The herders put the cows with a fever in the barn.

1. The cows had only stopped eating yesterday morning.
2. Standing around without eating any hay, the herders watched the sick cows.
3. One book that they consulted described a cure for feverish cows with diagrams.
4. The veterinarian told the herders how to examine feverish cows while they took a short coffee break.
5. The procedure would just take a minute.
6. The herders saw several drooling cows with binoculars.
7. They watched the sick cows sitting on the fence for an hour.

8. Then they noticed that the sick cows only ate from the first bin.

9. They found that the grain in the first bin had been contaminated by a pesticide by using the resources of the state university.

10. A clerk had mixed a pesticide in with the grain that is dangerous to livestock.

Problems with Squinting Modifiers

What modifier in the following sentence do you think would cause a problem for readers?

Large power plants that generate electricity normally are a source of thermal pollution.

The troublesome modifier is the adverb *normally*; it is a squinting modifier.

1 The Nature of Squinting Modifiers

The problem with **squinting modifiers** is that they can be read as modifying either a word or phrase that precedes them or a word or phrase that follows them. They squint: No one can tell if they look ahead or back. In the example given above, *normally* could be seen as modifying *generate:* The plants generate electricity normally. But *normally* could also be seen as modifying *are:* The plants normally are a source of thermal pollution.

2 Correcting Various Kinds of Squinting Modifiers

a. Adverbs

Many adverbs appear in positions where they squint:

INCORRECT: Power plants that discharge heated water into

  squinting modifier

  lakes often cause the death of aquatic plants.

Here *often* is a squinting modifier because readers cannot tell if it modifies *discharge (discharge often)* or *cause (often cause).*

28e
mod

If you discover such a modifier in one of your drafts, you must first specify what meaning you intend to convey. If you mean that some power plants discharge heated water often, you could correct the sentence as follows:

CORRECT: Power plants that often discharge heated water into lakes cause the death of aquatic plants.

If you mean that these power plants often cause the death of aquatic plants, you could correct the sentence in at least two ways:

CORRECT: Power plants that discharge heated water into lakes cause the death of aquatic plants often.

Often, power plants that discharge heated water into lakes cause the death of aquatic plants.

b. Prepositional Phrases

Prepositional phrases are sometimes left as squinting modifiers:

squinting prepositional phrase

INCORRECT: The plant director said after some study the situation would be corrected.

Here readers cannot tell whether *after some study* modifies *said (said after some study)* or *would be corrected (would be corrected after some study)*.

If you find such a squinting modifier in a draft, you must first specify what you intend the sentence to mean. If you intend *after some study* to modify *said,* you should move the modifier to the beginning of the sentence:

CORRECT: After some study, the plant director said the situation would be corrected.

On the other hand, if you intend *after some study* to modify *would be corrected,* you have at least two options:

CORRECT: The plant director said the situation would be corrected after some study.

The plant director said the situation would after some study be corrected.

c. Clauses

Some clauses appear as squinting modifiers:

squinting clause

INCORRECT: Some environmentalists I know would oppose that plan.

Does the writer mean *Some environmentalists I know* or *I know that some environmentalists would oppose that plan?* As the sentence stands, readers cannot tell.

If you find such a squinting clause in a draft, first decide which meaning you want to convey. If you want to write about some environmentalists that you know, you could correct the sentence by adding the appropriate relative pronoun:

> **CORRECT:**   Some environmentalists *whom* I know would oppose that plan.

To convey the other meaning, you could revise as follows:

> **CORRECT:**   I know that some environmentalists would oppose that plan.

Or you could set off the *I know* with commas, making it a parenthetical insertion in the sentence:

> **CORRECT:**   Some environmentalists, I know, would oppose that plan.

Exercise 5

Identify the squinting modifiers in the following passage, and then correct them in the way that fits the meaning of the passage best.

> **EXAMPLE:**   The first squinting modifier is the clause *I believe* in the second sentence. You could correct it by enclosing *I believe* in commas: Not enough people, I believe, are aware of the dangers this form of pollution causes.

Many tons of mercury, lead, and other heavy metals have been dumped into rivers across the country. Not enough people I believe are aware of the dangers this form of pollution causes. These heavy metals do not break down easily. Scientists say frequently these metals can remain dangerous for a long time. They settle in the mud and silt in river bottoms. There they can enter the systems of insect larvae. Scientists point out after some time the larvae emerge from the river bottoms and are easy prey for fish. Fish that eat these larvae sometimes build up large concentrations of heavy metals in their tissues. No one I trust would feel safe eating large quantities of these fish.

28e
mod

29

S P E L L I N G

I f the spelling system for English were perfect, each letter would always stand for the same distinctive sound, and each distinctive sound would always be symbolized by the same letter. Of course, the spelling system for English is not perfect. One letter can stand for more than one distinctive sound; note the sounds that *c* stands for in *ice* and *cookie.* One distinctive sound can be symbolized by more than one letter or set of letters; note how the hard *k* sound is symbolized in the following words:

cop   kid   pick   chorus   clique

And in certain words, some letters apparently stand for no sounds at all:

de**b**t   dum**b**   **gh**ost   is**l**and   **k**nife   **p**sychic   recei**p**t

It would be wrong of us, however, to suggest that the English spelling system is totally inconsistent and that you can do nothing to improve your spelling. The system has more regularities than is commonly acknowledged, and many people have found that by taking certain steps they can become better spellers.

Some of you might resist any urging to improve your spelling since you have had teachers who have not penalized you heavily or at all for misspelling. But in most writing tasks outside of college, misspellings will cost you dearly. Some of our students have been denied

442

job interviews because their letters of application contained a spelling error or two, and we often hear people label others uneducated because those others are poor spellers. So examine the strategies we describe in this chapter, and use those that seem likely to help you become a better speller.

29a

Strategies to Help You Identify Your Misspellings

In this section we describe some strategies that you can use to spot misspellings in various drafts that you have produced.

1 Proofreading Carefully

Before you submit an essay for evaluation, you should proofread it carefully. To become a good proofreader, you might have to change your normal manner of reading. When most people read normally, their eyes focus on a letter or a group of letters, and then their eyes jump along the line to a new letter or cluster of letters. They focus, skip over some letters or words, and focus again. This skipping is possible since within words it is often possible to predict what letters will follow others and since within phrases it is often possible to predict what words will follow others.

The trouble with a normal reading style for proofreading is obvious: You might skip over words and parts of words in which a spelling error occurs. A large part of learning to be a good proofreader involves slowing down your normal rate of reading and not skipping words and parts of words.

One way to do this is to examine a draft backward, from the last word to the first. This technique will force you to focus on only one word at a time, but the trouble is that you could focus on *there* and decide that it is spelled correctly even though in context *their* is the word you need.

Another technique is to take a ruler with an opening in it and slide it along the lines of your draft so that you can see only a few words at a time. Some good proofreaders place a ruler below a line of print and focus on words in that line one at a time.

29c
sp

2 Asking a Friend to Proofread for You

Many writers find that, no matter what they do, they are blind to some of their own spelling errors. If you are like these writers, it can help to have a friend proofread your essays for you. Or perhaps the members of a peer-review group could agree to proofread one another's essays.

3 Using a Spell Checker

If you use a computer to prepare your essays, you will probably have access to a program called a spell checker. A spell checker checks all the words in a document against the dictionary that has been programmed into the computer. If you activate a spell checker, it might scroll through the document and highlight all the forms that do not match anything in the dictionary. Or it might produce a list of all such forms.

In either case, you can then decide whether the words to which the spell checker has called your attention are actually misspelled or whether they simply have not been programmed into the dictionary. Spell checkers will not correct misspellings; you must do that.

You cannot assume that a spell checker will solve all your spelling problems. Most spell checkers are not programmed to determine whether a particular word fits its context or not. Therefore, most will not draw the word *it's* to your attention even though in context you need the word *its.*

Exercise 1

Identify and correct all fifteen spelling errors in the following passage. Also, indicate which of the misspelled words, if any, a spell checker would probably not help you identify.

One of the greater influences in standardizing the spelling of English was the invention of printing from movable type. The man who intraduced printing in England was William Caxton. While visiting Cologne, Germany, in 1471, Caxton presumibly learned of the printing press in existance there. Later he helped set up a printing press in Belgium. Using this press, in 1475 he issued what was definately the first book printed in the English langauge. One year later, Caxton brought this press with him to Westminster, England.

The principle advantage of the printing press was that it could easily produce multaple copies of a book at a comparitively small cost. Before the printing press, if people wanted more than one copy of a peice of litterature, they had to pay a scribe to make the additional copies. These scribes often felt that it was their priviledge to spell words as they wished. Any particular word could be spelled differantly by various scribes. With the easy multiplication of copies of a book that a printing press made possible, however, a printer could be instrumental in the maintainance of a system of standardized spelling.

Another effect of the printing press was that it made books accessable to more people than just the rich. Books became available for individual readers at relitively inexpensive prices.

Strategies to Help You Improve Your Spelling

1 Improving Your Visual Memory

To complete all your assigned reading in college, you probably have to move through it quite quickly. Yet when you come across new words or words that are difficult for you to spell, you should slow down and try to create a mental image of these words. Some people find that if they spell words aloud, the sounds reinforce the mental images.

29b
sp

2 Being Alert to Clues from Related Words

It often helps to put some words in pairs or in sets with related words. For example, if you relate *muscle* to *muscular* and *musculature,* you should more easily remember that *muscle* contains a *c.* Similarly, imagine that you are not sure which vowel fills the following slot: *imm_grant.* Relating this word to *migrant* can help you remember that an *i* is correct: *immigrant.* It helps many people to keep a list of such relationships.

Exercise 2

To which other words could you relate the following words in order to aid your memory about the presence of the letters in boldface:

civi**l**ian	hori**z**on	ma**l**ign
conde**mn**	hy**mn**	si**g**n

3 Tuning Out Distractions from Informal Speech or from Nonstandard Dialects

Some people's home dialects systematically repress the pronunciation of certain letters, such as the final consonant in a cluster of consonants, and most people at one time or another slur consonants or blur vowels. In informal situations, hardly anyone notices such practices. For some people, such careless pronunciations never cause spelling troubles. They can say or hear "goverment" and still write *government.* Other people, however, say or hear "mathmatics" and write *mathmatics,* not the correct form, *mathematics.* If you are one of those people who can be thrown off in spelling by how they say or hear words, you should start a list in which you note how you say or hear words and how those words are correctly spelled.

Exercise 3

How do you think the following words are most often misspelled? Why do you think they get misspelled in these ways?

> **EXAMPLE:** Some people misspell *quantity* as *quanity* because they do not hear or say the *t.* Some people spell *realtor* as *realator* because of how they say or hear the word.

1. accidentally	11. granted	21. prejudice
2. a lot	12. history	22. probably
3. arctic	13. incidentally	23. professor
4. athletics	14. irrelevant	24. representative
5. attract	15. library	25. sophomore
6. business	16. memento	26. strength
7. candidate	17. mined	27. strictly
8. contact	18. mischievous	28. temperament
9. current	19. no one	29. uncommon
10. disastrous	20. nuclear	30. veteran

4 Distinguishing American from British Spelling Patterns

The American system of spelling differs from the British system in a handful of ways. Generally, most of you will be using the American system of spelling. But if you work in a part of the British Commonwealth or submit some writing to a publisher in the British Commonwealth, then you will probably need to use the British system. The major differences between these two systems are listed on the following page.

American	British
-or	*-our*
honor	honour
neighbor	neighbour
o	*ou*
mold	mould
plow	plough
e **omitted**	*e* **present**
acknowledgment	acknowledgement
judgment	judgement
-er	*-re*
center	centre
meter	metre
l	*ll*
canceled	cancelled
leveled	levelled
-ize	*-ise*
apologize	apologise
capitalize	capitalise
e	*ae, oe*
encyclopedia	encyclopaedia
esophagus	oesophagus
im-	*em-*
impanel	empanel

**29b
sp**

ESL Consideration

AMERICAN AND BRITISH SPELLING SYSTEMS

Whether you are using the American spelling system or the British system, be consistent, especially with words derived from other words:

	Verb Form	Derived Noun Form
AMERICAN SYSTEM:	polarized	polarization
BRITISH SYSTEM:	polarised	polarisation
INCONSISTENT:	The two gases are polarised on the electrodes, and this polarization is the result of electrolysis.	
CONSISTENT:	The two gases are polarized on the electrodes, and this polarization is the result of electrolysis.	

5 Distinguishing Homonyms and Near Homonyms

Homonyms are words that have the same or very nearly the same sound but different spellings. *There, their,* and *they're* are homonyms. Homonyms are at the root of many spelling errors. Some people mean *you're* and write *your.* Near homonyms, or words that are similar in sound (such as *accept* and *except*), also cause many spelling errors. Keeping a list of homonyms and near homonyms that give you the most trouble may help you avoid errors. Here are some of the more commonly confused homonyms and near homonyms:

a		**d**	
accept	except	dairy	diary
access	excess	decent	descent
advice	advise	desert	dessert
affect	effect	device	devise
aid	aide	discreet	discrete
altar	alter	dual	duel
assistance	assistants	dyeing	dying
ate	eight		

b		**e**	
bare	bear	elicit	illicit
beach	beech	emigrate	immigrate
berry	bury	eminent	imminent
berth	birth		
board	bored	**f**	
born	borne	fair	fare
brake	break	flour	flower
bread	bred	formally	formerly
breadth	breath	forth	fourth
buy	by		

c		**g**	
capital	capitol	gorilla	guerrilla
cell	sell	grate	great
censor	censure		
cereal	serial	**h**	
coarse	course	hair	hare
complement	compliment	hardy	hearty
conscience	conscious	hear	here
council	counsel	heard	herd
		higher	hire

i

idle	idol
in	inn
instance	instants

k

knew	new
know	no

l

lead	led
lessen	lesson
loan	lone
loose	lose

m

made	maid
main	mane
meat	meet
medal	meddle
miner	minor

o

oar	ore
one	won

p

pain	pane
passed	past
patience	patients
peace	piece
peak	peek
pear	pair
personal	personnel
pier	peer
plane	plain
poor	pour
precede	proceed
presence	presents
principal	principle
profit	prophet

q

quiet	quite

r

rain	reign
read	red
right	write
role	roll

s

sail	sale
scent	sent
seem	seam
shone	shown
sight	site
sole	soul
son	sun
stake	steak
stationary	stationery
steal	steel
straight	strait

t

taught	taut
team	teem
than	then
threw	through
tide	tied
to	too

v

vain	vein

w

wander	wonder
waste	waist
way	weigh
weak	week
weather	whether
were	where
which	witch
wood	would
wrote	rote

29b
sp

In addition, you must distinguish forms such as *altogether (altogether fitting and proper)* and *all together (The members of the team were all together for a moment at the reunion)*. Here are some similar pairs:

already (We are already behind schedule.)
all ready (But we were all ready to leave on time.)

awhile (Sit down and stay awhile.)
a while (We can stay for a while.)

everyday (That was hardly an everyday event.)
every day (Every day cannot be exceptional.)

into (They walked into the negotiating room.)
in to (They gave in to the demands.)

maybe (Maybe we can buy a new estate.)
may be (That may be wishful thinking.)

It is also worth noting that *a lot* must never be written *alot.* The form *alright* is becoming acceptable in more informal situations; in your formal writing you should use *all right.*

29b
sp

Exercise 4

In each of the following sentences, select the word in parentheses that is correct. Be prepared to defend your choice.

> **EXAMPLE:** In 1755, Dr. Samuel Johnson published his *Dictionary of the English Language,* a work that has had significant (affects, effects) on the English language. [The correct word is *effects.*]

1. In this work, Johnson offers (advice, advise) about the spelling, meanings, and propriety of words.

2. It was Johnson's (personal, personnel) goal to "refine our language to grammatical purity, and to clear it from colloquial barbarisms, licentious idioms, and irregular combinations."

3. In matters of spelling, Johnson was conservative; rarely did he (altar, alter) the spellings that printers had agreed upon.

4. Johnson believed that one should not (medal, meddle) with the spelling of a word just because the pronunciation of the word had changed.

5. After all, he argued, he would be working in (vain, vein) if he tried to relate the spelling of a word to its current pronunciation, since pronunciations change.

6. Therefore, the word forms that Johnson (cited, sighted) were the ones he found in the literary products of the best English writers.

7. Johnson also gave good (council, counsel) about the primary and secondary meanings of words.

8. Some of his definitions, however, are (quiet, quite) difficult to understand—for instance, his definition of a network as "any thing reticulated or decussated, at equal distances, with interstices between the intersections."

9. And some of his definitions are so unusual that they have (passed, past) into the folklore of Western civilization; he defined oats as "a grain, which in England is given to horses, but in Scotland supports the people."

10. In most cases, however, Johnson's definitions give ample testimony to the (breadth, breath) of his reading.

6 Using Mnemonic Devices

Mnemosyne was the goddess of memory in Greek mythology, and the word *mnemonic* comes from her name. A **mnemonic device** is one that helps you remember something. Many people find mnemonic devices extremely helpful in remembering how to spell particular words, especially homonyms.

The mnemonic devices you use do not have to be logical or clever or widely appealing; they simply have to work for you. Some of our students remind themselves that *there,* which has to do with location, has *here* in it; and that *their,* which signals personal possession, has *i* in it, which they relate to the personal pronoun *I.* Still others say that *dessert* has two *s*'s, not one, since people hope for more of it.

29b
sp

7 Applying Some Rules

You may well be suspicious of the advice to learn some rules about spelling. You have probably been exposed to many spelling rules, all of which you could have handled if there were not so many exceptions to them. Still, we believe that knowing some rules will help you improve as a speller.

a. Deciding between *ie* and *ei*

Knowing the jingle about "*i* before *e*" can help you spell many words. Divided into sections, this jingle is as follows:

i before *e:*   apiece   fiend   frontier   grieve   priest   shriek

except after *c:*   ceiling   conceit   receipt

or when sounded as *ay:*   neighbor   weigh.

There are some exceptions to this rule; they are worth memorizing:

> *e* before *i* even though not after *c:* caffeine   either   foreign   height   leisure   neither   seize   weird
>
> *i* before *e* even though after *c:* ancient   conscience   science   species

Exercise 5

Add either *ie* or *ei* to each of the following in order to produce a correctly spelled word. Be prepared to explain your decisions.

> **EXAMPLE:**   To *f* _____ *rce* you would add *ie* (This slot does not follow *c*, and the appropriate sound is not "ay"): *fierce.*

1. repr _____ ve   3. perc _____ ve   5. fr _____ ght
2. _____ ght   4. dec _____ t

b. Making Nouns and Related Constructions Plural

(1) Most Nouns

To produce the plural form of most nouns, add *s:*

Singular	Plural
job	jobs
style	styles

(2) Nouns Ending in ss and Related Clusters of Letters

If a noun ends in sounds that are symbolized by *ss, zz, x, sh,* and *ch,* make the noun plural by adding *es:*

Singular	Plural
pass	passes
buzz	buzzes
tax	taxes
bush	bushes
church	churches

(3) Nouns Ending in y

If a noun ends in a *y* preceded by *a, e, o,* or *u,* make it plural by adding *s:*

Singular	Plural
day	days
key	keys
buoy	buoys
guy	guys

29b
sp

However, if a noun ends in a *y* preceded by a consonant, make it plural by changing the *y* to *i* and adding *es:*

Singular	Plural
beauty	beauties
nursery	nurseries

(4) Nouns Ending in f, fe, ff, or ffe

If a noun ends in *f* or *fe,* make it plural by changing the *f* to *v* and adding *s* or *es:*

Singular	Plural
loaf	loaves
wife	wives

Here are some exceptions to this rule:

Singular	Plural
belief	beliefs
chef	chefs
chief	chiefs
grief	griefs
motif	motifs
roof	roofs
safe	safes

If a noun ends in *ff* or *ffe,* make it plural by adding *s:*

Singular	Plural
staff	staffs
giraffe	giraffes

(5) Nouns Ending in o

If a noun ends in an *o* preceded by a consonant, the general guideline for making it plural is to add *es:*

Singular	Plural
tomato	tomatoes

But a few forms add only *s:*

Singular	Plural
banjo	banjos
piano	pianos
silo	silos

29b
sp

And a few nouns ending in *o* have two plural forms, one ending in *es* and one ending in *s:*

Singular	Plural
memento	mementos, mementoes
mosquito	mosquitos, mosquitoes

You should use whichever plural form your dictionary lists first.

If a noun ends in an *o* preceded by a vowel, make it plural by adding *s:*

Singular	Plural
cameo	cameos
radio	radios

(6) Nouns Borrowed from Greek or Latin

If a noun has been borrowed into English from Greek or Latin, you often have to use the plural form derived from the lending language:

Singular	Plural
alumna	alumnae (feminine)
alumnus	alumni (masculine)
basis	bases
crisis	crises
hypothesis	hypotheses
thesis	theses

As the English language continues to change, however, it is tending to develop two plural forms for some nouns borrowed from Greek, Latin, or French. One of these forms comes from the lending language, and one is a naturalized form. You should use the form that your dictionary lists first:

Singular	Plural as in the lending language	Naturalized plural
appendix	appendices	appendixes
chateau	chateaux	chateaus
focus	foci	focuses
index	indices	indexes
medium	media	mediums
memorandum	memoranda	memorandums
phenomenon	phenomena	phenomenons
radius	radii	radiuses
stadium	stadia	stadiums

29b
sp

(7) Nouns with the Same Form in the Singular and Plural

Some nouns have the same form in the singular and in the plural:

Singular	Plural
deer	deer
elk	elk
sheep	sheep
species	species

(8) Nouns with Irregular Plurals

A small number of nouns have plural forms that you could not predict on the basis of rules; you have to remember their irregular forms. Here are some examples:

Singular	Plural
child	children
goose	geese
mouse	mice
ox	oxen

(9) Abbreviations, Letters, Numbers, and Years

Make abbreviations, letters, and numbers plural by adding an apostrophe plus *s* to them. In most cases, if you were to omit the apostrophe, you would confuse readers. For example, if you wanted to refer to more than one *I* and added just an *s,* you would produce *Is,* which readers would probably see as a verb. The proper form for such plurals is as follows:

I's   *SOS*'s   *A.B.*'s   *6*'s

To form the plural of years, you can add either an apostrophe plus *s* (1960's) or just an *s* (1960s). This latter form is a possibility since there is little chance that anyone would misread it.

(10) Proper Names

You should make people's names and other capitalized names plural by adding *s* or *es:*

two Shirleys   three Mitches   two Americas

29b
sp

(11) Compounds

If the parts of a compound are roughly equal in significance, you make the compound plural by adding *s* to the last word, even if the compound is hyphenated:

Singular   **Plural**
breakpoint   breakpoints
city-state   city-states

However, if the parts of a compound are not roughly equal in significance, you make the compound plural in one of these ways:

1. By adding *s* to the part that is a noun:

Singular   **Plural**
in-law   in-laws
passerby   passersby
poet laureate   poets laureate

(One exception to this is the plural of *spoonful: spoonfuls.*)

2. By adding *s* to the noun that is more or most important:

Singular   **Plural**
sister-in-law   sisters-in-law

3. By adding *s* to the final part if no part is a noun:

Singular   **Plural**
also-ran   also-rans

**29b
sp**

Exercise 6

Write the plural form for each of the following, and be prepared to defend your decisions with references to rules.

EXAMPLE: *printing press*   *printing presses* [The word *press* is a noun, and *printing* was originally a participle. In such cases, you add *s* or *es* to the noun.]

1. pastel   4. bay   7. cuff   10. zoo   13. COD
2. porch   5. belief   8. potato   11. analysis   14. A (the letter)
3. strategy   6. leaf   9. piano   12. moose   15. green light

c. Spelling the Third-Person Singular Forms of Verbs Ending in *y*

With verbs that end in a *y* preceded by *a, e, o,* or *u,* spell the third-person singular form by adding an *s:*

I say, she says   we enjoy, she enjoys
you key in, he keys in   they buy, he buys

With verbs that end in a *y* preceded by a consonant, spell the third-person singular form by changing the *y* to *i* and adding *es:*

I hurry, he hurries   we tarry, she tarries

d. Adding Prefixes

Adding a prefix to a word does not change the spelling of that word. However, you have to be careful not to confuse some prefixes. Here is a list of some frequently confused prefixes; if you have trouble distinguishing some of these, it would be helpful to memorize them.

Prefix	Paraphrase	Example
ante-	before	antebellum
anti-	against, versus	antihero
hyper-	beyond, excessive	hypertension
hypo-	less than normal	hypothermia
inter-	between	interstellar
intra-	within	intramural
macro-	large-scale	macroeconomics
micro-	small-scale	microeconomics
super-	great, extraordinary	supertanker
supra-	above, over	supranational

29b
sp

e. Adding Endings to Words

(1) Dropping or Retaining the e Before an Ending

If you want to add an ending (a suffix or inflection) to a word whose last letter is *e,* should you drop or keep the *e* before adding the ending? To decide, ask yourself two questions: Is the *e* silent? Does the ending begin with a vowel? If you answer yes to both of these questions, you should drop the *e* before adding the ending:

fame + ous = famous   remove + able = removable

noise + y = noisy   write + ing = writing

One group of exceptions to this rule includes words in which a silent *e* is preceded by a *c* or a *g* and in which the ending begins with *a, o,* or *u.* In these cases, retain the silent *e* to signal that the sounds symbolized by *c* and *g* are soft:

advantage + ous = advantageous   service + able = serviceable

manage + able = manageable   notice + able = noticeable

Another group of exceptions to this rule includes words in which the *e* is retained to distinguish potentially confusing words or to help in the pronunciation of words:

dye + ing = dyeing, not dying (a different word)
singe + ing = singeing, not singing (a different word)
acre + age = acreage, not acrage (not a word)

The other side of the final *e* rule covers words that end in a silent *e* but add an ending that begins with a consonant. These words usually retain the *e:*

excite + ment = excitement   life + like = lifelike

There are a few exceptions to this rule in the cases of ordinal numbers and words with the ending *-ful, -ly,* or *-ment:*

nine + th = ninth   true + ly = truly
awe + ful = awful   judge + ment = judgment

(2) Adding an Ending to a Word That Ends in y

If you want to add an ending to a word that ends in *y,* should you keep the *y* or change it to *i* before adding the ending? If the *y* is preceded by a vowel, you should usually keep the *y:*

boy + ish = boyish   enjoy + ment = enjoyment

But if the *y* is preceded by a consonant, you should usually change the *y* to *i* before adding the ending:

icy + er = icier   mercy + less = merciless
pity + able = pitiable   solidify + cation = solidification

Remember, though, that if the ending itself begins with an *i,* then you must not change the final *y* to an *i,* even if the final *y* is preceded by a consonant:

baby + ish = babyish   carry + ing = carrying

(3) Deciding When to Double a Final Consonant in a Word Before Adding an Ending

If you want to add an ending such as *-ing* to a word like *stop,* should you first double the *p* or not? To decide, you should ask yourself the following three questions in order: Does the word end in a single vowel plus a consonant? Is the word a one-syllable word, or, if not, does the accent fall on the last syllable of the word? Does the ending start with a vowel?

If you answer yes to all these questions, then you should double the consonant before adding the ending:

admit + ed = admitted   regret + able = regrettable
begin + er = beginner   rid + ance = riddance

If you answer no to any one of the three questions, then you should not double the consonant before adding the ending.

Imagine that you want to add *-ing* to *stoop*. Does the word end in a single vowel plus a consonant? No. Therefore, you should not double the final consonant: *stooping*.

Imagine that you want to add *-ance* to *sever*. Does the word have only one syllable, or, if not, is it accented on its final syllable? The answer to both questions is *no*. Therefore, you do not double the final consonant: *severance*.

Finally, imagine that you want to add *-ment* to *equip*. Does the ending begin with a vowel? No. Therefore, you do not double the final consonant: *equipment*.

(4) Deciding Between -sede, -ceed, and -cede

To use the endings *-sede, -ceed,* and *-cede* properly, it helps to know the following facts:

- Only one commonly used word ends in *-sede: supersede*.
- Only three commonly used words end in *-ceed: exceed, proceed, succeed*.
- Several words end in *-cede*. The most common are *concede, intercede, precede, recede,* and *secede*.

If you memorize the spelling of *supersede, exceed, proceed,* and *succeed,* you should be safe in assuming that any other words that have the sound of these endings take the *-cede* form.

29b
sp

Exercise 7

Select the correctly spelled form in each of the following pairs.

EXAMPLE: irresistable, irresistible [*irresistible* is correct]

1. forceible, forcible
2. outrageous, outragous
3. shoeing, shoing
4. mileage, milage
5. sincerely, sincerly
6. fiveth, fifth
7. arguement, argument
8. duely, duly
9. coyness, coiness
10. defyance, defiance
11. occurrence, occurence
12. peepping, peeping
13. saddness, sadness
14. plausable, plausible

8 Charting Words That Give You Trouble

Another strategy that might help you spell correctly is to keep a chart of difficult words. Some of our students do this by writing down the words correctly, by highlighting the part or parts of the words that give them trouble, and then by trying to generalize about the source of the trouble. The treatment of one word on such a chart could look like this:

Correct spelling	Trouble spot	Nature of the problem
accident	accident	representing the schwa ("uh") sound

9 Memorizing Words That Give You Trouble

It takes some effort to memorize the spelling of words that you find difficult to spell, but the effort is usually worth it. Below we provide a list of frequently misspelled words. You might find it helpful to take a small group of these words and commit them to memory. After you have finished with one group, you can move on to another. Doing so will probably save you time and embarrassment later, and it should bolster your confidence in your spelling abilities.

29b
sp

a	anxious	autumn	brilliant
absence	apologize	auxiliary	bruise
abundance	apparent	average	budget
accelerate	appearance	awful	buoyant
accessible	appreciate		bureau
accident	approximate	**b**	bury
accommodate	arbitrary	baggage	business
accumulate	arctic	banquet	
achievement	argument	barrel	**c**
acknowledge-	article	becoming	cafeteria
ment	ascend	beggar	cancel
acquire	assassin	beginning	captain
admissible	athlete	behavior	carriage
advertise	attach	belief	categorical
aggravate	attempt	benefit	cemetery
agriculture	attendance	bicycle	certain
amateur	attitude	boundary	changeable
analysis	audience	breathe	character
announce	authoritative	brief	chief

choice
circular
civilization
clothe
coherent
collar
column
committee
communicate
competent
conceive
concession
condemn
confer
confidence
congratulate
conscience
consensus
considerable
consistent
continue
convenient
cooperate
correspondent
courage
courteous
criticism
curiosity
curriculum
custom

d
deceive
decision
defense
definite
delicious
dependent
descend
desert
desperate
dessert
develop

dictionary
difference
disappear
disappoint
discipline
discuss
distinguish
divide
divine
divisible
doctor
dominant
don't
doubt
duchess
duly
duplicate
during
dynamic

e
earnest
easily
efficient
eighth
either
eligible
embarrass
emphasis
encyclopedia
endeavor
enormous
enough
envelope
environment
equipment
equivalent
especially
essential
evidence
exaggerate
excellent
excessive

exercise
exhilarating
existence
expensive
explanation
explicit
expressive
extension

f
fallacy
familiar
famous
fascinate
favorite
February
fertile
fictitious
fierce
fiery
filth
finally
financial
flourish
foreign
fortunate
fountain
freight
fulfill
fundamental

g
garage
generosity
genius
ghastly
glorious
government
grammar
gratitude
grievous
guarantee

h
hammer
handsome
happiness
height
hesitate
hindrance
historic
honor
hospitable
hypocrisy

i
ignorance
illiterate
imagination
imitation
immediate
immense
impossible
incessant
incident
incompatible
inconvenient
incredible
independent
indispensable
inevitable
inferior
ingenious
intelligent
interrupt
irrelevant

j
jackknife
janitor
jargon
jealous
jewelry
journalism
journey
judgment

**29b
sp**

judicious
justice

k
karate
kennel
khaki
kidney
kindergarten
kitchen
knowledge
knowledgeable
knuckle
kudos

l
laboratory
language
league
leisure
length
liable
library
license
lieutenant
lightning
liquid
liquor
literary
literature
livelihood
loneliness
losing
lovable
loveliness
luncheon

m
magnificent
maintenance
manageable
marriage
mathematics
mercenary

metallic
mileage
miniature
minimum
mirror
miscellaneous
mischievous
miserable
missile
misspell
moccasin
momentous
mortgage
murmur

n
narrate
nautical
navigation
necessary
niece
nihilism
ninetieth
nonsense
noticeable
nuclear

o
occasion
occurrence
ominous
omission
opinion
opposite
optimism
oratory
origin
oxygen

p
pamphlet
paragraph
parallel
parenthesis

particular
peculiar
performance
permanent
permissible
persistent
persuade
pervade
phenomenon
physician
picnicking
pleasant
possession
practical
precede
preference
prejudice
preservation
prevalent
privilege
probably
proceed
prominent
pronunciation
psychology
pursuit

q
quaking
quality
quarantine
quarrel
quarter
questionnaire
quiescent
quiet
quorum
quote

r
really
rebut
recede
receipt

recognition
recommend
redundant
reference
relevance
religious
reluctance
remembrance
repetition
reservoir
respectful
responsibility
restaurant
rhythm
ridiculous
roommate

s
sacrifice
salary
scarcity
schedule
science
secretary
seize
separate
shepherd
siege
significant
similar
sincerely
solemn
sophomore
sovereign
species
speech
statue
strategy
strenuous
studying
subtle
succeed
sufficient
supersede

29b sp

surround
syllable
synonym
system

t
technique
temporary
tendency
terrible
thief
thorough
though
tongue
tragedy
truly

u
unanimous
undoubtedly
universal
university
unmistakable
unnecessary
upper
useful
usual
utterance

v
vacillate
variety
vehicle

vengeance
vicinity
villain
visible
voice
voluble
volume

w
warrant
weight
weird
which
width
withhold
won't

worst
wouldn't
writing

y and **z**
yacht
yawn
yearn
yeoman
yield
yoga
zealous
zenith
zephyr
zoology

29b
sp

Some Common Errors at the Sentence Level

See the Index of Common Errors (pages 884–886) for references to further discussions of these errors.

Sentence Fragment A group of words that is punctuated as if it were a sentence but that is not a sentence, usually because it lacks a subject, lacks a verb, or is a subordinate clause.

FRAGMENT: Looked for a motel in Ely.

CORRECTED: They looked for a motel in Ely.

Comma Splice A sentence in which only a comma appears between two or more independent clauses.

COMMA SPLICE: Billy could not face his accuser, he could only moan to himself.

CORRECTED: Billy could not face his accuser; he could only moan to himself.

Fused Sentence A sentence in which no mark of punctuation appears between independent clauses.

FUSED SENTENCE: The park is lovely it is also dangerous.

CORRECTED: The park is lovely; it is also dangerous.

Faulty Predication A sentence that brings together subjects, verbs, or complements that do not go together logically.

FAULTY PREDICATION: The most recent *theory* of language *thinks* about word origins.

CORRECTED: Developers of the most recent theory of language think about word origins.

Mixed Construction A construction that includes elements that do not go together grammatically.

MIXED CONSTRUCTION: *By hurrying* to turn their papers in on time *is* a practice of many sophomores.

CORRECTED: Hurrying to turn their papers in on time is a practice of many sophomores.

Faulty Parallelism The result of using different grammatical structures in the same kind of grammatical slot.

FAULTY PARALLELISM: They try *painting* realistic representations and *to sculpt* abstract figures.

CORRECTED: They try painting realistic representations and sculpting abstract figures.

continued

Faulty Comparison   A sentence with parts that are compared but that are incomplete, ambiguous, or illogical.

FAULTY COMPARISON: Rebecca finds the class as interesting as Ned.

CORRECTED: Rebecca finds the class as interesting as Ned does.

Faulty Agreement Between Subject and Verb   The error of not making subjects agree with verbs in person and number.

FAULTY AGREEMENT: *The admiral,* along with dozens of his cousins and aunts, *sing* about the Queen's Navy.

CORRECTED: The admiral, along with dozens of his cousins and aunts, sings about the Queen's Navy.

Shift in Tense   An error in which the verbs in a sentence unjustifiably shift from one tense to another.

SHIFT IN TENSE: Many authors *support* their case with the same passages but *interpreted* the passages differently.

CORRECTED: Many authors support their case with the same passages but interpret the passages differently.

Shift in Voice   An error in which the verbs in a sentence unjustifiably shift from the active voice to the passive, or from the passive to the active.

SHIFT IN VOICE: Gandalf *thought* deeply, and then a decision *was made* by him.

CORRECTED: Gandalf thought deeply, and then he made a decision.

Shift in Mood   An error in which the verbs in a sentence unjustifiably shift from one mood to another.

SHIFT IN MOOD: It is imperative that he *see* Andelain and *saves* it.

CORRECTED: It is imperative that he see Andelain and save it.

Split Infinitive   An infinitive with an adverbial modifier between the *to* and the base of a verb: to *really* win. Split infinitives can cause readers trouble if the adverbial material is long or hard to interpret.

SPLIT INFINITIVE: to *without any reservation whatsoever* trust

CORRECTED: to trust without any reservation whatsoever

Faulty Pronoun Case   The use of incorrect case forms of pronouns.

FAULTY CASE: They budget time as well as *me*.

CORRECTED: They budget time as well as I.

Faulty Pronoun Reference   A problem caused when writers do not make clear what the antecedent for a pronoun is.

FAULTY REFERENCE: After Evangeline talked to Fanny, *she* fell from power.

CORRECTED: After Evangeline talked to Fanny, Evangeline fell from power.

Faulty Agreement Between Pronouns and Their Antecedents The error that results when pronouns do not agree with their antecedents in number, person, or gender.

FAULTY AGREEMENT: Never again will *a person* experience such a great learning period as *they* do then.

CORRECTED: Never again will people experience such a great learning period as they do then.

Double Comparative or Superlative Form   An adjective or adverb with two signals of the comparative or superlative degree.

DOUBLE: *more* warm*er*, *most* fast*est*

CORRECTED: warmer, fastest

Double Negative   The use of two words with negative meaning in the same clause.

DOUBLE NEGATIVE: They did *not* get *no* warning about the oil spill.

CORRECTED: They did not get any warning about the oil spill.

Dangling Modifier   A modifier whose implied subject or actor is different from the subject of the clause the modifier is attached to.

DANGLING MODIFIER: *Covering the patient with a lead vest,* the machine took an x-ray.

CORRECTED: After the dental hygienist covered the patient with a lead vest, the machine took an x-ray.

continued

Misplaced Modifier   A modifier that, because of its placement in a
sentence, appears to modify the wrong words.

MISPLACED MODIFIER: They have an excellent discussion of
                      pollution *in their most recent work.*

CORRECTED: In their most recent work, they have an
                      excellent discussion of pollution.

Squinting Modifier   A modifier that can be read as modifying
either an element that precedes it or an element that follows it.

SQUINTING MODIFIER: Large power plants that generate electricity
                      normally are a source of thermal pollution.

CORRECTED: Normally, large power plants that generate
                      electricity are a source of thermal
                      pollution.

VIII

P U N C T U A T I O N

A N D   M E C H A N I C S

30

THE PERIOD,
QUESTION MARK,
AND EXCLAMATION
POINT

T he marks of punctuation can help you guide readers in several ways. Depending on the marks you use, you can signal where one grammatical unit stops and another begins, specify how grammatical units relate to each other in meaning, and enable readers to predict what kinds of structures and meanings will follow others. In addition, with some marks you can add stylish touches to your prose.

The marks of punctuation that we focus on in this chapter—the **period, question mark,** and **exclamation point**—are known mainly for their separating and specifying functions. Along with capital letters, they mark the separations between sentences. They also help readers determine whether a given sentence conveys information, asks them for information, or expresses strong commands or emotions.

30a

The Period

The main guidelines for using the period are as follows.

1 Use a Period After Statements and Mild Commands

Sentences consisting of a statement or a mild command should end with a period:

STATEMENT: They stopped in the middle of the road.

MILD COMMAND: Notice the single strand of gray hair.

When using a typewriter or a word processor, you should leave two spaces after the period at the end of a sentence.

2 Use a Period After Polite Requests

After sentences making a polite request, you should use a period if the request is rather routine and impersonal. The period is an indication that the writer does not expect an answer but rather the fulfilling of the request:

Kindly submit your course evaluations to the departmental secretary by December 16.

However, if the request is more personal and courteous, you should use a question mark:

Could you tell me, Spike, when our revisions are due?

3 Use a Period After Indirect Questions

Indirect questions imply a question or report on a question, but they do not themselves ask a question. After indirect questions you should use a period, not a question mark:

INCORRECT: They asked who thought of that design?

CORRECT: They asked who thought of that design.

4 Use a Period with Many Abbreviations

Many abbreviations require periods within them or after them. Some of these abbreviations appear before names:

Dr.   Mr.   Mrs.   Ms.   St.

Note that only one space follows such periods: *Dr. Jones.*
Some abbreviations appear after names:

Esq.   D.D.   Jr.   M.D.   Ph.D.   Sr.

30c
pqe

Note that there is no space after periods used within abbreviations:

Professor Jones, Ed.D., leaves for India tomorrow.

Some abbreviations appear only with figures:

33 B.C.   A.D. 1066   10:00 A.M./a.m.   11:59 P.M./p.m.

Some abbreviations are acceptable in addresses but should be spelled in full in ordinary writing:

Ave.   Blvd.   Dr.   St.

Finally, some abbreviations are acceptable in footnotes, bibliographies, and tables, but they should be spelled in full when they are used as separate words in ordinary writing:

etc.   p.   pp.   vol.

Unless you are certain about the form that an abbreviation takes, you should consult a good dictionary about that form, since many abbreviations require no periods within them or after them. It is conventional to use no periods in or after abbreviations for some technical terms, some signals in code, some organizations and political agencies, and the zip code abbreviations for states in the United States:

DNA   UFO   SOS   YWCA   YMCA
IBM   NASA   NATO   IA (Iowa)   IN (Indiana)

A final note about abbreviations: If a sentence ends with an abbreviation that requires a period after it, do not add a second period:

INCORRECT: They consulted Shelby Maugham, Ph.D..
CORRECT: They consulted Shelby Maugham, Ph.D.

5 Use Periods Within Parenthetical References to Plays and Long Poems

To indicate the source of part of a play or long poem that you have quoted, you should use periods to separate references to acts, scenes, and lines of plays, as well as to separate references to books and lines in long poems:

QUOTING FROM A PLAY: Many people have heard Desdemona's "Commend me to my kind lord" (*Othello* V.ii.123) and have wept.

QUOTING FROM A LONG POEM: Those people are still seeking "to justify the ways of God to men" (*Paradise Lost* I.26).

30a
bge

6 Use a Period with Decimals and Fractional Amounts of Money

You should use figures and periods to express decimals:

.05   9.9

Also, whenever you refer to fractional amounts of money greater than one dollar, you should use figures and periods:

$1.35 $9.95

Exercise 1

Explain why each of the following sentences is incorrect, and then correct each sentence.

> EXAMPLE: One student asked whether we would be reading some
> O. Henry stories? [This sentence is an indirect, not a
> direct, question. Therefore, it should be followed by a
> period, not a question mark: *One student asked*
> *whether we would be reading some O. Henry stories.*]

1. Kindly return the questionnaire to the dean's secretary?
2. Noam, do you know when the debate will be held.
3. We asked how that character could ever be considered an omniscient narrator?
4. Horace Hoffman, Ph D, writes about political issues.
5. They moved to Lansing, I.L., almost three months ago.

30b
pqe

30b

The Question Mark

The main guidelines for using the question mark are as follows.

1 Use a Question Mark After Direct Questions

After sentences that ask a direct question, you should use a question mark:

Is that narrator reliable?

What makes you think that they are major characters?

Sometimes you might choose to use a compound sentence in which the first clause makes a statement and the second asks a direct question. In this case, use a question mark after the sentence:

They claim that adolescents are irresponsible, but is all of their evidence valid?

If you quote someone else's direct question and add a designation of the speaker, you should use only a question mark, not a question mark and a comma, between the quoted question and the designation of the speaker:

INCORRECT: "Am I a fool?", asked Gimpel.

CORRECT: "Am I a fool?" asked Gimpel.

Similarly, if you make a statement that ends with a quoted question, use only a question mark at the end:

INCORRECT: Gimpel then asked, "Am I a fool?".

CORRECT: Gimpel then asked, "Am I a fool?"

(For more information on question marks and quotation marks, see **34b**.)

Finally, if a direct question ends with an abbreviation that requires a period after it, you should include a question mark after that period:

Is it clear and bright at 3:00 a.m.?

30b
pqe

2   Use a Question Mark After Questions Included in Statements

Whenever you include a question in a statement, you should use a question mark after the question. Sometimes the question is set off by dashes or parentheses:

We have not been able to find the time—and when will we ever find the time?—to do all the assigned reading.

Sometimes the question is not set off from the statement that contains it:

How are we to get along without her? is the question now.

One exception to this guideline concerns including one-word questions such as *how* and *why* in statements. When you include such a question, you should not follow it with a question mark, and you should not capitalize it. Instead, italicize or underline the one-word question:

The question now was *why*.

3 Use a Question Mark After Questions Included in Other Questions

If you write one question that has another question included at its end, you should use one question mark, not two, at the end of the entire structure.

INCORRECT: Why did the lecturer ask, Must a story have characters??

CORRECT: Why did the lecturer ask, Must a story have characters?

4 Use Question Marks with a Series of Questions

If a sentence contains several separate short questions in a row, each should be punctuated with a question mark. When your writing situation is quite formal, begin each question with a capital letter:

These characters are obviously searching, but we must ask, For what? How eagerly? and What chance of success do they have?

If the situation is less formal, do not begin each separate question with a capital letter:

Someone in our study group wondered, of what time? of what place? in what manner?

5 Use a Question Mark with Dubious Information

If you need to indicate that a date, figure, or word is dubious, put a question mark in parentheses after it:

She gave the number of a house on Aldersgate (?) Street.

If the dubious information is itself included in parentheses, then you should enclose the question mark in brackets:

Some commentators trace that technique all the way back to Edmund Spenser (1552[?]–1599).

30b
pqe

You should avoid using a question mark within parentheses to try to indicate sarcasm:

AVOID: As writers of grant proposals, they are flawless (?).

It would be better to express a sarcastic attitude by means of a technique such as understatement:

As writers of grant proposals, they are not without flaws.

Exercise 2

Explain why each of the following sentences is incorrect, and then correct each sentence.

> **EXAMPLE:**   The house is haunted, isn't it. [This sentence is incorrect. It asks a question and therefore should end with a question mark: *The house is haunted, isn't it?*]

1. Why did they all move west.
2. We know that geometry is important, but why do we have to spend two months studying it.
3. "Will you try to fly into the eye of the hurricane?", they asked.
4. Was the inquisition scheduled to begin at 10:00 a.m.
5. Juan's question to them was "Why did this happen to me?".
6. The snow appeared to be falling—Was this really possible—on every part of Ireland.
7. The question Daru faced was why?
8. How does Hemingway reveal what surgical procedure the man and woman are talking about is the question we have to answer.
9. At this point we must still ask, sharing what. with whom. and what is the secret.
10. Their commentaries are always very insightful (?).

30c

The Exclamation Point

Use an exclamation point only if the form it follows carries emotional force. Exclamation points can appear after many different forms:

Fine!	Aren't they great!
Not again!	Get out of our way!
It can't be true!	What a great idea that is!

In every case, the exclamation point is justified only if the form conveys a sense of astonishment, shock, joy, grief, outrage, or great irony.

You should avoid using an exclamation point after forms that often convey milder emotions or senses: *ok, goodness, well, yes,* and *no.* After such forms, a comma is usually sufficient:

> Yes, they could graduate after three years of study.

You will have occasion to use an exclamation point most often when you record speech. In other situations, you will rarely need an exclamation point. If you overuse the exclamation point, you can easily seem strident or insecure about your message.

When quoting or paraphrasing other writers, you might occasionally be tempted to use an exclamation point in brackets after a claim that you dispute. You should resist this temptation:

> **AVOID:**   According to Professor Bond, "Westervelt is a
> sensitive [!] character."

If you dispute a claim in a quotation but it is not clearly in error, you should present the quotation accurately and then argue against it in your own words. If a quotation contains an error, use *sic* (Latin for *thus*) in brackets immediately after the error:

> According to Professor Mancan, "When Katherine Anne Porter was born in 1790 [sic], the world of short fiction gained a skilled and sensitive model."

You should never combine an exclamation point with other marks of punctuation:

> **INCORRECT:**   They were enraged now. "We will squash you!",
> they roared.
>
> **CORRECT:**   They were enraged now. "We will squash you!"
> they roared.

If an exclamation point and another mark of punctuation are both called for at the same location, retain only the exclamation point, since it is the strongest punctuation mark of all:

> **INCORRECT:**   Who screamed, "Kill the beast!"?
>
> **CORRECT:**   Who screamed, "Kill the beast!"

(For more information on exclamation points and quotation marks, see **34b**).

30c
pqe

Exercise 3

Find at least five examples of published prose in which forms are followed by an exclamation point. Describe the kind of sense or emotion that each form conveys.

31

O n a scale measuring the separations that different marks of punctuation introduce between grammatical elements, the semicolon and
the colon rank just below the period, question mark, and exclamation
point. That is, the semicolon and the colon introduce slightly less than
a full stop. At the same time, the semicolon and the colon indicate
more specifically than do the marks of end punctuation how the elements on both sides of them are related to each other.

31a

The Semicolon

Some people associate the semicolon only with the most formal kinds
of writing, and they assume that they should rarely, if ever, use it. This
is a faulty and unfortunate assumption, for the semicolon fulfills important functions in many different kinds of writing.

1 Use a Semicolon Between Independent Clauses Not Joined by Coordinating Conjunctions

When you want to include two or more independent clauses in one sentence, you can link them with a comma and one of the coordinating conjunctions *(and, but, or, for, nor, so, yet)*:

> We needed some help finding information about world records, but all the reference librarians were busy.

However, you can also link such clauses with a semicolon:

> A student assistant was quite helpful; he showed us a good index.

In the next sentence, semicolons link three independent clauses:

> We proceeded to the seventh floor; we searched eagerly among the stacks of books; then we found what we needed.

You will find that in many sentences containing a semicolon the independent clauses are identical or very similar in form:

> We read about weather records; they read about human achievements.

In addition, the independent clauses linked with a semicolon will almost always be closely related in meaning. Four of the more common close relationships are illustrated below.

31c
sc

1. Clauses presenting alternatives

> The price for the edition with black-and-white photographs is ten dollars; the price for the edition with color photographs is fifteen dollars.

2. Clauses pointing out a contrast

> The Colombian city of Tutunendo averages 463.4 inches of rain per year; the Chilean Desierto de Atacama has a brief rain squall only occasionally each century.

3. One clause explaining material in the other clause

> People in that settlement rarely see the sun in the winter; they live very close to the North Pole.

4. One clause expressing a cause and the other revealing the consequence

> Each of them tried to break the record of eating thirty-eight soft-boiled eggs in seventy-five seconds; afterward, none of them ate another egg for five years.

Remember that, if you place an independent clause before a semi-colon, in all but a few cases you must do likewise after the semicolon. If you do not, you will be making an error in sentence structure that is nearly as serious as the error of using unjustified sentence fragments (see Chapter 22). Consequently, you should not use an independent clause on one side of a semicolon and a subordinate clause on the other.

INCORRECT:

independent clause

She ate 2,780 cold beans one by one in

subordinate clause

thirty minutes; although she used only a cocktail stick.

POSSIBLE CORRECTION: She ate 2,780 cold beans one by one in thirty minutes; she used only a cocktail stick.

Nor should you have an independent clause on one side of a semicolon and only a phrase on the other:

INCORRECT:

phrase

With only a little apparent effort; he ate

independent clause

seventeen bananas in two minutes.

POSSIBLE CORRECTION: He ate seventeen bananas in two minutes; he seemed to expend little effort.

Finally, you should not use an independent clause on one side of a semicolon and only a word or a series of words on the other:

two adjectives   independent clause

INCORRECT: Fresh, salty; the one hundred peanuts were eaten in forty-six seconds.

POSSIBLE CORRECTION: The peanuts were fresh and salty; they were eaten in forty-six seconds.

2 Use a Semicolon Between Long or Internally Punctuated Independent Clauses Even When They Are Joined by Coordinating Conjunctions

If one or both of the independent clauses that you wish to connect in a sentence are long or contain commas, you may choose to separate the clauses with a semicolon, even though you use a coordinating conjunction between them:

> Hetty Howland Green, who lived from 1835 to 1916, saved money by eating cold oatmeal for much of her life; and after her death, her estate, which included many different holdings, was estimated to be worth ninety-five million dollars.

The semicolon helps readers keep one independent clause and its parts distinct from the other and its parts.

3 Use a Semicolon Between Independent Clauses Joined by Conjunctive Adverbs or Transitional Expressions

Sometimes you might choose to make an explicit connection between one independent clause and another by using a conjunctive adverb (such as *however* or *moreover*; see **18a**) or a transitional expression (such as *for example* or *in addition*). You could, of course, express each independent clause as a separate sentence:

> They talked of trying to set a new record for wheelbarrow racing. However, they settled for an attempt on the record for swinging in a hammock.

But if you want to draw more attention to the close relationship between the two independent clauses, you can use a semicolon to link them within the bounds of one sentence:

31a
sc

> They talked of trying to set a new record for wheelbarrow racing; however, they settled for an attempt on the record for swinging in a hammock.

Note that generally a comma follows the conjunctive adverb or transitional expression. After only a few one-word adverbs or transitions (such as *thus, now,* and *hence*) is the comma often omitted:

> The speaker they invited had once given a speech lasting thirty hours; thus they did their best to make themselves comfortable.

You need to remember that conjunctive adverbs and transitional expressions linking independent clauses do not have to appear at the beginning of the second clause. The semicolon, on the other hand, must remain between the independent clauses, no matter where the conjunctive adverb or transitional expression is placed. Therefore, all of the following are correct:

> Attempting to eat six pounds of eels in a minute is not safe; in fact, doing so is extremely inadvisable.
>
> Attempting to eat six pounds of eels in a minute is not safe; doing so, in fact, is extremely inadvisable.
>
> Attempting to eat six pounds of eels in a minute is not safe; doing so is extremely inadvisable, in fact.

Likewise, a conjunctive adverb or transitional expression can appear in various positions in an independent clause preceding a semicolon:

> However, attempting to eat six pounds of eels in a minute is not safe; doing so is extremely inadvisable.
>
> Attempting to eat six pounds of eels in a minute, however, is not safe; doing so is extremely inadvisable.
>
> Attempting to eat six pounds of eels in a minute is not safe, however; doing so is extremely inadvisable.

In all our sample sentences containing a semicolon, an independent clause appears on both sides of the semicolon. It is an error to use a semicolon before a conjunctive adverb or transitional expression that appears within an independent clause:

31a
sc

> INCORRECT: Attempting to eat six pounds of eels in a minute; however, is not safe.
>
> CORRECT: Attempting to eat six pounds of eels in a minute, however, is not safe.

4 Use a Semicolon Between Long or Internally Punctuated Items in a Series

Consider the following sentence:

> The dignitaries visited the following universities: Harvard University, the oldest surviving American university, Brown University, a school that was once called Rhode Island College, and Yale University, an institution that once proposed a merger with Vassar College.

How many universities did the dignitaries actually visit? The *and* before the name *Yale University* probably leads you to conclude that both the name and the words *an institution that once proposed a merger with Vassar College* refer to one and the same institution. But how many institutions are referred to earlier—two, three, or four? Without additional knowledge, you cannot tell for certain. Semicolons would help clarify the meaning of this sentence:

> The dignitaries visited the following universities: Harvard University, the oldest surviving American university; Brown University, a school that was once called Rhode Island College; and Yale University, an institution that once proposed a merger with Vassar College.

To sum up, in a series you should use semicolons to keep each listed item and the elements that belong with it separate from all the other listed items and the elements that belong with them.

Here is another kind of list to which this guideline applies:

> On their summer trip, they stopped in the following places: Wilmer, Minnesota; Orange City, Iowa; Butte, Montana; and Spokane, Washington.

Exercise 1

Add semicolons and change commas to semicolons wherever necessary in the following sentences.

> **EXAMPLE:**   Katharine Hepburn has been nominated for an Oscar often, indeed, she has been nominated twelve times.
>
> Katharine Hepburn has been nominated for an Oscar often; indeed, she has been nominated twelve times.

**31a
sc**

1. Katharine Hepburn won her most recent Oscar in 1981, Gary Cooper won his last one in 1952.

2. Few actors have won as many Oscars as Katharine Hepburn has she has won Oscars for starring roles in four films.

3. Greer Garson spoke for over an hour and a half at the 1942 Oscar ceremonies, today, however, television producers impose time limits on all speakers at the ceremonies.

4. The youngest person ever to win an Oscar is Shirley Temple, with an honorary award at the age of five, the oldest is George Burns, for his role in *The Sunshine Boys* at the age of eighty.

5. That film about a foreign invasion of the Americas, which was released in the United States, struck many viewers as violent, and a study of the film, which attracted considerable attention, showed that the film portrayed 134 acts of violence per hour.

6. *Rescued by Power* is considered the least expensive commercial film ever made it was highly successful, however.

7. Some of the most frequently portrayed characters in film are the following: Sherlock Holmes, a character created by Sir Arthur Conan Doyle, Count Dracula, a terrifying figure created by Bram Stoker, and Frankenstein's monster, a figure created by Mary Shelley.

8. The Soviet Union claims to have 163,400 movie theaters, some of these, however, are only buildings that contain a movie projector.

9. The longest film ever shown is *The Longest Most Meaningful Movie in the World* it is forty-eight hours long.

10. *Heaven's Gate* was not an inexpensive film, it was, as a matter of fact, one of the most expensive films ever made.

Exercise 2

Write five original sentences, making sure that you use all four guidelines for semicolons.

31b

The Colon

The expectations that the colon creates in readers are usually even more specific than those the semicolon creates. When readers see a colon, they usually expect to see after it some material that defines, renames, explains, or illustrates the material before the colon.

Note that in almost all cases an independent clause must precede a colon (one exception, seen in this book, is the use of short words as labels—for example, *correct*—followed by a colon). Also note that only one space should follow a colon.

31b
sc

1 Use a Colon Before a List or Series

The most common function of the colon is to introduce a list or a series that follows an independent clause and clarifies a point in it. Often the list will be introduced by words such as *the following* or *as follows*, and the colon will appear immediately after these words:

> Some of the best-selling albums of all time are as follows: Michael Jackson's *Thriller*, Fleetwood Mac's *Rumours*, and Whitney Houston's *Whitney Houston.*

But words such as *the following* do not always precede the colon:

> They have collected some valuable albums: Nat King Cole's *King Cole Trio*, Pink Floyd's *Dark Side of the Moon*, and Rodgers and Hammerstein's *South Pacific.*

You need to make sure that you do not separate parts of an independent clause with a colon:

INCORRECT:	They enjoy composers such as: Mozart, Ravel, and Copland.
CORRECT:	They enjoy composers such as Mozart, Ravel, and Copland.
INCORRECT:	In that year, they had contracts with: RCA Victor, CBS Records, and Decca Records.
CORRECT:	In that year, they had contracts with RCA Victor, CBS Records, and Decca Records.

In some contexts, this version of the last sentence might be more emphatic:

In that year, they had contracts with all of the following: RCA Victor, CBS Records, and Decca Records.

Also remember that, in general, if you use more than one colon per sentence, you can create an awkward sentence and can easily confuse readers:

They love the following kinds of jazz: honky-tonk, swing, and especially the blues as performed on the following instruments: the alto saxophone, the trombone, and the piano.

This sentence could be revised as follows:

They love honky-tonk, swing, and especially the blues as performed on the following instruments: the alto saxophone, the trombone, and the piano.

2 Use a Colon Before an Element that Defines, Renames, Explains, or Illustrates the Preceding Independent Clause

Occasionally, you might choose to write an independent clause and then include an element that defines, renames, explains, or illustrates the material in the independent clause. For instance, after the first independent clause, you might include another independent clause:

They gave in to the temptation: They bought the compact discs.

Whether or not you capitalize the first letter of the word after the colon depends on how formal you think your writing situation is. If you

31b
sc

see the situation as quite formal, capitalize the first letter of the word after the colon. If you see the situation as not very formal, use a lowercase letter to begin the word after the colon.

The element after the colon could also be a subordinate clause, a phrase, or a single word:

> They hoped for a special time: when others would understand their music.

> They knew exactly what they wanted: to be appreciated.

> They needed one thing above all else: rest.

In all such cases, you must use an independent clause before the colon. With the colon, you mark a pause, creating expectations in readers; right after the colon, you fulfill those expectations.

3 Use a Colon Before a Formal Quotation

Introductions to quotations can often be set off with a comma:

> According to Professor Nagy, "Current college students have a speaking vocabulary of approximately five thousand words."

In some situations, however, a colon works better. Use a colon if an independent clause introduces the quotation. Most quotations introduced in this way will begin with a capital letter:

> The lecturer concluded with a sentence that many people did not understand: "The longest known palindromic word in English is *redivider*."

Also, use a colon if the quotation contains more than one sentence:

> In the words of Oliver Sacks: "Through experience, education, art, and life, we teach our brain to become unique. We learn to be individuals."

(See **34a** for information on using block format with very long quotations.)

4 Use a Colon in Some Conventional Positions

Various conventions call for colons in the following situations:

a. After Salutations in Formal Business Letters

Dear Dr. Gorp:

31b
sc

b. In Memorandums

To: Dean Benevlio
From: Dr. Bracken
Date: April 2, 1970
Re: The proposed open admissions policy

c. Before Subtitles of Books

Gender: An Ethnomethodological Approach
Orality and Literacy: The Technologizing of the Word

d. In Divisions of Time

9:20 a.m.
The runner crossed the line in 1:06:02.

e. In Biblical Citations

John 1:1
Romans 12:1

f. In Entries on Lists of References or Works Cited

Gardner, John. *On Moral Fiction.* New York: Basic, 1978.

(Modern Language Association—MLA—bibliographic format requires a colon between references to the place of publication and the publisher.)

Holland, Norman N. "Human Identity." *Critical Inquiry* 4 (1978): 451–469.

(MLA format requires a colon between references to the year of publication and the page on which the article appears.)

Miller, J. B. (1976). *Toward a new psychology of women.* Boston: Beacon.

(American Psychological Association—APA—format requires a colon between references to the place of publication and the publisher.)

Exercise 3

Add all necessary colons and delete all unnecessary colons in the following sentences.

EXAMPLE: Their team is strong in several events the steeplechase, the pole vault, and the shot put.

Their team is strong in several events: the steeplechase, the pole vault, and the shot put.

31b
sc

1. They decided to try to get tickets for: the long jump competition and the high jump competition.

2. They both had one main goal for the meet to finish in the top three in the mile run.

3. The coach was especially anxious about the following events the javelin throw, the hammer throw, and the marathon.

4. The coach gave: an explicit warning to his top two marathoners "Wait until the twenty-mile mark to make your move."

5. The members of the relay team are: Harrier, Swifte, Distons, and Slugg.

Exercise 4

Use a colon to combine the sentences in each of the following sets into one sentence.

EXAMPLE: The members of that student organization had one goal. They wanted to play basketball for more than 102 consecutive hours.

The members of that student organization had one goal: to play basketball for more than 102 consecutive hours.

1. Their grandparents particularly enjoy three games. They enjoy chess, cribbage, and Scrabble.

2. The doctor gave them a firm response. According to the doctor, "You are not in shape to play volleyball for 175 consecutive hours."

3. One of the games they had never heard of. That game was curling.

4. Two endurance records seemed unbreakable to them. One was the record for playing racquetball continuously. The other was the record for playing water polo continuously.

5. We still remember the coach's words. The coach said, "Stay within yourself." The coach also said, "Run your own race."

31b
sc

32

THE COMMA

T here are more guidelines for using commas than for using any other mark of punctuation. Moreover, not all established writers agree about which of these guidelines they should always follow and which they may occasionally ignore. Unfortunately, for many developing writers this situation causes confusion and anxiety. They come to see commas as threats or stumbling blocks, not as tools to help them shape and communicate meanings to readers.

If you have trouble deciding when to use commas, you need not abandon all hope. If you review the guidelines for using commas and carefully examine how other writers have used commas, you should at least be able to avoid making glaring errors with commas. At best, you should be able to see how others have used commas to convey extremely fine shades of meaning, and you should be able to convey such fine shades of meaning yourself. The main guidelines for using commas follow.

32a

Use a Comma Between Independent Clauses Linked by Coordinating Conjunctions

If two or more independent clauses are related closely enough in meaning that you want to link them within one sentence, a common way to do so is to use one or more commas and one of the coordinating conjunctions *(and, but, or, for, nor, so,* and *yet)*. Take care not to confuse these with conjunctive adverbs, such as *however* (see **18a**), and transitional expressions, such as *in conclusion.*

For example, if you wanted to link two independent clauses in one sentence with a coordinating conjunction, you could write the following:

coordinating
independent clause conjunction   independent clause

Clark tried to explain, but Lois had heard enough.

Note that the comma appears before, not after, the coordinating conjunction.

If you wanted to link three independent clauses in one sentence with coordinating conjunction, you could write the following:

independent clause   independent clause

Jimmy supplied the photographs, Lois wrote the story,

coordinating
conjunction   independent clause

and Clark did the proofreading.

In following this guideline, make sure that you are using a comma between two independent clauses, not between two parts of a compound predicate:

first part of predicate   second part
of predicate

INCORRECT: Clark ran to a phone booth, and emerged to defeat the villains.

CORRECT: Clark ran to a phone booth and emerged to defeat the villains.

If the two independent clauses you link are short (about five words long), roughly parallel in form, and approximately equal in rhetorical force, you may omit the comma that would otherwise link them:

The villain threatened but our hero scoffed.

Make sure, however, that you include a comma if omitting it could cause readers even momentary confusion. Consider this sentence:

The movie ended in disaster and sadness overcame us.

A reader may think, if only for a moment, that the movie ended in disaster and sadness. A comma prevents such a misreading:

> The movie ended in disaster, and sadness overcame us.

Sometimes you can omit the coordinating conjunction. When you link in one sentence three independent clauses that are short (about five words long), roughly parallel in form, and approximately equal in rhetorical force, you may rely on commas alone:

> They cajoled, they begged, they implored.

Finally, if one of the two independent clauses that you are linking is long or requires one or more commas within it, a semicolon may work better than a comma before the coordinating conjunction:

> The one film, which we both saw when we were twelve years old, made us laugh; but the other, which we did not see until we were in our twenties, terrified us.

Exercise 1

Add all necessary commas to the following sentences.

> EXAMPLE: The beaches were open but few people dared to go in the water.
>
> The beaches were open, but few people dared to go in the water.

1. One of the shark hunters relied on scientific instruments but the other relied on intuition alone.
2. They loaded the boat with supplies they checked the weather report and they headed out to sea.
3. They left the harbor and began to scan the horizon nervously.
4. They thought they saw something in the distance but it proved to be an illusion.
5. They hummed they paced they worried.

32b
com

32b

Use a Comma After Most Introductory Elements

Many kinds of elements can introduce a sentence: adverbs *(finally)*; conjunctive adverbs *(however)*; transitional expressions *(in the third place)*; participles *(stalling)*; infinitives *(to win)*; prepositional, participial, and infinitive phrases *(with the team, stalling for time, to win the tough games);* and full and elliptical adverb clauses *(after we arrived).* After most such introductory elements, you should use a comma:

> Stalling, he asked the doctors several questions. [comma after the introductory participle *stalling*]
>
> In the third place, he felt that his father's will was unfair. [comma after the introductory transitional expression *in the third place*]
>
> After he met with the doctors, he realized that he could not care for his brother properly. [comma after the introductory adverb clause *after he met with the doctors*]

In applying this second guideline, make sure that you do not treat part or all of a sentence subject as an introductory element. Some words and phrases can function either as introductory elements or as subjects, depending on their context. In the next sentence, *Promising to visit* has a comma after it since it is a participial phrase that introduces the sentence and modifies *he:*

> Promising to visit, he helped his brother board the train.

But in the following sentence, *Promising to visit* has no comma after it, for it is a gerund phrase used as the subject of the sentence:

> Promising to visit felt entirely natural.

32b
com

You may omit a comma after an introductory element when that element is short (two to three words) and when you judge that readers will not need a comma after that element to read the sentence correctly. For example, you need not use a comma after an introductory element like *On Tuesday* in the following:

> On Tuesday they found an inexpensive motel.

But you should use a comma after an introductory element like the one in this sentence:

> When those brothers read, mathematical equations dance in their imaginations.

The comma will keep readers from assuming, if only for a moment, that *mathematical equations* names what the brothers read.

Finally, remember not to use a comma after an introductory element that is immediately followed by a verb:

> introductory element   verb
> ⌒⌒⌒⌒⌒⌒⌒⌒⌒   ⌒⌒⌒⌒
> Into the room walked two strangers.

Exercise 2

Add commas wherever necessary in the following sentences. If you decide not to use a comma after an introductory element in a sentence, be prepared to justify your decision.

> EXAMPLE: After she stole the $40,000 the young woman fled.
>
> After she stole the $40,000, the young woman fled.

1. After driving for several hours she stopped at a deserted motel.
2. Driving for several hours will tire out most people.
3. However some people enjoy extended trips by automobile.
4. Overlooking the motel was an eerie Gothic house.
5. Growing behind the house a huge elm provided some shade.
6. Feeling too tired to drive on she decided to register for a room.
7. To register for a room she needed a credit card.
8. After she had registered for a room she decided to take a shower.
9. While looking around the room she thought of her friends.
10. Thinking of her friends was pleasant.

32c

Use Commas to Enclose Nonrestrictive Elements

Many words, phrases, and clauses can be either restrictive or nonrestrictive modifiers or renamers.

1 Modifiers of Nouns and Pronouns

Restrictive modifiers of nouns and pronouns are essential to the identification or definition of the noun or pronoun they modify. Therefore, they are critical to the proper interpretation of sentences. Restrictive modifiers do not take a comma before or after them. In this sentence, the adjective clause *who skip the film* is restrictive:

All students who skip the film will have to repeat the course.

This adjective clause is essential to the identification of those students who will have to repeat the course. Will all students have to repeat the course? No—only those who skip the film. Without the adjective clause, the sentence would read as follows:

All students will have to repeat the course.

The meaning of this sentence is vastly different from that of the sentence with the restrictive clause.

Nonrestrictive modifiers are not essential to the identification or definition of the noun or pronoun they modify. They can add interesting material about that noun or pronoun, but readers will not need that information to identify to whom or what the noun or pronoun refers. Nonrestrictive modifiers take a comma before and after them, unless they conclude a sentence; in that case, they are preceded by a comma and followed by a period:

> Alfred Hitchcock, *who was a genius in using trick shots,* portrays a chaotic universe.

The adjective clause *who was a genius in using trick shots* modifies a proper noun referring to someone easily identified, so the clause is nonrestrictive and therefore set off by commas. This does not mean that the information conveyed by the nonrestrictive clause is unimportant but simply that this information is not necessary for readers to identify Alfred Hitchcock.

2 Renamers of Nouns and Pronouns

Appositives are words, phrases, or clauses that appear after a noun or pronoun to rename it or identify it further. Appositives can be either restrictive or nonrestrictive.

32c com

If an appositive is restrictive, it is essential to the identification or definition of a person, place, or thing; restrictive appositives should not be set off with commas or with a comma and a period. Consider the following sentence:

> Tolstoy's novel *War and Peace* has been made into a film.

The appositive *War and Peace* should not be set off with commas because, as readers with some knowledge of Tolstoy's career are aware, he wrote more than one novel. The title *War and Peace* appears here to help readers pick out from all the novels he wrote the one to which the writer is referring. If you were to read *Tolstoy's novel has been made into a film,* you could not know which novel the writer has in mind.

Now consider this sentence:

> Herman Melville's white whale, Moby Dick, is an excellent subject for a film.

Is this sentence punctuated correctly? Readers with some knowledge of literature would understand what *Herman Melville's white whale* refers to without having to read the name *Moby Dick*. Since only one white whale is famous in Melville's writing, all anyone would have to do is refer to that whale in order for readers to identify it. Therefore, the words *Moby Dick* are nonrestrictive and should be enclosed in commas. The example as it appears above is correct.

Occasionally, you may have to do some research before deciding whether an appositive is restrictive or nonrestrictive. Consider this sentence:

John F. Kennedy's son, John, attended the reception.

Is this sentence punctuated correctly? In other words, in what situation would you need to use commas around *John?* You would need commas if your readers did not require the information supplied by *John* to identify John F. Kennedy's son. And they would not need this information if John F. Kennedy had only one son. Thus if you did not know how many sons John F. Kennedy had, you would need to do some research. Research would show that he had only one son, and therefore the information supplied by the name *John* is not necessary for the identification of John F. Kennedy's son. In the example, the name *John* is a nonrestrictive appositive and is correctly set off with commas.

Exercise 3

In each of the following sentences, an appositive or a modifier of a noun or pronoun appears in italics. Above each appositive or modifier, label each as restrictive or nonrestrictive, and then add all necessary commas to each sentence.

EXAMPLE: Ronald Reagan *who appeared in some films himself* visited the film museum.

nonrestrictive
Ronald Reagan, who appeared in some films himself, visited the film museum.

1. In that theater, viewers *who are noisy* are asked to leave.

2. The actor *who had recently won a prestigious award* was making a film in Italy.

3. Students *who are culturally illiterate* should take the course in film.

4. The city of New York *with its many movie theaters* is an excellent location in which to study film.

5. The film *to see when you are forty* is The Big Chill.

6. Shakespeare's play *Hamlet* has often been made into a film.

7. Dune *an intriguing novel* has been adapted for the movie screen.

8. Their brains *reeling with images* needed some rest.

32c
com

9. The city *with some unique movie theaters* is in Louisiana.
10. Actors and actresses *who have an abundance of talent* are in great demand.

3 Modifiers of Verbs

Many elements that modify verbs appear at the end of sentences. The usual question about punctuating these elements is whether to put a comma before them or not. These elements can be either restrictive or nonrestrictive.

If one of these elements is restrictive, it is essential to the meaning of a sentence; if it is omitted, the meaning of the sentence will change radically. A restrictive modifier of a verb should not be set off with commas. Consider the following sentence:

They will miss the beginning of the film if they hesitate.

Is this sentence punctuated correctly? The answer depends on whether the modifier *if they hesitate* is restrictive or not. The easiest way to find the answer is to leave the modifier out and see whether doing so radically changes the claim of the sentence:

They will miss the beginning of the film.

This sentence asserts that they will in fact miss the film, while the earlier one asserts that they will miss it only if they hesitate. These sentences have two very different meanings. The modifier *if they hesitate* is restrictive and should not be set off with commas. The first example above is punctuated correctly.

If a modifier of a verb is nonrestrictive, it can add interesting material to or comment on the information in a sentence, but deleting the modifier will not radically change the meaning or claim of the sentence. A nonrestrictive modifier should be set off with commas or with a comma before and a period after it. Consider this sentence:

They missed the film, even though they hurried.

Is this sentence punctuated correctly? Again, the answer depends on whether deleting the modifier *even though they hurried* radically changes the meaning of the preceding independent clause. It is clear from the original sentence that they missed the film, and leaving the modifier out of the sentence does not change that fact. Therefore, the final modifier is nonrestrictive and should have a comma before it. The example sentence as it appears above is correct.

ESL Consideration

UNNECESSARY COMMAS BEFORE ADVERB CLAUSES AND PHRASES

Frequently, writers mistakenly insert commas before adverb clauses and phrases that come at the end of sentences:

INCORRECT: I came to one of the American business schools, because they are internationally famous.

Commas setting off adverb clauses or phrases at the end of sentences are usually unnecessary:

CORRECT: I came to one of the American business schools because they are internationally famous.

The problem often occurs with adverb clauses using the subordinating conjunction *because.* You should also check clauses and phrases that use such subordinating conjunctions as *if, unless, though, although, even though, when, whenever, since, while, after,* and *before* to make sure they do not contain unnecessary commas:

INCORRECT: I buy anthologies of Native American literature, whenever I find them in bookstores.

CORRECT: I buy anthologies of Native American literature whenever I find them in bookstores.

32c
com

Exercise 4

In each of the following sentences, a modifier of a verb appears in italics. Above the modifier, label it as restrictive or nonrestrictive, and then add all necessary commas to each sentence.

restrictive

EXAMPLE: This film will attract many viewers *if it is marketed wisely.* [The sentence is correct as it stands.]

1. That film will win some major awards *provided the critics do not ridicule it.*
2. The other film is incoherent *although its editing is artistic.*
3. See that film *provided that you wish to be horrified.*
4. The alien will die *unless someone shows some compassion.*
5. The hero escaped from the jungle *even though hundreds of enemy soldiers were in pursuit.*

32d

Use Commas with Most Absolute Phrases

An absolute phrase consists of a noun or pronoun followed usually by a participle and possibly by some modifiers (*The sun sinking rapidly to the south of us;* see **14h**). If you use an absolute phrase to introduce a sentence, you should place a comma after the absolute phrase:

> absolute phrase
>
> His disguise approved by his roommate, Gus went to work as an actress in a soap opera.

If you use an absolute phrase within a sentence, you should set the phrase off before and after with commas:

> absolute phrase
>
> The two secret agents, their identities carefully concealed, played roulette together.

And if you conclude a sentence with an absolute phrase, you should use a comma before the phrase:

> absolute phrase
>
> The car returned from the future, its exterior covered with ice.

Exercise 5

Write three original sentences and punctuate them correctly. In the first sentence, use an absolute phrase as an introduction. In the second, use an absolute phrase between the subject and the verb. And in the third, conclude the sentence with an absolute phrase.

32d
com

32e

Use Commas with Elements That Interrupt or Stand Outside the Structure of Independent Clauses

Many kinds of elements either interrupt the structural pattern of independent clauses or stand outside that pattern. These elements are usually set off from independent clauses by a comma or by commas.

1 Elements That Usually Introduce Independent Clauses

Some elements that stand outside the structural pattern of independent clauses introduce those clauses. These elements take a comma after them.

a. Forms of Direct Address

If you address your readers directly at the beginning of a sentence, use a comma after the words of address:

Friends, we must go back to Woodstock.

b. Mild Interjections

Sometimes in informal writing, you may wish to introduce a sentence with a mild interjection such as *ah, oh,* or *well.* When you do, you should use a comma after the mild interjection:

Ah, those drive-in movies were important.

c. The Words *Yes* and *No*

When you begin a sentence with *yes* or *no,* you should normally use a comma after the *yes* or the *no:*

No, those reporters cannot divulge that information.

A dash is also correct. It draws a little more attention to what follows the *yes* or *no* than a comma does:

No—you are the one who is wrong.

2 Elements That Often Appear Within Independent Clauses

Many elements that stand outside the structural pattern of independent clauses appear within those clauses. When they do, a comma should both precede and follow them. Remember that some of these elements can also introduce sentences. When they do, they should have a comma after them.

a. Conjunctive Adverbs and Transitional Expressions

Whenever you use a conjunctive adverb (such as *however*) or a transitional expression (such as *in the last place*) within a sentence, you should both precede and follow it with a comma:

The mother's case for custody, *therefore,* is excellent.

32e
com

If you do not intend conjunctive adverbs to mark a break in continuity within independent clauses, you should not set them off with commas:

We *therefore* urge you to write a guide for tourists.

In this sentence, *therefore* modifies *urge*. In the earlier example, *therefore* modifies the entire clause in which it appears.

b. Writing About Writing

Sometimes, especially when you stand in a close relationship to your readers, you might include within sentences some words that you use to write about your own writing (see **38d**). Be careful with such words because in some contexts they are unnecessary verbiage. However, when you can justify using them, you should set them off before and after with commas:

words that emphasize

This film, it must be stressed, is not political.

words that hedge

This film, at least in my view, is not political.

c. Antithetical Phrases or Clauses

Whenever you include within a sentence words that show a contrast with readers' expectations, you should set those words off before and after with commas:

antithetical element

The wolf, not the scientist, staked out the territory efficiently.

Whenever you have two interdependent clauses within one sentence, you should usually separate them with a comma:

The more the power plant shook, the more terrified the reporters became.

However, if the clauses are short (about five words long), and if it is unlikely that readers will wonder where one clause stops and the other one starts, you may omit the comma:

The more they trained the faster they ran.

d. Complementary Expressions

When, after a word or a phrase, you use an expression that adds to or completes the meaning of the word or phrase, set off the expression before and after with commas:

complementary expression

A more important, if not the most important, character is Hal.

3 Elements That Appear at the End of Independent Clauses

Tag questions stand outside the structural pattern of the independent clauses they appear with. Tag questions appear after independent clauses and are preceded by a comma:

tag question

That business was risky, wasn't it?

Exercise 6

In the following paragraph from a personal letter, find all the elements that interrupt or stand outside the structural pattern of independent clauses. Add commas before, after, or before and after these elements, as necessary.

EXAMPLE: In the first sentence, *My fellow critics* is a form of direct address and should have a comma after it.

My fellow critics soon we assemble in Burbank for our annual convention. In my opinion we must discuss the current rating system for films. The rating system not any other subject deserves the greatest amount of our time and attention. Those who devised the current rating system it is true had good intentions. This system however has harmed both viewers and filmmakers. And such a situation I must emphasize cannot be left unchanged. No the system cannot be left unchanged. The more we delay changing the system the more harm we will allow it to do. And we are the people most capable of changing this situation. Join me in preparing to identify a better system won't you?

32f

Use Commas with Elements in a Series

If you join three or more words, phrases, or clauses in a series, you should use a comma after each part of the series except the last:

series of nouns

The rugby player spoke of loyalty to god, king, and country.

series of noun phrases

The champion's training program included walks on the beach, sprints around the track, and runs in the hills.

32f com

Make sure that you do not use a comma before the first element of a series:

INCORRECT: They ran in, rain, sleet, and snow.

CORRECT: They ran in rain, sleet, and snow.

If you link all the elements in a series with coordinating conjunctions, then you should use no commas between these elements:

Their opponents spoke of glory and riches and power.

When you use such a construction, you draw more attention to each separate element in the series than you would with the more common construction:

Their opponents spoke of glory, riches, and power.

It is common journalistic practice to omit the comma before the coordinating conjunction that appears just before the end of most series:

Their opponents spoke of glory, riches and power.

In some cases, this practice causes a problem. Consider the following sentence:

The group enjoyed exotic delights, hang gliding and cliff diving.

32f
com

What exactly does this sentence mean? Did the group enjoy three different things or activities—(1) exotic delights, (2) hang gliding, and (3) cliff diving? Or are the hang gliding and the cliff diving really the exotic delights? If the writer intended to list three different things, then he or she should have used a comma before *and:*

The group enjoyed exotic delights, hang gliding, and cliff diving.

And if the writer intended *exotic delights* to be a general term for *hang gliding* and *cliff diving,* then he or she could have made that unmistakably clear by writing as follows:

The group enjoyed exotic delights: hang gliding and cliff diving.

To make sure that your readers never have to wonder how to interpret a series of elements, you should consistently use the comma before the coordinating conjunction just before the end of the series.

Exercise 7

Combine all the sentences in the following sets into one sentence, and punctuate all series according to the formula *x, y, and z.*

> EXAMPLE: She investigated the police commissioner.
> She investigated the police captain.
> And she investigated several detectives.
>
> She investigated the police commissioner, the police captain, and several detectives.

1. Celie becomes a woman of wit.
Celie becomes a woman of pride.
Celie becomes a woman of self-assurance.

2. The military attorney discovered the truth about the murder.
The military attorney discovered the truth about relations between officers and enlisted men.
And the military attorney discovered the truth about race relations in parts of the United States.

3. The hero leaped through a window.
The hero stunned the villain.
And the hero rescued several of the paintings in the museum.

4. The apprentice had to sand wooden floors.
The apprentice had to paint a large gate.
And the apprentice had to wax a car.

5. People across the nation wanted to hear more from the gardener.
Many politicians asked for his advice.
But his wisdom consisted of nothing more than clichés from television.

32g

Use Commas with Coordinate Adjectives

Two or more adjectives preceding a noun can be either cumulative or coordinate. Here are two cumulative adjectives:

> unusual political strategy

The adjective *unusual* modifies the idea expressed by the adjective *political* and the noun *strategy* together. The entire phrase indicates that the political strategy referred to is unusual. In such a phrase, no comma should appear between *unusual* and *political.*

If two adjectives are coordinate, each one modifies the following noun separately:

> clean, quiet neighborhood

Here the adjective *clean* modifies *neighborhood,* and the adjective *quiet* modifies *neighborhood.* In such a phrase, a comma should appear between *clean* and *quiet.*

Two tests can help you distinguish coordinate adjectives from cumulative ones. First, coordinate adjectives will not sound strange if you insert an *and* between them, and cumulative adjectives will. The phrase *clean and quiet neighborhood* sounds fine, but the phrase *unusual and political strategy* does not. Second, coordinate adjectives can be reversed in order and still sound fine, but cumulative adjectives cannot be reversed and still sound fine. The phrase *quiet, clean neighborhood* sounds fine, but the phrase *political unusual strategy* does not.

Exercise 8

Add commas between whatever coordinate adjectives you find in the following sentences.

EXAMPLE: The movie had a complicated surprising plot.

The movie had a complicated, surprising plot.

1. Who was looking out the large rear window?
2. At the start of the film, she is an abused illiterate child.
3. The karate teacher tried an unusual defensive move.
4. Their loyalties were divided between the rugged stern sergeants.
5. The other basketball team was from a large urban center.

32h

Use Commas with Quotations

When you quote other writers directly, you will often need to use one or more commas. For example, you should use a comma to separate words that introduce a quotation from the quotation itself:

According to the scientist, "Some people have changed the course of events."

However, if the introduction to the quotation is an independent clause itself, or if the quotation includes more than one sentence, you should use a colon after the introduction:

The scientist was very clear about their dilemma: "The most insignificant action can affect the future."

If you interrupt a quoted sentence, perhaps to indicate who said or wrote it, you should set the interruption off with commas:

> "My brother and sister," whispered the time traveler, "are fading from the picture."

Note that the first comma appears inside the quotation marks.

If you quote a sentence and then indicate who said or wrote it, you will need to separate the quoted words from your own words with a comma:

> "The future will be wonderful," the scientist wrote.

(For more information on punctuating quoted material, see **34b**).

Finally, make sure that if you use words in quotation marks as parts of a sentence—for example, as a subject or predicate noun—you do *not* set off those words with commas:

INCORRECT:	"Always remember," were their last words.
CORRECT:	"Always remember" were their last words.
INCORRECT:	Their response was, "Persevere."
CORRECT:	Their response was "Persevere."

Exercise 9

In a review of the movie *Tootsie,* David Ansen writes: *"Tootsie* will make you very happy." Use Ansen's sentence as indicated below:

1. Write a correctly punctuated sentence in which you quote Ansen's sentence after the introduction *In the words of David Ansen.*

2. Write a correctly punctuated sentence in which you quote Ansen's sentence after the introduction *David Ansen gives the film high praise.*

3. Write a correctly punctuated sentence in which you quote Ansen's sentence but interrupt it where it seems most appropriate to add the words *according to David Ansen.*

4. Write a correctly punctuated sentence in which you quote Ansen's sentence but interrupt it where it seems most appropriate to add the words *in David Ansen's view.*

5. Write a correctly punctuated sentence in which you quote Ansen's sentence and then conclude with the words *writes David Ansen.*

32i

Use Commas in Some Conventional Settings

Various conventions call for commas in the following settings.

1 With Some Questions in Declarative Sentences

If you use a question as a subject or a complement within a declarative sentence, you do not need to set the question off with a comma:

What time is it? is the question they asked.

Their question was Who is the best attorney?

However, if you use a question as the direct object in a sentence, you should set it off with a comma:

They asked themselves, What can anyone do if the river rises?

2 After Salutations

After salutations in informal letters, you should use a comma:

Dear Ted and Alice,

3 With Titles and Classifications

You should use commas to set off titles for persons, designations of degrees, or references to job classifications that you include within sentences:

Jan Mimezist, Ph.D., will offer a course in short films as a political tool.

Of course, if the title, designation of degree, or reference to job classification concludes a sentence, then you need to use only one comma:

That decision was approved by J. H. Hochsteger, editor in chief.

4 With *Jr.* and *Sr.*

Use commas to set off the abbreviations *Jr.* and *Sr.* when they follow a name but do not conclude the sentence:

H. S. Klaus, Jr., will produce that film.

If a numerical designation such as *III* follows a name, do not set it off with commas:

They nearly forgot to consult S. Samson III.

32i
com

5 With Addresses and Political Subdivisions

Use commas to separate the elements of addresses and political subdivisions that appear in sentences:

They moved to 56 Blackstone Street, Chicago, Illinois 60637, after they sold their house.

That matter worries officials in Marin County, California.

6 With Dates

You may use commas to separate the elements of dates:

They began filming on Monday, June 10, 1991, and finished two weeks later.

Or if you do not name the day of the week, you may reorder the elements of the date and omit all commas related to the date:

They began filming on 10 June 1991 and finished two weeks later.

Remember that you should never use a comma within the designation for a year.

INCORRECT: 1,789
CORRECT: 1789

7 In Long Numbers

When you record numbers of three or fewer digits, you should use no comma between any of the digits. When you record numbers of four digits, you have a choice. You may use a comma or you may omit it:

1,001   1001

When you record numbers of more than four digits, you should use a comma after every three digits, counting from the right:

49,000   1,000,001

Exercise 10

Indicate which of the two sentences in each pair is correct.

EXAMPLE: In the following set, the second sentence is the correct one.
a. _____ Whose baby is it?, was their first question.
b. _____ Whose baby is it? was their first question.

32i
com

1a. _____ They asked themselves Who would leave a baby?

b. _____ They asked themselves, Who would leave a baby?

2a. _____ They decided to take a course in child psychology from B. F. Freed, Ph.D.

b. _____ They decided to take a course in child psychology from B. F. Freed Ph.D.

3a. _____ Also attending that class was I. M. Patern Sr.

b. _____ Also attending that class was I. M. Patern, Sr.

4a. _____ A cottage in Clearwater, Florida was available to them.

b. _____ A cottage in Clearwater, Florida, was available to them.

5a. _____ The baby was born on Tuesday, February 5, 1991, in Utah.

b. _____ The baby was born on Tuesday February 5 1991 in Utah.

32j

Use Commas to Prevent Misreadings

Occasionally, you will have to use a comma to prevent readers from misinterpreting a sentence. For example, you should use a comma to ensure that a string of words is not read as a sentence fragment:

INCORRECT: Days before Roxanne moved to town.

CORRECT: Days before, Roxanne moved to town.

Additionally, you should use a comma to help readers keep parts of sentences distinct from one another:

INCORRECT: After filming the director and her assistants needed a short break.

CORRECT: After filming, the director and her assistants needed a short break.

Using a comma in situations like this is particularly important when one part of a sentence ends with the same word that the next part begins with. For instance, instead of writing

What the noise is is of no significance,

you should write

What the noise is, is of no significance.

Finally, you should use a comma at points where you have just-ifiably omitted words. For example, you should use a comma after *others* in the following sentence to indicate that you have left *the film seemed* out:

> To some the film seemed comic; to others, grotesque.

Exercise 11

Add commas as necessary to the following sentences to prevent possible misinterpretations.

> EXAMPLE: Ever since the crew has been terrified.
>
> Ever since, the crew has been terrified.

1. Besides taking that specimen from the planet was a mistake.
2. Those who can see a movie each week.
3. Soon after the boxer fell to the mat.
4. What the proposal is is no concern of yours.
5. While they were eating the buffalo passed by to the south.

32k

Unnecessary Commas

In general, you should *not* use commas in the following positions, unless, of course, you need commas to prevent misreading:

1. Between a single adjective and a noun

   > INCORRECT: the deposed, ruler
   >
   > CORRECT: the deposed ruler

2. After a coordinating conjunction linking two independent clauses

   > INCORRECT: They returned to their hometown, but, the revolution had altered it radically.
   >
   > CORRECT: They returned to their hometown, but the revolution had altered it radically.

3. Between a preposition and its object or objects

   > INCORRECT: The long drive made her feel forever between, home and school.
   >
   > CORRECT: The long drive made her feel forever between home and school.

4. Between a subject and predicate

INCORRECT: The retired people, swam in the pool.

CORRECT: The retired people swam in the pool.

5. Between an auxiliary verb and a main verb

INCORRECT: They should, forget the club in Morocco.

CORRECT: They should forget the club in Morocco.

6. Between parts of a compound verb

INCORRECT: She stood, and criticized the training session.

CORRECT: She stood and criticized the training session.

7. Between a verb and a direct object

INCORRECT: They played, a game with a military computer.

CORRECT: They played a game with a military computer.

Take special note that, if the direct object is a noun clause, in most cases it still should not be preceded by a comma:

INCORRECT: They believed, that mermaids did not exist.

CORRECT: They believed that mermaids did not exist.

8. Between a verb and a predicate adjective or predicate noun

INCORRECT: The jeweled falcon was, exquisite.

CORRECT: The jeweled falcon was exquisite.

INCORRECT: Their crime was, doubting the government.

CORRECT: Their crime was doubting the government.

Exercise 12

Rewrite the following sentences, retaining all necessary commas and removing all unnecessary ones.

EXAMPLE: One of the characters, however, needed, a heart.

One of the characters, however, needed a heart.

1. The wicked, witch scared them at first, but they soon recovered.
2. They followed the correct road, and, they reached the city.
3. The wizard, it soon became evident, was hiding behind, a curtain.
4. The balloon rose and, soared out of sight.
5. Finally, they realized, that they were home again.

33

DASHES AND PARENTHESES

In general, dashes and parentheses set off similar kinds of elements in sentences: elements that usually interrupt the structural pattern of sentences and sometimes contrast with the main message of sentences. Occasionally, therefore, you will have the opportunity to exercise your personal taste in matters of punctuation by deciding between dashes and parentheses.

You should remember, though, that dashes usually call more attention to interrupting elements than parentheses. As Russell Baker notes, "The dash SHOUTS. Parentheses whisper." If you use these marks of punctuation with discretion, they can add some effective touches to your prose.

Dashes

If you are preparing a paper on a typewriter or a word processor, you form a dash by typing two hyphens with no separation between them or between them and the neighboring words:

```
Three strategies for helping deaf students--
teaching them lip reading and speech, teaching
them Manually Coded English, and teaching them
American Sign Language--will be discussed.
```

511

If you are writing in longhand, you form a dash by making one unbroken line about twice as long as you would make a hyphen and by leaving no spaces between the line and the neighboring words.

1 Use a Dash to Connect an Introductory List to the Rest of a Sentence

You may use a single dash to connect an introductory list to the rest of a sentence, which usually defines, explains, or clarifies that list:

> Facial expressions, distinctive gestures, and rules for combining gestures—all these are important in the system of American Sign Language.

A colon would also be correct in this situation:

> Facial expressions, distinctive gestures, and rules for combining gestures: All these are important in the system of American Sign Language.

But the dash appears more often than the colon in such positions in informal contexts. And the dash is more appropriate than the colon in more formal contexts when you want to invest a sentence with a greater sense of drama.

**33a
dp**

2 Use Dashes to Set Off Abrupt Interruptions Within Sentences

Whenever you include within a sentence some material that interrupts the structural pattern and perhaps the flow of meaning in that sentence, you should set that material off with dashes:

> Some ideas about educating the deaf—to put the matter bluntly but accurately—have destroyed lives.

Remember that the elements before and after the interruption must fit together grammatically:

> INCORRECT: They recommended American Sign Language because—and this is of the utmost significance— since it helps deaf children develop the basic rules for processing language.

If you read this sentence without the interruption, you will see that it moves from the word *because* to the word *since*. The sentence should be revised as follows:

CORRECT: They recommended American Sign Language because—and this is of the utmost significance—it helps deaf children develop the basic rules for processing language.

If the material you use to interrupt a sentence is itself an independent clause, you must bear in mind some special conventions about how to punctuate the interrupting clause. If the interrupting clause is a statement, you should not begin it with a capital letter or conclude it with a period:

The board of governors—they had discussed difficult issues for two consecutive days—adjourned early on Friday.

If the interrupting clause is a question, you should not begin it with a capital letter, but you should conclude it with a question mark placed immediately before the second dash:

Members of the board of governors—and who can blame them?—adjourned early on Friday.

Finally, if the interrupting clause is an exclamation, you should not begin it with a capital letter, but you should conclude it with an exclamation point placed immediately before the second dash:

Members of the board of governors—what remarkable workers they are!—adjourned early on Friday.

3 Use Dashes to Set Off Some Modifiers, Appositives, and Inserted Elements Within Sentences

33a
dp

You may use dashes to set off some modifiers, appositives (see **17e**), and inserted elements within sentences. These elements usually do not interrupt the structural pattern or meaning of sentences greatly. In fact, it would also be correct to set off most of these elements with commas:

modifier

American Sign Language, with its unique patterns of signs, is very different from Manually Coded English.

appositive

The other system, American Sign Language, makes extensive use of facial expressions.

inserted element

Lip reading, in their opinion, is not the best response.

But if you wanted to call more attention to the material set off with commas in the examples above, you could set it off with dashes. Notice how dashes focus your attention on the material between them:

American Sign Language—with its unique patterns of signs—is very different from Manually Coded English.

The other system—American Sign Language—makes extensive use of facial expressions.

Lip reading—in their opinion—is not the best response.

Dashes are especially helpful for readers when you use a series of three or more appositives. Consider the following sentence:

Various kinds of tragedies, neglect, faulty diagnosis, and shortsighted programs of education, have afflicted some deaf children.

When the sentence is punctuated in this way, it is difficult to interpret. Does it ask readers to focus on various kinds of tragedies, kinds of neglect, kinds of faulty diagnosis, and kinds of shortsighted programs of education? Or does it use one general term *(tragedies)* and then list three specific renamers of that term *(neglect, faulty diagnosis,* and *shortsighted programs of education)*? This latter interpretation seems probable, but to make this meaning clear to readers, dashes should set off the specific renamers:

Various kinds of tragedies—neglect, faulty diagnosis, and shortsighted programs of education—have afflicted some deaf children.

33a
dp

4 Use a Dash to Introduce a Concluding List, Explanation, or Summation

Occasionally you may want to conclude a sentence with a list, an explanation of an idea in that sentence, or a statement that sums up the meaning of that sentence. It is correct to introduce such a list, explanation, or summation with a colon:

These teachers need some special traits: patience, sensitivity, and determination.

But you could also introduce such elements with a dash. The dash functions in this way more often than the colon in informal situations. And the dash is appropriate in those more formal situations when you want to give a more emphatic introduction to concluding lists, explanations, or summations:

These teachers need some special traits—patience, sensitivity, and determination.

5 Use Dashes to Show Interruptions or Hesitations in Recorded Speech

When you record other people's speech or invent dialogue for a sketch or story, you may occasionally need to use one or more dashes to indicate halts, interruptions, or hesitations:

"It was a time of—uh—of emptiness—of nothingness," said Helen.

"Why don't you—" Anne began and then halted.

Note that in the second example no comma or period appears between the dash and the quotation mark.

If you need to indicate that a speaker trailed off and did not stop suddenly, then you should use ellipsis points (see **34c**):

"Well, well, well, I'll be. . . ."

6 Avoid Overusing Dashes

In most pieces of academic writing, especially in essays in the sciences and social sciences, the dash is relatively rare. So make sure that you can justify the dashes that you use in your academic essays. And no matter what kind of writing you are working on, you should not use dashes to link phrases and thereby avoid writing complete sentences. Moreover, if you use more than one set of dashes in a sentence, that sentence will probably strike readers as somewhat fragmented:

TOO MANY DASHES: That child seemed—we emphasize the word *seemed*—to be able to hear, and therefore the authorities recommended an educational program—we are kind in calling it educational—that left the child deprived—deprived of the chance to develop language without enormous impediments.

One way to revise this sentence would be to drop the first pair of dashes and the material between them or the second pair of dashes and the material between them. You could also transform the material after

33a
dp

the last dash into a separate sentence. This procedure has several benefits: (1) It reduces the number of dashes in the sentence, (2) it allows the original critical attitude to come through clearly, and (3) it stresses in a separate sentence the information about the child's being deprived of the chance to develop language without enormous impediments.

Exercise 1

Add dashes where appropriate in the following sentences. Also indicate what other marks of punctuation, if any, could be used instead of the dashes. If dashes and other marks of punctuation could be used in certain positions in these sentences, describe in what kind of situation you would choose dashes and in what kind of situation you would choose other marks of punctuation.

> EXAMPLE: American Sign Language, lip reading, and oral speech all of these are recommended by a prominent group of educators. [You could use either a dash or a colon after *speech*. The dash would probably be preferable in less formal situations; the colon, in formal situations.]

1. Those students proposed can you blame them that their school hire a deaf person as president.
2. The culture of the deaf with its rich perceptions and sensibilities has surprised many researchers.
3. The explanation was simple no one had identified the source of their difficulty correctly.
4. Several organizations the Alexander Graham Bell Association for the Deaf, the Convention of Institutes of the Deaf, and the National Association of the Deaf promote the employment of deaf people.
5. Diseases, birth defects, and accidents all these can cause hearing disorders.

**33a
dp**

Exercise 2

Find three sentences that contain a dash or a pair of dashes, and specify what kinds of information the dashes are being used to set off.

33b

Parentheses

You should never use only one parenthesis. Whenever you decide to set material off parenthetically, you must use two parentheses.

1 Use Parentheses to Set Off
Supplementary Information

You should use parentheses to set off information that may be helpful or interesting to readers but that is not central to the message of sentences. When you set off information with parentheses, you are suggesting that readers should treat the information as an aside. Specific kinds of information that parentheses often set off include the following:

1. An example

   Some inventions (for instance, the telephone) have changed the way people think of communication.

2. A specification of meaning

   MCE (Manually Coded English) is not endorsed by all members of the faculty.

3. An indication of birth date or life span

   Alexander Graham Bell (1847–1922) said he would like to be remembered as someone who had taught the deaf.

4. A cross-reference

   Bell was also interested in flying (see page 747).

In legal, business, and technical writing, it is common to use parentheses to enclose numerals that clarify or confirm a spelled-out number:

That copyright will expire in thirty-five (35) years.

In some cases, you could set off information within sentences with parentheses or with commas or dashes:

Some inventions (for instance, the telephone) have changed the way people think of communication.

Some inventions, for instance, the telephone, have changed the way people think of communication.

Some inventions—for instance, the telephone—have changed the way people think of communication.

Normally, the parentheses would call less attention to the information set off than the commas or the dashes would.

**33b
dp**

If you ever need to include supplementary information within some other bits of supplementary information, you should use brackets within parentheses:

Alexander Graham Bell's assistant (Thomas A. Watson [1854–1934]) played an important role in Bell's research.

Remember that the elements on both sides of parenthetical material must fit together to produce a grammatical sentence:

INCORRECT: The explanation we heard (that Bell had become interested in telegraphing speech while working with tuning forks) that was true.

If you read this example without the parenthetical information, you will discover that you are reading a sentence fragment:

FRAGMENT: The explanation we heard that was true.

To correct this error, you would have to omit the word *that.*

In almost all cases, no punctuation mark appears just before the first of a pair of parentheses. The second of a pair of parentheses should have a punctuation mark after it if the structure of the overall sentence calls for one there:

33b
dp

A COMMA: If the descriptions of Bell's experiments are accurate (see page 1875), we can call him a genius in designing experiments. [comma after an introductory adverb clause]

A SEMICOLON: The public judgments were positive (see page 1901); Bell, however, remained humble. [semicolon between two independent clauses]

A PERIOD: Some of the experimental reports are startling (see especially page 1910). [end punctuation]

If you enclose a statement within parentheses and use that parenthetical statement within another sentence, you should neither begin the enclosed statement with a capital letter nor conclude it with a period:

Our evaluation of Bell's achievements (it begins in the next section) is complex.

Parenthetical questions and exclamations, however, do take the appropriate mark of end punctuation:

Bell's experiments (how could one person perform so many?) have an interesting relationship to each other.

Bell's experiments (how intricately they are related to each other!) have inspired other scientists.

If you enclose a complete sentence within parentheses and have that parenthetical sentence stand outside other sentences, then you should begin the sentence with a capital letter and conclude it (within the parentheses) with a period, question mark, or exclamation point, whichever mark is appropriate:

> Bell talked of locating icebergs by recording echoes from them. (His idea is reflected in some recent inventions.)

2 To Enclose Letters or Numerals Marking Divisions in Lists Included in Sentences

Whenever you include lists of long or complex items in a sentence, you may use letters or numerals enclosed in parentheses to help readers keep the items on the list separate from one another:

> In sum, Alexander Graham Bell invented or described all of the following: (1) the telephone, (2) an electrical apparatus to locate metal in the body, (3) a method to extract fresh water from the vapor in the air, and (4) kites that could lift a person into the air.

Exercise 3

In each of the following pairs of sentences, incorporate the information from the second sentence into the first by means of parentheses.

> EXAMPLE: Prolonged exposure to loud noises probably causes tinnitus. *Tinnitus* refers to ringing in the ears.
>
> Prolonged exposure to loud noises probably causes tinnitus (ringing in the ears).

1. Many Americans have a noticeable hearing disorder. The number of Americans with a noticeable hearing disorder is approximately fifteen million.
2. Some diseases can damage the inner ear. Meningitis is an example of these diseases.
3. For more information about Ménière's disease, see the story about Ludwig van Beethoven. This story is found on pages 63–72.
4. Ludwig van Beethoven composed some of his best music after he had started to lose his hearing. Beethoven lived from 1770 to 1827.
5. Today deaf people can make and receive phone calls by using a TDD. TDD stands for Telecommunication Device for the Deaf.

Exercise 4

Write three sentences, including at least one pair of parentheses in each.

34

QUOTATION MARKS, THE SLASH, ELLIPSIS POINTS, AND BRACKETS

Each time that you quote other people's words and sentences, you must clearly distinguish their words and sentences from your own (see also **45c** and **45d**). As you do so, you signal that their words and sentences can be verified, and you acknowledge your intellectual debts. In this chapter, we explain the marks of punctuation that will help you indicate quoted words and sentences and help readers interpret these words and sentences correctly.

34a

Using Quotation Marks

Quotation marks function in the following ways.

1 Use Quotation Marks to Enclose Direct Quotations

Whenever you record words or sentences from other people, you are quoting these people directly. When you quote other people, make sure that you do so accurately, and punctuate these quotations as indicated below.

a. Double Quotation Marks

When you quote others' words, you must use double quotation marks around those words:

> "Everyone should read the account of the person with hardly any short-term memory," the therapist wrote.

Or

> According to the therapist, "Everyone should read the account of the person with hardly any short-term memory."

Note that in the first example the *t* in the final *the* is not capitalized. Also note that in the second example, the first letter of the quotation is capitalized even though this letter is not the first in the overall sentence. This practice is standard when the quotation does not function as a grammatical part (for example, as a direct object) of the overall sentence. When you use the quotation as a grammatical part of a sentence, you should not capitalize the first letter of the quotation, even if it was capitalized in the original source:

> The therapist stressed that "everyone should read the account of the person with hardly any short-term memory."

Here the quotation is the direct object in the overall sentence.

b. Single Quotation Marks Within Double Quotation Marks

Whenever you use a quotation that includes a second quotation, you should use single quotation marks around the inner quotation and double quotation marks around the outer quotation:

> According to Dr. Rem, "In the words of two of my patients, 'We remember all of our dreams.' "

Note that the period goes inside both the single and double quotation marks.

c. Double Quotation Marks Within Single Quotation Marks Within Double Quotation Marks

You should be cautious about including one quotation within a second, and the second within a third, since you run some risk of confusing your readers. But in some situations you might need to take

34a
qseb

that risk. In this case you should punctuate the quotations as follows:

> As our colleagues put it, "We were impressed when the professor said, 'The key to this puzzle lies in Bartlett's statement, "Images have fundamentally important parts to play in mental life." ' "

Note that the period goes inside all of the quotation marks.

d. Paragraphs to Mark Changes of Speakers in a Conversation

Whenever you quote a conversation involving two or more people, you should start a new paragraph each time a different person speaks:

> "Do you remember the first words you ever spoke?" asked Dr. Young.
> "Yes, I did not speak until I was four years old, but my first utterance was relatively long," Dr. Singleston replied.
> "It was?"
> "Yes, as I recall, my first utterance was a sentence exactly twenty-nine words long."

If you need to indicate that one person's quoted speech contains more than one paragraph, the start of each new paragraph should be marked by double quotation marks, but only the final paragraph should have double quotation marks after it:

> "As I mentioned," Professor Salance said, "psychologists usually divide the memory system of a human being into three stages.
> "The first stage is called sensory memory. In this stage, information lasts for only an instant or two.
> "The second stage is called short-term memory. Information in short-term memory lasts as long as the person keeps it at the forefront of consciousness.
> "The final stage is called long-term memory. If information moves into long-term memory, it can last for many years."

34a qseb

e. A Special Format for Quoting Long Prose Passages

Whenever you wish to record a quotation that would require more than four lines of typed or handwritten prose, you should display the quotation, according to the following guidelines:

1. Just before you start recording the quotation, double-space and begin recording the quotation on a new line.
2. Double-space throughout the quotation, and do not change your normal right-hand margin.

3. If the quotation consists of one paragraph or less, indent the first line of the quotation as well as all subsequent lines ten spaces from your normal left-hand margin.
4. If the quotation consists of two or more paragraphs, indent the first line of each paragraph thirteen spaces and all subsequent lines in each paragraph ten spaces from your normal left-hand margin.
5. After you have recorded the quotation, double-space once and begin working once more from your normal left-hand margin.
6. The only time you will have to use double quotation marks is when double quotation marks appear in the passage you are recording. Then you should include double quotation marks in your displayed quotation in the appropriate places.

Here is a displayed quotation that is less than one paragraph long:

Remembering almost always involves a process of construction or creation. Frederick Bartlett made this claim already in 1932:

> Remembering is not the re-excitation of innumerable fixed, lifeless and fragmentary traces. It is an imaginative reconstruction, or construction, built out of the relation of our attitude towards a whole active mass of organised past reactions or experience, and to a little outstanding detail which commonly appears in image or in language form.
> (213)

Since Bartlett wrote these lines, his claim has been reinforced by several different experimental psychologists.

f. A Special Format for Quoting More Than Three Lines of Poetry

If you wish to quote three or fewer lines of poetry, you should enclose the lines with double quotation marks and run the lines into the body of your essay. When you do so, you should mark the division between one line and another with a **slash** (/).

34a
qseb

You are probably most used to seeing a slash used to indicate alternatives *(a pass/fail course)*, overlapping times *(the Winter/Spring volume of a journal)*, measurements *(six feet/second)*, and fractions (1/16). In all these cases, there should be no space before or after the slash.

However, when you use a slash to mark separations between lines of poetry that you are quoting, you should leave a space before and after the slash:

```
Several modern poets have echoed Wordsworth when he
wrote, "But yet I know, where'er I go, / that there
hath past away a glory from the earth" ("Ode:
Intimations of Immortality from Recollections of
Early Childhood" 17-18).
```

When you quote more than three lines of poetry, you should display them. Adopt a new left-hand margin ten spaces to the right of your normal left-hand margin. Double-space the lines of poetry, and double-space before and after them. And try to display the lines as they appear in the source:

```
     Wordsworth introduces the themes of forgetting
and loss early in his ode:
          It is not now as it hath been of yore;--
               Turn wheresoe'er I may,
                    By night or day,
          The things which I have seen I now can
          see no more.
                    ("Ode: Intimations of
                     Immortality from Recollections
                     of Early Childhood" 6-9)
```

34a
jseb

Exercise 1

Practice using the various devices for punctuating quotations by following the various sets of directions below.

1. Write a sentence in which you first indicate who said or wrote certain words and then quote those words directly.

2. Write a sentence in which you first record another person's words directly and then indicate who that person is.

3. Write a sentence that includes one quotation within another.

4. Write a sentence that includes one quotation within a second and that second quotation within a third.

5. Record a short conversation between two or more people.

6. Make up or record a portion of one person's talk that includes more than one paragraph.

7. Write a sentence that introduces a passage of prose from someone else; the passage should require more than four lines of your paper and should consist of less than one paragraph. Display the quoted passage correctly.

8. Write a sentence that introduces a passage of prose from someone else; the passage should require more than four lines of your paper and should consist of more than one full paragraph. Display the passage correctly.

9. Write a sentence in which you quote two lines of poetry.

10. Write a sentence that introduces a quotation of more than three lines of poetry. Display the quoted lines correctly.

2   Use Quotation Marks to Enclose Certain Titles

Double quotation marks are also used around certain titles. In general, these are titles of works that are part of larger works and are not marketed or performed on their own. (Titles of larger works are usually italicized or underlined; see **37b**.) Specifically, quotation marks are used around titles of short or moderately long poems, short stories, sections of books, songs, sections of major musical compositions, speeches, episodes of television programs, and articles in magazines, newspapers, and professional journals. Here are a few examples:

**34a
qseb**

TITLE OF A POEM: "Memorial Verses," by Matthew Arnold

TITLE OF A SONG: "The Way We Were"

TITLE OF AN ESSAY
IN AN ACADEMIC JOURNAL: "A Study of Early Memories," by K. Gorden, in the *Journal of Delinquency*

TITLE OF A CHAPTER
IN A BOOK: "Incontinent Nostalgia," Chapter 16 in Oliver Sacks's *The Man Who Mistook His Wife for a Hat*

Note that if such a title contains a title already enclosed in double quotation marks, you should change the double quotation marks around the contained title to single quotation marks:

"Views of Mind and Brain in Penfield's 'Memory Mechanisms' "

Take special note that the title you give to one of your own essays should not be enclosed in double quotation marks on that essay. However, you might need to use double quotation marks in parts of your titles if they contain the titles of works that call for double quotation marks:

The Philosophical Foundation of Freud's "Screen Memories"

Finally, if you ever refer to the title of one of your own essays in a different essay, you should enclose that title in quotation marks.

Exercise 2

Practice using quotation marks for punctuating titles by following these five sets of directions.

1. Write a sentence in which you give the title of a short story.
2. Write a sentence in which you give the title of an article in an academic journal.
3. Write a sentence in which you give the title of a song.
4. Write a sentence in which you refer to an essay title that includes the title of a poem. Make up the essay title if you wish.
5. Create a title for an essay you have written or will write; in this title refer to the title of an article in a magazine.

3 Use Quotation Marks to Enclose Words Used in a Special Way

Whenever you use words in a special way, you should enclose them in double quotation marks. For example, you may need to use one or more words to define other words:

As a verb, *to effect* means "to bring about."

Sometimes you may employ quotation marks to put some distance between you and expressions you think are offensive or deceptive:

Many people cannot forget the pictures of "the final solution."

However, you should avoid using quotation marks around expressions that you know belong in the realms of slang or casual conversation:

AVOID: That teacher's ability to remember names is "awesome."

In general, words with connotations such as *awesome* carries in the example are rare in academic writing, but if they serve a good purpose in your prose, use them without the quotation marks, which draw special attention to them. If such expressions do not serve such a purpose, revise them.

Exercise 3

In the following paragraph, add double quotation marks around words that call for them, and cross out double quotation marks that appear where they should not. You may also have to revise some words.

> EXAMPLE: In the first sentence, double quotation marks would be likely to appear around *one who has a good memory* or *who has a good memory.*

According to most dictionaries, a memorist is one who has a good memory. Our ethics professor is the most remarkable memorist we have ever met; in fact, his abilities to recall things are "radical." In one case, we discussed how hospitals should take responsibility for lethal mistakes made by their staff members. Our professor said that many hospitals label such mistakes therapeutic misadventures. And without consulting any notes, he described dozens of cases in which hospitals had used this label. In another class, we examined the metaphors that the Nazis had used to persuade citizens to accept the final solution. Our professor was able to discuss more than twenty such metaphors without ever consulting his notes. We once asked him if he ever used devices that could be considered mnemonic (a word that means assisting or aiding the memory). He replied that he had never felt any need to use mnemonic devices. We concluded that his talents were truly "out of sight."

Using Quotation Marks with Other Marks of Punctuation

The following guidelines should help you decide whether a single or double quotation mark goes to the left or to the right of another mark of punctuation.

1 Periods and Commas Go Inside Quotation Marks

If you record a quotation and do not need to give a parenthetical citation of its source, and if a period or comma is called for near a quotation mark, always put the period or comma inside the quotation mark:

"One of the people whom A. R. Luria studied," the lecturer added, "could listen to as many as seventy words and numbers and then repeat them accurately."

If you record a quotation and give a parenthetical citation of its source, you should punctuate the material as follows (the examples illustrate the MLA citation form; see 45e):

When the person whom Luria studied read a passage of prose, "each word produced an image" (Luria 387), an effect that led later researchers to investigate what it means to see prose.

Or

According to Luria, the images that the man saw could "easily lead him astray" (387).

2 Colons and Semicolons Go Outside Quotation Marks

If you record a quotation and do not need to give a parenthetical citation of its source, and if you wish to use a colon or a semicolon near a quotation mark, put the colon or semicolon outside the quotation mark:

A few people have what the lecturer called "no measurable limits to the capacity of their memory"; even fewer experience no loss of memory traces.

Several people are well known among psychologists as "mnemonists": Arturo Toscanini, the Reverend Dryden William Phelps, and one of the people whom Luria studied.

If you record a quotation and give a parenthetical citation of its source, then you should punctuate the material as follows (the examples illustrate the MLA citation form):

When the person whom Luria studied read a list of words, "each word would elicit a graphic image" (Luria 386); the problem with the images is that they began to dominate the man's thinking.

Or

"What a crumbly, yellow voice you have" (Luria 386): This is how the man described L. S. Vygotsky's voice.

34b
yseb

3 Dashes, Question Marks, and Exclamation Points Can Go Either Inside or Outside Quotation Marks, Depending on the Situation

Dashes, question marks, and exclamation points appear inside quotation marks if they apply only to the quoted material, not to the overall sentence in which the quoted material appears:

> "I just lost the—" the assistant was interrupted suddenly.

> They replied, "How can she form a perfect image of any printed page she sees?"

> The researchers responded, "She can form a perfect image of a million dots in a random pattern!"

Note that the last two examples do not require a period in addition to the question mark or exclamation point. What might be seen as an exception to this rule occurs when a quotation is followed by a parenthetical citation:

> Professor Strohmeyer concludes by writing, "Can one synthesize an image of something not seen before?" (403).

> According to Wordsworth, "Heaven lies about us in our infancy!" ("Ode: Intimations of Immortality" 66).

If dashes, question marks, and exclamation points apply to the overall sentence in which quoted material appears, not to the quoted material itself, then these marks appear outside the quotation marks:

> "Truth is memory"—these words haunt some people.

> Do you know what she meant by writing "memory is truth"?

> That person has the nerve to write that "that is all you will ever recall"!

You might occasionally write a sentence that asks a question and that concludes with quoted material that also asks a question. Or you might write a sentence that is an exclamation and that concludes with quoted material that also is an exclamation. In such cases, you should use only one question mark or exclamation point, and you should place the question mark or exclamation point inside the quotation marks:

> Who originally asked, "How can anyone live without memories of childhood?"

> The outrageous nerve of them to chant, "Away with cultural memories!"

Exercise 4

Edit the following passage so that it is punctuated correctly.

EXAMPLE: The first sentence should read *A prominent psychologist gave a talk yesterday called "Amazing Memorists."*

A prominent psychologist gave a talk yesterday called "Amazing Memorists". Some of the more amazing stories she told were about the Reverend Dryden William Phelps, who was described in the psychological literature in 1929. According to the lecturer, if someone mentioned to the Reverend Phelps a date in the prior sixty years, he could state which day of the week that date had fallen on. When they heard this, many members of the audience turned to each other and said, "That man's memory was astonishing"! But the Reverend Phelps had other impressive abilities. In the words of the lecturer, once he heard a date, he could "give a brief weather report for that day;" moreover, he could mention something that happened on that day.

The lecturer also told some anecdotes about the conductor Arturo Toscanini. Before one concert, a bassoonist came to Toscanini and reported that the key for the lowest note on his bassoon was broken. Toscanini was silent for a moment and then said, "It is all right—that note does not occur in tonight's concert". Although some who attended the lecture called such anecdotes "too extraordinary to be true", other individuals could only shake their heads and ask, "Why can't I even remember where I put my car keys?"

34c
yseb

34c

Using Ellipsis Points

You might occasionally wish to omit some words, phrases, sentences, or even paragraphs from quotations. Of course, in omitting material you must never distort the meaning or the tone of the original passage. But you will be able to omit some kinds of elements without distorting original passages.

If the material you wish to omit appears at the beginning of a sentence in the original passage, simply omit the material and use quotation marks to show at what point in the original sentence you are beginning to quote. Here is a sentence from Gummerman and Gray's "An Uncommon Case of Visual Memory":

> Briefly, eidetic imagery refers to the ability, usually found in children, to retain a very vivid and faithful image of a scene that was viewed for only a number of seconds.

The sentence is quoted below with its beginning omitted:

> Psychologists commonly say that "eidetic imagery refers to the ability, usually found in children, to retain a very vivid and faithful image of a scene that was viewed for only a number of seconds."

To mark omissions from parts of sentences other than the beginning, you must use ellipsis points. Ellipsis points are three periods in a row, each period having a space before and after it. Note that you should never carry ellipsis points from one line to the next. You may use ellipsis points to signal the following kinds of omissions from quoted material.

1 Omissions of Material Within a Sentence

To signal the omission of material within a sentence, replace the material with ellipsis points. For instance, here is another sentence from Gummerman and Gray's "An Uncommon Case of Visual Memory," first quoted in full and then with material omitted:

> "Nancy's memory, as mentioned earlier, does not seem to be eidetic" (Gummerman and Gray 410).

> "Nancy's memory . . . does not seem to be eidetic" (Gummerman and Gray 410).

Note the spaces before and after each ellipsis point. Also note that the commas enclosing *as mentioned earlier* are omitted because to leave one or the other or both would make the sentence difficult for readers to interpret.

Now suppose that Gummerman and Gray had written this sentence on page 410:

> Since Nancy could not perform certain memory tasks, tasks described in detail earlier, she does not seem to be eidetic.

If you wanted to omit the material enclosed by commas in this sentence, you should retain the first comma before using ellipsis points. The comma will help readers see the proper grammatical relationship between the clauses of the quoted sentence:

> "Since Nancy could not perform certain memory tasks, . . . she does not seem to be eidetic" (Gummerman and Gray 410).

34c
qseb

2 Omissions of the End of a Sentence, of the Beginning of One Sentence Embedded in a Sequence of Sentences, or of Entire Sentences and Paragraphs

You may use ellipsis points to omit the last part of a sentence, the first part of a sentence embedded in a sequence of sentences, or entire sentences and paragraphs. To mark these kinds of omissions, you must use four periods: one period immediately after the last word before an omission to indicate that the sentence has ended, and three spaced periods to mark the omission. We illustrate this practice using the following original passage:

> Some people are able to memorize extremely long passages of prose, as we noted above. Once people memorize these passages, they usually are able to retain them for long periods of time. As you might expect, some examples will make these points clearer.
>
> One person who participated in our studies memorized Proust's *Remembrance of Things Past* and was able to write it with only a few errors thirty days after memorizing it.
>
> Some researchers dispute the report of this feat of memorization, but the feat was videotaped and later validated by several researchers not associated with our project.
>
> A second person who participated in our study memorized sixteen different fairy tales from the Grimm Brothers' collection and was able to write them from memory almost flawlessly sixteen days later.

34c
ʜseb

In the following quotation, the end of the first sentence is omitted:

> "Some people are able to memorize extremely long passages of prose. . . . Once people memorize these passages, they usually are able to retain them for long periods of time."

The beginning of the third sentence is omitted in the quotation below:

> "Once people memorize these passages, they usually are able to retain them for long periods of time. . . . some examples will make these points clearer."

If you wanted to quote the second sentence of the passage, omit the third sentence, and go on to quote the fourth sentence, you would use ellipsis points after the last word in the second sentence (*"time. . . ."*) and begin recording the fourth sentence.

Finally, if you wanted to quote all of this passage except the third paragraph, you would use ellipsis points after the last word in the second paragraph (*"it. . . ."*) and begin recording the fourth paragraph after a normal paragraph indentation.

If you ever omit the end of a directly quoted sentence that concludes with a question mark or an exclamation point in the original, you should record the question mark or exclamation point before the ellipsis, as illustrated below:

ORIGINAL SENTENCE:	How can people perform such feats, such amazing feats?
QUOTATION:	"How can people perform such feats? . . ."
ORIGINAL SENTENCE:	That feat was amazing, simply amazing!
QUOTATION:	"That feat was amazing! . . ."

3 **Omissions of One or More Lines of Poetry**

If you ever wish to omit one or more lines of a poem, mark the omission with a line of spaced periods about as long as the line or lines you omit. These four lines come from John Keats's "Ode on a Grecian Urn":

Heard melodies are sweet, but those unheard
  Are sweeter; therefore, ye soft pipes, play on;
Not to the sensual ear, but, more endear'd,
  Pipe to the spirit ditties of no tone:

If you wanted to omit the third line, you would quote as follows:

Heard melodies are sweet, but those unheard
  Are sweeter; therefore, ye soft pipes, play on;
. . . .
  Pipe to the spirit ditties of no tone:

34c
qseb

Exercise 5

Follow each of the numbered instructions, using ellipsis points as necessary.

1. Find a sentence in a book or article. Write a sentence in which you include a direct quotation of the sentence you found, omitting as much of the beginning of the sentence you found as seems appropriate.

2. Find another sentence in a source that is of interest to you. Write a sentence in which you include a direct quotation of the sentence you found, omitting as much from the interior of the sentence you found as seems appropriate.

3. Find another sentence in a source of interest to you. Write a sentence in which you include a direct quotation of the sentence you found, omitting as much from the end of that sentence as seems appropriate.

4. Find two sentences in a row in a source of interest to you. Write a sentence in which you introduce a direct quotation of the two sentences you found, omitting as much of the beginning of the second sentence as seems appropriate.

5. Find a paragraph in a source that interests you. Write a sentence in which you introduce a direct quotation of this paragraph, omitting one sentence from the paragraph. Remember to display the quotation if it requires more than four lines in your paper.

Using Brackets

Occasionally, you may need to add information to a quotation, yet you cannot simply insert your own words into other writers' sentences. What you must do is use brackets, [ ], to enclose the information that you add. If your typewriter or word processor does not include keys for brackets, you will have to draw them in on your paper in pencil or black ink.

Brackets are often necessary to perform the following tasks:

1. To identify who or what a pronoun in a quotation refers to

> "At one point in his life, he [Mozart] heard a song once and then went home and wrote it down from memory."

2. To give the reference of general nouns in quotations

> "According to some people [those with excellent visual memories], it is possible to invent extraordinarily detailed images of imaginary scenes."

(Note that the second bracket appears before the comma.)

3. To translate a foreign word or phrase that occurs in a quotation

> "All they could remember of that scene was that it looked *vies* [disgusting or offensive]."

4. To indicate that you have italicized or emphasized certain words in a quotation

> "People with excellent long-term memories *might* [emphasis added] be bothered by images they cannot forget."

Finally, if you find an error in spelling, wording, or grammar in a passage that you are quoting, you should record the passage as you found it and indicate that the error is not yours but occurred in the original. To mark an error, you should enclose the word *sic* (Latin for "thus") in brackets immediately after the error:

> "On the basis of many tests, researchers have deducted [sic] that few people have excellent long-term memory abilities."

If the error occurs in the last word of a quotation, the brackets and *sic* go before the mark of end punctuation and the final quotation mark:

> "When some people perform difficult memory tasks, they look as if they were unconscience [sic]."

You should never use brackets and *sic* after word choices or claims that you disagree with but that are not clearly erroneous.

Exercise 6

Use brackets to insert the necessary information into each of the following quotations.

> **EXAMPLE:** Use brackets to indicate that the year referred to in the following quotation is 1894:
>
> "In that year, Napoleon Bird played pieces on the piano from memory for forty-four hours."
>
> "In that year [1894], Napoleon Bird played pieces on the piano from memory for forty-four hours."

1. Use brackets to indicate that the four hours referred to in the following quotation occurred between 11:00 p.m. and 3:00 a.m.

   "For four hours, Bird played dance music for a large number of couples."

2. Use brackets to indicate that the phrase *such people* in the following quotation refers to those with the ability to remember many musical pieces.

   "Such people are not necessarily talented musicians."

3. Use brackets to indicate that the phrase *that part of England* in the following quotation refers to Cheshire:

   "In that part of England, Mr. Bird was a celebrity."

4. Use brackets to indicate that you have added the emphasis or the underlining to the word *hundreds* in the following quotation:

   "In the course of those forty-four hours, Mr. Bird played *hundreds* of piano pieces."

5. Use brackets and *sic* after the error in the following quotation:

   "People who witnessed parts of Mr. Bird's performance agreed that it was extrordinary."

34d
qset

35

According to John Benbow, author of a style manual, "If you take hyphens seriously you will surely go mad." We know a few people who drive others nearly to distraction by asking them to explain the precise difference in meaning between such forms as *slow-moving vehicle* and *slow moving vehicle.* But we hope to prove Benbow wrong. We think that you will be able to take hyphens very seriously and not weaken but strengthen your grip on reality.

35a

Use Hyphens with Some Compound Nouns

One kind of compound noun (the hyphenated compound) requires a hyphen in it. According to *Webster's Ninth New Collegiate Dictionary,* the compound noun formed from *cross* and *purposes* is hyphenated: *cross-purposes.*

In other compound nouns (open compounds), two words appear with a space between them. According to the same dictionary, the compound noun formed from *cross* and *fire* is an open compound: *cross fire.*

In still other compound nouns (closed compounds), two words are fused. According to the same dictionary, the compound noun formed from *cross* and *bow* is a closed compound: *crossbow*.

The question that you might face as you write compound nouns is which of these three forms these compound nouns take. Complicating this matter is the fact that not all dictionaries agree about which form a particular compound noun takes. In addition, compound nouns generally change their form over time. Most enter print as open compounds, change to hyphenated compounds, and end up as closed compounds. Therefore, in your treatment of compound nouns, you should follow the advice of a current dictionary, and you should do so consistently.

A related note here is that a pair or a series of compound nouns, or closely related forms, all of which have a word or two in common, can be shortened as follows:

eight- and nine-year-olds   psycho- and sociolinguists

Exercise 1

Predict what form the compound noun made from each of the following pairs of words takes. Then check your dictionary to see whether your predictions are correct, and compare your answers with those of classmates using dictionaries different from yours. Note that if the compound is not listed, it exists as two separate words.

EXAMPLE: *blue* and *moon* → *blue moon* (according to *Webster's Ninth New Collegiate Dictionary*)

1. *bunk* and *bed*
2. *cross* and *link*
3. *flood* and *water*
4. *get* and *together*
5. *head* and *ship*
6. *head* and *start*
7. *master* and *mind*
8. *pit* and *stop*
9. *goings* and *on*
10. *interest* and *group*

35b
hy

35b

Use Hyphens with Some Compound Modifiers

Whenever you combine two or more words into a single grammatical unit that appears before and modifies a noun or a pronoun, you should use hyphens between the parts of the modifying unit:

a *soon-forgotten* game   a *week-long* seminar

a *three-hour* movie   a *two-volume* set

Sometimes writers come up with some fairly long modifying units, especially in more informal situations:

They had the *end-of-a-losing-season* blues.

If you use two or more compound modifiers in a row, all of which have a word or two in common, you can shorten them as follows:

nine- or *ten-o'clock* bedtimes

In some cases, however, hyphens are not used with modifying elements.

1. When modifying units are easy for readers to interpret without ambiguity, they generally appear without a hyphen:

    senior high school   *life insurance* policy

2. Modifying units that are hyphenated if they appear before nouns or pronouns usually are not hyphenated if they appear after nouns or pronouns. All of the following, therefore, are correct:

    a soon-forgotten game

    a game soon forgotten

    The game was soon forgotten.

35b
hy

    The only exceptions to this note are the modifying units that are hyphenated in the dictionary. Here are a few examples from *Webster's Ninth New Collegiate Dictionary:*

    coarse-grained   general-purpose   well-favored

    Such modifying units should have a hyphen in them whether they appear before or after a noun or pronoun:

    a *coarse-grained* analysis

    The analysis was *coarse-grained.*

3. If one of the words in a modifying unit is an adverb ending in *ly,* do not use a hyphen between the words:

    a *barely suppressed* yawn   a *superbly planned* concert

4. If one word in a modifying unit is a comparative or superlative form of an adverb, do not use a hyphen between the words:

    a *faster developing* storm   the *fastest developing* storm

5. If one word in a modifying unit is a possessive form, do not use a hyphen between the words:

    a *long day's* journey   *one week's* pay

6. If the modifying unit is a phrase from a language other than English, do not use hyphens within the phrase:

an *ad hominem* attack   the *ex post facto* law

Exercise 2

In the following passage, cross out all unnecessary hyphens and add all necessary ones.

EXAMPLE: The following passage serves as a case study in a first year course in ethics.

The following passage serves as a case study in a first-year course in ethics.

Imagine yourself relaxing on a late summer afternoon. Imagine further that one of your good friends rushes into your apartment with a never to be forgotten look of terror on his face. He pleads with you to help conceal him, and then he scrambles into one of your poorly-lighted closets. A moment later, a man brandishing a machete staggers into your apartment. The fury in his eyes is more terrible than any other you have ever seen. "Where is he?" he screams. "He owes me at least three-days' wages." What should you do? Your mind races back through some of the lessons about lying that you once learned. They were easy-to-remember. But the lessons really do not help you decide whether to tell the truth at all times or to conceal the truth and try to save your friend's severely-threatened life.

35c

Use Hyphens with Some Prefixes and Suffixes

The following suffix usually requires a hyphen between it and the word it is added to:

-elect (as in *governor-elect*)

Some prefixes usually require a hyphen after them:

all- (as in *all-conference*)   quasi- (as in *quasi-legislative*)
ex- (as in *ex-governor*)   self- (as in *self-parody*)
half- (as in *half-truth*)

Other prefixes should be followed by a hyphen if they are added to certain kinds of elements. A prefix should be followed by a hyphen if it is added to a capitalized word or a date:

pre-Whitman   pre-1960

A prefix should also be followed by a hyphen if adding the prefix without a hyphen would produce an awkward combination of letters or a misleading word form:

de-emphasize (to avoid *deemphasize,* which could be mispronounced)

anti-intrusion (to avoid *antiintrusion,* which could be mispronounced and looks strange)

bill-like (to avoid *billlike,* which could be mispronounced and looks strange)

re-cover (which means "to cover again," not to be confused with *recover*)

re-create (which means "to create again," not to be confused with *recreate*)

re-form (which means "to form again," not to be confused with *reform*)

re-sign (which means "to sign again," not to be confused with *resign*)

Whenever you add a prefix to an open compound noun, you should use only one hyphen; that hyphen goes between the prefix and the first word of the compound:

pre-Gregorian calendar   post-grammar school

35c
hy

If you use two prefixes with the same base word, you should record the base word only once, after the second prefix. The first prefix should always be followed by a hyphen. The second prefix should be followed by a hyphen if your dictionary calls for one between it and the base word:

pro- and anti-imperialism

Exercise 3

In the following passage, cross out all unnecessary hyphens and add all necessary ones.

EXAMPLE: The following case study is the one our supervisor elect recommends.

The following case study is the one our supervisor-elect recommends.

Imagine that you have been appointed to propose some reforms in the code of ethics that medical doctors must commit themselves to. What response would you recommend to a doctor facing the following dilemma? A patient has worked for thirty years with the expectation of someday taking a trip around the world. The patient has no close-relatives. Looking ahead to a pre New Year's Day departure, the patient has a medical examination near the beginning of December. The doctor discovers that the patient has about two-months to live. Never in the doctor's post-1992 practice has the doctor faced such a dilemma. Should the doctor say anything to the patient? Should the doctor reveal the full truth? Should the doctor convey some half truths? What should the doctor do to keep self doubts from increasing?

35d

Use Hyphens to Divide Some Words at the End of a Line

If you need to prevent a word from running too far into the right-hand margin of a paper, you might be able to use a hyphen to divide it into two parts and then move the second part to the beginning of the next line. In general you should try to hold this practice to a minimum, but in some cases it is unavoidable.

In certain positions in papers, however, you should never divide a word and distribute its parts on two different lines. You should never leave part of a word at the end of the first line of an essay, at the end of any paragraph, or at the end of any page.

In addition, certain kinds of elements should never be divided:

Contractions *(wasn't,* not *was-n't)*

Numbers *(13,000,* not *13-000)*

Acronyms *(NATO,* not *NA-TO)*

Abbreviations *(a.m.,* not *a.-m.)*

One-syllable words *(armed,* not *arm-ed)*

Two-syllable words that, if divided, would leave fewer than three letters at the end or beginning of a line *(acorn,* not *a-corn)*

Words that, if divided, could be misinterpreted *(coop,* not *co-op)*

Words that can be divided at the end of a line should be divided between syllables:

consist → con-sist   formation → for-mation *or* forma-tion

If you have questions about syllabication, make sure to check your dictionary.

In the case of a compound word, divide it between the two words that are joined to form the compound:

blackout → black-out   setback → set-back

Finally, if the word you need to divide includes a prefix or suffix, divide the word by using a hyphen between the prefix or suffix and the word:

subsurface → sub-surface   nationhood → nation-hood

Exercise 4

Indicate whether it would be possible to divide each of the following words at the end of a line. If it would be possible, indicate where you would use a hyphen to mark the division.

EXAMPLE: *foreshadow* is possible to divide *(fore-shadow)*

1. couldn't
2. NCAA
3. b.c.
4. climbed
5. ocean

6. delicious
7. pickpocket
8. successful
9. maladapted
10. postgraduate

35e

Use Hyphens with Some Numbers and Spelled-out Numbers

In three instances, you should use hyphens with numbers or spelled-out numbers (see also **37d**). First, use a hyphen between the two words in the spelled-out forms of the numbers *21* through *99:*

twenty-one   ninety-nine

Numbers below *21* are spelled as one word, and those above *99* should be recorded as numerals:

seven   106

Second, you should use a hyphen between the spelled-out numerator and denominator of a fraction, unless the numerator or the denominator or both already contain a hyphen:

three-sixteenths   three thirty-seconds

Third, you should use a hyphen with numbers that show a range:

1949-1950 (but not in constructions such as *from 1949 to 1950*)

pages 6-83

Exercise 5

Practice using hyphens by following the directions given in each of the numbered sentences.

EXAMPLE: Write a sentence containing the spelled-out form of *25*.

Twenty-five people attended the dinner party.

1. Write a sentence containing the spelled-out form of *18*.
2. Write a sentence containing the spelled-out form of *59*.
3. Write a sentence containing the spelled-out form of *99*.
4. Write a sentence containing the spelled-out form of $\frac{5}{8}$.
5. Write a sentence containing the spelled-out form of $\frac{3}{22}$.

35e
hy

36

O ccasionally, we hear claims that apostrophes make no difference to readers' understanding of sentences. But the apostrophe can convey important meanings to readers, as we illustrate in this chapter.

36a

Use Apostrophes to Signal the Possessive Case

The main function of apostrophes is to signal the possessive case of nouns and indefinite pronouns. The possessive case is used mainly to show that someone possesses something *(the family's cottage)* or that one thing is closely associated with another *(Van Gogh's ears).*

Sometimes, of course, you can convey such meanings without using an apostrophe. Instead of writing *Van Gogh's ears,* you could write *the ears of Van Gogh.* This latter kind of construction is usually preferable when you are referring to things closely associated with inanimate objects. Many writers would choose *the advantages of this approach* over *this approach's advantages.*

1 The Possessive Form of Singular Nouns and Indefinite Pronouns

Different handbooks give different guidelines for forming the possessive of a singular noun or an indefinite pronoun. And sometimes different academic fields observe different conventions for forming such possessives. Therefore, it is possible for you to see forms such as *Moses'* and *Moses's* in print. We follow the recommendation published by the Modern Language Association; this recommendation is to form the possessive of a singular noun or an indefinite pronoun by adding *'s,* even if the noun or pronoun ends in *s*:

the witness's problem	the lawyer's files	Louis's story
Euripides's tragedy	anybody's guess	Sanchez's book

2 The Possessive Form of Plural Nouns

To form the possessive of plural nouns that end in *s* or *es,* you should add just an apostrophe:

the members' votes [the votes of more than one member; *member's votes* refers to the votes of one member]

cities' employees [the employees of more than one city; *city's employees* refers to the employees of one city]

You should also add just an apostrophe to form the possessive of plural proper nouns:

the Smiths' cottage   the Joneses' lawn

Note that you should not use an apostrophe with plural proper nouns that are not possessive:

INCORRECT: The Joneses' are on vacation.

CORRECT: The Joneses are on vacation.

To form the possessive of plural nouns that do not end in *s* or *es,* you should add *'s:*

children's rights   people's rights   deer's rights

3 The Possessive Form of Compound Elements

To form the possessive of compound elements such as *mothers-in-law* and *someone else,* make only the last word possessive:

mothers-in-law's response   someone else's idea

36a
ap

4 The Possessive Form of Nouns Linked by a Conjunction

To form the possessive of nouns paired up or linked in a series, you have to decide whether those named by the nouns possess something together (joint ownership) or whether each of those named possesses something individually (individual ownership).

To signal joint ownership, make only the last noun possessive:

Zellig and Sarah's proposals [Zellig and Sarah together make proposals].

To signal individual ownership, make each noun possessive:

Zellig's and Sarah's proposals [Zellig and Sarah each make a different proposal].

5 Unnecessary Apostrophes

The following personal pronouns are already possessive in form:

CORRECT: yours   his   hers   its   ours   theirs

To add an apostrophe to such a pronoun is incorrect because doing so signals possession twice:

INCORRECT: your's   his'   her's   it's or its'
                 our's   their's

Exercise 1

Supply the correct form in the blank spaces of the following grid. Then use each form in a sentence.

EXAMPLE:

Singular	Singular possessive	Plural	Plural possessive
driver	driver's	drivers	drivers'

Singular	Singular possessive	Plural	Plural possessive
_____	_____	officers	_____
witness	_____	_____	_____
_____	woman's	_____	_____
_____	_____	_____	fathers-in-law's

36a
ap

Exercise 2

In the following passage, correct all errors in the use of apostrophes.

EXAMPLE: In several scholar's opinions, the idea for a code of laws
originated in ancient Babylon.

In several scholars' opinions, the idea for a code of laws
originated in ancient Babylon.

In several scholar's opinions, the idea for a code of laws originated in
ancient Babylon. There a king called Ur-Nammu assembled the first
known code around 2100 B.C. The most famous and extensive code was
the Code of Hammurabi. In Hammurabi's Code, many punishments were
designed to fit the crime. For example, if a son struck his father, the sons'
hand was cut off. Or if a person spied on someone else's private matters,
the offenders' eyes were put out.

It is clear from the code that husbands' rights were more extensive
than were wives'. A husband could divorce his wife whenever he
pleased. She could sue for the restoration of what was hers', especially
her dowry. However, most wives were cautious about suing, for if they
were found to have failed in their duties, they would be sentenced to
death by drowning.

One issue that some legal scholars are exploring is the extent to
which elements of Hammurabi's Code influenced some of Moses' laws,
laws that were recorded around 1200 B.C.

36b

Use Apostrophes to Mark Omitted Letters
or Numbers

Apostrophes may signal that letters or numbers have been left out of
constructions. One case involves a small set of words and figures:

e'en (for *even*), e'er (for *ever*), o'er (for *over*), ma'am (for
madam)

'56 Ford (for *1956*), class of '72 (for *1972*)

You might associate words such as *e'en* with old poems and stories, and
in fact few writers use these words today unless they are seeking an
antiquated or quaint effect. The omission of the first two numbers in
dates is common only in informal writing.

Another case involves some set expressions:

o'clock (for *of the clock;* the full form is no longer used)

will-o'-the-wisp (for *Will of the wisp*)

Sometimes letters are omitted from words to record speech accurately or to capture the sound of regional or social dialects:

"We used t', when we's a'comin'up children—you see, they'd cut and thresh their wheat and rye ever'year. Well, y'see we'd fill our beds up ever'year. Ever'year. And now, since they quit that, why I had one full and I just kep' it. Just sun it and wash th'tick'n'things, and it's just as good as it ever was. I'm keepin' it for a keepsake."

Mrs. Pearl Martin, in *The Foxfire Book*

Finally, apostrophes indicate omitted letters in contractions. **Contractions** are the products of making one word out of two, and in the process leaving out one or more letters. Some contractions result from bringing the expletive *there* and a verb together:

there is → there's   there will → there'll

Combining a pronoun and a verb also produces contractions:

I am → I'm	it has → it's
I had → I'd	it is → it's
I have → I've	we are → we're
I would → I'd	we have → we've
you are → you're	we will → we'll
you have → you've	let us → let's
you will → you'll	they have → they've
he had, she had → he'd, she'd	they will → they'll
he would, she would → he'd, she'd	who is → who's
he is, she is → he's, she's	who has → who's
he will, she will → he'll, she'll	

Still others result from bringing two parts of a verb phrase together:

cannot → can't	might have (not might of) → might've
could have (not could of) → could've	should have (not should of) → should've
does not → doesn't	was not → wasn't
did not → didn't	were not → weren't
do not → don't	would not → wouldn't
is not → isn't	will not → won't

Two words of caution about contractions are necessary. First, contractions are not accepted in the formal writing of many academic disciplines. Therefore, you should ask your instructors whether contractions are acceptable in written work submitted to them. Second, you should take care not to confuse four common contractions with four possessive adjectives:

Contractions	**Possessive adjectives**
It's humid today.	*Its* hoof was bruised.
You're here early.	*Your* ticket is ready.
They're protesting.	*Their* farm is ruined.
Who's in charge here?	*Whose* fault was it?

Exercise 3

In each sentence, underline the word in parentheses that is correct.

EXAMPLE: The Hebrew people assembled most of (their, they're) religious and social laws into a code.

1. If people examine the code of the ancient Hebrews, they will see that (its, it's) roots were in the teachings of Moses.
2. These teachings are notable for (their, they're) moral content.
3. (Whose, Who's) duty was it to interpret all those teachings?
4. (Their, They're) not all equally easy to understand, are they?
5. When (your, you're) discussing the historical development of law, how will you judge the contribution of the laws of Moses?

Use Apostrophes to Form Some Plurals

36c
ap

To form the plural of letters, as well as of words referred to as words, italicize (underline) the letter or word and then add an apostrophe and an unitalicized (not underlined) *s*:

Your *i*'s are hard to distinguish from your *j*'s.

You use three *seem*'s in one sentence.

To form the plural of numbers, symbols, abbreviations, and references to decades and centuries, add just an *s*:

2s   fours   600s   &s   SATs   1960s

Exercise 4

Write five sentences, each including one of the following elements in plural form.

EXAMPLE: believe → They use three *believe*'s in one short paragraph.

1. e   2. probably   3. 3   4. IRA   5. 1950

3

F or the most part, the matters we focus on in this chapter are not marks added to prose; technically, therefore, they are not marks of punctuation. Rather, these matters are special treatments given to numbers, letters, and words in certain situations. They can best be classified as matters of mechanics. The word *mechanics* should not lead you to assume that these matters have an insignificant effect on readers. Consider these two sentences:

> Thirty students, along with their supervising professor, headed south on the *Polar Explorer* for a project that was scheduled to last twenty-three days.

> Thirty students, along with their supervising prof., headed South on the Polar Explorer for a project that was scheduled to last 23 days.

Though it is unlikely to mislead readers, the second sentence might make them judge the writer as unskilled or careless.

37a

Capital Letters

The following guidelines should help you decide when to capitalize a letter.

550

1 Capitalize the First Letter of Sentences

You should capitalize the first letter of each sentence you write:

The group planned to study cultural customs.

Were all the responsibilities clear?

How time-consuming that can be!

If you ever use a sentence fragment, make sure that it can be justified. But also remember that its first letter should be capitalized:

And now to the books.

There are a few situations in which you should think particularly carefully about whether to use capital letters (see also **30b**). For instance, occasionally you might pose a general question and then follow it with several specific questions. If these specific questions are complete sentences, you should capitalize the first letter of each:

What were their choices now? Could they cut the project short? Or could they ask for additional funding?

If the more specific questions are not complete sentences, then you have a choice between using capital and lower-case letters to begin them. If you see your writing situation as quite formal, you should begin each question with a capital letter:

What are some possible effects? Confusion? Panic? Chaos?

If you see your writing situation as less formal, you may begin each question with a lower-case letter:

What are some possible effects? confusion? panic? chaos?

When you use a complete sentence after a colon, you must decide whether to capitalize the first letter of that sentence. Generally, in a formal writing situation, you would capitalize the first letter of a sentence after a colon, whereas in an informal situation you would probably use a lower-case letter to begin it:

Their choice was clear: They had to examine their own prejudices.

Their response was predictable: they gave up.

Finally, if you set off a complete sentence with dashes, you should not capitalize the first letter of the sentence that you set off:

Their explanation—they said they had been careless—was an understatement.

37a
cian

❷ When Quoting, Generally Capitalize Words That Are Capitalized in the Source

Imagine that you are working with this sentence from page 25 of William J. Fielding's *Strange Customs of Courtship and Marriage:*

> Sealing the engagement pact with a ring or other token is a usage of great antiquity.

If you were to use this quotation in such a way that it is not a grammatical part (for example, a direct object) of one of your sentences, you should leave the capital letter exactly as it is in the original:

> According to William J. Fielding, "Sealing the engagement pact with a ring or other token is a usage of great antiquity" (25).

However, if you were to make the quoted sentence a grammatical part of one of your sentences, then you should change the capital letter to a lowercase letter:

> Some scholars point out that "sealing the engagement pact with a ring or other token is a usage of great antiquity" (Fielding 25).

In the overall sentence, the quotation functions as the direct object.

If you ever need to change a letter that was originally lowercase into a capital, you should enclose the capital letter in brackets:

> "[A] usage of great antiquity"—this is how William J. Fielding describes the practice of giving an engagement ring.

When you quote lines of poetry, you should capitalize exactly as the published version of the poem indicates. Often the first letter in each line of a poem will be capitalized:

> It little profits that an idle king,
> By this still hearth, among these barren crags,
> Matched with an aged wife, I mete and dole
> Unequal laws unto a savage race,
> That hoard, and sleep, and feed, and know not me.
>
> Alfred, Lord Tennyson, "Ulysses," 1–5

But not all lines of published poems begin with capital letters, and you must record lines exactly as you find them in the source:

I have descended millions of stairs with my arm in yours,
not, of course, that with four eyes one might see better.
I descended them because I knew
that even though so bedimmed
yours were the only true eyes.

Eugenio Montale, "Xenia II," 8–12 (trans. G. Singh)

3 **Capitalize the First Letter of Proper Nouns and Most Proper Adjectives**

a. Proper Nouns

Common nouns refer to a member or to members of a group or class of things. They are usually not capitalized: *person, city, car.* Proper nouns refer to specific and namable members of a group or class. They are usually capitalized:

Elizabeth Cady Stanton   Portland   Volvo

Sometimes common nouns are used as parts of proper nouns. In such cases, the common nouns should be capitalized:

Tremont Street   Hess Lake   Mount Rainier

When made plural, such common nouns are capitalized if they precede proper nouns but usually not if they follow them:

Mounts Rainier and Hood   Lakes Erie and Huron

Tremont and Beacon streets   Hess and Murray lakes

In certain geographical names, both the common and proper nouns are capitalized:

Hawaiian Islands   Appalachian Mountains

Sometimes names of people are followed by a title, in which case the main words in the title are capitalized:

Janel Barrest, Attorney at Law   Jan Feste, Professor of Art

More often names of people are preceded by a title, which is capitalized:

Professor Cerul   Doctor Menin

In such cases, the title and the name together are considered a proper noun. If you separate such a title from a name, then the title becomes a common noun, and it should not be capitalized:

G. W. Livingsturm, a professor at the state university, is scheduled to address our literary club.

**37a
cian**

The only exception to the preceding generalization involves the titles for unquestionably high offices:

> They threatened to write to the President of the United States.

Here are some examples of proper nouns you should capitalize:

Personal names

Father   Mother   Aunt Rose   Jacob

Note that if words such as *father, mother,* and *aunt* do not refer to specific people, they are not capitalized:

> She has three aunts.

Nor are they capitalized in constructions such as *my mother, your father,* and *their aunts.*

Races and nationalities

Hispanics   Kurds   Slavs

Languages

French   Welsh   Hopi   Tamil

Institutions and organizations

Howard University   National Merit Society   Peace Corps

Historical events and periods

Boston Tea Party   Dark Ages   Middle Ages

Philosophic and artistic movements

Dadaism   Impressionism   Modernism

Countries and geographical areas

Pakistan   Gulf of Oman   Central America

Religions and religious terms

Buddha   God   Islam   Taoism

Note that if you refer to more than one deity, you should not capitalize the word *god:*

> They studied several gods once worshipped in the Euphrates Valley.

Sections of the United States

the South   the West

Note that references to directions should not be capitalized:

> Turn south and drive for six miles.

Buildings

Carnegie Hall   Empire State Building   Sears Tower

Specific academic courses
Economics 301   History 110   Philosophy 511

Note that if you do not refer to specific courses, you should not capitalize words such as *history:*

She has taken eleven history courses.

Holidays
Memorial Day   Thanksgiving Day

Days of the week
Sunday   Monday   Tuesday

Months
September   October   November

But note that names of seasons are not capitalized:

spring   summer   fall   winter

Planets
Mercury   Venus   Jupiter

But note that *earth, sun,* and *moon* are not capitalized.

b. Proper Adjectives

Proper adjectives are derived from proper nouns. In many cases these adjectives are capitalized:

Swiss engineering   Brazilian exports

But some proper adjectives have become so familiar that they are now accepted as common adjectives and are not capitalized:

bohemian lifestyle   french fries   roman type

If you are unsure whether to capitalize a proper adjective, check your dictionary.

4 Capitalize All Significant Words in Titles of Artistic Works

Whenever you record titles of plays, poems, stories, novels, musical compositions, and productions of visual art, you should capitalize all significant words in those titles. The significant words are the first word, the first word after a colon, the last word, both parts of a hyphenated compound, and all other words except articles, short prepositions, and short conjunctions. A preposition or conjunction is short if it is made up of four or fewer letters. Thus, you need not capitalize *into,* but you should capitalize *through.*

37a
cian

5 Capitalize *I* and *O*

You should always capitalize the personal pronoun *I* and the word *O,* which always precedes immediately a noun of direct address:

"My friend, *O* my friend, *I* have not forgotten."

Capitalize the interjection *oh* only if it is first in a sentence:

"*Oh*, I hadn't realized that."

"That book? Yes, *oh* yes, I remember it well."

Exercise 1

Capitalize letters as necessary in the following sentences.

    EXAMPLE: They did fieldwork in the trobriand islands.
                They did fieldwork in the Trobriand Islands.

1. Some of their findings are difficult to interpret.
2. The deception—if it can even be called deception—was harmless.
3. Do michigan and rush streets run parallel to each other?
4. When they reached lake victoria, they headed south.
5. They hoped to hear doctor Esquentes, as well as two professors from duke university.
6. Their philosophy courses were challenging, and history 301 required that they do a great deal of reading.
7. Only a few people in that region south of the border can still speak hopi or navajo.
8. They founded the medievalist society to encourage the study of the literature of the middle ages.
9. The crew of the spaceship will travel from earth to pluto.
10. Her first novel is called *touchstones on the way.*

37b

Italics

The kind of type that you will usually find in books and magazines is called roman type:

    culture

Type that slants to the right is called italic type:

culture

As you write and type papers, you can indicate that a word is italicized by underlining it:

culture

1 Italicize Titles of Individually Produced Works

You should use quotation marks around some titles (see **34a**) and italicize others. In general, the titles of longer works are italicized and those of shorter works are enclosed in quotation marks. In addition, the works whose titles take italics are likely to be individually issued or produced (for example, a book or magazine). On the other hand, works whose titles should appear in quotation marks are likely to be issued or produced as parts of larger works (for example, a chapter in a book or an article in a magazine). The kinds of titles that should be italicized are as follows:

Titles of books, novellas, and plays

The Psychopathic God   *The Turn of the Screw*   *Hamlet*

But note that some very well known books (including all sacred writings) and long documents are not italicized:

the Bible   the Koran   the Bill of Rights

Titles of magazines, periodicals, professional journals, and newspapers

Seventeen   *Harvard Educational Review*   *Wall Street Journal*

Note that you should record the title of a newspaper as it appears on the masthead, but you should omit any introductory article:

New York Times, not *The New York Times*

Titles of long poems published separately

Paradise Lost   *Odyssey*

Titles of films

Rear Window   *Witness*

Titles of paintings, drawings, statues, and other works of art

Michelangelo's *David*
Van Gogh's *Wheat Field and Cypress Trees*

Titles of long musical compositions and record albums

Don Giovanni   *Sgt. Pepper's Lonely Hearts Club Band*

37b
cian

Titles of radio and television series

Nova   *All Things Considered*

If you ever need to embed one title in another, you should use roman type for the embedded title:

Power and Politics in King Lear

2 Italicize Names of Certain Vehicles and Scientific Names for Plants and Animals

Names of ships, trains, airplanes, and spacecraft

Titanic   *Orient Express*   *Memphis Belle*   *Apollo 2*

But note that the abbreviations *USS* and *HMS* are not italicized when they precede the name of a ship:

USS *John F. Kennedy*

Scientific names for plants and animals

the sugar maple (*Acer saccharum*)
the grizzly bear (*Ursus horribilis*)

**37b
cian**

3 Italicize Numbers, Letters, and Words Referred to as Such

Whenever you refer to a number as a number, a letter as a letter, or a word as a word, italicize the number, letter, or word:

Is that a *7?*

How many words have an *e* before *i?*

Did you use *alleged?*

4 Italicize Words and Phrases from Languages Other Than English

In most cases, when you use a word or phrase from a language other than English, italicize it:

The period of Spanish history that most fascinated her was the reign of Fernando and Isabel, *Los Reyes Católicos.*

If you think that your readers need a translation of the italicized word or phrase, include the translation in quotation marks:

> The period of Spanish history that most fascinated her was the reign of Fernando and Isabel, *Los Reyes Católicos* ("The Catholic Monarchs").

Some words and phrases originating in languages other than English have become so familiar to many speakers of English that these words and phrases are not italicized:

> blitzkrieg   junta   mea culpa   savoir-faire

Whenever you are uncertain whether words and phrases originating in languages other than English require italics, check your dictionary. If the words or phrases are listed, they have probably became familiar enough in English that you need not italicize them.

5 Italicize Quoted Words That You Wish to Emphasize

Occasionally, you might wish to emphasize a word or phrase in a quotation. You should use italics for this purpose. And after the closing quotation marks you should insert *emphasis added* in brackets:

> William J. Fielding notes that in some cultures, "at the time of childbirth, the *husband* takes to his bed and simulates the pains that the wife actually undergoes" [emphasis added].

6 Use Italics Sparingly to Emphasize Your Own Words

You may use italics to emphasize some of your own words. However, you should not overdo this practice since italicized words draw so much attention to themselves that they can make your style seem insincere, aggressive, or frenzied:

> Professors *simply must* understand that they should *in no cases* call on unprepared students in class.

Sometimes it is legitimate to use italics to emphasize some of your own words. For instance, you may want to stress the point of an important contrast:

> That was neither a prediction nor a hypothesis; it was a *guess.*

**37b
cian**

Exercise 2

Italicize (underline) words and phrases as necessary in the following sentences.

EXAMPLE: Did you read the short story in the recent New Yorker?

Did you read the short story in the recent *New Yorker?*

1. Each year several musical societies perform Handel's Messiah.

2. This year our discussion group will focus on a book by Nancy Chodorow called The Reproduction of Mothering.

3. Will your "O'Connor's Saints" appear in the next issue of American Literature?

4. They often heard the phrase ein wenig ("a little").

5. Did you know that the words catarrh and rhythm come from the same source?

Abbreviations, Acronyms, and Initialisms

When may you use abbreviations *(a.m.),* acronyms (formed from initials and pronounced as a word: *MADD*), and initialisms (formed from initials and pronounced letter by letter: *CIA*)? The answer depends on the situation in which you write.

1 Generally Accepted Abbreviations, Acronyms, and Initialisms

The following abbreviations, acronyms, and initialisms are accepted in nearly all kinds of writing:

Some abbreviations before names

Dr.   Mme.   Mr.   Mrs.   Ms.   Messrs.

But note that none of these abbreviations is appropriate if it is not followed by a name:

INAPPROPRIATE: The Dr. was not in last week.

APPROPRIATE: The doctor was not in last week.

Some abbreviations after names

D.D.   D.D.S.   Esq.   Jr.   LL.D.   M.A.   M.D.   Ph.D.   Sr.

Some abbreviations used with numbers

440 B.C.   A.D. 66   6:10 a.m.   7 p.m.   55 mph   200 rpm

But note that it is inappropriate to use these abbreviations without a number:

INAPPROPRIATE: It was early in the a.m. when they left.

Some acronyms and initialisms

Some acronyms and initialisms are so well known that they are acceptable in most kinds of writing:

AFL-CIO   EKG   SEATO   UNESCO

If you use a less familiar acronym or initialism, such as COMECON, you should identify the element parenthetically when it first appears:

COMECON (Council for Mutual Economic Assistance)

Thereafter, you can use just the acronym or initialism.

Abbreviations for places commonly known by their abbreviations

U.S.   D.C.   U.S.S.R.

Spacing and Punctuating Abbreviations

Remember that no space should appear between the parts of the abbreviation or initialism:

Ph.D.   CIA

This convention is different from the one governing the spacing of initials in people's names. Initials in people's names have a space between them:

T. S. Eliot

Finally, if you conclude a declarative sentence with an abbreviation that ends with a period, that period also functions as the sentence period:

The meeting is scheduled for 3 p.m.

But if you conclude a question or an exclamation with an abbreviation that ends with a period, you must use a question mark or an exclamation point after the period concluding the abbreviation:

Did they schedule the meeting for 3 p.m.?

No, they scheduled it for 3 a.m.!

37c
ciar

2 Abbreviations Acceptable in Footnotes, Reference Lists, and Lists of Works Cited

In some kinds of writing, such as most kinds done in the humanities, very few abbreviations are allowed. Yet even in these kinds of writing, certain abbreviations are appropriate in footnotes, reference lists, and lists of works cited:

Abbreviation	Meaning
anon.	anonymous
b.	born
c. or ca. (from *circa*)	about (with dates)
cf. (from *confer*)	compare
ch., chs.	chapter(s)
d.	died
ed., eds.	editor(s), edition(s)
e.g. (from *exempli gratia*)	for example
et al. (from *et alia*)	and others
etc. (from *et cetera*)	and so forth
f., ff.	and the following (page or pages)
ibid. (from *ibidem*)	the same
i.e. (from *id est*)	that is
l., ll.	line(s)
ms., mss.	manuscript(s)
N.B. (from *nota bene*)	note well
n.d.	no date
no., nos.	number(s)
p., pp.	page(s)
rev.	revised, revision
rpt.	reprint
sc.	scene
tr., trans.	translator, translated by
viz. (from *videlicet*)	namely
vol., vols.	volume(s)
vs.	versus

37c
cian

Occasionally, you will see some of these abbreviations (such as *cf.* and *i.e.*) in the body of an essay. But usually such essays will be fairly informal.

The abbreviations for months of the year are also accepted in footnotes, reference lists, and lists of works cited:

Jan.	Feb.	Mar.	Apr.
May	June	July	Aug.
Sept.	Oct.	Nov.	Dec.

Postal abbreviations for the names of states are also acceptable as you document your sources:

Abbreviation	State	Abbreviation	State
AL	Alabama	MO	Missouri
AK	Alaska	MT	Montana
AZ	Arizona	NB	Nebraska
AR	Arkansas	NV	Nevada
CA	California	NH	New Hampshire
CO	Colorado	NJ	New Jersey
CT	Connecticut	NM	New Mexico
DE	Delaware	NY	New York
DC	District of Columbia	NC	North Carolina
FL	Florida	ND	North Dakota
GA	Georgia	OH	Ohio
HI	Hawaii	OK	Oklahoma
ID	Idaho	OR	Oregon
IL	Illinois	PA	Pennsylvania
IN	Indiana	RI	Rhode Island
IA	Iowa	SC	South Carolina
KS	Kansas	SD	South Dakota
KY	Kentucky	TN	Tennessee
LA	Louisiana	TX	Texas
MA	Massachusetts	UT	Utah
ME	Maine	VT	Vermont
MD	Maryland	VA	Virginia
MI	Michigan	WA	Washington
MN	Minnesota	WV	West Virginia
MS	Mississippi	WI	Wisconsin
		WY	Wyoming

37c
cian

3 Abbreviations Acceptable Only
in Informal Writing

You should almost always avoid the following types of abbreviations, except when you are writing informal notes and—in the case of abbreviations for state names—lists of works cited and addresses.

Abbreviations for titles

Sen.   Pres.   the Hon.   Gen.

Abbreviations for names

Eliz.   Geo.   Robt.   Wm.

Abbreviations for cities, counties, states, provinces, and countries

Bos. (for Boston)   IN (for Indiana)   N.Z. (for New Zealand)
Ott. (for Ottawa County)   Ont. (for Ontario)

Abbreviations for days of the week, months, and holidays

Mon.   Oct.   Mem. Day

Abbreviations for parts of business names

Inc.   Bros.   Co.

These last abbreviations should be used only along with a company name and only if they are part of that name:

CORRECT: They founded Prime Manufacturing Co.

INCORRECT: They hoped to form a co.

Exercise 3

Describe a situation in which you could appropriately use each of the following abbreviations.

> **EXAMPLE:** *pp.*   You could use this abbreviation in a list of
> works cited in a humanities paper.

1. D.D.S   2. A.D.   3. ed.   4. IA   5. Inc.

37d

Numbers

When you need to mention a number in your writing, should you spell it out *(sixteen)* or use a numeral *(16)*? The answer depends on your writing situation and on where in a sentence you plan to record the number.

37c
cian

Numerals are common in certain kinds of writing. In technical, scientific, and journalistic writing, for instance, writers generally use numerals for all numbers above ten. However, as you prepare to write in such areas, it would be wise to consult the style manual or manuals accepted as standard in those fields.

Here we offer guidelines for recording numbers when you are writing in the humanities, for numerals are less common in writing in the humanities than in technical, scientific, and journalistic writing.

1 Spell Out Numbers from One Through Ninety-Nine

You should spell out most numbers from one through ninety-nine (see the end of this chapter for exceptions) and any of these numbers followed by the words *hundred, thousand,* or *million:*

one	thirty-seven	ninety-nine
six hundred	thirty-seven thousand	ninety-six million

Use numerals for other numbers (unless they begin a sentence):

106   1,037   137,096

Within sentences, you should try to avoid mixing spelled-out numbers and numerals. For example, if you wish to refer to the numbers *200, 239,* and *541* in a sentence, you should write *200, 239,* and *541,* not *two hundred, 239,* and *541.*

2 Always Spell Out Numbers at the Beginning of a Sentence

Even if you ordinarily would not spell out a number, you must spell it out if you use it at the beginning of a sentence:

One hundred and sixteen receipts were also missing.

If such a sentence strikes you as awkward, try to revise it so that the number can appear as a numeral:

Also missing were 116 receipts.

Because you always spell out a number at the beginning of a sentence, sometimes you may not be able to avoid mixing spelled-out numbers and numerals:

Two hundred and twenty people walked a total of 823 miles.

37c
cia

3 Use Numerals According to
Certain Conventions

It is conventional to record numbers as numerals in these
cases:

Addresses
437 Honeycreek Road

Dates
December 16, 1949   16 December 1949

Exact times of day
9:04 p.m.   10:12 a.m.

But note that you should spell out whole numbers if they appear before
o'clock, noon, or *midnight*:

one o'clock   twelve noon   twelve midnight

And you should spell out times of day if they are half or quarter
hours:

half past six   quarter after seven

Percentages, decimals, and fractions
68 percent   1.2   11/32

Ratios, scores, and statistics
3 to 1   100 to 99   N = 3

Identification numbers
Route 41   Apartment 5   Channel 35   104.1 FM

Pages and divisions of written works
Chapter 6   page 5   scene 2, lines 70–71

In the case of measurements, follow the earlier general guidelines
for numbers:

ninety-six degrees   seventy-two dollars
113 degrees   246 dollars

Exercise 4

Use each of the following numbers or sets of numbers in a sentence in
such a way that the sentences would be appropriate in a formal paper in
the humanities.

EXAMPLE: 14 → The panel selected fourteen editorials for awards.
1. 99   2. 300   3. 158   4. 300, 158, and 247   5. 2.3

Some Common Errors in Punctuation and Mechanics

See the Index of Common Errors (pages 884–886) for references to further discussions of these errors.

Question mark after an indirect question:

INCORRECT: They asked who thought of that prank?

CORRECT: They asked who thought of that prank.

Question mark and a comma after quoting a direct question and before adding a reference to the speaker:

INCORRECT: "Am I a fool?", asked Gimpel.

CORRECT: "Am I a fool?" asked Gimpel.

Semicolon between short independent clauses joined by a coordinating conjunction:

INCORRECT: We needed help in the library; but all of the librarians were busy.

CORRECT: We needed help in the library, but all of the librarians were busy.

Semicolon between a subordinate clause and an independent clause:

INCORRECT: Since they were late for the show; they had to wait to be seated until after the first scene.

CORRECT: Since they were late for the show, they had to wait to be seated until after the first scene.

Omitted mark of punctuation between independent clauses (fused sentence):

INCORRECT: They took a trip to Montana they especially liked hiking in the mountains.

CORRECT: They took a trip to Montana; they especially liked hiking in the mountains.

Colon after a construction that is not an independent clause:

INCORRECT: They enjoy composers such as: Mozart, Ravel, and Lennon.

CORRECT: They enjoy composers such as the following: Mozart, Ravel, and Lennon.

continued

Omitted comma between independent clauses joined by a coordinating conjunction:

INCORRECT: Clark tried to reassure the reporters and Lois called the police.

CORRECT: Clark tried to reassure the reporters, and Lois called the police.

Comma after a coordinating conjunction linking independent clauses.

INCORRECT: Clark tried to explain but, Lois had heard enough from him.

CORRECT: Clark tried to explain, but Lois had heard enough from him.

Only a comma between independent clauses (comma splice):

INCORRECT: Jimmy saw two people running from the bank, he could not describe them in detail.

CORRECT: Jimmy saw two people running from the bank, but he could not describe them in detail.

Comma between parts of a compound predicate:

INCORRECT: Clark ran to a phone booth, and emerged to defeat the villains.

CORRECT: Clark ran to a phone booth and emerged to defeat the villains.

Omitted comma after certain introductory elements:

INCORRECT: When those brothers read mathematical equations dance in their heads.

CORRECT: When those brothers read, mathematical equations dance in their heads.

Omitted comma or commas to set off nonrestrictive modifiers of nouns and pronouns:

INCORRECT: The government responded to Syria which had sent an important letter to the United Nations.

CORRECT: The government responded to Syria, which had sent an important letter to the United Nations.

Commas to set off restrictive modifiers of nouns and pronouns:

INCORRECT: All students, who skip the film, will have to repeat the course.

CORRECT: All students who skip the film will have to repeat the course.

continued

Comma before a restrictive modifier of a verb:

INCORRECT: They will miss the beginning of the film, if they hesitate.

CORRECT: They will miss the beginning of the film if they hesitate.

Omitted comma before the last item in a series, especially when misinterpretation could result:

INCORRECT: They enjoy exotic delights, hang-gliding and cliff-diving.

CORRECT: They enjoy exotic delights, hang-gliding, and cliff-diving.

Commas and periods outside quotation marks:

INCORRECT: "I, however", said the doctor, "never forget a thing".

CORRECT: "I, however," said the doctor, "never forget a thing."

Omitted apostrophe with the possessive form of a noun:

INCORRECT: No one could find the doctors briefcase.

CORRECT: No one could find the doctor's briefcase.

Apostrophe with a possessive adjective:

INCORRECT: The wolf was favoring one of it's hind legs.

CORRECT: The wolf was favoring one of its hind legs.

Hyphen between two modifiers, the first of which is an adverb ending in *ly*:

INCORRECT: The speaker noticed some barely-suppressed yawns.

CORRECT: The speaker noticed some barely suppressed yawns.

Capitalizing references to general areas of study:

INCORRECT: They decided to major in History.

CORRECT: They decided to major in history.

IX

S T Y L E

38

W hen people refer to the style of prose, they usually mean the way in which ideas are expressed. You perhaps are most conscious of style in your own prose as you make choices about sentence structures. In a particular context, should you write *I extinguished the fire* or *The fire was extinguished by me?* Does *I extinguished the fire* have a significantly different meaning from *The fire was extinguished by me?* Such a question is highly debatable. What is certain, though, is that the two sample sentences differ from each other in focus and emphasis. Such differences will affect how readers respond to the sentences. Making decisions about style, therefore, is an extremely important activity.

38a

Kinds of Situations and Levels of Style

As writers move from one writing situation to another, they usually vary the level of formality of their prose style. Sometimes they use **highly formal style.** You might use this style if you were asked to write the citation for someone receiving an honorary degree from your school.

Throughout your life, you will probably have many opportunities to use **formal style.** Most of the writing that you turn in for credit in college courses should be in formal style.

Other writing that you do will probably be in **consultative style.** You would probably use this style in a business letter addressed to people you do not know well.

Still other writing that you do will probably be in **informal style.** You would probably use this style in a letter to people you know quite well.

Finally, you will probably have many chances to use **familiar style.** This is the style that you would use in a letter to a very close friend or to a member of your family. Occasionally, **colloquialisms** slip into familiar style; these are words and phrases closely associated with casual conversation. If you were to write *I really messed up that time,* many readers would call *messed up* a colloquialism.

In the following pages, we indicate, whenever possible, how words and structures correlate with the levels of formality in prose style.

38b

Style and Sentence Subjects

As you examine your style, one part of sentences that you should pay close attention to is the subject. The complete subject of a sentence is important because it usually tells what the writer is focusing on and will inform readers about. In the rest of this chapter, we lead you through some questions about the subjects of your sentences, primarily the simple sentences, and we offer guidelines that can help you decide whether to revise your sentence subjects.

38c
sub

38c

Can You Justify Using Expletives?

An **expletive** is a word that is not the subject of a sentence yet appears at the beginning of a sentence, where readers expect to find the subject. An expletive is usually followed by a form of *be* and the subject of the sentence. The most common expletives in English are *it* and *there*.

1 Reasons for Caution in Using Expletives

You should be cautious about using expletives for several reasons. First, they can frustrate readers since they introduce a slight delay before readers can see the subject of sentences. Second, sentences with expletives are usually longer than their counterparts. Compare the following two sentences:

> It is necessary for school systems to identify functional illiterates [ten words].

> School systems must identify functional illiterates [six words].

Finally, even when expletives appear in sentences describing actions or processes, they introduce a static quality:

> There were some enraged students burning books on the steps of the library.

To help you decide whether you can justify expletives in a draft, we take a closer look at the two main expletives.

2 The *It* Expletive

The *it* expletive appears in two kinds of constructions. Sometimes *it* and a form of *to be* are followed by an adjective:

> It is *necessary* to realize that functional illiterates can read and write but not well enough to cope with their environments.

Sometimes *it* and a form of *to be* are followed by a noun phrase:

> It is *their job* to halt the spread of illiteracy.

When *it* appears in expletive constructions, many of these constructions should be revised. You should be particularly suspicious about sentences that contain references, perhaps somewhat masked references, to both an agent and to an action that agent performs or a state that agent is in. In many such sentences, you are better off expressing the agent in the subject and the action or state in the verb. Since the following sentence contains references to agents and an action, it can be revised as indicated:

> It is their [potential agents'] intention [a mental action] to learn how to sign their name.

> They intend to learn how to sign their name.

However, *it* expletives can sometimes improve the flow of sentences. Generally, sentences flow better when they move from shorter elements through longer ones. You could write the following:

> To watch them progress through the McGuffey reading books was exciting.

This sentence packs a great deal of information before the verb, perhaps too much for readers to take in well. In such a case, you could use an *it* expletive to move the sentence from shorter to longer elements:

> It was exciting to watch them progress through the McGuffey reading books.

Occasionally, you may wish to use *it* to keep the information carried by a subject near the end of a sentence, where it receives the greatest emphasis:

> It was disheartening *to see students lose self-esteem.*

This sentence would fit well in a passage in which you were stressing the dire consequences for these students. But if you wanted to stress how the students' loss of self-esteem affected observers, you could omit the expletive and write the following:

> To see students lose self-esteem was disheartening.

3 The *There* Expletive

When *there* appears as an expletive, it is usually followed by a form of *be* and a noun phrase:

> There are at least *five different views on literacy education.*

**38c
sub**

You should be cautious about using *there* expletives. This is particularly true if sentences with *there* expletives contain references, perhaps somewhat masked references, to an agent and to actions that agent performs. Many such sentences should be revised so that the agent is named in the subject, especially if references to that agent have appeared in prior sentence subjects. And the action should be described in the verb. Since the following sentence contains references to both an agent and an action, it could be revised as indicated:

> There was an intention [a mental action] by the governor [the agent] to support literacy workers.
>
> The governor intended to support literacy workers.

Some sentences might contain no references to agents, so if you revise them, you will have to refer to the appropriate agents:

> There was a vigorous debate [an action] in class about literacy training.

> Some students vigorously debated literacy training in class.

However, like the *it* expletives, *there* expletives, too, can sometimes be justified. For instance, *there* should be used when the only alternative would be to write that something exists and when it is not customary to think of that something as existing. Since people do not normally think of joy as existing, we prefer

> There was no joy in Mudville.

to

> No joy existed in Mudville.

A *there* expletive also helps make a point less personal and more general. You could make a personal point by writing

> I find much to admire in Spenser's style.

But to make the point more general, you could write

> There is much to admire in Spenser's style.

Of course, you must be able to back up such claims, since readers will be more likely to question the general claim than the personal one. Furthermore, writers often use a *there* expletive to present information to readers for the first time:

> There is a new kind of illiteracy in the Western world.

Presenting brand-new information in this way has the advantage of keeping sentences moving from shorter to longer elements.

A final and closely related point is that sometimes writers use a *there* expletive to present brand-new information to readers and then make that information the focal point of one or more paragraphs. Lewis Thomas begins his essay "Thoughts for a Countdown" with the following sentence:

> There is ambiguity, and some symbolism, in the elaborate ritual observed by each returning expedition of astronauts from the moon.

Thomas then goes on to devote more than a paragraph to this ritual.

Exercise 1

Count how many *it* and *there* expletives you used in one of your recent drafts. Then indicate how many of them you were conscious of using as you wrote the draft. Do you find now that your use of every one of them was justified? Explain in detail, specifying which ones you would still keep and why.

38d

Can You Justify Using *You, I,* or *We* as Subjects?

Sometimes the sentences that writers are criticized for have *you, I,* or *we* as subjects. You will certainly need to use these pronouns as subjects sometimes, but you must do so with care.

1 *You* as Subject

When developing writers make *you* a subject, they often mean by it "people in general." The trouble with this practice is that the message conveyed about the *you* may not apply to some people. Imagine reading the following:

You will gain financial security if and when you learn to write.

The writer is making a general point, but the *you* makes it too general, including readers for whom it is not true. Even if the writer wants to retain the point about financial security, he or she would be wiser to use a plural reference:

People will gain financial security if and when *they* learn to write.

You or a variant of it (such as *yours*) works best as a subject when it means "you, the reader." If you use it in that sense, make sure that what you write does indeed apply to your readers.

38d
sub

Exercise 2

Write three different sentences with *you* as the subject of each. In each sentence, use *you* in such a way that it could not apply to at least some people who might read it.

EXAMPLE: You are lashed to a raft and pushed out to sea after you die. [Many readers live in cultures in which this sentence could not apply to them.]

2 *I* and *We* as Subjects

You will probably use *I* and *we* as sentence subjects when you write in a diary or journal. However, *I* and *we* can also serve as sentence subjects in more formal kinds of writing—for instance, personal narratives, memoirs, and parts of descriptions.

Notice how often *I* appears as a sentence subject in this passage from *The Autobiography of Malcolm X:*

> There I was back in Harlem's streets among all the rest of the hustlers. I couldn't sell reefers; the dope squad detectives were too familiar with me. I was a true hustler—uneducated, unskilled at anything honorable, and I considered myself nervy and cunning enough to live by my wits, exploiting any prey that presented itself. I would risk just about anything.

To rewrite this passage without the *I*'s would destroy its point and poignancy.

Even in essays that do not focus primarily on you as the writer or writers, when you report on something you have done, it is usually better to do so directly *(I have found)* than indirectly *(One has found)*. However, we are concerned about the following two general practices associated with using *I* and *we* as sentence subjects.

a. When Writers Focus Too Narrowly

Sometimes, especially in response to test questions that call for essay answers, writers use *I* or *we* as sentence subjects over and over. They focus exclusively on themselves or their close friends and relatives:

> I am not sure about the general difficulties in learning to read and write. But I can answer for my own case. When I learned to read and write, I was only four years old. I learned to read by watching shows on public television.

Although such responses are fine in some situations, often readers look for broader perspectives. For example, they expect to read about injustice in general and would be exasperated by sentences such as this:

> I usually experience many little injustices from my roommates on Friday afternoons.

We suggest that you examine the situations in which you write. In some situations, it will be inappropriate for you to write about your own and your friends' experiences. But in other situations, you will be expected to use such experiences to support general points, and you may even be asked to focus on these experiences.

38d
sub

Exercise 3

Examine one of the essays you have written in response to an examination question. Approximately what proportion of your sentences make general points? Approximately what proportion of your sentences focus on your own and your friends' personal experiences? From your vantage point now, do you think your decisions about these proportions were wise?

b. When Writers Write Too Much About Their Own Writing

Sometimes writers use *I* and *we* in sentences in which they write about their own writing. What does this mean? As you write, it is possible to work on two different levels. On one level you convey information about your subject matter. On the other level you show readers how to read, react to, and evaluate what you have written about the subject matter.

There are different kinds of writing about your own writing, and some of them overlap. We illustrate several of these kinds by adding clauses of writing about writing to the following sentence:

More than 800 million people over the age of fifteen cannot read and write.

1. With **organizers,** you show readers how you are organizing your essay:

   I (We) will next point out that more than 800 million people over the age of fifteen cannot read and write.

2. With **action markers,** you announce what specific action you are performing. Writers argue, agree, conclude, promise, hypothesize, and the like:

   I (We) contend (conclude) that more than 800 million people over the age of fifteen cannot read and write.

3. With **truth markers,** you give a personal judgment regarding the truth or probability of the information about your subject matter. Sometimes you might hedge information:

   I (We) think it possible that more than 800 million people over the age of fifteen cannot read and write.

And sometimes you might emphasize that the information is true:

   I am (We are) absolutely certain that more than 800 million people over the age of fifteen cannot read and write.

38d
sub

4. With **source markers,** you let readers know who said or wrote something. For writing to fall into this category and not into the category of truth markers, the truth of the information must not be in question. Only the source of the information is in question. And if that source is you, you will use an *I* or *we* in sentence subjects:

> *I (We) have stated that* more than 800 million people over the age of fifteen cannot read and write.

5. With **attitude markers,** you reveal your attitudes toward your subject matter:

> *I (We) find it appalling that* more than 800 million people over the age of fifteen cannot read and write.

6. Finally, with bits of **commentary,** you communicate with readers as though you were in a direct conversation with them:

> *I (We) urge you to read about why* more than 800 million people over the age of fifteen cannot read and write.

You can probably guess why essays with much writing about writing are criticized. The sentences with writing about writing are longer than those with just the information about the subject matter, and they can seem excessively chatty and informal. Furthermore, these sentences can make readers wonder what the real subject matter of the essays is. About our examples, for instance, someone might ask whether the subject matter is the writer *(I)* or writers *(we)* or the large number of illiterates in the world.

But sometimes writing about your own writing is justifiable. In general, readers expect you to indicate where you found your information, unless, of course, that information is common knowledge. Readers also tend to accept organizers in introductions, in transitions between subsections of essays, and in conclusions. This is especially true of long and complex essays.

More specifically, whether you should use one or more of the various kinds of writing about your own writing depends on your particular writing situations. For instance, if you are writing about a controversial subject to readers who are somewhat negative about that subject, you would be wise to hedge a little now and then *(I believe* or *I think it possible that).* We suggest that you read many other writers, analyze the situations in which they write, see how often they write about their own writing, and then judge how effectively they do so.

38d
sub

Exercise 4

For each of the following sentences, identify the clause that the writers are using to write about their own writing; tell what purpose the clause serves; and describe both a situation in which the sentence might be inappropriate and a situation in which it might be appropriate.

> EXAMPLE: I now move to the point that the Industrial Revolution increased the need for literacy. [The clause *I now move to the point that* is used to write about writing. It may indicate what action the writer is performing, but it also shows how the writer is organizing the essay. These words would probably be inappropriate in a 250-word report to people who know a lot about literacy; however, they might be fitting in a 2,500-word persuasive paper directed at people who know little about this subject.]

1. I argue that with a low level of literacy a country will have difficulty finding skilled workers.

2. I tend to believe that a low level of literacy in a country will be associated with poor health-care practices.

3. We begin by noting that a country with a low level of literacy can hold no meaningful elections.

4. I have absolutely no doubt that a person could read and write and still not be able to function well in a technological situation.

5. We find it somewhat surprising that more women than men in the world remain illiterate.

38e

Do Most of Your Subjects Name Significant Characters in the Stories Your Sentences Tell?

38e
sub

We recommend that you view sentences as telling stories. In these stories, there are agents who do things or characters who play roles. These characters can be people:

> *Mr. Leseng* fought illiteracy.

They can be organizations or political entities:

> *Several states* have enacted minimum competency laws.

They can be things:

> *The laser printer* omitted every seventh word.

And they can even be ideas and abstractions:

> *This theory* has helped some students and hurt others.

Our point is that in general your sentences will be easier to read if you use their subjects to name significant characters. Then you would probably describe in the verb what the characters did.

However, two different constructions—nominalizations and noun strings—work against naming a significant character in sentence subjects. Therefore, you should be cautious in using them.

1 Nominalizations

Nominalizations are nouns that have been formed by adding a suffix to certain adjectives and verbs. Adding the suffix *-ness* to the adjective *murky* produces the nominalization *murkiness.* Adding the suffix *-ment* to the verb *establish* produces the nominalization *establishment.*

Notice how nominalizations push references to characters out of the sentence subject:

An analysis of the effects of home schooling was carried out by a teachers' committee.

The nominalization *analysis* is the subject. However, it does not name significant characters but rather refers to what the characters did. The actual characters are not named until the very end of the sentence, in the prepositional phrase *by a teachers' committee.* You could revise this sentence by naming a significant character in the subject and describing the action in the verb:

A teachers' committee analyzed the effects of home schooling.

38e
sub

Many nominalizations in sentence subjects should be revised since they serve only to confuse readers or slow them down. But some nominalizations are useful, even necessary. Here again you must evaluate your choices very carefully in context.

Some nominalizations make good substitutes for *the fact that.* You could write this:

The fact that I denied their request startled them.

But it would be less cumbersome to use a nominalization:

My denial of their request startled them.

Some nominalizations appear so often in print that they have almost become characters in their own right. Few people have trouble with nominalizations such as these:

freedom   revolution   hope   wisdom

Most important, some nominalizations function to wrap up in one word much preceding discussion. In a paper, you might have a section with several sentences beginning with *They believe that.* After these sentences it would work well to encapsulate the earlier information with the nominalization *beliefs:*

These beliefs lie at the heart of their views of the world.

Exercise 5

Revise each of the following sentences so that in each a reference to a character appears in the subject. In some cases, you might have to invent a reference to an appropriate character.

> **EXAMPLE:** In 1961, a closing of many schools was carried out in Cuba.
>
> In 1961, Cuba closed many schools.

1. At that time, a dispersing of teachers and older students to the rural areas occurred.
2. The hope on the part of these teachers and students was to teach many people how to read.
3. A utilization of many different methods of instruction by them was evident.
4. And a close examination of illiterates' learning styles was made.
5. At the end of the year, a reduction in the rate of illiteracy from 25 percent to about 4 percent was apparent.

2 Noun Strings

In most **noun strings,** one noun modifies another:

noun   noun
field   guide

Sometimes a noun string also includes one or more adjectives:

adjective   noun   noun
systematized   policy   awareness

Certain noun strings appear so often and name such easily recognized things that they cause few readers difficulty:

boat launch site   fall book sale

Many readers, however, will have trouble with noun strings in which the major character is hard to locate. If such a noun string functions as a subject in a sentence, it is difficult to figure out who or what

38e
sub

plays an important role in the sentence. Consider the following noun string:

late adolescence interaction pattern analysis

One difficulty centers on *late.* What is late? Adolescence? The interaction? The analysis? No one can tell. A greater difficulty is caused by the nominalization *analysis.* Who analyzes? In other words, what character or characters stand behind this noun string? Again, no one can tell.

To revise such noun strings, you usually have to start from the last word and work your way to the front, changing nominalizations to verbs and putting some nouns into prepositional phrases:

adjective   noun   noun   noun   noun
late adolescence interaction pattern analysis

prepositional   prepositional
phrase   phrase
verb   noun
analyzed patterns of interaction in late adolescence

To change the revised string into a full sentence, you would have to name a character or characters who did the analyzing:

Our team analyzed patterns of interaction in late adolescence.

We think that nearly all readers would find our revision easier to read and recall than the following:

Late adolescence interaction pattern analysis was carried out by our team.

38e
sub

Exercise 6

Revise each sentence so that a reference to a character appears in each subject and so that the noun strings are simplified. In some sentences, you will have to invent a character that could plausibly appear in them.

EXAMPLE: World literacy rates assessments have been carried out by the United Nations.

The United Nations has assessed rates of literacy in the world.

1. Data analysis and review reports have been written by researchers sponsored by the United Nations.
2. Preliminary data significance estimates have been prepared.
3. Initial data alarm reactions have been experienced.
4. Special illiteracy diagnosis and remediation programs have been established by the United Nations.
5. But program implementation quality control has been neglected.

38f

Do Most of Your Sentence Subjects Convey Old Information?

Most sentences after the first one in an essay convey two kinds of information—old information and new information. Old information is that which readers already know. It usually appears in the sentence subject. New information is that which readers learn as they read the sentence. It usually appears in the sentence predicate. In this section, we focus on the correlation between subjects and old information.

1 Kinds of Old Information

Some bits of information are old whenever they appear since they are parts of normal readers' general knowledge. Therefore, *The moon* in the following conveys old information:

old information   new information

The moon reflected just enough light for James to read by.

Other bits of information qualify as old in certain situations. The information may be obvious from the situation itself. Or the readers may be working in the same area of research as the writer and will therefore recognize many references.

Other bits of information qualify as old because they were mentioned in earlier sentences. Therefore, *It* in the second of the two following sentences conveys old information; *It* refers to the training program:

The training program was abandoned.

old infor-
mation   new information

It had become outdated.

Finally, some bits of information are old since readers can infer them from other bits of information. For example, if someone mentions the whole of something, you can, if you know about the thing, recognize references to its parts:

The book had to be discarded.

old information new information

Some pages were missing.

In most sentences in clear and memorable prose, the subject conveys old information. In fact, in many sentences there is a correlation between the subject, a significant character, and old information.

Exercise 7

Identify the old information in each sentence of the following passage, and indicate on what basis the old information can be viewed as old.

EXAMPLE: In *The sun shone bleakly on the town of Nils on Monday,* readers can take *The sun* as old information on the basis of general knowledge about the world.

1. The Nils Board of Education held an important meeting.
2. The president of the board had learned about an allusive poem being read.
3. The president called for censorship.
4. The meeting stirred up a great deal of controversy.
5. The poem became more widely read than ever before.

2   One Benefit of Old Information in Subjects: Short-to-Long Order in Sentences

Since you can almost always convey old information in fewer words than you can convey new information, if you have old information in subjects, those subjects will probably be relatively short. And readers have an easier time if they move from shorter subjects to longer predicates than if they move from longer subjects to shorter predicates. For example, which of the following pairs of sentences moves more gracefully?

38f
sub

The new methods caused several problems. Difficulty in understanding the role of the affective domain in cognitive learning was one of them.

The new methods caused several problems. One of them was difficulty in understanding the role of the affective domain in cognitive learning.

The second pair moves more gracefully than the first. The main reason is that the second sentence in the second pair moves from a short subject bearing old information to a longer predicate bearing new information. The second sentence in the first pair does just the opposite.

Sometimes, of course, you will not be able to write subjects that convey only old information. It is wise to review these subjects to make sure that they are not overloaded with information. The subject in the following sentence contains so much information that it is difficult to understand, probably even for experts in sociology:

> *Expression of the degree of overt recognition of social class distinctions necessary for correct usage of politeness formulae* changed over the nineteenth century.

The American Sociologist

3 Another Benefit of Old Information in Subjects: A Consistent Set of Focal Points in Passages

Not all of the subjects in an essay can or should be identical, but if they convey old information, they will usually keep readers focusing on a closely related set of things. Consider the following paragraph from a student's essay (all the complete subjects are in italics):

> *Light rock-and-roll* can be as comforting to a college student as classical music can be to a professor. *Most radio stations* play light rock-and-roll. *Themes about sex, alcohol, and violence* come up in the lyrics of light rock-and-roll. But *country music* deals with sex, alcohol, and violence too.

These subjects are not unrelated, but if you examine the paragraph closely, you will see that the writer misses chances to express old information in subjects. If we revise accordingly, we can produce a paragraph with a more coherent set of focal points (all the complete subjects are in italics):

38f
sub

> *Light rock-and-roll* can be as comforting to a college student as classical music can be to a professor. *Light rock-and-roll* is played on most radio stations. *The lyrics of light rock-and-roll* bring up themes about sex, alcohol, and violence. But *these themes* come up in country music too.

By making sure that most of your sentences move from old to new information, you take a significant step toward achieving coherence in passages.

Exercise 8

Revise the following paragraph so that as many sentences as possible move from subjects conveying old information to predicates conveying new information. Usually, you will be able to leave connectives (such as *therefore* and *and*) in their original position. You may assume that all of the information in the first sentence is new to readers.

> Currently, Locutus is the most popular word-processing program available. Other packages are not nearly as attractive as it. A mere fifty dollars is its cost. And several different versions are available for Locutus. Therefore, almost any major brand of personal computer can function with Locutus. The speed of all text-editing operations is the most desirable feature of Locutus. And yet it never sacrifices accuracy. Most major retail stores have Locutus available.

38g

How Varied Are the Beginnings of Your Sentences?

Our discussion of old information in sentence subjects might seem to contradict some advice you have probably heard: "Vary the beginnings of your sentences." We acknowledge that if sentences had no structural variety at their beginning, prose would get monotonous. But we resist this advice if it means changing sentence subjects around just to introduce variety.

If you think that the beginnings of your sentences tend toward monotony, you can, of course, check whether you can find synonyms for words in sentence subjects. But you can vary those beginnings without necessarily changing the subjects. Keep in mind, though, that the variations must be appropriate in context.

In some cases, you can move elements from later parts of sentences to the beginning:

38g sub

1. Adverbs

   They tried, *finally,* to add a word to the language.

   Finally, they tried to add a word to the language.

2. Conjunctive adverbs

   They tried, *however,* to add a word to the language.

   However, they tried to add a word to the language.

3. Adjectives

   The two inventors, *proud and persistent,* tried to add a word to the language.

   Proud and persistent, the two inventors tried to add a word to the language.

4. Prepositional phrases

> They tried, *as a last resort,* to add a word to the language.
>
> *As a last resort,* they tried to add a word to the language.

In other cases, you can introduce elements at the beginning of sentences. You can often use these elements to sum up what has gone before, to orient readers to time and place, or to lead readers through a passage. We will illustrate some of these elements by adding them to the following sentence:

> They tried to borrow some technical terms.

1. Coordinating conjunctions

> *And* they tried to borrow some technical terms.

2. Truth markers or attitude markers

> *Perhaps* they tried to borrow some technical terms.

Or

> *Unfortunately,* they tried to borrow some technical terms.

3. Infinitive phrases

> *To achieve this purpose,* they tried to borrow some technical terms.

4. Participial phrases

> *Having killed several metaphors,* they tried to borrow some technical terms.

5. Absolute phrases

> *Their experiment planned,* they tried to borrow some technical terms.

38g
sub

Exercise 9

Examine one of your recent essays closely. Make a list of all the sentence beginnings (all the words up to the verb). Does your essay have much structural variety in sentence beginnings? If not, could you increase the variety without changing sentence subjects? Be prepared to discuss these questions with your classmates.

39

REVIEWING AND REVISING VERBS

O ne of the following is the opening paragraph of Farley Mowat's *A Whale for the Killing*. The other is our alteration of that paragraph. Which do you think is which?

> A torment of sooty cloud scudded out of the mountainous barrens of southeastern Newfoundland. Harried by a furious nor'easter, eddies of sand-sharp snow beat against the town of Port Aux Basques; an unlovely cluster of wooden buildings sprawled across a bed of cold rock and colder muskeg. White frost-smoke swirled up from the water of the harbour to marry the cloud wrack and go streaming out across Cabot Strait toward the looming cliffs of Cape Breton and the mainland of North America.

> A torment of sooty cloud was visible out of the mountainous barrens of southeastern Newfoundland. The town of Port Aux Basques, an unlovely cluster of wooden buildings sprawled across a bed of cold rock and colder muskeg, was being hit by eddies of sand-sharp snow harried by a furious nor'easter. White frost-smoke came up from the center of the harbour to marry the cloud wrack and go streaming out across Cabot Strait toward the looming cliffs of Cape Breton and the mainland of North America.

The first paragraph is Mowat's. In altering his paragraph, we worked with the elements that many people say are essential to the effectiveness of prose—the main verbs. Mowat's main verbs describe actions precisely and vividly: *scudded, beat, swirled.* Our main verbs are not nearly as effective in bringing pictures to mind: *was, was being hit, came.*

In this chapter, we ask you some questions about the verbs in your drafts and offer some advice that might help you in revising.

Can You Justify Separating Subjects and Verbs from Each Other?

The connection between the subject and the verb is the main grammatical bond in a sentence. If you separate a subject from its verb, you might slow down and confuse readers:

> Rhea, whose sister, Avis, enjoys talking at length about how she got involved with the movement to save the cranes when she was a student in Nebraska, is my most trusted friend.

By the time readers get to the main verb, *is,* they might wonder for an instant who the trusted friend is.

If you ever separate subjects from verbs, you should try to do so with short elements. If you ever separate subjects from verbs with longer elements, you should have a good reason to use them.

1 Elements That Sometimes Appear Between Subjects and Verbs

39a
vb

Some words and short phrases commonly appear as parenthetical insertions between subjects and verbs:

> That species, *in fact,* has been extinct for fifty years.

Some elements that modify the subject also commonly appear between the subject and the verb:

> The dodos, *which were flightless,* were hunted for food.

Although elements that modify the verb are less graceful between the subject and the verb than are those that modify the subject, you will find examples of the former in published prose:

> The government, *to help some endangered species of birds,* has banned nearly all uses of DDT.

2 Some Reasons to Separate Subjects and Verbs

Writers often insert a parenthetical expression between a subject and verb to throw emphasis on the subject:

> Fifty species of birds, in fact, have become extinct in the last two hundred years.

The parenthetical insertion *(in fact)* focuses attention on *Fifty species of birds.*

When writers separate subjects from verbs with modifiers of the subject, they usually do so when they want to include the information the modifiers carry but judge that the information is not important enough to warrant its own sentence:

subject   modifier of the subject   verb

> The great auks, which lived in North America, died as
> a result of human activity.

The writer judged that the information about where the great auks lived was worth including but was not important enough to warrant a separate sentence. Thus, the writer expressed it in an adjective clause, where *is* has the feel of background information.

Another reason writers sometimes insert a construction between the subject and the verb is to call attention to the inserted construction. In the following sentence the inserted information draws great attention to itself:

subject   inserted information   verb

> The driver, very young and apparently drunk, was killed
> instantly. (Joan Didion)

Finally, sometimes writers separate a subject from its verb in order to whet readers' appetite for the information that follows. Notice how Donald R. Fleming delays information in order to pique readers' curiosity about how his point will be completed:

> A major theme in American history, evidenced by armed risings of
> the back country against the tidewater in the South and by the
> assault upon Eastern bastions of privilege by the Populists of the East
> and West, has been the recurring sense of regional deprivation as a
> deliberate infliction by favored regions upon the rest of the country.
>
> "The Big Money and High
> Politics of Science"

3 Separating Parts of Verb Phrases from Each Other

You should be very cautious about separating parts of verb phrases from each other since sentences with such separations can be awkward and difficult to read:

> Farmers may on or before May 1 at the State Agriculture Bureau nearest them return unused chemicals.

In this sentence, readers see *may* but then have to wait until they read the main verb, *return,* to learn what the predication is.

Although skilled writers occasionally do separate parts of verb phrases, they rarely insert long constructions. They insert short constructions when they want to call special attention to the inserted material:

> The Kirtland's warbler will perhaps survive the loss of habitat.

This sentence highlights the inserted *perhaps* and therefore the precariousness of the warbler's situation.

Exercise 1

Revise all the following sentences that need revision.

> EXAMPLE: That species of warblers, since it has not been sighted for several years in any of its former ranges, may be extinct.
>
> Since it has not been sighted for several years in any of its former ranges, that species of warblers may be extinct.

If you decide not to revise a sentence, be prepared to discuss your reasons.

1. The population of bald eagles, in fact, seems to be increasing.

2. The osprey, its great wings etched against the purplish blue of the sky, was a magnificent sight.

3. Trained ornithologists, to try to determine whether the Eskimo curlew is extinct or simply has avoided all contact with human beings in the last several years, have established several observation decks.

4. Officials at the zoo, when they learned that a California condor had been born in their facilities the prior night, called a news conference.

5. Destroying large tracts of tropical rain forest will inevitably lead to the extinction of some tropical birds.

39a
vb

39b

Can You Justify Using Passive Verbs?

Perhaps no other grammatical structure in English has been attacked more often than the passive-voice construction. In fact, some teachers order their students never to use passive verbs.

1 Reasons to Be Cautious with Passive Verbs

There are good reasons to be cautious about using passives. First, sentences with passive verbs are almost always longer than the corresponding sentences with active verbs:

PASSIVE: Ospreys were studied by Professor Coniformes.

ACTIVE: Professor Coniformes studied ospreys.

Second, passive verbs do not describe actions as directly and energetically as active verbs do:

PASSIVE: The eggshell was cracked by the baby eagle.

ACTIVE: The baby eagle cracked the eggshell.

Although both sentences describe the same activity, the passive sentence has more of a static quality than does the active sentence.

Third, passive verbs often allow writers to express something other than a significant character in the subject of a sentence. This practice makes the sentence more difficult to read and remember. Consider the following:

Analyses of the effects of DDT on eagles' eggs were carried out by Dr. Franceen.

The simple subject of this sentence is *analyses.* But *analyses* is not a significant character in the story this sentence tells. It names what action a character performed. In order to express a significant character in the subject, you would have to use an active verb:

Dr. Franceen analyzed the effects of DDT on eagles' eggs.

A sentence subject that does not name a significant character in the story the sentence tells will be particularly annoying when that character is obvious from the situation being described. For instance, you could begin a description of an evening walk with this sentence:

I tiptoed to the edge of the meadow.

39b
vb

If you were to follow this sentence with

Mockingbirds could be heard in the distance.

readers would probably wonder why you did not use *I* since you refer to yourself in the first sentence and are obviously doing the hearing in the second.

Similarly, the lack of a significant character in the subject of a sentence will be particularly noticeable if that character is named in the preceding and following sentence subjects:

Professors Smythe and Wessen collected data at four different sites. Then a review of the data was carried out. Finally, Smythe and Wessen made a startling announcement.

The passive verb in the second sentence has the nominalization *review* for its subject. *Review* does not name a character, a fact that stands out since the subjects of the first and last sentences do name characters.

The final reason why you should be cautious with passive verbs is that they can mask responsibility:

The toxic chemicals were marketed as environmentally safe.

The phrase indicating who marketed these chemicals is omitted. Who marketed the toxic chemicals? On the basis of this sentence, no one can tell. In some cases, then, people use passives to avoid revealing who the agents are. When the described actions approach the unethical, this use of passives does too.

2 Justified Passive Verbs

Passive verbs are not in the language just to make trouble for writers and readers. They have some important functions.

First, passive verbs are useful when you do not know and cannot find out who or what did something:

The bird-watching blind in Mackinaw Bay *had been burned.*

Second, passive verbs are useful when you could find out who or what did something but decide that mentioning the agent is not important:

Two large malls *were being built* on the coast.

Scientists often use passive verbs with the implication that they could name themselves as those who performed experiments, but they choose not to since they, as particular experimenters, are not important. Their experiment, so the implication goes, could be replicated by others.

39b
vb

Third, passive verbs are useful when you want to add general force to points or to make points that are general truths:

Laws of interacting with the environment *must be obeyed.*

Finally, and most important, passive verbs will help you express the old information in sentences near or at their beginning. Doing so will usually improve the overall coherence of the passage. Consider these two sentences:

Several developers have ignored published guidelines about how close to the coast to build condominiums. The Environmental Protection Agency has always defended these guidelines.

The second sentence moves from new information about the Environmental Protection Agency to old information about the guidelines. This sentence would move more effectively if a passive verb were used to switch the positions of the old and new information:

These guidelines *have* always *been defended* by the Environmental Protection Agency.

Exercise 2

Examine the following sentences and the descriptions of the situations in which they are used. Then indicate whether you think the uses of the passive verbs are warranted; be prepared to justify your decisions.

EXAMPLE: A newspaper report of an accident includes the sentence "The victim's relatives are being notified." [The passive is justified since mentioning who did the notifying is not important in this situation.]

39b
vb

1. A team of scientists begins the methods section of a research report with the following sentence: "Two vials of distilled water were boiled."

2. In a report on great explorers, a student writes the following: "Burton and Speke made some gross miscalculations. Indeed, huge mistakes were made. And they paid for them dearly."

3. An article in a newspaper concludes with this sentence: "An autopsy will be performed."

4. In a descriptive paper, a student writes the following: "I caught a glimpse of a scarlet tanager, and I wanted to get a closer look. I sneaked up on it, step by quiet step. Its bright colors could be plainly seen. But then I stumbled on an ivy vine."

5. A media relations specialist for the Pentagon writes the following in a press release: "The decision to shoot down the foreign airliner was made. The missiles were launched. And the plane was destroyed."

39c

Can You Justify Using Forms of *Be?*

Recently, one of our students who was preparing for a job search wrote a brief autobiography and asked a job placement adviser to look it over for her. When she got it back, she found that he had written a note instructing her to eliminate all forms of *be* in her writing. Like many others today, he was acting as if the verb *be* should not be in the language.

1 Situations in Which You Should Revise Forms of *Be*

The main traditional complaint against forms of *be* is that they show no action and therefore bring no energy and movement to prose. Not all verbs have to show action, of course, but this complaint is valid when forms of *be* are used in certain ways.

First, sometimes writers use forms of *be* to list examples:

Some examples of animals I would like to see *are* the Bengal tiger, the Asiatic lion, and the blue whale.

In nearly all contexts it would be better to revise as follows:

I would like to see the Bengal tiger, the Asiatic lion, and the blue whale.

Second, sometimes writers use forms of *be* to list qualities or traits:

Some qualities I admire *are* grace and perseverance.

Again, in nearly all situations it would be better to revise as follows:

I admire grace and perseverance.

Third, often writers use a form of *be* to link a subject to a predicate noun:

        subject   predicate noun

The California grizzly *was* the loser.

But using a different verb to capture the meaning of both the original verb and the predicate noun has the advantages of shortening the sentence and supplying action:

The California grizzly *lost.*

39c
vb

Finally, sometimes writers use a form of *be* to link a subject to a predicate adjective:

subject   predicate adjective

That pesticide *will be* harmful to ospreys.

Here, too, using a different verb to capture the meaning of the original verb and the predicate adjective can shorten the sentence and supply action:

That pesticide *will harm* ospreys.

2 Situations in Which You Can Justify
Forms of *Be*

Forms of *be* are in the language because they have important roles to play. One of these is to introduce characteristics of people and things. In some situations, of course, instead of saying that someone is kind, it is wise to describe that person performing kind actions. But sometimes you will not be able to afford the space that such descriptions require. And sometimes adjectives carry information that is difficult to convey with verbs. So you will want to list characteristics, and forms of *be* allow you to do so:

The candidate for the position *is* very shortsighted.

Another function of *be* is to make powerful equations:

In their treatment of the natural world, many human beings seem to be saying, "We *are* gods."

You will also need forms of *be* to discuss ideas, abstractions, and qualities. Throughout your college career, you will probably find yourself writing about such abstractions as beauty, justice, knowledge, and reality. In these cases, you will probably have to rely fairly heavily on forms of *be*. Here are three sentences from Ralph Waldo Emerson's "Nature," where he uses forms of *be* to discuss ideas, abstractions, and qualities:

But to a sound judgment, the most abstract truth is the most practical.

Beauty is the mark God sets upon virtue.

All good is eternally reproductive.

Finally, if you were to ban all uses of forms of *be,* you could not read and write all those metaphors that depend on a direct equation. If you had been Henry David Thoreau's editor for *Walden,* you would

**39c
vb**

have had to tell him to revise all sentences such as the one in which he states that time is a stream he fishes in.

> *Exercise 3*
>
> Revise each of the following sentences by changing the form of *be* and whatever other elements you think need to be changed.
>
> > **EXAMPLE:**   Draining that swamp will be a threat to the ibises that live there.
> >
> > Draining that swamp will threaten the ibises that live there.
>
> 1. If the government builds that dam, everyone will be a loser.
> 2. The dam would be the ruin of several unique habitats.
> 3. At least three different species of lizards would not be survivors of the rising water.
> 4. Some examples of what we would lose are vast tracts of wilderness and several inspiring waterfalls.
> 5. Such losses will be irritating to those who knew the river valley in its natural state.

39d

Are Your Action Verbs Specific Enough?

Whenever you use a verb that describes an action, you will have to decide whether it describes that action specifically enough. The word *specific* is commonly defined in association with the word *general.* As action verbs become more general, they apply to more actions. As action verbs become more specific, they apply to fewer actions. Action verbs are more or less general or specific in relation to other action verbs. *Move* is more general than *walk,* and *walk* is more general than *strut. Move* applies to several actions; *strut* applies to fewer.

1 Reviewing *Do, Give, Have,* and *Make*

We suggest that you pay close attention to *do, give, have,* and *make.* Writers sometimes use these rather general verbs in connection with nouns:

They will *do a study* of the wetlands.

They will *give consideration* to the levels of pesticides.

They will *have a gathering* after the study.

They will *make a recommendation* for preservation.

But a more specific verb could replace the more general verb and the noun:

> They will *study* the wetlands.
>
> They will *consider* levels of pesticides.
>
> They will *gather* after the study.
>
> They will *recommend* preservation.

Using the more specific verbs will save you some words and help you describe actions more precisely.

2 Senses and Emotions

Another advantage of using more specific verbs to depict specific actions is that they usually appeal to readers' senses. If we write that someone moved, what image does *moved* bring to your mind? Probably not a very clear one. But if we write that someone sauntered, you probably develop quite a clear mental image. When readers' senses are affected, they usually react emotionally. More general words tend to appeal to readers' intellects.

In describing a duckling, you could write the following:

> The duckling moved along the beach.

For readers to react with some emotion to this sentence would not be unusual, since it focuses on a baby of a species. But if you wanted to intensify the emotion for readers, you could use a more specific verb:

> The duckling limped along the beach.

Limping, of course, brings a clear picture to readers' minds, and it suggests injury and hardship and vulnerability. Therefore, most readers would react with a more intense emotion to the second sentence than to the first.

You will have to decide when such appeals to readers' emotions will be appropriate. Some writing tasks call for an appeal primarily to readers' intellects. Others call for an appeal primarily to readers' emotions. And still others require both an appeal to readers' intellects and the support of that appeal with appeals to readers' emotions. We suggest that you watch how other writers respond to writing tasks similar to those you face. Knowing about generality and specificity in action verbs should help you achieve particular goals in particular situations.

Exercise 4

Replace each italicized word or group of words in the following paragraph with an action verb that is quite specific. Add additional words if you think your new verbs require them.

EXAMPLE: The crippled owl *moved* its wings against the bars of its cage.

The crippled owl *drummed* its wings against the bars of its cage.

Visiting the government laboratory where birds born with deformities are taken was a distressing experience for us. In one room we saw a green heron that was missing an eye. It continually *made strange motions with* its head, trying to see everything around it. We also saw a baby great blue heron that had one leg shorter than the other. We watched sadly as it *moved* around in its pen. A double-crested cormorant was in a worse state. The top part of its bill *had a curve* down and around the bottom part. The cormorant could therefore not open its bill; it could only *move* one side of its bill against the other. Finally, we saw a bald eagle that had only a feathery stump where one wing should have been. It *gave us a threatening look* from its perch, but the attempted threat seemed pathetic as the eagle flapped its one wing but apparently did not dare leave its perch.

39c
vb

REVIEWING AND REVISING SENTENCE ENDINGS

Is there any significant difference between these two sentences?

Tomorrow night we will fly to Stockholm.

We will fly to Stockholm tomorrow night.

Although both have exactly the same words and convey essentially the same information, the two sentences would not work equally well in some contexts. Consider the following short passage:

Tomorrow we will be very busy. In the morning we must meet with an expert in international protocol. Tomorrow afternoon we will have to get some vaccinations. And . . .

Which of the two sample sentences fits better at the end of this passage? The first one does. In fact, if you read the passage with the second sentence at the end, you probably feel a slight letdown as you see the words *tomorrow night,* which in this passage carry little news for you.

The two sample sentences show how important the end of a sentence is. In this chapter, we ask you some questions about the sentence endings in your drafts and give you some general guidelines for possible revisions of those endings.

40a

Do the Ends of Your Sentences Convey the Most Important Information in Those Sentences?

You should try to express the most important information in a sentence at its end, which is often called its stress. If a sentence is made up of one main clause, you should identify the most important information in that clause and try to express it at the end. If a sentence is made up of more than one clause, then you have two tasks: (1) try to express the most important information in each clause as near the end of each clause as possible, and (2) try to express the clause that is most important at the end of the overall sentence.

Our advice rests on the fact that readers pay particularly close attention to the ends of structures—great attention to the ends of sentences but also significant attention to the ends of clauses in sentences.

The most important information in a clause or overall sentence is usually the new information. Often it is the information that you will expand upon the most in later sentences. Or you could say that the most important information in a sentence usually communicates the point of the entire sentence. The point of *We wrote that novel as a group* has to do with the reference to a group. The point of *As a group we wrote that novel* has to do with the reference to a novel.

40c se

Exercise 1

Give the main point of each of the following sentences, and write a question to which the sentence would be a good response.

EXAMPLE: The point of *We received the letter yesterday* has to do with the reference to yesterday. This sentence would be a good response to *When did you receive the letter?*

1a. The new secretary delivered the letter.
 b. The letter was delivered by the new secretary.
2a. The first to show some enthusiasm was Jacques.
 b. Jacques was the first to show some enthusiasm.
3a. We assembled excitedly in the conference room.
 b. In the conference room, we assembled excitedly.
4a. With a grin, our team leader waved the letter in the air.
 b. Our team leader waved the letter in the air with a grin.
5a. Because the letter promised to be the most important one we would ever receive, we debated who should open it.
 b. We debated who should open the letter, because it promised to be the most important one we would ever receive.

1 Elements That Usually Should Not Appear at the Ends of Sentences

We can advise you to be cautious about leaving the following kinds of elements at the end of a sentence, since it is difficult to imagine them as the most important information in a sentence.

a. Old Information

Old information in a sentence is that which readers already know about or which they can infer. The customary position for old information in a sentence is an early position, usually the subject. In that position, old information helps readers connect that sentence to preceding sentences.

But most writers occasionally produce sentences such as this:

Eager anticipation is another normal response.

The word *another* shows that old information appears at the end. This sentence could be revised so that old information precedes new:

Another normal response is eager anticipation.

b. Orienters

Orienters give readers directions about where or when something took place, or they establish the framework in which a sentence should be interpreted. They are elements such as *In their 1990 study, in many sectors,* and *from an aesthetic standpoint.* Usually such elements set the information of a sentence in a context, and such context-setting is most helpful to readers when it happens early in sentences. In most cases, therefore, a sentence such as

Our novel is a masterpiece from an aesthetic standpoint

should be revised into

From an aesthetic standpoint, our novel is a masterpiece.

c. Writing About Your Own Writing

Sometimes people express writing about their own writing at the ends of sentences. The kinds of writing about writing that we sometimes see at the ends of sentences are:

ACTION MARKERS: Our novel deserves a Nobel Prize, *we concluded.*

TRUTH MARKERS: Our novel qualifies as the great American novel, *I believe.*

SOURCE MARKERS: Our novel has an exquisite style, *according to at least two critics.*

These examples seem especially weak in their endings. The writing about writing comes almost as a letdown. It is easy to revise these sentences:

We concluded that our novel deserves a Nobel Prize.
Our novel, we concluded, deserves a Nobel Prize.

I believe that our novel qualifies as the great American novel.
Our novel, I believe, qualifies as the great American novel.

According to at least two critics, our novel has an exquisite style.
Our novel, according to at least two critics, has an exquisite style.

d. Qualifiers

Qualifiers are elements such as *to some degree* and *to an extent.* Such elements often reveal writers concerned not to overstate their case, especially when treating controversial topics. In such cases, using these phrases is commendable. But even then the phrases often do not carry the main point of a sentence. Often they add a qualifying note to that point and should not appear last. But you will always have to decide how to place qualifiers on the basis of the situation you are working in. In some situations, you might wish to use a sentence such as this one, which stresses the word *helpful:*

To some degree, the debate about our novel was helpful.

In other situations, you might want to stress a limitation on that helpfulness:

The debate about our novel was helpful to some degree.

**40a
se**

Exercise 2

Read the following sentences and (1) identify each sentence that ends with information that usually should not appear at the ends of sentences, (2) identify the word or words that probably should appear at the ends, and (3) provide at least one revision for the sentence.

EXAMPLE: The letter might be a disappointment, according to the secretary.

The words that probably should not be stressed are *according to the secretary.* These words serve only to give the source of the judgment. The word in that judgment that probably should be stressed is *disappointment:*

According to the secretary, the letter might be a disappointment.

1. A disappointing letter could lead the team to abandon additional efforts, it seems likely.

2. Such a result would be a modern tragedy, at least in some people's opinions.

3. Our only choice was to open the letter.

4. The honor of opening the letter fell to our team leader.

5. The room became hushed and tense at this time.

6. She looked up from the letter with an expression of joy, it seemed to me.

7. Then she announced that we had won the Nobel Prize for literature.

8. Our first reaction was a tinge of disbelief.

9. Great joy was our second.

10. We looked like children at a birthday party, according to several spectators.

2   Strategies for Positioning Elements Wisely

With elements other than bits of old information, orienters, kinds of writing about writing, and qualifiers, we cannot recommend caution about using them at the ends of sentences. How should you decide which of these two sentences you should write?

We will travel to Stockholm as a group.

As a group we will travel to Stockholm.

40a se

Such a question is impossible to answer in the abstract. You will have to determine in context what is old information and what is new information. In a context in which you have mentioned traveling to Stockholm, one of the examples above is more appropriate than the other:

We will travel to Stockholm as a group.

This sentence saves the new information about going in a group for the end.

Sometimes your decision will rest not so much on what is old and new information as on what information you most want readers to remember, which you would express at the end of your sentence.

As most writers review their drafts, they find sentences in which the most important information is not at the end. They cannot always make changes, for some word orders are awkward and others are ungrammatical. Often, however, you will be able to revise sentences so that the most important information appears at the end.

a. Eliminate Redundant Material at the End

In some sentences, the most important material does not appear at the end because it is followed by redundant material:

The Swedish academy was most impressed by our narrative techniques in the ways we constructed a story.

Since *in the ways we constructed a story* adds very little to the information carried by *our narrative techniques,* you could revise this sentence by cutting out the redundancy at the end:

The Swedish academy was most impressed by our narrative techniques.

b. Move Less Important Material to the Left

Some sentences end with a modifier that does not carry the most important information:

Some Nobel laureates have received standing ovations after their speeches.

In reviewing such a sentence, you might well decide that you should stress *standing ovations,* not *after their speeches.* After all, it is almost predictable that if the laureates are to receive standing ovations, it will be after their speeches. You could revise this sentence by moving *after their speeches* to the left:

After their speeches, several Nobel laureates have received standing ovations.

c. Move the Most Important Information to the Right

Sometimes you may discover that you have expressed the most important material in sentences too early in those sentences:

At two years of age, she was reading books on the craft of fiction.

This sentence stresses what the person was reading—books on the craft of fiction. In some situations, this might be exactly right. It would be right, for instance, in a passage detailing how she prepared herself throughout her life to write fiction. But if instead you wanted to call the most attention to when she did the reading, you would have to revise:

She was reading books on the craft of fiction at two years of age.

40a
se

This sentence would work well in a passage stressing how soon she started to read challenging material. (Expletives can also help you move material to the right in a sentence; see **38c**.)

d. Use Reversals

With some verbs (forms, for example, of *be, lie, rest, sit, hover,* and *stand*), you can reverse the positions of subjects and complements. You would do this, of course, if you wanted to place near or at the end of a sentence what originally appeared in a subject. Consider this sentence:

> Deciding where to hold a press conference was our second major responsibility.

The information carried by *our second major responsibility* is old information, since one would ordinarily not mention a second responsibility without having earlier mentioned a first. You could use a reversal to get the old information away from the end:

> Our second major responsibility was deciding where to hold a press conference.

With many comparisons, you can go through a kind of reversal process by switching the terms of the comparison:

> Our novel costs more than Faulkner's.

> Faulkner's novel costs less than ours.

e. Use Passive Verbs

You can reverse the positions of subject and object in many sentences by changing the verbs from the active to the passive voice. The passive would be useful in revising a passage such as this:

> The draft of our acceptance speech was stirring. Conrad had written it.

In the second sentence, *it* carries old information, referring to the acceptance speech. The new information is carried mainly by *Conrad.* You could use a passive verb to get the old information at the beginning of the sentence and the new information at the end:

> It had been written by Conrad.

f. Changing One Sentence into Two

Sometimes you may discover that one of your sentences contains at least two bits of information that you want to stress. In such a case, the sentence should have those bits of information at the ends of clauses. But some sentences have two or more important bits of information in positions where at least one of them does not get the stress it deserves:

> Our rivals decided to order the least expensive tickets to Stockholm, with the result that they would probably arrive late for the awards ceremony.

Of course, someone might want to leave this sentence as it stands because it stresses the probable late arrival. However, a writer might also want to stress the *least expensive tickets,* perhaps in order to comment on these people's spending habits. One way to do so would be to separate the one sentence into two:

> Our rivals decided to order the least expensive tickets to Stockholm. As a result, they would probably arrive late for the ceremony.

Another option is to join these two clauses with a semicolon and leave them as parts of one sentence:

> Our rivals decided to order the least expensive tickets to Stockholm; as a result, they would probably arrive late for the ceremony.

Exercise 3

Revise each of the following sentences so that the italicized word or words appear at the end. You may have to introduce additional words into the sentences.

> **EXAMPLE:**   *Our hotel reservations* were made by Vladimir.
>
> Vladimir made *our hotel reservations.*

1. *After a great deal of difficulty,* he was able to reserve sixteen separate rooms.
2. But it was important that we stay *together* at one hotel.
3. *We could inform each other of important events* if we stayed at one hotel.
4. *The reception given by the king* was one event that we were expected to attend.
5. *Many international dignitaries* would attend this reception.
6. *For us to be seen together as a group* would be important.
7. We will have to learn to respond to questions with *noncontradictory answers* that do not clash with each other.
8. And we will have to be patient if we happen to be asked *repeatedly* the same question.
9. *Our desire to act like worthy award winners* was the focus of our preparations for the ceremonies.
10. We will be representing *our country* and our university.

40a
se

Exercise 4

Examine the sentence endings in one of the essays you have written recently. Does each sentence stress the information that it should? Be prepared to discuss your answers to this question with your classmates.

If You End a Sentence with Several Similar Elements of Equal Importance, Have You Arranged Them from Shortest to Longest?

Occasionally you might choose to conclude a sentence with two or more of the same kind of element. If one of these elements is more important than the other for your purpose, you should place that one last. If you do not, you risk writing a sentence that ends anticlimactically:

> Getting to Stockholm late would mean that we would miss the Nobel ceremony and that we would have to wait in a line at the hotel.

In the context of missing the Nobel ceremony, the matter of waiting in line at the hotel seems almost laughable.

But what if the elements are equally important? How should you order them? Sometimes, of course, these elements will refer to events that happened in a certain order, and you will probably want to represent that order in your sentence. Such an order, however, will not always come into play. Then you should arrange elements from shorter to longer or from shortest to longest. This practice rests on the fact that in most cases the longer the sentence element, the more informative it will be. You will be placing the more or the most informative element at the end. Therefore, you would write

> We planned to sign autographs outside our hotel and in the center of the foyer of the assembly hall.

And not

> We planned to sign autographs in the center of the foyer of the assembly hall and outside our hotel.

Of course, you would have good reason to ignore this advice if you were seeking a humorous effect. Moving from the serious to the slight or from long to short can be comical:

> We expected to join the ranks of frequently quoted figures: the sublime poet of Avon, William Shakespeare; the famous psychoanalyst, Sigmund Freud; and Casey Stengel.

Finally, as you review sentences that conclude with similar elements, take care not to end a sentence with too many adjective clauses. When you end a sentence with more than two adjective clauses, the sentence will seem somewhat unwieldy and sprawling. Consider the following example (the first word in each adjective clause is in italics):

> Our novel was compared with the book *that* had been reviewed by several critics *who* had formed a group to promote works *that* organizations of parents had banned from reading lists *that* teachers consulted.

Exercise 5

If you decide that any of the following sentences needs revision in order to have a more effective ending, give your reasons, and then revise the sentences.

> EXAMPLE: At our last meeting before leaving for Stockholm, our assistant came into the room with another letter from the Swedish academy and with a few memos.

The information about the letter seems more important than that about the memos. And the phrase about the letter is longer than the one about the memos. Suggested revision:

> At our last meeting before leaving for Stockholm, our assistant came into the room with a few memos and with another letter from the Swedish academy.

1. Our assistant also had some records to bring up to date, and he did so with an accuracy that had grown out of years of attention to details and with speed.

2. Our assistant remembered to draw attention to the letter from Stockholm and to distribute some reminders about air travel.

3. The leader of our group opened the letter, turned pale, and slumped into her seat.

4. She mumbled that this news might kill her, drive her insane, or cause her to lose sleep.

5. The members of the Swedish academy wrote to express their wish that we would not be disappointed and to state that their prior announcement of our winning a prize had been a serious error.

40b
se

41

I n Act III of Richard Sheridan's *The Rivals,* Mrs. Malaprop says the following to Captain Absolute about her niece Lydia Languish, who follows her heart in love rather then Mrs. Malaprop's instructions:

> You are very good, and very considerate, Captain. —I am sure I have done every thing in my power since I exploded the affair! long ago I laid my positive conjunctions on her, never to think on the fellow again;—I have since laid Sir Anthony's preposition before her;—but, I am sorry to say, she seems resolved to decline every particle that I enjoin her.

Even though the speech appears out of context, you certainly must wonder about Mrs. Malaprop's choices of words. For instance, she apparently thinks of a word such as *proposal* or *proposition* but says *preposition* instead. And she makes such errors so often that we now have in the language the term *malapropism,* the name for a word that sounds like the correct one but that is ludicrous in context.

Sheridan uses Mrs. Malaprop's faulty diction intentionally and comically. However, if you make faulty choices of words in essays, the effect on your readers will almost certainly be negative. In this chapter, we ask you several questions about your diction, and we give you guidelines for revising it.

41a

Enriching Your Vocabulary

The larger your working vocabulary is, the easier it will be for you to judge the effectiveness of your word choices. As you read and as you listen to others speak, it is a good idea to make note of the words that are new to you and of the contexts in which you encounter those words. We recommend that you keep a list of such words and their definitions, along with notes about typical contexts for them. Here is one example of an entry on such a list:

> *innominate* (adj.): having no name. Context: *An innominate fear overcame them.*

You can also strengthen your working vocabulary by learning some common prefixes, roots (words or parts of words that are used to build other words), and suffixes, which we list below:

Prefix	Meaning	Example
ante-	before	antecedent
anti-	against	anti-apartheid
bi-	two	bipolar
de-	from, away from	decelerate
dis-	deprive of	disbar
il-	not	illegal
in-	not	insincere
mis-	wrong, bad	misanthropic
neo-	new	neologism
non-	not	nongenuine
omni-	all	omniscient
pre-	before	premature
re-	again, back	reaffirm
semi-	half	semicircle
sub-	under	subhuman
super-	above, over	supernatural
tri-	three	tricornered
trans-	across, over	transcontinental
un-	not	undaunted
uni-	one	unicycle

41a
dic

Root	Meaning	Example
-audi-	to hear	audiometer
-bene-	good	benefactor
-bio-	life	biosphere
-geo-	earth	geology
-graph-	to write	photograph
-luc-	light	translucent
-manu-	hand	manuscript
-phil-	love	philology
-port-	to carry	portage
-psych-	soul	psychology
-scrib-, -script-	to write	manuscript

Suffix	Meaning	Example
-dom	place, state	kingdom
-en	cause to become	lighten
-ful	having the quality	colorful
-ic	related to	tragic
-ist	one who	pianist
-ity	the quality of	tenacity
-ive	having the nature of	creative
-ize	cause to become	terrorize
-less	without	mindless
-ment	condition of	endowment
-ness	state of being	laziness
-ship	condition, position held	scholarship, fellowship

41a
dic

Exercise 1

Use each of the following words appropriately in a sentence. Consult your dictionary as necessary.

EXAMPLE: antedates   This urn antedates the Iron Age by a century.

1. grapheme   3. tripartite   5. enhancement
2. subscript   4. transcription

Are Your Words Accurate and Precise?

The **denotation** of a word is its dictionary meaning—what all or a great majority of people would say it means. One of the beauties of English is that, largely because of its borrowings from other languages, it has many sets of words that mean nearly the same thing. The challenge is to use the words that have precisely the denotations you need.

Consider *procrastinate* and *dawdle.* These words have similar denotations: They both describe actions that are not completed as quickly as some people might wish. But to procrastinate is to put off a task that one could complete. It fits well in a sentence such as this:

> They got into academic difficulty because each time they received an assignment they procrastinated.

It does not fit well in a sentence such as this:

> QUESTIONABLE: They procrastinated down the trail, stopping occasionally to admire the flowers.

On the other hand, to dawdle has more to do with slow and seemingly aimless movements. *Dawdle* fits well in this sentence:

> They dawdled down the trail, stopping occasionally to admire the flowers.

But it does not fit as well in this sentence:

> QUESTIONABLE: They got into academic difficulty because each time they received an assignment they dawdled.

41b
dic

You should read your drafts carefully, paying particularly close attention to the content words (nouns, verbs, adjectives, and adverbs). Ask yourself whether these words convey precisely the shades of meaning that you intend.

When writers fail to use accurate and precise words, they fail most often in one of three ways, each of which we examine below.

Exercise 2

Use a form of each word in the following pairs appropriately in a sentence. Consult a dictionary if you wish.

EXAMPLE: suggest, insinuate

They *suggested* that we sample some of their new cheeses.

Are you *insinuating* that my alibi is not believable?

1. lumber (verb), saunter (verb)
2. use (verb), exploit (verb)
3. assertive, aggressive
4. satiric, sardonic
5. confident, sarcastic

6. obscene, profane
7. eager, anxious
8. reprimand, chide
9. impediments, delays
10. inconsistent, incongruous

1 Incorrect Words

Sometimes writers use an incorrect word because it sounds similar to the correct one. Here is a sentence cited in *The Chronicle of Higher Education:*

> The new main lodge for Minnowbrook Conference Center, opening this month, will be equally elegant yet have a more restive atmosphere.

The writer needed a word such as *restful* but settled on *restive* instead. However, *restive* usually applies to unruly or restless people or situations; it means the opposite of what the writer wanted.

Exercise 3

The following are slightly modified forms of sentences that Mina Shaughnessy cites in *Errors and Expectations.* Each contains at least one word that is incorrect in context. Identify these words, and revise each sentence so that it means what you think its writer intended it to mean.

> EXAMPLE: Our students must make an effort to make the necessary transgressions to fulfill their needs. [The incorrect word is *transgressions.* The writer probably meant to write *Our students must make an effort to make the necessary transformations* (or *transitions*) *to fulfill their needs.*]

41b
dic

1. The program uses a new floormat.
2. They used him as an escape goat.
3. They are eliminating waste and gas from combining with air.
4. Once his father demonstrates between the two birds, this little boy will not have any problems.
5. I think psychology has increased my mind.
6. The demand for jobs has prolifically declined.
7. That is why one must construct a child's mind before it gets set.
8. Not speaking English proposed difficulties for them.
9. Many students portray immature concepts.
10. Through education a person's financial well-being is enlightened.

2 Vague Words

If you use vague words, you convey such a wide range of meanings that readers can be unsure of your message. In Chapter 39, we discussed vague verbs such as *do* and *make*. Here we add that you should take care that your nouns and adjectives are not vague.

Take the adjective *funny,* for example. Something that is funny could be amusing, laughable, odd, different, or peculiar. In most contexts, the precise meaning of *funny* would probably be clear; but if it is not, you should choose a more precise adjective. Other adjectives worth paying close attention to are *bad, fine, good, interesting, moving,* and *nice.*

Some nouns that you should review carefully are *thing, way,* and *area.* Consider the use of *things* in the following:

On that fitness trail, we did most of the things the signs directed us to do.

This sentence would be more precise if it were revised as follows:

On that fitness trail, we did most of the exercises the signs directed us to do.

Exercise 4

Each of the following sentences contains at least one vague word. Identify these words and revise them so that each sentence is more precise.

> EXAMPLE: They promised to report to training camp in shape, a thing that would be difficult to honor.
>
> They promised to report to training camp in shape, a pledge that would be difficult to honor.

41b
dic

1. Their throws from the outfield were nice.
2. Watching the car go through the guard rail and into Gonner's Gulch was moving.
3. I would have thought it funny that the back door was ajar.
4. In preparation for ballet class, we do most of the things that our instructor suggests we do.
5. Writing a good poem is an area I have always been interested in.

3 Obscure Words

Readers today are bombarded by words and phrases whose meanings they cannot figure out. Hospitals release reports referring to "therapeutic misadventures" (in other words, someone made a mistake and a patient died on the operating table). And energy companies inform people that "plutonium has taken up residence" (in other words, the companies had a catastrophic radiation leak).

Probably very few of you intentionally use obscure language in order to confuse readers. But all writers must be on guard against such language, for it is becoming so common that it can easily slip into essays now and then. There is also the temptation to equate obscure and difficult language with profundity. In your own writing, you should be on guard against the following common kinds of obscure language:

a. Euphemisms

The term *euphemism* literally means "good speech" or "good-sounding speech." **Euphemisms** are neutral or even pleasant ways to refer to processes and things that are frightening, sad, dangerous, disgusting, or terrifying. For example, many people do not say that a friend died; they say that the friend passed on or left this vale of tears.

Euphemisms can serve as notes of tact and civility in a society. We have no quarrel with such euphemisms. But they can also serve to glorify the common or the ugly and to distort the truth. Should citizens allow a government to refer to a tax increase as "revenue enhancement"? We do not think so. We recommend that you leave in your drafts the euphemisms that ease pain but revise the euphemisms that inflate and distort.

b. Ornate Words

Throughout its history, the English language has borrowed many words from Latin, Greek, and French. Generally, these words have more formal or ornate associations than do the words of Anglo-Saxon origin. These words have their place, particularly in the writing of specialized academic disciplines. But writers can also use these words to puff themselves up, and in so doing they often confuse readers. They might write about "organoleptic analysis" rather than about smelling or sensing something. In this process, the writers work directly against the possibility of communicating information to others.

c. Circumlocutions

To use a **circumlocution** is literally to talk around a subject. Writers using circumlocutions express in ten words what others could express in two or three. For instance, we once heard someone say that some of his statements were not lies; in his view, they offered "a different version from the facts." Take care to revise any such constructions in your drafts, unless, of course, you are using them to imitate the speech or writing of someone who regularly uses circumlocutions.

d. Jargon

The term *jargon* has many different meanings in our culture. In this book, **jargon** refers to the specialized words and phrases of particular groups and professions. For instance, certain kinds of chemists work with "multiphoton ionization." When it is used by writers within a particular group, jargon is not bad. However, if you use the jargon of a particular field with readers who are not familiar with that field, you will have to translate the jargon. Otherwise your writing will mean little or nothing to those readers and will probably irritate them.

Exercise 5

The following sentences come from a section called "Faking It: The Art of Obfuscation" in *The Ultimate College Student's Handbook.* Translate them into more easily understood sentences. Use a dictionary if necessary. You should be able to revise most of them into sentences two to four words long.

EXAMPLE: "Indefeasible difficulties necessitate a reassessment of allotted time parameters vis à vis the restructuring of predesignated completion goals."

It will be late.

1. "Phrenialogically speaking, the aforementioned subject ineluctably eluded my short-term mnemonic functions, resulting in an unaccountable cognition void."

2. "Indivertible circumstances misdirected the successful ensconcement of the errant property rendering possessorship inoperative."

3. "The variable achievement gradient assiduously ascribed a regrettably unpropitious exponential symbol to the diagnostic instrument which I benignly submitted for judicious academic consideratory purposes."

4. "The overwhelmingly addictive character of televised divertissements short-circuited my ambitionary regard for the apprehension and retention of the opusculatory material now under consideration."

5. "Notwithstanding the scintillating repartage concomitant to this scholastic assemblage, intransigent preternatural biologic functions conspired to surmount my fragile resolve, plunging consciousness beneath my direct autonomy and thus insuring a rapid decline into somnolency."

**41b
dic**

Have You Selected Words with Appropriate Connotations?

Connotations are the associations and suggestions that a word brings to mind. Usually, they are intertwined with people's emotions. As you review the words in your drafts, you should check that the connotations of those words are consistent with your overall purposes for the drafts. In *The Fatal Shore,* Robert Hughes contrasts the "rich man's four tipples" to the poor person's gin. *Tipples* is a marvellous word here. Hughes is showing how the upper-class elegance and grace of Georgian England was only a thin veneer over the degeneration of the lower classes. According to *Webster's Ninth New Collegiate Dictionary,* the denotation of *tipple* is "an intoxicating beverage; DRINK." For most people it carries connotations of lightness, gaiety, elegance, and control. All these stand in stark contrast to the place of gin in the lives of the poor. They drank a lot of it, they did so out of desperation in slum-like surroundings, and it turned them into a sodden mob.

You will not be able to choose only words with connotations as appropriate to a purpose as those of *tipples* are appropriate to Hughes's purpose. But you should be alert for words with connotations that will help you achieve your purposes.

You should also avoid words with connotations that might offend readers or raise distracting questions for them. Recently, some friends of ours received a letter in which a president of a school board asked for funds for his school. He gave several reasons why the school deserved monetary gifts. One reason was that the school "serviced 375 children from 6:30 a.m. until 6:00 p.m." The connotations of the word *serviced* alienated our friends somewhat. The writer wanted to make them think of a nurturing environment, but *serviced* made them think of a very impersonal and mechanical situation. *Service* is a word they associate with the work mechanics do on cars. They did not send the school any money.

To increase your sensitivity to the connotations of particular words, you might look them up in a dictionary or thesaurus and also pay close attention to how skilled writers use these words.

Exercise 6

Generalize about how the words in each of the following sets differ from each other in connotations. Then use each in a sentence in which the word's connotations are appropriate.

EXAMPLE: skinny, svelte

Both of these words have to do with thinness, but *skinny* is quite negative in connotations: *Until I began to work out in the strength-fitness room, I was a skinny weakling.* *Svelte* is much more positive, connoting sleekness and grace: *The pictures of all those svelte models in magazines can contribute to the eating disorders of teen-agers.*

1. stocky, obese   4. brave, bold
2. entertain, amuse   5. wisdom, prudence
3. lady, woman

Are Your Collocations Correct?

Collocations are words that conventionally go together. For instance, people write of *making mistakes,* not of *doing* them. Our main concern in this general area is with the prepositions that are associated with certain nouns, verbs, and adjectives. We frequently read faulty constructions such as the following:

INCORRECT: repugnance at (correct: *repugnance to*)

respond on (correct: *respond to*)

Many errors of this kind occur when writers use *of* although another preposition is needed:

INCORRECT: sequel of (correct: *sequel to*)

enthusiasm of leaving (correct: *enthusiasm for leaving*)

And sometimes other prepositions appear where *of* ought to:

INCORRECT: total disregard to (correct: *total disregard of*)

regardless to (correct: *regardless of*)

Choosing the appropriate preposition or prepositions can be particularly challenging when you coordinate two words, each of which requires the addition of a preposition. Sometimes writers err in using a single preposition when each of the coordinated words requires a different one:

INCORRECT: qualified and interested in a new job
CORRECT: qualified *for* and interested in a new job

INCORRECT: respond and comment on the paper
CORRECT: respond *to* and comment on the paper

ESL Consideration

MANAGING PREPOSITION COLLOCATIONS

One effective way of managing the diverse preposition collocations in
English is to keep lists of the collocations according to structural
categories. These lists can make the task of editing collocation
problems easier. Here are two well-established categories that cause
frequent problems:

CATEGORY 1:   Form of *be* + Adjective + Preposition
is absent from, is different from, is worried about

CATEGORY 2:   Verb + Noun + Preposition
has access to, has patience with, takes pride in

It is difficult to pair nouns, verbs, and adjectives correctly with
prepositions because the pairings follow no general rule. Any of the
following entries are worth memorizing if they give you trouble:

They *acceded to* our wishes.

They were *accompanied by* two bodyguards.

They were *accompanied with* a new proposal.

According to an unnamed source, the debt is huge.

They were *accused of* a crime.

But they were *acquitted of* the charge.

We *adapted* these charts *from* their sources.

They can *adapt to* new situations.

This situation *admits of* several alternatives.

They never will *admit to* a mistake.

We all *agree in* principle.

Can we *agree on* a plan of attack?

We will never *agree to* that proposal.

We heartily *agree with* you.

They were *angry at* such treatment.

They were *angry with* us.

They are *capable of* several surprises.

How much will they *charge for* repairs?

Were they *charged with* embezzlement?

41d
dic

Compare this apple *to* that one. [The two are in the same category.]

That is like *comparing* apples *with* oranges. [The apples and oranges are in different categories.]

We *concur in* that judgment.

We rarely *concur with* you.

You can *confide in* us.

But you should not *confide* that *to* us.

The two buildings are *connected by* a walkway.

We are *connected with* that group.

We will *contend for* that principle.

Must we *contend with* you?

We *differ about* three separate issues.

They *differ from* their neighbors in appearance.

We will always *differ on* that question.

I thought we were *freed from* bondage.

They are now *free of* their oppressors.

Their program is *identical to* [or *with*] ours.

We are all *impatient for* improvements.

Have you become *impatient with* your parents?

We are *independent of* the university.

Their program is *inferior to* ours, of course.

What have you *inferred from* my remarks?

Come *join in* the fun.

Join with us in this campaign.

We have *joined* one *to* the other.

There is no *necessity for* you to hesitate.

There is no *necessity of* your hesitating.

We *object to* that conclusion.

Those seats are *occupied by* dignitaries.

They are *occupied in* research.

They have been *occupied with* that project for several years.

They were *overcome by* the terrible sight.

They were *overcome with* remorse.

They found it difficult to *part from* their cousins.

They rarely *part with* any possessions.

41d
dic

The first option is *preferable to* the second.

Prior to our arrival, they had hidden the clues.

They were *receptive to* our comments.

We were *rewarded by* the psychologist.

We were *rewarded for* running the maze.

We were *rewarded with* a sum of cash.

They were *superior to* their opponents.

We are most *thankful for* the help.

We are especially *thankful to* you.

These projects really *vary from* one another in scope.

They also *vary in* size.

Their tolerance level *varies with* the circumstances.

Wait at home patiently.

Wait for a taxi.

We should *wait on* this customer first.

Your idea is *worthy of* consideration.

A good dictionary will also help you make pairings such as those illustrated above. But your best option is to listen to and read as much as you can.

Exercise 7

Supply the correct preposition for each of the following blanks.

> **EXAMPLE:**   The Academy of Lagado was housed ____in____ several buildings.

1. One professor confided _____ us that he was trying to extract sunbeams from cucumbers.

2. Another professor had agreed _____ a proposal to build houses by starting with the roof and working to the foundation.

3. "After all," he said, "bees and spiders are capable _____ accomplishing such feats."

4. Another professor considered ploughing with cattle inferior _____ his approach.

5. According _____ him, it was more efficient to plough with hogs.

6. In one room, Gulliver was nearly overcome _____ a horrible smell.

7. His guide warned him, however, that any offense would be highly resented, and he was nearly overcome _____ remorse.

8. In the part of the academy where professors specialized in speculative knowledge, some professors were impatient _____ some additional improvements in their own language.

9. Prior _____ our arrival, they had begun a project to eliminate all verbs from their language.

10. They were receptive _____ and thankful _____ our suggestions.

41e

Have You Selected Words from Appropriate Levels of Formality?

Many English words differ from one another in their level of formality. Some strike readers as very formal, learned, ornate, even ceremonial. Others strike readers as much more informal and down to earth.

You should make sure that in their level of formality your words fit your writing situations. If you were writing about a serious subject on a serious occasion to people you do not know well, it would be a mistake to use very informal words. On the other hand, if you were writing a letter to your best friend about matters that are important to you, it would be surprising and probably alarming to that friend if you used highly formal language. Below we describe some levels of formality present in the vocabulary of English, and we comment on some of the situations in which it would be appropriate to use words from these levels.

41e
dic

1 The Highly Formal Level

Among the most formal words in English are words borrowed from Latin:

ascend, conflagration, interrogate, probity, regal, trepidation

They sound learned and somewhat heavy. Writers use such words most often in very serious or ceremonial situations. If you had to prepare the text for the dedication of a building on your campus, you probably would use several highly formal words.

These words will necessarily appear now and then in the writing you do in college. But too many students assume that the greater the number of highly formal words they use, the more intelligent they will sound. They assume that they should always write *ascertain* instead of *find out*. In so doing, they can lose all sense of their own voice.

2 The Formal Level

To an extent, we associate the formal level of diction with borrowings from French. These are words such as the following:

mount, question, royal, terror, virtue

These, too, sound learned, but often not to the extent that the borrowings from Latin do.

You will probably use these words often in your academic writing. In fact, it is difficult to write anything at all about some subjects, such as politics, foods, and religion, without using borrowings from French. But be careful not to use formal diction too heavily. On a short quiz, for instance, formal diction could make your teachers think you are trying too hard to sound impressive.

3 The Informal Level

Many of the words on the informal level are derived from the languages the Angles, Saxons, and Jutes spoke when they settled in England in the fifth century after Christ. These are words such as the following:

ask, fear, goodness, kingly, rise

These often have an earthy, everyday quality.

These words do not usually fit well in very formal or ceremonial settings. They are the words you would depend on in letters to people you know a little. And these words will do much of the work you need to do in academic papers.

4 The Familiar Level

The familiar level of diction, the level you would use with friends and relatives, includes many words derived from the languages of the Angles, Saxons, and Jutes. But it also includes at least two other kinds of expressions:

a. Colloquialisms

Colloquialisms are words and phrases that people associate with casual conversation:

barf, hassles, have it made, messed up, OK, snooze

b. Slang

Slang refers to colorful and vivid words and phrases invented and used by a group of people usually in order to identify themselves as a group. As we were writing this book, some high school and college students were using the slang expressions *popping junk* (gossiping), *crib* (house or apartment), and *get cazh* (to relax and let down one's hair).

Most academic writing does not call for familiar language. However, you may draw on it when you write dialogues, personal essays, satiric essays, and the like; just be sure that you can justify its use.

Your main task with regard to levels of formality in diction is to try to match the level of your words to your readers' knowledge of the subject matter and to the situation in which you write. But you must also avoid mixing levels of diction without good reason. Here is a portion of a newspaper sermon that Robert Graves and Alan Hodge found:

> It is one of the mysteries of that inner life of man (one so replete with mysteries hard to accept or solve) that some of us are clearly, as it were, freeborn citizens of grace, whilst others—alas! many others—can only at great price buy this freedom. Of this there can be no doubt. The Gospel appointed for to-day reports to us, in the words of our Lord Himself, a story at once simple and mystifying, about day-labourers in an Eastern vineyard. Some of them had worked a full day, whilst others had only "clocked in," so to speak, when it was nearly time to go. Yet each received from the employer the same flat rate of remuneration—a Roman penny. Our Lord said that was all right, which must be enough for us.

As Graves and Hodge point out, the language of this sermon shifts from highly formal theological language—"It is one of the mysteries of that inner life of man (one so replete with mysteries hard to accept or solve) that some of us are clearly, as it were, freeborn citizens of grace"—through some informal language ("Some of them had worked a full day"), to the familiar ("Our Lord said that was all right"). Such shifts are sufficiently jarring that it is difficult to imagine many people reacting positively to this sermon.

41e dic

Exercise 8

Use the words in each of the following groups in a sentence that is appropriate to the level of formality of the words. Change the forms of the words if you wish.

EXAMPLE:	delay, account	*They have delayed liquidating the balance of their accounts.*
	dillydally, tab	*They have dillydallied around and not covered their tab.*

1a. abduct, gentleman
 b. snatch, guy
2a. acknowledge, films
 b. own up, flicks
3a. betray, athletes
 b. doublecross, jocks

4a. unintelligent, damaged
 b. stupid, screwed up
5a. capitulate, viands
 b. give up, grub

41f

Have You Used Abstract and General Words in Appropriate Proportions to Concrete and Specific Ones?

**41f
dic**

When you choose words, especially nouns, you will have to decide whether to use abstract or concrete ones. The words *abstract* and *concrete* are usually defined in relationship to each other. The **abstract** is that which exists only in your mind. It includes the names of feelings, qualities, conditions, states of being, classes of things, ideas, theories, fields of inquiry, and relationships. The **concrete** is that which you can know directly through your senses. You can see aspen leaves, taste apple cider, and feel frost in the air.

The words *general* and *specific* are also usually defined in relationship to each other. The more **general** the reference of words, the more things they refer to. The more **specific** the reference of words, the fewer things they refer to. Therefore, words can be more or less general or specific relative to other words. *Recreational activities* is more general than *sports*. *Sports* is more general than *racquet sports*.

Abstract words often go with general ones. Concrete words often go with specific ones. As you write and revise, you will have to decide how many abstract and general words you use relative to concrete and specific ones.

Abstract and general words have some important advantages. They can refer to intricate ideas and package a great deal of information for evaluation. They can also be used to make claims that apply to many people and situations. Besides, they appeal to the intellect. For example, how do you react to the following sentence?

> Perseverance is the ability to accomplish tasks, even when the obstacles are formidable.

Most people probably experience little emotional reaction to this sentence. Rather, they think about what the terms mean, try to understand the overall claim, and decide if the claim is true or false.

The chief advantage of concrete and specific words is that they are vivid and emotionally moving. Instead of writing about *perseverance* and *ability* and *formidable obstacles,* we could depict fifteen-year-old Melissa Sue Pelligrino finishing the Paavo Nurmi Marathon in Hurley, Wisconsin, in three hours and fifty minutes, even though she had fallen at the twenty-mile mark and severely scratched her palms and knees. We made all these details up, but we hope the point is clear. Reading about a specific young person finishing a marathon with torn and bleeding hands and knees does move many people to feel sympathy and admiration for her.

You have probably read writers who use mainly abstract and general words. They can classify lots of information, make large generalizations, and narrate on a sweeping scale. But their prose can seem somewhat remote.

You have probably also read writers who use mainly concrete and specific words. Their prose can be vivid, moving, and memorable. But if all the specificity or concreteness does not catch readers' attention, the readers can simply dismiss it.

Therefore, in most cases you should seek appropriate proportions between the abstract and general words and the concrete and specific words in your essays. In many college writing situations, skilled writers use abstract and general terms early, late, and at important junctures in essays. They use specific and concrete terms to illustrate, enliven, and substantiate the abstract and general claims.

If you follow our advice about balancing the terms you use, you will have a good chance to make significant points and to move readers to think that the points apply to them. If you appeal only to their intellects, they may accept your claims but not act on them. If you appeal only to their emotions, they may act on your claims without thinking about them very carefully. If you appeal to your readers' intellects and their emotions, they can act on your claims with good reason.

41f
dic

Exercise 9

Each of the following sentences uses abstract and general words to make a general claim. Add at least one sentence after each of the following to support, enliven, or illustrate the general claim.

EXAMPLE: Honesty is the best policy

Honesty is the best policy. Last week my roommate, Jack, cheated on a calculus test. Professor Tangent accused him of cheating, but Jack denied it. Since then, Jack has lied so often that he has to keep track of all of his lies in a special journal.

1. Greed causes trouble.
2. Political posturing by world leaders can be dangerous.
3. Humor helps teachers on any level.
4. Sarcasm only causes harm.
5. Repressing emotions can be harmful.

Is Your Figurative Language Fresh, Appropriate, and Consistent?

As you review your drafts, you will have to decide how much figurative language to use. Most of your language will be literal; it will refer to things in themselves. Figurative language or figures of speech present one thing in terms of another; they push into the realm of the pictorial.

Three of the more common figures of speech are simile, metaphor, and personification. With **similes,** writers make comparisons between two things, using *like, as,* or *as if.* Describing a particular cast used in fly fishing, Norman Maclean writes the following:

> The cast is so soft and slow that it can be followed like an ash settling from a fireplace chimney.

With **metaphors,** writers make direct comparisons between things. Describing an old and emaciated woman in a hospital, Richard Selzer writes:

> Her hands were spiders at the ends of sticks.

With **personification,** writers treat abstractions, objects, and animals as if they were human. You could personify conscience as the "counsellor looking over your shoulder."

Figures of speech can bring a fresh perspective to ideas. Writers can use them to help readers imagine what they know little about, identify more parts of something than they ever noticed before, and see something in a new way. Figures can also add flair to prose. But figures are not appropriate in all contexts, for they can open up several ways in which to see things. When precision of reference and description is a major goal, such opening up may be dangerous.

41g
dic

1 Are Your Figures of Speech Fresh?

If you decide to use some figures of speech in an essay, you should use fresh ones. You should avoid dead metaphors such as *a bed of roses, the day's grind, to lap up the miles, raining cats and dogs, the staff of life,* and *to wolf something down.* You should also avoid worn-out similes such as *blind as a bat, fit as a fiddle, fresh as a daisy, hard as a rock,* and *tight as a drum.*

You should seek new and vivid figures or find ways of reviving old ones. The chapter title "A Horse Foaled by an Acorn" in *The Fatal Shore* by Robert Hughes is an elaborate metaphor that Hughes resurrects from eighteenth-century England. When readers first see this title, they wonder how an acorn can give birth to a horse. As they read the chapter, they learn that the metaphor had its origin in old names for the gallows.

As Hughes puts it, "Being a construction of three parts linked by a cross bar, the gallows was the three-legged mare . . . being made of oak, it was the wooden mare, and to die on it was to 'ride the horse foaled by an acorn.'" This metaphor first catches readers' attention. Then it leads them to see the great difference between riding a horse and being hanged. When they grasp this difference, they are probably amazed at the people who could talk of dying in terms of riding a horse. Or they may see the apparent bravado as a mask for terror. In either case, they will think about hanging and the psychological effects of its threat for actual or potential criminals in eighteenth-century England very deeply—precisely what Hughes is aiming for.

2 Are Your Figures of Speech Appropriate?

41g
dic

Sometimes writers produce inappropriate figures of speech when they compare two things that do not have enough in common to reveal something interesting to readers. Imagine reading that someone has a "stable of videotapes." Does this comparison describe the videotapes in a revealing and interesting way? We have a difficult time imagining how. When the items compared do have something in common but that something is not relevant or revealing, the result may be strained figures of speech. One could describe a small cloud as a piece of white peppermint. But outside of some special situation, few readers would say that this figure leads them to see clouds in an interesting new way. Strained figures may also result when the terms of the comparisons do not fit writers' overall purposes. You could describe the pleasurable process of reading a spellbinding book as a race:

The book was so interesting that I sprinted from page to page.

But the more you bring in images of exertion, the more you work against your purpose of depicting the reading as pleasurable:

> As I reached the last chapter, my breathing became painful, and I strained for the finish.

3 Are Your Figures of Speech Consistent?

Sometimes writers start to compare one thing to another in a figure of speech, but before they have finished spelling out the terms of the comparison, they move into a new comparison. This happens most often with metaphors; in such cases, one says that writers have produced mixed metaphors. Here is one example:

> A dictionary is not a book one goes to as a last resort but rather a wonderland of images, a valve for the outlet of the imagination.

The writer compares a dictionary to a wonderland of images and then to an outlet valve; these points of comparison do not go well with one another.

Exercise 10

Explain why the figures in the following sentences are inappropriate or mixed metaphors. (All the sentences are taken from Richard Lederer's *Anguished English.*)

EXAMPLE: "A U.S. senator created a new animal when he exclaimed, 'That's a horse of a different feather.' " [In this sentence the senator begins with a metaphor involving a horse but then extends the figure illogically with the reference to feathers.]

1. ". . . a national newscaster announced that 'the political football is now in the Polish government's court.' "

2. "And from Lou Brock, the great St. Louis Cardinals outfielder: 'I always felt I was a guy who had the ability to light the spark of enthusiasm which unlocked the hidden geysers of adrenalin that causes one to play at the summit of his ability.' "

3. "Milwaukee is the golden egg that the rest of the state wants to milk."

4. "The idea was hatched two years ago, but it didn't catch fire until two months ago, when the co-director jumped in feet first. Since then, things have really been snowballing for the two."

5. "She was a diva of such immense talent that, after hearing her perform, there was seldom a dry seat in the house."

41h

Have You Avoided Sexist Terms?

Until relatively recently, many people used the pronouns *he, him,* or *his* to refer to a person whose sex was unknown. If they referred to a doctor and a nurse, they assumed that the doctor was male and the nurse female. And when they referred to all people or to people in general, they used *man* or *mankind.*

However, many girls and women have said that these practices demean them, discourage them from going into certain professions, and exclude them from their rightful place in humanity. Therefore, to be honest and true in representing humanity, and to avoid having a negative effect on girls and women, you should avoid words that demean or exclude them.

It is true that there are also terms that demean or exclude men and members of various races and ethnic groups. But the demeaning or excluding terms that probably are used most frequently today are those referring to girls and women. Therefore, you should be particularly careful to follow these five guidelines:

1 Avoid Demeaning References to Women

Many terms for women demean them by referring to them as children *(babes, girls),* as animals *(chicks, foxes),* or as parts of their anatomy or clothing *(tail, skirt).*

2 Avoid Calling Attention to a Woman's Gender or Marital Status

Sometimes writers refer to Graham Greene as Greene and then to Flannery O'Connor as Miss O'Connor. Why should they call attention to the fact that O'Connor was a woman, and a single woman at that? They should not. If one person (a male) deserves to be referred to by his first and last names or just his last name, then so does another person (a female). When courtesy titles are necessary (in letters, for example), many women prefer *Ms.* rather than *Miss* or *Mrs.*

3 Avoid Stereotypes

There is a story about a man and his son, both of whom were in an automobile accident. The father died, but the boy survived and, critically injured, was taken to a hospital. As the boy was brought into the emergency room, the doctor exclaimed, "Oh God, it's my son!" The question is this: What is the relationship of the doctor to the boy?

If you had some trouble responding that the doctor is the boy's mother, then you can understand all the better how strongly some stereotypes about the sexes and some occupations control people's thinking. Today, at least in most parts of North America, nearly all occupations are open to both men and women. Thus, you should not refer to a person of a particular occupation as *he* unless you know that the person is male.

4 Avoid *Man, Men,* and *Mankind* for References to People in General

If you use the terms *man, men,* or *mankind* to refer to people in general, many women will feel excluded. It would be better to use the words *humankind* or *humanity.*

Similarly, you should find a replacement for many of the words that end in *-man* or *-men*. For example, you could change *chairman* to *chairperson.* This word is becoming widely accepted, but if it strikes you as awkward, you could substitute *chair* or *head.* In another case, we prefer *police officer* to *policeperson* as a substitute for *policeman.* Your own sense of what is awkward, as well as some dictionaries of nonsexist language, should help you make such decisions.

5 Avoid Forms of *He* When Referring to a Person of Unknown Gender

One problem with the English language is that it has no singular third-person pronoun that refers to a person of unknown gender. Therefore, writers can face dilemmas such as these:

Everyone should have (his? her?) dictionary here.

An excellent teacher reveals (his? her?) own views in lectures.

Everyone is conventionally considered to be singular, and at one time most writers used *his* in such a sentence. At one time most writers used *his* in the second example also. But you cannot use *his* in either sentence without excluding women. Therefore, we recommend the following three strategies:

a. Try to Change the Pronoun to an Article

In some cases, the easiest solution is to insert *a, an,* or *the* where the pronoun appeared:

Everyone should have (his? her?) dictionary here.

Everyone should have a dictionary here.

b. Use the Plural

If inserting *a, an,* or *the* does not work, see whether you can change the singular word (such as *everyone*) to a plural. Then you should use a plural pronoun as well:

Everyone has his day.

All people have their day.

c. Use a Form of *He or She*

Finally, in some cases you will have to use a form of *he or she:*

The composer who wins the competition will conduct (his? her?) symphony in next week's concert.

The composer who wins the competition will conduct his or her symphony in next week's concert.

But repetitions of this practice in the same sentence or in different sentences that are close to each other will seem at least somewhat awkward:

> SOMEWHAT AWKWARD: An excellent teacher reveals his or her own views in his or her lectures.

And each repetition increases the awkwardness:

> MORE AWKWARD: An excellent teacher reveals his or her own views in his or her lectures to his or her students.

41h
dic

Exercise 11

If any of the following sentences display sexism, rewrite them to eliminate the sexist references.

> EXAMPLE: When a dental hygienist works, she must focus all her attention. [The writer of this sentence unjustifiably assumes that a dental hygienist is female (note the pronoun *she*). Possible revision: *When dental hygienists work, they must focus all their attention.*]

1. Henry James and Mrs. Wharton are often studied concurrently in courses in American literature.

2. Several students in that dormitory select only those courses that are likely to have good-looking babes in them.

3. One course in that department has the title "The Sufferings of Mankind in Literature and Film."

4. When the dean evaluates proposals for new courses, he checks the course subtitles carefully.

5. Several scholars have studied the function of colons in the titles of articles in professional journals.

41i

Have You Avoided Distracting Sound Patterns?

Many skilled writers and speakers occasionally use sound patterns to reinforce or vivify a message. They may repeat a word, as Franklin D. Roosevelt does in his famous statement:

> The only thing we have to *fear* is *fear* itself.

Or they may choose words that begin with the same sound. Note how Winston Churchill uses the *g, w,* and *wh* sounds in the following:

> We will have no truce or parley with you [Hitler], or the *g*risly *g*ang *wh*o *w*ork your *w*icked *w*ill.

41i dic

You should be alert to such possibilities in your own prose.

On the other hand, you should eliminate from your essays sound patterns that might distract readers from your message. For instance, repeating sounds too close to each other can be annoying:

> This is a *hitch which* attaches to the frame of the car.

You could revise this sentence by substituting *that* for *which.*

Repeating individual syllables or clusters of syllables too close to each other can also be irritating:

> This *exam exam*ines only lower-order thinking.

You could revise this sentence by changing *examines* to *tests.*

Finally, sometimes writers repeat individual words too close to each other:

> *In* "*In* a Different World," they debate the merits of the fantastic in literature.

The first *In* could be replaced with *Throughout.*

One of the better ways for you to discover whether you have left distracting sound patterns in drafts is to read the drafts aloud, listening for these sound patterns, or to ask your friends to do this for you.

Exercise 12

If you find a distracting sound pattern in any of the following sentences, revise the sentences.

> EXAMPLE: *This test tests the material we studied last week* has a distracting sound pattern in *test tests.*
>
> *This test covers the material we studied last week.*

1. Today is an especially special day in your career.
2. They use passive verbs too to an extent.
3. In *In Our Inmost Thoughts,* they explore modern epic poetry.
4. Their citation of the student evaluation of the administration was a miscalculation.
5. Do some people with enormous vocabularies stutter?

41i
dic

42

REVIEWING AND REVISING TO COORDINATE EFFECTIVELY

N ear the beginning of *The Decline and Fall of the Roman Empire,* Edward Gibbon includes the following sentence:

> The principal conquests of the Romans were achieved under the republic; and the emperors, for the most part, were satisfied with preserving those dominions which had been acquired by the policy of the senate, the active emulation of the consuls, and the martial enthusiasm of the people.

This sentence, like many others in Gibbon's masterpiece, shows a noticeable amount of coordination.

Coordination is the linking of two or more words, phrases, or clauses so that they can function together grammatically. In Gibbon's sentence, the independent clause before the semicolon is coordinated with the independent clause after the semicolon. And the second independent clause ends with three coordinated prepositional phrases.

Coordination usually helps writers achieve balance, order, and even elegance in their prose. But when elements lacking any logical connection are coordinated, the result is illogical or vague. And coordination of many elements in one sentence after another can make the writing seem strained and artificial.

In this chapter, we ask you two basic questions about elements that you might coordinate. We also give you some guidelines to use in revising coordinated elements.

42a

Have You Used Compound Sentences Effectively?

1 Identifying Compound Sentences

When you join two or more independent clauses and have no subordinate clauses in a sentence, you form a compound sentence (see **21a**). The independent clauses in compound sentences can be linked by three different marks of punctuation: commas, semicolons, or colons.

a. Commas Linking Independent Clauses in Compound Sentences

When commas link independent clauses in compound sentences, they are nearly always accompanied by either coordinating or correlative conjunctions (see **21a**). Here is one example of a compound sentence with a comma and a coordinating conjunction:

               independent clause   coordinating conjunction

Gibbon suffered from many illnesses, and

           independent clause

several times he almost died.

The next example is a compound sentence with a comma and correlative conjunctions:

correlative conjunction   independent clause

Either Gibbon had an inborn taste for history,

correlative conjunction   independent clause

or he developed this taste under his aunt's guidance.

b. Semicolons Linking Independent Clauses in Compound Sentences

Many compound sentences are formed by the linking of two independent clauses with a semicolon:

        independent clause   independent clause

Gibbon's mother ignored him; his aunt cared for him.

42a
co

In some compound sentences, however, the semicolon is followed by a conjunctive adverb, and the conjunctive adverb is usually followed by a comma:

independent clause   conjunctive
                                                  adverb
Gibbon wanted to marry Suzanne Curchod; however,
           independent clause
his father opposed the engagement.

c. Colons Linking Independent Clauses in Compound Sentences

A colon, too, can link independent clauses in a compound sentence, most often when the second independent clause explains or elaborates on the first clause:

independent clause   independent clause
Gibbon's decision was painful: He broke off his engagement.

2 The Effect or Force of Compound Sentences

Sometimes you will think of two different clauses and realize that you can either coordinate them or subordinate one to the other. You could write

independent clause   coordinating
                                     conjunction
Gibbon had to accept his father's judgment, or
          independent clause
he would have lost his inheritance.

Or you could write

subordinate clause
If Gibbon had not accepted his father's judgment,
          independent clause
he would have lost his inheritance.

Since the logical relationship between the two clauses is the same in both cases, how should you decide between them? As usual, the deciding factor will be the specific context in which you are working, but we can offer you some general advice.

42a
co

When you coordinate clauses, you are letting your readers know that the clauses have approximately equal significance. You want readers to see both clauses as standing in the foreground:

> Gibbon had to accept his father's judgment, or he would have lost his inheritance.

But should you want the information in the first clause to stand in the background relative to that in the second clause, you would choose this version, which subordinates one clause to the other:

> If Gibbon had not accepted his father's judgment, he would have lost his inheritance.

Why would you place some information in the background? Most often you would do so because it is old information (see **38f**), as in this context:

> Gibbon obeyed his father because of the price he would have had to pay if he were to rebel. If Gibbon had not accepted his father's judgment, he would have lost his inheritance.

In sum, if you decide to coordinate two clauses, they should be closely related in meaning, and you should have a reason for giving them equal prominence.

Several kinds of close relationships commonly characterize the clauses in compound sentences. Some important ones are listed below:

UNFOLDING OF EVENTS:	Gibbon accepted his father's judgment, and he never again thought seriously about marriage.
ALTERNATIVES:	Gibbon could have written about the liberty of the Swiss, or he could have focused on Greek civilization.
EXPLICIT CONTRASTS:	Gibbon's work on the Byzantine Empire is good, but his work on the Roman Empire in the West is far better.
QUALIFICATIONS OF CLAIMS:	Gibbon interpreted some phenomena incorrectly, but many sources were not available to him.

**42a
co**

Well-written compound sentences often have a balanced and stately rhythm and sound definitive. They leave the impression that they contain all the important information about a subject. For this reason, compound sentences are wonderfully appropriate vehicles for proverbs:

> The kisses of an enemy may be profuse, but faithful are the wounds of a friend. (Proverbs 27:6, NIV)

Exercise 1

Form compound sentences by adding one or more independent clauses to each of the following independent clauses. To link the clauses, try to use all the means discussed in this section.

> EXAMPLE: Our history professor assigned us parts of Gibbon's history.
>
> Our history professor assigned us parts of Gibbon's history, but some students ignored the assignment.

1. The next day our professor marched authoritatively into class.
2. She asked a question about Gibbon's view of barbarism.
3. Gibbon had some interesting views on the effects of barbarism on a political body.
4. Some of us could only guess about those views.
5. Then our professor made a surprising decision.

3 Some Pitfalls to Avoid in Writing Compound Sentences

There are five common pitfalls to avoid in writing compound sentences.

42a co

a. No Apparent Relationship Between the Independent Clauses

How would you react to the following compound sentence?

QUESTIONABLE: Gibbon lived for some time in Lausanne, and his history had a successful reception.

You would probably say that there is no apparent connection between these independent clauses. Your reaction would probably be justified, for these two clauses, at least out of context, are not closely related. You should avoid joining such clauses in a compound sentence unless your context makes clear the connection between them.

We can imagine such a context for the sample sentence:

> I can recall only two things about Edward Gibbon. Gibbon lived for some time in Lausanne, and his history had a successful reception.

But such a context is more the exception than the rule.

Sometimes writers form independent clauses into a compound sentence because the clauses are closely related in their minds. But they neglect to provide the information that would show readers how the clauses are related:

QUESTIONABLE: Gibbon was a captain in the South Hampshire militia, and he wrote insightfully about the fall of Constantinople.

Readers who know a good deal about Gibbon's life could supply the connection between the second clause and the first, but the writer does not make it. In most cases, however, readers would not know the connection, and the writer needs to inform them:

Gibbon was a captain in the South Hampshire militia, and this experience of men and war camps helped him write insightfully about the fall of Constantinople.

b. Illogical Relationships Between the Independent Clauses

Sometimes the problem with the clauses in a compound sentence is that they are related in a way different from the relationship signaled in the sentence:

ILLOGICAL: Some of Gibbon's adversaries hoped for dismal sales of his history, and it sold very well.

These clauses are related through contrast, and that relationship ought to be signaled properly:

Some of Gibbon's adversaries hoped for dismal sales of his history, *but* it sold very well.

c. Vague Relationships Between the Independent Clauses

When the coordinating conjunctions linking independent clauses are vague, they can produce ambiguity:

AMBIGUOUS: In 1793 Gibbon returned to England, and his health declined.

Does this sentence mean that Gibbon returned to England and later his health declined? Or does it mean that Gibbon returned to England and as a result his health declined? Without knowing more about the details of Gibbon's trip to England, one can only guess at the meaning. But if

42a
co

the *and* is supposed to carry the first meaning we mentioned, then that meaning should be made clear. Here is one way to do so:

> In 1793 Gibbon returned to England, and subsequently his health declined.

On the other hand, if *and* is supposed to carry the second meaning we mentioned, that meaning should be made clear:

> In 1793 Gibbon returned to England, and consequently his health declined.

Both of these revisions are compound sentences. Of course, the context of the original sentence may suggest that subordination is the better option. For example, if the information about Gibbon's return to England has preceded the sample sentence, you would probably want to subordinate that information when you bring it up again. If you originally intended *and* to mean *and subsequently,* you could revise and subordinate as follows:

subordinate clause   independent clause

After Gibbon returned to England in 1793, his health declined.

If, however, *and* was to mean *and consequently,* you could revise and subordinate in this way:

subordinate clause

Because Gibbon returned to England in 1793,

independent clause

his health declined.

**42a
co**

Whether you coordinate the clauses or subordinate one to the other, the point is that you should signal as precisely as possible how the clauses relate in meaning. Sometimes a coordinating conjunction (particularly *and*) is not the most precise signal.

d. Faulty Parallelism Between the Independent Clauses

According to the principle of parallelism, whenever you coordinate or compare elements, you should try to give them the same grammatical form. By and large, people think of parallelism in regard to coordinated or compared elements within one clause. But parallelism also applies to elements within the clauses of compound sentences. For example, if you write a compound sentence including two independent clauses, with each of these clauses having a compound direct object, you should try to make all the direct objects parallel in form:

> FAULTY PARALLELISM: We do not like *typing* and *editing,* but we do like *to read* and *to compose.*
>
> PARALLEL: We do not like *typing* and *editing,* but we do like *reading* and *composing.*

If you write a compound sentence in which the independent clauses are exactly or nearly parallel in all elements (they have the same kinds of units, equally long, in all grammatical slots), you have produced a balanced sentence. Here is one from Alice Walker:

> We look for signs in every strange event; we search for heroes in every unknown face.

Sometimes in balanced sentences writers introduce two terms in the first clause and then reverse the order of these terms in the second. This technique is called **chiasmus,** from *chi,* the name for the twenty-second letter of the Greek alphabet, which was symbolized by χ, suggesting a crossing over. Here is an example from John F. Kennedy:

> Let us never negotiate out of fear, but let us never fear to negotiate.

All balanced sentences, and especially those with chiasmus, convey a sense of orderly, poised, elegant completeness. They have a reflective turn and are thus often used to express general points or truths. Your challenge in writing compound sentences is not to let readers suspect that you could have balanced out the clauses within them better than you actually did.

**42a
co**

e. Too Many Compound Sentences Close to One Another

If you use several compound sentences, particularly balanced compound sentences, close to one another, your style might strike readers as artificial and even ponderous or monotonous. This passage, which we borrowed from Gibbon and altered, can give you a sense of the effect that a series of compound sentences can produce:

> It is not alone by the rapidity or extent of conquest that we should estimate the greatness of Rome, for the sovereign of the Russian deserts commands a larger portion of the globe. In the seventh summer after his passage of the Hellespont, Alexander erected the Macedonian trophies on the banks of the Hyphasis, and within less than a century, the irresistible Zingis, and the Mogul princes of his race, spread their cruel devastations and transient empire from the sea of China to the confines of Egypt and Germany. But the firm

edifice of Roman power was raised, and it was preserved by the wisdom of ages. The obedient provinces of Trajan and the Antonines were united by laws, and they were advanced by arts. They might occasionally suffer from the partial abuse of delegated authority, but the general principle of government was wise, simple, and beneficent. They enjoyed the religion of their ancestors, and in civil honours and advantages they were exalted, in just degrees, to an equality with their conquerors.

This is a paragraph of only moderate length, but you can sense from it what happens to style when a writer tries too hard for a balanced structure. Some readers even say that this paragraph has a singsong effect. Here is the way Gibbon wrote the paragraph:

It is not alone by the rapidity or extent of conquest that we should estimate the greatness of Rome. The sovereign of the Russian deserts commands a larger portion of the globe. In the seventh summer after his passage of the Hellespont, Alexander erected the Macedonian trophies on the banks of the Hyphasis. Within less than a century, the irresistible Zingis, and the Mogul princes of his race, spread their cruel devastations and transient empire from the sea of China to the confines of Egypt and Germany. But the firm edifice of Roman power was raised and preserved by the wisdom of ages. The obedient provinces of Trajan and the Antonines were united by laws and adorned by arts. They might occasionally suffer from the partial abuse of delegated authority; but the general principle of government was wise, simple, and beneficent. They enjoyed the religion of their ancestors, whilst in civil honours and advantages they were exalted, by just degrees, to an equality with their conquerors.

42a co

This paragraph shows a great deal of coordination, and at least one sentence comes close to being balanced. But Gibbon does not coordinate clauses nearly as much as we did in our alteration. You can learn from him to be cautious about using several compound sentences close to one another.

Exercise 2

Identify which of the compound sentences in the following passage illustrate one or more of the pitfalls described in **42a**. Then revise each of the flawed sentences.

EXAMPLE: Our history professor stressed that we should read Gibbon's *Decline and Fall,* but we read it in its entirety. [These clauses are related illogically. Possible revision: Our history professor stressed that we should read Gibbon's *Decline and Fall,* and we read it in its entirety.]

Our history professor stressed that we should read Gibbon's *Decline and Fall,* but we read it in its entirety. This history falls into two distinct parts, and it is coherent. Its coherence stems from its treatment of the Roman Empire as a single entity. Additionally, its coherence stems from its focus on how the Roman Empire gradually lost political and intellectual freedom.

A few of our fellow students read Gibbon too hurriedly, and they missed some of his best insights. They viewed the assignment with some distaste, and they read Gibbon extremely hastily. Most of us, however, read him with care and appreciation. We completed the assignment faithfully, and Gibbon wrote about the fall of Constantinople brilliantly. We were intrigued with his description of what he called "the triumph of barbarism and religion." We were fascinated by his treatment of Roman law. And we were amazed at his insight into religious sects. Reading this work took an enormous chunk out of our schedules, and completing the assignment was easily worth the time.

42b

Have You Coordinated Elements Within Clauses Effectively?

When coordinated elements within clauses give readers trouble, it is usually for one of the reasons we discuss in this section.

Order of Coordinated Elements

42b
co

Often writers coordinate parts of a clause without thinking about the order of those parts. As you review your drafts, you should pay attention to the elements that you coordinate and make sure that you have ordered them in the way that will be most meaningful and stylistically pleasing to readers.

One approach is to coordinate elements in the order in which they occurred. For instance, consider this sentence:

Samuel Johnson lived in Litchfield, Oxford, and London.

The order of the coordinated city names reflects the temporal order in which Johnson lived in these cities.

If a consideration of time does not affect coordinated elements, then you may want to list elements in climactic order, from less or least important to more or most important. Consider this sentence:

Disregarding the rules could result in death, a fine, or a scolding.

It seems almost ludicrous to end the sentence with *a scolding* rather than *death*. The following arrangement would be more effective:

> Disregarding the rules could result in a scolding, a fine, or death.

But what if you cannot discover some principle of time or importance to use in arranging coordinated elements? If they are all about equally long, then you can order them however you choose. For example:

> Johnson frequently conversed with Reynolds, Burke, and Goldsmith.

> Johnson frequently conversed with Burke, Goldsmith, and Reynolds.

Other variations, too, are possible, as long as one conversation did not precede the others and as long as one of these names is not more important in context than the others.

If the coordinated elements differ in length, however, you should arrange them from shorter to longer or from shortest to longest. This order is justified by the fact that longer elements usually carry more information than shorter ones and that you should try to get the most informative or important element in a sentence as close to the end as possible. If you were to find a sentence such as the following in a draft, you should ask yourself if the order of elements at the end of the sentence is justified:

> Johnson's essays are noted for their penetrating moral and literary insights, stylistic polish, and humor.

42b
co

Perhaps in some context this order reflects the importance of the elements for your purpose. In many contexts, however, these elements would all be equally important. Then you should choose the more graceful order of shortest element to longest:

> Johnson's essays are noted for their humor, stylistic polish, and penetrating moral and literary insights.

If possible, too, it is best to coordinate after the subject more often than within the subject, for then sentences will tend to move from shorter to longer elements. Of course, you will always want to conclude sentences with the information that is most important or that you want to expand on. But otherwise you should choose the more graceful order—like that in the first sentence below rather than in the second:

> Johnson's most famous works are *Rasselas,* the *Dictionary of the English Language,* and *The Lives of the English Poets.*
>
> *Rasselas,* the *Dictionary of the English Language,* and *The Lives of the English Poets* are Johnson's most famous works.

Exercise 3

Revise the sentences in which the coordinated elements are not arranged in the most justifiable order.

> EXAMPLE: Samuel Johnson was a critic, the greatest conversationalist of the eighteenth century, and an essayist.

Since there is no context to tell us whether Johnson's being an essayist is more important than the other references, we can revise the sentence so that it ends with the longest element:

> Samuel Johnson was a critic, an essayist, and the greatest conversationalist of the eighteenth century.

1. As a child, Johnson suffered from weak eyes and a tubercular infection in the glands of his neck.
2. Johnson's *Dictionary* surpassed earlier dictionaries in its apt citations of words and its bulk.
3. Some of Johnson's more memorable definitions are of *oats, excise,* and *pension.*
4. Johnson published *The Lives of the English Poets* in 1781, *Miscellaneous Observations on the Tragedy of Macbeth* in 1745, and an edition of Shakespeare in 1765.
5. Near the end of his life, Johnson was a victim of a paralytic stroke, asthma, and dropsy.

42b
co

2 Parallelism Between Coordinated Elements

Whenever you coordinate or compare elements within a clause, you should try to use the same kind of word, phrase, or clause. Doing so produces parallel structures (see **24e** and **24f**). These similarities in form call attention to similarities and differences in meaning. Here is a sentence lacking parallelism and clarity:

> FAULTY PARALLELISM: Johnson was a man with the ability to work rapidly but also tending to procrastinate badly.

If one introduces parallelism into this sentence, the sentence flows more smoothly and communicates its meaning more clearly:

> Johnson was a man with the ability to work rapidly but also the tendency to procrastinate badly.

The next example, from a modern literary critic, demonstrates how effective parallelism can be in the hands of a skillful writer:

> He [Sidney Hook] was humorless, but never petty; obstinate, but not malicious; domineering, but not self-centered. (Alfred Kazin)

Exercise 4

Revise the following sentences so that they exhibit proper parallelism.

> EXAMPLE: Johnson was a man of penetrating insights and who expressed himself vividly.
>
> Johnson was a man of penetrating insight and vivid expression.

1. The careers Johnson tried ranged from teaching to a writer.
2. Johnson's household showed his attempts to avoid solitude and at escaping melancholy.
3. *Rasselas* shows both how extensive Johnson's imagination was and the nature of his spiritual life.
4. In Johnson's view, actors should recite their lines with fitting gestures and modulating elegantly.
5. His method of quoting literary figures was more helpful than a hindrance.
6. Johnson's secretaries worked skillfully and with a great deal of care.
7. Johnson knew and had admiration for the ancient writers.
8. As a young man, Johnson earned some money by translating the classics for booksellers and through satires for the public.
9. Johnson wrote in favor of order in the state, guarded by and with the defense of citizens.
10. Johnson's life was filled with art, his art full of life.

3 Possible Ambiguities Within Coordinated Elements

As you review coordinated elements, you have to make sure that you do not leave ambiguities. Consider this sentence:

> Johnson frequently had great compassion for old men and women.

Does this sentence mean that Johnson had sympathy for old men and old women? Or does it mean that he had sympathy for old men but for women of various ages? If this sentence is supposed to have the first meaning, it would be better in this form:

> Johnson frequently had great compassion for old men and old women.

If the sentence is supposed to have the second meaning, it would be better in this form:

> Johnson frequently had great compassion for women and old men.

The next sentence, from one of our students, also has an ambiguity caused by coordinated elements:

> What about surgical removal of one cerebral hemisphere and language?

Surely the sentence does not mean what it says; "surgical removal of language" makes no sense. To carry the intended meaning, the sentence might be revised as follows:

> What effect will the surgical removal of one cerebral hemisphere have on a person's language capabilities?

Exercise 5

Each of the following sentences contains coordinated elements that can be read in more than one way. Describe at least two meanings for each sentence, and then revise each sentence to eliminate any ambiguity.

EXAMPLE: *Johnson and Boswell won a prize* could mean that they jointly won a prize or that each one won a prize. To convey the first meaning, we can revise as follows: *Johnson and Boswell together won a prize.* The second meaning can be conveyed as follows: *Johnson won a prize, as did Boswell.*

1. At one time, Johnson worked at translating and writing satires.
2. Samuel Johnson and Sir Joshua Reynolds wrote a book.
3. Members of the club offered critiques of poems and dramas.
4. Johnson apparently intended many of his works as instruction in morality and encouragement.
5. One member of the club called a long poem by Dryden partially logical and moral.

42b
co

4 Presentation and Punctuation of Coordinated Elements

If you coordinate two elements within a clause, you will usually need no punctuation between them:

INCORRECT: Toward the end of his life, Johnson enjoyed *fame, and a comfortable income.*

CORRECT: Toward the end of his life, Johnson enjoyed *fame and a comfortable income.*

In a few cases, you might choose to use a comma between two coordinated elements. The comma draws attention to the second coordinated element:

His habits were endearing, *and costly.*

You can also use a comma if you are contrasting two coordinated elements with the words *not . . . but:*

It was not Johnson, but Reynolds.

Finally, if the elements you coordinate—for example, two noun clauses—are long in themselves, you may choose to put a comma between them to help your readers keep them apart:

Johnson argued that his foe's proposal would be harmful to the system of education commonly used in England, and that the proposal could lead to a loss of intellectual freedom among people on several levels of society.

**42b
co**

If you coordinate three or more elements within a clause, usually you would present and punctuate them as *x, y,* and *z* (see also **32f**):

The members of the club enjoyed *civilized delights, food, and drink.*

It is journalistic practice to skip the second comma:

The members of the club enjoyed civilized delights, food and drink.

But we urge you to retain the second comma so that your readers will not be tempted to interpret *food and drink* as a unit, in this case a unit specifying what civilized delights the writer means. The original sentence means that members of the club enjoyed three different things or groups of things: (1) civilized delights, (2) food, and (3) drink. And to make sure that you convey that meaning, you should retain the second comma.

Should you ever present a series of coordinated items as *x and y and z and . . . ?* Here is a title from John Dewey:

The Child and the Curriculum and the School and the Society

The effect of this presentation is to give more emphasis to each individual reference. It is as if Dewey is saying, "In the matter of education, each one of these references is extremely important."

Another common effect of presenting a series of items in the form *x and y and z and . . .* is to suggest a piling up, a massing of things. Note this sentence by Donald Hall:

> Never before have men been exposed to so many words—written words, from newspapers and billboards and paperbacks and flashing signs and the sides of buses, and spoken words, from radio and television and loudspeakers.

Hall makes readers focus on each of the coordinated items in each series. And as the references pile up, the effect is to mirror what Hall is writing about—the masses of words that people are exposed to today.

Linking elements in a series with one *and* after another is not a strategy that you will want to use often, primarily because it is unusual enough to draw attention to itself. But used occasionally, for a special purpose, the strategy can be very effective.

Exercise 6

Write a sentence in which you present a series of elements using the formula *x and y and z and. . . .* Be as specific in your own mind as possible about the effect you hope the sentence will have on readers. Then take the sentence to your composition class and see whether your peers say that the sentence has the intended effect on them.

42b
co

43

H ere is part of a story written by a six-year-old:

> Maybe I could go back in dinosore time I maybe could go back in dinosore time and I was riding in a hot air balloon but a terodecklo poped my hot air balloon I jumped out I was so weak and I rode on a trisrotops he killed a tiranosores rex he was big I went back in my own time with the trisrotops my mom and dad let me keppe him

We hope that as this young writer grows older he never loses his whimsical imagination, adventurous spirit, and sense of voice. But he obviously must still master some skills involved in writing. One of these is knowing when to subordinate one clause to another. For example, the clause

I maybe could go back in dinosore time

should probably appear as one of the following:

If I could go back to dinosaur time
If I could

In this chapter, we ask you some questions about the material that you subordinate and do not subordinate in your drafts, and we also give you some guidelines for revising.

43a

Can You Identify Subordinate Elements?

1 Subordination as a Grammatical Relationship

Subordination is a grammatical relationship in which a word, phrase, or clause is dependent on another word, phrase, or clause. For this reason, subordinated elements are often called dependent elements. They cannot appear by themselves but have to be related to one or more other elements. Usually, they modify another element or function as single parts of speech do within sentences. The following clause is a subordinate clause:

After we decided to take a photography class

This clause cannot stand by itself. If a writer were to punctuate it as a separate sentence, readers would consider it a sentence fragment (see **22a**). Normally, such a subordinate clause is acceptable only when it is joined to an independent clause:

subordinate clause
After we decided to take a photography class,
independent clause
we examined some college catalogues.

2 Some Kinds of Subordinate Elements

Some very common subordinate elements are subordinate clauses, which come in three varieties. Adverbial clauses modify verbs, adjectives, adverbs, or independent clauses:

Since we considered ourselves excellent prospects, we applied only to top photography schools.

Adjective clauses modify nouns or pronouns:

The school *that we like best* is in New York.

And noun clauses function within sentences just like individual nouns:

What we applied for was a fellowship.

Some other subordinate structures are the various kinds of phrases, including absolute, participial, gerund, infinitive, and preposi-

43a
sub

tional phrases. Here are examples of a participial phrase and a gerund phrase, respectively:

> *Hoping to learn how to unleash our talents,* we were eager to be accepted into a top school.
>
> *Refining our talents* should be easy to do.

Still other subordinate elements are the appositives. These are nouns or noun phrases that appear after another noun or a pronoun in order to rename or further describe whom or what the noun or pronoun refers to:

> Georgia, *our leader,* was always the most confident of us all.

Finally, there are single-word modifiers, the adverbs and adjectives. In the preceding example, *confident* is an adjective, and *always* is an adverb.

As you move from the level of subordinate clauses down to the level of single-word modifiers—that is, as you move from a clause such as *After we decided to apply to a top school* through *After our decision* to *Afterward*—each subordinate structure respectively expresses less and less information explicitly. At the same time, each structure respectively presupposes more information. For example, once they have provided the proper context, writers could use *Afterward* instead of *After we decided to apply to a top school,* for the readers would be able to fill in the unstated information.

Exercise 1

**43a
sub**

Revise each of the following sentences by changing the subordinate element in italics to a shorter subordinate element.

> **EXAMPLE:** *If you want to build a camera obscura,* you will need a huge box.
>
> To build a camera obscura, you will need a huge box.

1. The words "camera obscura," *which mean "dark chamber,"* are appropriate.

2. A camera obscura is a huge box *that has a tiny opening in one side.*

3. On the side of the box opposite the opening, the light forms an inverted image of the scene *that is outside the box.*

4. *Because it is large enough for a person to enter,* the camera obscura is sometimes used by artists as an aid in sketching.

5. *The outline of the image formed inside the box having been traced,* the artists can color in the picture.

3 Common Functions of Subordinate Elements

In general, subordinate elements move information out of the foreground and into the background of readers' attention. A sentence with subordinate elements uses its form to direct readers how to attend to its parts. Subordinate elements, the form implies, deserve somewhat less attention. This general principle should become clearer as we consider the kinds of information that subordinate elements typically convey.

a. Old Information

Many subordinate elements convey old information (see **38f**). A typical example appears in this short passage:

> We applied for admission to several top schools as early in the academic year as October. Although we applied very early, we were not admitted until five months later.

In the second sentence, the subordinate clause *Although we applied very early* conveys old information.

One important question to ask about subordinate elements that convey old information is whether they are needed. In the passage above, for instance, the second sentence could appear without the subordinate clause and still be properly understood:

> However, we were not admitted until five months later.

The answer to this question depends on rhetorical situations. Writers might keep the subordinate clause if they need to provide a fairly large stepping-stone from one sentence to the next for their readers. But otherwise, they would do better to replace the subordinate clause with *however*.

**43a
sub**

b. Information About Interpretive Frameworks

Some subordinate elements carry information about the framework in which the main point should be interpreted or evaluated:

> *If people were to judge our photographs from the perspective of painting,* they would miss the essence of our work.

c. Background Information

Many subordinate elements convey information that writers consider to be background information. This information may be interesting, entertaining, and enriching, but it is not what writers want their readers to focus on at a particular point in a passage. Consider the following sentences:

> Edward Steichen, who was a member of the Photo-Secession group, never colored his photographic images. He promoted photography as an independent art form.

In this context, the subordinate clause *who was a member of the Photo-Secession group* carries information that the writer wishes to place in the background relative to the information about not coloring pictures and about photography as an independent art form.

However, what is in the background in one context might need to be in the foreground in another. In discussing schools of photography, a writer might want to express the information about the Photo-Secession group in an independent clause:

> *Edward Steichen, who never colored his photographic images, was a member of the Photo-Secession group.* He opposed the work of the pictorial photographers.

Through subordinate elements, you can convey all kinds of background information, including information that shows times, qualifications, causes, manners, conditions, reasons, and the like. You will be able to decide what should be in the foreground and what should be in the background only if you keep your purpose for a piece of writing clearly in mind.

Exercise 2

**43a
sub**

Use subordination to combine all the clauses in each of the following groups into one sentence. Make the italicized clause in each group the main clause of the sentence. You may have to alter some words.

> EXAMPLE: *We often compared ourselves to artists.*
> These artists had broadened people's conceptions of photographic possibilities.
>
> We often compared ourselves to artists who had broadened people's conceptions of photographic possibilities.

1. *Margaret Bourke-White photographed many dramatic events for illustrated magazines.*
These magazines appeared during the 1930s.

2. Henri Cartier-Bresson used a miniature camera.
He was able to photograph people at important but fleeting moments in their lives.

3. *Dorothea Lange's documentary photographs aroused concern about the plight of migrant farmworkers.*
Many of these photographs are now preserved in the Library of Congress.

4. Richard Margolis uses special lighting techniques to photograph landscapes.
He is an American photographer.
His landscapes look deeply mysterious.

5. Color film has been commercially produced since 1935.
Color film was not widely used by professional photographers until the 1970s.
In the 1970s photographers such as Marie Losindas used color film for still lifes and portraits.

43b

Have You Avoided Some Common Problems with Subordination?

1 Failing to Subordinate Old and Background Information

One error that writers make is failing to subordinate what is obviously old or background information in context. Consider these sentences:

> I ran out of film and decided to go to the photography store for more. I went to the photography store, and I found that all the good film was gone.

43b
sub

The first clause in the second sentence conveys primarily old information. It is possible that because of some aspect of the situation in which these sentences will be used, this old information is necessary. But this old information does not seem important enough to be expressed in an independent clause. This sequence of sentences should probably be revised as follows:

> I ran out of film and decided to go to the photography store for more. When I got there, I found that all the good film was gone.

Consider another sequence of sentences:

> Edward Steichen never colored his photographic images. He was born in 1879. He promoted photography as an independent art form.

Compared to the information in the other sentences, the information in the second sentence seems to belong in the background. In fact, it seems to belong so far in the background that you might wonder whether it should be expressed at this point. But in some contexts— for example, a context in which you are tracing the history of photography as an independent art form—you might decide to include it. In that case, you might subordinate it as follows:

> Edward Steichen, who was born in 1879, never colored his photographic images. He promoted photography as an independent art form.

Exercise 3

Revise the following paragraph by subordinating whatever is obviously old or background information in context.

> **EXAMPLE:**   The second sentence begins with an independent clause: *We applied to these schools early.* In context, this clause expresses old information. Possible revision: *Since we applied to these schools so early, we expected to have our applications acknowledged.*

We applied to several top schools very early in the academic year. We applied to these schools early, and we expected to have our applications acknowledged. But for many months we heard from no schools. Finally, we started to receive rejection notices. These were obviously form letters. We began to wonder how so many different schools could overlook our stellar qualifications. We decided that these schools were using faulty criteria in the admissions process. We decided this, and we expected better news in the future. Finally, we received a letter from a school offering admission to all of us. This school was in Nevada. We were happy with everything about the letter except the news that our admission was conditional on our taking some classes in basic photographic techniques. The school placed this condition on us, but we accepted the offer of admission.

43b
sub

2 Illogical Subordination

Illogical subordination often involves introducing adverb clauses with a subordinating word that signals an illogical relationship between the adverb clause and an independent clause:

> **ILLOGICAL:**   Because the battery in her camera was low, the shutter still worked properly.

This sentence makes the claim that a low battery caused the shutter to work properly. But anyone who knows something about battery-powered cameras realizes that there is no cause-effect relationship between these two clauses. The clauses should be related as follows:

> *Although* the battery in her camera was low, the shutter still worked properly.

3 Thwarted Subordination

Thwarted subordination occurs when a writer uses *and* or *but* before a subordinate clause linked to part of an independent clause:

> **THWARTED:**   They decided to try the new color film, and which had just become available.

The *and* before the subordinate clause thwarts initial attempts by readers to relate these clauses properly. As the example stands, it is not grammatical. To revise such a sentence, drop the *and:*

> They decided to try the new color film, which had just become available.

4 Vague or Ambiguous Subordination

Vague or ambiguous subordination is the result of introducing a subordinate element, usually a clause, with a word that can be interpreted in more than one way. One such word is *as:*

> **VAGUE OR AMBIGUOUS:**   As Escher was focusing on the structure, he tripped.

Does this mean "when Escher was focusing" or "because Escher was focusing"? As the sentence stands here, no one can tell how the *as* should be interpreted.

If you find such a sentence in a draft, you should revise it in either of these ways so that your meaning is clear:

> When Escher was focusing on the structure, he tripped and fell.

> Because Escher was focusing on the structure, he tripped and fell.

Some other subordinators that can produce vagueness or ambiguity are *along the lines of, being as, in terms of, since,* and *while.*

43b
sub

5   Excessive Subordination

Excessive subordination usually means that subordinate elements contain unimportant or irrelevant information:

EXCESSIVE: Before leaving for photography school, I packed
             my new camera, plenty of film, and my leather
             camera bag, which my great-aunt Dorthea gave me
             for my twelfth birthday.

In some contexts, perhaps, the information about the writer's great-aunt Dorthea and the twelfth birthday might be worth including. But in many contexts it will not be needed:

Before leaving for photography school, I packed my new
camera, plenty of film, and my leather camera bag.

Another problem is subordinating so much different information within one sentence that the sentence seems unfocused:

EXCESSIVE: If I could afford a new camera, I would do some
             serious work in wildlife photography as long as I
             could get time off work and although I would
             need some additional training before I could be
             considered an original talent.

One way to bring some order into such a mass of clauses is to break the whole structure into two or more sentences:

If I could afford a new camera and could get time off work, I
would do some serious work in wildlife photography. Before I
could be considered an original talent, though, I would need
some additional training.

The kind of excessive subordination that confuses readers the most, perhaps, involves several adjective clauses piled up at the end of a sentence:

EXCESSIVE: They tried a photographic technique that they had
             learned in a class that has been offered at several
             institutions that are scattered around the part of
             the country that people consider the Southeast.

Some sentences of this sort are virtually impossible to understand. Others are understandable but end with information that is only remotely related to the information with which they begin. Usually, you can

43b
sub

revise such sentences by omitting irrelevant details and shortening some subordinate clauses to phrases:

> They tried a photographic technique that they had learned in a class offered at several institutions scattered around the Southeast.

Exercise 4

Revise the following paragraph by correcting all the errors in subordination.

> EXAMPLE: So that we had taken a course in photography, our photographs seemed fuzzy.
>
> Although we had taken a course in photography, our photographs seemed fuzzy.

So that we had taken a course in photography, our photographs seemed fuzzy. This fuzziness was frustrating to us since we worked hard to focus our camera lenses precisely. Sometimes we would focus on a subject, look away briefly, and then focus again. But many of our photographs still seemed somewhat unclear and fuzzy. Finally, we decided to ask one of our teachers to help us as we were struggling with this problem. She asked us to describe the decisions we made as we prepared to expose the film. She discovered that we did not think about the size of the aperture, and which is the opening controlling the amount of light that strikes the film. She recommended that we always select an appropriate aperture size, which will affect the depth of field, which is an area of sharpness, which extends in front of and behind the point of focusing, which we had shown a little skill in selecting.

43c

Have You Presented Subordinated Material Appropriately?

1 Adverbial Elements

Many adverbial elements can appear in several different places within a sentence:

> *Later* we decided against their proposal.
> We *later* decided against their proposal.
> We decided *later* against their proposal.
> We decided against their proposal *later*.

Writers would need to select the sentence that best suits their purpose in context, but all these forms are grammatical.

Many adverbial clauses can also appear in more than one position in a sentence:

> *After we considered it thoroughly,* we decided against their proposal.

> We, *after we considered it thoroughly,* decided against their proposal.

> We decided against their proposal *after we considered it thoroughly.*

Mostly, though, adverbial clauses appear first or at least early in sentences. These clauses usually express old or background information, and the beginning of a sentence is where such information typically appears.

However, some adverbial clauses are subordinated not because their information is old or not very important, but because writers typically subordinate information that stands in certain logical relationships to other information. For instance, information about the conditions for an action is usually subordinated to information about the action itself:

> *If you pose for me,* I will create a photograph with excellent balance among line, space, and tone.

If the subordinated information is the most important in a sentence, the adverbial clause containing it can be placed at the end:

> I will create a photograph with excellent balance between line, space, and tone if you pose for me.

When deciding where to place an adverbial clause, you generally have to consider the context you have built up. For example, if in context you are stressing information about kinds of equipment, you should write

> The price is $500 if you want the telephoto lens.

But if you are stressing information about prices, the following sequence would be more appropriate:

> If you want the telephoto lens, the price is $500.

Exercise 5

For each of the following sentences, write a question to which the particular sentence would be an appropriate response. The questions should focus on the information expressed at the end of the sentences. Feel free to modify the sentences that appear here if that seems necessary.

EXAMPLE: *We will discuss printing color film tomorrow* is a good response to *When will we discuss printing color film?*

1. We will try some wide-angle lenses later.
2. Later we will try some wide-angle lenses.
3. We must mix the chemicals properly this time.
4. This time we must mix the chemicals properly.
5. They checked the film with great care.
6. With great care they checked the film.
7. The film will be ruined if you turn on the light.
8. If you turn on the light, the film will be ruined.
9. We came over to the darkroom because you called.
10. Because you called, we came over to the darkroom.

2 Adjectival Elements

Adjectival elements generally occur as close to the word they modify as possible. Nevertheless, some adjectival elements are almost as mobile as many adverbial elements:

Glowing with satisfaction, the class members examined the photographs.

The class members, *glowing with satisfaction,* examined the photographs.

The class members examined the photographs, *glowing with satisfaction.*

43c
sub

Writers can select the form that best suits their purpose in context. They need to be aware, though, that the last form would not work if photographs could glow with satisfaction.

Unlike the phrases in the examples above, adjective clauses always appear after the words they modify. Most writers try to place them immediately after the word they modify. Occasionally, you might see a sentence with a word or two between an adjective clause and what it modifies:

QUESTIONABLE: The camera is lost that I liked the best.

Such a sentence is likely to raise questions, so it would be better to revise it:

The camera that I liked the best is lost.

If writers separate an adjective clause from what it modifies by more than two words, they make it very hard for their readers to interpret the sentence:

> **VERY QUESTIONABLE:**   The camera will probably never be found that I liked the best.

Many readers would call such a sentence ungrammatical.

Exercise 6

Combine all the clauses in each of the following groups into one sentence. Use the first clause in each group as an independent clause and turn the other sentences into subordinate adjectival elements. Experiment with different kinds of adjectival elements and different positions for them.

> **EXAMPLE:**   We left the classroom with several cameras. The cameras had been donated to the school.
>
> We left the classroom with several cameras that had been donated to the school.

1. We hiked to a part of campus.
That part of campus was deserted.
That part of campus seemed forlorn.
That part of campus was called "the speakers' corner."

2. The instructor asked us for ideas.
The instructor wanted ideas about fundamental concerns in photographing the speakers' corner.
The instructor looked somewhat impatient.

3. One student offered an answer.
She took a deep breath.
The answer was that we should seek striking contrasts between light and shadow.

4. Another student proposed a different idea.
This student was standing in the rear of our group.
His idea was that we should integrate form and feeling in the photographic texture.

5. The instructor was looking for a different response.
He was shaking his head back and forth with dismay.
The response centered on focusing the camera properly.

43c
sub

3 Nouns, Noun Phrases, and Noun Clauses

Generally, when nouns and noun phrases appear in sentences as appositives, they immediately follow another noun or a pronoun. As noted earlier (**17e**), appositives identify further what that noun or pronoun refers to. Here is an example:

> Our photography instructor, *Dr. Fernsehen,* seemed able to see things that we could not.

Noun clauses function within sentences as individual nouns do—as subjects, direct objects, and the like:

noun clause as subject

What the instructor wanted first was technical skill.

noun clause as direct object

The instructor demanded that we practice our technique.

Exercise 7

Write a noun clause to replace each of the italicized nouns and noun phrases in the following sentences.

> **EXAMPLE:**   *Her suggestion* was helpful.
> What she suggested was helpful.

1. The instructor then inquired about *our thoughts.*
2. Is the focal point in a scene *an obvious feature to all onlookers?*
3. Would one photographer necessarily agree with *another's choice?*
4. *Our ultimate response* showed that in some ways we were moving beyond our instructor.
5. Our instructor saw *our learning* as impressive.

4 **Using Cumulative Sentences Skillfully**

43c
sub

When you compose a sentence in which you express a main clause first and then follow it with subordinate elements, you are writing a **cumulative,** or loose, **sentence.** Technically, if you end a sentence with only one subordinate element, you have produced a cumulative sentence. But most people reserve this name for the sentences that end with two, three, or more subordinated elements. The modifying elements accumulate at the end. Here are two examples, with the subordinate elements in italics:

> We would become more skilled photographers *if we learned to interpret contours better and if we became better able to capture the free play of light.*

> Some of our peers were very careless, *jumping to conclusions, selecting improper shutter speeds, forgetting to seek the abstract essence of a scene.*

If you practice with various kinds of cumulative sentences, your stylistic repertoire will grow enormously. Cumulative sentences have a natural flow like that of sentences in natural conversation. They work especially well, therefore, to break up a passage in which the rhythm threatens to become monotonous. They also will help you make a point and then refine and sharpen it at the end of a sentence, the part of a sentence that readers focus on most intently.

However, if you really pile up the subordinate elements at the end of a sentence, you can obscure readers' focus, not sharpen it. And as with all slightly unusual structures in prose, you should not use so many cumulative sentences that you call attention to what you are doing.

If you use cumulative sentences to sharpen or elaborate points, readers can see a cumulative sentence every page or so and not think that you are overdoing it. In fact, they will probably come to view your style as mature and skillful.

Exercise 8

Add subordinate elements to the end of each of the following independent clauses. Experiment with different kinds of subordinate elements in different orders.

    EXAMPLE: We made a decision.

               We made a decision, casting aside all advice to be cautious, trusting our own emotions and intuitions.

1. We announced our decision to our classmates.
2. We were going to produce a show of our photographs.
3. Our classmates looked a little surprised.
4. We began to seek sponsors for our show.
5. We were ready to face the critics' judgments.

43c
sub

5   Using Periodic Sentences Skillfully

In a **periodic sentence,** the predication of the main clause is not completed until the very end of the sentence. In one kind of periodic sentence, subordinate elements, sometimes several subordinate elements, precede the main clause:

Reclining in chairs near the entrance to the gallery, casting nonchalant glances toward those viewing our photographs, six of us waited for the critics' evaluations.

In another kind of periodic sentence, the first part of the main clause (usually the subject) appears, then one or more subordinate elements appear, and finally the verb and complements of the main clause appear at the end:

> The two critics, conceding that we might have grand artistic visions and that we certainly knew how to talk about contours, contrasts, and creativity, said that our pictures showed serious technical flaws.

As you can sense, the effect of a periodic sentence is very different from that of a cumulative sentence. A periodic sentence puts off completing the main point until its end. But when the main point does come, it comes with a good deal of force.

Periodic sentences work especially well when you want to create suspense, when you want to draw special attention to a point, or when you want to mirror the process of discovering or working out an idea. If you are aiming for such an effect, use a periodic sentence. If not, hold off on periodic sentences. They are more unusual in structure and more difficult to read than cumulative sentences.

Exercise 9

Write two periodic sentences, one that creates suspense and surprises readers at its end and another that mirrors the process of solving a difficult problem.

**43c
sub**

X

THE RESEARCH REPORT AND WRITING IN DISCIPLINES

44

C O N D U C T I N G

P R I M A R Y   A N D

S E C O N D A R Y

R E S E A R C H

44a

General Procedures for Researching

1 Defining Research

Researching, evaluating, and writing are all investigative processes. Consequently, researching requires the same learning skills that you use to evaluate issues and to write documents. But researching also requires you to go beyond your intuitions and your present knowledge. It means discovering facts and searching for the bases of views and assessments. It requires preparation: determining the subject, audience, objective, and scope for the research project and figuring out what and how much information you need. It also means ferreting out reputable sources, ideas, and evidence and comparing them in order to arrive at perceptive interpretations. Once you have marshaled your material, you need to outline, draft, and revise your research project.

Regardless of their field, active researchers refer to any ventures that lead them to greater understanding of data and phenomena as "doing research." They try to unravel problems by collecting information: They speculate from experience or study other researchers' descriptions, explanations, and conclusions. The raw data—or first-hand information—that they accumulate is routinely called **primary information** and includes findings amassed from experiments, observations, interviews, surveys, and the like. It is unanalyzed information, typically recorded in journals and notebooks or consisting of tape-recorded interviews or unedited transcripts. **Secondary information** is categorized, appraised data and typically includes judgments published in books, brochures, essays, reports, manuals, and dissertations.

From primary and secondary data, researchers fashion tentative resolutions to situations or issues and then proceed to test these hypotheses. Doing primary research requires the same mastery of critical thinking needed to identify and solve almost any problem, and gauging secondary research demands the same acute critical reading skills required for college courses and professional life. Hence, one way to look at research is to realize that whenever you read, ask questions, debate ideas, or write about a subject, you are doing research. Likewise, every time you research, you are applying your systematic critical thinking and reading skills.

2 Self-Initiated Research

When you say to yourself "Gee, I'd like to know more about that," you are aspiring to research. Issues and upsetting concerns are everywhere around you, demanding attention. You start asking questions about an event such as *Why did this occur this way at this time? How did this happen? How many times could it happen again? Who was involved in the event and why did some people seem to be more important than others? What is its significance as an event or phenomenon? How does it compare with similar phenomena? Does it have any broader significance?* The bothersome aspects pique your curiosity, and, after you have exhausted what you know about the issue, you go to other sources—either knowledgeable people or printed material—looking for informed explanations. This is self-initiated research of questions you raise. These questions can vary from the mundane to the cosmic and can pertain to disciplines as diverse as the theoretical and laboratory sciences, behavioral sciences, and the humanities.

44a
psr

3 Assigned Research

You probably will face a situation or question that someone else thinks is important, and you will need to find an answer that resolves the problem with reasoned, supportable arguments. This type of research in colleges is familiar to anyone who has written a laboratory report or library report and in industry to anyone who has grappled with a feasibility memorandum, proposal, technical description, analysis, or conference report. You will find that research documents typically fall into one of three very broad categories: explanatory reviews, evaluative arguments, and explanation-evaluation reports.

Explanatory Reviews

Explanatory reviews explain published research, opinions, or facts on a specified topic. These reviews are valuable only if the writer has identified the most important investigations on a topic and interpreted these investigations in ways that highlight any salient connections or controversies. Explanatory reviews report currently accepted wisdom on a topic and are invaluable to researchers needing quick overviews of a subject.

Evaluative Arguments

Evaluative arguments propose a problem and argue for a particular solution or complex of solutions. Evaluative arguments present the writer's perspective, and their relevance lies directly in a writer's ability to persuade. For example, as a scholar in political science, you might decide that Americans are still divided along the political lines that separated the Union from the Confederacy, and this thesis would become the central argument of a series of articles that you planned to write. Or you might want to point out to the National Science Foundation that your original grant was only "seed money" and that you need more funding to complete your investigations. Your implied thesis—that the NSF should extend your grant—is based on your evaluation and requires a detailed, factual argument to be convincing.

Explanation-Evaluation Reports

44a
psr

Most of the time, research reports merge explanation and evaluation: They propose a problem, critique relevant research on it, and argue for a solution based on a combination of accepted wisdom, primary and secondary research, and innovative argumentation. The explanation sections of both the Civil War articles and the statement to the NSF would acquire an objective tone from a fair review of sources that both support and oppose contemporary positions. Not every college professor or student believes that the Civil War was that important, and many researchers heatedly debate—among themselves and in print—the value of certain research projects. A study that combines explanation and evaluation is both objective and persuasive. Most readers expect balanced arguments and are positively influenced by writers who offer both explanations and sufficient primary or secondary research.

4 Researching and Writing

Because researching and writing up your research follow the same fundamental processes of inventing, drafting, revising, and publishing, the same premises and advice presented in Chapters 6 through 12 hold true. Whatever type of writing you have to do, you need to prepare adequately, think imaginatively, and confirm your hunches. But research writing has a few twists that do not apply to essay writing. It requires additional approaches to gathering ideas: for example, consolidating a series of experiments, interviewing experts, compiling bibliographies, and conducting secondary research.

As you are drafting your research report, you may find that you need to interview one more expert, gather more information or update some of it, or perhaps check the procedures on your experiment one more time. You may also find yourself skipping some of the steps that you would normally follow when drafting an essay. For example, as you gather your research, you may unconsciously shape that information into a plan and arrange your notes into an informal outline. Thus, you may omit a formal outline because you have already organized the material.

Furthermore, in research writing you have to keep careful records of whose ideas you are using, whose words you are citing, and where others can find the sources. Inadequate documentation can lead readers to conclude that your report is sloppy or, worse still, plagiarized.

44b

Conducting Primary Research

1 Observation

Observation is the most basic way of gathering firsthand information and the initial step of researchers' scientific method. As you watch people interact, plants or animals function, or machinery or processes operate, you gain greater understanding of the activity. And, as you question why people act the way they do, what significance certain plant or animal behavior has, or what goes into a certain process, you are evaluating what you have seen and generalizing from your observations. Observing is relatively easy, but evaluating what you observe is more difficult because you have to decide what you can ignore and what you should focus on. The real talent you need for successful observation is knowing what to question.

This talent evolves as you gain experience with an issue or field of study. However, even trained investigators sometimes miss obvious questions. The discovery of penicillin is a case in point. Early twentieth-century biologists, searching for a cure for infectious diseases, were baffled because their cultures kept getting contaminated by a mold. Years passed before Alexander Fleming thought to ask the obvious: What was the mold and how did it affect the cultures? His questions and insights changed other scientists' perception of the problem and eventually led him to penicillin.

Firsthand observation affords researchers several advantages. You are present for an event and can record exactly what you see. You can also observe particular environments and note when conditions vary. But firsthand observation has disadvantages as well. Since the soundness of any observation depends on the perspective of the observer, one observer's report will likely differ from another's. Multiple witnesses to an accident, for instance, rarely give identical reports. Furthermore, you may not be able to get permission to observe some people or organizations, or to control the circumstances of a phenomenon or the amount of data it suggests. And your presence may change the dynamics of the situation or the participants' actions, which may lead you to ask unsuitable questions. When you use firsthand observation in your research, plan thoroughly: Pick your location and time with care, secure necessary authorizations, keep meticulous records, and resist the temptation to interpret as you observe.

2 Experimentation

Observation leads directly to a second type of primary research, experimentation. Once you have observed something and speculated about how and why it happens, you will want to design a trial that tests and verifies the links between the observed phenomena and your preliminary speculations or hypotheses. To design and carry out satisfactory experiments, you will need inventiveness, patience, and, more than likely, help from others in the discipline. Although there is no single best outline for designing experiments, you should be aware that with any experiment you need to take three standard elements into account: constants, variables, and parameters.

A **constant** is a factor, condition, or quality in any specified circumstances that maintains the same value. A **variable** is a phenomenon, subject to change, that an experimenter wants to measure. A **parameter** is an arbitrary constant, one that has a particular value for a given experiment but may have a different value in another design. For example, in an atmospheric experiment, one constant would be the presence of gas; the variables could be the measurable air pressure or

44b
psr

barometric pressure because they differ in degrees; and the parameter could be the time of the experiment (for example, between the hours of 10:00 A.M. and 10:00 P.M., June 5, 1992) or the temperature (for example, between 7° C and 37° C). Even some studies in the humanities and literature use constants, variables, and parameters. A historical study of a word such as *you* would set that specific word as the constant. The parameter might be Shakespeare's play *As You Like It,* a comedy written as Middle English faded completely into Modern English, and different grammatical forms of the word *(you, ye)* or its different syntactic placements (for instance, as subject, direct object, or predicate noun) might be the variables. Identifying constants, variables, and parameters is vital to any experiment, for modifications or imprecisions in these elements can critically affect the accuracy of the test results—and, therefore, your reliability as a researcher.

The purpose of an experiment is to measure the variables of a constant within stipulated parameters. But something can always go awry and force you to redesign the experiment or redefine the constants, variables, or parameters. Yet with all its challenges and dilemmas, experimentation is the most convincing type of primary research that can be presented as evidence for a perspective. You are performing the research, rigidly overseeing the procedures governing it, and meticulously recording and reporting its results.

However, the advantages of experimentation also point to its drawbacks. At best, you are making a good guess and then testing and retesting that guess. Errors can creep into even the most controlled experiments, causing undetected flaws in the test that can frustrate the results. Even more troublesome is the urge, felt by many investigators, to work longer on the experiment than on the writing. Too much time spent creating experiments or replicating those of others can defeat the purpose of gathering information.

3 Interviews, Surveys, and Questionnaires

44b
psr

One of the most common ways people learn is by asking others for information. One version of this type of research is the interview. An interviewer's goal is to transmit information from a source to others whom it might interest. To obtain that information, an interviewer must ask pertinent, well-researched questions and follow the respondent's answers with additional questions. Hence, before asking their first questions, interviewers should know their respondent's upbringing and training, current interests and vocational duties, career plans and personal aspirations, and, if possible, biases. Knowing this background also has a benefit for you as a writer: It not only helps you decide what questions you should ask, but—given your respondent's answers—also suggests various avenues you can take when you write the results of your exchange.

Designing an interview means learning something about secondary research. For example, you can find common background information on a topic or expert in the *Encyclopedia Americana, Encyclopaedia Britannica, Collier's Encyclopedia,* or any general readership encyclopedia that features signed articles. Try specialized encyclopedias, almanacs, atlases, biographical dictionaries, government documents, statistical yearbooks, and bibliographies for more specific information. (Selected listings of such materials appear later in this chapter, on pages 683–687.) When you have exhausted these resources, check bibliographies that index essays and research documents (see pages 687–691). You can find quick summaries on notable people in the *Who's Who* series (for example, *Who's Who in America, Who's Who in Finance and Industry, Who's Who of American Women,* and *Who's Who of Medical Specialists.* For the most current material, go through newspaper indexes such as the *New York Times Index, Los Angeles Times, Wall Street Journal,* or the *Washington Post.* Finally, ask other practitioners in the discipline or reference librarians at your college or public library—professionals willing to help anyone who is serious about research.

Steps in Conducting Interviews

- Investigate your subject thoroughly.
- Make an appointment in advance with your interviewee at his or her convenience. Identify yourself and the nature of your research when setting up the appointment. Ask if the interviewee minds being tape-recorded.
- Prepare your questions. Keep them short, and don't be afraid to ask for further information.
- Appear on time for the interview. Dress appropriately, and bring a tape recorder or paper and pen. Start with easy questions that show your research and interest in the topic, gain the interviewee's trust in you, and guide the interview. Move to tougher questions, and end with ones that signal a conclusion. Use a matter-of-fact tone.
- Leave when the interviewee has had enough. Thank him or her, and offer to send copies of your report after it is written.

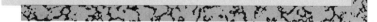

Surveys and questionnaires are also forms of interviewing. Social scientists and political pollsters conduct numerous telephone queries and one-on-one conversations with people at voting precincts, shopping centers, and other public facilities. Their questions survey respondents' immediate reactions, including potentially meaningful nonverbal behaviors, and permit them to interact—though briefly—with each respondent. By means of questionnaires, which are forms sent to selected respondents seeking their answers to a set of questions, researchers can collect abundant data about a society's overall preferences and prejudices without having to question an entire population.

As forms of primary research, interviews, surveys, and questionnaires have various advantages and disadvantages. Interviews, for instance, are remarkably flexible because you control the questions and can switch directions or topics quickly if you see changes in your respondent's answers and nonverbal behaviors. This flexibility—along with people's natural willingness to talk more than needed—lets you glean more information from an interview than from observation or experimentation. But an interview is only as successful as your preparation. You need to do some investigating beforehand so that you are knowledgeable about the particular subject. Moreover, interviews take up time and may tax your interviewee's good will if the two of you do not get along. Hence, coordination and rapport are also essential. The same holds true for surveys and questionnaires: They provide substantive information for a researcher only if they are carefully designed and measure consistently and completely what they claim to measure.

Developing a survey or questionnaire parallels the writing process in some ways: You brainstorm ideas based on the information you want to survey (your topic), propose and arrange different questions (your initial draft), and restructure and rearrange those questions as you rethink your purposes in gathering the information (your revised drafts).

Questionnaires use two basic types of questions: objectively scored questions, which yield succinct data that can be easily compared with other data, and open-ended questions, which ask for opinions rather than countable information. Objectively scored questions are easily standardized, so you can put the details you collect into tables. But although such questions are less complicated to analyze and report, they do not give you as much evaluative information as open-ended questions. On the other hand, open-ended questions can leave you with unusable data if the questions are confusing or if they ask the people completing your questionnaire for information that they do not have.

It is best, therefore, to test the questionnaire before using it to collect information. Ask yourself what the questionnaire is supposed to

44b
psr

find out, how in-depth the information needs to be, how clearly you have asked for this information, and how well the people answering the questionnaire will know this information. You should also consider whether the people you question will be relying on their memories or their immediate observations. Memories always change more rapidly than direct observations; consequently, information based on memories may seem less valid in your report.

44c

Conducting Secondary Research

1 Initiating Library Reports

Primary research can be engrossing, particularly when you uncover something no one else has yet noticed. However, secondary research—analyzing and integrating other researchers' primary data—is the backbone of most research. Research documents generally combine primary and secondary research because the projects they report on require information from both sources. For instance, essays printed in journals ranging from *The Journal of the American Medical Association* to *The Journal of Verbal Learning and Verbal Behavior* and *Research in the Teaching of English* routinely begin by introducing necessary background information or reviewing pertinent literature. These commentaries and critiques are examples of secondary research. As introductions to a research writer's perspective, they prove to readers that the writer is qualified to debate a topic. Literature or background reviews display the writer's knowledge of the topic and show that the writer has taken these findings and conclusions into consideration before writing down his or her perspective. For these reasons, knowing how to conduct secondary research is vital for any academic or professional pursuit.

44c
psr

If you are unfamiliar with library resources, conducting secondary research for a library report can be a daunting experience. The best way to face any library report is with a plan and the equipment necessary to accomplish that plan. (See page 696 for a suggested schedule.) Gather together a notebook or note cards to keep your materials organized, pencils or pens, paper clips, rubber bands, and a supply of change for the copying machines. Schedule enough time for your search, and begin your investigations early. If your library does not own the particular book, journal, or document you need, you may be able to get it from another library. But securing interlibrary loans—borrowing documents from another library—takes time. Most serious researchers scan dozens of articles, reports, and books and spend several days—not just a few hours—before finding what they need to write an acceptable report. Expect to look at twenty-five to fifty sources and to spend more than two working days in the library. Whether your report is due in two weeks, two months, or two years, start it the day you get the assignment. Remember that doing secondary research means capitalizing on critical reading skills and that part of critical reading is allowing yourself time to make the material intelligible. So budget your time and energies carefully.

Above all, be willing to persevere, because you may not find exactly what you are seeking on your first try. Consider yourself a detective who knows what the issue is but wants to know the motive (why it occurs), means (how it occurs), and opportunity (under what conditions it occurs). Don't be afraid to ask a librarian for help. Librarians are veteran researchers, and reference librarians in particular are expert at finding information. Nevertheless, because you are the research writer, you are responsible for locating sufficient resources, evaluating them, summarizing or paraphrasing their details, and avoiding any suggestion of plagiarism.

2 Secondary Sources in the Library

Listing every resource available to you in a library is beyond the scope of this or any handbook. The amount of information is too vast. Librarians, for example, review sources and bibliographies and answer countless inquiries every day about an incredible variety of subjects. Yet even the most expert librarian does not know everything in a library. Therefore, we can give you only an overview of the basics of secondary research: the card catalog system, standard reference resources, general and some specialized indexes, government documents, and some of the on-line computer data bases. Librarians can always fill you in on more specialized resources.

Card Catalog

Library Classification Systems

Libraries categorize and shelve books and journals by subject, using either the Dewey decimal system or the Library of Congress system or both. This classification information, summarized in the work's **call number,** appears in the upper left-hand corner of the book's catalog card and on the book's spine; it allows you to find the work on the shelf in the library.

44c
psr

A library's card catalog is an index to the materials that that particular library owns. The catalog is usually a collection of cards located in cabinets near the circulation or reference areas in the library, but in some libraries you will find this information in bound volumes, or, increasingly, on computer terminals. The card catalog lists materials such as books, bound periodicals, tapes, microforms in alphabetical order by the author's last name **(author cards)**, the first important word in the title **(title cards)**, or the first word of the general subject **(subject cards).** A card catalog is not the best place to look for journals, magazines, newspapers, or government documents because it does not index individual essays or government publications. Articles in journals are found by using the indexes to the journals. (See pages 690–691 for indexes.)

Each author, title, and subject card in the catalog gives you the source's call number (in the upper left-hand corner) and its author, title, edition, publisher, place and date of publication, number of pages

LIBRARY CATALOG CARDS

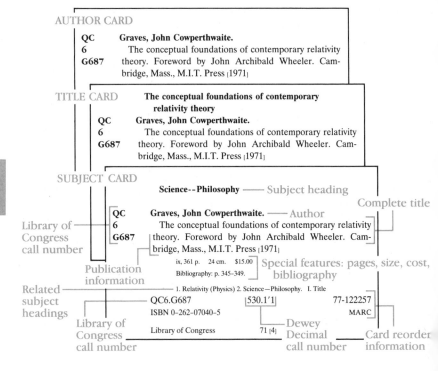

and any special features (for instance, book size, illustrations, maps, charts, or computer disks); it also tells you whether the book includes an index or a bibliography. The call number indicates where the material is shelved in the library. At the bottom of each card you will find a list of at least three related subject headings, which can lead you to other materials on the same topic.

If you know the subject of your report, but not the authors or titles that you should be consulting, look through the catalog cards in the subject index. If you are unsure about how the Library of Congress system labels a subject, look in the multivolume *Library of Congress Subject Headings* (the *LCSH*), which catalogs the subject headings, related subjects (marked with an *sa*), related but broader categories (marked with an *xx*), and terms (marked with an *x*) not used to categorize materials.

Most academic, industrial, and medical libraries have transferred unwieldy card catalog files into computer files and, consequently, cut the time that most researchers spend hunting through cards for materials. You get the same information from an on-line search that you find in a card catalog, although the printout may look somewhat different. (See page 692 for searches on computerized data bases.)

Standard Reference Sources

Perhaps your own bookshelves already contain some common reference sources, such as a desk dictionary, a thesaurus, an encyclopedia, and a dictionary of quotations. Standard reference works also include almanacs, atlases, biographical dictionaries, dictionaries, encyclopedias, handbooks, manuals, statistical sources, and yearbooks (see listings by discipline on pages 685–687), as well as bibliographies and indexes (see listings by discipline on pages 687–691). However, when you start your search for standard reference sources, you will quickly discover an annoying problem: Reference works sometimes use titles that bewilder apprentice researchers. Looking through the current edition of Eugene P. Sheehy's *Guide to Reference Books,* a reference source that catalogs and describes general and specialized reference works in all disciplines, will save you time and, perhaps, a few headaches.

44c
psr

Almanacs and Yearbooks

Almanacs are annual compilations of factual data, often represented in charts, lists, or statistical tables. Yearbooks record information that happens in a particular year in a specified discipline. Here is a sampling of the major almanacs and yearbooks:

Britannica Book of the Year
Bureau of the Census Catalog

Facts on File Yearbook
Guinness Book of World Records
Statistical Abstract of the United States
United Nations Statistical Yearbook
World Almanac and Book of Facts

Atlases and Gazetteers

An atlas is literally a bound collection of maps of countries, counties, oceans, and even planets. Besides providing topographic information, these maps broadly survey the physical and governmental boundaries of the areas or focus on specifics such as climatic and environmental conditions, agricultural products and crop rotations, migration patterns, and the like. A contemporary atlas can also be a volume of tables, charts, or other visual aids illustrating a particular subject. Another type of atlas is a **gazetteer,** which is a geographic dictionary or index.

Rand McNally Cosmopolitan World Atlas Rev. ed. 1987.
The Times Atlas of the World. 2nd rev. ed. 1983.

Biographical Dictionaries

Biographical dictionaries retell the lives and give the credentials and accomplishments of notable people. Like encyclopedias, they either give general information about notable people in several fields or focus on significant people in particular disciplines or from certain historical periods.

Current Biography
The McGraw-Hill Encyclopedia of World Biography
James, Edward T., and Janet W. James, eds. *Notable American Women: 1607–1950.* 3 vols.
Sicherman, Barbara, et al., eds. *Notable American Women: The Modern Period.*
Who's Who
Who's Who in America

**44c
psr**

General Encyclopedias

General encyclopedias are good for nonspecialists as broad overviews of diverse people, places, ideas, and subjects. Because they are so far-reaching, they are useful only if you know almost nothing about a topic or need chiefly background information on it. The most helpful general encyclopedias provide cross-references to related subjects and articles within the series. A very few also provide brief bibliographies.

Some general encyclopedias are multivolume works, such as the following:

Collier's Encyclopedia. 24 vols. 1981 ed.
Encyclopedia Americana. 30 vols. 1977 ed.
Encyclopaedia Britannica. 30 vols. 1987 ed.
World Book Encyclopedia. 22 vols. 1987 ed.

Others, such as *The New Columbia Encyclopedia* (1975) or the *Random House Encyclopedia* (1983) are single-volume works and, consequently, are more limited.

Discipline-Specific Dictionaries, Encyclopedias, and Handbooks

Specialized dictionaries, encyclopedias, and handbooks provide detailed information pertaining to a particular field of study or discipline. You will immediately grasp the differences between these reference sources and generalized dictionaries when you look up a term or concept. For example, a good desk dictionary such as the *American Heritage Dictionary of the English Language* gives you the definition, pronunciation, origin, and changes in meaning for a word, as well as suggests its appropriate usage. It also offers a brief definition of a concept, such as the Heisenberg uncertainty principle. On the other hand, a specialized dictionary, such as *Chambers Science and Technology Dictionary,* supplies a complete description and explanation of Heisenberg's postulate but does not define words such as *certainty, dictionary,* or *postulate.*

The number of specialized encyclopedias, dictionaries, and handbooks reaches into the thousands. The following list, organized by discipline, is selective. The best ways to find reference sources pertinent to your report are to ask a reference librarian and to spend time perusing the resources. Experience with the abundant resources in a discipline will teach you which are valuable and which are not.

44c
psr

Suggested Sources for Humanities

General Sources and Guides

Barzun, Jacques, and Henry G. Graff. *The Modern Researcher.* 4th ed.
Carter, Warren, ed. *Guide to World Literature.* 1980.
Jones, L. *Art Research Methods and Resources: A Guide to Finding Art Information.*
New Cambridge Modern History.
The Reader's Adviser. 6 vols.
Wilson, F. P., and B. Dobree, eds. *Oxford History of English Literature.*

Almanacs and Yearbooks

Hughes, Catherine. *American Theater Annual.*
International Television & Video Almanac.

Atlases and Gazetteers

Barraclough, Geoffrey, ed. *The Time Atlas of World History.* 3rd ed.
Shepherd, W. R. *Historical Atlas.*

Biographical Dictionaries

*Contemporary Authors: A Biographical Guide to Current Authors and Their
    Works.* 123 vols.
Dictionary of Literary Biography. 33 vols. and supplements.

Dictionaries, Encyclopedias, and Handbooks

Apel, Willi. *Harvard Dictionary of Music.*
Brandon, S. G. F., ed. *A Dictionary of Comparative Religions.*
Delpar, Helen. *An Encyclopedia of Latin America.*
Friedel, Frank, and Richard K. Showman, eds. *Harvard Guide to American
    History.* Rev. ed. 2 vols.
Langer, William L., ed. *An Encyclopedia of World History: Ancient, Medieval,
    and Modern.*
Leach, Marie, and Jerome Fried, eds. *Funk & Wagnalls' Standard Dictionary
    of Folklore, Mythology, and Legend.* 2 vols.
Morris, Richard B. *Encyclopedia of American History.* 6th ed.
Myers, B., ed. *McGraw-Hill Dictionary of Art.*
Stambler, Irwin. *Encyclopedia of Pop, Rock, and Soul.* Rev. ed.

Suggested Sources for Science and Technology

General Sources and Guides

Grogan, D. J. *Science and Technology: An Introduction to the Literature.* 3rd
    ed.
Smith, Roger C., W. Malcolm Reid, and Arlena E. Luchsinger, eds. *Guide to the
    Literature of the Life Sciences.* 9th ed.

Almanacs and Yearbooks

McGraw-Hill Yearbook of Science and Technology.

Atlases and Gazetteers

Gerlock, Arch C., ed. *National Atlas of the United States of America.*
National Geographic Atlas of the World. 5th ed.

Biographical Dictionaries

Dictionary of Scientific Biography.
Ireland, Norma Olin. *Index to Scientists of the World from Ancient to Modern
    Times: Biographies and Portraits.*

44c
psr

Dictionaries, Encyclopedias, and Handbooks

Carter, E. F. *Dictionary of Inventions and Discoveries.* 2nd ed.
Gray, Peter, ed. *The Encyclopedia of the Biological Sciences.* 2nd ed.
McGraw-Hill Encyclopedia of Science and Technology. 15 vols.
Ralston, Anthony, ed. *The Encyclopedia of Computer Science and Engineering.*

Suggested Sources for Social Sciences

General Sources and Guides

Holler, F. L. *The Information Sources of Political Sciences.* 2nd ed.
White, Carl M., et al. *Sources of Information in the Social Sciences: A Guide to the Literature.* 2nd ed.

Almanacs and Yearbooks

Barone, M., and G. Ujifusa, eds. *The Almanac of American Politics.*
Congressional Quarterly Almanac.
Washington Information Directory.

Atlases and Gazetteers

Brace, C. Loring, et al. *Atlas of Human Evolution.* 2nd ed.
Hawkes, Jacquetta. *The Atlas of Early Man.*

Biographical Dictionaries

Dictionary of American Biography. 21 vols.
Stephen, Leslie, and Sidney Lee. *Dictionary of National Biography.* 22 vols.

Dictionaries, Encyclopedias, and Handbooks

Encyclopedia of Sociology.
Laqueur, William Z. *A Dictionary of Politics.*
Sills, David L., ed. *International Encyclopedia of the Social Sciences.*
Wolman, Benjamin B., ed. *Dictionary of Behavioral Sciences.* 2nd ed.

44c
psr

Bibliographies and Indexes to Periodicals

General and Discipline-Specific Bibliographies

A bibliography you survey for sources is similar to the one you must compile for your research report. Any bibliography is simply a list of books, journal articles, essays from periodicals, and other research materials that interested scholars can find and read for themselves. If the purpose of your research report is to survey general ideas on a topic such as college football, your bibliography will be a generalized one. If, on the other hand, your purpose is to investigate a particular subject, such as the medical instances of arthritic conditions in professional football players, you will benefit more from specialized discussions. The same holds true for bibliographies. A general bibliography is useful if you are browsing or consider yourself a nonspecialist in a field. Discipline-specific bibliographies focus on research materials required by specialists in a field of study.

At the beginning of each bibliography—or at the beginning of the first volume in a multivolume bibliography—you will find instructions on how to use the reference source. The most serviceable bibliographies are **critical bibliographies.** These annotated lists summarize or evaluate each entry and can save you time in the library, for they let you judge whether a source is valuable for your research project. However, no matter how carefully done, a critical bibliography cannot take the place of your analysis of a research document because you and not the bibliographer know what perspective you want to advance.

Suggested General Bibliographies

Besterman, Theodore. *A World Bibliography of Bibliographies.* 5 vols. 4th ed.
Books in Print. (Offered as on-line data base through DIALOG.)

Suggested Bibliographies for Humanities

Bateson, F. W., ed. *New Cambridge Bibliography of English Literature.* 5 vols.
Essays and General Literature Index.
M[odern] L[anguage] A[ssociation] *International Bibliography of Books and Articles on the Modern Languages and Literatures.* (Offered as MLA, 1976–, an on-line data base.)

**44c
psr**

Suggested Bibliographies for Science and Technology

Durbin, Paul T., ed. *A Guide to the Culture of Science, Technology, and Medicine.*
Smit, Pieter, *History of the Life Sciences: An Annotated Bibliography.*

Suggested Bibliographies for Social Sciences

Foreign Affairs Bibliography. 5 vols.
Harmon, Robert Bartlett. *Political Science Bibliographies.*

Indexes to Periodicals

Periodical is a broad term for a publication issued at regular intervals. Newspapers, popular magazines, and professional journals are periodicals that may publish information on the same topic but present it in vastly different ways. Newspapers such as the *New York Times,* the *Chicago Tribune,* or the *Washington Post* may report a recently announced scientific advance but leave out all but the most dramatic details of its discovery. Magazines such as *Commentary, Discover, Newsweek,* or *Time* publish essays for nonspecialists. Each expands newspaper discussions of a discovery by reviewing its controversial aspects or mentioning its cultural, fiscal, or political implications, but none goes into much more depth. Journals such as the *American Psychological Association Journal, Language and Society,* or *Physiological Zoology* recount the primary research that resulted in a new approach. The data they publish are intended for specialists in the discipline. Such professional journals are indispensable sources of the most current information in narrowly defined research areas. Their articles, however, may sometimes be difficult for nonspecialists to understand.

The hard way to find information in periodicals is to scan the tables of contents or a year-end index for every issue of every periodical. The easier way is to locate discipline-specific indexes and, based on the information they provide, retrieve only the studies needed for your research. **Periodical indexes** are reference tools that enable you to locate articles on specific subjects in various periodicals. Although individual indexes cover different periodicals, each typically lists entries by author, subject, and title. Instructions on how to use a specific index appear at the beginning of the volume or, more typically, at the beginning of the first volume in a series.

Once you have identified the essays you want to review and the periodicals they appear in, you need to find the call numbers for the periodicals in the card catalog or, at larger research libraries, in the serials listings. Most libraries bind several issues of a periodical together and shelve the volumes separately from the general collection. Many libraries have replaced individual issues and older, bound volumes with microforms. If your library does not own an index you need or does not subscribe to an essential periodical, consult a reference or periodicals librarian for help. You may be able to get the needed book or article through interlibrary loan services. As is true of critical bibliographies and many technical documents, periodical indexes that include **abstracts,** or summaries of ground-breaking articles, save you time and energy.

44c
psr

LISTINGS FROM THE *READERS' GUIDE TO PERIODICAL LITERATURE*

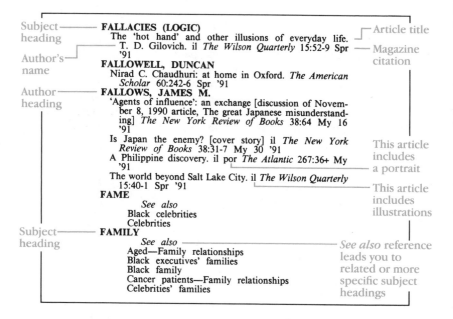

Subject heading — **FALLACIES (LOGIC)** — Article title
The 'hot hand' and other illusions of everyday life.
Author's name — T. D. Gilovich. il *The Wilson Quarterly* 15:52-9 Spr — Magazine citation
'91
FALLOWELL, DUNCAN
Nirad C. Chaudhuri: at home in Oxford. *The American Scholar* 60:242-6 Spr '91
Author heading — **FALLOWS, JAMES M.**
'Agents of influence': an exchange [discussion of November 8, 1990 article, The great Japanese misunderstanding] *The New York Review of Books* 38:64 My 16 '91
Is Japan the enemy? [cover story] il *The New York Review of Books* 38:31-7 My 30 '91 — This article includes
A Philippine discovery. il por *The Atlantic* 267:36+ My '91 — a portrait
The world beyond Salt Lake City. il *The Wilson Quarterly* 15:40-1 Spr '91 — This article includes illustrations
FAME
See also
Black celebrities
Celebrities
Subject heading — **FAMILY**
See also — *See also* reference leads you to related or more specific subject headings
Aged—Family relationships
Black executives' families
Black family
Cancer patients—Family relationships
Celebrities' families

Suggested General Periodical and Book Review Indexes

Book Review Digest.
Book Review Index. (Offered as on-line data base through BOOK REVIEW INDEX, 1969–.)
Readers' Guide to Periodical Literature.
New York Times Index.

44c
psr

Suggested Indexes and Abstracts for Humanities

Abstracts of English Studies.
Art Index.
Communication Abstracts.
Film Literature Index.
Guide to the Performing Arts.
Humanities Index.
Music Index.

Suggested Indexes and Abstracts for Science and Technology

Biological Abstracts. (Previously called *Bioresearch Index* [1967–1979].)
Garfield, C., ed. *Science Citation Index.*
General Science Index.

Suggested Indexes and Abstracts for Social Sciences

Educational Resources Information Center (ERIC). Previously called *Resources in Education (RIE).*
Psychological Abstracts. (Corresponds to on-line data base *PsychINFO* in DIALOG, 1967–.)
Public Affairs Information Service Bulletin. (Corresponds to on-line data base *PAIS International,* 1972–.)
Social Sciences Citation Index. (Corresponds to multidisciplinary on-line data base *Social Scisearch.*)
Women's Studies Abstracts.

Government Documents

Researchers have found that government documents—books, fliers, magazines, and pamphlets published by federal and state governments—include valuable information for all the sciences and social sciences and a surprisingly rich amount of material on the humanities. Because governments collect and publish so much information, not all these documents are available at all libraries, and none are cataloged according to the Dewey or the Library of Congress systems. Some large, regional libraries are depositories for federal documents, as well as state documents. Most libraries have subject indexes to government documents that you can use to identify government publications relevant to your research. Once you have pinpointed in an index entries that look promising, take the index to the government documents librarian, who can help you either find the publication in the library or secure it through interlibrary loan.

44c
psr

Suggested Indexes for Government Publications

American Statistics Index
Congressional Information Service
Government Publications Index
Index to International Statistics
Index to U.S. Government Periodicals
Monthly Catalog of United States Government Publications

On-line Data Base Searches

On-line searches provide access to thousands of electronically stored sources and data bases, many of which are generated from existing printed indexes on general and discipline-specific subjects. Furthermore, computer-based searches also save time, for they list the citations (some with abstracts), thus furnishing you with an electronically generated bibliography appropriate to your research topic. Because these services are sold to libraries, you will need a reference librarian skilled in searching computer data bases to help you, and you can expect a charge of $5 to $20 for using the data bases. Given their speed and convenience, however, data base searches are well worth the fees.

CD-ROM Data Base Searches

CD-ROM ("compact-disk, read only memory") are periodically updated, do-it-yourself data bases recorded on laser-read compact disks capable of accommodating up to one-half of a gigabyte of information. From CD-ROM files, you can retrieve various types of information from bibliographic citations. Depending on the company producing the disks, you can also retrieve information ranging from detailed abstracts, journal articles, and reference documents to directory listings of public companies, maps, and listings of government documents. You can literally save hours of searching through equivalent printed indexes by using CD-ROMs. However, because these are self-help data bases (and therefore mostly available without charge), you must pay careful attention to the informational guides that explain how to use them.

44c
psr

Suggested General On-line/CD-ROM Data Bases

DIALOG Information Service.
Infotrac Magazine Index Plus.
Newspaper Abstracts Ondisc.
Readers' Guide to Periodical Literature.

Suggested On-line/CD-ROM Data Bases for Humanities

Arts and Humanities Search.
Humanities Index.
MLA Bibliography. CD-ROM.

Suggested On-line/CD-ROM Data Bases for Science and Technology

Biosis Previews.
NTIS (National Technical Information Service)
PC Globe and *PC USA.*
Science Citation Index-CD Edition (SCI CD)

Suggested On-line/CD-ROM Data Bases for Social Sciences

ERIC (CD-ROM and on-line)
PAIS International.
Social Science Index.

Interlibrary Loan Services

Libraries cannot own every book, journal, magazine, pamphlet, or government document printed. Therefore, most libraries participate in a lending program called **interlibrary loan services.** With this service, your library borrows for you, for a limited time, a text from another library. The librarians will locate the libraries that own the book or journal you need, but you must tell them the name of the work, its author, needed page numbers, and necessary publication information. Interlibrary loan services sometimes carry a fee, to cover the lending library's cost of mailing the material to your library, as well as the cost of any copying.

44c
psr

45

45a

Planning a Research Project

1 Establishing and Maintaining a Schedule

That widespread human characteristic, procrastination, can stop you dead in your researcher's tracks. You may believe that you are just lazy or that you work "better" under pressure or that you have to be gripped by the topic or that, no matter how gripped you think you are, you still don't have enough "smarts" to write it. But each reason is wrong. Procrastination is linked directly to writer's block. (See **6b** for more on writer's block.) Motivation and curiosity don't precede researching and writing; they grow from those processes. The lines of a song, that you have to "prime the pump before you're worthy to receive," hold true: You can't write a comprehensive, readable research report unless you get started and stick to it. Success breeds success, particularly in writing research documents. Once you begin, what you accomplish will spur you on to do even more.

When you receive the assignment for the report, put the final due date on your calendar, and draft a schedule for the project. (See the suggested schedule at the end of this section.) As you sketch out what you have to do, remember that writing a research report parallels the typical phases of the writing process. Be realistic about your time, resources, and ability to handle this process. If the project is due in two weeks, you can't schedule ten days for researching and still leave yourself enough time to organize your materials and write a sensible first draft. Nor can you assume that you will get materials ordered on interlibrary loan immediately. Instead, estimate your time by recognizing your individual writing habits and staying flexible. Even though you may not be able to predict exactly how long your research will take, you can reasonably calculate that you will spend between 35 and 40 percent of your time researching and between 60 and 65 percent writing and revising.

As a general guideline, reserve most of your time for generating a preliminary thesis statement, reading and evaluating research materials, and drafting an initial version of the report. Then you should have sufficient time to handle any unexpected situations, such as changes in your perspective or thesis. Leave your second largest blocks of time for revising and editing, and the least time for finding note cards, pens, paper clips, rubber bands, or change for copying machines. One easy way to keep to a schedule is to carry these items with you so that you are ready to work on the project at any time.

2   Choosing a System of Note Taking

You can also save time if you adopt an organized system of taking notes. Many researchers record bibliographic information, research activities, and evolving thoughts about a project on note cards or in a research journal, a bound, spiral, or loose-leaf notebook that organizes your notes for a research study. A few use lap-top computers to enter information directly into a data base.

Note cards have the advantages of being portable and forcing you to summarize in order to fit everything you need on a few cards. Additionally, you can keep material separate by recording reference information for bibliographies on three-by-five-inch index cards and research notes on larger four-by-six-inch cards. You can also shuffle note cards into various combinations when you start organizing and composing your first draft. Research journals let you chronicle your primary research results, record your secondary sources, and write out ideas, conclusions, or recommendations for the final report. But if your research is elaborate or comprehensive, you may find it time consuming to subdivide journal notes. As for computers, some libraries have adapters that permit library patrons to copy information directly from a data base into a lap-top computer. While this procedure is quick, you could lose material (that is, "crash" the disk). Whatever method you pick, use it consistently and take precautions to protect your notes. That way you save yourself time, confusion, and frustration.

45a
Irr

696 Launching a Research Report

Schedule of Tasks and Due Dates

PROJECT DUE DATE: _____

Tasks   **Scheduled Due Date**

Initial Tasks
Limit designated topic   _____
Identify and profile audience   _____
Draft preliminary thesis statement   _____
    Outline initial perspective
    List questions demanding additional
       research
Gather tools for project   _____

Research Tasks
Begin research
    Compile working bibliography   _____
    Consult sources (no writing)   _____
    Compile notes   _____
    Recheck documentation information   _____

Drafting Tasks
Compose first draft
    Structure reference information
        Outline ideas   _____
        Shuffle note cards   _____
        Write first draft

Revising Tasks
Revise draft
    Review overall plan   _____
    Review or restructure ideas   _____
    Check unattributed statements against
       research notes   _____
Document sources   _____
Revise entire document   _____

Publishing Tasks
Edit entire document   _____
    Check mechanics
    Check visuals
    Check printing facilities and deadlines
Review final copy   _____
Submit final copy   _____

45a
Irr

45b

Narrowing a Subject and Formulating a Preliminary Thesis Statement

1 Limit the Research Topic

Whoever assigns you a research report has some limit in mind but may not always give you the guidelines. (See **44a** for the distinctions between assigned and self-initiated research projects.) Your first step, therefore, is to assess the assignment or research project using whatever you already know about the subject and whatever you find in a preliminary survey of the research materials. (**6d** illustrates various invention techniques that can help you tap into the knowledge you already have about a subject; Chapter 7 is a general guide to restricting writing topics. Skim these discussions before starting your research because the same generalities that apply to generating ideas for an essay apply to research writing.)

If, for instance, your instructor gives you the broad assignment to research a controversial aspect of bilingual education, ask yourself what the term *bilingual education* means to you. If you are unsure, check a dictionary or encyclopedia for general information. Ask yourself what major controversies mark general discussions of education and what extraordinary controversy bilingual education suggests. On individual note cards, write down several possible argumentative issues and your immediate reactions to them. You are now better prepared to look through the card catalog or specialized indexes for information on these issues.

Next make educated guesses about how much of the information you have discovered your audience wants. If your assignment is to demonstrate that you understand the basic issues in bilingual education, investigate your library's resources. You may find a ready-made organizational strategy as you investigate; that is, your library may not have sufficient resources about some aspects of the topic. Therefore, a least-to-most important structure, based on the amount of information you can find, may be best.

Finally, shape a preliminary thesis statement. Brainstorm about your subject. Consider the most daring reaction to a topic that you can. Then try to frame this reaction as a question, a problem you have unearthed, or a potential disagreement. For example, could bilingual education actually be a farce? Should it, instead, be the mainstay of your community's educational programs? The chances are that your reactions will suggest an approach to the project that your audience will also find informative.

2 Consider Possibilities for a Preliminary Thesis Statement

A thesis statement (see **8a**) tells the reader what your perspective is. You might think it paradoxical to write a thesis statement before you have seriously begun a research project, but that is the best time. A preliminary thesis statement describes what you have in mind. It is also evaluative in that a research report is analogous to a hypothesis: It is a guess, a supposition that you take as likely and therefore provable for the purpose of your argument.

Whether the report is assigned or self-initiated, try following a plan for inventing a preliminary thesis statement.

Restate Your Topic as a Simple Issue

If you were assigned a topic, reduce it to a simple statement. If you must define the topic, choose a subject that interests you, narrow it to a specific topic, and write that topic out as a simple statement. For example, the topic *bilingual education in my monolingual community* restricts the subject *bilingual education* to your school or school district.

Directly State That Issue

Consider your simple statement, and write in one short sentence what you believe about that topic. Your goal is to estimate the most common reaction to your topic in as brief a sentence as you can manage, for instance, a sentence such as this one: *Most people believe that only people who don't speak English need bilingual education programs.*

Add a New Twist to a Common Reaction

Let your creative juices flow. Play with your sentence until you find a different approach to the topic. Here are some approaches you can take:

1. Argue the opposite side. For instance, contest your sentence by arguing that *Bilingual education should be mandatory for all high school students.*

2. Consider an unstated meaning. Look for what your sentence implies—for example, that *Bilingual education teaches more than grammatical terms, new words, and facts about America.*

3. Look for an unexpected cause. Suggest an original reason for the reaction your sentence sums up, such as *Native speakers of English need bilingual education more than those who speak English as a second language* or *Bilingual education is a wrong-headed attempt that deprives people from other countries of their national identity.*

4. Find a weakness. State why the reaction is questionable or even unacceptable; for example, *Bilingual education promotes stereotyped ideas* or *Educators scared of bilingual education should rethink what they want students to learn.*

List Your Grounds

Take the most promising idea or intriguing twist that you come up with and brainstorm a list of reasons that support this approach. Once you have listed all you can think of, you will have both a preliminary thesis statement and a rough synopsis of supporting ideas. You are ready to research the idea in the library.

Preliminary thesis statements can—and probably must—change as you learn more about your subject and challenge yourself. Each revision should refine your perspective. When you finally sit down to compose your first draft, you should have confidence that you can express your interpretation of the subject and your reasons for your position. Always remember that flexibility is the norm for critical thinking and perceptive writing.

3 Profile Your Audience

Once you have a preliminary thesis statement, seriously rethink your intended audience. You want to consider how much information you will need for certain audiences and how best to identify and handle an audience's biases on a topic. (Chapter 7 outlines audience analysis strategies.) Most academic research reports are written for an audience of one—the professor who assigned the report. It is safe to assume that an instructor knows the subject area, is reasonably intelligent, and has a keen interest in the accuracy of your research. It is also safe to assume that the professor will have to read numerous reports, so part of your job as a writer is to make yours stand out. The specific assignment and the professor's course objectives clarify your guidelines when writing for this audience, but whenever you are unsure, ask the professor.

45b
Irr

Research documents written by professionals are seldom restricted to one audience. More frequently, a supervisor or manager commissions a report that is later circulated to other, perhaps less well identified, audiences. A diverse audience challenges you because you have to figure out what to include or not include and how much professional jargon you can use. Novice readers expect more explanations, definitions, and ancillary interpretations than do experts. Furthermore, an unconvinced audience requires a research document with a substantially different tone than that needed for an already persuaded audience.

4 **Survey Your Resources**

Next briefly glance at the possible sources of information about your subject or its central issue. Scan reference works, books, essay collections, professional journals, popular magazines, and newspaper reports, remembering to record (on cards or in a journal) necessary bibliographic information on promising sources. This way you can quickly return to these sources. If you see disagreement shaping up, write out your understanding of its facets in your research journal *in your own words.* This way you assure yourself that you understand what the disagreement really is. Putting ideas into your own words clarifies what you understand about the issues; keeping ideas in another writer's words denies you your perceptions.

If this preliminary work intrigues you, then your research will be easier because it is rewarding. If you cannot find information on an issue, let a reference librarian steer you toward related issues. If the project promises only boredom, talk to a practicing professional who might be able to stimulate your interest. You may simply need assistance in stating the thesis or finding a library with more technical or contemporary resources. Your boredom might be due to overextension or a basic unfamiliarity with a subject. Again, a reference librarian can show you elementary discussions of a subject. By skimming these, you can better determine whether the subject engages you.

A professional can suggest a different focus on a subject and may be willing to help you understand a subject that seems overly complex. Give yourself and the topic some time before abandoning it for another one. Workable topics are more than just those subjects on which your library has research materials; they spark your intellectual interest and lure you into subsequent research projects. Unworkable topics are too broad, too controversial, or too esoteric.

45b
Irr

5 Create a Working Bibliography

Whether you use a research journal or note cards, your first step in accumulating research materials is creating a **working bibliography.** Working bibliographies—preliminary lists of sources that you want to consult—are like outlines because they are fluid drafts rather than publishable products. You can add to a working bibliography at any time, rearrange its entries under different headings as you find out more about individual reports, or delete entries your library does not have or cannot obtain. Record all the publication information that you will need for your final bibliography, but don't let perfect bibliographic form overtake the bibliography's purpose. You are the only one using this working bibliography; therefore, at this stage, publishable form is helpful but not mandatory.

The best way to prepare a working bibliography—and save yourself valuable time in the library—is to develop a common-sense search strategy. Take your packet of note cards or your journal and record each entry on a separate card or sheet. Cards have an advantage over journal sheets or computer entries, for prior to preparing your final bibliography, you can discard cards dealing with sources that you did not consult.

Consider leaving the card catalog for later in your search. You may be overwhelmed by the number of books and collections you find and spend hours recording sources that you will not need to consult or that will not be helpful for your project. Start instead with general, background sources and move to more discipline-specific ones. Dictionaries, encyclopedias, and biographies are good first steps because they give you the major players, as well as key terms, issues, trends, and controversies. Move next to indexes that list reviews of the discipline's literature or to issue-based research reports. Either will give you a good idea of the current state of research on your topic. Once you have a sense of the general outline of your research topic, investigate specialized bibliographies and indexes to recent journal articles, books, and reviews.

45b
Irr

When you have a good idea of the contours of your research topic and some understanding of contemporary approaches to it, check the card catalog for books and collections about the topic. Now, at least, you have criteria for selecting among the sources that you will find. Finally, consider whether you will need to undertake any primary research or require any original documents (such as plays, novels, and reports). Primary research arises from what you already know. Original documents are works that secondary documents evaluate, and secondary documents are valuable preliminaries to any primary work—no matter what the research project.

Taking Notes

1 The Suppositions to Follow in Taking Notes

Researchers take notes to summarize and record information they find in source material and to remember what they have read. Taking notes is condensing someone else's ideas in your own words, without misinterpreting those ideas. Success in taking notes depends on your skills in critical reading and thinking: To digest someone else's ideas you first have to understand them. (Look over Chapters 2 and 3 for critical reading and thinking strategies.)

Taking notes on factual data is easier than taking notes on concepts, opinions, and judgments. With facts, brief notes suffice. (As with all notes, make sure you put quotation marks around directly cited information so that you will remember that you quoted rather than summarized it.) With concepts, very brief notes may not be enough to help you remember the concept later on. Read all source material with an eye to how its information contributes to your report and to what your audience needs to know about your perspective. Err on the side of recording too much information rather than too little. If you comment on the idea as you are taking notes, set up a system so that you can tell weeks later which ideas are yours and which came from the source material. Try writing your summaries in black ink and your reactions in red. Or print the summaries on one side of a card and write your reactions on the other. Remember, it is far more trying and time consuming to locate a source a second time, reread it, and take new notes than it is to discard information or reactions while you are drafting the report.

45c
lrr

2 The Strategies to Follow in Taking Notes

Evaluating Research Sources

It is seldom a good idea to rely on just one source. To do so implies that the one source has fully addressed your point of view. Moreover, using only one source could call into question the completeness or objectivity of your report. Expect to survey many more sources than you will use for your final report. Find recognized standard sources for the background materials in your report, and use the most current sources you can for the more argumentative sections. Evaluate each source critically. Do not be satisfied until you determine what is the best one for your report.

Evaluating research sources requires reading the work for its timeliness, authoritativeness, and objectivity. Five criteria can help you assess a source: its **relevance** to your topic; its **recency;** the author's **status** in the field; the **balance of presentation;** and the **evidence or reasoning.** You can't rely on a title to tell you what a source is about. First of all, then, scan the introductions, tables of contents, indexes, and any abstracts, if provided. These will indicate whether the document is relevant. Even better, consult works about the work you are appraising. Book reviews tell you other people's interpretation of a book's currency. Bibliographic surveys of a topic typically mention the most influential articles and reports on that topic and why they are significant.

Second, consider how recently the book, article, or report was written. If you are investigating a historical or literary topic, such as nineteenth-century literary plagiarists, then documents that are contemporary with the allegedly plagiarized works or contemporary authors' public statements about plagiarisms are important; it is not critical that they be recent. However, scientific, medical, and political research requires the most up-to-date sources.

Third, question an author's credentials. Practicing professionals are typically most current on research. Obtaining information about an author is relatively simple. Many professional journals, for example, list the academic affiliation, publication record, or research interests of the writers published in that issue. Book publishers do the same in the publicity notices, or blurbs, found on book jackets. If this information is missing, ask other professionals in a discipline about a writer, or check the biographical sources for that research field. (See suggested sources in **44c.**)

Check the nature and prestige of the publishing source. A popular journal is a good source of general or background information, whereas scholarly sources, particularly those with recognized reputations in a field, try to print in-depth assessments of current research. Again, ask other professionals or reference librarians for help.

Fourth, as you learn more about a research field, you become better able to judge a writer's biases. A text reflects the way its writer views the world. You have to judge the writer's biases from what you know of the discipline and from the writer's evidence and arguments. Is the work in the discipline's mainstream? Does it illuminate pertinent controversies ignored by others in the field? Ask yourself whether the

45c
Irr

source depends on the writer's beliefs, verifiable facts, or closely argued judgments. Is there an objective analysis or an offhand dismissal of conflicting perspectives? If you determine that a printed source is questionable, label it that way and go on. If the work is balanced, you are in a better position to incorporate it and reject works with obvious partialities.

Finally, consider how useful this information will be, given the topic you are researching. No matter how fascinating a project is or how skillfully a writer turns a phrase, if the project information or phrase is not pertinent to a report, the information source is not useful. Discard it. Look for material that advances your topic and perspective. Ultimately, your report will be effective only if its information accomplishes your objectives and informs your audience. Packing it with interesting but unrelated tidbits of knowledge defeats those objectives and leaves your audience unenlightened.

Strategies for Evaluating Reference Sources

45c
Irr

1. **Relevance.** Consider whether the source discusses an issue, fact, statistic, or perspective connected to your issue, question, or research topic.
   Is it useful?

2. **Timeliness.** Consider the date of your source. Historical and literary topics can benefit from contemporary reports, and scientific, medical, and political subjects from current reports.
   Is it dated?

3. **Source's status.** Consider the author's credentials in the field, the prestige and nature of the journal or publishing body, and the reception other specialists in the discipline accord it.
   Is it reliable?

4. **Balance.** Consider whether the document agrees or disagrees with other sources and how controversial it is.
   Is it objective?

5. **Support and reasoning.** Consider whether the source presents necessary and sufficient evidence or conclusive reasoning.
   Is it conclusive?

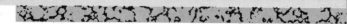

Armed with your abilities to read and think critically and a knowledge of what resources libraries can offer, you are ready to plan your
research project, assemble your working bibliography, compile and
integrate your sources, and write a credible research essay.

Quoting Sources Directly and Indirectly

When you copy a writer's words, you are quoting directly. It is
your responsibility to quote accurately and perceptively. Your quotation has to reproduce your source material exactly, down to the spelling, capitalization, and internal punctuation. Check your notes against
the original, then recheck them. Check your typed report against your
notes for accuracy.

Use quotations sparingly. Your research report integrates other
writers' ideas and facts with your own information and interpretations;
it does not merely string quotations together. (See **46a** for weaving quotations and restatements into a research report.) So quote when your
source's idea is stated in such distinctive, lyrical, or pithy words that a
summary would not do justice to the idea. Or quote when a summary
would take up too much space in your text. You should also quote
when you intend to argue with and eventually defeat the source's contentions. Quoting when the source material supports your contentions
gives your report additional credibility in your audience's eyes.

Guidelines for Direct Quotations

- Choose quotations that express your idea succinctly or
  support your perspective directly. Avoid restating an
  argument if it is not immediately relevant to your
  position.
- If quoted material includes an obvious error or
  questionable material, put *sic,* enclosed in brackets, right
  after the particular word or words to show that the
  quotation is exact and that you recognize the error or
  questionable point. (See **34d** for use of brackets.)
- Quote from the most reliable sources you find. Judge
  their reliability by their relevance to your topic, recency,
  author's reputation, balance of presentation, and
  evidence and reasoning.
- Use quotations sparingly.

45c
Irr

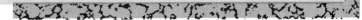

Indirect quotations paraphrase direct quotations. For example, this material is quoted directly:

> In the debates that surround studies of literary plagiarism, one critic writes, "[T]o see the similarities, without seeing the differences, seems . . . a dangerous game" (Chesterton 20–21).

For an indirect quotation, you would rephrase the information in your own words, introduce the indirect quotation with the word *that*, and omit any separating punctuation:

> In the debates that surround studies of literary plagiarism, one critic warns about the risks of stressing how books resemble each other without taking into account how they diverge (Chesterton 20–21).

Summarizing Sources

An essential form of note taking, **summaries** describe or abstract someone else's research, omitting your reactions or interpretations. Summaries objectively state the gist or main points, rather than the subtleties, of a source's actual statements. They reflect the tone and emphases of the source but do not follow its organization. In addition, they omit the examples, illustrations, direct quotations, and other details that make a source interesting. Because they leave out detailed information and your evaluations, summaries are always shorter than either the original source or a paraphrase of that source:

45c
Irr

ORIGINAL:
Despite the pressures to accept mass-communicated political reality, people have the capacity to resist. The capacity to reject distorted pictures of the world is greatest in a liberal political system like that of the United States, which has not yet taken the final turn toward the totalitarian world of *1984*. American citizens are still free, within limits, to think what they like and say what they think. Nevertheless, the degree of freedom that remains in American society is deceptive in that it leads people to doubt the need for vigilance and personal courage. It is tempting to think that there are more important things in life than politics. It is tempting to trust our political affairs to a government that spends a great deal of energy inviting our trust and presenting political issues as too complex and technical to warrant our concern. (W. Lance Bennett, *News: The Politics of Illusion*)

SUMMARY:
U.S. citizens have the right and the duty to reject misleading images that the media present about politics and political leaders. Citizens who don't exercise that right and who accept what the media present may misunderstand important, complex issues.

Strategies for Summarizing

1. Read and reread the source material carefully.
2. Separate the main points from the supporting evidence and any speculative digressions.
   a. Circle the subjects and main verbs in the sentences.
   b. Underline key repeated words, or put notes in the margins of the work. These tell you what the central concepts are.
   c. Find the thesis statement and highlight it.
   d. Find the topic sentences in the paragraphs. Determine how these topic sentences explain the thesis statement and how the writer has sequenced these explanations.
3. Looking only at the highlighted information or your marginal notes, write down, in your own words and sentences, the major points as you remember them.
4. Put the original aside and reread your summary. Smooth out the language.
5. Check the summary against the source material to make sure that you have captured only the main points. Delete any of your interpretations from your summary. (A complete summary is usually about one-third the length of the original text.)
6. Copy on the summary the original writer's name, the title of the work, the publication information, and the page numbers that you have summarized.

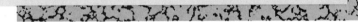

Paraphrasing Sources

Direct quotations can carry authority but can also be awkward. Summaries, because they are abbreviated versions of main ideas, reorganize the source's material and leave out nuances. When you need a restatement in your own words of another researcher's ideas that follows the researcher's organization, you should paraphrase.

Paraphrases restate another writer's thoughts without altering the original's organization, emphasis, or tone, but they do not repeat the source's word choice or sentence structure. Acceptable paraphrases restate a source's ideas and organization in words and sentences that differ from the original because, in part, they fit the stylistic demands of your research report. Select synonyms for terms and phrases in the source material and alter the sentence structure, using your research goals as your criteria. If you find yourself writing down key words and expressions, put quotation marks around them. That way you will remember what you have paraphrased and what you have quoted. Like direct quotations and summaries, paraphrases do not include your reactions to a source's perspective.

Strategies for Writing Paraphrases

1. Read and reread the source carefully.
2. Separate the main points from the supporting evidence and any speculative digressions.
   a. Circle the subjects and main verbs in the sentences.
   b. Underline key repeated words and terms, or put notes in the margins of the work.
   c. Highlight the thesis statement and topic sentences.
   d. Notice the writer's style (that is, the preferred level of diction, sentence structures, patterns of development).
3. Put the source material aside, and write in your own words what you remember from what you read.
4. Check your statement against the source to determine
   a. if you have accurately captured the source material's major ideas in the presented order.
   b. if you have reproduced the ideas in your own words.
5. Copy the writer's name, title of the work, publication information, and page numbers of the information you have paraphrased.

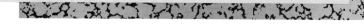

45c
Irr

It is unacceptable to retain the original writer's *words and sentence structures* in your paraphrase. Changing only a few words from the original makes a paraphrase unacceptable because that is the same as plagiarizing the source:

ORIGINAL:
Though ours is an age of high technology, the essence of what engineering is and what engineers do is not common knowledge. (Henry Petroski, *To Engineer Is Human*)

PLAGIARIZED VERSION:
In our age of high technology, the nature of engineering and the jobs engineers do is not well known.

To avoid this situation, put the source away before you start to write your paraphrase. That way you will be less tempted to "copy" what you have just read. For example:

ORIGINAL:
The most characteristic shrub of the Salt-Desert area is Shadscale. This species can be found mixed in with Big Sagebrush on many sites; its greater tolerance to salinity, however, allows it to be the dominant species over vast areas of the moderately saline soils found in valley bottoms. Shadscale is an important browse plant for livestock, especially when it bears succulent young stems and leaves. (from James A. MacMahon, *Deserts*)

PARAPHRASE:
The Shadscale shrub is well adapted to the Salt-Desert because it can tolerate the mildly salty soil of that valley. The shrub's immature leaves and stems make it an important food source for livestock.

3 The Mechanics to Follow in Taking Notes

Time-Saving Steps for Taking Notes

Just as no two writers use the same composing strategies, no two researchers record notes in the same way. Some scrupulously make notes in research journals, keeping individual sources on different pages. Others separate bibliographic material from reference information by putting documentation and publication information on three-by-five-inch index cards and textual notes on four-by-six-inch cards. Some researchers assign a separate colored note card for each source when they know they won't need numerous sources for a report.

If you use note cards, put an identifying label (for example, the author's name, the work's abbreviated title, page numbers, and a number that corresponds to the appropriate bibliography card) on one corner of the top of the card. On the other side, jot down an outline heading. This way you won't forget where or why you got the information. If the passage you are using is long, consider photocopying it and then taping it to cards or into your research journal. (See information on photocopying below.) Remember that if you use more than one page or card for an entry, you should number them consecutively.

Don't start taking notes until you understand what you are reading. Without having a clear sense of what the source is proposing, you may write down an idea and later forget whether it was your own or someone else's. Consequently, you might end up plagiarizing a work. If you take your notes carefully and document your sources

45c
Irr

conscientiously, you will avoid such problems and write a report that reflects your understanding and perspective.

A few standard procedures will make your work go more quickly.

1. Copy all necessary information the first time you look at a source. A real time saver is to document your sources in the format of the style manual that you will be using for your research paper. When you type your "Works Cited" list, you will already have the bibliographic citations in the proper form. Nothing is more frustrating than to have to return to the library because you have forgotten the page numbers for a reference.

2. Skim the table of contents, index, preface or foreword, and, if available, the abstract of the source. This "quick read," done once, will orient you to the writer's position and tell you whether the source is worth more of your time. If the work seems pertinent to your topic and perspective, then read and evaluate the material. Review Chapter 2, on critical reading, for helpful strategies. To judge a source, use your own perspective on the topic and the knowledge you gain from your study.

3. Jot down key words and concepts that relate to your topic. Then, as briefly as possible, quote directly, paraphrase, or summarize the original's interpretation of those terms and ideas. Record only the most important facts and ideas rather than everything the source presents, and enclose direct quotations in quotation marks. It is easier than you may think to overquote when you are taking notes. You can skirt this problem by avoiding quoting more than one paragraph from each source and by paraphrasing or, better yet, summarizing what you have read. Paraphrases and summaries lead you away from overquoting. Just be sure to identify summaries and paraphrases with subheadings at the top of the note card or journal page.

45c
Irr

4. In your summaries and paraphrases, create a shorthand that you will understand later (for example, *ltr* for *later*, *wrds* for *words*, *bk* for *book*). Use symbols or abbreviations for common words (for example, *&* for *and*, *%* for *percent*, *w/* for *with*, *w/out* for *without*, *+* for *plus*, *=* for *equals*, *>* for *greater than*, *<* for *less than*), and use Arabic numerals for written numbers *(2, 4, 15* for *two, four, fifteen)*.

5. Annotate your note cards or journal pages. If a source is particularly important, put * at the top. If it is questionable, put ??; if it is confusing, gloss it differently (for instance, *?). If it repeats information, set up a cross-referencing system.

6. Before returning a source to the library staff, recheck your note cards. Make sure that you have correctly recorded all the material you need and only the material you need.

BIBLIOGRAPHY CARD

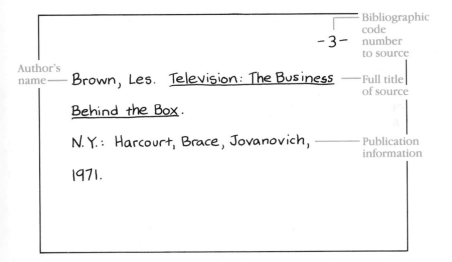

Author's name —— Brown, Les. <u>Television: The Business</u> ——Full title
of source

<u>Behind the Box</u>.

N.Y.: Harcourt, Brace, Jovanovich, ——— Publication information

1971.

- 3 -   Bibliographic code number to source

BIBLIOGRAPHY CARD

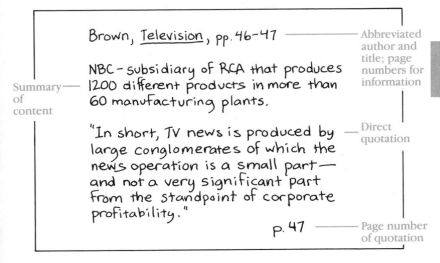

Brown, <u>Television</u>, pp. 46-47 ——— Abbreviated author and title; page numbers for information

Summary of content —— NBC - subsidiary of RCA that produces 1200 different products in more than 60 manufacturing plants.

"In short, TV news is produced by large conglomerates of which the news operation is a small part— and not a very significant part from the standpoint of corporate profitability." — Direct quotation

p. 47 ——— Page number of quotation

45c
Irr

CONTENT CARD

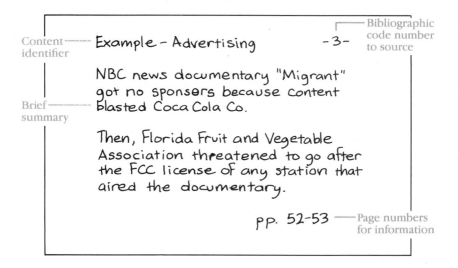

Content identifier ——— Example - Advertising   -3-   Bibliographic code number to source

NBC news documentary "Migrant" got no sponsors because content blasted Coca Cola Co.

Brief summary

Then, Florida Fruit and Vegetable Association threatened to go after the FCC license of any station that aired the documentary.

pp. 52-53 ——— Page numbers for information

Photocopying Source Material

More and more often, researchers photocopy articles, sections of reports, and book chapters so that they can read them later at their convenience. This duplication method is a popular short cut. You can gather your research materials together, copy pertinent sections, and record bibliographic information on the back of the copies. Later, you can scrutinize the material, write in the margins of the copies, and assure yourself that anything you quote is accurate. Photocopying is especially comforting for those researchers who continually forget to write down page numbers; with a photocopy, you have the correct page numbers for your "Works Cited" list.

45c
Irr

But photocopying source material can lead to plagiarism if you try to draft the report from the copies. Copying source material is not reading critically, interpreting ideas, or incorporating those interpretations into your perspective. Therefore, whether you duplicate materials or not, it is best to transfer relevant information to a journal, loose-leaf pages (stapled together so that you don't lose any parts), or note cards. If you must use a quotation, cut it out of the copy and paste it on a note card. (Do not forget to label the card so that you remember where the quotation came from.) This way you can integrate quotations into your summaries and paraphrases.

BIBLIOGRAPHY CARD AND PHOTOCOPY

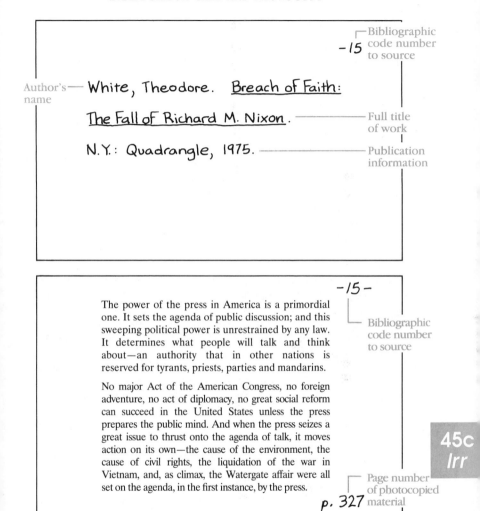

┌─Bibliographic
─ 15 code number
to source

Author's— White, Theodore. Breach of Faith:
name

The Fall of Richard M. Nixon. ————— Full title
of work

N.Y.: Quadrangle, 1975. ————— Publication
information

─/5─

The power of the press in America is a primordial one. It sets the agenda of public discussion; and this sweeping political power is unrestrained by any law. It determines what people will talk and think about—an authority that in other nations is reserved for tyrants, priests, parties and mandarins.

Bibliographic
code number
to source

No major Act of the American Congress, no foreign adventure, no act of diplomacy, no great social reform can succeed in the United States unless the press prepares the public mind. And when the press seizes a great issue to thrust onto the agenda of talk, it moves action on its own—the cause of the environment, the cause of civil rights, the liquidation of the war in Vietnam, and, as climax, the Watergate affair were all set on the agenda, in the first instance, by the press.

Page number
of photocopied
p. 327 material

45c
Irr

4 The Precautions Needed to Avoid Plagiarism

Intentional plagiarism has very serious consequences. Scholars have been discredited; researchers have lost grants from irritated and embarrassed funding agencies. Employees are fired for plagiarizing documents, and students are expelled from college for copying printed sources or letting friends write reports for them.

However, sometimes students and professionals find that they have plagiarized unintentionally. There are several ways you can plagiarize unintentionally:

1. Sometimes, novice research writers misunderstand the correct documentation style for their report. You should start by locating the style manual particular to a relevant discipline and remember a few simple guidelines for documenting material. Specifically, whenever you write down the exact words another writer has used, you are quoting directly. You must put quotation marks around the material and add either an in-text citation (with accompanying bibliographic source) or an endnote or footnote. What may be less obvious is that you must also provide in-text citations and bibliographic notes when you quote indirectly, summarize, or paraphrase because indirect quotations, summaries, and paraphrases report another writer's ideas.

   The only exception to this rule occurs when you report **common knowledge.** Learning to read critically means that you inevitably make some ideas your own. They become "common" to you. For example, a physics student familiar with Heisenberg's principle of indeterminacy or Newton's second law customarily does not document that information in a report written for readers who are professionals in physics. However, if this same physics student analyzes the quest motifs found in John Barth's novel *The Sot-Weed Factor* and does not know about quest motifs, the student will need to document whatever source provides those particulars.

   Additionally, many ideas are common knowledge because they are commonly available in several sources. These ideas do not need to be cited in your research report. Common knowledge ends when you report a writer's specific opinion about a subject or the reported results of a particular experiment, interview, observation, questionnaire, or study.

2. Misunderstanding the nature of the assignment can also lead you to plagiarism. You are most challenged when you receive an academic research assignment that specifies the number and kind of resources. In this case, the mechanics of the assignment appear to take over the information potential of the report. But don't let yourself be fooled. The reader may have designated the number and kind of sources, but, if you are to write an informative and interesting text, you need to look at more resources than you will eventually use for the report.

45c
Irr

3. Inexperience in analyzing what you read and synthesizing it with what you think can also lead you to unintentional plagiarism. You read a passage, note the information in very similar terms, then forget to document—or document incompletely—a paraphrase, idea, or citation that comes from another writer. When that happens, you can't tell from your notes what parts were the other writer's and what were your interpretations, and so you run the risk of presenting the other writer's words or ideas as your own. **Analyzing** what you read means taking it apart and discovering what the ideas are and how they are individually related to one another and to the author's perspective. **Synthesizing** means integrating several writers' ideas, including your own, to create a new perspective. In fact, synthesizing ideas means making those ideas your own. And this process is common with processes of active researchers. They find, after a time, that they automatically tie what they are currently reading with what they have previously read and thought. However, synthesizing does not mean forgetting to credit the sources that gave you those ideas to begin with.

4. Time pressures can also lead to inadvertent plagiarism. Writers who fail to budget adequate time for various writing projects find themselves with too much to write and revise before a deadline. Literally, they lack the time to think about what they have read and integrate that knowledge with their own. In a rush, they forget that they have copied directly out of a text. Or, worse yet, they talk a friend into reviewing an assignment for them and copy the friend's comments directly rather than take those comments as strategies for further revisions.

Such copying, however, is deliberate plagiarism. Sometimes writers fear that their own ideas are not worthwhile, so to ensure a passing mark from their teachers, they sometimes paraphrase ideas from "crib" notes, critical essays, or plot summaries and present these ideas as their own. Needless to say, such plagiarism is usually dealt with severely, if discovered.

45c
Irr

Although you are not plagiarizing when you collaborate with another writer, have a friend review your work, or use the same report for two classes, you are not being fair. Before collaborating, getting peer review, or double-submitting a research report, check with your instructor. You are plagiarizing when you quote, restate a unique idea, summarize a specific concept, or paraphrase another individual's main points and perspective *without documenting the original source material.*

Strategies for Avoiding Plagiarism

1. Develop a method of taking notes that includes putting quotation marks around any group of three or more words that you copy from a source, highlighting specific ideas taken from a source, and copying full publication information for a source.

2. Never copy information from another student's work or allow another student to copy yours.

3. Check your summary or paraphrase against the original. Find synonyms for words that you have copied directly; find sentence structures that differ from the original writer's sentences.

4. Check your written text against any photocopies of sources before submitting your text.

5. When in doubt, reference the source.

45d

Understanding Documentation Styles and Formats

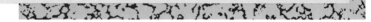 **1** Why Cite Reference Sources?

45d
Irr

Your research report is due this week. Your professor or supervisor will not agree to an extension. You suddenly find that you have forgotten to write down the location of a publisher or the page numbers for a reference. You also face the tedium of triple-checking the numbers you assigned to the references cited in your report against your list of "Works Cited." It is times like these that cause even experienced researchers to wonder why they should cite references at all.

Despite the headaches, there are several compelling reasons for citing references fully and accurately. First, the one place you can go wrong in a research report is plagiarizing—not giving due credit to original sources for ideas, facts, data, or words. Citing every source you use does not suggest that you have patched together ideas without analyzing them or integrating them with yours. Solid research reports are seldom patchworks because you have read, evaluated, and modified what you have used. You make yourself a knowledgeable resource to readers because you have done the hard work of research.

Second, citing reference sources allows your readers to do just what you did when you began your research: to find and evaluate pertinent information about a topic. No researcher is able to include in any report every idea from every document examined. Some concepts are omitted because they are not immediately relevant; others, because they are outlandish. But if your readers want to follow up on a point you make, you owe them the professional courtesy of providing a full reference citation so that they can find and study the original source for themselves.

Third, by citing reference sources, you substantiate your claim and strengthen your argument. Moreover, you need to cite your references in the format appropriate for the particular profession. Documentation customarily includes these two elements: (1) either a parenthetical citation or a footnote and (2) a list of works cited. By using the format particular to your field, you indicate your membership in that profession and enable other professionals (that is, your readers) to find the sources and further validate your claims. Hence you need to make sure that your reference citations are correct.

2 Recognizing Different Documentation Styles

Documentation style—the way in which you describe your sources—differs among disciplines and can even be inconsistent within one discipline. However, every documentation format demands the complete title of a reference work, the name(s) of its author(s), and publication information, including the work's edition, reprint number, the date and place of publication, and the publisher's name. What varies is how this information appears in the report, how it is specified, and how it refers readers to the report's bibliography. For example, the favored documentation style for business and economics reports consists of parenthetical, in-text citations and an alphabetized list of references at the end of the report. This style is also used in many research documents compiled for science and technology.

The *MLA Handbook for Writers of Research Papers,* the standard style manual for reports in the humanities, endorses an in-text, parenthetical format with a "Works Cited" list but allows a footnote or endnote format. Social science and psychology also favor an in-text, author-date method, illustrated in the *Publication Manual of the*

45d
lrr

American Psychological Association. Because most instructors assigning reports prefer the documentation formats sanctioned by the Modern Language Association of America (MLA) or by the American Psychological Association (APA), the following pages illustrate citations and bibliographic entries from the third edition of the *MLA Handbook* and the third revised edition of the APA *Manual.* Be aware, however, that preferred documentation or style manuals exist for virtually every discipline and should normally be followed in research reports for advanced college courses and in professional reports. (Check John Bruce Howell's *Style Manuals of the English-Speaking World* for a comprehensive list of style manuals.)

Parenthetical Documentation

Parenthetical documentation is a simple in-text citation format that provides readers with a shorthand reference to a source. You use in-text citations immediately after the summary, quotation, or paraphrase of a source. Parenthetical citations usually give just the authors' last names and the page numbers of the source material; the full citation appears at the end of the report, in a separate list of the works cited. The general rule for parenthetical documentation is to give readers enough information so that they can locate a work in the list, where complete information is provided. Parenthetical documentation has the advantage of not distracting a reader's attention.

Endnote and Footnote Documentation

Another common documentation format uses superscript numbers that refer the reader either to endnotes or to footnotes. These numbers are positioned immediately after the source material. Endnotes and footnotes replace parenthetical notes or citations, but they supply complete bibliographic information (that is, the authors' full names, the full title of the work, publication information, and page numbers). Endnotes begin at the end of a report on a page entitled "Bibliography," "Endnotes," "Notes," "Works Cited," "Literature Cited," or "References." Footnotes are reference entries placed at the bottom of the page, generally four spaces (two double spaces) below the text.

Some reports require notational documentation other than reference endnotes or footnotes. These **content notes** supplement information in the text by expanding points, defining terms, stating proofs, identifying frequently cited primary sources, explaining supplementary derivations, or directing readers to related matters, comparative studies, or other sources. Content notes can be grouped together as

45d
Irr

endnotes or typed below the text on appropriate pages. Some writers put lengthy explanations in appendices rather than breaking up the information into content notes. Again, as a rule of thumb, use content notes if the data in the notes reinforce your perspective. Information fundamental to your report should always be included in the text rather than in content notes.

45e

Documenting Your Research Report by MLA or APA Format

Careful scholars credit other writers and researchers. You have to acknowledge other writers and researchers whenever you use their language, approach, factual data, or original ideas. (For more on quoting, paraphrasing, and plagiarizing, see pages 713–716.) Unlike most of the other challenges writing poses, knowing how to write a reference is a relatively simple matter. In this section, we give an overview of when to use parenthetical citations and offer a brief list of models that follow MLA and APA guidelines for parenthetical citations. The models illustrate the types of sources you are most likely to use in an academic research report. For additional information about MLA and APA styles, see the *MLA Handbook for Writers of Research Papers* (third edition) and the *Publication Manual of the American Psychological Association* (third edition, revised), respectively.

1   Parenthetical Citations Following MLA Style

Citing an Entire Work by a Single Author

You do not have to provide a parenthetical citation when you refer to an entire work and its author in your report:

A former Carter administration cabinet officer turned consumer advocate, Dr. Sidney Wolfe in Women's Health Alert compared, state by state, warranted surgeries and medically questionable procedures and concluded that many medical professionals take advantage of uninformed patients.

When you refer to an entire work but not to its author, you must provide the author's last name in the citation:

> The basic argument in The True and Only Heaven details why pessimists from both sides of the political spectrum optimistically continue to believe that economic and technological developments are both beneficial and inevitable (Lasch).

When you cite a section from a longer work, you must include both the author's last name and the page number for a reference, but you do not use any punctuation between them:

> The extraordinary geologist who "discovered" the Burgess Shale, Charles Doolittle Walcott, left a far greater mark on science through his administrative efforts than through his paleontological research (Gould 242).

Citing a Passage from a Single Work by One Author

When you refer to a specific passage from a work and include the author's name in your text, you need to put only the page number in your citation:

> William W. Warner suggests that the Chesapeake Bay will continue to suffer as the population around the Bay increases at about "1.7 percent, or twice the national average" (258).

When you refer to a specific passage from a work but do not mention the author, you must include both the author's last name and the page number in your citation:

> Verloc, chagrined, believes that as a trusted secret agent who "flaunts his achievements before the public eye" he courts personal disaster for himself and his unsuspecting family, but his discovery is more ironic than instructive (Conrad 180).

Citing from Two or More Works by One Author

When you use material from several works by the same writer, provide a brief version of the title of the work to which you are referring so that readers can identify the appropriate publication in your "Works Cited":

45e
lrr

> John Gardner finds that all competent fiction
> starts with a basic plot structure and then
> complicates that structure--and enhances the
> work's literary merit--by dramatizing the
> characters' motivations (On Becoming 54). Gardner
> offers much the same argument in his earlier "New
> Critical" evaluations of literature (Forms of
> Fiction).

Citing a Passage from a Work by Two or Three Authors

When you use a specific passage from a work written by two or
three authors, include all the authors' last names and the page number
of the passage in your citation:

> If the sample population is large and the value
> of r small, then the sampling distribution of the
> coefficient of correlation will be normal
> (Arkin and Colton 16).

Citing a Passage from a Work by More than Three Authors

When you use a specific passage from a work written by more
than three authors, include the first author's last name, the abbreviation *et al.* (*et alii*, a Latin phrase meaning "and others"), and the page
number of the passage:

> Despite the short-term devastation nuclear war
> would cause, many scientists fear that "the
> disruption of the global ecosystem" would ravage
> human life for centuries (Turco et al. 37).

2 Parenthetical Citations Following APA Style

Citing an Entire Work by a Single Author

You do not have to provide a parenthetical citation if both the
author's last name and the work's publication date appear in your
text:

> For a 1991 consumer affairs report, Dr. Sidney
> Wolfe, a former Carter administration cabinet
> officer, compared, state by state, warranted
> surgeries versus medically questionable procedures
> and concluded that many medical professionals take
> advantage of uninformed women patients.

However, even if you include the author's name in your text, the APA style, unlike that of the MLA, requires the work's publication year in the reference citation:

> A former Carter administration cabinet officer turned consumer advocate, Dr. Sidney Wolfe (1991) compared, state by state, warranted surgeries versus medically questionable procedures and concluded that many medical professionals take advantage of uninformed women patients.

When you refer to an entire work but not to its author in your report, you must provide—in parentheses placed close to the reference—both the author's last name and the publication date, separated by a comma:

> A recent state-by-state comparison of warranted surgeries versus medically questionable procedures (Wolfe, 1991) calls into question the surgical advice some professionals give to uninformed patients.

> The basic argument in The True and Only Heaven (Lasch, 1991) details why pessimists from both sides of the political spectrum continue to believe optimistically that economic and technological development are both beneficial and inevitable.

Citing a Passage from a Work by One or More Authors

When you refer to a specific part of a work, you must include the author's last name, the publication year, and (using the appropriate abbreviation) the page, chapter, or visual graphic number; all these elements are separated by commas:

> Verloc, chagrined, believes that as a trusted secret agent who "flaunts his achievements before the public eye" he courts personal disaster for himself and his unsuspecting family, but his discovery is more ironic than instructive (Conrad, 1907, p. 180).

When you include the author's name in the text, put the publication year and page number, separated by commas and with the standard abbreviation, at the appropriate place in your text:

> William W. Warner (1977, p. 258) suggests that the Chesapeake Bay will continue to suffer as the population around the bay increases at about "1.7 percent, or twice the national average."

45e
Irr

Citing from Two or More Works by One Author

You distinguish material from two or more works by one author by the publication year:

> John Gardner (1983, p. 54) finds that all
> competent fiction starts with a basic plot
> structure and then complicates that structure--and
> enhances the work's literary merit--by dramatizing
> the characters' motivations. He outlines much the
> same argument in his earlier literary evaluations
> (1962).

Citing a Passage from a Work by Two or More but Fewer than Six Authors

When you cite specific material from a work written by more than two but fewer than six authors, include in your first reference all the authors' last names, the publication year, and the page number(s) —all separated by commas. In your report, use an *and* before the last author's name, but in your in-text citations and list of references, use an ampersand (&). Use the first author's last name, et al. (not underlined), and specific page numbers in any subsequent citations. In citing a work by just two authors, always repeat both last names, separating them with an *and* or an ampersand depending on the location:

> Despite the short-term devastation nuclear war
> would cause, many scientists fear that "the
> disruption of the global ecosystem" would ravage
> human life for centuries to come (Turco, Toon,
> Ackerman, Pollack, & Sagan, 1984, p. 37). In
> subsequent research, Turco et al. (1984) found
> that . . .

Citing a Passage from a Work by More than Six Authors

Rather than interrupt the flow of your report with a citation including seven or more last names, supply readers with the first author's last name followed by et al. (not underlined), the publication year, and page reference. Provide all the authors' full names in the "Works Cited":

> Researchers designed their laboratory procedures
> specifically so that they could identify any
> possible correlations between the molecule
> structure of fibroid tissue and pituitary
> prolactin (Chapitis et al., 1988).

45e
Irr

3 Bibliographic Entries Formatted According to MLA and APA Styles

After incorporating your research into your report through parenthetical citations, you need to give readers the documentation that explains those in-text citations. Unlike other aspects of researching and writing, documenting sources is simply a matter of following the prescribed formats outlined in either the *MLA Handbook* or the APA *Publication Manual*. However, you have to remember to copy all the necessary publication information and page numbers from your reference sources when you first look at them. And you need to keep the format of your references consistent with the style manual you are using.

Whichever style manual you follow, the basic information that you need for a reference citation for a book includes the following elements:

1. The full names of the author(s), editor(s), or translator(s). You can omit titles and degrees such as "Professor," "Doctor," or "Ph.D." from your reference. Use the abbreviations "Jr.," "Ed.," "Trans.," and "Comp." for, respectively, junior, editor, translator, or compiler.

2. The full title of the work, including its subtitle. If the work is a subsequent or revised edition, catalog it by its edition number (for example, 2nd ed., 3rd ed., 4th ed.), revision (Rev. ed. for *revised edition*), or year (for example, 1991 ed.). If you use part of a book (such as the preface, introduction, or a specific chapter, essay, poem, or story), record this information.

3. The publication information, including the city where the work was published, the name of the publisher, and the publication year. Use abbreviations *n.p.* (no publication place), *n.p.* (no publisher), *n.d.* (no date), and *n. pag.* (no pagination) when source material lacks this type of information.

For an article in a periodical, you will also need the following data:

4. The name of the publication as it appears on the title page of the journal.

5. The volume number and issue number (if the journal paginates each issue independently) and page numbers of the articles you have cited.

The following review of models summarizes only a few of the many types of works referenced, discussed, and illustrated in the MLA and APA style manuals. When in doubt, go to your library or bookstore, find the style manual you are following, and double-check there what information you need to supply and how you should format it.

45e
lrr

45e
Irr

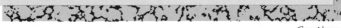

Continued

BIBLIOGRAPHIC MODELS FOR BOOKS

1. A BOOK BY ONE AUTHOR

MLA   Wolfe, Sidney M. Women's Health Alert.

Reading: Addison, 1991.

Lasch, Christopher. The True and Only Heaven:

Progress and Its Critics. New York:

Norton, 1991.

- Separate the author's name (reversed for alphabetizing), the book's title, and publication information with periods.
- Separate the title and subtitle with a colon and a single space. Single-space between colons and any following information.
- Capitalize the first word, the last word, and every significant word in the title.
- Separate the place of publication and the publisher's name with a colon, followed by a single space.

45e
Irr

- Shorten the form of a trade company's name, and use standard abbreviations such as *UP* for *University Press* (for example, Harvard UP or U of New Mexico P).
- End the citation with a period.

APA   Wolfe, S. M. (1991). Women's health alert.

Reading, MA: Addison-Wesley.

Lasch, C. (1991). The true and only heaven:

Progress and its critics. New York: Norton.

- Separate author's name, publication date, title, and publication information with periods.
- List publication year in parentheses immediately after the author's name.
- Separate titles and subtitles with a colon. Single-space between colons and any following information.
- Capitalize only the first word of the title and subtitle and any proper nouns and adjectives.
- If a city is not well known, add the name of the state, using U.S. Postal Service abbreviations.
- Shorten the form of a trade company's name. Spell out the names of association and university presses (for example, Harvard University Press or the University of New Mexico Press).
- End citation with a period.

2. A BOOK BY TWO OR THREE AUTHORS

MLA   Arkin, Herbert, and Raymond R. Colton. Tables

for Statisticians. New York: Barnes,

1963.

Monroe, Judson, Carole Meredith, and Kathleen

Fisher. The Science of Scientific

Writing. Dubuque: Kendall, 1977.

- Separate authors' names with commas and use an *and* before the last author's name. Separate authors' names, title, and publication data with periods.
- List authors' names in the order found on the title page. Reverse the first author's name for alphabetizing; list the other authors' names in normal order.
- If more than one publication location is given, use the first city only.

45e
Irr

APA   Arkin, H., & Colton, R. R. (1963). <u>Tables for statisticians</u>. New York: Barnes & Noble.

Monroe, J., Meredith, C., & Fisher, K. (1977). <u>The science of scientific writing</u>. Dubuque: Kendall/Hunt.

- List authors' names in reversed, alphabetizing order.
- Separate authors' names with commas, and use an ampersand before the last author's name.

3. A BOOK BY MORE THAN THREE AUTHORS

MLA   Quirk, Randolph, et al. <u>A Grammar of Contemporary English</u>. London: Longman, 1972.

Quirk, Randolph, Sidney Greenbaum, Geoffrey Leech, and Jan Svartvik. <u>A Grammar of Contemporary English</u>. London: Longman, 1972.

- List first author's name, reversed for alphabetizing, and either add *et al.* for the other authors *or* list all the other authors' names as they appear on the title page.

APA   Quirk, R., Greenbaum, S., Leech, G., & Svartvik, J. (1972). <u>A grammar of contemporary English</u>. London: Longman.

- Regardless of the number of authors, spell out each author's surname. List each name in reverse order, separated by commas. Use an ampersand between the last two authors' names.

45e
lrr

4. A BOOK BY A CORPORATE AUTHOR

MLA   United Nations Educational, Scientific, and Cultural Organization. <u>A Framework for Improvement of the Educational and Vocational Guidance Services for Girls and Women in Asia and the Pacific</u>. Bangkok: UNESCO Principal Regional Office for Asia and the Pacific, 1987.

- Spell out the full name of the corporation, commission, association, or committee as listed on the title page.
- If the corporate author is the publisher, you may abbreviate the publisher's name in the publication information.

APA   United Nations Educational, Social, and
        Cultural Organization. (1987). A framework
        for improvement of the educational and
        vocational guidance services for girls and
        women in Asia and the Pacific. Bangkok:
        Author.

- Spell out the full name of the corporation, commission, association, or committee. Alphabetize in references by the first significant word in the corporate author's name.
- If the corporate author is the publisher, put "Author" in the publication information.

5. TWO OR MORE BOOKS BY ONE AUTHOR

MLA   Gardner, John. On Becoming a Novelist. New
        York: Harper, 1983.

        ---. On Moral Fiction. New York: Basic, 1978.

        Gardner, John, and Lennis Dunlap, eds. The
        Forms of Fiction. New York: Random, 1962.

- List author's full name for first reference only. In subsequent references, put three hyphens (---) and a period, double space, and then give the next work's title. List the works in alphabetical order.
- If a subsequent work is co-authored or co-edited, list both author's names.

APA   Gardner, J. (1978). On moral fiction. New
        York: Basic Books.

        Gardner, J. (1983). On becoming a
        novelist. New York: Harper & Row.

        Gardner, J., & Dunlap, L. (Eds.). (1962).

        The forms of fiction. New York: Random House.

45e
Irr

- List author's name in each reference entry.
- Order multiple works by the same author by publication dates, earliest year first. Works by that author and a co-author or co-editor follow the listing of works by the author alone, regardless of publication date.
- Unless the works are articles in a defined series, alphabetize multiple works by the same author(s) if all the works were published in the same year.

6. A BOOK WITHOUT A LISTED AUTHOR

MLA   The New York Public Library Desk Reference. New York: Simon, 1989.

- Do not use *Anonymous* or the abbreviation *Anon.* Begin the citation with the work's title.
- Alphabetize in the "Works Cited" by the first significant word in the title.

APA   The New York Public Library desk reference. (1989). New York: Simon & Schuster.

- Cite the work in your text using the title and publication year.
- Do not use *Anonymous* or the abbreviation *Anon.* in the "Works Cited." Use just the work's title.
- Alphabetize in "Works Cited" by the first significant word in the title.

7. AN EDITED BOOK (See 15)

MLA   Lasch, Christopher, ed. The Social Thought of Samuel Adams. New York: Bobbs, 1965.

Connors, Robert J., Lisa S. Ede, and Andrea A. Lunsford, eds. Essays on Classical Rhetoric and Modern Discourse. Carbondale: Southern Illinois UP, 1984.

- Use lowercase abbreviations *ed.* or *eds.* for the editor or editors.
- Separate *ed.* or *eds.* from names with a comma.

APA   Lasch, C. (Ed.). (1965). The social thought of Samuel Adams. New York: Bobbs-Merrill.

Connors, R. J., Ede, L. S., & Lunsford, A. A.
(Eds.). (1984). Essays on classical
rhetoric and modern discourse. Carbondale:
Southern Illinois University Press.

- Capitalize the abbreviations *Ed.* and *Eds.* and put the abbreviations in parentheses immediately before the publication year.

8. A BOOK WITH AN AUTHOR AND AN EDITOR

MLA   Blake, William. Complete Writings. Ed.
Geoffrey Keynes. London: Oxford UP, 1972.

- Put the author's name before the title when you are citing the author's work in an edited work.
- Precede the editor's name with the abbreviation *Ed.,* or *Eds.* for multiple editors.

Keynes, Geoffrey, ed. Complete Writings. By
William Blake. London: Oxford UP, 1972.

- Put the editor's name before the title when you are citing the editor's work.

APA   Blake, W. Complete Writings (G. Keynes,
Ed.). London: Oxford University Press,
1972.

- Put the editor's name after the title, in parentheses, using the abbreviation *Ed.*
- Put a period after the information about the editor, not after the title of the work.

9. A TRANSLATION

MLA   Calvino, Italo. Cosmi-comics. Trans. William
Weaver. New York: Harcourt, 1968.

- Put the author's name before the title and the translator's name when you are citing the author's work.
- Put the abbreviation *Trans.* (for "Translated by") before the translator's name (listed in normal order).

Weaver, William, trans. Cosmi-comics. By
Italo Calvino. New York: Harcourt, 1968.

45e
Irr

- Put the translator's name and the abbreviation *trans.,* separated by a comma, before the title when you are citing primarily the translator's commentary.
- Put *By* before the author's name.

> Rossellini, Roberto. The War Trilogy. Trans. Judith Green. Ed. Stefano Roncoroni. New York: Grossman, 1973.

- If the work has both a translator and an editor, put the editor's name after the translator's preceded by the abbreviation *Ed.*

APA   Calvino, I. (1968). Cosmi-comics (W. Weaver, Trans.). New York: Harcourt Brace.

> Rossellini, R. (1973). The war trilogy (J. Green, Trans. S. Roncoroni, Ed.). New York: Grossman.

- Put the translator's name in parentheses after the title. Do not separate with other punctuation.

10. A LATER OR REVISED EDITION

MLA   Copi, Irving M. Introduction to Logic. 3rd ed. New York: Macmillan, 1968.

> Gross, G., ed. Editors on Editing: An Inside View of What Editors Really Do. Rev. ed. New York: Harper, 1985.

- Put the edition number after the title and separate it from the publication information with a period.
- Abbreviate the edition number (2nd, 3rd, 4th, and so on) or use *Rev. ed.* for "Revised edition."

APA   Copi, I. M. (1968). Introduction to logic (3rd ed.). New York: Macmillan.

> Gross, G. (Ed.). (1985). Editors on editing: An inside view of what editors really do (rev. ed.). New York: Harper & Row.

45e
lrr

- Indicate the edition number or revised edition in parentheses immediately after the title.
- Don't separate the edition information from the title with punctuation.

11. A REPRINT OF A PREVIOUSLY PUBLISHED BOOK; A REPUBLISHED EDITION

MLA   Reade, Charles. The Autobiography of a Thief and Other Stories. 1896. New York: AMS, 1970.

- For an essay reprinted in a collection, follow the basic format for works published in anthologies and collections. (See 16 and 17.)
- For a reprint with a new title, follow the original publication information with the abbreviation *Rpt. as* (for "Reprinted as") and the new title and publication information.
- For a republished book, cite the original publication year after the title. Complete the citation with the publication information for the edition you are citing.

APA   Reade, C. (1970). The autobiography of a thief and other stories. New York: AMS. (Original work published 1896)

- Put the original publication date of a reprinted book in parentheses at the end of the citation.
- Put the abbreviation *rev. ed.,* in lower-case letters and parentheses, immediately after the title of a republished, revised edition of a work.

12. A MULTIVOLUME WORK

MLA   Sewall, Richard. The Life of Emily Dickinson. 2 vols. New York: Farrar, 1974.

Niebuhr, Reinhold. Human Destiny. New York: Scribner's, 1964. Vol. 2 of The Nature and Destiny of Man. 2 vols.

- List the volume number and its publication information in the reference citation if you use material from only one volume in a series. Omit the volume number from parenthetical citation.

- List the total number of volumes in the series between the title and the publication information if you use material from two or more volumes. Include the volume number in your in-text parenthetical citation.
- Use Arabic numerals for Roman numerals no matter what the publication uses.
- If the cited volume has a title, list that title first. Follow the publication information with the abbreviation *Vol.,* the volume number, *of,* and the complete work's title. End the citation with the total number of volumes and the inclusive publication dates.

APA   Sewall, R. (1974). The life of Emily Dickinson.
     2 vols. New York: Farrar.

     Niebuhr, R. (1964). Human destiny (Vol. 2). New
     York: Scribner's.

- If you cite information from one volume of a series, put the volume number you have used in parentheses after the title.

13. A BOOK WITH A TITLE WITHIN A TITLE

MLA   Gallacher, Patrick J.   Love, the Word, and
     Mercury: A Reading of John Gower's
     Confessio Amantis.   Albuquerque: U of New
     Mexico P, 1975.

     Adelman, Janet.   The Common Liar: An Essay on
     Antony and Cleopatra.   New Haven: Yale UP,
     1973.

- Omit underlining the title of a long work if that title falls within the name of the book you are citing.
- Keep the quotation marks around the title of a short story or poem if it is a part of the book's full title. Underline the entire work.

45e
Irr

APA   Gallacher, P. J. (1975).   Love, the word, and
     Mercury: A reading of John Gower's Confessio
     Amantis.   Albuquerque: University of New
     Mexico Press.

Adelman, J. (1973). The common liar: An essay on
Antony and Cleopatra. New Haven: Yale
University Press.

14. A BOOK IN A SERIES

MLA   Gillon, Adam. Joseph Conrad. Twayne's English
Authors Ser. 333. Boston: Hall, 1982.

- Include the name of the series after the title of the work.
- Omit the editor's name.
- Use the abbreviation *Ser.* for "series."

APA   Gillon, A. (1982). Joseph Conrad. Boston:
G. K. Hall.

- Omit the name and number of the series and the general editor's name.

BIBLIOGRAPHIC MODELS FOR SELECTIONS FROM BOOKS

15. INTRODUCTION, PREFACE, FOREWORD, OR AFTERWORD

MLA   Atwan, Robert. Foreword. The Best American
Essays 1989. Ed. Geoffrey Wolff. Boston:
Houghton, 1989. ix-xii.

Green, Rayna. Introduction. Pissing in the
Snow and Other Ozark Folktales. By Vance
Randolf. New York: Avon, 1976. 11-30.

- Follow the author's name with the section of the cited work labeled Introduction, Preface, Foreword, or Afterword. Omit underlining or quotation marks for the cited section.
- If the writer of the section did not write or edit the entire work, include the writer's name in normal order after *By* or the editor's name in normal order after the abbreviation *Ed.*
- End the citation with the page numbers of the cited section.

APA   Atwan, R. (1989). Foreword. In G. Wolff (Ed.),
The best American essays 1989 (pp.
ix-xii). Boston: Houghton Mifflin.

45e
lrr

Green, R. (1976). Introduction. In V. Randolf, Pissing in the snow and other Ozark folktales (pp. 11-30). New York: Avon.

- Omit quotation marks around the selection's title.
- Observe the format for an article or chapter cited from an edited book.
- Follow the name of the section cited with *In,* the author or editor's name, the full title of the book, and the page numbers of the section in parentheses and preceded by the abbreviation *p.* for "page" or *pp.* for "pages."

16. SELECTION(S) FROM AN EDITED COLLECTION

MLA   Cherniak, Christopher. "The Riddle of the Universe and Its Solution." The Mind's I: Fantasies and Reflections on Self and Soul. Ed. Douglas R. Hofstadter and Daniel C. Dennett. New York: Basic, 1981. 269-75.

- Put quotation marks around the essay or selection's title.
- Follow the name of the individual essay or selection with the name of the book and its editor(s).
- End the citation with the page numbers of the essay or selection.
- Omit the abbreviations *p.* or *pp.* before the listed page numbers.

APA   Cherniak, C. (1981). The riddle of the universe and its solution. In D. R. Hofstadter & D. C. Dennett (Eds.). The mind's I: Fantasies and reflections on self and soul (pp. 269-275). New York: Basic Books.

- Omit quotation marks around the essay or selection's title.
- Follow the selection's title with *In,* name(s) of the editor or editors, a space, the abbreviation *Ed.* or *Eds.* in parentheses, the book's full title, a space, and the selection's page numbers preceded by the abbreviation *pp.*
- End the citation with the city and publisher.

17. SELECTION(S) FROM AN ANTHOLOGY OR COMPILATION

MLA   Cavafy, C.P. "The City." The Complete Poems of
            Cavafy. Comp., trans., and ed. Rae
            Dalven. New York: Harvest, 1961. 27.

- Use the abbreviations *Comp., Trans.,* and *Ed.,* respectively, for "compiler," "translator," and "editor."
- If one person compiled and edited the anthology, preface the name with *Comp.* and *ed.*
- After the publication date, double space and list the selection's inclusive page numbers. Omit any abbreviation for "page" or "pages."

APA   Cavafy, C. (1961). The city. R. Dalven.
            (Comp., ed., trans.) The complete poems of
            Cavafy (p. 27). New York: Harvest.

18. SELECTION(S) REPRINTED IN AN ANTHOLOGY OR COLLECTION

MLA   Steele, Shelby. "On Being Black and Middle
            Class." Commentary 85 (January 1988):
            42-47. Rpt. in The Best American Essays
            1989. Ed. Geoffrey Wolff. Boston:
            Houghton, 1989. 234-46.

        Beerbohm, Max. "Savonarola Brown." Seven
            Men. London: Heinemann, 1950.
            233-45. Rpt. in The Brand-X Anthology of
            Poetry. Ed. William Zaranka. Cambridge:
            Apple-Wood, 1981. 53-69.

45e
Irr

- First list the complete publication information for the selection's original publication.
- After the abbreviation *Rpt. in* ("Reprinted in"), list the title of the collection, the editor's name, and the publication information.
- Complete the citation with the inclusive page numbers.

APA   Beerbohm, M. (1981). Savonarola Brown. In W.
        Zaranka (Ed.), The brand-X anthology of
        poetry (pp. 53-69). Cambridge:
        Apple-Wood. (Original work published 1950)

19. SELECTION(S) FROM REFERENCE WORKS

MLA   "Genes." Van Nostrand's Scientific
            Encyclopedia. 5th ed. 1976.

        Kalish, Donald. "Semantics." Encyclopedia of
            Philosophy. Ed. Paul Edwards. 8
            vols. New York: Macmillan, 1967.

- Follow the general format for selections in an anthology or
  collection.
- If the article is unsigned, start with the title. If the article is
  signed, give the author's name first.
- If the reference work lists selections alphabetically, omit the
  specific volume and page numbers.

APA   Genes. (1976). In Van Nostrand's Scientific
            Encyclopedia (5th ed.).

        Kalish, D. (1967). Semantics. In P. Edwards
            (Ed.), Encyclopedia of philosophy (pp.
            348-358). New York: Macmillan.

- List immediately after the reference work's title the volume,
  edition, or inclusive page numbers to aid in identification and
  retrieval of the information.

45e
lrr

BIBLIOGRAPHIC MODELS FOR SELECTIONS FROM PERIODICALS

20. ARTICLE FROM A JOURNAL PAGINATED BY VOLUME

MLA   Sauerberg, Lars Ole. "Literature in Figures: An
            Essay on the Popularity of Thrillers."
            Orbis Litterarum: International Review of
            Literary Studies 38 (1983): 93-107.

Chapitis, Jane, Daniel H. Riddick, Lorraine M.
    Betz, John R. Brumsted, Mark Gibson,
    Jerilynn C. Prior, and Peter W.
    Gout. "Physicochemical Characterization
    and Functional Activity of Fibroid
    Prolactin Produced in Cell
    Culture." <u>American Journal of Obstetrics
    and Gynecology</u> 158 (1988): 846-52.

- In the case of works with multiple authors, MLA format also allows listing the first author's name and then *et al.,* as in the following: Chapitis, Jane, et al. "Physicochemical Characterization and Functional Activity of Fibroid Prolactin Produced in Cell Culture." American Journal of Obstetrics and Gynecology 158 (1988): 846–52.
- Usually journals that appear quarterly use continuous pagination. For the publication information, list the name of the journal as it appears on the title page, the volume number, the year, and the inclusive page numbers.
- Omit punctuation and the abbreviation *Vol.* between the journal's title and the volume number.
- Put the publication year in parentheses. Follow it with a colon, a single space, and the page numbers. Omit the abbreviations for "page" or "pages."
- Omit the issue number, listed on the journal's title page, from your citation if the journal uses continuous pagination.

APA Sauerberg, L. O. (1983). Literature in figures:
    An essay on the popularity of thrillers.
    <u>Orbis Litterarum: International Review of
    Literary Studies,</u> <u>38</u>, 93-107.

Chapitis, J., Riddick, D. H., Betz, L. M.,
    Brumsted, J. R., Gibson, M., Prior, J. C., &
    Gout, P. W. (1988). Physicochemical
    characterization and functional activity of
    fibroid prolactin produced in cell culture.
    <u>American Journal of Obstetrics and
    Gynecology,</u> <u>158,</u> 846-852.

45e
Irr

- Use Arabic numbers for the volume number. Underline that number, but omit the abbreviation *Vol.*
- Omit the abbreviations *p.* or *pp.* when citing the page numbers of an article in a journal using continuous pagination.
- Separate the publication information with commas.

21. ARTICLE FROM A JOURNAL PAGINATED BY ISSUE

MLA   Plax, Martin J. "Jews and Blacks in Dialogue."

Midstream. 28.1 (1982): 10-17.

- Some journals begin each issue on page 1. In such cases, follow this sequence: the volume number, a period, the issue number, date, and selection's page numbers.
- Omit underlining the volume and issue numbers, and omit the abbreviation *Vol.*
- Put a period between the volume and issue numbers (7.2 means volume 7, issue 2).

APA   Plax, M. J. (1982). Jews and blacks in

dialogue. Midstream. 28(1), 10-17.

- Underline the volume number; omit abbreviation *Vol.*
- Put the issue number in parentheses immediately after the volume number.
- Separate the volume and issue numbers from the inclusive pages with a comma.

22. MORE THAN ONE ARTICLE BY AN AUTHOR

MLA   Stedmond, J. M. "Genre and Tristram

Shandy." Philological Quarterly 38

(January 1959): 37-51.

---. "Sterne as Plagiarist." English Studies.

41 (1960): 308-21.

- Cite the author's full name for the first entry only. Afterward, use three hyphens, a period, and a double space.
- If a subsequent article is co-authored, type both authors' full names for the entry. (See 5.)

APA   Stedmond, J. M. (1959). Genre and "Tristram

Shandy." Philological Quarterly, 38, 37-51.

Stedmond, J. M. (1960). Sterne as

plagiarist. English Studies, 41, 308-321.

45e
Irr

23. ARTICLE FROM A WEEKLY OR BIWEEKLY PERIODICAL

MLA   Springen, Karen. "A 100 Mile Race? No
Sweat." Newsweek 31 Dec. 1990: 84.

"The Talk of the Town: Fanciers." The New
Yorker 31 Dec. 1990: 28-29.

- List the date of the article immediately after the name of the magazine.
- If the article is unsigned, begin the citation with the selection's title. Alphabetize the entry in the "Works Cited" by the first significant word in the title.
- List the page number(s) for the selection immediately after the publication date. Separate the date and pages with a colon and a single space. Omit abbreviations for "page" or "pages."
- If a multipage article appears on nonconsecutive pages, put a plus sign (+) after the first page number and omit other page numbers.

APA   Springen, K. (1990, December 31). A 100 mile
race? No sweat. Newsweek, p. 84.

The talk of the town: Fanciers. (1990, December
31). The New Yorker, pp. 28-29.

- Include the month and day of a weekly publication in parentheses with the publication year.
- Use the abbreviations *p.* or *pp.* before listing the selection's page numbers.

24. SIGNED AND UNSIGNED EDITORIALS; LETTERS TO THE EDITOR; PUBLISHED AND UNPUBLISHED LETTERS

MLA   Koch, Ron A. "Activism vs. Apathy."
Editorial. U. The National College
Newspaper 15 Mar. 1991: 6-7.

"Power Merge." Editorial. Wall Street Journal
7 Mar. 1991, Western ed., sec. A: 14.

Le Carré, John. Letter. The [London] Times 17
Mar. 1981: 13.

45e
Irr

- Begin the citation with the author's name if the editorial is signed. If it is unsigned, begin with the editorial's title.
- Put the word "Editorial" immediately after the title to label the selection. Do not underline or use quotation marks around the word.
- Follow the name of the magazine or newspaper with the publication date, a colon, space, and the page number(s) of the editorial. Omit the abbreviations *pg.* or *pp.*
- Indicate the edition of the newspaper. (See the paper's masthead.)
- If the newspaper is divided into sections, indicate the section with the abbreviation *sec.*

APA   Koch, R. A. (1991, March). Activism vs. apathy [Editorial]. U. The National College Newspaper, pp. 6, 7.

Power merge. (1991, March, 7). [Editorial]. The Wall Street Journal, p. 14.

Le Carré, J. (1981, March 17). Unlicensed to quote. [Letter to the editor]. The [London] Times, p. 13.

- Identify the work by putting either [Editorial] or [Letter to the Editor] in brackets after the title.
- If a multipage article appears on nonconsecutive pages, list the individual page numbers. Separate with commas.

MLA   Gordon, George (Lord Byron). "To John Murray." 21 Feb. 1820. Letter in Lord Byron: Selected Poems and Letters. Ed. William H. Marshall. Boston: Houghton, 1968. 469-73.

Labov, William. Letter to the author. 23 July 1989.

- Format published letters as if they were selections in a collection.
- Identify research information you receive in personal correspondence.

45e
Irr

APA   Gordon, G. (Lord Byron). (1968). Letter to John
          Murray. In W. H. Marshall (Ed.), Lord Byron:
          Selected poems and letters (pp.
          469-473). Boston: Houghton Mifflin.

- Format published letters as selections in a collection.
- Cite personal correspondence in the text, not in the "Works Cited."

25. BOOK REVIEWS

MLA   Mitgang, Herbert. Rev. of Savage Inequalities,
          by Jonathan Kozol. New York Times 25 Sept.
          1991, sec. C: 21.

       Henry, William A., III. "Going Beyond Brand
          Names." Rev. of Extenuating
          Circumstances, by Jonathan Valin. Time 3
          Apr. 1989: 81-82.

- List the reviewer's name first. If the review is unsigned, list the title first.
- Follow the title with the abbreviation *Rev. of* ("Review of"), the underlined title of the work reviewed, a comma, and the work's author.
- For a newspaper review, put the page number(s) of the review immediately after the section designation. Separate the elements with a colon.

APA   Mitgang, H. (1991, September 25). [Review of
          Savage Inequalites]. New York Times, p. C21.

       Henry, W. A., III. (1989, April 3). Going
          beyond brand names [Review of Extenuating
          circumstances]. Time, 81-82.

- If the review is untitled, use the information in the brackets as a title. Retain the brackets.
- Omit the abbreviations *pg.* or *pp.* before the page number(s).

45e
Irr

BIBLIOGRAPHIC MODELS FOR OTHER PRINT SOURCES

26. GOVERNMENT PUBLICATIONS

MLA   United States. Cong. Senate. Committee on Governmental Affairs. <u>Infrastructure Problems and Intergovernmental Solutions: Hearing Before the Subcommittee on General Services, Federalism, and the District of Columbia.</u> Washington: GPO, 1989.

New Mexico. Cooperative Extension Services. <u>Suicides in New Mexico by County.</u> By Leo Yates and Byron B. King. Las Cruces: New Mexico State University, 1978.

Rockwell, David C. <u>Water quality in the middle Great Lakes: Results of the 1985 USEPA Survey of Lakes Erie, Huron, and Michigan.</u> Chicago: United States Environmental Protection Agency and Great Lakes National Program Office, 1989.

- If no author is cited, begin the reference with the name of the government (national, state) and agency issuing the document. If an author is cited, list the name with *By* after the title or begin the entry with the author's name.
- List the title of the publication, underlined, after the agency.
- If known, list the edition (with the abbreviation *ed.*) or number of volumes (with the abbreviation *vols.*).
- Follow the abbreviations *S* (Senate), *H* (House), *S. Res.* (Senate Resolution), *H. Res.* (House Resolution), *S. Rept.* (Senate Report), *H. Rept.* (House Report), *S. Doc.* (Senate Document), and *H. Doc.* (House Document) with their identifying numbers.
- Use the abbreviations *GPO* (Government Printing Office) or *HMSO* (Her Majesty's Stationery Office).

APA   United States Congressional Committee on
         governmental Affairs.   (1989).
         Infrastructure problems and
         intergovernmental solutions: Hearing before
         Subcommittee on general services,
         federalism, and the District of
         Columbia.   Washington, DC: U.S. Government
         Printing Office.
      New Mexico Cooperative Extension Service.
         (1978).   Suicides in New Mexico by
         county.   Las Cruces: New Mexico State
         University.
      Rockwell, D. C. (1989).   Water quality in the
         middle Great Lakes: Results of the 1985 USEPA
         survey of Lakes Erie, Huron, and
         Michigan.   Chicago: United States
         Environmental Protection Agency and Great
         Lakes National Program Office.

* List the author's name first if known.
* If the government agency assigned the report a contract number, monograph number, or report number, include that information, in parentheses, after the work's title. Omit any punctuation between the title and the contract, monograph, or report
  number.

27. PUBLISHED PROCEEDINGS OF CONFERENCES

MLA   Littlefield, James E. , and Magdolna Csath,
         eds.   Marketing and Development: Issues
         and Opinions: Proceedings of the Second
         International Conference on Marketing and
         Development.   Blacksburg: Dept. of
         Marketing, Virginia Tech, 1988.

* Consider individual selections from the published proceedings
  of a conference as works in an anthology or collection.
* Consider published proceedings of conferences as books.

45e
Irr

APA   Littlefield, J. E., & Csath, M. (Eds.).
(1988). Marketing and economic development:
Issues and opinions: Proceedings of the
second international conference on marketing
and development. Blacksburg: Dept. of
Marketing, Virginia Tech.

- Consider individual selections from the published proceedings of a conference as works in collections.
- Consider regularly published proceedings as periodicals.

28. PUBLISHED DISSERTATION OR THESIS

MLA   Stoutenburg, G. A Psycholinguistic Approach to
Study the Language Deficits in the Language
Performance of Deaf Children. Diss.
Syracuse U, 1971. Ann Arbor: UMI,
1982. 72-6631.

Scharnhorst, Gary F. Good Fortune in America:
The Life of Horatio Alger. Diss. Purdue
U, 1978. Boston: Hall, 1980.

- Follow the abbreviation *Diss.* with a double space, the name of the degree-granting institution, and the dissertation's date.
- For a dissertation later published as a book, end the citation with the city, publisher, and date of publication.

45e
Irr

APA   Stoutenburg, G. (1971). A psycholinguistic
approach to study the language deficits in
the language performance of deaf children
(Doctoral dissertation, Syracuse
University, 1971). Dissertation Abstracts
International, 32, 6104B-6105B. (University
Microfilms No. 72-6631)

Scharnhorst, G. F. (1980). <u>Good fortune in</u>
<u>America: The life of Horatio Alger</u>. Boston:
G. K. Hall.

- Treat a published dissertation as a book unless you obtained the copy from University Microfilms.
- Do not underline the titles of dissertations published by University Microfilms.
- If you refer to the microfilm version of a dissertation, include the microfilm's number, as well as the volume and page numbers where you found the reference in *DAI.*

29. ABSTRACTS FROM *DISSERTATION ABSTRACTS INTERNATIONAL*

MLA   Griffin, Patricia C. "The Impact of Tourism and
Development on Public Ritual and Festival:
St. Augustine, Florida, 1821-1987." <u>DAI</u>
8908233 (1988): 185A. U of Florida.

- *Dissertation Abstracts (DA)* became *Dissertation Abstracts International (DAI)* in 1969 with volume 30.
- Volumes 27–36 were paginated with the abbreviations *A* for humanities and social sciences and *B* for sciences.
- Starting with volume 27, *DAI* added a third section for European dissertations, paginating it with *C.*
- Follow the abbreviation *DAI* with the dissertation's number, its year (in parentheses), a colon, and the page number in *DAI.*
- End the citation by identifying the degree-granting institution.

APA   Griffin, P. C. (1989). The impact of tourism
and development on public ritual and
festival: St. Augustine, Florida,
1821-1987. (Doctoral dissertation,
University of Florida, 1988). <u>Dissertation</u>
<u>Abstracts International</u>, 50, 185A.

- Omit University Microfilm information if you obtain a copy of a dissertation from the degree-granting institution.
- If the dissertation's publication and completion dates differ, cite both dates in the report.

45e
Irr

30. PUBLISHED AND UNPUBLISHED INTERVIEWS

MLA   Greene, Graham. The Other Man: Conversations
          with Graham Greene. By Marie-Françoise
          Allain. Trans. Guido Waldman. London:
          Bodley, 1981.

       Tarn, Nathaniel. Telephone interview. 27 Nov.
          1990.

* Begin citation with the interviewee's name followed by the title of the interview. If the interview is untitled, label the work *Interview.* Omit underlining or quotation marks around the label.
* Include the interviewer's name(s) if given in the publication.
* Complete reference citation with publishing information.

APA   Allain, M. (1981). The other man:
          Conversations with Graham Greene (G. Waldo,
          Trans.). London: Bodley Head.

* Use the format that matches the published source for the interview. Thus for newspapers, use an editorial or letter-to-the-editor format; for books, use the book citation format.
* Incorporate references to personal or telephone interviews in the report's text. For example: N. Tarn (personal communication, April 27, 1990). Omit listing in the "Works Cited."

31. MAP OR CHART

MLA   New Mexico. Map. Santa Fe: New Mexico State
          Highway Dept., 1981.

       Hearing, Language, Social Skills, Motor
          Skills. Chart. Duluth: U of Minnesota,
          Dept. of Communicative Disorders, 1981.

* Format maps and charts as if they were anonymous publications.
* Use the labels *Map* and *Chart,* respectively, to identify maps and charts. Omit underlining or quotation marks around the label.

APA   New Mexico. [Map]. (1981). Santa Fe: New
      Mexico State Highway Department.

Hearing, Language, Social Skills, Motor
      Skills. [Chart]. (1981). Duluth:
      University of Minnesota, Department of
      Communicative Disorders.

BIBLIOGRAPHIC MODELS FOR NONPRINT SOURCES

32. MUSICAL COMPOSITIONS; WORKS OF ART

MLA   Mozart, Wolfgang Amadeus. Piano Concerto No. 20
      in D minor.

Beethoven, Ludwig van. A Beethoven
      Ceremonial. New York: Fox, 1971.

O'Keefe, Georgia. Blue and Green Music. Art
      Institute of Chicago, Stieglitz
      Collection, Chicago.

- Omit underlining and quotation marks for instrumental compositions identified only by form, number, and key.
- Format a published score as a book publication.

APA   Mozart, W. Piano Concerto No. 20 in D
      minor. [Musical composition].

Beethoven, L. (1971). A Beethoven
      ceremonial. [Musical score]. New York: Sam
      Fox.

O'Keefe, G. Blue and Green Music. [Art
      work]. Chicago: Art Institute of Chicago.

- Label the medium in brackets after the work's title (for instance, art work, audiotape, musical composition, musical score, slide, videotape).

33. UNPUBLISHED LECTURES, SPEECHES, AND PUBLIC ADDRESSES

MLA   McQuade, Donald. Address. Opening General
        Sess. Conference on College Composition
        and Communication. Chicago, 22 Mar. 1990.

45e
Irr

- If the presentation is untitled, label the talk as an *Address, Keynote speech,* or *Lecture.* Omit underlining or quotation marks around these descriptive labels.
- If the presentation is titled, put quotation marks around that title. Follow the title with the conference title, city, and date.

APA   McQuade, D. (1990, March 22). <u>Opening general</u>
<u>session address</u>. Paper presented at the
Conference on College Composition and
Communication, Chicago, IL.

34. MOVIE OR TELEVISION PRODUCTIONS

MLA   <u>The Invasion of the Body Snatchers</u>. Dir. Don
Siegel. With Kevin McCarthy and Dana
Wynter. Allied Artists, 1956. Black and
white, 80 min.

Siegel, Don, dir. <u>The Invasion of the Body</u>
<u>Snatchers</u>. With Kevin McCarthy and Dana
Wynter. Allied Artists, 1956. Black and
white, 80 min.

- Underline the title of films.
- If you are referencing the film, start with its title. Include the director's and distributor's names and the release date. Include other identifying information (such as actors' names, physical characteristics) if pertinent to your report.
- If you are referencing the director, producer, or major actor, start with that person's name.

<u>Adam Clayton Powell</u>. Narr. Julian Bond. Prod.
Richard Kilberg and Yvonne Smith. Dir.
Richard Kilberg. The American
Experience. WNET. KNME, Albuquerque. 17
Feb. 1991.

- If you are citing a single program, list this title (underlined), the network, local station and city, and broadcast date.
- If you are referencing an episode from a television series, list its title (in quotation marks), narrator, producer, and director before the title of the program.

APA   Wanger, W. (Producer), & Siegel,
            D. (Director). (1956)The invasion of the
            body snatchers. [Film]. Hollywood: Allied
            Artists.

- Identify the medium in brackets immediately after the title.

        Kilberg, R. (Director). Bond,
            J. (Narrator). (1991, February 17). Adam
            Clayton Powell. [Television program].
            Albuquerque: KNME, The American
            Experience.

- Identify the production by putting in brackets an identifying label (such as television program, film).

35. INFORMATION SERVICES

MLA   Hall, Christian, and Karen Sunde. Text
            Linguistics and Composition. ERIC,
            1985. ED 272 863.

        McPartland, James M., and Robert E. Slavin.
            Increasing Achievement of At-Risk Students
            at Each Grade Level. Policy Perspectives
            Series Rept. 15-90-985. Washington:
            Office of Educational Research and
            Improvement, 1990. ERIC ED 317656-318
            838.

45e
Irr

- Include the program name and report number, if given; the location and name of the educational institution; and the publication year for any ERIC (Educational Resources Information Center) or NTIS (National Technical Information Service) document.
- List the service's identifying number for the report.
- If the document was previously published, list this information before the service name and identifying number.

APA McPartland, J. M., & Slavin, R. E. (1990).
     <u>Increasing achievement levels of at-risk
     students at each grade level</u>. (Report No.
     15-90-985). Washington, DC: Office of
     Educational Research and Improvement. (ERIC
     Document Reproduction Service No. ED
     317656-318 838)

     Hall, C., & Sunde, K. (1985). <u>Text linguistics
     and composition</u>. (ERIC Document
     Reproduction Service No. ED 272 863)

36. COMPUTER SOFTWARE

MLA <u>PC Tools Deluxe</u>. Vers. 5.5. Computer
         software. Central Point Software,
         1989. MS-DOS 3.2 or higher, 512K, disk.

- List the software program's author first if known. If that is
  unknown, list the program title (underlined) and the version, a
  descriptive label without underlining or quotation marks (for
  example, Computer software), the distributor's name, and the
  year.
- Separate the items with periods except for the distributor's
  name and the year. Separate those items with a comma.
- End citation with relevant operating information (such as system size, kilobytes number, form of program).

APA <u>PC tools deluxe</u>. Vers. 5.5 [Computer
         software]. (1989). Central Point
         Software. MS-DOS 3.2 or higher. 512K, disk.

- List the software program's author first if known. If unknown,
  start with the program title (underlined), version, and date of
  issue. Put a descriptive label (for instance, Computer software)
  in brackets following the title and version.
- Complete citation with distributor's name and relevant operating information.

45e
lrr

46

46a

Composing a First Draft

An engaging research report isn't a mere list of other people's investigations. It's an essay that presents your perspective in a thesis statement, integrates pertinent quotations and restatements with that thesis, and draws conclusions based on your synthesis of the research you have done. Start with a tentative framework for the report, sort your note cards to fit this framework, and write the first draft. Use a separate sheet of paper for each paragraph in the report, and list each paragraph's topic at the top of the sheets. This method is particularly helpful when you draft special paragraphs such as the introduction, conclusion, and those paragraphs that include quotations and paraphrases of the research you have industriously gathered. Additionally, using individual sheets of paper insures that each paragraph develops one idea and lets you easily verify the documentation for each quotation and paraphrase. This method helps you check individual paragraphs for unity and coherence and revise and edit a bit at a time for style and grammatical correctness.

1 Writing the First Draft

Research is seductive. Once you start looking for information, it is hard to stop. Eventually, you have to start writing. Start your first draft by reviewing your thesis statement. If it is a complex statement, simplify it. Break it down into its individual parts, number the parts, and move them around. Determine what unifies those parts, restate this generality, and use it to redraft your tentative thesis into a simple, declarative sentence.

Start writing the overall information for your report by first quickly jotting down a summary. *Don't start writing your introduction.* Put down your major points, what you hope to prove about them, and suggest their support. Get the thesis statement in shape early. Use the main points (that is, those indicated by Roman numerals) from your outline as topic sentences for individual paragraphs. Proceed by developing the first major point. State your claim for this point and, if you think readers will question or doubt what you are stating, offer proof in the form of authority, details, facts, figures, evidence, observations, or parallels. These are the persuasive strategies of logical reasoning. Details always keep readers alert. If you use a direct quotation or paraphrase, staple the note card with the material and its source to the sheet of paper and go on. You will save time, avoid misstating the quotation or confusing the paraphrase with your own ideas, and keep the citation and its bibliographic information where you want it. Concentrate on presenting your perspective—not on polishing your style.

Repeat the process of stating a main point, developing it, and incorporating quoted and paraphrased information until you have exhausted your outline. If you want to add information to a unit, you can do so on extra pages, marked with the appropriate page number and a letter—for example, 2a, 2b, and so on (2a follows 2 and precedes 2b). If you do so, you will not need to wonder where an insert belongs when you are revising. Amend the outline as you write by crossing out material, drawing arrows from one item to another, and adding side notes. Finally, don't expect to develop more than one long section of a report at a time. You are integrating an outline, research material, and your perspective into a fluid research document.

46a
drr

2 Weaving Quotations, Paraphrases, and Summaries into Research Reports

One of the most important skills you can develop is weaving quotations, paraphrases, and summaries smoothly into research reports. Poorly integrated quotations and restatements misrepresent the message of the original source and can suggest to readers that you are padding your report. They also put you at risk of plagiarizing. Borrowings skillfully blended into your text pinpoint an exact meaning or condense, in a pithy statement, an idea particularly relevant to your perspective.

You began integrating quotations, paraphrases, and summaries before you started drafting. You analyzed what a quotation says and how it says it by looking carefully at the source's perspective, tone, and style. Then you considered whether you would paraphrase the information or broadly summarize it. Now you have to combine quotations and restatements with your prose so that the syntax, verb tenses, pronouns, and so forth of both merge into a logical, seamless text.

There are several ways you can blend direct quotations into your report. Try always to provide a context for the quotation that suggests to your readers what connects your material and the cited information. Quoted material should illuminate your points; readers should not be left wondering why a particular quotation appears.

One way to weave quotations into text is to mention the writer's name or the title of the work before quoting:

ORIGINAL:
Personalized news encourages people to take an egocentric rather than socially concerned view of political problems. Moreover, the focus on attractive political personalities encourages a passive attitude among a public inclined to let those personalities do their thinking and acting for them. (W. Lance Bennett, *News: The Politics of Illusion*)

CITED IN REPORT:
W. Lance Bennett, a political science professor critical of today's network newscasts argues against human-interest stories: "Personalized news encourages people to take an egocentric rather than socially concerned view of political problems" (23).

If the quoted information is a partial sentence, match the grammatical construction of your framing sentence with that of the quotation:

CITED IN REPORT:
W. Lance Bennett, a political science professor, contends that the American public loses sight of governmental, political, and world events when its attention is diverted by entertainment masquerading as news. Commercial pressures encourage viewers "to take an egocentric rather than socially concerned view of political problems" and "a passive attitude" that prefers to let others do the thinking for them (Bennett 23).

46a
drr

Techniques for introducing quotations can become awkward and redundant if you use them too often. Try varying your sentence structure or relying on paraphrases and summaries more than quotations to avoid monotony.

Integrating Quotations into Research Reports

1. Use only quotations that fix your meaning, set up a position that you are contradicting, or state a point in unusually forceful or well-chosen language.

2. Never distort a source's meaning by quoting out of context or deleting pertinent information.

3. Introduce a quotation into your text by mentioning the writer's name or the title of the work that you are quoting from, or by working the quotation into the grammar of your sentence.

4. Always put quotation marks around direct quotations, unless you set them off from your text as block quotations (see 5). Use a colon to introduce a quotation that defines what you have just said. (For example—Even movie buffs deride Howard Hughes's movie *The Outlaw:* "Inconsistent and poorly directed.") Use a comma to introduce short quotations. (For instance, "A prime example," X claims, "is Y.") Omit the comma before quotations introduced by *that.*

5. Set off from your text quotations of more than four lines as a block, by indenting each line of the quotation ten spaces (five spaces for APA style) from the left margin. Double-space such quotations but do not use quotation marks around them.

6. Always include a citation and bibliographic reference for a quotation.

46a
drr

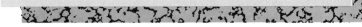

A quotation must appear in the original writer's exact words and (with some exceptions) follow his or her spelling, capitalization, and interior punctuation. Further, you must either enclose the quotation in quotation marks or set it off from your own prose, and you must have a bibliographic reference that tells interested readers where to find the original. You may make some slight changes in quoted material. These changes usualy involve changing capitalization so that a quotation will blend smoothly into your own prose. See **37a** for advice on capitalization in quoting.

There are two cautions to keep in mind as well. Avoid putting your arguments in explanatory comments within a quotation. You will write a more readable report if you argue with a source after you have given the quotation. Even more important, never twist a source's meaning by omitting information.

Direct quotations are often better for reports in the humanities because the quotations are from primary sources, such as literary texts or historical documents. Summaries and paraphrases are more common in business, science, and social science reports.

Finally, you use the same basic strategies to weave paraphrases (indirect quotations) and summaries into your report that you use to integrate direct quotations.

As you are drafting, reread the quoted, paraphrased, or summarized material, and ask yourself what significance it has for your perspective. Whether you use a quotation, a paraphrase, or a summary, you want only material that crystallizes your point, sums up a body of data, provides an original example supporting your claim, or points to trends or advancements important to this claim.

Revising Your Research Report

 Drafting Introductions and Conclusions

Introductions

Because introductions are maps to the content of your research report, they should be written after you know what your report is about. In other words, *write your introduction last.*

Unlike conclusions, introductions are seldom a discrete element of your research report. In easing readers toward their conclusions, some writers break up their reports into units with subheadings. Although they commonly label the section that presents their judgments as "Conclusion," they avoid calling the beginning of a report section an "Introduction." Instead, they usually label such preliminary sections "Background," "Statements" or "Definitions of the Problem," "Specifications," and so forth. These subheadings describe a report's content succinctly and identify its topic. They also indicate why the report was written and suggest the author's perspective.

Your introduction may describe the problem that you have researched, referencing the situation leading up to it and profiling the major questions it raises; or it may pose a question that your report answers or debates. Both of these techniques funnel information from a broad statement to a restricted thesis statement. By starting in general terms and narrowing to specifics, you familiarize your readers with your whole report and give them enough understanding to appreciate its content. Introducing the context for your research or posing salient questions works to your advantage when your audience is relatively uninformed and needs some background in order to understand the research project.

However, not all research documents require introductions. If your audience is already familiar with the topic and with your perspective, an introduction to either is superfluous. In such cases, a definition, some interesting detail, a list of recommendations, or an anecdote better illustrates your perspective and takes your readers immediately into the research subject.

Introductions can do more than present your perspective to your readers. They can also familiarize your readers with new terms, acronyms, and initials that the readers must know in order to read your report intelligently. Finally, an introduction introduces you. Therefore, you should revise your introduction's style until you appear as objective and knowledgeable as possible. This strategy induces your audience to read on and may help you convince it of your conclusions.

Conclusions

Conclusions to research reports briefly restate your research question and your results in the light of your audience's needs and the report's purpose. The conclusion reintroduces your opening perspective and shows how the evidence supports your thesis. Conclusions also point out the implications of your research and can suggest directions for future researchers. Conclusions are not the place to introduce problems that you have avoided in the report or hypotheses or findings that defeat your report's objectives. If you have not dealt effectively with such issues, revise your report.

**46b
drr**

2 Revising Your Report's Informational and Cohesive Patterns

Revising your drafted report calls directly upon your critical reading skills. *Challenge everything.* Review the report's information and then its cohesive structure to see if you have written readable, coherent prose. Review the graphics and bibliographic information as well, using the same strategies. (See Chapter 11 for global revisions and the chapters in Unit 9, Style, for stylistic revisions.) Revisions take less time than drafts. Nevertheless, sections of your report may require several revisions. In addition, you need to check the quotations, paraphrases, summaries, and bibliographic information at least twice.

46c

Preparing Ancillary Materials for Your Research Report

1 Informational and Descriptive Abstracts

Abstracts recapitulate a report's information, identify keywords, and highlight the conclusions. They are self-contained summaries, written in nonevaluative prose. You place an abstract after the report's title page and before the table of contents and list of illustrations or figures to help readers determine what your topic is and whether your report would be of interest to them.

A **descriptive abstract** is a short overview that reads almost like a table of contents to your report:

A series of experiments tested the effects of temperature on color changes with Hyla crucifer. Experimental results showed that temperature and substrate significantly influenced color changes.

An **informational abstract,** on the other hand, is longer because it includes not only major points but also the scope of your report, its findings, conclusions, and recommendations:

46c
drr

This report describes two factors that influence the color changes of the spring peeper. The relevant information for the report came from a series of experiments that tested the effects of temperature and substrate on color changes with Hyla crucifer. The results of these experiments contradict published studies on the relationship of temperature to color variation.

Informational abstracts are generally about 3 percent as long as the report or, at most, about 200 to 250 words. Descriptive abstracts are about half this length.

2 Table of Contents

A **table of contents** lists the headings and subheadings in long or complex research reports. By this means, it gives readers the gist of a report and tells them where to find particular information.

You prepare a table of contents by listing the major headings *in the same words that you use in your report.* After each major heading, alternate periods and spaces until you are within two inches of the right margin. Then list the page number for each heading. Indent any subheadings from your report under the appropriate main headings, and put their page numbers after a series of periods and spaces. Specify the illustrations, figures, and tables separately, in a "List of Illustrations" immediately after the table of contents.

3 Graphics

Graphics are **visual aids** that condense numerical information, present sparse or monotonously repetitive data, or portray useful details or connections. **Tables** summarize quantitative data; **figures** depict relevant information through charts, diagrams, graphs, photographs, or other illustrations. You can create a graphic from the research you collect. You can also use graphics printed in other sources, but you must cite the source and give a complete reference in your bibliography.

Graphics summarize any information, trends, or correlations discussed in a research report and can be persuasive supplements to the text. Yet no matter how precisely drafted or artistically illustrated, a graphic cannot make your data more important than they are or take the place of your written explanations. Therefore, when you have finished revising the text of your report, arrange charts, figures, illustrations, or tables to match the information in your report and on your storyboards. Then consider each graphic separately for its density, that is, how much information it presents; its simplicity, that is, how directly it presents the data; and its impact, that is, the effect it will have on the audience. Tables, for example, are usually filled with information and so are considered dense graphics. Line drawings are relatively uncomplicated when compared with annotated photographs. Pie charts may present less information than tables but usually make a greater impact on audiences, particularly when they are in color.

46c
drr

46d

Formatting and Publishing Your Research Report

Your report is written, revised, and edited. You have prepared necessary graphic aids and rechecked each citation and bibliographic entry. Now you need to type a final draft or review your computer copy before you print it. Like bibliographic entries, formatting requirements vary with the style manual you follow. The general recommendations offered here are based on the *MLA Handbook for Writers of Research Papers* (third edition) and the *Publication Manual of the American Psychological Association* (third edition, revised). Always check your discipline's style manual for specific guidelines.

1 General Standards

Use 8½-by-11-inch heavy white bond paper rather then erasable or colored paper. Put a new ribbon in your typewriter, and if you use a printer, it should be one with letter-quality rather than dot-matrix type. You want your audience to be able to read your report without having the paper tear, the print smear, or the typeface be difficult to decipher. Leave a 1½-inch left margin and make the remaining margins 1 inch wide. (APA recommends that all margins be 1½ inches.) Indent the beginnings of paragraphs five spaces, and indent block quotations ten spaces (five spaces for APA style). Double-space the entire text, including blocked quotations and the bibliography.

You should be able to type twenty-four to twenty-five lines per page. The *MLA Handbook* recommends numbering every page in your report consecutively by putting an Arabic numeral—along with your last name—in the upper, right-hand corner of each page. Omit the abbreviation *pg.* before the page number. APA style substitutes the short title for the author's name and omits page numbers only for figures. The APA *Manual* assumes that research reports have title pages; the *MLA Handbook* does not recommend them. On the first page of a report formatted according to MLA guidelines, type your name flush with the left margin, one inch from the top of the page. Double-space and type your audience's name, the course number, and the date, with double spacing between each part. Both the MLA and the APA manuals recommend centering your report's title and typing it in upper- and lower-case letters without quotation marks or underlining.

46d
drr

Type secondary headings in upper- and lower-case letters, and place them in the left margin. (Underline secondary headings for APA format.)

Center other headings, including "Works Cited" or "References," and type them in upper- and lower-case letters. Put the first line of each bibliographic entry flush with the left margin and indent all subsequent lines of an entry five spaces from the left margin. Begin each appendix on a separate page, and double-space any written text in an appendix.

2 A Final Review of the Finished Report

Before handing it in, review how your research report looks. It should be carefully edited and proofread. It should also be neat and legibly typed or printed. If you must make corrections, insert them in ink and use a caret ($\wedge$) to indicate where the additional material should appear.

Make sure that your formats for headings, subheadings, and graphics are consistent and that every citation has an accompanying bibliographic reference formatted according to the appropriate style manual. Check to ascertain that you have numbered the pages and graphics consecutively and labeled and titled any appendixes. If your audience demands it, include an abstract, a separate title page, table of contents, and list of figures. Then put the report in an appropriate binder. You are ready to submit it.

46d
drr

Karen Brophy and Alexander Pottston, college undergraduate students, wrote the following reports for a research assignment. The issue is television news, and the course is a sophomore/junior class entitled Communications 321. Brophy argues that television newscasts have changed for the worse because corporations favor profit over the information. Pottston, on the other hand, argues that entertaining newscasts keep viewers watching the news. He implies that the more Americans watch the news, the more they learn about their increasingly chaotic world. Brophy, a humanities major, chose *MLA Handbook* format for her report, while Pottston, a psychology student, preferred *APA* style.

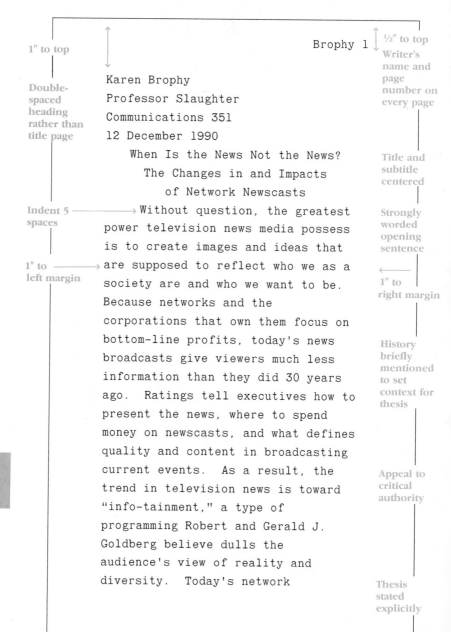

1" to top

Double-spaced heading rather than title page

Indent 5 spaces

1" to left margin

½" to top
Writer's name and page number on every page

Title and subtitle centered

Strongly worded opening sentence

1" to right margin

History briefly mentioned to set context for thesis

Appeal to critical authority

Thesis stated explicitly

Brophy 1

Karen Brophy
Professor Slaughter
Communications 351
12 December 1990

When Is the News Not the News?
The Changes in and Impacts
of Network Newscasts

Without question, the greatest power television news media possess is to create images and ideas that are supposed to reflect who we as a society are and who we want to be. Because networks and the corporations that own them focus on bottom-line profits, today's news broadcasts give viewers much less information than they did 30 years ago. Ratings tell executives how to present the news, where to spend money on newscasts, and what defines quality and content in broadcasting current events. As a result, the trend in television news is toward "info-tainment," a type of programming Robert and Gerald J. Goldberg believe dulls the audience's view of reality and diversity. Today's network

47
srr

Brophy 2

newscasts threaten to overpower
reality and create passive viewers
with narrow outlooks who
misunderstand issues and public
debates.

    Interestingly, American nightly
newscasts began strictly as a public
service. Since it was created, the
Federal Communications Commission
(FCC), the government agency allowed
to grant licenses to television and
radio stations, required networks to
allot a specified amount of time to
public service programming.
Television news was considered a
public service and so met the FCC's
licensing requirements. Thus, as
long as the television companies
produced news shows, the FCC had no
objections to the huge profits that
the companies' entertainment
divisions made.

    The first nightly news service,
launched by the Columbia
Broadcasting System (CBS) in the
summer of 1948, was typical of the
emerging pattern for all newscasts.
Broadcasts were usually fifteen

Introduction of history of newscasts with facts discussed in the course

Factually stated analysis

Specific event to characterize general trend

First 22 years of newscasts summarized in one paragraph

47
srr

Brophy 3

minutes long and consisted of a
conservatively dressed man reading
news reports and showing a few,
sometimes crudely produced graphics.
Over the next twenty years
television newscasts grew to
half-hour shows with "news
anchors"--serious looking men reading
and telling the news--and dramatic
footage of the stories they
reported. During the 1960s, 93
percent of the American population
watched a nightly newscast every
evening, and over one-third of those
viewers watched the Texaco-sponsored
Huntley-Brinkley Report (Goldberg and
Goldberg 68).

Huntley-Brinkley's popularity
set the stage in the 1970s for CBS's
newscaster Walter Cronkite. To gain
a bigger audience, CBS officials
created the image in viewers' minds
that Cronkite was "the most trusted
man in America" (Goldberg and
Goldberg 68). In what reviewers now
see as the newscasts' heyday, news
anchors prided themselves on
delivering accurate, informative

Summary statement of factual information

Source and exact page number given without abbreviations "p" or "p 6."

Historical overview continues

47
srr

Direct quotation with quotation marks blended into text

Brophy 4

reports, and networks "devoted
resources to investigative stories
and didn't condescend to their
audience--they dared to be boring"
(Friend 158). American viewers'
trust in the information these news
anchors presented drew their
attention to the news anchors'
particular stations and networks.
In the early 1980s, when Walter
Cronkite stepped down, the
television news saw an end to this
era of analytical, if somewhat
colorless, newscasts.

    Starting in the 1980s and
continuing today, network news
decisions have focused on profits
and ratings, the means by which
networks set their advertising fees.
Networks shifted from giving
information to a more entertaining
format for news. The change
occurred largely because the three
major networks were bought by large
businesses concerned more with net
worth than with network news. For
example, at present the American
Broadcasting Company (ABC) is owned

Direct
quotation
with
quotation
marks
blended
into text

Less
objective
language
introduced

Thesis again
suggested

Causal
connection
suggested

47
srr

Abbreviations
placed after
first
mention of
full name

Brophy 5

by Capital Cities, CBS by Loews, and
the National Broadcasting Company
(NBC) by General Electric (GE)
(Goldberg and Goldberg 33). The

First argument suggested

goals company executives continue to
seek are to maximize profits and to

Factual material paraphrased from original source

minimize costs. This situation is
clearly illustrated by the fact that
NBC receives one page in GE's annual

Abbreviations used for rest of report

stockholders' report and NBC's news
division, whose profits represent
less than .5 percent of GE's annual
earnings, is not mentioned at all
(Friend 158). Those charged with
putting these goals into practice
increasingly question whether it is
the news executives' "job to cover
the story or to look good--to look
lean--to their corporate masters"
(Goldberg and Goldberg 110). While

Cause-effect connection stated directly

they worry that the FCC might refuse
to renew a network's license if it
cancels all its news broadcasts,
corporations demand profits. These
demands actually explain the shift
in attitude about newscasts. To

Restatement of connection in writer's words

stay on the air, news must be
attention-grabbing if not
sensational.

47
srr

Brophy 6

Chain of
cause-effect
connections
set up

In order to increase company profits, news shows must <u>acquire</u> advertising dollars. The only way to rationalize charging large sums for advertising--as high as $275,000 for 30 seconds of prime air time--is to maintain high viewer ratings (Teague 215). Therefore, producers must blend into news programs the characteristics of the shows that receive high ratings. This argument gives enormous power to ratings services that measure how large a share of the viewing audience each network show has. When they started, ratings were gathered from diaries kept by selected viewers across the country. Now the major rating service, the Nielsen, monitors viewing habits by installing recording boxes in designated viewers' homes. The Nielsens produce influential numbers. As Richard Wald, senior vice president of ABC News, comments, "the Nielsens represent a necessary mythology that the business couldn't do without. Those are the only

Factual data and paraphrase blended in one sentence

Direct quotation introduced

47
srr

Brophy 7

rules. We have to live with them"
(qtd. in Goldberg and Goldberg 33).

Ratings control advertising
rates and, therefore, have become
the measure by which major
programming and personnel decisions
are made. In the 1980s, for
example, ABC News was so desperate
to improve its Nielsens that it
hired Barbara Walters for $1 million
a year. Walters, a well-known
celebrity interviewer with no news
experience, became co-anchor with
respected television journalist Harry
Reasoner (Goldberg and Goldberg 71).
Such decisions make economic sense
to executives who realize that one
rating point can mean up to $1
million in advertising revenue
(Athiede 59). Concern with news
content gives way to "the business
of delivering people to advertisers.
The shows are merely the bait"
(Brown 15-16). News producers, the
people who put the reporters'
stories together with the footage,
are faced with corporate executives
examining profit margins and a

Brophy 8

viewing audience that has decreased over 30 percent since 1980 (Friend, 156). Producers scramble to attract more viewers and more money by making changes in their newscasts' formats that seldom improve how viewers get their news.

Multiple sources blended together in one paragraph

Second argument for thesis

The concern with profits has changed the traditional standards for newsworthy reporting. Previously, broadcasters adopted the standards of print media that judged a story's value by its relevance and potential to affect the public, its political balance, and its freshness and timeliness (Warner 163-65). Today, whatever increases ratings or cuts costs controls what stories appear on the air as news and how they are reported. Private research at NBC, for example, concluded that the "three most important factors that influence ratings are the lead-in audience from local newscasts; the anchor; and last and least content" (Friend 162). In a survey of more than a dozen media observers, Joanmarie Kalter and Jane

47
srr

Brophy 9

Marion found that network
newscasters prefer to avoid
controversial issues such as race or
class and to present journalists as
interesting personalities rather than
"news gatherers and reporters"
(3-4). And Edwin Diamond discovered
that news is chosen more for its
footage and entertainment value than
for its significance to the general
public. He reports that two
executives in New York watched all
three network newscasts one night.

> There had been a fire at a
> Roman Catholic orphanage on
> Staten Island. One
> executive complained that a
> rival station had better
> coverage. "Their flames
> are higher than ours," he
> said. But another
> executive countered: "Yes,
> but our nun is crying
> harder than theirs"
> (Diamond xi).

By standards like these,
putting the national news after
local newscasts, airing sensational

Page citation only when author's name is mentioned in the sentence

No quotation marks with block quotations

Double-spaced block quotation

Indent 10 spaces

Transition paragraph linking corporate decisions with damaging results to newscasts

Writer's summary of major causes

47
srr

Brophy 10

stories, hiring a celebrity anchor,
and keeping news stories
disconnected are smart economic
moves. However, applying these
standards to news reporting
decreases the amount of information
viewers see and inevitably leads to
several disruptions in news
programs. It makes a national
anchor more important than the
story. It promotes local events
over costly and often more critical
international stories. It elevates
scandals, gossip, and entertainment
reports over in-depth analyses of
major political and international
events. It also lessens newscasts'
public service mission.

Corporate executives, and the
news producers they employ, infer
from the ratings that American
viewers want entertainment rather
than substance. NBC Nightly News
with Tom Brokaw is a prime example
of a newscast that favored such
corporate decisions. As Tad Friend
recounts, in an attempt to move the
newscast out of its last place

Effect of
causes
listed

Consequences
to specific
newscast
and
network
examined

47
srr

Brophy 11

rating, GE executives put the Nightly News in the hands of Steve Friedman, the executive producer legendary for pulling the Today Show out of its slump. Friedman saw the news as entertainment, a view of programming that worked for the Today Show. He attempted to create a more popular news show by adding weekly human interest features on power, guns, and drugs and by curbing expenses by cutting stories, analyses, commentary and some staff (e.g., reporters, producers, researchers).

Friedman saw the Teenage Mutant Ninja Turtles and the singing group "New Kids on the Block" as more worthy news items than some foreign news stories that he felt did not "really matter to the American people" (Friend 162). One time he ordered a story on Soviet President Mikhail Gorbachev's negotiations with officials from the Baltic States cut from a ninety-second story to a fifteen-second voice-over placed fourteen minutes into the broadcast.

e.g., abbreviation for Latin *exempli gratia* (for example)

Decision made for entertainment contrasted to decision made for news value

47
srr

Brophy 12

The event was a two-column head story the next day in the New York Times and the lead-in story that evening on the ABC World News Tonight.

Friedman's staff reductions followed his news philosophy; he warned that the news business was moving away from the old tradition of journalism. "Everyone who's gnashing their teeth about the death of the [Edward R.] Murrow tradition has 'former' in front of their name, they're just not in business anymore" (Friend 164). By this reasoning, reporters wedded to the older standards of television journalism were no better than extinct dinosaurs.

Friedman's changes, however, backfired, leaving the Nightly News at times shallow, its staff demoralized, and its ability to track breaking news stories seriously delayed. Staff cutbacks, for example, made gathering news during the 1989 San Francisco earthquake nearly impossible. While

Brackets enclose information not found in source material

Writer's analysis colorfully stated

47
srr

Brophy 13

ABC, CBS, and Cable News Network
(CNN) were rushing to San Francisco
to find spots from which to report
the event, NBC staff were stuck in
New York, unable to contact their
anchor, Tom Brokaw, or to get their
reporters into position. NBC news
covered the earthquake 50 minutes
later than any other network, and
Brokaw did not go on the air until

Analysis linked to factual information from course

the next day (Goldberg and Goldberg
24-29). Worst of all, despite the
changes, NBC's Nightly News has not
climbed out of its third-place
ranking in the Nielsen ratings.

These changes in approach to
and content of television news have
substantial consequences for American
citizens. W. Lance Bennett, a
political science professor, contends
that the American public loses sight
of governmental, political, and
world events when its attention is
diverted by entertainment
masquerading as news. Commercial
pressures encourage viewers "to take
an egocentric rather than socially
concerned view of political

Major consequence of changes stated

Non-media insider's position stated first

47 srr

Brophy 14

problems" and "a passive attitude" that prefers to let others do the thinking for them (Bennett 23). The result of this trend is that Americans who get their news primarily from television will not be capable of understanding the world and of participating in democratic processes.

Major point of writer's thesis restated

Media insiders' position stated second

Strong criticism of the "info-tainment" trend exists within the industry as well as without. Fred Friendly, former President of CBS News, resigned when network executives refused to interrupt I Love Lucy reruns for the Congressional hearings on Vietnam. Noted broadcast journalist Eric Sevareid labels celebrity anchors as people who "are acting the news . . . Journalists . . . trying to be stars" (qtd. in Teague 217). CBS news anchor Dan Rather fears that network news shows could become more of a newsreel that may package both local and national news in a one-hour format (Friend 156). CBS National Correspondent Bernard

Sources blended together to emphasize thesis

47
srr

Brophy 15

Goldberg, however, goes the furthest
in admitting why the change has
happened and what has to be done to
reverse it: "We better start
thinking about making the news more
important to people. The reason
we're losing viewers is because of
what we've defined as important"
(Goldberg and Goldberg 373).

Some critics who question the
consequences of this shift in
priorities have also proposed
solutions for the future shape of
network newscasts. Robert and
Gerald Goldberg conclude that
newscasts should be formatted
thematically. A broadcast could
cover daily events in the first half
of the program and then provide a
context for one or two of these
events during the second half of the
newscast. This format would allow
for more analysis and better
investigation and explanation of
complex issues.

Any substantial changes that
improve television newscasts must
begin with the attitudes of both the

Sources
blended
together to
emphasize
thesis

One
suggestion
for change
reviewed

More
consequential
suggestions
for change
introduced

47
srr

Brophy 16

producers who assemble the newscasts
and the audiences that watch the
programs. Television news media
must take responsibility for what
they put on the air. They must
resist corporate influence and
return to the idea that news is a
public service that is important to
viewers. The producers must
remember their shows inform the
public of many and different values
and ideas and also give viewers some
knowledge so they can understand
events and make informed judgments.

The networks are not solely
responsible for making these
changes, as those who protested
Steve Friedman's changes at NBC
know. Television audiences must
also take the initiative. Viewers
must make the effort to understand
what is happening not only in their
local communities but also
nationally and internationally.
They must demand that news programs
report both sides of a controversy
and that the programs give some time
to speakers representing the

Recommen-
dations for
action to
conclude
report

47
srr

Brophy 17

opposing viewpoints of an issue.
They must insist that networks
provide adequate staff to report
events fairly and completely. And
they must make their demands and
opinions known to corporations by
writing to the executives who make
decisions about news programming.
This type of an active interest in
what is on the television helps both
to inform viewers and to empower
them.

47
srr

Brophy 18

Works Cited

Atheide, David L. _Creating Reality:_
How TV News Distorts Events.
Vol. 33. Beverly Hills: Sage
Library of Social Research,
1976.

Bennett, Lance W. _News: The Politics_
of Illusion. New York: Longman,
1988.

Brown, Les. _Television: The Business_
Behind the Box. New York:
Harcourt, 1971.

Diamond, Edwin. _The Tin Kazoo:_
Television, Politics, and the
News. Cambridge: MIT P, 1975.

Friend, Tad. "Would You Buy a Used
TV-News Show from This
Man?" _Esquire_ 11 Feb. 1990:
155-66.

Goldberg, Robert, and Gerald Jay
Goldberg. _Anchors: Brokaw,_
Jennings, Rather and the Evening
News. New York: Birch Lane,
1990.

Kalter, Joanmarie, and Jane Marion.
"The Big Stories TV News is
Missing--and Why." _TV Guide_ 22
July 1989: 2-5.

Brophy 19

Teague, Bob. <u>Live and Off-Color:</u>
    <u>News Biz</u>. New York: A & W,
    1982.
Warner, Malcolm. "Decision Making in
    Network TV News." <u>Media</u>
    <u>Sociology</u>. Ed. Jerry Turnwall.
    Chicago: U of Illinois P, 1970.

2 spaces

1 space

Television News

1

½″ to top
Running head and page numbers start on title sheet

The Good News About Television News
Alexander Carl Pottston
The University of Northern Arkansas

Title, writer's name, and school centered on page

47
srr

Running head: TELEVISION NEWS

Abbreviated title used as running head

Television News

2

The Good News About Television News

<u>Background</u>

Several media critics charge that television news focuses too much on "soft" news--i.e., entertainment and human interest--and not on "hard" news. For example, political science professor W. Lance Bennett (1988, p. xi) condemns television news for its shallowness because news programs "cover only a narrow range of issues, from the viewpoints of an even narrower range of sources, with emphasis placed on drama over depth, human interest over social significance, and formula reporting over perceptive analysis." He goes on to wonder "How can anything so superficial be so central to our lives?"

Bennett is not alone in this criticism. Robert and Gerald Goldberg (1990) label today's television newscasts as "info-tainment." Even television insiders like former news anchor David Brinkley agree. Teague (1982) reports Brinkley's acid comment

---

Start title and page number in upper right-hand corner

Title, first-level heading, in upper- and lower-case, centered

Second-level heading flush with left margin, in upper- and lower-case, underlined

Introduction begins survey of opposing positions

Reference in text followed by date and page of quotation in parenthesis

Date in parentheses for reference without quotation

Reference and date before quotation

47
srr

Television News

3

about television news: "I really
don't give a damn and I can't
believe anyone else does about a lot
of things they put on the air. It
has no effect on people's lives.
There's no meaning. It has no
significance" (p. 220). Brinkley
goes on to suggest that television
newscasts have lost the ability to
"put the world in context for their
viewers" as the successful "Texaco
Huntley-Brinkley Report" did in the
1960s and his own news programs did
in the 1970s.

History of Format Changes

      Bennett, the Goldbergs, and
Brinkley are partially correct that
the shift in priorities for
television newscasts takes time away
from reporting and analyzing the
many events that happen every day
around the country and the world.
However, they and other critics
neglect two important points.
First, the format of older news
broadcasts would be judged as boring
by today's standards and, second,
contemporary television news

Page number of direct quotation after reference

Opposing critics' viewpoint acknowledged

Two major points of disagreement cited

47
srr

Television News

4

programs, by becoming more
entertaining, actually inform people
better and put issues in context
more effectively than earlier
newscasts did. American attitudes
and needs have changed over the past
twenty to thirty years, and what was
considered interesting news coverage
in the 1960s and 1970s would not be
considered engaging now. Today,
viewers demand that their news be
current, informative, and relevant
to their everyday lives. When a
crisis happens, they want accurate,
immediate reports. And when events
lead to puzzling, complex issues,
they want to know about the human
consequences so they can understand
how the issues will have an impact
on their lives.

> Statement setting context for thesis

> Most-to-least-important organizational structure implied

Today's news programs, ————
especially the major networks'
evening newscasts, effectively
combine "hard" news with human
interest stories. As a result they
are informative programs that strive
to keep people informed by
increasing the time spent on

> Two-sentence thesis statement expressing writer's perspective

47
srr

Television News

5

analyzing stories and putting issues
into context by relating them to our
lives. Most importantly, today's
television news is an accurate
representation of American society
and its diverse realities. These
basic changes in direction make
television news programs a competent
source of information for the
American public.

Pressures to Change

　　Television news has faced
several setbacks in the past ten
years that have resulted in news
shows giving more emphasis to their
ratings and profits. Corporations
took over the three major networks
in the 1980s and put in place tight
budgets and strict cost-controlling
measures that resulted in closed
offices and reduced staffs (Diamond,
1991, p. 34). During the same ten
years, the ratings for network
newscasts dropped 30%, presumably
because most of the viewers who had
previously relied on network
newscasts had "already learned 'the
news' from CNN [Cable News Network]

Thesis suggested again

Summary of source material with author-date reference citation in parentheses

**47
srr**

Identifying information, added by writer, in brackets

Television News

6

or their local news broadcasts"
(Friend, 1990, p. 156). Because CNN
runs live 24 hours per day, it can
give viewers a "constant diet of
fresh news" (Diamond, 1991, p. 33).
Because the nightly newscasts on the
American Broadcasting Company (ABC),
the Columbia Broadcasting System
(CBS), and the National Broadcasting
Company (NBC) are still 22-minute
summaries of a day's events, they
could not effectively compete with
this constant flow of information.
Caught between the management of
bottom-line oriented companies and
forward competitors like CNN, news
shows needed various measures to
increase viewership.

Most successful newscasters
began to pay attention to what the
viewers wanted to see rather than
primarily to what older newscasters
recommended producing. The outcome
has been a shifting in priorities in
which human interest stories have
been increasingly promoted as a
means of attracting viewers. The
shift has somewhat helped the major

Topic
sentence
ends
paragraph

47
srr

networks keep their audiences and
regain some viewers they had lost
(Goldberg & Goldberg, 1990). But
the shift has been more beneficial
for the viewing public that demands
programming relevant to their
everyday lives. For example,
viewers need only look at the
nightly newscasts to see that the
shows do tell the public the day's
most important stories. Recently
the New York Times writer Walter
Goodman (1991) surveyed the
transcripts of the nightly newscasts
of each major network for the week

Data from
figures in
the article
summarized
and
highlighted

June 17-21. Goodman found that,
with only slight changes, the
newscasts emphasized similar areas.
At most, network newscasts spent a
little over two minutes on
entertainment-related, human interest
stories, and "non-news" such as
greetings and sign-offs. Most of
the newscasts were devoted to
in-depth stories on social issues.
ABC's World News Tonight, for
example, devotes an average 9.9
minutes to reporting social issues,

47
srr

6.56 minutes to national news, 4.37 minutes to international news, and only 1.08 minutes to "soft" and "non-news" material.   CBS's Evening News and NBC's Nightly News focus more time on national and international news, a total of 14.02 minutes, respectively.   CBS gives 6.73 minutes to in-depth reports. Goodman admits that these figures vary from week to week as the quantity of important national and international events fluctuates. The numbers reveal, however, that television newscasts do concentrate time and resources on "hard" news and do make a substantial effort to inform their viewers by spending most of their time on various national and international issues.

Setting Context for News

Reporting national and international news events, however, is not all that the major networks hope to accomplish.   More and more network newscasts are characterized by in-depth analysis of issues and feature stories that attempt to

Writer's conclusion drawn from references and numerical data

Second point of thesis restated

Television News
9

contextualize and personalize issues for the viewing public. Each major network newscast highlights a nightly segment that delves into

Specific examples listed

important issues such as the status of homeless people; controversies surrounding abortion, the AIDS epidemic, and euthanasia; or the crises in American education, medical care, and business. As Goodman's survey documents, between June 17th and 21st ABC's World News Tonight opened several broadcasts with human interest segments including an ambitious series of reports entitled "Children in Crisis." NBC Nightly News'

Source material paraphrased

five-part series about middle-class America surveyed a range of problems from the economic hardships Americans are suffering to a review of America's traditional family values. And "Eye on America," a regular 5-minute segment on The CBS Evening News, focused on a variety of stories including looks at political correctness, the ethics of keeping comatose patients alive, and

47
srr

the ways some New Yorkers are overcoming their prejudices about AIDS by helping their afflicted neighbors (Goodman, 1991, p. 23).

The practice of illustrating major events with feature stories weds the information value of newscasts with the entertainment value that corporate executives know is necessary to keep news programs profitable. More importantly, by explaining such issues directly, feature segments direct their viewers' attention to issues that might otherwise be overlooked.

Feature segments also point out a related value of television news to its viewers. Hard news helps viewers understand the facts that make up an issue, how one group of facts may contradict another group, and how these facts can create different sides to an issue. But it is equally important for viewers to know how a given issue goes beyond statistics or objectively stated positions and affects the human beings involved.

Writer's conclusion stated

Related point emphasized

Writer's interpretation concludes section

Television News
11
Beyond the Nightly News
       Corporate executives, guided by
the news staffs they employ and the
ratings services they review, have
committed resources to giving viewers
a broader understanding of events and
issues. In addition to features on
their nightly newscasts, each network
airs weekly investigative shows and,
periodically, documentary reports
that explore vital topics further.
My informal survey of one week's
offerings revealed CBS airs two
weekly news shows, NBC one news/human
interest show, and ABC three weekly
series and one special (see Table 1).

Table 1
Survey of Weekly News Programs,
September 6-13, 1991
        Weekly Series Special Reports
CBS 60 Minutes
     48 Hours
NBC Real Life with
     Jane Pauley
ABC 20/20   A Line in the
     Nightline   Sand: What Did
     Prime Time   America Win?
     Live

Third point of thesis restated

Writer's primary research introduced

Heading Table and title of visual aid appear before table

Double-space between visual aid and continued text

47
srr

Television News

12

Several of these programs, including CBS's <u>60 Minutes</u> and ABC's <u>Nightline,</u> consistently rank high in the television rating services.

Although the networks differ in how many weekly news specials and documentaries they air, the overall number of shows indicates that the networks have made a commitment to such programming. Investigative shows, documentaries, and feature reports mean that networks can cast critical glimpses at and personalized views of certain controversial events and complex issues.

<u>Television News as a Maturing Force</u>

Finally, television news accurately represents our society's diverse nature and the sometimes overwhelming rush of events that happen daily. Humanities professor Camille Paglia (Paglia & Postman, 1991) asserts that television in general mirrors the images that are prevalent in our varied culture and that television newscasts in particular present life as viewers

Writer interprets data for reader

Transition *Finally* signals last point of thesis

Two-author citation with date and page reference

47
srr

Television News

13

experience it every day. She argues
that

> There's no sense to reality.
> It simply happens. Television
> is actually closer to reality
> than anything in books. The
> madness of TV is the madness of
> human life [because] TV is
> creating a picture of the world
> that is simply true to life
> (p. 54).

Paglia justifies her position
by analyzing television newscasts.
These programs paste together an
assortment of images from
cataclysmic natural disasters to
multi-cultural interpretations of
issues to humorous twists on
everyday problems. Along the way,
the programs break up their various
reports with commercials. This type
of collage requires a certain amount
of detachment by viewers, who must
shift from watching a report of an
earthquake that killed thousands to
watching a commercial selling Downy
Fabric Softener. Paglia suggests
that this detachment is part of a

Blocked quotation of 40 words or more, indented, double-spaced, without quotation marks

Page citation ends direct quotation

Source material's argument summarized and exemplified

47
srr

Television News

14

maturing process that every normal
adult goes through today (Paglia &
Postman, p. 54).

Paglia goes on to argue that in
order to deal with the amount of
tragic news events that happen
daily, people must learn to separate
themselves from the events if they
are to look at them in a less
emotional context. Television
newscasts, "by moving from disaster
to commercial," create "the effect
of Greek Tragedy: emotion, then
detachment; contemplation of loss,
then philosophical perspective"
(Paglia & Postman, p. 55). With
this perspective come ways to figure
out solutions or actions that each
of us can take when crises do arise.
Television news, by duplicating real
life, gives viewers the information
they need and may suggest some
solutions to world and local
problems. More importantly
newscasts allow viewers to think
about issues and formulate ideas
about what approaches to dealing
with pressing concerns are best.

Use of critic
as authority
for writer's
position

Television News

15

Second-
level
heading

Conclusion

As television journalist Bob Teague comments, "Watching the news is one of the very few things that all of the American people do together. . . . [I]t is very important and it should not be corrupted" (Teague, 1982, p. 218). Critics already realize that network news is a business that is sometimes limited by certain financial and time constraints. But they should also realize that viewers' time is equally limited and that viewers still want and need to know and understand the events that make up their society and world. Television newscasts are meeting viewers' needs even with the pressures of budget and time.

Television news has become a primary source of information for Americans because it is capable of keeping its viewers apprised of current events even as they are happening around the world. But newscasts also give viewers a context for interpreting problems,

Source cited
to introduce
conclusion

Thesis
restated

Conclusion
boldly
asserted

47
srr

Television News

16

for analyzing complex issues, and
for personalizing events. Perhaps
most importantly, television news
mirrors life and gives valuable
insights that can help viewers
bridge the gaps among issues,
peoples, and societies.

Television News
17

References

Bennett, W. L. (1988). News: The
politics of illusion (2nd ed.).
New York: Longman.

Diamond, E. (1975). The tin kazoo:
Television, politics, and the
news. Cambridge: MIT.

Goldberg, R., & Goldberg, G.J.
(1990). Anchors: Brokaw, Jennings,
Rather and the evening news. New
York: Birch Lane.

Goodman, W. (1991, July 7). Nightly
news looks beyond the headlines.
the New York Times, pp. 23, 24.

Paglia, C., & Postman, N. (1991,
March). She wants her TV! He
wants his book! Harper's
Magazine, pp. 44-51, 54, 55.

Teague, B. (1982). Live and
off-color: News biz. New York: A & W.

Bibliographic references with author's name, date, work, and publication data

Full date with month and day included for newspapers and magazines

First-level heading centered

First word of title and first word after colon capitalized

47
srr

48

48a

The Common Ground of Writing in All Disciplines

Writing in different disciplines—that is, writing in the various courses that you take in college—does not require that you learn a different writing process for each or that you discover and complete a blueprint particular to each subject. When you write in any discipline, you think critically, consider your understanding of audience, and observe, contemplate, and research. Writing in different disciplines almost invariably involves research. Research is not strictly scientific or technological or discipline-related. Research is a process, not a goal. Its aim is to discover, relate, and evaluate ideas, data, and other types of information. Humanists research ideas just as physicists research molecular structure or sociologists research cultural standards. As a process, research is exploratory: It involves not only library work but also personal analysis, empirical observation, and critical thinking.

    Writing in different disciplines also requires you to distinguish one field of study from another. And the differences among fields center most significantly on the questions asked by specialists in any particular field. Researchers in the three broad academic fields—social sciences, humanities, and natural sciences—ask different questions about their material. Different disciplines report their answers in formats and specialized vocabularies that distinguish their individual fields of study. Chapters 44 through 46 offer intensive research strategies common to all disciplines.

Writing in the Social Sciences

The social sciences (which include such disciplines as psychology, political science, sociology, anthropology, and communications) concern themselves with behavior—of individuals, organizations, and societies.

Researchers in the social sciences typically work with such questions as the following:

- What causes the observed behavior? How long has it existed? Does it represent change? Is it part of a trend, or an anomaly? That is, what is the history, and what are the causes?
- What hypothesis might explain this behavior?
- What kind of data are available? What are their sources: polls, surveys, long- or short-term studies, secondary research in the literature?
- What are the effects of this behavior? And what are the short- and long-term consequences likely to be? Who is most affected, and why?

Research reports in the social sciences can be straightforward *reports,* presenting the researcher's observations, analyzing them and other data, and stating a conclusion. Or they can function more as inquiries into the *significance* of behavior, arguing hypotheses and seeking to understand the relationship of causes and consequences. Chapter 47 presents two research reports of the latter type. The reports, written for a course in communications, argue opposite positions on the same topic—television news—and are annotated, so you can see the kinds of approaches, content, and presentation required in writing in the social sciences. The paper by Alexander Pottston is documented in American Psychological Association style, the most prevalent style for the social sciences.

The remainder of this chapter presents two research reports from the other two broad academic fields, the humanities and the natural sciences. Each report was written for a specific course: contemporary literature and introductory zoology, respectively.

48b
wd

48c

Writing in the Humanities

Specialists in the humanities (that is, disciplines such as philosophy, literature, history, and art history) study what makes people tick: what their values, capacities, and achievements are; why people debate one another; what defines a culture; where ideas come from and what impact those ideas have on people. Where a scientist will ask, What do my investigations prove about my hypothesis? a humanist will wonder, What do my observations tell me about human nature, its limits, or its interests?

One common type of report in the humanities is an interpretation and evaluation of a work of literature. Broadly defined, literature includes just about any text from nonfiction works (such as essays, biographies, editorials, news reports, and history) to plays, poetry, and imaginative prose fiction (such as epics, myths, novels, parables, romances, and short stories).

Some essays on literature limit themselves to summarizing what other writers have said about a literary work. These surveys are much like the "reviews of the literature" you find in business and economics, science and technology, and the social sciences. Most essays on literary works, however, combine primary with secondary research; that is, the writer integrates his or her reactions to a work of literature with the reactions of other writers, often literary scholars.

Usually, writers judging literary works ask questions about the principal aspects of a work, including

- *plot:* What conflict is set up in the text? Who are the protagonists (i.e., main characters or heroes) and the antagonists (i.e., characters opposing the protagonists)? How is the conflict developed and resolved? What goals, values, issues, or perspectives does the conflict bring out?
- *character:* What determines a character's major trait or traits? What are the character's qualities, strengths, and weaknesses?
- *setting:* Where does the work take place? Is the setting believable (i.e., does it have verisimilitude)? Is the setting relevant?
- *theme:* What is the central idea, concept, thought, or principle of the work?
- *point of view:* What voice (i.e., first person, second person, third person) does an author use in a work? Who tells the story, presents the arguments, describes the action, interprets the conflict, or expresses the emotions?

- *problem:* Did the author set out to propose a solution to a problem with this work?
- *style:* How has the author arranged the events and speeches? What do repeated patterns of words or expressions (i.e., rhetorical figures or rhetorical devices) tell us about the plot, conflict, characters, theme, point of view, or problem?

Notice how, with only slight changes in the wording, these questions could be asked by psychologists, sociologists, philosophers, historians, cultural anthropologists, and others interested in the humanities.

Rebecca Falb wrote a report about Toni Morrison's novel *Song of Solomon.* Falb traced the word *mercy* and all its various forms through Morrison's novel and decided that Morrison made *mercy* a part of the conflict and theme as well as a major trait for the characters. Falb used what other critics had written to set the context for her discussion of mercy in the book. Her report, written for a course surveying contemporary novels, follows the author-date citation form from the *MLA Handbook.* The page numbers without an author reference indicate where Falb found her evidence in Morrison's novel.

Merciful Knowledge
Toni Morrison's third novel, Song of Solomon, studies the dislocation and humiliation blacks encounter when removed from their nature-bound world and forced to exist within a white urban culture (Otten 45-62). The seed for the novel, a Gullah folktale, retells how African-born slaves release themselves from their bondage to fly back to Africa, the source of forgiveness and peace (Blake 78). The journey major characters take follows a mythic pattern (Harris 69-76). In her trials, one of the novel's main characters, Pilate, embodies redeeming spiritual values and, through her almost transcendent power, attempts to kindle these values in all around her, particularly her nephew Milkman Dead (Atlas 10). Milkman's journey toward decency, caring, a communal sense and, above all, mercy is what concerns Morrison here.
Cries for mercy imbue the stifling, ginger-laden atmosphere of Song of Solomon. Pilate demands it at Hagar's funeral. Clad in wings of blue silk, Robert Smith leaps from Mercy Hospital, asking for forgiveness. Inebriated and weeping for love, Porter appeals for mercy from his roof-top. We want justice, we want to be treated fairly, we

48c
wd

want to be loved, plea the people of Not Doctor
Street and Southside. Their laments are ignored,
however, by a merciless white society and by each
other. Instead of forgiveness, compassion, and
relief, the only thing blacks can count on,
according to Railroad Tommy, is a broken heart
(60). Faced with this despairing situation Pilate
chooses to show mercy rather than add to the misery
of the world, and Milkman, through his mythic
journey to self-identity, learns to be merciful.

The lack of mercy in Song of Solomon is
established in the first startling scene as Robert
Smith jumps from the cupola of Mercy Hospital.
Unable to continue killing for the Seven Days and
burdened with collecting insurance fees from his
poor neighbors, Smith drops his sorrows off the
side of the hospital with the request "Please
forgive me. I loved you all" (3). Mercy towers as
an impregnable symbol of the merciless attitude of
whites towards blacks (true to Morrison's inversion
of meaning in names throughout the novel), a
charity hospital that will not admit those most in
need of charity because of their colored skin.

The people of Southside, however, treat Smith
just as mercilessly. As he teeters atop the
hospital, they shake their heads in judgment and
murmur, "you never really do know about people"
(8). Porter receives similar treatment when he
climbs to his roof, drunkenly laments his great
love, and begs for mercy from God. How do his
neighbors respond? With taunts and laughter.
Macon confronts him with a demand for rent money
rather than an urgent appeal that he save his life.

Macon is consistently unforgiving in his
attitude toward others. He is curt and abrasive
and unwilling to compromise in dealing with his
tenants. He turns Mrs. Bains and her grandchildren
out in the street, causing Mrs. Bains to sadly
observe, "A nigger in business is a terrible thing
to see" (22). Why terrible? Because for a black
person to attain any success in the business world,
he or she has to suffer the abuses of racism.
Every person needs a release for their suffering,
and the easiest release is found in turning on
those subordinate to you--in this case, Macon's poor

48c
wd

tenants. Dr. Foster, though denied access to Mercy
hospital because of his colored skin, detests other
blacks, whom he refers to as "cannibals." Lack of
mercy multiplies in cruelty when those who share a
common attacker choose to attack each other.
    Mercilessness is formalized in the Seven Days.
Repeatedly, Guitar or one of the other members of
the group observes that there is no fair court
system for blacks. Because there is no justice,
there is no chance for mercy. After Emmet Till's
death, Guitar affirms "Ain't no law for no colored
man except the one that sends him to the chair"
(82). The Seven Days believe, then, that they are
justified in killing innocent whites. However,
these murders also lead one black man to brutalize
another as Guitar eventually shoots both Pilate and
Milkman in merciless loyalty to the Seven Days.
    Despite the absence of mercy in both the black
and white societies of Song of Solomon, one person
does show compassion and forgiveness--Pilate. At
her birth and pronouncement of her name, Circe
breathes, "Jesus have mercy" (19). But Jesus
doesn't seem to hear--Pilate's mother dies before
she is born, her father is shot by malicious
whites, she is abandoned and disdained because of
her missing navel, and her brother Macon snubs her.
"Every other resource was denied her: partnership
in marriage, confessional friendship, and communal
religion" (148).
    Pilate, however, chooses not to respond to the
injustices in her life by being merciless to
others. "When she realized what her situation in
the world was and would probably always be she
threw away every assumption she had learned and
began at zero . . . [she] acquired a deep concern
for and about human relationships" (149–150).
Pilate has to teach herself to offer love for hate,
to unlearn vengeful prejudices, and to learn to
show kindness and tolerance. The world will always
be merciless, but instead of forsaking life with a
plea for understanding as Smith did, she is
fiercely determined to savor life, sustaining its
vigor by forgiveness and compassion.
    Pilate's decision to live in mercy is in
obvious contrast to the harsh atmosphere of

48c
wd

Southside and its people. Her house is described as a "safe harbor" where there are no flies on the flypaper that hangs from the ceiling (135). She is one of the few in the crowd of spectators at Smith's suicide who shows compassion for the winged jumper. She releases Reba's abusive boyfriend even though he attacks her most beloved possession, her child, and she attempts to bring love back into Macon's marriage despite his hateful attitude toward her.

She offers her greatest deed of mercy when Milkman and Guitar steal her "inheritance." Macon coerces his son, as they lunch across from Mercy Hospital, to swipe the gold suspended in Pilate's green sack. When Milkman, Guitar, and the stolen tarpaulin are apprehended by the police, Pilate is summoned to the station. Here are two men she befriended as boys, one of them a treasured nephew, guiltily holding her inheritance. Once again, life is unfair--she has given them love, and this is how they respond. But instead of hurling vindictive accusations, Pilate slumps into her ignorant Aunt Jemima act: "It was this woman, who he [Milkman] would have knocked senseless, who shuffled into the police station and did a little number for the cops--opening herself up wide for their amusement, their pity, their scorn . . . whatever would be useful to herself and himself" (211).

Pilate gives, heals, forgives, embraces, and overlooks, never asking for mercy in return, until Hagar's funeral. Pilate adores Hagar and, upon her granddaughter's death, realizes that despite her love, Hagar will suffer severe judgment from the other Southside residents. The ladies at Lilly's Beauty Parlor, for example, say Hagar should be ashamed for fooling with her cousin and offer her no consolation for her broken heart. Few attend her funeral, and most of those who are there appear more out of embarrassed duty than out of compassion for the dead. Pilate defiantly marches into the church commanding "Mercy" for the meek, unforgiving mourners. She reiterates her demand and then sings with Reba:

48c
wd

In the nighttime.
Mercy
In the darkness.
Mercy . . . (321)

Because of Pilate's interest in human relationships and her compassionate heart, she seeks to help Macon and Ruth, a "Jocasta type" (Frederick 536), in their festering marriage. She gives Ruth a love potion and Milkman is conceived. He is "born in Mercy" (9), signifying not only that he was the first colored baby born at the charity hospital but also that, due to Pilate's merciful intervention, he was not aborted. When Freddie witnesses the boy suckling at Ruth's breast, his alarmed response echoes Circe: "Have mercy" (14).

Milkman's childhood is more materially privileged than Pilate's, and he has a home and family. However, he hates his status as the "plain" across which his parents wage their abusive battles and wants to escape from his past because "the knowledge Ruth and Macon had given him wrapped his memory of it [childhood] in septic sheets, heavy with the odor of illness, misery, and unforgiving hearts" (181). He believes that the "cards are stacked against him" as Guitar says (88), and laments the lack of kindness shown to him. Nonetheless, at this point, he deviates from Pilate's path and chooses to live in selfishness and self-pity instead of merciful action.

Milkman's relationship with Hagar exemplifies his lack of clemency. After twelve years, Hagar is expectant and possessive, while he coldly regards her as a "third beer." She is completely under his power, placed there by her own willingness to sacrifice her independence and self-identity for his love. Milkman abuses his power and terminates their relationship without a scrap of compassion. Six months later, as Hagar stands over him with a knife, opening her hollow, loveless eyes to admire his beauty, he caustically advises her to jam the blade into her vagina. His inability to concentrate on anything but his own self-pity renders him unable to be merciful to the suffering Hagar.

48c
wd

The journey to Danville and Shalimar leads Milkman to discover who he is, and, upon this discovery, he learns to be merciful in a merciless world. While hunting with Omar, Calvin, and the other men of Shalimar, Milkman leans against a tree and contemplates what he deserves and what others deserve from him:

> It seemed to him that he was always saying or thinking that he didn't deserve some bad luck, or some bad treatment from others. He'd told Guitar that he didn't "deserve" his family's dependence, hatred, or whatever. That he didn't even "deserve" to hear all the misery and mutual accusations his parents unloaded on him. Nor did he "deserve" Hagar's vengeance. But why shouldn't his parents tell him their personal problems? If not him, then who? And if a stranger could try to kill him, surely Hagar, who knew him and whom he'd thrown away like a wad of chewing gum after the flavor was gone--she had a right to try to kill him too. (280)

Self-identity is imperative to the ability to show mercy. In abandoning her assumptions and starting at zero, Pilate evaluates who she is and what is important to her before opting to live in kindness and forgiveness. Similarly, as Milkman slowly accumulates the pieces of his family's history and formulates a sense of self-identity, he is able for the first time to appreciate the problems of others and to judge with compassionate understanding. He acknowledges that his mother's life has been difficult (as his would be were he to be celibate for twenty years) and recognizes that his father values the same things his grandfather, Macon I, valued--property and ownership. He also admits to treating Hagar shamefully and resolves to amend their relationship. His understanding of himself and his actions allows him to empathize with the pain that those around him experience and to act mercifully on that empathy. Perhaps he doesn't deserve to suffer, but neither do they.

48c
wd

Milkman travels home and then returns to
Shalimar with Pilate to bury the bones of her
father. Both characters who had mercy breathed
over them at birth and who learned to show mercy in
life receive eternal relief at the burial site.
Pilate is given the chance to put to rest the
remains of her beloved father and to understand
what he meant by "You can't just fly off and leave
a body." When she is gunned down by Guitar, a bird
carries her earring, her identity, to heaven.
Jesus did listen to Circe's plea. Milkman realizes
the beauty in surrender and forgiveness and offers
his life to Guitar. He is granted the final mercy
of knowing who he is, enabling him to embrace his
alter ego Guitar (Bruck 300) and to drop his
burdens to the earth and fly.

Works Cited

Atlas, Marilyn Judith. "A Woman's Both Shiny and
    Brown: Feminine Strength in Toni Morrison's
    Song of Solomon." Society for the Study of
    Midwestern Literature Newsletter 9 (1979):
    8-12.
Blake, Susan. "Folklore and Community in Song of
    Solomon." Journal of the Society for the Study
    of Multi-Ethnic Literature of the U.S. 7
    (1980): 77-82.
Bruck, Peter. "Returning to One's Roots: The Motif
    of Flying in Toni Morrison's Song of Solomon."
    The Afro-American Novel Since 1960. Ed. Peter
    Bruck and Wolfgang Karrer. Amsterdam: Gruner,
    1982. 289-305.
Frederick, Earl. "The Song of Milkman Dead." Nation
    19 November 1977: 536.
Harris, A. Leslie. "Myth as Structure in Toni
    Morrison's Song of Solomon." Journal of the
    Society for the Study of Multi-Ethnic
    Literature of the U.S. 7 (1980): 69-76.
Morrison, Toni. Song of Solomon. New York: Knopf,
    1978.
Otten, Terry. The Crime of Innocence in the Fiction
    of Toni Morrison. Columbia: U of Missouri P,
    1989.

48c
wd

48d

Writing in Science and Technology

Scientists are interested in the processes, events, and structures that underlie the empirical world. Most scientists define their discipline by asking questions that define all critical thinking: Why? and How? do things happen. The specific questions scientists and technologists often include in their reports are as follows:

- What is the pattern that characterizes an event, phenomenon, experiment, or dynamic?
- What mechanisms generate the pattern?
- How does this pattern come to occur over time?
- Why does this pattern exist at all?
- Have investigations yielded firm evidence?
- Were the study designs adequate to test the hypothesis proposed? Can the study be replicated?
- Were the results of the study properly interpreted?
- What are the conclusions?

Scientific and technological writing (unless it is deliberately personal and essayistic, as is the style of such writers as Carl Sagan, Lewis Thomas, and Richard Selzer) usually relies on the scientific method and on a style of writing that favors an objective presentation of subject matter over the writer's own perspective and voice. The typical format for a scientific or technical report is as follows:

- an introduction stating the writer's hypothesis;
- a review of other scientists' relevant opinions;
- a review of methods and materials so others can replicate the writer's experiment;
- a report of the writer's results (often with references to tables and figures placed at the end of the report);
- and a discussion of the significance of the results, their connection to other scientists' results, and a conclusion about whether the results support or weaken the original hypothesis.

Lee Kats, an undergraduate biology major, wrote the report reprinted below. He combines primary research—that is, an experiment he designed, performed, and evaluated—with published conclusions; his results contradict those of other researchers. His introduction states the project, his hypothesis, and a brief summary of his experiment. He then moves to a discussion of the materials and methods he used for his experiment. And he ends with a discussion of his experiment and an assessment of his results that tied his experiment and conclusions to those of other people interested in this one area of zoology. Kats followed *The Council of Biological Editors Style Manual* for his citation and bibliographic format, although he knew that, if he wanted to submit his essay for possible publication, he would have to follow the format of the specific journal to which he sent the report.

AN EXPERIMENTAL STUDY OF THE EFFECT OF TEMPERATURE ON THE COLOR CHANGES OF THE SPRING PEEPER (HYLA CRUCIFER)

ABSTRACT
The purpose of this study was to test the variation in color value and notation of Hyla crucifer. Experiments using 90 individuals placed on different color substrate, reveal that the spring peeper changes to a more cryptic color when put on a non-matching substrate. Results indicate that temperature plays a far more important role in the color changes of H. crucifer than previously published research would suggest and that color changes occur rapidly with temperature variations.

INTRODUCTION
The ability to change color through the movement of pigments has been widely observed among animals (Prosser, 1973). Many times this change in color is such that the organism better matches the background on which it rests, possibly providing crypsis from a potential predator or from a potential prey. Substrate color-matching changes have frequently been observed in many reptiles and amphibians including the genus of frogs, Hyla (Nielsen and Dyck, 1978).

METHODS AND MATERIALS
The experiments were performed on a total of 90 frogs that I collected on several different occasions from a small pond in Kent County, Michigan. Each night's collection of frogs was kept overnight in the biology lab, half of them in a 20-gallon aquarium with a black bottom and the

48d
wd

other half in a white plastic gallon container. A
preliminary experiment had shown that these
conditions would give light and dark frogs. After
being observed for one trial, the frogs were
released back into the pond.

    To begin the experiment I removed the frogs
from their holding containers and estimated their
color by comparing each frog's color to that on a
Munsell color chart. I used one page of the chart
that had a consistent hue. I recorded the colors
using a first notation called value that measures
lightness and a second notation called chroma that
measures the saturation. The system measured as
follows: The higher the value, the lighter the
color; and the higher the chroma, the more reddish
the color.

    For colored backgrounds, I placed the frogs in
round, plastic containers that were 8 cm deep and
that tapered from 7.5 cm in diameter at the top to
5.5 cm at the bottom. I observed the frogs in
white containers, about 8/1 on the color scale, and
in containers painted black, about 2.5/2 on the
color scale. I placed the frogs individually into
the containers along with about 1 ml of deionized
water. I placed cellophane over the top of the
containers and matching paper tube extensions
around the top. These tubes, which extended
approximately 5 cm above the top of the containers,
were an attempt to prevent the frogs from looking
horizontally from the container and thereby
possibly matching some other color besides the
container they were in.

    I observed light frogs, those with values of 6
or 7, in dark containers and, as a control, in
light containers. I observed dark frogs, those
with values of 3 or 4, on the same two background
colors. These four different trials were used
taking frogs at a room temperature of 23°C (± 1°)
and observing them at 21°C and 10.5°C. I also
tested a group at 10.5°C after the frogs had been
acclimated for 48 hours at 9°C. During all trials, I
tested the frogs in their containers in a "Percival
E-30B" control-led environment chamber. I recorded
the color of each frog at the times 0, 7.5, 15, 30,
and 45 minutes.

48d
wd

RESULTS

In the conditions of this experiment, <u>Hyla crucifer</u> changes to a more cryptic color when put on a non-matching substrate. However, the frogs never completely matched the backgrounds of white or black. I found that the chroma notation did not change significantly, but that the value of the colors changed to a large extent. It appears that the frogs had a maximum lightness, about a value of 7, and a maximum darkness, a value of 3.

The value of the light frogs on the black backgrounds at 21°C decreased on an average of about 2.5 by the 30-minute mark, leveling off completely after that (Figure 1). The value of the light frogs at 10.5°C decreased about 1.6 after 45 minutes, and the value of those that had been acclimated decreased about 1.3. The controls for all the groups, dark individuals on black backgrounds, remained dark.

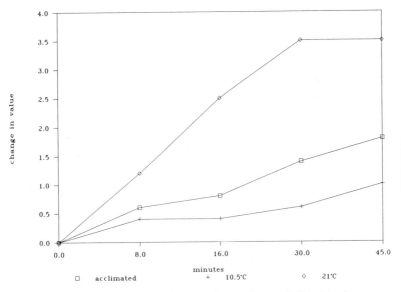

Figure 1: The average change in value of light frogs on black backgrounds with time for the 21°C, 10.5°C, and acclimated groups.

The difference in the values at 45 minutes between the non-acclimated frogs at 10.5°C and the acclimated frogs was not statistically significant using the Mann-Whitney U-test (one-tailed, $P > 0.469$) (Siegel, 1956). However, the differences in values between the 10.5°C non-acclimated and acclimated compared to the frogs at 21°C was statistically significant ($P < 0.002$).

Dark frogs on white backgrounds showed the most change. The greatest change in values came from the group of frogs tested at 21°C, with an average increase in value of over 3 in 30 minutes (Figure 2). Again, in control trials, dark frogs on black backgrounds, there is no color change. The difference in values at 45 minutes among all three groups was statistically significant ($P < .03$).

DISCUSSION

Unlike Conant (1975), who states that H. crucifer does not exhibit profound variation in color, I found that H. crucifer is capable of

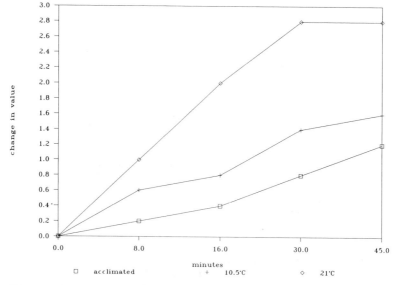

Figure 2: The average change in value of dark frogs on white backgrounds with time, for the 21°C, 10.5°C, and acclimated groups.

changing its color from almost black to light tan
when placed on a white background and the reverse
(i.e., light to almost black) when placed on a
black background. I found, however, that the
greatest changes came in the color notation of
value, which measures lightness. This same
adaptation to the lightness of the background while
lacking other significant color adaptations has
also been reported for H. cinerea (Nielsen and
Dyck, 1978).

Several investigators (Fingerman, 1963;
Norris, 1972) have reported that color changes in
amphibians are rather slow compared to other
animals, saying that extensive color changes take
anywhere from several hours to days. As can be
seen in Figures 1 and 2, I observed quite extensive
color changes in only 30 minutes, especially for
those frogs tested at 21°C.

Norris (1964) reports that temperature plays a
significant role in color change and that low
temperatures induced darkening in H. versicolor on
account of thermoregulatory control. In fact,
Porter (1972) says that in lizards temperature
relationships take precedence over concealment
coloration. This observation might explain why the
two cooler trials described in Figure 2 remained
much darker than those at 21°C. However, in Figure
1, one would expect to see the cooler trials turn
dark even faster in response to thermoregulatory
control. This did not happen.

I had expected that the frogs acclimated at
the cool temperature would change color in a
comparable rate to the group at 21°C. However, this
did not happen. In fact, the acclimated group was
not even significantly different from the
non-acclimated (Figure 1). Acclimated individuals
were significantly different from the 10.5°C group
(Figure 2), but they still did not have the extreme
change that those tested at 21°C had.

These data seem to indicate that H. crucifer
changes color to match its background at about one
half the rate at 10.5°C than those at 21°C. It
would seem that the frogs should match their
background quickly at all temperatures in their

48d
wd

activity range. Conant (1975) reports that H. crucifer may be clearly seen during the day on the forest floor, and I have seen this activity in the fall. The spring peeper is very active during the cool early spring, but most of this activity is nocturnal and limited to small ponds. One might hypothesize that rapid color matching in H. crucifer is more important in the avoidance of predators during its fall diurnal activity than during its nocturnal spring activity.

I believe that this small study has brought up many interesting questions not only about H. crucifer's ability to adapt to its background but also about the relationship temperature has on this ability. These questions may well deserve a deeper look.

LITERATURE CITED

Conant, R. 1975. A field guide to reptiles and amphibians. Houghton Mifflin Co., Boston.

Fingerman, M. 1963. The control of chromatophores. Macmillan Co., New York.

Nielsen, H.I.; J. Dyck. 1978. Adaptation of the tree frog, Hyla cinerea, to colored backgrounds, and the role of the three chromatophore types. J. Exper. Zool. 205: 79-94.

Norris, K.S.; C.H. Lowe. 1964. An analysis of background color-matching in amphibians and reptiles. Ecology. 45:565-580.

Porter, K.R. 1972. Herpetology. W.B. Saunders, Philadelphia.

Prosser, C.L. 1973. Comparative animal physiology. W.B. Saunders, Philadelphia.

Siegel, S. 1956. Nonparametric statistics. McGraw-Hill, New York.

48d
wd

G L O S S A R Y   O F

U S A G E

This glossary of usage provides a very selective listing of words, word forms, and phrases that writers should be aware of in revising and editing their prose. By using this glossary, you can continue to refine the choices you make as you try to avoid common usage errors or as you try to become more precise.

Writers make usage choices and distinctions at all levels of their writing. This glossary, however, is aimed at assisting you in the kind of writing you will do in college, which is generally a mixture of formal and consultative (middle) styles and tones.

The glossary is limited in at least two other ways. First, it contains approximately 115 items or pairs, whereas a comprehensive dictionary of usage may have well over 2,000 entries. Second, usage is fluid: Some of the distinctions described in this glossary will almost certainly disappear or change in the next years or decades. Therefore, if you take writing seriously, you must develop strategies for staying current with various levels of contemporary usage so that you can make usage choices appropriate to context, audience, genre, and subject matter. The best such strategy is wide and varied reading of good contemporary prose. But good current dictionaries, and especially dictionaries of usage, are valuable aids for even well-read writers.

a, an   The article *a* is used before words beginning with a consonant sound, including the "y" sound, which begins such words as "Europe," "unit," and "usage": *a book, a unit, a usage problem.* The article *an* is used before words beginning with a vowel sound: *an orange, an hour, an MTV special.*

accept, except   *Accept* is a verb meaning "to receive" or "to regard as true or right." When *except* is used as a verb, it means "to exclude." *Except* as a preposition (its more common use) means "with the exclusion of" *(All except Ann accepted the explanation).*

A.D., B.C.   *A.D.* (from the Latin phrase *anno Domini,* "in the year of the Lord") usually comes before the year *(A.D. 1948 was a very good year),* but it often follows the word *century (She lived in the twelfth century A.D.). B.C.,* which means "before Christ," ordinarily follows the year it refers to *(The dispute began in 93 B.C.).*

advice, advise   *Advice* is a noun *(She gives good advice); advise* is a verb *(We advised him to listen to what she says).*

affect, effect   When *affect* is used as a verb, it usually means either "to pre-

817

tend or feign" *(He affected ignorance),* "to have an influence on" *(The decision affected everyone in the organization),* or "to have an emotional effect on" *(Her singing affected me deeply). Affect* as a noun is a term specific to psychology. *Effect* as a verb means "to bring about or accomplish" *(That policy will effect real change). Effect* as a noun means "result" or "outcome" *(What was the effect of that policy?).*

aggravate, irritate   *Aggravate* can share with *irritate* the meaning "to annoy," but many usage authorities advise writers to restrict the use of *aggravate* to the meaning "to make worse," as in *Stress aggravated his delicate medical condition.*

agree to, agree with   The verb *agree* changes its meaning slightly when it is used with different prepositions: *Agree to* usually indicates consent *(I agree to the terms of the settlement); agree with* indicates harmony or concurrence *(I agree with your analysis).*

ain't   *Ain't* is a nonstandard contraction of *am not, is not, are not, has not,* and *have not.* Do not use this contraction in your writing except in dialogue or in direct quotation.

allude, elude   To *allude* to something is to refer to it indirectly or in passing. To *elude* someone or something is to avoid or escape from that person or thing.

allusion, illusion   An *allusion* is an indirect reference to something *(They never notice literary allusions).* An *illusion* is an erroneous perception of reality *(My neighbor has the illusion of being well educated).*

alot, a lot   The four-letter version is not an accepted spelling of this phrase; do not use *alot.* The correct version is *a lot,* but this is a vague and weak indicator of quantity or frequency; find a substitute, unless you are referring to a parcel of real estate.

already, all ready   *Already* is an adverb; it means "previously" or "by this time." *All ready,* when used in sentences such as "The dinner is all ready now," means "completely ready."

alright, all right   Avoid the use of *alright* in formal writing; it is not a generally accepted spelling of *all right.*

altogether, all together   *Altogether* means "entirely," "in all," or "on the whole" *(The customer was altogether satisfied). All together* refers to closeness or unity *(The students were all together to hear the news).*

alumnus, alumna   *Alumnus* is the masculine singular form; *alumni* is the masculine plural. *Alumna* is the feminine singular; *alumnae* is the feminine plural. However, *alumni* is also commonly used as the plural form to refer to all graduates of a college, university, or other organization. See also the entry for *criteria* for other foreign plural forms.

a.m., p.m.   The abbreviation *a.m. (ante meridiem)* means "before noon"; the abbreviation *p.m. (post meridiem)* means "after noon." Do not double the information by writing "9:30 a.m. in the morning"; write "9:30 a.m." or "9:30 in the morning."

among, between   Generally speaking, you should use *between* when you refer to two things or people, and *among* when you refer to three or more.

gu

Thus, you would write *between you and me* but *among several alternatives*. However, it is appropriate to refer to treaties, pacts, and agreements *between* more than two persons, entities, or nations.

amount, number   Use *amount* when referring to things that are not countable *(a large amount of water, the specific amount of suffering)*; use *number* when referring to countable things *(a number of oceans, the number of crimes)*.

an   *See* a, an.

and etc.   This is redundant; use *etc.* by itself, since *et cetera* means "and others of the same kind." But it would be better to include all the information referred to by the *etc.*, or to refer to the totality in another way.

and/or   This is a common usage in legal and business writing *(Jill and/or Elaine)*, but you should not use it in other contexts. Write out the options separately *(Either Jill or Elaine will administer the test, or both of them will)*.

and which, and who   Use these constructions only when they are parallel with an earlier construction *(Lisa Brown is a student who knows how to study* and who *keeps her priorities straight)*.

anymore, any more   Either spelling is acceptable for this adverb, although the one-word form is more common. In formal writing, this word is used primarily in negative constructions *(We don't go to movies anymore)*; avoid its use in positive constructions *(It costs too much to go to movies anymore)*.

anyone, everyone, someone   These indefinite pronouns should not be confused with *any one, every one,* or *some one.* The indefinite pronouns refer to one person *(Was anyone there?)*. The two-word forms are not indefinite pronouns; they refer to a person or thing that belongs to a group already referred to, implicitly or explicitly *(Here are five books that include the poem; you should feel free to take any one of them. Every one of you should study the poem for tomorrow's class)*.

anyway, anyways   *Anyway* means "in any case" or "nevertheless." *Anyways* is a colloquial form that is not acceptable in formal written work.

apt, liable, likely   These adjectives are not fully interchangeable versions of one another. In the context of formal writing, *likely* is most often used to communicate a positive meaning, and *apt* and *liable* are most often used to communicate a negative meaning: *She is likely to be judicious; I am apt to jump to conclusions; he is liable to be vindictive.* However, some usage commentators insist that *liable* be used only in contexts in which it means "legally responsible": *I am liable for all of his debts.*

as   This conjunction can mean either "when" or "because"; if the context does not make the meaning clear, use "when" or "because" instead.

as, like   For formal writing, avoid using *like* as if it were a conjunction; use *as* or *as if* instead, and use *like* as a preposition: *He looks like me; he looks as if he had seen a ghost.*

assure, ensure, insure   Although these words are interchangeable in many contexts, *insure* is preferred when referring to guarantees against risk, and

gu

assure is used to refer to a person's state of mind: *I can insure your home and business, but I cannot assure you that you will live forever.* Consult an unabridged dictionary for examples of these distinctions.

awhile, a while   Use *a while* after prepositions *(Stay for a while)* and before *ago (She came a while ago)*; use *awhile* when it can be translated as "for a while" in context *(Sit awhile)*.

bad, badly   Use *bad* as an adjective, *badly* as an adverb: *The tire hit a bad pothole, and the car lurched badly to the left.*

B.C.   *See* A.D.

because, since   When used as a conjunction, *since* can indicate either time ("during the time after which") or cause ("as a result of the fact that" or "because"): *Since she left, I'm leaving, too; since she left, three of her friends have called to invite her to the reading.* These two uses of *since* are seldom misunderstood in context, but you must be sure that your reader is not misled by your choice of conjunction.

being that, being as (how)   These are nonstandard or colloquial substitutions for the conjunction *because;* do not use them in formal writing.

beside, besides   Both forms can be used as a preposition meaning "except": *No one beside(s) me knew what a dingbat really is.* But often these words have distinct meanings. *Beside* means "next to" *(The chair beside me was empty)*; *besides* means "in addition to" or "other than" *(We noticed many other problems besides his attitude).* As an adverb, *besides* means "furthermore" *(He should leave; besides, he wants to leave).*

bring, take   In general, use *bring* to refer to movement toward the speaker *(Please bring me the newspaper)*; use *take* to refer to movement away from the speaker *(Please take these reports to the office).*

but what   This is a colloquial usage; avoid it in edited prose.

can, may   For formal writing, you should use *can* to indicate ability and *may* to indicate permission *(I can make the distinction, but I'm not sure that I may, given the context).*

capital, capitol   *Capital* refers to cities, money, and upper-case letters; *capitol* refers only to the building where legislatures assemble *(When we arrived in the capital, we decided not to visit the Capitol).*

censor, censure   *Censor,* as a verb, means "to examine and remove or suppress sensitive or objectionable material"; *censure,* as a verb, means "to blame or condemn officially."

center around   Use *center on* in your formal writing: *Interest centered on one issue.*

cite, site   *Cite* is a verb meaning "to quote" or "to commend"; *site* is a noun referring to a place or a plot of land.

complement, compliment   *Complement,* as a noun and a verb, is connected to the meaning of "complete"; *compliment,* as a noun and a verb, refers to acts of praise or admiration.

conscience, conscious   *Conscience* is a noun referring to the ability to distinguish right from wrong; *conscious* is an adjective referring to a state of awareness, wakefulness, or intention.

consensus of opinion, general consensus   For brevity's sake, use *consensus* alone, since in most contexts the single word carries with it the meanings of the longer phrases.

continual, continuous   In most contexts, *continual* means "recurring," and *continuous* means "without interruption." But check an unabridged dictionary if you want to be sure about your specific use of these terms.

could of   *See* of, have.

criteria, data, media, phenomena   These are the plural forms of *criterion, datum, medium,* and *phenomenon.* These plural forms are often used as if they were singular, though usually you should treat them as plural nouns in formal writing.

data   *See* criteria.

different from, different than   Generally, *different than* should not be used when a noun or noun phrase follows; use *different from* instead *(He and I are different from you).*

differ from, differ with   In general, use *differ from* to mean "to be unlike" *(Boston differs from New York);* use *differ with* to mean "to disagree with" *(We differ with one another frequently).*

disinterested, uninterested   Although these words have become almost interchangeable in speaking and in informal usage, you should observe the traditional distinction of meanings in formal writing: *disinterested* means "impartial," hence neutral and fair; *uninterested* means "unconcerned" or "indifferent."

don't, doesn't   *Don't* is the contraction for "do not"; *doesn't* is the contraction for "does not."

due to   In formal writing, use this preposition if it follows a linking verb *(The cancellation was due to the weather);* otherwise, use the preposition *because of (I cancelled class because of [not due to] the bad weather).*

emigrate, immigrate   *To emigrate* means "to leave one country or region to settle in another." *To immigrate* means "to enter and settle permanently in a foreign country." These two meanings are reinforced by the prepositions that these verbs ordinarily take: emigrate *from,* immigrate *to* or *into.*

ensure, insure   *See* assure.

enthused, enthusiastic   *Enthusiastic* is the preferred adjective in formal writing; *enthused* is informal or colloquial.

equally as   This usage is considered colloquial. Change "He is equally as intelligent" to "He is just as intelligent" or "He is as intelligent as you are."

etc.   In formal writing, use "and so forth" or "and so on" rather than the abbreviation, or write out the complete list if it is not too long. *See also* and etc.

everyday, every day   *Everyday* is an adjective meaning "ordinary" or "usual." *Every day* is an adjective-noun combination. It is used as a noun phrase *(Every day is a gift)* or as an adverb telling how often something is done *(We come here every day).*

gu

everyone, every one   *See* anyone.

except   *See* accept.

explicit, implicit   *Explicit* refers to something that is directly stated; *implicit* refers to something that is not directly expressed but can be understood nonetheless.

farther, further   In general, *farther* is used to indicate distance, whereas *further* is used to indicate degree or quantity *(He can walk no farther; there is nothing further to be done)*. But only *further* is used as a sentence adverb *(It is certain, further, that he will not make it to the end)*.

fewer, less   *Fewer* is used as an adjective to modify countable nouns *(fewer fish)*; *less* is used as an adjective to modify uncountable nouns *(less time, less flour)*.

firstly   In American usage, it is most common to use *first, second, third, . . . , finally*. If you use *firstly*, be consistent and use the other *-ly* forms as well.

former, latter   Use these substitutions only if they will not confuse or unduly tax your reader.

fun   Avoid using *fun* as an adjective in formal writing.

further   *See* farther.

good and   *Good and* is used as an intensifier *(good and ready)*, but it is not an advisable usage in formal writing; use *very* or some other intensifier instead.

good, well   *Good* is used as an adverb only colloquially. In formal writing, you should use it as an adjective *(She does good work)* or as a noun *(The good she does is remarkable)*. *Well* is the modifier to use when an adverb is required *(She does well in everything)*. *You look well* indicates a state of health; *You look good* indicates attractiveness.

hanged, hung   In formal writing, observe this distinction: *Hanged* is the form used to refer to execution by hanging, and *hung* is the form used for other meanings.

hisself   *Hisself* is a regional but nonstandard variant of *himself*. Do not use *hisself* in formal writing unless you do so to record dialogue.

hopefully   *Hopefully* means in one sense "in a hopeful manner" *(We waited hopefully for his response)*. But it is also used as a sentence modifier, meaning "it is to be hoped" or "it is hoped" *(Hopefully, it won't rain tomorrow)*. The second usage is common in speech and in informal writing, but it has been very controversial in formal writing; some commentators, in fact, have been outraged by this use. They prefer to indicate *who* hopes for a particular situation or outcome *(I hope that it won't rain tomorrow)*. If you use *hopefully* as a sentence modifier, you should be aware of the passions it may arouse.

hung   *See* hanged.

immigrate   *See* emigrate.

imply, infer   *Imply* means "to express indirectly, to suggest without stating"; *infer* means "to draw a conclusion." Speakers or writers imply; hearers or readers infer.

gu

in, into   Generally, the preposition *into* is used with verbs that express motion *(They went into the classroom)*. The preposition *in* is used with verbs that indicate location or condition *(They are in the room)*. However, both prepositions exist in so many idiomatic expressions that you should consult an unabridged dictionary to be sure of appropriate and idiomatic usage.

incredible, incredulous   *Incredible* means "unbelievable" or "hard to believe"; *incredulous* means "unwilling to believe" or "expressing disbelief."

infer   *See* imply.

insure   *See* assure.

irregardless   Use "regardless"; although *irregardless* has some currency in spoken English, it is not acceptable in edited writing.

irritate   *See* aggravate.

is when, is where   In formal writing, avoid these constructions in your definitions of words or phrases. If you have written such a definition ("A split infinitive is when [is where] you allow a modifier to unnaturally break up an infinitive"), revise it ("In a split infinitive, a modifier is inserted between the 'to' of the infinitive and its verb form").

its, it's   *Its* is the possessive form of the pronoun "it." *It's* is the contraction of "it is" or "it has." The two forms are not interchangeable.

kind, sort   In general, use the singular forms "this" and "that" with *kind* and *sort (this kind of text; that sort of instruction)*. Use the plural forms "these" and "those" with *kinds* and *sorts (these kinds of students; those sorts of answers)*.

kind of, sort of   These imprecise intensifiers *(He was kind of crazy, but sort of sweet)*, although common in speech and in informal writing, should be used sparingly, if at all, in formal writing.

latter   *See* former.

lay, lie   In formal writing, *lay* is most often a transitive verb; it means "to place, put, or prepare (something)," and its principal parts are *lay, laid, laid. Lie* is the intransitive verb meaning "to recline"; its principal parts are *lie, lay, lain.*

liable   *See* apt.

lie   *See* lay.

like   *See* as.

likely   *See* apt.

literally   In formal writing, do not use *literally* as a modifier meaning "actually" *(He was sleeping so soundly that he was literally dead to the world)*. Many readers will assume that you meant to write "figuratively" but suffered a lexical lapse. Write instead "He was sleeping so soundly that he seemed dead to the world."

loose, lose   *Loose* is sometimes used where *lose* is intended. In such contexts, remember that the verb *lose* is spelled with one *o.*

lots, lots of   *See* a lot.

gu

maybe, may be   *Maybe* is an adverb meaning "perhaps" or "possibly." *May be* is a verb phrase.

media   *See* criteria.

might of   *See* of, have.

moral, morale   The adjective *moral* refers to ethics or conduct *(the moral consequences);* the noun *moral* refers to the central lesson of a story *(the moral of the story). Morale* refers to the *esprit de corps,* the mental condition of a person or group, with respect to cheerfulness or confidence.

most   In formal writing, do not use *most* as a substitute for *almost (She knows almost [*not *most] everyone).*

must of   *See* of, have.

myself, yourself, himself   Although these forms are used in speech as substitutes for the personal pronouns, in formal writing you should use them as reflexive or intensive pronouns only.

nohow   Do not use this expression in formal writing.

nowheres   Nonstandard for *nowhere.*

number   *See* amount, number.

of, have   Although the pronunciation of *could've, must have, would have,* and *should've* may suggest that these words end in *of,* you must write these verbs with either *have* or its contraction, *'ve.*

OK, O.K., okay   All three forms are in general use; the third form may be slightly more common because its plural form and its verb forms are relatively standard. But use this word (noun, adjective, verb, or adverb) sparingly, if at all, in formal writing.

only   This wandering adverb is often placed directly before a word or phrase that it is not intended to modify. Although such misplacement seldom causes miscommunication, you should, in formal writing, place it immediately before the word or phrase you want it to modify *(I'll give you only one more chance).*

phenomena   *See* criteria.

plenty   In formal writing, use *plenty* as a predicate adjective *(Fifty dollars is plenty)* meaning "sufficient." Do not use *plenty* as an adjective before a noun *(plenty money);* use it as a noun instead *(plenty of money).* Do not use *plenty* as an intensifier *(We did plenty well).* And unless you use *plenty* to mean "abundance" *(a land of plenty),* use the word very sparingly.

plus   Avoid using *plus* as a conjunction in formal writing.

p.m.   *See* a.m., p.m.

precede, proceed   *Precede* means "to come before in time, order, or position"; *proceed* means "to go forward or to undertake an action."

predominant, predominate   *Predominate* is most often used as a verb, but it can also be used as an adjective; its adverb form is *predominately.* However, the more common adjective form is *predominant,* and the more common adverb form is *predominantly.*

principal, principle   As a noun, *principal* means "leader" or "money"; as an adjective, it means "leading" or "chief." *Principle* is a noun; it means "general law" or "rule of action or conduct."

proceed *See* **precede.**

quotation, quote In formal writing, use *quote* as a verb but not as a noun meaning "quotation" or "quotation mark."

raise, rise *Raise* is a transitive verb *(He raised an objection)*; its principal parts are *raise, raised, raised. Rise* is an intransitive verb *(She rises at dawn)*; its principal parts are *rise, rose, risen.*

real, really In formal writing, do not use *real* as an adverb to replace *really (That theory is really controversial). Really,* however, is an ineffective intensifier when used to replace "very"; find a better word.

reason . . . is because Avoid this construction in formal writing. "The reason I left is because I was angry" should be revised: "I left because I was angry."

rise *See* **raise.**

set, sit *Set* is most often a transitive verb *(He set the oranges on the table)* meaning "to place or put (something)"; its principal parts are *set, set, set. Sit* is almost always an intransitive verb *(She sits in the same chair every day)*; its principal parts are *sit, sat, sat.* Consult an unabridged dictionary for idiomatic and other uses of these verbs.

shall, will These auxiliaries are today chiefly distinguished from one another when they are used in questions. *Shall (or should) I listen?* is a request for advice or opinion. *Will I listen?* is a request for a prediction.

should of *See* **of, have.**

since *See* **because, since.**

sit *See* **set.**

so Avoid *so* as a simple intensifier when it means "very" *(She is so wonderful)*; replace *so* with a more expressive or exact intensifier, or complete the comparison *(She is so wonderful that few have noticed her codependency). See also* **such.**

someone, some one *See* **anyone.**

sort, sort of *See* **kind, sort** and **kind of, sort of.**

such Generally, *such* is considered to be a weak intensifier in formal writing. Although it is acceptable as an adjective *(in such contexts),* you should avoid using it to mean "very" *(He's such a good boy)* unless there is a full adverb clause in the offing *(He's such a good boy that no one in the neighborhood likes him). See also* **so.**

supposed to, used to The sound of the *d* at the end of *supposed* and *used* is often lost in spoken English. But remember to include the *d* when you write these phrases.

sure Do not use *sure* as a replacement for *surely:* "He *surely* [not *sure*] is prolific."

sure and, try and In formal writing, use *sure to* and *try to* when another verb follows *(I'll be sure to wear boots, and I'll try to be on time).*

gu

than In formal writing, *than* is used most often as a subordinating conjunction with or without the following adverb clause fully expressed *(She is taller than I [am tall])*. But *than* is also often used as a preposition, in which case only a noun or noun phrase follows *(She is happier than me)*. The prepositional use of *than* has been controversial, however; in formal writing, it is used more often as a conjunction.

that, which, who Use the relative conjunctions *that* and *which* to introduce restrictive clauses; *which* introduces nonrestrictive clauses. *That* is used to refer to things and humans; *which* refers to things and to collectives of people; *who* refers to persons (and sometimes to animals).

theirselves *Theirselves,* a dialectal variant of *themselves,* should not be used in formal writing except to record dialogue.

there, their, they're *There* is most often an adverb *(Put it there)* or an expletive *(There are too many spelling errors in that text)*. *Their* is the possessive form of "they" *(I drove their car)*. *They're* is the contraction of "they are."

thusly In formal writing, do not use *thusly* as a substitute for the adverb *thus.*

till, 'til, until *Till* and *until* are interchangeable as prepositions and as conjunctions; *'til* is not an accepted spelling of *until.*

to, too, two *To* is a preposition or the sign of the infinitive; *too* is an adverb; *two* is a number.

toward, towards Both spellings are acceptable, although *toward* is the more common spelling in American writing.

try and *See* sure and.

unique In formal writing, avoid using *unique* as a synonym for "unusual." Because it means "one of a kind," do not use comparative or superlative forms with it (avoid "most unique"), and do not use intensifiers with it (avoid "very unique").

used to *See* supposed to.

very Use this overworked intensifier sparingly in formal writing.

well *See* good.

which *See* that, which, who.

who *See* that, which, who.

who, whom *Who* and *whoever* are nominative case forms; *whom* and *whomever* are objective case forms. In formal English, these distinctions must be observed.

who's, whose *Who's* is the contraction of "who is." *Whose* is a possessive pronoun.

would of *See* of, have.

you're your *You're* is the contraction of "you are." *Your* is a possessive pronoun.

gu

GLOSSARY OF GRAMMATICAL TERMS

Absolute adjective Absolute adjectives name qualities that have no degrees. Examples: *round, unique, infinite.*

Absolute adverb Absolute adverbs describe manners of acting that have no degrees. Examples: *invisibly, matchlessly, uniquely.*

Absolute phrase An absolute phrase consists of a pronoun or noun phrase usually followed by a participle and possibly by some modifiers. Example: *The bank having closed early, we could not cash our checks.*

Abstract noun *See* Noun.

Active voice *See* Voice.

Adjective Adjectives modify nouns and pronouns, often by answering one of the following questions: Which one(s)? What kind? How many? Examples: *our car, lovely flower, several proposals.* (*See also* Descriptive adjective and Limiting adjective.)

Adjective clause *See* Subordinate clause.

Adjective phrase Adjective phrases contain an adjective, which may have a modifier before and after it and may be followed by a word, phrase, or clause that completes its meaning. Example: *very happy indeed to see you.*

Adverb Most adverbs are simple adverbs, which modify verbs (nonchalantly *wrestled*), adjectives (extremely *funny*), and other simple adverbs (unusually *quickly*).

Adverb clause *See* Subordinate clause.

Adverbial complement Adverbial complements are adverbial elements that complete the meaning of certain verbs, usually by conveying information about time or location. Example: *My keys are in the car.*

Alternative question Alternative questions seek a reply that isolates one of two or more options. One form is similar to that of yes-no questions: *Should the government raise or lower taxes?* The other form is similar to that of *wh*-questions: *Which do you prefer, a lemon or a lime?*

Antecedent An antecedent is the noun phrase that names what or whom a pronoun refers to. In *After the two scholars studied several cultures, they made a report,* the antecedent for *they* is *the two scholars.*

Appositive Appositives are nouns, noun phrases, and noun clauses that appear after nouns or pronouns in order to rename or further identify what the nouns or pronouns refer to. Example: *Batman, the Joker's nemesis, disappeared.*

Article   *A* and *an* are indefinite articles; *the* is a definite article.

Auxiliary verb   *See* Verb.

Clause   Clauses are groups of words that have a subject and a predicate. *See also* Independent clause and Subordinate clause.

Collective noun   *See* Noun.

Collocation   Collocations are words that conventionally go together. People write of *making mistakes,* not of *doing* them.

Common noun   *See* Noun.

Comparative form   Adjectives and adverbs have comparative forms, used when two things or processes are compared. (A comparative form of an adjective: *greener;* a comparative form of an adverb: *more wonderfully.*)

Complete predicate   *See* Sentence predicate.

Complete subject   *See* Sentence subject.

Complete verb   *See* Intransitive verb.

Complex sentence   Complex sentences have one independent clause and one or more subordinate clauses. Example: *While they were on the island, they heard the roar of cannon.*

Compound-complex sentence   Compound-complex sentences have two or more independent clauses and one or more subordinate clauses. Example: *Although the debaters were not fully prepared, they debated well, and the judges complimented them on their skills.*

Compound noun   Compound nouns are nouns formed by putting together two or more words. Compound nouns can be open compounds *(cross section),* hyphenated compounds *(cross-purposes),* or closed compounds *(crossbow).*

Compound object   When one kind of object is coordinated with another object of the same kind, the result is a compound object. The following sentence contains a compound indirect object: *This invention will save* them *and* us *some time.*

Compound predicate   *See* Sentence predicate.

Compound sentence   Compound sentences have two or more independent clauses, usually joined by a coordinating conjunction *(They made a fashion statement, but no one understood it)* or by a semicolon *(They made a fashion statement; no one understood it).*

Compound subject   *See* Sentence subject.

Concrete noun   *See* Noun.

Conjunction   Conjunctions connect words, phrases, and clauses. The most common conjunctions are coordinating conjunctions and subordinating conjunctions.

Conjunctive adverb   Conjunctive adverbs modify one independent clause while putting it into a logical relationship with an earlier independent clause. Examples: *consequently, however, moreover, nevertheless, therefore.*

gt

Connotation   Connotations are the associations and suggestions that a word brings to mind. For most people, the connotations of *home* center on comfort, security, and familial happiness.

Contraction   A contraction is one word made out of two, with one or more omitted letters marked by an apostrophe: The contraction *shouldn't* comes from combining *should* and *not.*

Coordinate adjectives   If two or more adjectives are coordinate, each of them separately modifies the noun that follows. Coordinate adjectives take a comma between them. Example: *clean, quiet neighborhood.*

Coordinating conjunction   The coordinating conjunctions, which link elements of equal grammatical rank, are *and, but, or, for, nor, so,* and *yet.*

Coordination   Coordination is the linking of two or more words, phrases, or clauses so that they can function together grammatically. In *fire and steam,* the noun *fire* is coordinated with the noun *steam.*

Correlative conjunctions   The correlative conjunctions, which occur in pairs and link elements of equal grammatical rank, are *both . . . and, either . . . or, just as . . . so, neither . . . nor, not only . . . but also,* and *whether . . . or.*

Count noun   *See* Noun.

Cumulative sentence   A cumulative sentence is one in which an independent clause appears first and is followed by subordinate elements. Example: *Some of our peers were very careless, hurrying to focus their cameras, forgetting to seek the abstract essence of a scene.*

Declarative sentence   Declarative sentences make statements. Example: *Nick walked away from Seney.*

Demonstrative pronoun   The four demonstrative pronouns *(this, that, these,* and *those)* carry a sense of pointing to someone or something. Example: *Those on the wall have to be moved; these here should not be touched.*

Denotation   The denotation of a word is its dictionary meaning, that is, what a great majority of people would say that it means.

Descriptive adjective   Descriptive adjectives attribute a quality or condition to nouns and pronouns. Example: *the forlorn moors.*

Direct object   A direct object is usually a noun or pronoun occurring after a transitive verb and naming who or what receives the action of that verb. Example: *Stradivarius made a violin.* Usually, the direct object answers the question *what?* of the verb. What was made? A violin.

Double possessive   The double possessive involves the use of two signals of the possessive case, an apostrophe plus *s* and an *of* phrase: *that serve of Maggie's.* The double possessive helps to avoid the ambiguity in such phrases as *Acton's picture. The picture of Acton* refers to an image of Acton; *the picture of Acton's* refers to a picture belonging to Acton.

Elliptical clause   Adverb clauses of comparison are frequently elliptical, that is, parts of them are omitted. In *Alice was smarter than the King,* there is an elliptical clause: *than the King.* The full form of this clause is *than the King was smart.*

gt

Euphemism   Euphemisms are neutral or pleasant ways of referring to processes and things that are deemed unpleasant, offensive, or terrifying. Many people do not say that a friend died; they say that the friend "passed on."

Exclamatory sentence   Exclamatory sentences (or exclamations) express how much a speaker or writer is struck by something. Example: *How well you sang today!*

Expletive   Expletives occur where readers expect to find subjects of sentences, but they are not subjects. The most common expletives are *there (There are several people at the door)* and *it (It is necessary to define functional literacy).*

Finite verbs   Finite verbs (such as *rose*) describe definite and limited actions, processes, occurrences, or conditions.

Gender   The three genders in English are masculine, feminine, and neuter. There is a form of the third-person, singular personal pronoun for each gender: *he, she, it.*

Gerund   A nonfinite verb (or verbal), the gerund has several different forms: *waving, being waved, having waved, having been waved.* Within sentences, gerunds function as nouns. Example: Waving *is not polite.*

Imperative mood   *See* Mood.

Imperative sentence   Imperative sentences express a command. Example: *Be happy!*

Indefinite pronoun   Indefinite pronouns refer to indefinite persons or things. Examples: *anybody, nobody, anything, everything, nothing, something.*

Independent clause   An independent clause has a subject and a predicate, and it is grammatically independent of other structures. An independent clause that appears by itself as a sentence is a simple sentence.

Indicative mood   *See* Mood.

Indirect discourse   Indirect discourse is the reporting, not the quoting, of what others have said or written. Example: *The emperor claimed that he could predict the future.*

Indirect object   Indirect objects appear between verbs and direct objects. They indicate to whom or for whom the action of the verb is performed: *Scrooge gave* them *a small gift.* A good way to identify the indirect object is to ask to whom? or for whom? of the verb. Gave to whom? To them.

Indirect question   Indirect questions imply or report on a question, but they do not ask a question. Example: *They asked who thought of that design.*

Infinitive   A nonfinite verb form (or verbal), the infinitive generally consists of the word *to* followed by the base form of the verb: *to examine.* Infinitives function within sentences most often as nouns, adjectives, and adverbs. Infinitives can have a subject (*We wanted* them *to win*) and an object (*We wanted them to win* the game).

Infinitive phrase   Infinitive phrases consist of an infinitive, an object or objects of the infinitive, and perhaps one or more modifiers of the object or objects. In the following example, the infinitive phrase modifies *way: The best way* to solve that problem *is simple.*

Intensive pronoun   The intensive pronouns are *myself, yourself, himself, herself, itself, ourselves, yourselves,* and *themselves.* These forms intensify the focus on a noun or pronoun. Example: *Henry* himself *prefers lobster.*

Interjection   Interjections are words that express strong emotions: Ouch! *I smashed my thumb!*

Interrogative adverb   Interrogative adverbs *(when, where, why,* and *how)* begin questions about specific bits of information. Example: When *did you leave?*

Interrogative pronoun   Interrogative pronouns *(who, whose, whom,* and *which)* are used to ask about persons and things. Example: Who *will volunteer?*

Interrogative sentence   Interrogative sentences request information. Example: *Did you march on their headquarters?*

Intransitive verb   Intransitive verbs do not signal the transfer of action from a subject to an object. There are two different kinds of intransitive verbs. Intransitive complete verbs can make a complete predication on their own: *Caged birds never* sing. Linking verbs connect a subject to a word in the predicate that either renames it or describes it. Forms of *be* are the most common linking verbs: *Ulysses* was *crafty.*

Irregular verb   With irregular verbs, you cannot predict by formula how the past-tense and past-participle forms are produced. Example: *swim, swam, swum.*

Limiting adjective   Limiting adjectives point out particular nouns and pronouns or indicate the number of people, places, things, or ideas referred to. There are eight kinds of limiting adjectives: possessive adjectives *(my, your, his, her, its, our, their);* demonstrative adjectives *(this, that, these, those);* cardinal adjectives *(one, two, three . . .);* ordinal adjectives *(first, second, third . . .);* relative adjectives (words such as *whichever* and *whatever*); indefinite adjectives (words such as *another, every,* and *several*); interrogative adjectives *(which, what, whose);* and proper adjectives (words such as *Brazilian* and *Tahitian*).

Linking verb   *See* **Intransitive verb.**

Mass noun   *See* **Noun.**

Modal verb   *See* **Verb.**

Modifier   A modifier is a word or group of words that limits or qualifies the meaning of another word or group of words. The most common modifiers are adjectives *(a* wonderful *meal)* and adverbs *(ran* effortlessly*).*

Mood   Mood refers to the changes in the form of a verb that show how the writer regards the action, process, occurrence, or condition. There are three moods in English. The indicative mood is used to make statements of fact and ask questions about facts: *The times are changing.* The imperative mood is used to make commands: *Stop it right now!* The subjunctive mood is used to express wishes, recommendations, speculations, and the like: *I recommend that you* be *quiet on that point.*

gt

Nominalization   Nominalization refers to a noun that is derived from a verb or an adjective. For example, the noun *analysis* is derived from the verb *analyze,* and the noun *cheerfulness* comes from the adjective *cheerful.*

Nonfinite verbs   Nonfinite verbs (such as *rising*) describe unfinished actions, processes, occurrences, or conditions. There are three kinds of nonfinite verbs (or verbals): infinitives, participles, and gerunds.

Nonrestrictive modifier   Nonrestrictive modifiers may convey interesting and useful information, but they are not essential to the identification of what they modify. In the sentence *Abraham Lincoln,* who had several matters on his mind, *boarded the train for Gettysburg,* the part set in regular type is a nonrestrictive adjective clause. Note that it is set off with commas, as all nonrestrictive modifiers should be.

Noun   Nouns refer to persons *(teacher),* places *(mountain),* things *(trees),* qualities *(softness),* actions *(collecting),* events *(game),* and concepts *(justice).* Nouns are commonly divided into several different categories. Common nouns refer to a member or to members of a general group or class of things: *city.* Proper nouns refer to a specific and namable member of a group or class: *Seattle.* Collective nouns refer to collections of people, places, and things in their entireties: *team.* Concrete nouns refer to things that people can perceive with their senses: *basketball.* Abstract nouns refer to concepts: *mercy.* Count nouns refer to things that can be counted: *toes.* Mass nouns refer to things or substances that cannot be counted: *slime.*

Noun clause   *See* Subordinate clause.

Noun phrase   A noun phrase has a noun or a word that functions as a noun (such as *speculating*) as its head word. The head word is often preceded by an article *(a, an,* or *the).* Frequently, too, the head word is modified before, after, or both before and after. Examples: *quiet desperation, a pickerel in a pond.*

Noun string   In most noun strings, one noun modifies another *(field guide),* but sometimes a noun string includes one or more adjectives *(systematic policy awareness).* Some noun strings can be very difficult for readers to interpret: *late adolescence interaction pattern analysis.*

Number   Nouns, some pronouns, and, to an extent, verbs show distinctions between singular number and plural number.

Objective complement   Objective complements appear after and complete the meaning of direct objects, either by identifying or by describing direct objects. In the following sentence, an objective complement further identifies the direct object: *They made David* the champion.

Parallelism   The principle of parallelism holds that whenever you coordinate or compare elements, you should make them have the same form: not *We do not like* typing *and* to edit but *We do not like* typing *and* editing.

Participial phrase   Participial phrases include a participle, an object or objects of the participle, and perhaps one or more modifiers of the object or objects: Seeing little white stars, *he decided to stay on the wrestling mat.*

Participle   A nonfinite verb (or verbal), the participle has several different forms: *waving, waved, having waved, being waved,* and *having been waved.* Within sentences, participles function as adjectives: Being waved, *the flag was clearly visible.*

Passive voice   *See* Voice.

Periodic sentence   In a periodic sentence, the main thought or the full independent clause does not appear until near the end. Example: *Noses testing the wind, ears tensed for signs of danger, the deer walked from the safety of the cedars into the field of corn.*

Person   Personal pronouns show a distinction between first person *(I, we),* second person *(you),* and third person *(he, she, it, they).*

Personal pronoun   Most of the personal pronouns take the place of nouns that refer to people. The subjective forms of the personal pronouns (those that could be used as a sentence subject) are *I, you, he, she, it, we, you,* and *they.* The possessive forms of the personal pronouns (those that could substitute for constructions such as *my car)* are *mine, yours, his, hers, its, ours,* and *theirs.* The objective forms of the personal pronouns (those that could be used as an object) are *me, you, him, her, it, us,* and *them.*

Personification   With personification, writers treat abstractions, objects, and animals as if they were human. Example: *Conscience is the counselor looking over our shoulders.*

Phrasal adjective   Phrasal adjectives are made up of two or more words, yet they function as one-word adjectives do. Phrasal adjectives are usually hyphenated when they precede the words they modify: up-to-date *records.*

Phrasal preposition   Phrasal prepositions consist of two or more words, yet they function as one-word prepositions do. Examples: *prior to, in addition to,* and *on behalf of.*

Phrase   A phrase is a group of words lacking a subject, a predicate, or both. A phrase usually functions within a sentence as single words do.

Possessive case   Nouns and some pronouns have a possessive case form to show possession or close association. Example: Isaac's *song is not quite finished;* hers *will be performed tomorrow.*

Predicate adjective   A predicate adjective follows a linking verb and describes the subject. Example: *Homer is* astute.

Predicate noun   A predicate noun follows a linking verb and renames or refers to the subject. Example: *Roger is* the boss.

Prefix   A prefix is a letter or cluster of letters added to the beginning of words to produce other words. For example, the prefix *en-* is added to *dear* to produce *endear.*

Preposition   Prepositions show relationships between words, often relationships of time and space. Examples: *above, around, below, during, inside, over, up, without.*

Prepositional phrase   Prepositional phrases consist of a preposition, the object or objects of the preposition, and any modifiers of the object or objects. Example: *in the tall grass.*

gt

Pronoun   Most pronouns substitute for nouns and noun phrases. For example, in *Currer saw Ellis and thanked her,* the pronoun *her* substitutes for *Ellis.* The different kinds of pronouns are as follows: personal pronouns, reflexive pronouns, intensive pronouns, reciprocal pronouns, relative pronouns, demonstrative pronouns, indefinite pronouns, and interrogative pronouns (see the individual entries for each of these).

Pronoun-antecedent agreement   Pronouns must agree with their antecedents in number *(the people . . . they),* person *(the car . . . it),* and gender *(Anne Hathaway . . . she).*

Pronoun case   The case of a pronoun is the form it takes to show how it relates to other parts of a sentence. Many pronouns can appear in three cases: the subjective *(we),* the objective *(us),* and the possessive *(our).*

Proper nouns   *See* Noun.

Reciprocal pronouns   The reciprocal pronouns are *each other* and *one another;* they mark reciprocal actions. Example: *The contestants quizzed each other.*

Reflexive pronouns   The reflexive pronouns are *myself, yourself, himself, herself, itself, ourselves, yourselves,* and *themselves.* Reflexive pronouns often reflect back on the subject of a sentence, indicating that the action passes back to the subject. Example: *They congratulated themselves.*

Regular verb   Regular verbs have past-tense and past-participle forms that end in *d* or *ed: roll, rolled, rolled.*

Relative adverb   Relative adverbs introduce relative (or adjective) clauses. Example: *She remembered a time* when *she scrubbed floors.*

Relative pronoun   The most common relative pronouns are *who, which, what,* and *that.* Relative pronouns introduce relative (or adjective) clauses. Example: *They wrote to the people* who *lived on the coast.*

Restrictive modifier   Restrictive modifiers are essential to the identification of that which they modify. In the sentence *All students* who skip the examination *will have to repeat the course,* the part in regular type is a restrictive adjective clause. Without it, readers would be unable to tell precisely which students are being referred to.

Root   Roots are words or parts of words used to build other words. Example: *bene-,* as in *benefactor.*

Sentence adverb   A sentence adverb modifies an entire sentence by commenting on its form or content. Example: Fortunately, *they escaped.*

Sentence predicate   The simple predicate of a sentence includes all the verbs (*see* Verb): *The principal of that school* has carried *a baseball bat.* The complete predicate includes the simple predicate and all the words that modify or complete the meaning of the verbs; it also includes all the words that modify those modifiers. In the earlier example, the complete predicate is *has carried a baseball bat.* In some sentences, two or more complete predicates are linked to form a compound predicate: *Julie* dipped her net into the water *and* caught a minnow.

Sentence subject   The simple subject of a sentence is usually the single noun or pronoun that names the thing or person who acts, experiences something, is described, is identified further, or is acted on: *The older* people *from the delta saved the village.* The complete subject includes the simple subject and all the words that modify it or one of its modifiers. In the earlier example, the complete subject is *The older people from the delta.* In some sentences, two or more complete subjects are linked to form a compound subject: The school board *and* a community group *raised money.*

Simple predicate   *See* Sentence predicate.

Simple sentence   A simple sentence has a subject and a predicate and is grammatically independent of other structures. A simple sentence is an independent clause punctuated as a sentence (*see* Independent clause). Here is an example of a simple sentence, with the subject separated from the predicate by a slash (/): *He / wrote about a river.*

Simple subject   *See* Sentence subject.

Standard Edited English   The variety of English used in most public documents written in the United States.

Subjective complement   A subjective complement follows a linking verb and completes the meaning of the subject by renaming or describing the subject. If the subjective complement renames the subject, it is a predicate noun: *Diogenes was a* cynic. If the subjective complement describes the subject, it is a predicate adjective: *Ulysses was* bold.

Subject-verb agreement   In Standard Edited English, subjects agree with verbs in person *(I am, it is)* and in number *(it is, they are).*

Subjunctive mood   *See* Mood.

Subordinate (or dependent) clause   A subordinate clause has a subject and a predicate, but the clause is subordinate to other constructions. Subordinate adverb clauses are usually subordinate to the verbs they modify: When you leave the room, *close the door.* Subordinate adjective clauses are usually subordinate to the nouns or pronouns they modify: *Those* who have finished the test *may leave.* Subordinate noun clauses are subordinate to other clauses in which they function as nouns: *They like* what no one else likes.

Subordinating conjunction   Subordinating conjunctions link adverb clauses to independent clauses. Examples: *until, since, unless, although, if, while.*

Subordination   Subordination is a grammatical relationship in which a word, phrase, or clause is dependent on another word, phrase, or clause. In *After it rained, the game resumed,* the clause *After it rained* is a subordinate adverb clause.

Suffix   A suffix is a letter or a cluster of letters that is added to the end of words to produce new words. For example, the suffix *-ize* is added to *trivial* to produce *trivialize.*

Superlative form   Adjectives and adverbs have superlative forms, used when three or more nonidentical things or processes are compared. Examples: the superlative form of the adjective *green* is *greenest,* and the superlative form of the adverb *rapidly* is *most rapidly.*

gt

Tense   The tense of a verb relates the time of an action, process, occurrence, or condition to a point of reference, often the time of writing. There are six tenses in English: present *(we work)*, past *(we worked),* future *(we will work),* present perfect *(we have worked),* past perfect *(we had worked),* and future perfect *(we will have worked).*

Transitive verb   Transitive verbs signal the transfer of action from the subject noun or pronoun to another noun or pronoun (which is called the direct object). In *Stradivarius made a violin,* the verb *made* is transitive.

Verb   Verbs describe mental or physical actions *(think, evade),* processes *(melt),* occurrences *(fall),* or conditions *(am).* Every simple sentence has at least one main verb, which refers to the primary activity in that sentence. The main verb can be accompanied by one or more auxiliary verbs, which express shades of meaning having to do with the time and nature of actions, processes, occurrences, and conditions. The four kinds of auxiliary verbs are forms of *be* (was *tagged*), forms of *have* (have *given*), forms of *do* (did *save*), and modal verbs, which have to do with matters of possibility, probability, and permission (might *win*).

Verb phrase   A verb phrase has a main verb as its head word. Sometimes this is all that a verb phrase contains. But the main verb may be accompanied by one or more auxiliary verbs. The full verb phrase includes the main verb and all the auxiliary verbs. Examples: *ambled, could have been ambling.*

Voice   Voice is a grammatical category that applies only to transitive verbs. With verbs in the active voice, the subject performs the action: *Elliot* praised *the kazoo band.* With verbs in the passive voice, the subject receives the action: *The kazoo band* was praised *by Elliot.*

Zero relative pronoun   The zero relative pronoun is a relative pronoun that has been omitted from a sentence. In *This is the mystery novel I like,* the relative pronoun *that,* which could appear after *novel,* has been omitted.

gt

INTRODUCTION TO DICTIONARIES

In *Memoirs of a Superfluous Man,* Albert Jay Nock writes that for "sheer casual reading matter, I still find the English dictionary the most interesting book in our language." You might find this claim somewhat extreme, but we hope that you will increasingly come to value dictionaries as resources for your reading and writing.

Choosing a Dictionary

If you have not already done so, you should add a good dictionary to your reference library. As you examine dictionaries, you will find that you can choose from among at least three different kinds.

1. Abridged Dictionaries

The kind of dictionary that is likely to suit most of your needs is an abridged dictionary, often also called a desk or college dictionary. The word *abridged* indicates that these dictionaries are shortened versions of much longer dictionaries. Abridged dictionaries usually list and define between 150,000 and 200,000 words.

The leading abridged dictionaries include the following:

The American Heritage Dictionary. 2nd college ed. 1982.   This dictionary lists the more nearly central meanings of a word before the other meanings. It includes extensive explorations of synonyms and provides more usage notes, as well as more illustrations, photographs, and maps (about three thousand), than any other abridged dictionary.

Concise Oxford Dictionary of Current English. 7th ed. 1982.   This dictionary lists the more common meanings of a word before its less common meanings. It provides British, as well as American, spellings of words but offers little help about matters of usage and contains no illustrations.

Gage Canadian Dictionary. 1983.   This dictionary provides information on how words are spelled, pronounced, and used in Canada. It has a significant number of usage notes and explorations of synonyms; it also includes about four hundred illustrations.

Random House Webster's College Dictionary. 1991.   The most recently published of the abridged dictionaries, this one lists the more common meanings of a word before its less common meanings. Whenever possible, it also includes the date for the first appearance in print of a word. It has a moderate number of usage notes, many explorations of synonyms, and about eight hundred illustrations.

Webster's New World Dictionary of American English. 3rd college ed. 1988.   This dictionary lists the older meanings of a word before the more recently developed ones. By means of stars, it calls attention to words that originated in the United States. It applies usage levels to particular words, includes more explorations of synonyms than any other abridged dictionary, and contains about 650 illustrations.

Webster's Ninth New Collegiate Dictionary. 1983.   This dictionary lists the older meanings of a word before the more recently developed meanings and, whenever possible, includes the date for the first appearance in print of a word. Although it does not provide usage notes or usage labels as often as some of the other abridged dictionaries, it does offer a substantial number of explorations of synonyms and about six hundred illustrations.

All these dictionaries differ from one another in more ways than are touched upon here. Before buying a dictionary, you may find it helpful to consult several other people about which dictionary they prefer and why they prefer it.

2. Unabridged Dictionaries

Unabridged dictionaries list and define many more words than do abridged dictionaries. The shortest well-known unabridged dictionary has about 315,000 entries; the longest well-known unabridged dictionary has about 616,500. Unabridged dictionaries are too expensive for most people to consider buying for their reference libraries. And they are too bulky to carry around.

However, they are magnificent resources, and you should know where in your public or school library you can find one. They define words that are too rare to be found in abridged dictionaries. They can help you understand rare uses of words. And one of them—*The Oxford English Dictionary (OED)*—provides detailed histories for many of its 616,500 entries. The editors of the *OED* have tried to collect a citation of the first, or at least a very early, occurrence in print of most words. After these early citations, the editors have arranged other citations in chronological order. Thus, you can get a good idea of how long a word has been in the English language, you can trace how the meanings of a word have changed through time, and you might be able to relate these changes in meaning to social and cultural attitudes and practices.

Two other well-known unabridged dictionaries are *Webster's Third New International Dictionary of the English Language* (with about 470,000 entries), which is famous for its descriptive rather than prescriptive stance on usage, and *The Random House Dictionary of the English Language,* Second Edition (about 315,000 entries).

id

3. Specialized Dictionaries

At some point, you may decide to add to your reference library one or more of a number of specialized dictionaries, each of which focuses on a specific area of interest. Here are several examples, with dictionary titles, names of editors or compilers, and dates of publication provided:

Dictionaries of Etymology

Dictionary of Word and Phrase Origins. William Morris and Mary Morris. 1977.

Origins: A Short Etymological Dictionary of Modern English. Eric Partridge. 1966.

The Oxford Dictionary of English Etymology. C. T. Onions. 1966.

Dictionaries of Foreign Terms

Dictionary of Foreign Phrases and Abbreviations. 3rd ed. Kevin Guinagh. 1983.

Dictionary of Foreign Terms. Mario Pei and Salvatore Romandino. 1974.

The Harper's Dictionary of Foreign Terms. 3rd ed. C. O. Eugene Ehrlich. 1987.

Dictionaries of Idioms

A Concise Dictionary of English Idioms. William Freeman. 1976.

Handbook of American Idioms and Idiomatic Usage. Harold C. Whitford and Robert J. Dixson. 1987.

Dictionaries of Regionalisms

A Dictionary of Americanisms on Historical Principles. Mitford M. Matthews. 1951.

Dictionary of American Regional English. Frederic Cassidy. 1985.

Dictionaries of Slang

Dictionary of Slang and Unconventional English. Eric Partridge. 1985.

The New Dictionary of American Slang. Robert Chapman. 1986.

Dictionaries of Synonyms

Roget's International Thesaurus. 4th ed. Rev. by Robert Chapman. 1984.

Webster's Dictionary of Synonyms. 1951.

Dictionaries of Usage

A Dictionary of Modern English Usage. 2nd ed., rev. H. W. Fowler, 1983.

Webster's Dictionary of English Usage. 1989.

Harper's Dictionary of Contemporary Usage. William and Mary Morris. 2nd ed. 1985.

Guides to Nonsexist Language

The Handbook of Nonsexist Writing. Casey Miller and Kate Swift. 1980.

Without Bias: A Guidebook for Nondiscriminatory Communication. J. E. Pickens, P. W. Rao, and L. C. Roberts. 1977.

id

Using Your Dictionary

Most dictionaries are excellent sources of information on a wide variety of subjects—the history of the English language, dialects, usage, biographical names, geographical names, names of colleges, and the like.

However, you will probably use your dictionary most often to check on the forms and meanings of words. To review how a typical abridged dictionary conveys such information, we examine the entry for the word *contemporary* in *The American Heritage Dictionary*. Here is a reproduction of the entry, with numbers associated with its various parts:

1.   2.   3.

con·tem·po·rar·y (kən-těm′pə-rěr′ē) *adj.* **1.** Belonging to the same period of time: *a fact documented by two contemporary sources.* **2.** Of about the same age. **3.** Current; modern: *contemporary trends in design.* —*n., pl.* **-ies. 1.** One of the same time or age. **2.** A person of the present age; a modern. [Med. Lat. *contemporarius* : Lat. *com-*, same + Lat. *tempus*, time.] —**con·tem′po·rar′i·ly** (-těm′pə-râr′ə-lē) *adv.*

— 4.

— 5.

— 6.

Synonyms: *contemporary, contemporaneous, simultaneous, synchronous, concurrent, coincident, concomitant.* These adjectives mean existing or occurring at the same time. *Contemporary* and *contemporaneous* have this basic sense usually with reference to an age or period; *contemporary* applies especially to persons, and alone has the sense of modern or present-day. *Simultaneous* more narrowly specifies occurence of events at the same point in time. *Synchronous* generally refers to exact correspondence of events in time or rate of occurrence over a short period: *synchronous movements of dancers. Concurrent* usually refers to correspondence of events over a longer period; often it implies parallelism in character or length of the events involved: *concurrent prison terms. Coincident* applies to events occurring at the same time, without implying a relationship between them. *Concomitant* refers to coincidence in time of events so clearly related that one seems attendant on the other.

— 7.

Usage: When *contemporary* is used in reference to something in the past, its meaning is not always clear. *Contemporary critics of Shakespeare* may mean critics in his time or critics in our time. When the context does not make the meaning clear, misunderstanding may be avoided by using such phrases as "critics in Shakespeare's time" or "modern critics."

— 8.

1. The Entry Word

Entry words are alphabetized throughout dictionaries. The particular form shown here illustrates the correct spelling for *contemporary*. If two spellings are about equally common, some dictionaries will list both forms, joining them with *or*. Other dictionaries list the forms as separate entries with cross references between them. If one spelling of a word is less common than another, many dictionaries list them together, with the more common spelling first: "**rhyme** also **rime**." You are safest using the first form that your dictionary lists.

id

The dots within the entry word show how the word is properly divided into syllables. This information will be particularly useful to you if you have to decide how to divide *contemporary* at the end of a line of script or type. Since you should never leave only one or two letters from a word at the end of a line or carry over one or two letters of a word to the beginning of a new line, you could divide *contemporary* between any of the syllables except the last two. It would be best, however, if you could divide this word after either the second or the third syllable.

2. Pronunciation

The symbols enclosed in parentheses after the entry word show how the word is pronounced. A full explanation of all the pronunciation symbols appears in the front of the dictionary. In addition, examples of how these symbols should be pronounced are given below the entry words on each set of facing pages. The bold ' after *těm* indicates that that syllable should receive the main stress when *contemporary* is said aloud. The lighter ' after *rěr* indicates that that syllable is the second most heavily stressed syllable when this word is said aloud.

Occasionally, you will find two pronunciations given for a word. For example, *contemplative* can be pronounced with a short *a* and the main stress on the syllable *tem*. Or it can be pronounced with a long *a* and the main stress on the syllable *pla*. In general, the pronunciation that the editors list first is the one they have judged to be preferred, but you should use the pronunciation you hear most commonly in your area.

3. Part of Speech

The abbreviation *adj.* indicates that the editors have judged that this word appears most commonly as an adjective. The dictionary lists no different forms for this adjective in the comparative or superlative degree; this lack of forms indicates that if it is ever appropriate to use this adjective in either the comparative or superlative degree, you should add *more* or *most* to it.

If you look among the definitions for *contemporary,* you will see that this word can also be used as a noun. Since *contemporary* as a noun does not form its plural simply through the addition of *s*, the proper plural ending (*-ies*) is also listed.

If the entry word has been a verb, this dictionary would have listed its various forms (for example, *sing, sang, sung, singing, sings*) and would have indicated whether the verb is transitive (*tr.*), intransitive (*intr.*), or transitive in some cases and intransitive in others.

4. Meanings

The meaning that the editors consider most nearly central to *contemporary* as an adjective appears first. The meanings that they see as farther from the center follow. After two of the first three definitions, illustrative examples appear. These can help you distinguish fine shades of meaning.

After the meanings for *contemporary* as an adjective, the meanings for *contemporary* as a noun appear. Again, the meaning that appears first is the one the editors see as most nearly central to the word when it is used as a noun.

5. Etymology

The material in brackets gives the etymology for *contemporary.* Such material is provided for all words whose etymologies are known and yet not obvious. The material here indicates that *contemporary* developed from the Medieval Latin form *contemporarius,* which derived from the two Latin forms *com-* (same) and *tempus* (time). If you ever need help understanding abbreviations that appear in etymologies, check the explanatory material given early in your dictionary, before the entry words appear.

6. Related Forms

The adverb *contemporarily* was obviously derived from *contemporary.* The editors have decided that since the essential meaning of this adverb is very close to that of the adjective they need not allot a separate entry to *contemporarily.* They can save space by listing it as a form closely related to *contemporary.*

7. Synonyms

This section, often called a synonym study, lists several words closely related in meaning to *contemporary* and then suggests how they differ in meaning. Sometimes dictionaries will also list the antonyms (words with opposite meanings) for particular entry words.

8. Usage Note

The advice in this section reflects the opinions of a panel of teachers, writers, and editors that the publishers of *The American Heritage Dictionary* have assembled. This panel offers advice about how words in certain senses should or should not be used in certain situations.

Since *contemporary* is not a part of any common idioms, no idioms are listed as part of this entry. Whenever an entry word is a part of an idiom, that idiom will be listed and defined. For example, the idiom *at hand* is defined as "close by" or "near" toward the end of the entry for *hand.*

Also not listed in the entry for *contemporary* are some labels that the editors use to convey additional information about words.

Some of these labels are called field labels; they indicate that one or more meanings of a word have their primary application only in certain areas. For example, in *The American Heritage Dictionary,* one of the meanings for the word *jam* ("to play jazz improvisations") is accompanied by the label *mus.,* designating the field of music.

Other labels are stylistic labels; they convey the editors' judgment that certain words should be limited to certain levels of style. Such labels include the following:

Nonstandard (language that is not acceptable to educated speakers)
Informal (the language of conversation)
Slang (the colorful language that groups use to identify themselves)
Vulgar (language that violates social taboos)
Obscene (language that violates standards of decency)
Offensive (language that is insulting and derogatory)

Two common labels having to do with time are obsolete and *archaic.* If a word is labeled *obsolete,* that word is no longer in active use. If a word is labeled *archaic,* that word was once common but is now rare.

Finally, some words also have a regional label attached to them, indicating where in the United States a word in American English is common (for example, *New England*) or where in the world a word in English is likely to be used (for example, *Chiefly British*).

id

While you are a student you may find yourself writing certain forms of business correspondence: a job application letter, résumé, and memo. These forms are briefly discussed, with examples, in the following pages.

Résumés

A résumé is a brief outline of your academic and work history and usually includes a statement of your relevant skills and interests. Résumés are usually organized topically by headings (for example, Education, Work Experience, Achievements, and Skills) and present concise accounts of your experience in each category.

A résumé should preferably not exceed one page in length. Use heavy bond or other high quality paper and type neatly; if you are working on a word processor and have access to a laser printer, print copies of your résumé on it. If you cannot produce clear, crisp copies yourself, have your résumé prepared by a professional copy service.

The main features of a résumé are as follows (see the sample on page 847):

- **Heading:** Include your name, current mailing address, and telephone number.

- **Objective:** Your résumé should include a statement of objective if you are applying for a specific job or type of job. State concisely your particular goals, taking care to avoid being so general that you could seem to be applying for any position or so specific that you sound uninterested in any position other than the one you name. If you are sending out your résumé to various employers in diverse businesses, you will probably not be able to state a general objective, so you can omit the category from your résumé. You should remember, however, in creating both a résumé and a job application letter, to tailor the documents to your audience as much as possible, by emphasizing relevant aspects of your education or work experience or by citing skills you possess that are pertinent to the job you seek.

- **Education:** Organize this category chronologically, beginning with your college education and ending with your high school experience if the latter is still recent (that is, if you are still a freshman or sophomore in college) or relevant (if, for example, you are applying for a summer job in your home town or city). Give the name of your college or university and indicate the year in which you will receive your degree, the type of degree (B.A., B.S., etc.), your major subject (you can note specialization if it is relevant to the job for which you are applying), your grade point average, if it is especially good, and any honors you may have won.

- **Work experience:** Again, organize this category chronologically, making sure that the dates of employment for each of your jobs are clearly indicated. Give the name and address (city and state) of each employer and state briefly the nature of the position you held, its responsibilities, and any major activities you carried out.

- **College achievements:** If you have had experiences or held positions in college that have some bearing on the job for which you are applying, list them.

- **Skills and interests:** List only those skills that actually relate to job performance (for example, typing speed, familiarity with types of software, knowledge of spreadsheets, etc.). In an increasingly multicultural society, it is a good idea to note whatever languages you may speak or write. As for interests and hobbies, again, be sparing: List only those that are pertinent to the job or that are of considerable importance to you, ones that suggest interesting aspects of your personality or special skills you possess.

- **References:** Generally, list the placement office of your college or university, which will furnish your transcript and other documents, such as letters of recommendation, to potential employers upon request. If there are particular persons from your work or academic experience—a supervisor, perhaps, or a professor whom you know well—you might want to ask if they will permit you to list them as references. If so, provide their names, titles, professional or academic affiliations, mailing addresses, and telephone numbers.

Letters of Application

An application letter is the natural accompaniment of your résumé when you are applying for a job. In fact, you should never send your résumé to a prospective employer without including a carefully composed letter of application. Without that letter, your résumé may very well end up on the unread stack. A compelling application letter—one that engages the reader's attention and presents a strong and articulate statement of your objectives and a sense of your personality—will almost certainly ensure that your résumé is given serious attention.

In format, a letter of application follows the standard conventions for business letters, using either the block form (all elements flush with the left margin) or partial block form (return address, closing, and signature aligned at the right of the page). The standard elements of a business letter (and, in this case, a letter of application) are as follows (see the sample on page 848):

Irm

- **Return address:** Give your address and the date on which you are writing the letter.
- **Inside address:** Include the name, title, company or institution, and full mailing address of the addressee of your letter.
- **Salutation:** The salutation is the formal greeting; it appears two lines below the inside address. A salutation addresses the recipient of the letter by title and ends with a colon. It is always best to write a letter of application to a specific person, not to a department. If you do not have and cannot find a name, use a generic title *(Dear Personnel Director, Dear Managing Editor)* or *Dear Sir or Madam (Dear Sirs* is generally considered a sexist usage). Use *Ms.* when addressing a woman unless you know for certain that she prefers *Miss* or *Mrs.,* and address women by their own first names, not those of their husbands *(Ms. Katherine Guy,* not *Ms. Douglas Guy).* When addressing an academic, use *Professor* or *Dr.* (many people prefer the first).
- **Body:** The body of the letter (typed in block paragraphs flush left; do not indent paragraphs) presents your particular situation in writing the letter. In the case of a job application letter, state that you are applying for a particular position, give a brief account of your interest, experience, and skills, and indicate when you are available for an interview and/or where you can be contacted for further discussion.
- **Closing:** The closing follows the body after a space of two lines. *Sincerely* or *Sincerely yours* (only the first word of a closing is capitalized) are perhaps the most serviceable all-purpose closings, although you may also use *Truly, Yours truly, Cordially,* and *With best regards* (the last two are somewhat more personal than the first two). Type your name four spaces below the closing; sign your name as you typed it in the space above.

Memos

Memos are the standard form used to communicate information within companies and organizations. They are usually, though not always, addressed to one person but are often read by a number of people. There is very little "format" to a memo: It includes the following elements (see the sample on page 849):

- **Date:** This is obviously important, as memos often serve as status reports or updates of ongoing situations or projects.
- **Names of sender and recipient (*To and From*):** These are self-explanatory. Very often writers of memos simply use first names in these slots, which makes sense, considering that many memos are written for an audience the writer knows well. If, however, you think your memo might be read by other people or might become part of a project file, you should consider using full names.
- **Subject:** State the subject as succinctly as possible, but be specific.
- **Body:** It is almost impossible to give guidelines for writing memos. A good memo accomplishes its writer's purpose, but there are many purposes for memos—to inform, to persuade, to report, to argue, to summarize, etc.— and thus many kinds of memos. Generally, a memo should be as concise as possible, but it should likewise give all relevant information and background, which sometimes takes multiple pages.

Irm

```
                    ANGELA KALAW
                   40 College Street
                   Oberlin, OH 44074
                    (216) 775-6789


OBJECTIVE
     To secure a summer internship in book publishing

EDUCATION
     Oberlin College, Oberlin OH (1989-present)
     Candidate for B.A. degree in English, May 1993
     Currently a junior
     3.3 GPA. Dean's list.

WORK EXPERIENCE
     Contributor, The Somerville Globe, Somerville, MA (Summer
1991)
     Published two articles in the community newspaper.

     Office Assistant, The Somerville Globe (Summers 1990 and
1991)
     Maintained office files, operated two phone lines, and
     proofread articles.

     Volunteer, Somerville Elder Services (Summer 1989)
     Assisted the community outreach committee at special
     events.

COLLEGE ACHIEVEMENTS
     Assistant Editor, Plum Creek Review (1990-1991)
     Selected fiction and poetry contributions for
     publication, consulted with printers, and maintained
     files.

     Reporter, Oberlin Review (1989-1990)
     Wrote weekly features of campus events.

     Treasurer, Oberlin Writers' Society (1990-1991)
     Coordinated annual budget and helped organize society
     events.

SKILLS AND INTERESTS
     Typing:    70 words per minute
     Computers: familiarity with Newsroom Pro software
     Language:  Spanish
     Hobbies:   poetry writing, piano
```

lrm

40 College Street
Oberlin, OH 44074
October 1, 1991

Align return
address
and date
at center

One to five
spaces

Inside
address

Ann Fallon
Senior Editor, College English
Houghton Mifflin Company
One Beacon Street
Boston, MA 02108

One space

Saluta-
tion

Dear Ms. Fallon:

One space

I am writing you regarding Houghton Mifflin's
summer intern program, for which I would like
to apply. As an English major in college
considering a career in publishing, I felt that
a summer internship at a major publisher would
be the best way to gain insight into the
business.

One space

As you can see from my enclosed résumé, I am
currently in my junior year at Oberlin, and I
am due to receive my B.A. degree in English in
May of 1993. In addition to my studies, I have
involved myself in extracurricular activities
related to my career goals since I began
college, as a reporter, Assistant Editor, and
Writers' Society coordinator. I also possess
strong typing and organizational skills, as
well as a familiarity with Newsroom Pro
software.

I will be in the Boston area during my fall
break, October 15 to October 22, and will be
available for an interview anytime during that
week. Please contact me in Oberlin at (216)
775-6789 or in Somerville at (617) 664-1123 if
you would like to speak with me about the
internship. Thank you very much for your time,
and I look forward to hearing from you.

One space

Sincerely yours,

Angela Kalaw

Angela Kalaw

Complimentary
closing

Four spaces
for signature

Typed name

lrm

August 20, 1992

TO: Ann Fallon

FROM: Angela Kalaw

SUBJECT: Status of Latin American
        Authors List

I just want to let you know that I have almost
completed the Latin American authors list,
which you asked me to put together.

As you suggested, I contacted Professor Carlos
Rioja at the University of New Mexico, and he
will not only send a list of major translators
of Latin American writers but will also be a
consultant on the book. Also, I checked at the
library and came up with a list of Latin
American women writers, since you thought you
might want to have an additional section in the
anthology emphasizing these writers.

I have all the materials together and just need
to type them up. I expect to have the list to
you by tomorrow morning.

Irm

Learning to write with a computer is not unlike learning to ride a bicycle: You learn best by actually doing it, not by reading about it. Although various kinds of computer hardware (for example, MacIntosh or IBM) and software programs differ from one another in sometimes significant ways, what you need to do to master any of them is simply to practice—and practice a lot.

Your college or university may very well have "computer literacy" requirements; even if not, some of your instructors may require that you write papers on a computer. Beyond your college career, you will almost certainly find yourself in a profession or business in which using a computer is standard procedure.

The kinds and quantity of writing you are asked to do in college are ideally suited to word processing, so if you do not already write with a computer, now is a good time to learn. The computer facilities on your campus are staffed by individuals who can provide you with a general overview of writing with a computer, answer questions, and probably allow you some time on a computer. If you are thinking of buying your own computer, they can give you informed assessments of the advantages and disadvantages of various models and of various types of software.

The following brief discussions are intended only as descriptions of the processes you can perform in drafting and revising with a computer. For a thorough introduction to computers and writing on them, visit your computer lab, or consult any of many excellent books and manuals available in bookstores or in your college library.

Writing Drafts

WC

Many writers find the computer a far more comfortable medium for composing papers, letters, and other documents than pen and paper or the typewriter. Although computers do not replace longhand writing and typewriting altogether—you would probably not write a grocery list on the computer, for example, and at times a typewriter is the only means of producing an addressed envelope or label—they do permit considerably more flexibility. You can begin a document, change your mind about what you are saying, move blocks of prose around, delete a word, or delete everything, all without crossing out sentences, tossing out sheets of paper, or getting writer's cramp.

You can turn down the monitor on the computer and write on a dark screen, a method (often called "invisible writing") of warming up and uncovering ideas that many writers find especially freeing. Such practice allows you to concentrate on the essence of what you want to say without concern for the way the words look or possible grammatical or syntactical errors. This sense of playfulness, which increases as you write more regularly with a computer, is a definite benefit. It allows you to experiment without penalty and to revise without writing your document all over again, an experience both frustrating and often boring enough to lead to carelessness.

You should always take care to save—that is, file—your text at frequent intervals; further, it is wise to make backup copies of major texts, in case something happens to your disks, and to keep a file of printed copies as well. Label your computer files as precisely as possible, so you can retrieve your notes and drafts easily.

Revising and Editing

For many if not most writers, these functions are the major advantage of writing with a computer. The computer gives you the ability to add and delete copy, to move text around, and above all to exercise your options—to think and rethink and make changes as a natural process of your writing, while you are actually doing the writing. This fluidity not only saves you the mechanical work of retyping or rewriting an entire paper. Equally as important, it enables you to be more imaginative and expansive as you shape a piece of writing. Because you can make changes so easily, you can also try out various ways of accomplishing your purpose. You can write multiple thesis statements, file them away and come back to them later, choosing the one that seems most persuasive. You can set up various organizational plans and adapt or rethink them if your ideas change. You can combine portions of separate drafts. You can write the body of a paper and return to write a more powerful introduction after you have developed the paper to your satisfaction.

Although the computer allows you great flexibility in working out ideas for a piece of writing, you should remember that your writing is always in your control, not in the machine's. Revision, as it was described in Chapter 11, is a process of "re-seeing," not merely reorganizing or even retooling important components like introductions and conclusions. Once you have drafted a piece of writing, you need to see it whole—and the screen is not the best medium for doing so. Print out a paper copy of your text and evaluate it carefully in terms of your perspective, the evidence you have used, your organization, and your sense of what your audience needs. Consult the revision worksheet on pages 154–155; it offers a systematic approach to revising. Note on paper the changes you want to make, *then* return to the screen and put them into effect, by adding, deleting, rewriting, and moving prose.

You should resist the temptation to edit—the line-by-line reading and polishing of your sentences—while you are still drafting or doing large-scale revision. After you are certain that you have established the final perspective and shape of your paper, then turn to its individual sentences. Again, editing on the

WC

screen is not necessarily the best practice, though many writers do become fairly proficient at it. But most people agree that they overlook errors when reading on the screen, especially in long texts. Print out a copy and note your editing changes there; then key them into the computer.

After you are certain that you have revised and edited to your best ability and are ready to submit your work to its audience, introduce a final note of skepticism: Print the final text one more time and proofread it scrupulously, looking for any remaining typographical errors or other lapses.

Storing Files

Because the computer has storage capacity, you can use it in effect as a kind of filing cabinet, keeping your work neatly stored in labeled files and readily accessible. Thus, not only do you have a record of what you have written, as well as the opportunity to make copies whenever you choose; you can also return to a piece of writing and revise it long after originally writing it. And you can store files that function as notebooks, jotting on the screen various ideas that you may want to return to for development later.

Special Aids

Software programs generally offer a variety of features that can help you in drafting and revising your writing. Among the most common of these are spelling checkers, electronic thesauruses, and style checkers. All can be useful, but all have limitations. A *spelling checker* scans your manuscript for misspellings and highlights errors. You should remember that spelling checkers contain a limited number of entries in their dictionaries, generally do not recognize proper nouns (although they will, with unintentional comic effect, at times suggest common nouns quite inappropriate in meaning as replacements), do not recognize compound nouns or verbs except word by word, and may not recognize alternate spellings (for example, *sceptic* for *skeptic*).

Much the same is true of *electronic thesauruses,* which supply lists of synonyms. When you are really stuck trying to find a compelling word or when you need to provide some variety in an extended description, a thesaurus can be a helpful aid. But generally you should use it sparingly, instead searching your own imagination and vocabulary for variety and freshness. First drafts, of course, almost invariably contain an overabundance of generic or vague words (for example, *interesting, very, unusual*). Above all, when you revise, resist the temptation to use the electronic thesaurus to change all these words, for in such wholesale substitution you run the risk of overdoing the changes or of choosing an inappropriate synonym. Look at your word choices in the context of each sentence; often you can simply delete a generic or vague use.

Style checkers can tell you only whether your writing conforms to broad, basic conventions of acceptable usage. Use a style checker if you think you have written ungrammatically or have failed to punctuate properly but cannot diagnose the problem. But do not rely upon it to rewrite for you, or to give your prose the distinctiveness of your own voice.

MANUSCRIPT

FORM

It is always a good idea to check with your instructors about their preferences concerning manuscript preparation (for example, some instructors will not accept papers written in longhand).

The following are standard conventions for preparing manuscripts for the papers you write. (For guidelines in preparing a research report, see the discussion and sample papers on page 763 and pages 764–799.)

Medium of Preparation

Generally, you should word process or type the papers you submit in your courses. If you do not have access to a computer or typewriter, make certain that your instructor will accept a paper written in longhand; if not, arrange to have your paper typed or word processed.

If you are writing with a word processor, be sure the printer you use yields clean, dark copies with no smears or uneven inking. Avoid dot matrix printers if possible.

If you are typewriting, be sure that your ribbon is clean and relatively new. If you must use correction fluid, do so carefully and sparingly. For major corrections, retype.

If you are handwriting, use a good pen with black or blue ink; do not use other colors. Be especially careful to write legibly.

Paper and Lines

Use sturdy white bond paper (not photocopy paper or onionskin, and not colored paper), 8½ × 11 inches, for both word processing and typing. Double-space.

For handwriting, used ruled white paper, 8½ × 11 inches, and write on every other line.

mf

Margins

Leave an inch margin on each side of the page and approximately an inch and a half on the top and bottom.

Title and Name

If your paper does not have a separate title page, type your name, the name of your instructor and course, and the date (all on separate lines) flush with the *left* margin, an inch and a half from the top of the page. Double-space and type the title, centered between the right and left margins. Type the title in capital and lower-case letters (see **37a** for guidelines); do not underline it or place it within quotation marks.

Double-space between the title and the first line of text.

Page Numbers

A number on the first page is optional; if you use one, center it two lines below the last line of text, an inch and a half from the bottom of the page.

Type your name and the page number—using arabic, not roman, numerals (for example, 6, not vi)—at the top of each page after the first page. Position the name and numeral in the upper right-hand corner, flush with the right margin and an inch and a half from the top of the page.

Spacing

Paragraphs: Indent five spaces.

End punctuation (period, question mark, exclamation mark): Leave two spaces after these marks.

Internal punctuation (commas, semicolons, colons), closing parenthesis, and brackets: Leave one space after these marks.

Dash or hyphen: Leave no space on either side.

mf

Acknowledgments (continued from page iv)

Eugenio Montale: *New Poems*. Copyright © 1972 by Eugenio Montale and G. Singh. Reprinted by permission of New Directions Publishing Corporation.

George Orwell. "Shooting an Elephant" from *Shooting an Elephant and Other Essays* by George Orwell, copyright 1950 by Sonia Brownell Orwell and renewed 1978 by Sonia Pitt-Rivers, reprinted by permission of Harcourt Brace Jovanovich, Inc., the Estate of the late Sonia Brownell Orwell and Martin Secker & Warburg Ltd.

Camille Paglia and Neil Postman. Excerpt from "She Wants Her TV! He Wants His Book!" Copyright © 1991 by *Harper's Magazine*. All rights reserved. Reprinted from the March issue by special permission.

Diane Ravitch. From "Back to Basics" by Diane Ravitch, *The New Republic*, March 6, 1989. Reprinted by permission.

David J. Vogel. From David J. Vogel, "Business Without Science," *Science Digest*, July 1981. Reprinted by permission of the author.

Elizabeth Whelan. Excerpt from "Big Business vs. Public Health: The Cigarette Dilemma," *USA Today*, May 1984. Used with permission of Dr. Elizabeth M. Whelan.

E. B. White. Excerpt from "Once More to the Lake" from THE ESSAYS OF E. B. WHITE. Copyright 1941, © 1977 by E. B. White. Reprinted by permission of HarperCollins Publishers Inc.

Marie Winn. Excerpts from "Television and Violence: A New Approach" and "Reading and Television." From THE PLUG-IN DRUG by Marie Winn. Copyright © 1977, 1985 by Marie Winn Miller. Used by permission of Viking Penguin, a division of Penguin Books USA Inc.

INDEX

a, an, 817, 828
Abbreviations
  for academic degrees, 560
  in bibliographic entries, 562, 724
  with business names, 564
  for days, 564
  for geographical names, 561, 563, 564
  for holidays, 564
  in informal writing, 564
  lists of, 562, 563
  for months, 563
  for names of people, 564
  with numbers, 561, 562
  periods with, 471–472, 561
  plurals of, 455, 549
  postal, 563
  spacing of, 561
  for titles with names, 560
Absolute adjectives, 424, 827
Absolute adverbs, 428–429, 827
Absolute phrases, 234, 498, 827
Abstract(s), 18
  bibliographic formats for, 747
  descriptive and informational, 759–760
  as research sources, 690–691
  sample, 811
Abstract vs. concrete words, 628–630
Abstract nouns, 832
Academic courses, capitalization of, 555
Academic tone, 137
Accent, fallacy of, 126
accept, except, 448, 817
Accident, fallacy of, 130
accordingly, as conjunctive adverb, 283
Acknowledgement of sources
  necessity for, 520
  using footnotes or endnotes, 714
  using MLA style, 487
Acronyms
  commonly used, 561
  spelled out within parentheses, 517, 561
Action markers, 579, 604
Action verbs, 599–601

Active voice, 268. *See also* Passive voice
A.D. and B.C., positioning of, 561, 817
Adams, Robert M., 17–18
adapted from, to, 622
Addition, conjunctions indicating, 176(box)
Additive phrases, 371
Address (street, city, and state)
  numerals in, 566
  punctuation of, 507
Ad hominem argument, 132–133, 134
Adjective(s)
  absolute, 424
  vs. adverbs, 421–422, 425–426
  comparative form of, 423, 467
  compound. *See* Compound modifiers
  coordinate, 503–504
  cumulative, 503, 504
  defined, 270, 827
  demonstrative, 273
  descriptive, 273
  fronted, 307–308
  identification of, 270–272
  incomplete comparisons with, 422–423
  introducing noun clauses, 319
  limiting, 273–274, 831
  after linking verbs, 421–422
  nouns as, 583–584
  participles and participial phrases as, 259, 276–277
  phrasal, 833
  possessive pronouns that function as, 240
  predicate, 292
  proper, 274, 555
  in subordinate clauses, 230
  superlative form of, 423, 467
  transitional, 176(box)
  types of, 273–275
  See also Modifiers
Adjective clauses
  comparative vs. superlative forms of, 271–272
  in complex sentences, 317–319
  defined, 317

857

ind

ind

ind

ind

ind

ind

ind

ind

ind

ind

ind

ind

ind

ind

E S L   I N D E X

*This index references discussions of sentence construction and usage
that are of particular interest to second-language speakers. Special
topics are given highlighted coverage in "ESL Consideration" boxes,
noted here by **boldfaced** page references and the word* **box.**

esl

*This index references the most common errors in sentence structure, diction, and punctuation. References in **boldface type** are to "Quick-Reference" boxes, which give incorrect and corrected examples.*

err

err

Preface